❧❧

Van Morrison: Astral Weeks To Stardom, 1968-1972

"I was a kid then. I didn't know anything about anything, I was just spinning off the top of my head."

VAN IN CONVERSATION WITH RTE'S MIRIAM O'CALLAGHAN, 2018

ॐ

"I don't intellectualize music. For me that spoils it, … It takes away whatever you connect with."

VAN IN CONVERSATION WITH MICHAEL HANN, 2017

ॐ

"I was reading Allen Ginsberg … I was definitely influenced by William Blake."

VAN IN CONVERSATION WITH ROLLING STONE'S DAVID FRICKE, 2016

ॐ

"When I get people saying 'that's my favorite album' my feeling is that I was just a kid when I made that record; I didn't know what was going on."

VAN IN CONVERSATION WITH RICHARD PURDEN, IRISH NEWS, 2018

ॐ

"People tell me Astral Weeks changed their lives. But it didn't change my fucking life."

VAN MORRISON IN CONVERSATION WITH JON WILDE, UNCUT, 2005

VAN MORRISON:
ASTRAL WEEKS TO STARDOM, 1968-1972

HOWARD A. DEWITT

With the editorial and layout assistance of
Scott Amonson

HORIZON BOOKS
P. O. BOX 4342
SCOTTSDALE, AZ 85261

ISBN: 978-0-938840-07-7 (Paperback)
Library of Congress Number: 2020908268
Printed by Kindle Direct Publishing in the USA.
Edited, Cover Art & Layout by Scott Amonson

Published By:
Horizon Books
P. O. Box 4342
Scottsdale, AZ 85261
www.howardadewitt.com

To request permissions, contact the publisher at: Howard217@aol.com

THIS BOOK IS DEDICATED TO:

PAT THOMAS: The master writer who convinced me to finish the multi-volume biography.

᙭

SIMON GEE: The force behind the first book thirty-seven years ago and Wavelength.

᙭

STEPHEN MCGINN: The Van Morrison Newsletter kept me on course.

᙭

ART SIEGEL: The hidden resource who knows everything positive about Van The Man.

᙭

JOHN GODDARD: The owner of Village Music; he found everything I needed on Van and other artists.

᙭

DENNIS LOREN: For starting my career as a rock music writer.

᙭

MARC BRISTOL: For publishing more than 100 articles in Blue Suede News.

ROCK N ROLL BOOKS BY HOWARD A. DEWITT

❖ **Searching For Sugar Man II: Rodriguez, Coming From Reality, Heroes & Villains** (2017)

❖ **Searching For Sugar Man: Sixto Rodriguez' Mythical Climb To Rock N Roll Fame and Fortune** (2015)

❖ **Van Morrison: Them and the Bang Era, 1945-1968** (2005)

❖ **Stranger In Town: The Musical Life of Del Shannon** (with D. DeWitt (2001)

❖ **Sun Elvis: Presley In The 1950s** (1993)

❖ **Paul McCartney: From Liverpool To Let It Be** (1992)

❖ **Beatle Poems** (1987)

❖ **The Beatles: Untold Tales** (1985, 2nd edition 2001)

❖ **Chuck Berry: Rock 'N' Roll Music** (1981, 2nd edition 1985)

❖ **Van Morrison: The Mystic's Music** (1983)

❖ **Jailhouse Rock: The Bootleg Records of Elvis Presley** (with Lee Cotton) (1983)

HISTORY AND POLITICS

❖ **Trump Against The World: Foreign Policy Bully, Russian Collusion** (2018)

❖ **Sicily's Secrets: The Mafia, Pizza & Hating Rome** (2017)

❖ **Meeting Hitler: A Tragicomedy** (2016)

❖ **Obama's Detractors: In The Right-Wing Nut House** (2012)

❖ **The Road to Baghdad** (2003)

- ❖ A Blow To America's Heart: September 11, 2001, The View From England (2002)

- ❖ Jose Rizal: Philippine Nationalist As Political Scientist (1997)

- ❖ The Fragmented Dream: Multicultural California (1996)

- ❖ The California Dream (1996)

- ❖ Readings In California Civilization (1981, 4th edition revised 2004)

- ❖ Violence In The Fields: California Filipino Farm Labor

- ❖ Unionization (1980)

- ❖ California Civilization: An Interpretation (1979)

- ❖ Anti-Filipino Movements in California: A History, Bibliography and Study Guide (1976)

- ❖ Images of Ethnic and Radical Violence in California Politics, 1917-1930

- ❖ 1930: A Survey (1975)

NOVELS

- ❖ Stone Murder: A Rock 'N' Roll Mystery (2012)

- ❖ Salvador Dali Murder (2014)

- ❖ SPORTS BOOKS

- ❖ The Phoenix Suns: The View From Section 101 (2013)

TABLE OF CONTENTS

PREFACE

"The only thing that bothers me is that I don't really know why I became famous, because I wasn't one of those people that wanted it."

VAN MORRISON IN CONVERSATION WITH Q MAGAZINE, APRIL 1997

"I write from a different place. I do not even know what it is called or if it has a name."

VAN MORRISON IN CONVERSATION WITH CHRIS NEIL, 2009

"I am an artist. I should be exempt from shit."

P. J. PROBY

This book is the second in a five-volume biography of Van Morrison's life. The era from 1968 through 1972 witnessed Morrison's evolution from a pop artist known for "Gloria" and "Brown Eyed Girl" into a mystical cult figure who did it his way. His wave of hits for Warner Brothers in the early 1970s brought mainstream stardom and monetary rewards.

If this book has any use, it is to analyze a microscopic period in Morrison's life. The inability of Van's biographers to look deeply into his personality and to understand why he is shy, private and tyrannical with those who invade his space is a problem. His biographers over analyze him in-depth (think Clinton Heylin and Johnny Rogan), those who admire his intellect (think Brian Hinton, Peter Mills, Greil Marcus or Erik Hage) or the biographers who attempt to place him in the larger picture (think Ritchie Yorke, John Collis, Ken Brooke, Steve

Turner and Howard A. DeWitt). They offer varied interpretations of Van's life. His interpreters provide the footprint to his life.

The list of Morrison inspired books on interpretive subjects with a narrow focus is helpful to the biographer. The best is Ryan H. Walsh, **Astral Weeks: A Secret History of 1968**. This is a major book suggesting how and why 1968 Boston was the final influence on the Belfast Cowboy's **Astral Weeks** album. Often overlooked are Martin Buzacott and Andrew Ford's **Speaking in Tongues: The Songs of Van Morrison,** which is a marvelous analysis of the music to 2005 and Ken Brooks, **In Search of Van Morrison**. Gerald Dawe's **My Mother City, Belfast** includes a section on Morrison. Dawe's **The Rest Is History**, which arrived in 1998, is a brilliant quirky piece of literature not aimed at the rock and roll crowd. The first chapter, which is required reading in Irish literature classes at major universities, discusses Belfast's history through Morrison's life and music. As a professor at Trinity College, Dublin, Dawe's work is personal, autobiographical and informative placing Morrison in the center of Irish literature. Dawe is a major poet and his best piece on Morrison **In Another World: Van Morrison & Belfast** relives the Belfast 1950s and 1960s music scene. This set the stage for Van's career.

Gerald Dawe has insights few can match. He describes "Cyprus Avenue" as a "childlike vision leaping into view." The heart-breaking lyrics he ascribes to Morrison highlights his songwriting genius. Not surprisingly, Dawe connects Morrison to the beat poets. This suggests why Van is bored with convention. The sense of romanticism running through Morrison's oeuvre is another facet of his public persona. The James Joyce stream of consciousness in lyrical form defines Morrison's songs.

The use of Irish settings is another Morrison trademark. In "Madame George" he writes of Sandy Row, which is a Protestant working-class section of Belfast. It is in the inner city. The simple working-class life style is a theme continually running through Van's songs.

Last but not least in the specialized books is the often cranky, but brilliant, study by David Burke **A Sense of Wonder: Van Morrison's Ireland**. The Protestant-Irish influences that are part and parcel of

Morrison's music are featured in a book arguing Morrison's songs are a map to his life.

The first Morrison biography Ritchie Yorke's **Into the Music**, published in 1975, benefitted from Van's in-depth interviews. Why did Van agree to talk to Yorke? The Canadian journalist told me when he called Van, they talked music. When they met, Van loved Yorke's lack of a tie, a sport coat or a white shirt. He had on a Ronnie Hawkins t-shirt. The next time they got together Yorke was shirtless. He told Van about his 8-track collection. He complained he couldn't find many of Van's 8-tracks. He told Van he had just found the **His Band and the Street Choir** album on 8-track. This conversation broke the ice. Van sat for a lengthy interview. This became the basis of Yorke's biography. Yorke also wrote two brilliant articles on Van. The sad thing is no one took rock biography seriously in the mid-1970s.

In 1983 my book **Van Morrison: The Mystic's Music** arrived after I spent more than a decade following Van around the San Francisco Bay Area. I never interviewed Van. I talked to him once at the Great American Musical Hall. I was a regular at his father's record store. I can remember John Goddard driving up in his Cadillac with a box of records for George Morrison. Shana sat at the cash register playing Kiss records. Like Van, George was grumpy in a friendly way. Van's mother, Violet, often came into the store. I talked to them over the years. I found both of Van's parents delightful. They were proud of their son. When my book went out of print, I planned a multi-volume biography. It took me until 2005 when **Van Morrison: Them and the Bang Era, 1945-1968** appeared as the first of a five-volume biography totaling more than 3,000 projected pages. Why did Van never sit down with a biographer again after Yorke's 1975 book?

The answer is a simple one. He believes the press misquotes him. The facts reported in articles and books are often at variance with his version of the truth. Van complains the story was never told the way he states it. As a shy, private person Van kept biographers from his sacrosanct life.

One author will talk about his music. Another will discuss Belfast. Another will only analyze the albums. Fortunately, there is one author with two books who has told the story brilliantly, honestly, in depth, with excellent research and his writing shows the facile pen of the poet.

That author is Johnny Rogan. **Van Morrison: A Portrait of an Artist**, arrived in 1984 and another volume **Van Morrison: No Surrender**, came out in 2005. Van has responded in key interviews to discuss his biographers. He gives forth his opinions about the press and those in the academic community. Since 2008 Van has been kind to his critics. The war on the press was over thanks to Rogan. Van increasingly talked to reporters to correct what he termed "fiction over fact." Johnny Rogan changed how the Van Morrison biographical tomes were conceived, written and accepted. His work also opened up Morrison. In the last decade his personal reflections tell one a great deal about his musical mission but keep away from his personal life.

What did Rogan do to change Van's mind? Nothing. Van simply took his case directly to selected reporters. Although Rogan produced two excellent books, Van thought they were fiction. They weren't. Rogan's books contained material Van couldn't fathom. The problem was Van couldn't figure out how and why Rogan wrote of his life employing selected parts of Irish history that Van had no interest in or knowledge of. Van has had no contact with Irish political movements. Morrison lived outside of Ireland for much of the period. Rogan overemphasized Irish political history. Why did this dismay Van? Who knows! Only Van can answer that question. Rogan's book, those close to Van told me, caused Morrison to scratch his head. He asked his friends: "Couldn't the biographers get it straight?" Van only wanted two things. He desired to establish his music for a broad-based audience. He went to war with what he said were the corrupt and deceptive record labels. His second wish was to be recognized as a hard-working blue-collar musician.

There is one early biography Morrison liked. Steve Turner's **Too Late to Stop Now**, published in 1993, is a lavish, coffee table book with wonderful illustrations. This was unfortunate as it prompted some to ignore the high level of research and the beautiful writing endemic to Turner's book. He writes with a skilled pen. John Collis' 1996 **Inarticulate Speech of the Heart** is a workmanlike look at Van's life with some interesting observations. Brian Hinton's 1997 **Celtic Crossroads** brought Morrison's writing into an interpretive intellectual framework. Patrick Humphreys, **The Complete Guide to Van Morrison**, is a brief 1997 book containing wonderful material.

Clinton Heylin's **Can You Feel the Silence? Van Morrison, A New Biography**, released to critical acclaim in 2002, is the best Morrison book. But it is marred by a proclivity to disparage, criticize and degrade the Belfast Cowboy. The research and the writing are superb. The mano-a-mano testosterone driven arguments detract from an otherwise brilliant piece of journalism.

In 2005 Howard A. DeWitt's encyclopedic **Van Morrison: Them to the Bang Era, 1945-1968** told the inside story of how he became a cultural icon. It is an in-depth, fact laced examination of the early years.

Then the professors weighed in on Erik Hage's **The Words and Music of Van Morrison** published in 2009. It is an incisive academic critique of the music with little attention to his life. It is a brilliant analysis of how and why Morrison makes music. The following year Greil Marcus' **When That Rough God Goes Riding** analyzed Morrison's early music with the touch of a skilled literary critic.

Peter Mills is the professor with the deft analytical touch as his 2010 book **Hymns to the Silence: Inside the Words and Music of Van Morrison** tells the reader how and why Van Morrison made his music. The beauty of the Belfast Cowboy's music is it is open to many interpretations.

ASTRAL WEEKS AND VAN'S LEGEND

In 1968 Van Morrison's **Astral Weeks** album was released to critical acclaim and miniscule sales. He released four more Warner Brothers albums by 1972. Van evolved into an established rock and roll star. His distinctive voice is like no other performer. His songwriting is mystical. His lyrics are filled with literary illusions. He isn't Bob Dylan. The comparison makes him uncomfortable. He has a whole lot more perspective and direction than most rock performers. Bruce Springsteen, John Fogerty, Bob Seger and John Cougar Mellencamp have taken Morrison's critical angst to the bank.

From 1968 to 1972, Morrison evolved from a cult artist into a mainstream commercial star. When the Belfast Cowboy found fame and fortune, he hated it. The initial five years with Warner were tumultuous ones. By 1972, Van was in the first stage of mastering the intricacies of the business side of the industry. After the cult album, **Astral Weeks**, he turned out a series of vinyl masterpieces with hit records.

Earlier biographies emphasize Van's negative personality. He wasn't the miscreant Clinton Heylin portrays. He wasn't the easygoing personality that seeps through in Steve Turner's brilliant coffee table biography. Van was like any other person in his early twenties attempting to make it in the music business. He was at times testy. He was at other times friendly. The evolution from cult artist to mainstream stardom is the story in these pages. The back-story is Morrison was not the incarnation of a weird genius. He was simply a working musician. He was a singer-songwriter on his way to fame and fortune. His volatility toward the music business was real. He needed to have his music his way to survive artistically.

It is almost impossible, if not impolite, to begin a discussion of Van Morrison without analyzing his productivity. Like fellow performer Bob Dylan and actor, composer, musician, poet and writer Sam Shepherd, Van never stops working. His legacy is tied to productivity.

Morrison's literary-intellectual foundation was laid in 1968 in **Astral Weeks**. It took some time for the music to be embraced by a wider commercial audience. It was only the second album released by Van Morrison. He remarked it would take some time for his audience to get on the same wavelength.

While he remains a brilliant songwriter, a consummate musician-performer and a continually evolving intellectual, his roots are in Belfast. He is Irish to the core. He tried living in Woodstock. He spent some time in Boston and New York. Marin County was his home base during his marriage to Janet Planet and for a long time after the divorce. His home at the top of a beautiful hill outside Fairfax was a dream cottage. He still has a Mill Valley home where his daughter, Shana, lives.

By 1972 his life was a rich one. Fame and stardom were not blessings. How did stardom impact Morrison? He made a lot of money. He was forced to periodically hide out from the press, the fans and the pressures of the rock and roll life. He said in numerous interviews fame is not good for creativity. In an interview with Fintan O'Toole, Van observed: "You don't have the anonymity which is important for creativity."

Morrison is a blue-collar worker. He turns out an album almost every year. He maintains a firm commitment to intermittent concerts, charity events, and a personal life that is rich and varied. Since he is the ultimate contradiction, there are periods in his life where he has taken time off to recharge his creative juices. It is impossible to predict what Van will do next. That is the beauty of Morrison's enigmatic career.

The bottom line is he loves to work. From his garage band, Them, until the present, he has produced a vast catalogue of recorded gems. There is enough unreleased material in Morrison's vault for at least fifty new albums. The biographical material in his songs is rich. He discusses every part of his life. There is often frustration in Van's voice during interviews. The reason is a simple one. He has difficulty talking about and explaining his music. Since the release of **Astral Weeks**, journalists, rock historians and those who make a living dissecting rock music have pestered Van with questions and presumptuous conclusions. For a time, he drifted into a shell due to inane and inarticulate questions. Clinton Heylin describes this as maladjusted.

He can't accept he is famous. He has trouble justifying his enormous wealth. It makes him nervous. He is a man of contradictions. He hasn't escaped the haunting specter of the early Warner Brothers albums. The critics and the fans often remark nothing compares to **Astral Weeks**. For a time, it was the bar by which all future Morrison albums were judged. He is still persistently dogged by questions surrounding **Astral Weeks**. While this is in some ways unfortunate, it suggests the depths of his songwriting genius. Perhaps this is why he revisited it in 2008 performing and recording it live in the Hollywood Bowl.

Astral Weeks earned Van critical acclaim. Monetary rewards followed. He promptly went off on a hit record cycle before pulling away from the concert stage in the mid-1970s. Van is a man of mystery. His personality is one of multiple contradictions.

Morrison remains dedicated to his craft. He is an intricate and often complex craftsman. Van has mastered the nuances of the business ends of the industry. One of the sub-themes of this book is

Morrison's handling of his business affairs made him a multi-millionaire. He has said the period from 1968 through 1972 was the most difficult of his creative life. During the early 1970s, he educated himself on how to beat the record companies at their own game. It was this obsessive-compulsive drive to fame, monetary gain and stardom that guaranteed mainstream commercial success.

From 1968 to 1972, Van Morrison achieved a degree of fame and a bit of fortune. During this era, he reinvented himself many times. The music reached into a new direction. If it didn't improve for the critics, it did for the fans. No one knew what to expect. That is Van's charm.

Van hates the term "mainstream music." That is where he gravitated from 1968 to 1972. Blues, jazz and pop sounds influenced his artistic direction. His biggest worry remains not being paid.

Van Morrison and Bob Dylan mid-1980s

Clinton Heylin's **Van Morrison: Can You Feel The Silence?** is arguably the best Morrison biography. Heylin doesn't understand Morrison personally. He is angry Van sued him. When he wrote about Van's reaction to the other artists he influenced, he failed to realize from Van's point of view his talent was borrowed without compensation.

Van ignored Springsteen's career until the 1980s. He hadn't listened to the Bosses songs. When he did, he was outraged. He wrote of Springsteen: "He definitely ripped me off ... I mean he's even ripped my movements as well ...." Heylin continually berates Morrison for his views.

What does Heylin miss? Everything! He doesn't understand Morrison's obsession with royalties. Heylin wrote Morrison showed "evidence of a truly paranoid perspective." (p. 392) This is of course nonsense. Heylin continued his attack suggesting Van was "less and less stable" on tour. This is absolutely untrue. Some band members told me Van was so tight musically in concert due to constant practice and the presence of former James Brown saxophonist Pee Wee Ellis. The twelve Morrison shows I attended in 1986 were ones in which Van used saxophonist Pee Wee Ellis, guitarist John Platania and keyboardist Jeff Labes to play off him. Van also incorporated cover songs like "Send In the Clowns" to make his shows middle of the road mellow. Heylin failed to understand Van was now an in-concert act who could sell out and perform in larger venues. This is something he was working toward since the early 1970s.

Van was a songwriter who went on stage. He was uncomfortable in concert. He had an inordinate case of stage fright. From the earliest Them days, he had difficulty performing. He also didn't care to be interviewed. When comfortable he was calm and introspective. He was also friendly to select media and record company types. No one was ever sure how to get to Morrison. These contradictions made it difficult to pinpoint his personality or career direction.

Van's songs make for poetic reading. While he is not a rock singer, some of his music is in that genre. It is from that field his fame has sprung. For the most part his songs are the product of personal insight, literary preoccupation and blues-jazz influences.

The problem with a biographical study is his diverse personality traits. While this has kept his music fresh, it reflects his mercurial life. He has studied more religions, types of mediation, romantic poets, obscure philosophers, and Hindu Holy men disguised as gurus, channeling gurus and cults than is seemingly possible. This is integral to his search for truth.

There have been periods of writer's block and inactivity. He always rebounds with a batch of new songs. He sought and achieved an orderly and rational life. His closest friends maintain he is well adjusted and sometimes boring.

The breadth and scope of Morrison's music is amazing. He has recorded every type of music. He toured when he felt like it. He changed musicians. He altered his musical style. He eschewed the trends. Van did it his way. The critics have never left him alone. They love to tweak him. He ignores them. He also reads everything written about those interpreting his career. He is a harsh critic of those who analyze his music. He often takes exception to articles about his creative direction. It is not just the rock press he abhors. Mainstream newspapers have been known to receive a corrective missive. The press is often petty and juvenile.

Van occasionally made references to writer's block. He hasn't had the problem since sorting out his business affairs. There are boxes of unreleased songs, according to one musician, that are warehoused in Sausalito. Van can tap into this archive at any time. He maintains a full-time employee to select material for a long-planned box set.

He realizes he works in an industry where survival is difficult. Although he has had a long and profitable relationship with Warner Brothers, they tried to nickel and dime him to death. When they stored his voluminous tapes, the expenses were excessive. Van threatened to sue Warner Brothers. He suggested the money charged to store his materials was excessive. He won the battle with Warner Brothers. Van organized his recording career with a strong business sense. Warner executives were incensed. No one was more incensed than Mo Ostin. He was an accountant looking at the bottom line. Profit! The accountant, as Morrison labeled him, became the head of Warner eventually firing Van. He never forgot how Van wanted to fight him at a dinner party in his home. Ostin exacted revenge for Van's behavior. Morrison said in retort he fired Warner.

Van does not suffer fools well. He refuses to answer questions about his personal life. He says it has nothing to do with his music. He isn't interested in reliving his past. He has a stock answer. Respect my privacy. He wants to talk about "Van the industry." The business side, the recording side, the musical side, and the concert side are the subjects he will discuss at length.

Van's writing is a big part of his creative genius. From the time he arrived in London to record with Sir Edward Lewis for Decca, with Them, he demonstrated his use of language. It was the key to his future success. He is an unparalleled wordsmith. With little formal schooling, he left a proper education at fourteen, Van was not restricted by the University education that taught a person what to say and what not to say. He has his own vision of what prose should accomplish. He is determined to write his lyrics and perform them his way. He is also a reader with an inquisitive mind. He was only fourteen when he started playing with his neighborhood bands. He was in a show band by seventeen. There is a sense of Oscar Wilde to Van's lyrics. He has an aestheticism that is profound. He moved in a field where musical lyrics were often trite and dull. On Hyndford Street as a youth, Morrison was a child prodigy. He would lie on his back in the front room of his Belfast home and play the saxophone for hours. The neighbor, Molly Fee, told me of his dedication. Van is driven. This combined with a blue-collar work ethic to produce his legendary career. Van has many standards. None is stricter than his monetary concerns. Because he signed some unfortunate contracts and lost some control over his early songs and albums, he has taken a hard line on business. This policy has made him a rich man. Unlike many creative artists, Van has never disintegrated. Drugs and alcohol never got him. He was never a failure who had to turn to the oldies circuit to make a living. If he is described as difficult, it is to protect his financial interests. But make no mistake he is difficult.

Journalists who hound his trail suggest his life periodically spins out of control. Van is always in control. This has caused the record executives, the booking agents and his lawyers a great deal of concern. He makes his own deals. There is little compromise.

Van has never been dazzled by his own persona. He has his feet on the ground. He has worked to make his career a lengthy one. The result is a wide and varied selection of songs and albums. Over time, Van has received the recognition he so richly deserves. The Cleveland-based Rock and Roll Hall of Fame enshrined him. He continues to be recognized for his songwriting and performing. In his early music, Van was an apprentice. It was with **Astral Weeks** the legend took shape. Since this book covers the period beginning with the seminal **Astral Weeks** LP, there is a sense of his legendary accomplishments.

The narrow confines of Van's world invariably causes him problems. He has explained time and time again fame led to a constricted world. One in which he is constantly struggling to maintain his integrity, his honesty, his sense of his surroundings and his private life. Morrison has carved out his own special world. It is in this place he creates his art. He is adamant the critics, the professors, the journalists and others say little, if anything, about his private life. This is of course impossible. He is a public figure. As such he is fair game for the biographers and the general press. This book makes no excuses for Van's at times boorish behavior. He is known for his temper tantrums, his firing of musicians, his sacking of business managers, his mistreatment of booking agents, his cavalier attitude toward friends and his frequent public tiffs with a wide variety of people. By examining the pressures brought to bear on his life, these incidents explain integral parts of his personality. His work habits derive from his private time. The demands upon his time, his creative energy and his future are enough to make anyone cranky.

If Van had recorded only **Astral Weeks**, he would be considered a musical genius. He has amassed a body of work creating an alternate musical universe. It is a form of musical Neverland with great rewards. Because Van inspires a vast following of obsessive fans, they fantasize about his personal space. Van leads a routine and at times boring life. He is as normal as they come. Which is why he explodes over media accounts of his private life. There are no horror stories from his youth. He didn't suffer as a child. He came from a loving home. His parents doted on him. His dad used his vast record collection to educate his son. While Van didn't go to Oxford, in fact he left school at fourteen, he did receive a fine education. It was in music, in the books and magazines he found in Belfast's Smithfield Market.

Morrison's two themes are finding love and understanding religion and mysticism. His writing, his songs, his career direction and his personal life are infused with these themes.

His daily goal is to write and create. He is able to leave behind emotions and responsibility. He does this by stepping on stage, wandering into a recording studio or practicing with his band. He is hard-working continually looking to create. He has put in thousands of hours on his career. In 2015 Morrison reflected on his work ethic in an interview with Fintan O'Toole.

Van Morrison: "There's a guy that has a book out. I forgot what it's called [Malcolm Gladwell's **Outliers**, with its theory that virtuosity comes from 10,000 hours of practice], … Germany is really what did it for me. … It was really training, boot camp." This is a reference Van made to his nine months playing six nights a week with a show band, the Monarchs, prior to forming with Them.

He told O'Toole he puts his music at the full disposal of an adoring public. He also speaks of his private life, his opinions, his fears, his phobias, his concerns and his future. In his songs, he provides a history of his life. In the interview he provides lost facts, opinions and influences. Van remains, and will always be, a contrarian. Although biography is an inexact science, Van's life was fashioned by the people around him. Bert Berns, at Bang Records, was malevolent in business matters. This helped to make Morrison the consummate businessman. Mervyn Solomon taught Van humility. Phil Solomon taught him key business lessons. Countless others, including Sir Edward Lewis, Bob Schwaid and Lewis Merenstein, contributed to his early business education. One of the problems with rock music biographies is there are no personal papers or archives. In Van Morrison's case this material exists. It is in a brief but informative biography, **Reliable Sources**, which his Caledonia Productions Company put together in the 1970s. It is a major source. There is also an abundance of newspaper, magazine, Internet articles and interviews. These are combined with a number of excellent biographies and numerous in-depth studies of his music to produce a complete picture of Morrison's life. The interviews for this book were often conducted with people requesting anonymity. Why? They feared Van's wrath. Fortunately, half the people interviewed allowed the use of their names.

Religious themes are an important part of Morrison's musical direction. He has also mined the life of the average person. He is much like the English writer, V. S. Pritchett, who went to work writing his stories until his death in 1997 at the ripe old age of 97. Pritchett presented a view of every day English life. Much like Pritchett, Van has had to fight daily to keep his ideas and his music in front of the general public. It has not been easy in an industry rife with corruption, greed and dishonesty. In the early 1970s, Van strove for financial stability. He quickly earned it.

One of the problems with a Morrison biography is his relationship with other people. There are two stories. The first comes from his Irish cohorts. They remark he is friendly, seldom nasty, and he has a sense of duty to his friends. The other set of stories are from musical associates and the non-Irish. One former Morrison friend remarked: "He fired his band, he fired his wife, he dismissed his manager, he fired his publicist and sometime in the 1990s he fired his mother." This humorous reference to an argument with his mother suggests how difficult he is at times.

Van is an ironic writer. In one song, "Whatever Happened To P. J. Proby," he discusses a teen idol that eclipsed Van in popularity for a few years. This tune reminded the critics Morrison has never gone away. He continues to make new music. Whatever happened to P. J. Proby? That is the question. Most of Van's songs are intricate stories. They reflect his likes, his dislikes and his influences. He has frequently said by listening to his music one can understand his life. Some of Van's lyrical criticism is directed toward the record labels. In "Big Time Operators," he gives us his version of how Bert Berns and Bang Records treated him. It is not a pretty picture. Through the turmoil, the emotional and psychological difficulties and the problems with his record labels, his managers, the media as well as his booking agents, Van has tasted success. His life is a continual triumph over adversity.

Ricky Nelson described Van in his song "Traveling Man." With stints living in Belfast, London, New York, Cambridge, Boston, Bath, Los Angeles, Woodstock and Fairfax-Mill Valley, Morrison is a peripatetic figure who relocates for intellectual inspiration. During his years in each location, he developed different parts of his musical repertoire. He has used literary, personal, historical and local symbols in his music. Not long after moving to America, he created a new sound. One completely different from the Them hits "Gloria" and "Here Comes The Night." With Bert Berns' Bang Record label, he recorded "Brown Eyed Girl." This was a pop hit. Van detested it. He worked hard on an alternative to anything remotely connected to Bert

Berns. That creative drive led to **Astral Weeks**. The cult Morrison was born.

There is a frustration in writing about Morrison. His close friends will speak on and off the record. But they are generally wary. His enemies and even a few friends will speak into the night about his difficult personality. He is often called a great Irishman. In the next instance, he is labeled a prig. There are two Van's. One hangs out with his friends. The other is a source of irritation to musicians, managers, bookers, record executives and even occasionally to zealous fans. It is the contradictions that make him an interesting person. The music is brilliant. His life is a long soap opera. He shows no signs of slowing down.

The most fascinating aspect of writing this book was to spend time with people in and around Van's personal life as well as those in the industry who have worked with him. As a noted record executive remarked: "I said hello to him in the elevator at Warner Brothers, he looked at me like I was from Mars. He had no idea who I was or why I was talking to him." The executive was Ray Ruff who booked Morrison and Them on their first American tour. When Ruff saw Van, a year later, he said: "Hello." It had only been four year since the Them tour. Van walked away. Van was already in the artistic fog defining his life. Or was it the pressure dealing with Warner Brothers? Van Morrison's life is not a rags to riches saga. He was born and raised lower Irish middle class. Van's story comes with a cautionary note. The riches robbed Van of his freedom. Fame intruded upon his daily life. He is not happy about it.

When he was born in August 1945, Ireland was in the throes of one of its worst economic crises. He was not born to a socially prominent family, nor did he live on an important street but food was on the table and the house was warm. He might have grown up to be an electrician like his dad. But Van had a talent that could not be denied. He also had an intellect different from his contemporaries. Although he left school at fourteen, Van read voraciously. He kept a notebook handy long before fame intruded.

His home on Hyndford Street was a constant reminder of where he came from and where he might return. "I think Van was driven by his birth home," Mervyn Solomon told me.

There is another side to Morrison's life biographers have ignored. Van is first and foremost a leading figure in the studio freedom that rock musicians found in the 1970s. Without this freedom **Astral Weeks** would not have been recorded. As this volume will show, he is at the center of the independent revolt of the singular artist. As the omnivorous biographer, Greil Marcus, has noted: "Van Morrison's music … holds a story - a story made of fragments." His lyrics are the key to his life. They are the story of his daily life. Over the years there has been a great deal of material on how Morrison's music evolved, how he writes and how he lives his life. Van was also the antidote to the British Invasion. When he arrived in America, as the lead singer of Them, he was incensed the group was labeled a British act. He took exception to that category. He created a sense of his own songwriting and performing. He defined his unique lyrical direction. His personal eccentricities are another reason to study his art and life. Van wants only his art studied. He prefers his private life be left alone. The problem is his private life invariably influences, directs and drives his art.

The ups and downs of Morrison's career have done little to stifle his creativity. He remains an artist vanishing down a rabbit hole to reinvent himself. Among the wellspring of Morrison influences are Huddie Ledbetter, known as Lead Belly, and W. B. Yeats. These are not the typical influences for rock musicians. This book will show how the small moments in Van's life led to the bigger triumphs. The most important aspect of this book is it neither deflates Morrison nor excessively praises him. That is the problem with Morrison biographies. They are alternately too critical or too praiseworthy. He sees his writing and performing as that of a blue-collar musician. He says he is nothing special. I disagree. This book describes five years of his extraordinary talent maturing from 1968 through 1972.

The sub-theme to this book is the difficulty Morrison had in his career getting to the point of making **Astral Weeks**, and then he was faced with a battle with Warner Brothers for survival. He realized hit records kept him in the mainstream. Van's plan was to build a large body of work with hit records and personal lyrical touches as he moved toward attracting a mainstream audience. This seemed impossible in

1968. By 1972, he was a successful mainstream artist. Today the brand that is Van Morrison owes its origins to the 1968 to 1972 era.

BIBLIOGRAPHICAL SOURCES

For the notion Bruce Springsteen ripped off Morrison see Clinton Heylin, **Van Morrison: Can You Feel The Silence, A New Biography** (London, 2002), pp. 391-392. Also see Peter Mills, **Hymns To The Silence: Inside The Music of Van Morrison** (London, 2010), pp. 121-122 for the best explanation of why and how Morrison wrote "A Town Called Paradise" and how it influenced Bruce Springsteen. Also see Howard A. DeWitt, **Van Morrison, The Mystic's Music** (Fremont, 1983) passim.

The psychological and emotional make-up of Van's early years is detailed in Howard A. DeWitt, **Van Morrison: Them and the Bang Era, 1945-1968** (Fremont, 2005). Interviews with former Paul Butterfield pianist Mark Naftalin, former Van drummer Tony Dey, former Van guitarist Chris Michie, former Van guitarist John Platania, Marin County musician Mitch Woods, hit maker formerly of the Paul Butterfield band, Elvin Bishop and Jeff Labes rounded out the introduction.

The material on how Van progressed in Belfast's music scene, why he left it and how he viewed the American music scene resulted from half a dozen interviews with Mervyn Solomon in Belfast. Mervyn marched me through the former haunts and clubs that were instrumental to Morrison's decision to pursue a solo career. Phil and Dorothy Solomon had me over to their Bournemouth home for lunch and a four-hour marathon conversation on how and why Morrison survived as a solo artist. Steve Rowland in numerous interviews described and analyzed the London music scene. Conversations with Shel Talmy, Ray Ruff, Sir Edward Lewis, Molly Fee and Dan Bourgoise were important to this book.

See Fintan O'Toole, "Van Morrison: Being Famous Is Not Great For The Creative Process, Not For Me Anyway," **The Irish Times**,

August 29, 2015. https://www.irishtimes.com/culture/music/van/van-morrison-being-famous-is-not-great-for-the-creative-process-not-for-me-anyway-1.2332216

O'Toole is not a rock journalist. He is a respected and much sought after national and international writer with a reputation for superior work and careful conclusions. He felt honored to interview Van. O'Toole has won the Orwell Prize and the European Press Prize. The level of sophistication in O'Toole's questions impressed Morrison. He opened up to him. There is a Byronesque tone to Morrison's personality. He uses rage to mask his insecurities. The mask of alienation and self-sufficiency Van employs seldom is missing during interviews, radio and television appearances and in social settings. Morrison's resentment has cooled over the years, but in the period from 1968 through 1972 the mask of rage continued to fuel his career. In his private life, according to family and close friends, he would rage on for as long as a year. Why is this important? For the biographer this is a telling point. Van is fond of labeling biographers "lazy." Why? He wants to control the story. The problem for the biographer is to resist hagiography, as well as to prevent Morrison from writing his life. There are few overtures of friendship from Van. That character trait prevented his most perceptive biographer, Clinton Heylin, from understanding how rage and a tough character helped Morrison take his music to fame and fortune.

Van Morrison's approach to the media took a turn for the better in 2008. Since that time major journalists, not rock and roll hacks, have increasingly interviewed Van. We know more about his life and his times. The result is we now know how and why Van considered his war on the music business was necessary to artistic survival.

Johnny Rogan's **Van Morrison: No Surrender** is the archetypical paranoid Morrison biography. Rogan argues: "An important caveat to any serious, well-researched biography or study of Morrison's life is that the reader should be aware that a number of allegations against the subject cannot be featured in print for legal reasons. The author may feel that the final portrayal is far too flattering in certain places, while the reader who neglects to read between the lines may think the biographer could have been a little more sympathetic. "Death alone will open Pandora's box." This quote comes in response to Morrison's comment: "Rogan's got something to hide. What's he hiding? I'd like to do a book on him." There needs to be an adult in the room. The irony is Rogan has written two of the most in-depth, well researched tomes on Morrison. His co-biographical conspirator, Clinton Heylin, is equally paranoid. Van will do that to you.

"For a biographer, Clinton Heylin takes a curiously sarcastic approach to his subject ..." Kevin Mitchell wrote in the **London Independent**. In doing so Heylin failed to recognize Morrison's talented songwriting and performing. It is a shame Morrison's law suit and disparaging remarks tilted Heylin's biography toward the pathetic. Poisonous prose and faulty conclusions obscure an otherwise well-researched and cogently written biography. None of us who write on Van can excuse his bad manners and selfishness. As a journalist, a storyteller and a retired professor there is another side to the Belfast Cowboy's story. In the period from 1968 through 1972 he went from a singer with a Top Ten pop hit "Brown Eyed Girl" to a renegade producer, Bert Berns and a failing record label, Bang Records, and, finally, to a major label, Warner Brothers, where he dealt with industry insiders determined to control, own and legally hijack Morrison's intellectual property. He didn't allow this and went to battle with the industry. He won. That is what this book describes.

See Gerald Dawe, **The Rest Is History** (Abbey, 1998) for a bridge between Belfast's Irish influences and the Americana themes in Van's music. Also see, Gerald Dawe, **In Another World: Van Morrison & Belfast** (Newbridge Co. Kildare, 2017) and Gerald Dawe, **The Cambridge Companion To Irish Poets** (Cambridge, 2018). Dawe describes "Madame George" as "a dream or vision in Irish folklore."

David Burke, **A Sense of Wonder: Van Morrison's Ireland** (London, 2013) is the best book on Belfast's influence. For Morrison's school years see Johnny Rogan, **Van Morrison: No Surrender** (London, 2005) and Steve Turner, **Van Morrison: It's Too Late to Stop Now** (New York, (1993).

ঙওঙ

PROLOGUE

"Hell is a city much like London -

A populous and smoky city;

There are all sorts of people undone,

And there is little or no fun done; ..."

SHELLEY

"He extends himself only to express himself."

JAY COCKS ON VAN MORRISON

ঙওঙ

Like the poet Percy Shelley, Van Morrison was influenced by the city. It wasn't Shelley's London; it was Northern Ireland's Belfast. Van is alternately pleased and unhappy with his birth city. It forms an indelible influence upon his character. The neighborhood he grew up in is the East Belfast section known as Bloomfield. It was here he came of age in a small, shotgun style home. It was a Protestant neighborhood with a feeling of failure and a decided lack of opportunity.

His bedroom looked out onto a depressing street. Most days the sun was hidden behind Belfast's darkened sky. It is a narrow street amid a cluster of shotgun houses. It is a depressing place to grow up. George Ivan Morrison loved it. It helped form his personality. East Belfast became a barometer for his moods.

Northern Ireland was in Van's soul. He was through and through an Irishman. When he was home in Belfast, he could hear his father, George, rustling around the house. In sharp contrast, his mother, Violet, continually talked with the neighbors. His neighbor, Molly Fee, was usually out in the front of her house talking about the neighborhood news. It was a quiet, orderly and a well-adjusted neighborhood. Van preferred it that way. He was for all intents and purposes a homebody. This presents another side to the Morrison legend. He is shy. He is unassuming. He is private.

He has not lived the raucous life the media portrayed early in his career. Rather, he was a self-indulgent young man with a penchant for intellectual stimulation. His personality is a strange one. He is not cruel. He often ignores the feelings of others. He is completely self-absorbed. He often has visions. He talks of channeling his music. Initially, Van knew very little about William Blake, but he had many of this writer's experiences. There was no vision more persistent than that which came down the street near his home. It was a mystical vision that scared and inspired him. This vision persisted as it drove his creative impulses.

Morrison said a light flashed down the narrow confines of Hyndford Street. This took place early one morning as Van walked up to his home at 124, as the sun peaked through to light the windows. He took that as an omen. Good things were about to happen. As a young man, he couldn't tell people about his mystical images. Later in life, he would confess they had occurred. In interviews. Van talked about how visions inspired his songwriting.

To his friends, the ideas of special dreams, mystical experiences and poetic images were hard to fathom. In his youth, Van had no idea who William Blake was or why he was important. In time, he would forge an eerie identification with this writer.

For Van, Belfast played another role. It provided a sense of nostalgia. This had a dramatic impact upon his personality. Over the years, he would recall the good old days, even if they weren't the best of times.

NOSTALGIA FOR THE OLD BELFAST DAYS

When he lived in the San Francisco Bay Area in the early 1970s, his Irish heritage made him critical and judgmental. It also accentuated his mercurial personality. It intensified his penchant for blowing things out of proportion. The curse of the Irish created problems in his personal relationships. These conflicts carried over into his business life. To some, Van appears selfish and self-indulgent. To others he seems an artist needing his personal space. To still others, he had a personality much like his dad. He was diffident. These traits would not go away. By the age of twenty-one, Van had led his band, Them, to a series of hit records including "Here Comes the Night" and "Gloria." Yet, he made very little money. He was reduced to living for a time with his parents. It was at this point he decided to opt for a solo career.

When he was in Belfast, Van frequently walked down to the Smithfield Market. He went through the small stalls that sold records, sheet music and musical instruments. It was here he bought his first guitar. Then he would wander over the Dougie Knight's bicycle shop and talk to his friends about music.

During these brief trips home, Van often visited with Mervyn Solomon. He was the person who single-handedly placed Them on Decca Records, by introducing the band to Sir Edward Lewis. Mervyn then convinced his brother, Phil Solomon, to manage the band. For his advice and time, Mervyn wanted nothing more than to see Van and Them succeed in the music business. "He possessed an immense talent," Mervyn said.

Van said his father had gone to Detroit to work. He returned home with a cache of jazz and blues records, thereby whetting Morrison's appetite for American music. Van fanaticized about the American life. Van's dad, George, told stories of the music scene in and around Detroit. This was an early catalyst to Van's insatiable interest in the blues.

While he was back in Belfast, Van was fascinated with the local nightlife. The club scene remained vibrant. The musicians appeared to be having fun. There was a sense of new musical directions. At night Van would walk down to the Bloomfield Community Center. As a teenager he played in this nondescript hall. The image of these teen appearances occupied a special part of Van's psyche.

When he walked down to Orangefield School, Van had a fleeting sensation about the old days. In the schoolroom, he paid very little attention. Now he longed for an academic challenge. He was always a voracious reader. He educated himself in historical, religious and literary matters.

With his strong Scottish-Irish accent, Americans had trouble understanding Morrison. It took many years for Van to feel comfortable in the American setting. Once he settled into the Fairfax house north of San Francisco, he became increasingly comfortable.

For Van, Fairfax was a blessing. The town had no parking meters. He frequented the local bookstore, which also sold coffee. There were small restaurants, a softball field where the Grateful Dead played the Jefferson Airplane. The nearby Lion's Share in San Anselmo presented the San Francisco Bay Area's best bands. Van would perform there as he called the club a day before or on the day he wanted to appear. KSAN and college radio stations announced the show. The tickers were gone in an hour. The clubs were not the only Marin County draw. There were songwriters, sound engineers, technicians, roadies, musicians, arrangers, industry insiders and a group of business folks looking to help a fledgling rock star. Van had everything at his fingertips to perfect his music career.

THE SENSE OF AN ULTIMATE OUTSIDER

From the time he began playing in show bands, Van was the ultimate outsider. He considered himself the Ulsterman who didn't want to compromise. The obsessive-compulsive drive to maintain and his musical independence made Van personally difficult.

There was always the sense Van didn't fit into the rock music industry. He didn't label himself a rock and roll singer. He spent the remainder of his career complaining about inaccurate descriptions of his music and persona. He wrote letters to London newspapers from his Holland Park or Notting Hill residences complaining about the inaccurate depictions of his music and career.

It was the sense he was the ultimate outsider that drove Morrison toward success. He continually felt slights. The real and perceived slights drove his lyrical magic. He believed he was not taken seriously. He would show them his talent. He would earn praise from the prurient critics.

While growing up in Belfast, Van had an angelic childhood. He wasn't threatened by the problems the Irish faced. His parents, George and Violet, were important in forming his intellectual core. He had a sense of education without the formal degrees.

When he lived in America, Van's childhood on Hyndford Street seemed far away. The analytic nature of Van's mind developed during these years. He was a thinker. He had the capacity to describe the influences of his Irish heritage in song. The post-war Irish economy and the conflicts inherent in Northern Ireland proved to be the key to his developing personality. Since Van was born in 1945, the year that World War II ended, this impacted his personality. What he read, what he thought, what he ate, what he wore and what he envisioned for the future were locked into this post-World War II era.

BELFAST COME HITHER AND PROTECT ME

Belfast was the ballast to Van's life; he took strength from his birth city. While East Belfast is a depressing area of terrace type houses, it provided Van with a sense of security.

The Protestant streets of Bloomfield were safe and secure. When his parents married on Christmas day 1941 the pattern was set. They isolated themselves from other people. They possessed a strong, insular self. This gave Van an inner strength and a strong feeling of family. When fame and fortune arrived, his Belfast days acted as a buoy to avoid sinking into the morass of fame and fortune. He remained centered.

Van's Scottish-Irish heritage was an integral part of his personality. He was dour, careful with the dollar, opinionated and wary of strangers. His father, George, came from a lineage that emphasized diligence, hard work and honesty. These were important traits manifested in Van's character and personality.

There were also diversions. He would ride his bike down to a path at Orangefield and slowly pedal around the area. Cyprus Avenue, with its opulent homes and middle-class lifestyle, was a favorite stopping point. The park in and around Orangefield was the ballast separating the social-political differences between Protestants and Catholics.

The Protestant area, Orangefield, became an increasingly important symbol in Van's life. He could always depend upon it to calm his nerves. The green grass, the rainy winter days, and the brief moments of sunshine reflected his personality. It was in this environment Morrison began thinking of himself as a mystic.

Sometime in the late 1960s and early 1970s, William Blake provided him with an explanation for his visions. It was Blake who saw religious icons and influences from supernatural phenomena. Van realized he wasn't imagining things. He had the same visions. It was this special way of looking at things as a child that set Van apart from his contemporaries.

He often had anxiety attacks. He told a number of interviewers he didn't think he would live very long. For this reason, he considered entering a monastery.

He was a typical East Belfast young man. He attended services at the Brethren Gospel Hall, when he was very young, and there was always a religious element in his life. As a religious thinker, Van was never dogmatic. Like his mother Violet, he remained a free spirit. Since the Protestant pressures and the Orange Halls were everywhere, Van followed these symbols for a time.

The elegant spire of St. Donard's Church of Ireland looms over East Bloomfield. It casts a pale over the small houses. It is the Protestant reminder of the power of the church. Like a magnificent edifice to religious thought, St. Donard occupies a special place in East Belfast. It also serves as a reminder of the importance of faith. A lesson Van never forgot.

The Protestant Ethic was so strong if you hadn't shopped for food by Saturday, you had to wait until Monday. Catholics had their shops open in the afternoon. This duality puzzled Morrison. He saw it for what is was; the clash of ideology and narrow thinking. Van ignored these problems. He refused to be drawn into arguments on religious subjects. There was a sense of toleration to Morrison. There was also a sense of intellectual isolation.

VIOLET MORRISON AND HER SON'S MUSICAL GENIUS

George Morrison receives the credit for exposing his son to the jazz, blues, country, traditional Irish music and a few pop tunes that defined his musical interests. His mother, Violet, was instrumental in developing his singing talents. She provided the somewhat amateur, but personal, musical performances that inspired her son.

After George and Violet were married, they settled into 124 Hyndford Street. There was always music in the house. It was Violet who continually prodded her son to explore his musical directions. She saw a young boy who needed to be happy. She realized music was the only way to euphoria. She also experimented with religion and urged him to study the paths of different faiths.

Violet Stitt Morrison was born on September 24, 1921 with a mid-wife in attendance at the family home at Belfast's 47 Connswater Street. In **Van Morrison: No Surrender**, Johnny Rogan makes a number of key points about Morrison's mother. The most telling is her artistic and musical ability. Rogan concludes she is the source of Van's creativity. He suggests, via an interview with cousin Jackie Stitt, Van had political interests. Nothing is further from the truth. Van had no political interests.

Van's mother was intellectually inquisitive. She took the message of a large number of preachers and, according to Molly Fee, she believed in faith healing. This wide-ranging intellectual curiosity enabled her to seek out a diverse intellectual life.

Violet Morrison was a free spirit who lacked inhibition. These were not traits that carried over to Van. He remained shy, constrained and at times reclusive. She had the opposite personality.

HOW FAME CAME AND LEFT: 1968 ASTRAL WEEKS

George Ivan Morrison was now known as Van Morrison. He was a solo act no longer fronting the rock band Them. He had a number of hit records. He left the group, Them, and he began his solo career with Bang Records, which yielded the enormous pop hit "Brown Eyed Girl." His association with the label and its chief producer, Bert Berns, soon soured. He was back in Belfast broke, depressed and seemingly at the end of the line.

In 1968, Morrison's career looked like he had hit rock bottom. The short period with Bang Records was controversial with no sign of altering the contract binding him to the label. He felt like a chattel slave. Then Joe Smith of Warner Brothers came to the rescue. He secured a fair and equitable Warner Brothers contract. At least this is what Van thought. It didn't take long for him to realize he didn't control the material on the first three Warner albums. The loss of revenue and control intensified Morrison's desire to control his product. From 1968 to 1972 he did that by evolving into a mainstream act.

When the reissue of **Moondance** came out his ex-wife, Janet Planet, chided her ex-husband for ranting and raving about the reissue. She told Van to get over it. He owned all of his material after the first three Warner albums. He didn't get over it. He continues to complain about lost royalties. Getting paid was the mantra from 1968 to 1972. That was still the case forty years later when he performed **Astral Weeks: Live At The Hollywood Bowl**. When it comes to royalties Van is a one trick pony.

The contradiction in Van's character is he would write a Top 40 hit record and then turn out a tune that had little chance of hitting the charts. This was Van Morrison. He was a bundle of contradictions in a million-dollar songwriting body.

INTO LATE 1967 AND THE TRANSITION TO SOLO STARDOM

In late 1967, Van was tired of Belfast. The weather was cold. His friends lacked talent. They also lacked ambition. He was frustrated. He had lived in Belfast his entire life. With the exception of traveling with the various show bands and going to America for the 1966 Them tour, he returned to Northern Ireland broke. There were other conflicts.

The religious differences in and around Belfast had an impact upon young Morrison. When Van performed with the Regency Show band, he watched the Protestants and Catholics fight each other. This reinforced Van's resolve to remain apolitical. He was a person who had little, if any, interest in politics. He was obsessed with his music, his career and the next phase of his life. He had big plans for recording in America. He decided not to sign with the English Philips label. Then he traveled to America to record for Bert Berns' Bang Records.

Phil Coulter, who would go on to become a popular musician and major BBC presenter in Ireland, recalled Van was torn between remaining in Belfast and moving to London or New York. It was Van's interest in rhythm and blues music that prompted him to sign with Berns and relocate to America.

Coulter was also a musician, songwriter and record producer. He was a traditional Irish musician with a folk-pop sound based in a defined Irish heritage. It was Coulter who alerted record industry insiders to Morrison's multiple talents. Although he was one of Morrison's staunchest supporters there were others who came to the fore. In Belfast Mervyn Solomon and Solly Lipsitz also praised his unique talent.

A persistent myth is Phil Solomon wished Morrison no success in his solo career. The reverse is true. Solomon gave the Belfast Cowboy his blessing. He also released him from a binding contract. No one in London, including Dick Rowe, believed Morrison had a lengthy solo career. There was no reason for Solomon to be hostile to Van. He didn't expect his career to continue to flourish after Them. Solomon was also a wealthy man. He and his wife, Dorothy, were shrewd money managers, excellent judges of talent, and they had a reputation for spotting pop hit making artists. "We didn't need Van Morrison," Phil told me over lunch in his Bournemouth penthouse apartment. "We liked Van, the drama was too much for us," Dorothy smiled and agreed.

In 1983 I sat in Phil Solomon's penthouse apartment in Bournemouth as the Filipino maid served us lunch. Long since retired from the London music scene, Phil, talked at length with his wife, Dorothy, providing comments. They were both happy Morrison was an international star. They wanted the best for him. Phil paused as he ate his salmon. He looked up, like a smiling cherub, he said: "I thought that Van's inability to deal with people would derail his career. I was wrong." For the remainder of the lunch Phil and Dorothy regaled me with stories of how tough it was to make it in the London music business in the mid-1960s. Van made it. They were overjoyed. There were others who talked of the difficulty young artists had surviving in London's musical jungle.

There were musician friends who were important to Morrison. Mick Cox was the most significant fellow musician. It was 1967, Van was not confident about his songwriting. Cox worked with him on his writing. They were close friends. One day Cox was returning from a series of small shows at local Irish country halls with a three-piece band. As they arrived at Van's house at midnight, the Belfast Cowboy's parents were dressed up ready to leave to hear some music. Van and Cox jumped into the Morrison's car. They were off to listen to the McPeake Family. At five in the morning the McPeake Family finished singing traditional Irish songs. Cox observed that this is one of the influences forming Van's musical persona.

In 1967 Cox witnessed Morrison's evolving talent. He recalled that when "Brown Eyed Girl" was released, Van showed up at his apartment on Limestone Road in London unannounced with a 45 in his hand. It was a copy of "Brown Eyed Girl." Cox commented: "This was Morrison's ambition come full circle."

At this point Van wrote Janet Planet he was returning to America. He believed stardom was on the horizon. When the **San Francisco Chronicle** interviewed Janet Planet about hearing "Brown Eyed Girl" on the radio, she remarked: "I sat there in Marin County ... turned on my radio and listened every day."

VAN AND MICK COX: LETTERS EXPLAINING HIS SOLO FUTURE

The Mick Cox friendship was special. Why? It survived because Cox was mellow, non-judgmental and he never said a negative word about the Belfast Cowboy. He was shy. He was quiet. He was much like Van. They were close enough for Morrison to write letters from a New York Hotel. Van talked about his dreams and hopes for the future. Van reminisced at length in one letter about how he wrote his songs in the New York environment.

Van Morrison: "I come into those dimly lit afternoons alone avenues to encounter new dreams one more I answer to myself the selfish self." In this letter Morrison states, he [*sic*] "paralysed right in my own mind." This undated letter was written from the King Edward Hotel in New York. It indicated the depth of his friendship with Cox.

While in New York, Boston, Woodstock and later in Fairfax, California, Morrison kept in touch with Cox. There were six letters Van wrote to Cox while in the U.S. These letters indicate how difficult the early New York, Boston and Woodstock period was for Morrison. He complained about having to stay with friends. He said: "There are about 50 different directions to go." This was in reference to his attempt to create a solo career. In these letters, Morrison described a clear picture of his future.

Van Morrison: "Basically I'm trying to establish something musically and take it from there. … I want to form a happy harmonious band that grooves with each other and enjoys playing the kind of music which they like playing which sounds very complicated …." It wasn't. Van had a vision that turned out to be **Astral Weeks**. In these letters he screams out about Bert Berns. On his Bang Record contract, Van wrote: "I think it's sufficient to say Bert Berns & Bang was a FUCKED UP BAD SCENE."

In these letters there is a Christmas card signed: "Van and Brenda." There are also unpublished pictures of Morrison. Some were taken as the Belfast Cowboy stood behind Jimi Hendrix. The friendship with Cox continued until the former Alleykatz and Eire Apparent member died in 2006. The 1990 Cox album **Compose Yerself** features Van on harmonica.

Van's letters to Cox provide a clue to where he lived for a time in Boston. The address for one letter was 549 Franklin Street in Cambridge Massachusetts. This allows one to identify where he hung out, where he ate and where he lived in the area. Cox visited Morrison until his death. He was tight lipped about their friendship.

This is not the usual relationship Morrison had with friends. He was a lone wolf. He took his time to bond with people. Cox, like Phil Coulter, was an exception. They would get together with their guitars to write, play and record into the night. In later years, Cox would come to New York, Woodstock, the south of France and the San Francisco area to play and live with Morrison. It was in the early to mid-1970s the friendship nurtured Morrison's embryonic talent.

When he settled in Boston for eight months, Van frequently wrote to Cox complaining about lack of money. He wrote: "I'm at present staying at the home of a friend who is interested in management." This letter was written from 549 Franklin Street in Cambridge. Of his new album in progress, which was **Astral Weeks**, Van observed: "I want it to be a lasting thing and not a flash in the pan."

In and around Belfast, Van was too intense for many of the locals. He had a manic drive for success. This did not go over very well with the lazy loafers who hung out in the cafes and music halls. While Van loved Belfast, he has always had a disdain for the local's lack of drive.

Tales of heavy drinking was another aspect of Morrison's last few years in Belfast. While these tales have been blown out of proportion by most of Van's biographers, they offer a window into his personality difficulties. Despite these tales a large number of people in and around Belfast describe Van as quiet, thoughtful and sweet. He is a man of multiple contradictions. This is a key to his songwriting prowess. He weaves lyrical tales reflecting his Irish heritage. The lyrics look deeply into his life. The personality defects many biographers describe are a window into his complex character.

FROM 1968: THE TALENT ROLLS ON

From 1968 to 1972, Van experimented with a wide variety of musical styles. At times influences from the music business darkened and distorted his songwriting. These influences eventually turned out to be a gold mine. Using his life as the catalyst to songwriting, Van's highly personal writing style exploded with emotion. It was a path that led to commercial success.

Morrison was born in an age of musical upheaval. By the 1960s the personal themes, the rock operas, the social freedoms and the growing popularity of rock music helped his career flourish. He had trouble trusting industry people. He found it difficult to secure reliable management, as well as equitable recording contracts. Despite his talent, Van fought to survive in the corporate musical jungle. He had to become a businessman.

When he signed with Warner Brothers, Morrison entered the big time. The label had merged with Seven Arts Productions and the newly named company turned into Warner Bros.-Seven Arts. In many ways it was no longer a music label. Lawyers, movie producers, people who produced cartoons and executives who bankrolled Stanley Kubrick's "Lolita" operated in a corporate atmosphere where the executives knew little to nothing about rock and roll music. They knew even less about Van Morrison.

The most remarkable aspect of Morrison's early career is he survived the one-sided royalty contracts, the outright contract manipulation of his early Warner Brothers albums, and the business tricks that turned profitable rock acts into paupers. He was a business musical neophyte challenging the record industry. Why? He was upset with the general abuse of young artists. He fought back. He mastered the record business. He became a multi-millionaire.

He had a brief marriage to Janet Planet and critics, like Lester Bangs, assumed that his divorce forced him to write hit records. This is another myth. Janet had plenty to do with his hit records. He wrote many of the songs for her. After the divorce he wrote other love songs. It was Van's writing that created his legend. A plausible explanation is the hits were always there. He could turn them on. He could turn them off.

AN IRISH REVOLUTIONARY: BUT NO ONE KNEW IT

The Irish in Van is an integral part of his personality. He is an Irish visionary. This is evident in the images he employs in his lyrics. He has a sense of the Emerald Island, both its past and future. He is a bard emphasizing his Celtic heritage. Whether it is in song, in concert or in interviews, Morrison is always Irish.

Initially, the rules of the rock music world prevented him from emphasizing his Irish heritage. Those who describe Van, as Irish born, but British influenced and American polished, haven't recognized his continual debt to all things Irish. He has had to deal with institutional violence, domination from England, cultural castration from other parts of Ireland and the onus of being a Protestant. These forces coalesced to shape his character. They determined his intellectual direction.

He was also aware of the class differences in and around Belfast. One only has to listen to "Cyprus Avenue" to envision the humiliation, the slights and the sense of inferiority that cropped up from time-to-time because of the Belfast social structure.

Van Morrison has a strong claim to being one of the best songwriter's in rock history. He takes exception to that description. His work is all about story telling. It is in the pleasure of these tales he entertains and educates his fans. Although Morrison has spent his entire career denying his rock and roll roots, they are evident in his music. The problem is he is so diverse, so eclectic and so determined to avoid the mainstream there are often periods, where he is under appreciated.

For those who prefer lyrical beauty, Van is the artist of choice His sense of poetry carries a literary focus. When did Van start writing the poetry that became his legendary cache of songs? In an interview with Fintan O'Toole in 2015, he recalled his early writing days.

Van Morrison: "I was writing poems when I was in school, but I wasn't connecting them to songs yet…. The poems I was writing weren't really songs. They were more like observations, … First there was the poems, and then there were the songs …."

He lacks the usual rock star ego. He is quiet, often self-effacing. Who is Van Morrison? He is the remote provider of intensely pleasurable songs. He is an author whose songs are constantly analyzed for meaning and deep insight. There is a kind of exhaustion and bewilderment when one examines Van's work. It is an oeuvre which has been extensively analyzed to death. It is also a huge body of work. Van doesn't want it interpreted.

The songs he writes are more like literary novels than simple-minded rock and roll. Van battled his labels to make sure his music translated into his final vision. He continually berates the distasteful promotions, the juvenile advertising and the idiotic hype that is a part of rock music. The machinations of the record labels receive the brunt of his criticism. He is concerned his message will go unnoticed. His musical tales leave no place to hide. What he says in song is real and sometimes hurtful. For fifty plus years, Van's tunes have hit the mark.

He provides the critical elements for subliminally intelligent rock music. His growth as an artist from 1968 onward suggests his metamorphosis into a superb creator. The complexity of his songs moves him into new directions. From time-to-time he has dabbled in rockabilly, blues, country, rhythm and blues, Celtic, jazz and good old rock and roll.

THE LITERARY AND MORAL VAN MORRISON

In 1964, Van Morrison met Mervyn Solomon. They struck up an immediate friendship. Solomon became Van's earliest mentor. Not only had Solomon played drums in a show band, he was a mover and shaker in local entertainment circles. He owned a series of record stores; an Irish record label, Emerald, and he was Elvis Presley's first Irish RCA distributor. Solomon provided an entre card for Morrison into the record business. Solomon was the first person to suggest the literary side of rock and roll. "When I mentioned his gift with words," Mervyn told me, "Van was nervous. He didn't like praise." While Solomon talked with Solly Lipsitz they often had coffee or drinks visiting over Morrison's writing capabilities. They agreed he was a monster talent. This was in the mid-1960s long before fame and fortune thrust that mantle on the Belfast Cowboy.

I spent a number of days in Solomon's home listening to early Van Morrison tapes. He was not only a fan, he helped Morrison's career quietly remaining in the background. With his stately appearance, good manners and encyclopedic knowledge of the Belfast music industry, Solomon had an unblemished reputation. This wasn't the case in the U.K. music scene.

Why did Morrison confide in and talk openly with Solomon? Solomon's integrity impressed Morrison. He pursued an equitable and moral vision in the entertainment business. Mervyn told Van that equitable contracts led to a lengthy career. Long before they talked music, Mervyn talked business. Van never forgot the lessons. Solomon was the type of person Van could emulate. He did!

After some time, Mervyn introduced Van to his brother, Phil, and the result was Van's garage band, Them, signed with the Solomon Organization. This quickly led to a contract with Decca Records. From their offices on London's New Oxford Street, Phil and his lovely wife, Dorothy, began merchandising Them and Van's music. It wasn't long before the rock and roll world was referring to the lead singer and songwriter, Van Morrison, as a literary figure.

During the early part of his career, Van wittingly established a literary persona. It is in the use of language Morrison is most adept. He writes in **Astral Weeks** of entering the "viaducts of your dreams." The idea he was born again, not only runs through the song, it posits he is entering another world. That world is about to emerge in New York, Boston, Woodstock and Fairfax. It is as a writer, not necessarily as a performer, Morrison envisioned his future. "To be born again," Van writes, is what kept him alive in the transition from anonymity to stardom.

In the 1970s, Van's life took on the perplexity of a three-ring circus, as he began weaving his dreams into song form. The result is a complex musical environment. He rejected predictable notions of stylistic unity. His tunes are a wild, gorgeous ride through intricate themes. These themes are woven into Van's life. They are the central reason for his existence.

Van writes from a spiritual and moralistic world. This moralism reflects the problems and tensions of the day. When Van talks about entering a monastery, he demonstrates the perils and pitfalls of being a rock star. His poetic gifts and spiritual resilience forged a fifty-plus year career knowing few boundaries. He started writing from a very early age. He maintains notebooks to the present day. In these pages, he jots down ideas, he begins new songs, and he places his images into the public domain. It is his way of maintaining his sanity in the rock and roll marketplace. Even though he screams out that he is not a rock artist.

His songs are so esoteric they are open to multiple interpretations. Van claims he is little more than a cipher. He channels his feelings. He refuses to describe himself as a song poet. That is a job he leaves to the professors. He remarks there are many different forms of inspiration. Even he doesn't understand the forces shaping his music. There is a muse somewhere, Van has stated repeatedly during interviews, that muse drives his songwriting.

Van Morrison's position is a lonely one. He never rides with the trends, nor takes advantage of all of his commercial opportunities. This is one of the paradoxes of his life; he has received honors, acclaim and recognition. These accolades make him uncomfortable. Fame has been a mixed blessing. Because of what he calls "the fame game," Van continually changes his career and musical direction.

THE VAN MORRISON MODE

There is the Van Morrison mode. That is the man who sees life through his work. His life is his oeuvre. There is a vivid and tangible direction to his music. He has become famous while remaining a curmudgeon. Working primarily in England, Ireland and America, he has established an unrivalled musical legacy. His music is always fresh. He continually creates new intellectual directions. Van has paid the price for this success. Fame has robbed him of his privacy. He lives in a veritable cocoon.

He is a virtuoso musician whose recordings fill a special niche in the music business. His sublime and beautiful song sketches tell us a great deal about his world. He dabbles in forms of literature. He is a critic of things personal. Morrison is witty and penetrating. He is also a confirmed romantic. He ponders problems in his writing. His critics use his life to define his songs.

From 1968 through 1972, Van Morrison transcended age, generational division and changes in popular tastes to remain in the vortex of the music industry. Van continued to develop themes of religion, loneliness and despair in much the same way Frank Sinatra had in the 1940s and 1950s.

It was in the half dozen years after leaving Bang Records that Van developed into a consummate showman. The reviewers early on failed to recognize his in-concert brilliance. He remained at times temperamental. To the fans, however, it is a religious experience to attend a Morrison show. As Van said many times, he works to attract a loyal audience. "Otherwise they will want the flavor of the month," he told guitarist Chris Michie. He had a spiritual sense of his future.

Religion was a ballast to Morrison. It allowed him to focus upon what was important in his life. With extensive reading in Buddhism, the Jehovah's Witness sect, Scientology and various forms of Christian theology, Van reached an intellectual maturity rare in the rock music field. The Van Morrison mode is complex.

THEMES OF A MATURING ARTIST

The years from 1968 through 1972 saw Van mature as a writer, a performing artist and as a person. He was often rude, arrogant, prone to temper tantrums, and he had difficulty getting along with people. At the next moment he can be a prince. He is a person of multiple contradictions who matured. He is not the hopelessly diffident person many journalists perceive. There is another side to the Belfast Cowboy.

Interviews with those close to Van tell another story. While he changes managers, booking agents, musicians, girlfriends and record companies at will, he has remained loyal to his old Belfast, London, Cambridge, Woodstock, San Francisco, Bath and Dublin friends. Van is a more complicated individual than biographers suggest.

There are two themes running through Van's work, mysticism and religion. Or is this one theme? Built into this is a newfound appreciation for romantic poetry and a reflective philosophy. Evelyn Underhill's book on mysticism, published in 1911, was one of the first to intrigue Morrison. The Underhill book had a message impacting Morrison's thought. She wrote: "We are all the kindred of the mystics. … Strange and far away from us though they seem, they are not cut off from us by some impassable abyss." Where and when did Van discover the Underhill book?

It was when he visited the home and studio of an old Belfast friend, Cecil McCartney, that Van adopted the term mysticism. McCartney has said his paintings, his life style, his reading habits and his over the top abstract painting made a lasting impression upon Morrison. Van denies this characterization.

In 1963 Morrison met McCartney. They became acquaintances. Van was eighteen and McCartney was twenty-four. For the next twenty-five years they had an occasional drink. They were not close friends. Cecil McCartney was the type of hanger-on Morrison detested. Cecil was a pop artist. He dabbled in music with an album **OM** released on Columbia in 1968. He was no more than a petulant sideshow in the

London scene. What is the point of Cecil McCartney's friendship? He was the type of person driving Morrison crazy trying to hang on to the celebrity train. This explains why Van at times is irritable and cranky.

When Cecil and Van ended their friendship in 1989, they were drinking at the Crawforsburn Inn in County Down, Northern Ireland. They began discussing a murder case involving Myra Hindley. She was a murderess who became a Christian. McCartney questioned her religious conversion. Van took exception. He told McCartney Christianity could provide a new life. Then Van threw his keys at his friend and left the pub. They never spoke again. McCartney has gone to the press offering a painting as a peace offering. Van never responded. He didn't need friends using him for celebrity purposes.

The tall tales Cecil McCartney spun did little to endure him to Morrison. Steve Turner, one of Morrison's most perceptive biographers, relayed McCartney's story that some of his drawings had an astral projection. This is nothing more than self-serving drivel. What makes McCartney odious is he continually re-invented the story and improved upon it. It was well thought out nonsense. It appears Steve Turner bought McCartney's story hook, line and sinker.

HOW AND WHY VAN MATURED AS AN ARTIST

How did Van evolve into one of the most acclaimed entertainers in the business? The reason is talent and a blue-collar work ethic. He has matured as a songwriter. As a performer he continued to fine tune his concert act. Van's transcendent maturity is ignored at times by reviewers. This is because of his penchant for tirades. While not always warranted, these outbursts suggest his hostility to the print media. He reads everything biographical about his career. When a book or article delves into his private life he explodes. Sometimes he can't contain his disdain for the opinions of others. At other times he pursues legal action. He sued Clinton Heylin over his biography. Lawsuits in the U.K. and the U.S. failed to prevent publication of Heylin's biography. They continue in a war of words to the present day.

One of Van's personality traits is his ability to criticize. He is a cogent critic of what goes on around him. Much of what passes for literary rock and roll criticism these days is self-aggrandizing nonsense.

Witness the recent rumor that Bono was to head the World Bank. He would have trouble locating it. In pompous surrealistic tones, Bono stated he was ready to take over. Fortunately, Van does not take himself as seriously, hence, he does not wind up looking like a fool.

Morrison's intricate and self-assured songs tell us a great deal about his life. There are organizing themes in Van's work. The notion of religious influences, lost love, puppy love, found love, as well as betrayal, disrespect and false friends run through his lyrics. He comes from a background of intense, precise and picturesque observations of life. His lyrics and music exist in the borderlands between realism and romance. He combines these themes time and time again. Van argues his songs are an exercise in realism.

He is an impulsive writer with an intense view of the world. He has few close friends. He often equates friendship with a desire to know him because of his fame. He is alternately paranoid and pleasant with friends. No one seems to know the real Van. Which may suggest his mood swings prevent him from establishing a clear and predictable personality. What is ironic about Van is he is a moralistic crusader on a personal stage.

If any rock musician has earned the right to occasional pomposity, it is Van Morrison. This is a small price to pay for the exchange of marvelous music and inspiring concerts. Morrison uncensored is what his career became from 1968 to 1972. He found his commercial niche in the music business. He could do as he pleased. He has!

LITERARY BIOGRAPHY: IS ALL BIOGRAPHY FICTION?

When Samuel Johnson wrote his terse sentences on the English poets, the tangled lives of the Romantic literary generation, he became a publishing phenomenon. Then the literary biographers exhausted their material. This led to the rise of fictional biography bringing a new dimension to the genre. Van Morrison states his biographers practice a form of fiction. While this is not generally true, it does make a point. What are the methods of rock biographies?

The rock biographer faces challenges. There are few archival letters. For this book I quoted for sale Morrison letters from auction houses employing fair usage. There were also letters shared with me written by and to Morrison from close associates. The rock and roll press, and in Van's case the mainstream media is filled with material. Band members, roadies, producers, engineers and industry insiders cooperated. To Van all biography is fiction. He believes if he doesn't write it, there is no need for the book.

A. S. Byatt's **Possession** and Julian Barnes' **Flaubert's Parrot** challenged biographical methods, as they examined lives from a fictional viewpoint. Once again Van's notion that all biography is fiction comes to mind. When James Boswell wrote his biography of Samuel Johnson, he was a celebrity stalker. Once again Morrison charges that this is the case among his biographers. It is a solid point. Is the archival past real or imagined?

The answer to that question is a complicated one. The recollections of friends, colleagues and those who wish him ill makes the biographical record vague. Van hates Clinton Heylin's biography. He loves Steve Turner's book. Why? Heylin was hypercritical. Turner is a Christian writer who was more charitable toward Morrison. Those close to Van said he was flummoxed by the Johnny Rogan and Greil Marcus studies. He couldn't make heads or tails of either book. He loved Peter Mills' account. Brian Hinton's study brought approval from Van. It came out at a time Van was experimenting with different religions.

WHAT IS MORRISON'S SEMINAL INFLUENCE?

What is Van's seminal influence? It is one with multiple answers. First, he is the consummate songwriter. Second, he evolved into the ultimate performer. Third, he took care of business. Fourth, he approached the industry on his own terms. Fifth, he became one of the earliest rock and roll writers to use literary themes. Sixth, he took over the role of record company executive to run his own empire. Seventh, he became his own publicist while complaining about and controlling a large part of the rock and roll press.

The richness and vitality of Van's music continues as he evolves into his mid-70s. He shows no sign of slowing down. He encourages others to depart from time tested and simplistic musical themes. This is an insight into his longevity. He has never traveled the hit waters. Rather Van's seminal influence is on the genre. That genre is the singer-songwriter who continues as a performer.

His songs are a short story into his life. His reverberating images contain the essence of his life. It is an act of musical faith when he writes a song.

SEARING AMBITION AND AN AVERAGE LIFE

Van Morrison, the singer, deserves praise for his lyrical interpretations, his musical fortitude and his battles to retain his intellectual property. He is prone to personal attacks. He continually complains about lost royalties. He has a penchant for overstatement.

In numerous interviews, Van stated he lives an average life. He is a person who likes to go to the same coffee shop, reads the same newspapers, and scours the same type of books as he develops his intellect. He leads a controlled and healthy life.

He is a wonderful person with his daughter, Shana, and the two children he had with Michelle Rocca. He has never shirked his family obligations. He shares custody of the two children with Michelle Rocca. His ex-wife has been unfair by looking at Van's touring schedule and telling him he can have the children during those times. It is a testy relationship. The divorce threw Morrison into his blue-collar work mode. He needed more money to pay for Michelle's over the top demands. She filed a motion to have his Mill Valley home placed in her name. Shana lives there. Rocca didn't get the house. Van's lawyers didn't beat down the requests for nannies, maids, yard workers, personal shoppers and who knows what else. Michelle Rocca has never worked a day in her life. There are two previous long-term relationships that were financially beneficial to Rocca. The stress and financial machinations from the divorce took five years. The finalization of the divorce wasn't until February 2018. Van is a good father sharing custody of his two young children while living a busy Belfast life. Here lies the contradiction. He is a warm family man. He is a staunch friend who is a lion with those who engage him in the music industry. His searing ambition knows no compromise.

1

There is no soft pedaling the periodic rages that are in Morrison's psyche. He will at times complain to someone for some time if he is talked about without his permission. When Janet Planet discussed **Astral Weeks**, Van was at times testy with family and friends. His raging has declined with age and maturity.

If Van has a problem it is with his career. He doesn't see his fame and his place in the music industry. He still visualizes the dollars that he has missed collecting, the slights that attempt to marginalize his music and the nasty critics who simply don't get his musical direction.

The use of language is one of Van Morrison's signature talents. He is an extraordinarily talented writer. How and why did this take place for a young man who left school at fourteen? The answer is not a simple one. Van is a historian disguised as an observer. He was able in lyrical song form to take Irish sensibilities and translate them to the American shore.

BIBLIGRAPHICAL SOURCES

During interviews Van is often not forthcoming. That has changed since 2008. One of the best interviews took place when an Irish journalist sat down in 2015 for a relaxed and lengthy talk. See Fintan O'Toole, "Van Morrison: 'Being Famous Is Not Great For the Creative Process. Not For Me, Anyway'," **The Irish Times**, August 29, 2015. https://www.irishtimes.com/culture/music/van/van-morrison-being-famous-is-not-great-for-the-creative-process-not-for-me-anyway-1.2332216

This prologue was helped by conversations over the years with Molly Fee, Chris Michie, Simon Gee, Shel Talmy, Steve Rowland, P. J. Proby, Violet Morrison, Phil Solomon, Mervyn Solomon, Tony Dey, Mark Naftalin, Art Siegel, Pat Thomas, Terry Rissman, John Platania and Haik Arakail.

See David Burke, **A Sense of Wonder: Van Morrison's Ireland** (London, 2013) for a wonderful book exploding myths about his career. He sees Belfast and Ireland as a mythical place. This attitude obviously influenced Morrison.

On the controversy or the friendship with Cecil McCartney see, for example, Henry McDonald, "My Peace Offering To Van Morrison," **London Guardian**, February 11, 2006.

https://www.theguardian.com/uk/2006/feb/12/arts.artsnews Also see a record that shows another side of this ubiquitous artist, Cecil McCartney, "Hey Alethia, I Want You + Liquid Blues, 1968." https://www.youtube.com/watch?v=Tp-o3nau5Mc This song was on an early and very rare early 1970s album **OM** and McCartney also had two singles. He was dismissed as attempting to ride in on the coattails of his distant cousin Sir Paul McCartney. Although it is a brief description of Cecil McCartney's bluster, swagger and piffle see David Burke, **A Sense of Wonder: Van Morrison's Ireland** (London, 2013), pp. 197-98. McCartney is a case study of those who hang out with Van and then suggest they have influenced his art. Whether or not Cecil McCartney is even a distant relative of Sir Paul McCartney is in serious question. What he represents is the hanger-on types driving Van Morrison to bluster and call out the phonies in his private life and in song. What is tragic concerning McCartney is his mania to present Van with an eight foot by four-foot painting to somehow repair their ruptured friendship. Rather than approach Van, this wanker, Cecil McCartney, cries out to the press that he can't understand why Morrison is furious. Cecil's comments to the press suggest one reason why Van is difficult and how his personality is volatile at times. When the **London Guardian** editorialized McCartney was the artist who inspired **Astral Weeks** and influenced the **Enlightenment** album, Van went bonkers. He wasn't sure whether he was angry with the **Guardian** or with McCartney. One can only speculate he was furious with both of them.

See Steve Turner, **Too Late To Stop Now** (London, 1993), p. 89 for the Cecil McCartney revelations. Also see Paul Szabady, "Astral Weeks By Van Morrison," **Stereo Times**, May 9, 2012. This article originally was published in 2004.

Van Morrison's mysticism is a well-known aspect of his music. It is also an integral part of his personality. See Evelyn Underhill, **Mysticism: A Study of the Nature and Development of Man's Spiritual Consciousness** (New York, 1911, 12th edition, 1930) and Underhill's **Practical Mysticism** (New York, 1914, Vintage Reprint New York, 2003). Underhill is one of the hidden influences in Van's intellectual maturation and her books increased the sophistication in his songwriting. Underhill popularized Western Mysticism. Another important influence on Van Morrison is the 16th Century Spanish mystic and poet St. John of the Cross whose poem "Dark Night Of The Soul" is captured in a number of Van's songs. When Morrison writes about the "dark night of the soul" in "Tore Down A La Rimbaud" on the **A Sense of Wonder** album and "Give Me My Rapture" on **Poetic Champions Compose** he paid tribute to these influences. "Tore Down A La Rimbaud" takes its title from the French poet Arthur Rimbaud. Van said it took him eight years to write the song. "I'd been reading him [Rimbaud] when I got the original idea. The idea is ten or twelve years old, and I just rewrote it." Also see, John Collis, **Inarticulate Speech of the Heart** (Boston, 1996), pp. 160-162. In "Tore Down A La Rimbaud," Morrison wrote: "Won't you guide me through the dark night of the soul." These thoughts and lyrics were percolating in his psyche from 1968 to 1972 as he continued to write in his notebooks. The creative brilliance of this half a decade period set the stage for the large number of unreleased songs, the cache of ideas for new songs that are in his notebooks and the roadmap for his future. The Mystic's Music is not a misnomer. Van Morrison's blue-collar hard-working mentality was a key to his future success. That success was guaranteed with his 24/7 workaholic habits from 1968 through 1972.

The Van Morrison letters quoted in this chapter were put up for public auction in the U.K. They were from the estate of Mick Cox, 1943-2008. One of the most interesting is a letter from the Meriton Hotel, 58th West Street, New York City. It was in this letter that Van poured out his heart and soul about Bert Berns betrayal, his plans for a new band, his ideas on music and the difficulty he had living in the U.S. The London agent Bonhams put the material up for auction in 2013. The asking price was from $1900 to $2600. No public information is available on the sale or the buyer. Another London memorabilia agent, The Saleroom.com placed a two-page letter from Morrison to Cox up for auction in 2016. This letter is valuable as it shows Cox wrote to Van who was moving continually in the U.S. These letters offer rare insights into the struggles, the innate difficulties and the manner in which Morrison beat the music industry at its own game.

PART I

THE BACKGROUND TO A SOLO CAREER: WHY
AND HOW VAN'S LIFE IS MISINTERPRETED

CHAPTER 1

VAN BACKSTAGE AT ASTRAL WEEKS LIVE: FINALLY, ROYALTIES ON HIS CLASSIC ALBUM

"He seeks to transcend the apparent boundaries of any given song."

GREIL MARCUS

"T. B. Sheets is a great album of which seven of the eight songs are about Van Morrison and a girl he loves."

JESSICA HOPPER

"Beyond the back door was a view of mountainsides in the moonlight. I let out a yahoo. The night was on."

JACK KEROUAC, ON THE ROAD

❧❧

The announcement Van Morrison would perform his legendary **Astral Weeks** album live forty years after its release surprised everyone. That is everyone except Morrison. He had thought of reinventing it for years. By 2008 his body of work was legendary. Nothing eclipsed **Astral Weeks**. His four live albums were well received, but the anticipation of **Astral Weeks: Live At The Hollywood Bowl** was over the top.

Why **Astral Weeks Live**? The album was owned by Warner Brothers. For forty years Van talked about the pain and the turmoil associated with a cult album that didn't sell but went on to define his career. He was still pissed about the money. Or the lack of it from Warner Brothers. One of Morrison's dominant personality traits is to stew, complain and carry on about a slight real or imagined. This one was real. He had to give up a portion of control of his songwriting and publishing royalties to escape the prison the Bert Berns' Bang Record contract placed him in during the late 1960s. In 1968 when Warner signed him to a label friendly agreement, Van was promised creative control. That didn't happen. Now it was time to get even. He would perform **Astral Weeks** the way it was originally intended.

As he planned for the album the decision was made to piece two live shows together. These were the Hollywood Bowl shows. Hence, the title **Van Morrison: Astral Weeks, Live At The Hollywood Bowl**. There was only one rehearsal prior to the shows. Van told the band there would be no post-production engineering.

Van Morrison: "The Hollywood Bowl concerts gave me a welcome opportunity to perform these songs the way I originally intended them to be … There are certain dynamics you can get in live recordings that you cannot get in a studio recording … There was a distinct alchemy happening on that stage in Hollywood."

In 2008 Morrison was a grizzled veteran of the rock and roll world. He knew the importance of a compliant media. This began the new Van Morrison. A whirlwind interview schedule in 2008-2009 inaugurated a rock star eager to let the press know their past mistakes were forgiven. Van wanted to correct the record. Along the way Van provided personal insights into his career. With some journalists, butter would not melt in his mouth. Van's interviews at the swank Beverly Hills Hotel were forthcoming ones. He also found a brilliant and fair-minded journalist in the **Los Angeles Times'** Randy Lewis. For the next decade Van gave some of his best interviews to Lewis. The reason? It was simple! The Belfast Cowboy wanted to set the record straight.

Van found Lewis so knowledgeable he hired him as a consultant to his **Listen To The Lion Records** label. This journalist became an adviser in the production of the album and the DVD. It was money well spent.

Van wondered why the biographers had failed to consult him for their lengthy books. He appeared to be talking about Johnny Rogan's

Van Morrison: No Surrender, published in 2005. Or perhaps the 2002 Clinton Heylin biographical hit piece. He remarked to **Los Angeles Times** reporter Randy Lewis, as well as Scott Foundas, that he couldn't understand why those who wrote books didn't contact him. The biographers mystified him. Those of us who write about Van have more of a chance to talking to the Pope than to Morrison. That is fine. The lyrics in his songs as well as observations in interviews suggest how and why Van has this skewered view of the biographical process.

VAN SITS DOWN WITH THE PRESS EXPLAINING WHY ASTRAL WEEKS, 2008

When asked: "Why **Astral Weeks Live**?" Van responded: "I had always wanted to do these songs fully orchestrated and live." When a **Los Angeles Times** reporter asked: "What's your thought ... about the boldness of a 22-year-old ... with some rock hits ... going into a New York studio with the likes of Downbeat's jazz bassist of the year (Richard Davis), the Modern Jazz Quartets' drummer Connie Kay and one of Charlie Mingus' collaborators guitarist Jay Berliner?" Without missing a beat Morrison responded: "The music on Astral Weeks required these great musicians." It was a concept album. It was like no other in rock history. Playing with legendary jazz studio and solo artists was not on the landscape for rock musicians. Morrison made it his mantra. Van didn't lose touch with these jazz greats. Connie Kay played drums on "Tupelo Honey" and "Listen to the Lion." Van Morrison: "Connie was the best drummer I have run across yet." He continues to praise them, to hire them and to make sure the world knows they were important in his rise to commercial prominence. The pain from the early **Astral Weeks** failure remains a constant.

As Morrison sat with a **Los Angeles Times** reporter forty years after **Astral Weeks**, he reflected on the original album. Van said he had misgivings about Bert Berns, the Bang years and even the first Warner Brothers album. On Lewis Merenstein, Van observed: "I did not have a choice at the time. I was all the way on the ground." Van elaborated stating his New York life was a precarious one. He had no money. He had few friends. He had gangsters hanging out daily at his hotel. He spent his time preparing the songs for **Astral Week** in New York. They were still unfinished when he relocated to Boston. After eight months in Boston it was back to New York. The planning and formalizing of the final product took place over a three-year period from 1965 to 1968. As Van recalled the seminal year was 1968, but it was the eight months in Boston where the precision in rewriting the songs, setting the music and planning the sequencing of tunes made **Astral Weeks** work. As Van spoke there was a sense of past memories and anger in his voice. After forty years he still felt the **Astral Weeks** album did not belong to him.

Did Van Morrison write his songs years before he produced them and does he continue to collect and archive his material? Yes! He continues to have material in his archives from that period. He said a number of songs with drummer Connie Kay remain unreleased.

During conversations with a number of journalists, Bert Berns and Lewis Merenstein were criticized. On Merenstein's production, Van denied it. "I wrote it all, put it all where it needed to be." He respected Berns' abilities. He said Berns was interested only in pop hits. He had a coterie of bookies, pimps, record industry criminals and other unsavory characters hanging around him. Berns and his friends made Van nervous. They frightened Janet Planet. The mob compromised Berns' reliability and tainted his artistry.

When asked if his second Warner album, **Moondance**, was a sharp departure, Morrison said: "First of all 'Moondance' was written by me in 1965, as an instrumental ..." That said Morrison explained there is no sequencing to his songs or his albums. He concluded: "I have always played what I feel like playing whenever I feel like playing it."

Since he would perform **Astral Weeks Live**, Van reflected on the album forty years later, as he prepared for the live shows. The songs, according to Van, were "poetry and mythical musicians channeled from my imagination." He continued to use the same techniques in 2008. He said **Astral Weeks** is "sort of like "Astral Decades ...."

During an interview with Randy Lewis, Van didn't hesitate when asked what the lyrics to **Astral Weeks** meant. This is a question he abhors. The new Van reiterated the spiritual connection the music has is with his psyche. He did have one regret. He wished he had "the timbre of John Lee (Hooker) and I wouldn't mind I sounded like Lead Belly." Van's roots continued to define his musical soul.

As he reminisced about musicians, Van said he would have "loved for Miles Davis to have played on a record of mine."

COMPLAINING ABOUT LEWIS MERENSTEIN FORTY YEARS LATER AND OTHERS

There are few slights, mistakes or poor decisions in Morrison's career he doesn't revisit. In doing so he shares his anguish. In the case of Lewis Merenstein, he told the **Los Angeles Times** "Merenstein came about when my back was against the wall." He observed: "When success comes 'the sharks in disguise' show up to derail your career." This was a reference to the hardball legal tactics Ilene Berns played with Van after Bert's death. She forced him into a compromise settlement on the Bang contract. This deprived Morrison of some of his royalties in a deal favorable to her interests. Van was upset losing out to Bert Berns' widow.

He let the **Los Angeles Times** know the critics had it wrong about **Astral Weeks**. Those who said it was conceived in Boston, those who said it was written on the spur of the moment in New York and those who gave Lewis Merenstein too much credit, they were all wrong.

Van Morrison: "**Astral Weeks** are little poetic stories I made up and set to music. The album is about song craft for making things up and making them fit to a tune I have arranged." To quiet the critics as to how, when and why he wrote his legendary album which was inherently different from anything on the market, Van said: "Astral Weeks' songs were written over a period of time—some early 1966—and evolved musically." Then he made it clear he had a plan for reinventing **Astral Weeks Live**.

THE INITIAL PLAN FOR ASTRAL WEEKS LIVE

The initial plan was to have Van appear on November 7 and 8, 2008 at the Hollywood Bowl along with one or two original musicians. Morrison's production company, **Listen To The Lion Records**, announced a DVD of the concert as well an album that would be released in 2009. The show was carefully scripted and advertised. The

New York Daily News announced the album was "one of the five most anticipated pop events of 2009."

Although there was only one rehearsal prior to the show, one musician told me he had never met Van. That musician said he had not met Van but could follow him with the charts. He did not need more than one rehearsal. Morrison wanted the CD and DVD to sound like it did when the audience sat listening to it.

The Hollywood Bowl shows were so well received, Morrison scheduled two concerts at the WaMu Theater at Madison Square Garden. He continued the live shows on March 3 and 4, 2009 at New York's Beacon Theater. Along the way he spoke with journalists, he appeared on Late Night With Jimmy Fallon performing "Sweet Thing," as he finished this whirlwind promotional, love fest with the media. **Astral Weeks** was back. Van Morrison owned it.

After the two Hollywood Bowl shows, Van continued to perform twenty-one versions of **Astral Weeks Live**. It was artistically successful. He finally received his just royalties. When Morrison took **Astral Weeks Live** to London in early 2009, he sat down with the **London Telegraph's** Scott Foundas. Morrison's explanation covers a lot of ground concerning the re-emergence of **Astral Weeks**.

Van Morrison: "I've never played live with any of the people who were on the original recording; I've never done any live gigs with those people. … this recording keeps coming up all the time-in top tens and polls and various things. There's a demand for it from the audience. There're loads of reasons why. That's enough for me, …"

ASTRAL WEEKS IS BACK: NOVEMBER 2008

Why did Van Morrison decide to redo his **Astral Weeks Live**? He wanted the material broadcast over a Public Radio Broadcasting outlet. The shows, from the Hollywood Bowl, were scheduled to be broadcast live over KCRW. This is not only the first live international broadcast from the Hollywood Bowl; it is the first time Van agreed to a live international broadcast.

KCRW 89.9 on the FM dial was an odd choice to broadcast the concert. It is a Santa Monica based public radio station. This was in line with Morrison's thinking. He wanted a non-commercial outlet.

His company, "Listen To The Lion Records," filmed the show for a DVD. The subsequent release **Astral Weeks Live At The Hollywood Bowl** was critically acclaimed. There is a promised documentary that has yet to hit the marketplace. The album rose to number one on the **Billboard Internet** album listing. It was thirty-three on the U.S. **Billboard 200** and number thirty-six on the Austrian album chart.

The Hollywood Bowl shows received extensive publicity as the original bassist, Richard Davis and guitarist, Jay Berliner were announced to recreate their parts. Davis had a family emergency. He didn't appear. There were other changes. Peter Erskine was scheduled to appear on drums as Connie Kay, the Modern Jazz Quartet's drummer, passed away in 1994. Bobby Ruggiero replaced Erskine. The two-set concert featured a band of musicians familiar with Morrison's music including bassist David Hayes, drummer Rick Schlosser, flutist and saxophonist Ritchie Buckley and organist and horn player Paul Moran. Tony Fitzgibbon was brought in on violin and viola. In Van's search for new musicians, Michael Graham was hired to play cello. Graham is a Yale University graduate. He is a master teacher at a number of universities. He is also a member of the Oakland Symphony.

Roger Kellaway, the former music director for Bobby Darin, led the band. Not surprisingly, Van had another band ready if this one didn't work.

The second band featured Jay Berliner on guitar, David Hayes on bass, Bobby Ruggiero on drums as well as Buckley, Moran, Fitzgibbon and a string section. Why two bands? Van hasn't answered that question.

After forty plus years **Astral Weeks** continued to achieve cult status. According to Steven Van Zandt, the album was a guiding point for bands from Bruce Springsteen and the E Street Band to U-2. Looking back from the vantage point of 2008, Van told **Rolling Stone:** "The album is sophisticated poetry that I set to multilayered musical arrangements, dynamic melodies coarse through every song."

In the week prior to the Hollywood Bowl shows, Van met with the press. He began the interview by calling "Brown Eyed Girl," "the money song." Van smugly remarked: "They got the money and I got none." This was a swipe at Bert Berns. It made everyone chuckle. Van made it clear the **Astral Weeks Live** CD would be a project standing on its own merits. "I am not revisiting it really, as this is a totally different project."

Van sat down with the alternative or counter culture newspaper, the **Los Angeles Weekly**, for a rare one on one interview to promote the November 2008 **Astral Weeks** concerts. The first point Morrison made was this was not ancient history. It was a new twist on past material.

During the **Los Angeles Weekly** interview, Van vented concerning his biographers. This interview with the **Los Angeles Weekly** took place at the posh Beverly Hills Hotel. Morrison showed up resplendent in unfriendly behavior by lumping all of his books into "unauthorized pseudo-biographies." He spent an hour with the reporter. He made a strong case for reinterpreting **Astral Weeks**. He also talked about how his audience helps him stretch out his material. Van is famous for a ninety-minute set as required by the contract. From time to time, he will continue on for another ten or fifteen minutes. As Van concluded this interview, he reminded the reporter that his job was "to turn lead into gold." Obviously, the Belfast Cowboy in 2008 was supremely confident about his ability to reinterpret **Astral Weeks Live**.

ASTRAL WEEKS LIVE: THE PRODUCTION AND VAN'S COMMENTS

Once **Astral Weeks Live** was announced, Morrison was prepared for the moment. The one rehearsal was a perfect way to set up the material. He would open with a series of random songs. Then after the intermission **Astral Weeks Live** took center stage. Morrison emphasized he was the producer. After forty years he remained angry over Merenstein's post-production alterations. He had other thoughts on live recordings. "There are certain dynamics you can get in live recordings that you cannot get in a studio recording. ... There was a distinct alchemy happening on that stage in Hollywood. I felt it."

Jessica Pilot asked: "How long did it take to write the material?" Morrison said of the songs: "These were written prior to '68 over a period of five years." That ends the notion he wrote the songs in Boston. He did add the finishing touches to **Astral Weeks** in Boston.

Morrison worked on **Astral Weeks** for half a decade. He presented the material to Bert Berns. The Bang Record chief wasn't sure the songs were commercial. Lewis Merenstein was the only person who believed in the concept. Why? Merenstein was a jazzman. He loved the jazz implications. Warner Brothers management had no clue as to Morrison's genius. The sessions were inexpensive ones. Schwaid-Merenstein bore some of the studio costs. Forty years later, Warner Brothers looked like a genius label. That wasn't the case.

As he looked back on forty years of **Astral Weeks**, Van reflected: "I have always been my own producer, so everything has always been in my hands. I have always had the say. … My music has a life of its own that does not take well to other people's ideas …" That said Van closed the interview with the observation: "I am a writer; therefore, I write." For the next decade he has shown this statement to be true. When Jessica Pilot concluded the interview asking about new albums, Van characteristically responded: "I may switch around musicians, as my music requires keeping the sound where it needs to be." In 2018 the collaboration with Joey DeFrancesco paid tribute to that quote.

As Van prepared for the Hollywood Bowl shows, he sat down with Scott Foundas, an Englishman living in Los Angeles, who wrote for the **LA Weekly**, for a lengthy interview. They talked in depth. Foundas showed up with a photographer, Kevin Scanlon, who got along well with Morrison. Scanlon was invited to take photos of the shows. Then he traveled with Van to the New York City and London performances. He was also part of a proposed documentary. Van said he was producing "**To Be Born Again**." The proposed documentary has not seen the light of day.

Rolling Stone reviewed the **Astral Weeks Live** shows and predicted the documentary **To Be Born Again** would highlight the entire year-long process of "rediscovering the record." Darren Doane, who Van hired to complete the documentary, told **Rolling Stone**: "The film is about exposing and tearing down all the myths about Van Morrison and the music industry as a whole."

THE HOLLYWOOD BOWL SHOWS: GREAT AND NEW

Morrison opened the show at seven in the evening as the sunset floated over the Hollywood Hills with "Wavelength." The audience approved with rapturous applause. The first half of the show was a warm up for the live **Astral Weeks** material. The first set was highlighted by versions of "St. Dominic's Preview," "Brown Eyed Girl" and "Gloria." After a fifteen-minute intermission, Van came out to perform the **Astral Weeks** material.

The thirteen musicians on stage knew the material inside out. When the album was finished Van lit up the audience with a rousing version of "Listen To The Lion." He ended the show with "Common One." Not bad for a forty-year-old album with bonus songs thrown into the mix.

The list of honors for **Astral Weeks** goes on forever. In the United Kingdom, **Mojo** ranked the LP number two. In the U.S. **Rolling Stone** had a nineteen listing of all-time rock LPs. The somewhat staid **Time** magazine called it rock and roll's third best album. Most of the critics ranked it with the Beach Boys' **Pet Sounds** and the Beatles **Sgt. Pepper's Lonely Hearts Club Band**. **Q** magazine called it the sixth best English LP.

The rankings and listings could fill a page. It was the previously hostile critics who recognized taboo points such as death, nostalgia for childhood, lost love, Celtic music and ennui as serous subjects for rock and roll musicians.

Astral Weeks was not folk, jazz, blues or rock and roll. It was a combination of these influences with literary musings. This is what created **Astral Weeks**. It was Van Morrison inventing a personal way to interpret his music.

The question on everyone's mind was: "What were the **Astral Weeks** Shows like?" The answer was the critics, with some humorous and unforgiveable caveats, praised them. When he performed at the WaMu Theater in New York the **New York Times** critic chided Van for an opening set of what the critic deemed "leftovers." They weren't. Van performed some tunes he rarely played. The second part was **Astral Weeks** prompting the audience to roar approval.

THE CRITICAL REACTION TO ASTRAL WEEKS LIVE

There was universal praise for **Astral Weeks Live At The Hollywood Bowl**. David Wild, in **Rolling Stone**, observed Van remained unhappy with Warner's inability to promote the original release. He continued to discuss the lack of royalties forty years later.

The Wild interview is an important one. Morrison opens up about fame, the problems surviving in the music business and how MTV and other industry changes impact his life, his career and his perception of the business. This interview indicates he had thoughts of redoing **Astral Weeks** for almost two decades. One of Van's industry traits is to think out, plan out and carry out ideas over a long period of time. Hence, **Astral Weeks Live**.

Jim Fusili's **Wall Street Journal** review is one of the best reviews of **Astral Weeks Live**. Fusili talked to Morrison. Van said he hadn't listened to the album in forty years. Then they had a mutual love fest discussing his songs. Randy Lewis, in the **Los Angeles Times**, labeled **Astral Weeks Live** "a faithful re-creation of the original." He praised the February 10, 2009 release of the live album on **Van's Listen To The Lion Records** label. He pointed out the show would move on to New York due to the positive publicity. The February 27 and 28, 2009 Madison Square Garden performances were on the way to selling out as the Fusili story appeared. During an interview Van said: "I wanted to end the **Astral Weeks** set with 'Madame George.' I wanted to tell people at the end these songs are a 'train of thought'." Then Van added: "I think 'Lion' is all me, as well, so I ended with that. ..."

Jim Fusili: "The new recordings from these shows captures a fascinating performance by an incomparable artist." That said Fusili, like other critics, recognized the re-interpretation for what it was, that is a new rendering of a classic album.

After thinking about the show, Van added: "I do not consciously aim to take the listener anywhere. If anything, I aim to take myself there in my music." As Lewis left the interview with Van, he observed Morrison's religious instincts. As they parted, Van said: "I think God must have wanted it to happen-my higher power instinct .... It is a matter of getting back to doing 'me'-what I like." The **Los Angeles**

Times reporter left to file his story. He had a tape full of quotes. This was the new Van Morrison.

David Germain, writing in the **Cincinnati Enquirer**, was one of many reporters who said Morrison finally got the chance to get it right. In an interview Germain asked Van: "Why is there a second **Astral Weeks** album?" Van said: "I didn't do exactly what I wanted to, because I didn't have the support, and I didn't have any money." Van continued the phone interview from London. Van added: "I didn't really have the freedom." On **Astral Weeks**, forty years later, Van clarified his view of his cult album: "Basically it's short stories, it's fiction, and it means something different to each person."

Greg Kot in the **Chicago Tribune** observed: "Van Morrison finally got around to revisiting the album that many consider his masterpiece."

NOVELISTS AND CRITICS ON VAN MORRISON'S MUSIC

Van Morrison's **Astral Weeks** influenced a host of novelists. When Steve Erickson's 2012 **These Dreams of You** was released to critical acclaim the title was from a Morrison song. Lester Bangs summed up Morrison's appeal to a select group of writers when he observed: "Van Morrison is interested, obsessed, with how much musical or verbal information he can compress into a small space, and, almost conversely, how far he can spread one note, word, sound or picture."

Lucy Caldwell is a thirty-eight-year-old award-winning playwright and novelist born in Belfast. She grew up listening to Van Morrison. How did this impact her work? It was Van's images of the Irish countryside, his remarks on Irish history, his reflections on love and his literary presence guiding Caldwell's writing to literary prominence. Her 2017 collection of essays, **Multitudes**, bears the mark of themes resplendent in Morrison's later songs. The pain of heartache and the tenderness of life are described in her tribute to Morrison's lyrical magic.

In a 2016 interview with the **Irish Times**, Caldwell observed: "The music of Van Morrison … and Astral Weeks … is something of a guiding spirit in my stories." Caldwell writes about her East Belfast childhood. One much like Morrison's. It was **Hymns To The Silence** that formed Caldwell's literary pictures of Belfast. "My Belfast … is not that of Van Morrison's … But mine wouldn't exist without his." That said it all. A best-selling novelist looked to her muse. It was Van Morrison. The result is Caldwell's prose reflects Belfast's rich heritage and Van's inspiration.

THE STORY OF THE ASTRAL WEEKS LIVE AT THE HOLLYWOOD BOWL: DVD

Van's company, **Listen To The Lion Records**, produced the album and there was an exclusive deal with Amazon for a brief period. The DVD is a bonus for the fans containing Morrison being interviewed by Scott Foundas. He explains the meaning behind some of the songs. The DVD had post-production engineering making it a rare treat.

There were bonus tracks. The inclusion of versions of "Common One" and "Gloria" were rare treats. The trailer features "To be Born Again" which is an interview with Morrison. He explains how and why much of the planning took place. The meaning of Van's songs and what took place behind the scenes made **Astral Weeks Live At the Hollywood Bowl** a gem. Mike Clark, writing in **USA Today,** observed: "A preservation of last year's rhapsodically received … performances, kinetically photographed and edited for an even more succulent taste."

VAN SHOULD HAVE THE LAST WORD

Van had the last word on **Astral Weeks**. This Q and A with the **Los Angeles Free Press** opened up the Morrison mystique as Van attempted to correct past errors, challenge mythical reporting and explain his reasons for recording **Astral Weeks Live**. Perhaps Van said it best when he told **Rolling Stone** of **Astral Weeks:** "It received no promotion from Warner Brothers—that's why I never got to play the songs live." Now Morrison believes he reclaimed a lost masterpiece. **Rolling Stone** observed Morrison is now pulling out underappreciated songs and performing them in concert.

Van Morrison: "*Astral Weeks* songs ... were from another sort of place—not what is at all obvious. They are poetry and mythical musings channeled from my imagination. ... [They] are little poetic stories I made up and set to music. The album is about song craft for me—making things up and making them fit to a tune I have arranged. The songs were somewhat channeled works—that is why I called it 'Astral Weeks'. As my songwriting has gone on, I tend to do the same channeling, so it's sort of like 'Astral Decades', I guess."

As Van ended his November 8 concert at the Hollywood Bowl, he remarked to the audience: "You've made a happy man very old." **Billboard** wondered what Van meant? The thirteen-piece band, the string section and the flawless execution was not lost on the Bible of the music business. They noticed Van sternly guided some musicians.

When the brief intermission ended the recreation of **Astral Weeks** was not note for note. It was a new album. Despite a large group of musicians, a strong string section and the energy that came with the recreation, there was a sense of historical revision. As Van walked slowly off the stage with a scat vocal the audience was standing in gleeful applause. The Hollywood Bowl was filled with people watching a never to be repeated historic event.

BIBLIOGRAPHICAL SOURCES

See Jim Fusili, "Van Morrison Revisits' Astral Weeks," **The Wall Street Journal**, February 24, 2009 http://online.wsj.com/article/SB1235432248786353835.html for the best review of the album. See Tom Moon, 1,000 Recordings To Hear Before You Die (New York, 2008) and "The Immortals: The First Fifty," **Rolling Stone**, 2008, for an appreciation of Morrison's albums.

For Van's explanation of why he decided to re-record **Astral Weeks Live** see, Randy Lewis, "Van Morrison's Full Q & A on 'Astral Weeks'," Los Angeles Times blogs.latimes.com, October 31, 2008. Also see Randy Lewis, "His 'Astral Projection': Morrison Links Live Album To A Spiritual Journey," **Los Angeles Times**, January 9, 2009. Van was at ease with Lewis and during two separate interview sessions he talked at length about **Astral Weeks**' spiritual nature. Also see Randy Lewis,

"The Earthly Days of 'Astral Weeks'," **Los Angeles Times**, November 1, 2008. http://articles.latimes.com/2008/nov/01/entertainment/et-morrison1

The literary side of **Astral Weeks** is examined in Tobias Carroll, "Van Morrison, Unlikeliest of Literary Muses: On The Outsize Influence of Astral Weeks," **Literary Hub**, April 26 2018.

A wonderful book of criticism is Jessica Hopper: **The First Collection of Criticism By A Living Female Rock Critic** (Chicago, 2015). It is an interesting collection paying tribute to Morrison's records where she makes use of Van's lyrics to frame her beautifully written and thoughtful rock music critiques. Her analysis of **Astral Weeks** is personal and heartfelt. She begins her book with a paean to **Astral Weeks.**

See, Ryan H. Walsh, **Astral Weeks: A Secret History of 1968** (New York, 1968), passim. The Walsh book is a brilliant one. He documents how and why Boston-Cambridge influenced Morrison's seminal album. He also presents the cast of characters and the influences leading one of the Belfast Cowboy's most productive periods. From 1968 to 1972 chart hits, best-selling albums and excellent concerts helped to bring Morrison into the commercial mainstream.

See, Lester Bangs and Greil Marcus, editor, **Psychotic Reactions and Carburetor Dung, The Work of A Legendary Critic: Rock 'N' Roll As Literature and Literature As Rock 'N' Roll** (New York, 1988) and Lester Bangs, **Main Lines, Blood Fests And Bad Taste: A Lester Bangs Reader** (New York, 2003). For Bangs' extraordinary life and how Van Morrison fit into his psyche and guided much of his early writing see, Jim DeRogatis, **Let It Blurt: The Life and Times of America's Greatest Rock Critic** (New York, 2000).

Lucy Caldwell, "Streets Like These: Lucy Caldwell on Van Morrison's Influence," **The Irish Times**, September 28, 2016 https://www.irishtimes.com/culture/books/streets-like-these-lucy-caldwell-on-van-morrison-s-influence-1.2808591 is another example of how Van's music influenced a writer. See Lucy Caldwell, **Multitudes** (London 2017) for eleven short stories that are not only brilliant but they bear an influence from Morrison's music. She grew up in East Belfast and her view of the area is one influenced by Morrison's lyrical magic.

For a lukewarm view of the **Astral Weeks Revisited** see Jon Caramanica, "A Precise, But Mirthless Tribute To 'Astral Weeks'," **The New York Times**, March 1, 2009.
https://www.nytimes.com/2009/03/02/arts/music/02van.html?rref=collection%2Ftimestopic%2FMorrison%2C%20Van&action=click&contentCollection=timestopics&region=stream&module=stream_unit&version=latest&contentPlacement=9&pgtype=collection

For a phone interview after the **Astral Weeks Live** shows, see David Germain, "Van Morrison Records New 'Astral Weeks' Live," **The Cincinnati Enquirer**, February 20, 2009.

Greg Kot, "Astral Weeks' Is Not Rock: It's Not Jazz-Just Timeless," **The Chicago Tribune**, February 8, 2009 is a well thought out piece on the music. Also see Dean Goodman, "Van Morrison Returns Triumphantly To Early Commercial Setback," **Reuters Gazettes**, June 13, 2009. The large number of phone and personal interviews for **Astral Weeks Live** prompted Morrison to complain about Warner Brothers, to ask why his biographers don't contact him for interviews and he stressed he was finally going to get paid for **Astral Weeks.**

For the 2008 **Astral Weeks** show at the Hollywood Bowl see, David Wood, "Forty Years Later, Van Morrison Returns To 'Astral Weeks' In L. A." **Rolling Stone**, No. 1065, November 13, 2008, p. 26. Also see, "Van Morrison Discusses 'Astral Weeks,' Which He'll Perform At The Hollywood Bowl," **Los Angeles Times**, November 1, 2008

There is a lengthy literature on **Astral Weeks** turning fifty. Since Greil Marcus described the album as a "beacon, a light on the far shores of the murk," there have been hundreds of articles. One of the best comparing Van's debut Warner Brothers album with **Moondance** and then he goes on to articulate a full biography of Morrison's career, see, Steven Hyden, "Van Morrison Is More Than 'Astral Weeks'-And He Damn Well Knows It," **The Ringer.com**, November 28, 2018.
https://www.theringer.com/music/2018/11/28/18115160/van-morrison-life-career-albums-astral-weeks As Hyden discusses most of Van's work he comes to the conclusion that Morrison doesn't care what anyone thinks, and he has disdain for those who ripped him off. Hyden talks about Bruce Springsteen ripping off Van Morrison and he uses the Belfast Cowboy's words to great effect. "For years people have been saying to me-you know …. Have you heard this guy Springsteen?" Morrison continued. "And he's definitely ripped me off … (and) I feel pissed off now that I know

about it." There is no reticence to Morrison. He calls it as he sees it. The anti-commercial attitudes that Van fostered toward the record industry have not gotten their full due. He has helped to change the culture for artists who are no longer dictated to by the industry. Van didn't do it alone but his contribution helped the artist to develop his or her own persona. This allowed Morrison to make personal records, some of which sold very well others didn't. As Hyden points out this is the beauty of Van Morrison. He does it his way. The rest of you can kiss his ass if you don't like it.

The 2008 **Astral Weeks Live** is a major turning point in Morrison's relationship with the press. He went out of his way to complete interviews stating how and why he decided to take the album live. It wasn't just about the royalties as some have contended. Van said a reinterpretation of **Astral Weeks** finally made the album his own. That is, it went beyond royalties as he suggested there was a theme or content change as he reinvented the material.

When the **New York Daily News** on January 4th, 2009 named the show one of the five most anticipated pop music events for the year, Van had made his point. He owned the literary and creative side of the legendary album and he mentioned he was happy to receive royalties. See Jim Farber, "Five Most Anticipated Pop Music Event For 2009," **New York Daily News**, January 4, 2009. https://www.nydailynews.com/entertainment/music-arts/anticipated-pop-music-events-2009-article-1.420360 For a less than enthusiastic review of **Astral Weeks Live** see, Andy Whitman, "Old Fart Roundup: Van Explodes, Brooooce Implodes," **Paste**, January 21, 2009. https://www.pastemagazine.com/blogs/whitman/2009/01/old-fart-roundup-van-explodes-brooooce-implodes.html

See Mike Clark, "New on DVD Morrison Concert …" **USA Today**, May 22, 2009. The Clark review is an excellent one. For the proposed documentary **To Be Born Again** see "Van Morrison Rediscovers 'Astral Weeks' In 'To Be Born Again' Doc, **Rolling Stone**, August 17, 2009. https://www.rollingstone.com/movies/movie-news/van-morrison-rediscovers-astral-weeks-in-to-be-born-again-doc-245955/ The documentary which was scheduled for a 2010 release has never seen the light of day.

See Shannon Vale, **Astral Weeks Live: A Fan's Notes** (Anthem Books, 2011). This book is a wonderful read combining personal insight with great reporting. It is well written in a style appealing to

Morrison's fans. It is filled with a useful appendix and key facts about the shows.

For information on the life shows see Guenter Becker's recommended website **Vanomatic**. http://ivan.vanomatic.de Also see blogger Pat Corley for excellent insights and great information. http://patrickmaginty.blogspot.com The Van Morrison mailing lists are also important. When Pat Corley's **Vanatic: The Story Of A Van Morrison Fan**, appeared in 2016, it provided the creative insights of a forty-three year Morrison fan. It was fantastic. It was even handed and well written. The 86,000 words are gold and the 292 pages provide marvelous conclusions.

In the Shannon Vale book, she lists the songs performed and there were some surprises in the twenty-three **Astral Weeks Live** shows. He only performed "T. B. Sheets" once and that was due to Ilene Berns once owning a portion of the royalties. The presence of "Gloria" twenty times in twenty-three concerts tells one Van had strong commercial instincts.

For the **Billboard** story, see, "Van Morrison", November 8, 2008 (Hollywood Bowl), November 14, 2008.
https://www.billboard.com/articles/news/1043494/van-morrison-nov-8-2008-los-angeles-hollywood-bowl

One of the ironies of the live concert is the DVD "Van Morrison, Astral Weeks: The Concert Film" is out of print as this book goes to press. There is footage for the November 6 2008 rehearsal with versions of a truncated "Moondance" at less than two minutes and "Have I Told You Lately that I Love You," checking in at just over two minutes.

See David Wild, "A Conversation With Van Morrison," **Rolling Stone**, August 9, 1990. https://www.rollingstone.com/music/music-features/a-conversation-with-van-morrison-232640/

The reflective atmosphere forty years later on **Astral Weeks** prompted many reassessments. One of the best is Sean O'Hagan, "Is This The Best Album Ever Made?" **London Guardian**, November 1, 2008. https://www.theguardian.com/music/2008/nov/02/vanmorrison-popandrock The O'Hagan story is an interesting one. He reports that Alfie Walsh, the lead singer of a Belfast showband, the Olympics, came to Van's house to pick him up for a show. His mother, Violet, told Alfie Van couldn't come to the gig. He was staying home to write poetry. O'Hagan uses this story suggesting when Van recorded **Astral Weeks**, he wasn't in awe of his session mates. O'Hagan writes of the Los Angeles concerts in 2008 "I hear he is going to record the concerts for a live album … I have mixed feelings about that." O'Hagan called it "too magical to recreate." He was wrong. When O'Hagan recalled interviewing Morrison in 1987 at the Chelsea Arts and how difficult he was during the interview. "He arrived very late and for the first hour was tight-lipped and combative. It was only when we moved off the subject of his music that he began to open up." It was at this point that O'Hagan recalled Van talked but how he was a typical Irish writer. He wasn't difficult. He was Irish. The quest for the homeland is a part of Van's larger work and O'Hagan does an excellent job pointing out this theme. By evoking the manes of John Donne, W. B. Yeats, T.S. Eliot and Seamus Heaney, Van swims in the mainstream of a literary tradition few rock artists embrace. By employing Romanticism, theosophy and esoteric literary themes in his songs, Van is atypical of his genre. O'Hagan should not have been surprised he was atypical during interviews.

One critic, Rosemary Rogers, wrote of Morrison: "Van was a stubby fireplug in a porkpie hat, usually full of booze, would stop a performance to get into a fistfight with a club manager over money. Or, just because he felt like it would finish his set by lying on the floor hanging on to his microphone. In short, he was, as Yeats would put it, 'A drunken vainglorious lout." Rogers goes on to suggest Janet Planet and the medium, Georgie Hyde-Lees, helped Van to "engage in automatic writing, the process of writing while channeling the supernatural …" She was the wife of William Butler Yeats. Van identified with her. Somewhere in this criticism Van Morrison is lost to analysis. This is exactly his complaint. For the review of Ryan H. Walsh's **Astral Weeks: A Secret History of 1968** which Rogers uses to make these observations, Rosemary Rogers, "The Sacred Text Of Rock 'n' Roll," **Irish America.** https://irishamerica.com/2018/11/the-sacred-text-of-rock-n-roll/ Rogers is a mainstream journalist. She is typical of Irish journalists who never interviewed Van. They are news not music writers. Her questions and general approach differed from rock and roll journalists as they were less contentious. Hence, Morrison's cooperation with the press in the last decade. Yet, she was as critical but also more insightful than the typical rock music journalists or the intellectual ciphers like Greil

Marcus who attempt to make Morrison a literary figure. Van is literary but not in the Marcus mode. The press deserves some of the blame for helping to create Van's negative reaction to interviewers. Yet, there is no excuse for his at times nasty behavior.

The video of **Van Morrison: Astral Weeks Live** ends with Van thanking his mother for the inspiration, the talent and the ability to follow his dream.

CHAPTER 2

BIOGRAPHY TWO: FROM CULT TO MAINSTREAM STARDOM

"Man can embody truth ... but not know it."

W. B. YEATS

"Morrison remains a singer who can be compared to no other in the history of rock & roll."

GREIL MARCUS

"Van has been known to get a little grumpy towards the end of a long evening."

SALMAN RUSHDIE

ﻌﻌ

When Vladimir Nabokov sailed to America in 1940, he wrote a novel about biography and art, **The Real Life of Sebastian Knight**. In this novel he stated: "remember that what you are told is really threefold: shaped by the teller, reshaped by the listener, concealed from both by the dead man of the tale." In researching and writing a biography of Van Morrison the subject is alive. His foibles are ignored. Most biographers understand his quirks. Clinton Heylin still refers to Van in unfriendly terms. Johnny Rogan is more at ease with the cranky Irishman. Steve Turner sees a Christian philosopher. Peter Mills examines the roots of Morrison's early music with the skill of a novelist and the penetrating eye of a seasoned musician. Brian Hinton sees literary influences and a host of other biographers have varying views. It is as if Morrison is an elusive personality. He isn't! He is a contrarian. He is a multi-talented writer. He is a charismatic performer. He is a private individual. He is a successful businessman. The problem is combining these traits into a readable biography.

There is another caveat to a Morrison biography. That is the tales of drinking. Heylin and Rogan spend too many pages on the problems with alcohol. At times they are spot on. He was in his early years an ornery drinker. Is this a problem? It was at times. It wasn't really much of a problem in his professional life. In 1971-1972, when Van performed largely in the San Francisco area, his shows were increasingly professional. The local San Francisco press mentioned Morrison's drinking when at times he didn't appear to be drinking. He performed well. In those days some shows were great while others were average. Van was temperamental. I saw about twenty-five shows in those two years. I never thought his on-stage performance was compromised by drinking. It was as often boisterous concert goers who hollered "Brown Eye Girl." When he performed at Frenchy's in Hayward, they served drinks and dinner. At the table next to me a young lady swilled down half a dozen drinks, ate a $2.95 steak and as Van came on stage she was talking loudly. Fortunately, the music drowned her out. After Van performed a couple of songs she stood up. She shouted: "Oh, shit." Then she threw up all over the table. Van didn't notice nor did he seem to care. It was a strange night.

Joey Bebo, Van's drummer in Boston in 1968, pointed out Van was stage shy. "I saw him down a bottle of Southern Comfort before one show. This is why he liked Janis Joplin. She drinks Southern Comfort. Socially, I seldom saw Van have more than a beer. He wasn't a social drinker," Bebo continued. "He drank to escape his stage fright."

Van Morrison: "You're Irish, number one and you're a drinker number two." When Morrison joined Alcoholics Anonymous in 1985, he quickly departed the organization. Why? No one knows! The speculation is everyone wanted his autograph. Alcohol didn't derail his career nor did his adversely influence his writing.

What is the importance of the alcohol question? It isn't drinking that has caused Morrison problems. It is a prickly, unpredictable personality. Unfortunately, Clinton Heylin's hit piece blames the bad behavior on booze. It might just be Van's personal behavior.

Irish poets and literary figures were not exactly teetotalers. Van's biographers need to consider if alcohol influenced his literary flair.

THE CHALLENGE OF A MULTI-VOLUME BIOGRAPHY

The challenge of a multi-volume Morrison biography is sorting through the myths and discovering the realities. The mass of gossip, the misconstrued facts, the interviews with those who have an ax to grind, and the constant musings of the rock and roll press make this biography a difficult task. The sheer mass of material in six decades of rock and roll history makes Van a subject hard to understand and comprehend. There are many different musical Van Morrison's. His art, his writing, his concepts and his views continually change. This is the primary reason for a fifty plus year legendary career.

How does one write a Van Morrison biography? How does one begin? Van Morrison was born George Ivan Morrison. He became another person to reach musical stardom. The choices for Morrison biographers are limitless. Yet, there is a similarity to the biographies. Clinton Heylin sees Van as the ultimate artist who has had enormous difficulties in the real world. Johnny Rogan sees Van through the eyes of Irish history. Steve Turner sees Van through a Christian focus. Brian Hinton directs his attention to Morrison's music as art. Ritchie Yorke tries to tie in numerous interviews with the Belfast Cowboy to make him appear human. Greil Marcus ties Van's music primarily to **Astral Weeks**. He also suggests that for the next decade Van was at his peak. No one disputes this obvious point. Howard A. DeWitt is interested in the early music. Ken Brooks dissects the key songs. John Collis concentrates on the Belfast Cowboy's personality, and he is able to garner insights that others have missed. Peter Mills presents the music through the artist's eyes, experiences and the myriad outside influences. Which biographer has the essence of Morrison? The obvious answer is none. Yorke, Collis, Heylin, Rogan, Hinton, Mills and Turner come closest to describing Morrison accurately. Some critics disagree. They don't see anyone defining Morrison's quixotic musical journey.

There is one biographer who has gotten into Morrison's head. That is the English academic Peter Mills. Unlike many writers, Mills has academic and music credentials. He was the lead singer of Innocents Abroad. Their two albums remain cult collector pieces. Mills does not consider his book a biography. It is a study of the music, the songwriting and the live performances. It is in fact one of the best biographies on Morrison. The reason is a simple one. He compartmentalizes Van's life and career in defined areas such as the Irish influence, the songwriting, the recording studio and the art of composition. All of these are necessary to understanding the Belfast Cowboy.

Morrison's personality creates problems for the biographer. He is never consistent. There is a moody countenance making him unpredictable. While this is not a trait unique to Morrison, it creates interpretive problems.

Van Morrison's life is one of contradictions. "He is a conflicted soul," Pete Vanrosendael commented. Like many people who follow Van's career Vanrosendael complains: "We need to find out who the real Van is, a biographer needs to take off the gloves." The public persona is gruff and uncompromising. The private side is that of a man who is kind, compassionate and loyal to his friends. The two sides of Morrison's personality seldom come together.

There are other problems in a Morrison biography. The Belfast Cowboy has a sense of wanderlust. He has lived in Belfast, Dublin, London, Bath, New York, Boston, Cambridge, Brentwood in Los Angeles, Fairfax, Mill Valley and Woodstock. His creativity depends upon the local landscape. His songs are filled with images from Belfast's Cyprus Avenue, Fitzroy Avenue and his home on Hyndford Street. These are contrasted with images of Woodstock and San Francisco. Van is a visual writer. He describes the local environment. This presents the biographer with many problems. Foremost among the biographer's difficulties is how to portray the Belfast Cowboy.

BEFORE HE WAS VAN MORRISON

When George Ivan Morrison was born on August 31, 1945, in Belfast, Ireland, it was a poor country with political problems. By 1969,

BIOGRAPHY TWO: FROM CULT TO MAINSTREAM STARDOM

Van Morrison emerged as the leading exponent of literary rock and roll. By Van's own account, he is not a rocker. He was a kid in Belfast with a penchant for listening to obscure blues, country and jazz sounds. He was also imbued with a strong work ethic. The combination of a lower middle-class Irish background, leaving school at fourteen and rising to the top of the music business left scars on the Belfast Cowboy's psyche and personality.

Van Morrison is a rare phenomenon. He is a serious, but popular, artist with an at times commercial direction. He is Irish to the core. His best work took place in America. He is known everywhere as "Van the Man." He is a wealthy man who has owned homes in California, Dublin, Belfast, Bath, London and rumor has it in the French countryside.

How does Van view biography? He disdains it. That is, it fails to meet his criteria for objectivity, factual truth and interpretive wisdom. He doesn't talk to his biographers. Van fears a biographer would sit back and watch him do the work. He is intentionally obtuse. There are few heart to heart interviews about his life. That said, he is often open and opinionated in interviews since the late 1990s. That is the period in which he quit drinking. His early Belfast friends describe Morrison as "a most precious little boy."

His family background influenced Van Morrison. How has it impacted his life? He is formed and directed by the Belfast Hyndford Street house. It was in this small two-floor home, with a shotgun feel, belonging more in Memphis than to Belfast, where Van spent his formative years.

His father, George, was a hard-working electrician with a large record collection. His mother, Violet, was bright and free spirited. She had inordinate intellectual curiosity. The genetic outcome was inevitable. Van was a blend of two bright people with different passions. Not only did father and son connect musically, they had a strong personal bond. One in which their personalities blended. Friends have said when you meet George, you have also met Van.

George was a gruff, no-nonsense guy with a penchant for confrontation. Van's mother was the opposite. Van was able to pursue musical interests. Early on he had a preoccupation with contrarian ideas. He left school at fourteen. This has been a bone of contention with him. He never excelled educationally in the halls of academe. His songwriting and performing demonstrate a level of personal knowledge due to reading, thinking and addressing the issues of the day. His ability to educate himself is unparalleled. His intellect is enormous and beyond comparison. There is no subject Van can't master.

While his parents were not people of letters, they were bright, intellectually curious and provided young Van with the stimulus he needed to develop. They fostered an atmosphere nurturing his creative side. His neighbor, Molly Fee, recalls he had all the benefits of a single child. Whatever Van wanted is what he got. This turned into a lifelong passion for music and reading thereby creating a philosophical bent.

THE DIFFERENT DIRECTIONS OF VAN'S BIOGRAPHERS

The different directions for Morrison's biographers suggests the complexity of the subject. Where does one start? The answer is Belfast. Where does one end? The answer is Ireland. There is no such thing as objective biography. There are various interpretations and a host of myths. Realities do abound. They have different meanings. In interviews with family and friends, he is described as "generous, kind and considerate." In talking to music people, Van is often described as "arrogant, explosive, angry and suspicious." In talking to his friends, the word they use to describe him is "compassionate." In the industry the word is business minded.

As he aged, mellowed and reflected, Morrison is eager to discuss his career. In 2015 Van sat down with Fintan O'Toole for an interview with the **Irish Times**. O'Toole commented he was aware of the Belfast Cowboy's reputation. It was a few days before Van's seventieth birthday. O'Toole wasn't sure what he would discover. He was shocked. Van was a gentleman. "I find him courteous, engaged oddly straightforward. All he asks for is a cup of coffee and that we sit in the window of the hotel where we meet with a view of the Belfast Lough," O'Toole observed. This interview is a penetrating window into Morrison's psyche.

BIOGRAPHY TWO: FROM CULT TO MAINSTREAM STARDOM

The extraordinary sense of intimacy Van's fans feel for his music and his life adds a great deal to a serious book. The drinking, the periodic raging, the quirky shows, the later in life banning of alcohol at concerts don't detract from his journey, but this suggest the quirky nature of a brilliant artist. Biographers are supposed to know their subjects, as well as they know themselves. In Van's case, this is difficult. Biography attempts to tell the reader that a life can be analyzed, summed up, written and sold. Van spent most of his life condemning biography. He calls it half-truths. In a number of songs, notably "New Biography," he pleads to be left alone.

RUMOR, MYTHS AND HALF TRUTHS

Rumors, myths and half-truths are some of the reasons Morrison is hostile to the biographical process. Van is an autobiographer in songwriting. He does this in his lyrics. From time to time, the rumor of his impending autobiography surfaces. One year it was announced at the Frankfurt Book Fair. It has yet to appear.

His writing is a commentary not only upon his life, but also about those around him. His prose is a storehouse of his memories. Often, he writes about his Irish heritage. There is no way of predicting where his mind will wander or what his lyrics will describe.

The biographer must look at Van Morrison and write about the outer self as well as the inner soul. There are two Morrison's. One is a public figure. The other is a private person. One has little in common with the other. The obscure areas of personality are most important in defining Morrison. Throughout this book there are references to the obscure Van. This term highlights his music and personality.

When people describe their conversations with Van, they invariably comment on his analytical intelligence. He does not suffer fools very well. He has a penchant for sharp criticism. He doesn't see this as being rude. It is simply an integral part of his personality. He is a person always seeking answers.

Why does Van fear biography? Only he can answer that question. He often says it is an invasion of privacy. He sometimes suggests the facts and interpretation are incorrect. He argues he is the only one who can tell the real story. The truth is he wants to control the facts, the writing and the interpretations. That is not an unusual trait among celebrities. At times it leads to a tug of war between fact and fiction.

THE TUG OF WAR BETWEEN FACT AND FICTION

It is the tug between fact and fiction that drives Morrison crazy. He has trouble seeing the facts. He envisions fiction in writing about his career. If you put Van Morrison's songs and interviews together, they provide not only a biography, his words suggest a penetrating analysis of the music industry. He complains about those who misrepresent him, Van at times is purposely obtuse to confuse the meaning in his personal life.

He maintains a vast personal musical archive. From time to time, Van is seen in record stores like John Goddard's Village Music in Mill Valley. He would purchase a large amount of records. Then Van would head down to the Depot Bookstore and Café. He would look in the philosophy section and purchase a book. He would head to the coffee shop which is inside the store and order tea and a scone. He would sit in the corner reading, slowly drinking his tea and writing in a notebook. Even when he was relaxing, Morrison was working. He is invariably looking for blues LPs. He also possesses a large collection of vinyl albums, cassette tapes, unreleased recordings, experimental music and CDs, as well as some records that provide a large repository of his music. It is an archive that is unrivaled.

It is the latent autobiographical prose that provides the primary source material for a Morrison biography. In "Just Like Greta," Van sings about his desire to become reclusive as he complains about fame and fortune. He has repeated this mantra many times.

THE THREE MAIN VAN BIOGRAPHIES AND COUNTLESS OTHERS: CAN ANYONE TOP THESE?

There are three excellent Van Morrison biographies. They are in-depth biographical tomes that have a likeness in interpretation and attitude. The critics, however, dislike most of the biographies. "He has been poorly served by biographical studies," Kim Larsen writes in **Wavelength**. Really! This is the tact taken by Van's fans. This conclusion ignores the irascible nature of Morrison and the difficulty in writing about him.

The main complaint from Van fans is most books are a cut and paste job from the popular musical press. Some studies fit these criteria. Others books like those of Peter Mills, Clinton Heylin, Johnny Rogan, Eric Hage and Steve Turner present copious personal interviews from a wide variety of sources. Brian Hinton focuses with a college professor's fanaticism upon the art in Morrison's life and songs. Ken Brooks and Patrick Humphries look at the music. Contrary to the critics, there is broad and thoughtful analysis of Morrison's music and life.

Johnny Rogan and Clinton Heylin provide the most thoughtful biographies. Rogan's erudite work traces Van's career in tandem with Ireland's political and social problems. This approach befuddles the critics.

Rogan uses Morrison's apolitical nature to contrast his life to the Troubles in Northern Ireland. This is a brilliant way of getting inside Van Morrison's mind. Unfortunately, the critics want more analysis of "Brown Eyed Girl." When Rogan uses the sub-title "No Surrender," to showcase his brilliant second volume on Van Morrison, he employs the slogan of the Protestant minister and radical politician Ian Paisley. What this does is to place Morrison in the context of his Northern Irish heritage. This is brilliant analysis. It is contrary to the facts. Van had little to say about the problems in Northern Ireland. In discussions with those close to him I was told he was "heart broken and distraught with thoughts of Belfast."

What was it about the Troubles that drove Van to America for a decade in exile? It was the religious divisions, it was the constant security checks, it was the presence of British troops, it was the changes in local culture. These forces made America look like the Garden of Eden. It turned out it wasn't.

Rogan's use of sources is wide and inclusive. He gets to the core of those around Morrison. Kim Larsen, in a review of Rogan's book, labels these folks "informants." This is the crux of the problem. Some fans and many of the reviewers believe that anyone who grants a personal interview about Morrison is an "informant." George Orwell would be proud of these folks.

The Larsen review gives Rogan credit for purposeful analysis. Larsen, a psychologist, came closest to anyone in understanding what Rogan attempted. It was to write an honest thoughtful book.

Clinton Heylin's biography arrived in 2002 and was the most balanced book to date. Heylin's volume was filled with new material. That is the good news. The bad news is he had a vendetta against Morrison. For some reason Heylin had a blistering hatred for Van. This was due to his media comments and impending lawsuit.

IS VAN ANYTHING BUT CONSISTENT?

Johnny Rogan argues in his superb biography, **Van Morrison: No Surrender**, published in 2005, Morrison's personality has taken on an "Ulster-like intransigence, strangely in keeping with the political ethos of East Belfast." This volume argues to the contrary. Van is anything but consistent. He has little interest in the politics from East Belfast or Northern Ireland. Or anywhere else!

From 1968 to 1972, Morrison matured as an artist and as a person. The problems with fame and fortune intensified his reclusive nature. The idea Van reinvents himself time and time again is a tried and true cliché. A simple explanation is he is an artist who has continued to grow and mature. It is Morrison's differences with the media that prompted biographers to intensify their criticism.

Morrison's personal behavior provided plenty of critical ammunition. When the Belfast Blues Society attempted to honor him with a plague, Morrison threatened a lawsuit. With journalists, he often insists on a half hour time frame. He delights in being difficult. When he is amongst fans, however, he is at times gracious. The contradictions never cease to exist.

Like many of his Ulster contemporaries, Morrison has a stubborn nature. One that is not compromising. So, who knows, maybe Johnny Rogan is right. This volume argues otherwise.

WHAT ARE THE DISTORTED FACTS IN VAN MORRISON'S LIFE?

There is a notion among some Morrison's biographers Van felt like a second-class Irish citizen. This was because he believed Belfast was second to Dublin on the historical landscape. This is pure nonsense. There is nothing more Northern Irish than Morrison. The poet, Gerald Dawe, has addressed this issue with clarity and precision. The Belfast Cowboy is and has always been culturally Irish. Van told Mervyn Solomon, Phil and Dorothy Solomon, Sir Edward Lewis and Solly Lipsitz he felt a sense of personal freedom coming from Belfast. It was the center of his intellectual universe. The irony is Morrison's early material was written, recorded and performed in the U.S. It was still Irish. The most distorted fact interpreting his life is the lack of Irish influences in his early years.

The notion he is difficult in the studio doesn't on the surface appear to be a distorted fact. It is! If you listen to Van, he explains his music has to be done his way. Is he is difficult in the studio? The musicians I interviewed said if so, there is a good reason. Today he cuts the record, owns the master tapes and leases them to a major label. He believes his producers, advisers, engineers, technicians and anyone else in the recording studio may not understand his direction and methods. He doesn't see himself as difficult. He says he is an artist going his own way.

Belfast Protestantism was not solely a religion; it was a way of life. "We didn't go to church all the time, but it was a very churchy atmosphere in the sense that's the way it is in Northern Ireland," Van said. He didn't consider the local music scene to have anything to do with London. There was interest in traditional Irish music and American rhythm and blues. "Maybe a third of the people that are into R & B would go to hear the McPeakes," Van commented to **Rolling Stone** in July 1970.

Many biographers speculate on his inability to develop lasting personal relationships. This is a myth. With band members like John Allair, John Platania, Jay Berliner and David Hayes among others he has had a long term personal and professional relationship.

VAN MORRISON HAS THE LAST WORD ON HIS BIOGRAPHERS

The aversion Morrison has to biography has deep roots. He wants his private life left untouched. He wants to direct the story. If a song has meaning he will inform you. If not, don't write about it. He is alternately rude and charming during interviews. He refuses to accept he is a public figure open to scrutiny. A small group of perhaps a few thousand fans subscribe to this notion. Let's look at what Van has said about his biographers.

"You get these biographies that claim to be about me. They come up with stories and some of it is partial truth, some of it's completely made up. It's all third-party stuff. They interview people from years ago who know nothing about me and probably didn't know much about me then. Then there's book that say things about my music, like they know where the songs come from. It's all bullshit," Van remarked to **Uncut** in 2005. The conclusion is there is no biography satisfying the Belfast Cowboy.

Van doesn't understand research. I don't blame him. How many different opinions does a biographer find? Hundreds! Sifting through the evidence is fun. Not according to Morrison. "I think the guys who wrote the last couple of books were complete ignoramuses, not qualified for the job. If anybody told them anything, they believed it, they didn't question it," Van remarked to **Mojo** in 2006. His anger was directed at Johnny Rogan's **Van Morrison: No Surrender**. This is a marvelous piece of scholarship. Rogan writes with a literary flair. He mixes Irish history with Van's personal life. Of all the Morrison books it is the most intellectual. Rogan also corrected many of Clinton Heylin's misinterpretations. His book lacks the syrupy attempts by other authors to win Morrison's favor. Rogan has an interpretive, if misguided one, employing Irish politics in a microscopic view of the Belfast Cowboy.

What is the truth of Van Morrison's personality? When David Burke told a close friend, he was writing a book about Van Morrison, a friend said: "I hope you have a good lawyer." When the Belfast Blues Appreciation Society announced it would erect a plague outside his childhood home on Hyndford Street, Morrison threatened legal action. Van is cranky. He is authoritarian. He is difficult. He does explain it. "There's no mystery. What I do is very simple. My songs, my music, my whole shtick is not something that's mysterious," Van told **Mojo**.

Why is Van difficult? He sees his art as that of a simple songwriter. Myth doesn't interest him. He defines reality. He hates to read about "his legend." "All I can do is be me," Van continued. "I write songs because nobody says I can't." That is Van. I am writing this book because nobody says I can't. So enjoy it. I will leave out Van's personal life. The one hundred and twenty-nine people I have talked to since the early 1970s have conflicting stories. I will do my best to keep them straight.

The Morrison story is that of an enigma. Who is the reporter who got it right in London? Barry Egan, **The Sunday Independent** columnist in Ireland, is accurate, sympathetic and interesting to read. There are too many Egan stories to tell but the ones that are most significant connect Van with an intellectual stream. In one column he said Morrison made use of a Nineteenth Century Austrian philosopher, Rudolf Steiner, on the importance of "thinking with the heart and feeling with the mind." Egan was making reference to a 1987 Morrison song "I Forgot That Love Existed." This is the reason one writes about the Belfast Cowboy. He has an intellect and a way with words few possess.

Van Morrison's art invites admiration and ardor. In person Van is a contradiction. He is sullen, angry and difficult at one moment. In the next he can be friendly, candid and forthcoming. Why is this important? The biographer has two paths. One is to fully document who Morrison is, what he does personally and how this influences his art. The second path is to ignore his difficult moments, to minimize the personal fights and to simply praise his music. This path leads to hagiography. This book takes the first path without touching on any form of scandal. Morrison's war against the record labels, his fight to preserve his copyrights, his ability to overcome the criminals, crooks, sharks and low lives who populate the record industry are connected to his unwavering creativity that never abates. This is the backbone to this book.

As I followed Van from Belfast to London to New York to Boston to Woodstock to San Francisco and back to Belfast with stops along the way in Brentwood, Notting Hill Gate and Bath, I realized geography had an impact upon Morrison.

David Burke's **A Sense of Wonder: Van Morrison's Ireland** answers the question of North Ireland's influence upon the Belfast Cowboy. Surprisingly, Burke claims it is "patently ridiculous to label Morrison a poet." That conclusion is at odds with this book. He is also critical of Van who claims: "My songs are better than Yeats." Humility is not a Morrison virtue.

While Burke's book is an excellent one, it suffers from a heavy dependence upon Clinton Heylin and Johnny Rogan both of whom have axes to grind.

The usefulness of Burke's magnificently written volume is his ability to place the stamp of Northern Ireland's Irishness on the Belfast Cowboy. Burke argues Van is the "archetypical hard done-by Northern Irish Protestant." I am not sure what this means. Perhaps it is that Morrison is a cranky bastard at times. That is not the tone and direction of this book.

By traveling Van's footsteps, I have interpreted his life. While not as accomplished as some fans, notably Art Siegel, Bernard McGuinn, Simon Gee, Michael Fishman, Boom Baker, Pat Corley, Russ Dugoni, Michael Seltzer, Ron Sexton, Pat Thomas and a host of others I fail to mention, I have followed Van around since the Them days. My two previous books were attempts to look inside his soul. Now with three more volumes planned I will complete my multi-volume biography. The first volume **Van Morrison: Them and the Bang Era, 1945-1968** introduced his early years. This volume covers five key years, 1968-1972. They are important ones. This is the period Van Morrison established his brand, his independence and the path of his future.

The problem of contemporary biography is to blend the subject with his life. The Bang and Warner record deals explain, but fail to excuse, his at times boorish behavior. His biographers have sensationalized and over reported his drinking. His early life was not recognized for its intellectual brilliance. That is not until Johnny Rogan's 1984 biography set the tone for the intellectually minded Morrison.

BIBLIOGRAPHICAL SOURCES

An excellent and thoughtful analysis of Morrison biographies is Kim Larsen, "Johnny Rogan: Van Morrison, No Surrender," **Wavelength: The Unofficial Van Morrison Magazine**, no. 34, September 2005, pp. 32-36. The Larsen review is an exceptional and thoughtful piece of criticism that gets to the heart of the problems writing a Morrison biography.

The Morrison biographies used for this chapter include Ken Brooks, **In Search of Van Morrison** (London, 1999), John Collis, **Van Morrison: Inarticulate Speech of the Heart** (London, 1996), Howard A. DeWitt, **Van Morrison: The Mystic's Music** (Fremont, 1983), Howard A. DeWitt, **Van Morrison: Them and the Bang Era, 1945-1968** (Fremont, 2005), Clinton Heylin, **Van Morrison: Can You Feel The Silence? A New Biography** (London, 2002), Brian Hinton, **Celtic Crossroads: The Art of Van Morrison** (London, 1997, revised edition, 2000), Patrick Humphries, **Van Morrison** (London, 1997), Johnny Rogan, **Van Morrison** (London, 1984), Johnny Rogan, **Van Morrison: No Surrender** (London, 2005) and Steve Turner, **Van Morrison: Too Late To Stop Now** (New York, 1993).

Also see some of the specialized studies on Van's music; these include Martin Buzacott and Andrew Ford, **Speaking In Tongues: The Songs of Van Morrison** (Sydney, 2005), Ken Brooks, **In Search of Van Morrison** (London, 1999) and Patrick Humphries, **Van Morrison** (London, 1997).

For a look at the forces that influenced Morrison it is essential to view some Irish history. See Donald S. Connery, **The Irish** (London, 1968) for some of the forces influencing Morrison. Also see Gerald Dawes, **The Rest Is History** (Dublin, 1998) for a look at the Irish character and a chapter on Morrison. Also see Colleen Taylor, "Gerald Dawe: Music Notes," **Irishecho.com** March 22, 2017 for how the poet Dawe relates Belfast's history, influence and ambiance to Van Morrison's music. This was a reaction to a new Dawe book on Van Morrison **In Another World**.

See Peter Mills, **Hymns to the Silence: Inside the Words and Music of Van Morrison** (New York, 2010) for the best biographical study of Irish influences, his writing, and his work in the studio and his place in the music industry. Mills is unusually perceptive and analytical concerning the formation and execution of Morrison's music. See Gerald Dawe, **In Another World: Van Morrison & Belfast** (Dublin, 2017), passim.

See Fintan O'Toole, "Van Morrison: Being Famous is Not Great For The Creative Process. Not For Me, Anyway," **Irish Times**, August 29, 2015, for an in-depth interview where Van opens up concerning his personal life and career. Talking to a Northern Ireland reporter, Morrison opened up about his career. https://www.irishtimes.com/culture/music/van/van-morrison-being-famous-is-not-great-for-the-creative-process-not-for-me-anyway-1.2332216

Also see Erik Hage, **The Words and Music of Van Morrison** (Westport, 2009). See the brilliant blog spot for some of the best comments on Van. http://patrickmaginty.blogspot.com/

The transition to a solo career was the next step after Them. For material on that transition see, for example, Daniel Kreps, "Van Morrison Details 'Authorized Bang Collection'," **RollingStone**, March 30, 2017. https://www.rollingstone.com/music/music-news/van-morrison-details-authorized-bang-collection-117565/ The importance of the Kreps articles is Van explains why the three disc set of material from Bert Berns' Bang label was released. In the process one can see the transition to a solo career. Members of Them pointed out in numerous interviews they saw Van's solo direction as early as 1966.

For Morrison's comments on those who have completed biographical studies, see, David Burke, **A Sense of Wonder: Van Morrison's Ireland** (London, 2013), pp. 10-11. For Morrison's comparison to a Vienna philosopher, see Barry Egan, "On His Classic I Forgot That Love Existed, Van Morrison Makes Use of 19th-Century Austrian Philosopher Rudolf Steiner's ..." **Dublin Sunday Independent**, February 21, 2010. https://www.independent.ie/lifestyle/through-the-eyes-of-a-dragon-26634131.html One of the more penetrating interviews with Van Morrison came at a time when he was sixty years old and he was beginning a new era with the press. Van believed that by attempting to explain his life the media coverage would be fair and accurate. See Paul Sexton, "Van Morrison: Seeking The Man Inside," **London Independent**, April 7 2006.

BIOGRAPHY TWO: FROM CULT TO MAINSTREAM STARDOM

https://www.independent.co.uk/arts-entertainment/music/features/van-morrison-seeking-the-man-inside-6104374.html What sets this interview apart from others is Morrison attempts to explain his life. The writer also reflects on a 1986 interview he had with Morrison. The result is a thorough and often revealing look at how the Belfast Cowboy thinks and views the world. There are some penetrating insights into an evening he had with Bono and Salman Rushdie. The over interpretation of Van's broad body of work is one of the Belfast Cowboy's constant complaints. "I'm basically an introvert and that's OK," Van remarked. He also looks back upon the beginning of his career with a fondness for electric music. "There wasn't a lot of electric music going on," Van said of the 1950s. He vowed to correct that fact. He also said he looked to perfect his vocal styling. He did so my listening to Louis Prima and Johnny Ray. He discussed his fondness for country music. Hank Williams and Merle Kilgore were two of many country performers that Morrison followed. The large number of interviews Van has given on his musical influences are important in reconstructing what he listened to, how it influenced his writing and why and how he adapted some of these performers stage presence.

A telephone interview with P. J. Proby helped this book and this chapter. In Palm Spring legendary record producer cum actor Steve Rowland helped to fill in key parts of the story as it pertained to the recording industry and its idiosyncratic behavior.

Since 2008 Van has consistently speculated on the why and how of his early years. In various interviews he has looked back with comments on what he read, how his voracious reading habits influenced his music and how and why he reacted to the foibles of early rock and roll journalism. For an example of the new Morrison in an interview looking back, see, **Van Morrison interview with Marty Whelan 4th Nov 2016**. https://www.youtube.com/watch?v=ZBbNsPbqbKU In this interview Morrison talks about the influence of short story writer-novelist Roald Dahl and philosophical-mystic author Colin Wilson. This interview is unusual and provides insights into what Morrison read, thought and conceived from 1968 to 1972. "It's my duty to keep singing," Morrison remarked to Whelan. "I've always identified as an outsider," Morrison observed. He talked in this interview of not succumbing to conformist behavior. The focus of this book is on Van's rage with the music business which he explains with clarity in the Whelan interview. Van said he was enjoying the journey of life concluding he wasn't searching any longer; he had arrived. The Whelan interview is a brilliant and personal look back by Morrison.

See Bob Stanley, **Yeah! Yeah! Yeah!: The Story of Pop Music From Bill Haley To Beyoncé** (New York, 2013), pp. 91-91 for an identification of Morrison with the English beat groups. Morrison would take issue with Stanley's conclusions. But the Stanley book is the best one on how and why pop music brought Morrison's talents to the general public. "Brown Eyed Girl" was the key to Morrison's ascendancy.

For Van's ban on alcohol later in his career and the role alcohol has played in his career, see, for example, "Van Morrison's Alcohol Ban," **Boston.com**, September 15, 2008. http://archive.boston.com/ae/celebrity/articles/2008/09/18/van_morrisons_alcohol_ban/ In 1985 Morrison joined Alcohol Anonymous. It is best to let Morrison explain his drinking demons in his own words. Van Morrison: "The heaviest dope I ever did was alcohol. I've done stuff like hash and grass, which isn't really heavy dope. But alcohol is a different story—it's a real heavy drug, a real motherfucker ... In Ireland, everybody drinks. Nobody gives it a second thought. You're Irish, number one, and you're a drinker, number two."

For the role of the, see, for example, Christopher Hill, **Into The Mystic: The Visionary and Ecstatic Roots of 1960s Rock and Roll** (New York, 2017) is indispensable. This is a study of the spiritual and mystical influences of the Grateful Dead, the Beatles, the Rolling Stones, Bob Dylan, Van Morrison, the Incredible String Band, the Left Banke, Lou Reed and the Velvet Underground among others on pop culture.

One of the best biographical essays on Morrison is a book review, See Pat Thomas, "The Van Morrison Bible Has Just Been Written By Peter Mills, Read It Now, While Swinging Down At The Kingdom Hall," February 4, 2011. https://www.facebook.com/notes/pat-thomas/the-van-morrison-bible-has-just-been-written-by-peter-mills-read-it-now-while-sw/10150144880970460/ The genius of Thomas's prose is he equates Morrison's darkest music with cult legend Nick Drake. That sets the stage for pointing out how and why Peter Mills analysis of Morrison's music fills a historiographical void. Where Van received his inspiration and the artists who provided it is a major part of Mills book and Thomas reminds us of how these influences provides us with a view into Morrison's soul.

The question of Morrison's drinking, which has been overblown, was placed into perspective by interviews with Joey Bebo in the 1960s, Mark Naftalin in the 1970s and Chris Michie in the 1980s. None of these sources described excessive drinking. The only book that harps on the drinking is the Clinton Heylin biography. While Johnny Rogan discusses the issue, he does so with an intellectual detachment that Heylin lacks. This is the major source of Morrison's disdain for the media.

To understand the Trouble as they relate to Van Morrison, see, Roddy Doyle, "Say Nothing: A True Story of Murder and Memory In Northern Ireland," **The New York Times**, February 22, 2019. This is a review of Patrick Radden Keefe's book and Doyle's personal prose adds to the Van Morrison story. What Van thinks of the Troubles remains an enigma.

CHAPTER 3

THE TRANSITION TO A SOLO CAREER, 1967

"It takes Life to love Life,"

EDGAR LEE MASTERS

"I play in a free form, inspired style; I have no choice but to change it up according to the vibe."

VAN MORRISON

"It was a rare interview for Van.... When I finally met him, he struck me as a shy blues-man, far apart from the ego-driven world of rock & roll."

CAMERON CROWE

❧❧

The transition from fronting a rock group, Them, to that of a solo performer was a move Van Morrison planned with precision. He made it clear to the other members of Them, he had a musical vision apart from the beat group sound. Billy Harrison said Van treated his band mates as if they were hired hands. He wanted a backup band. He didn't want to be in a group. Harrison's comments are not the norm. To a person those working with Van during his solo years describe the Belfast Cowboy as paying a high wage, demanding perfection but never disrespecting the musicians and he is unusually quiet and self-effacing. There is no mystery why Van made the transition to a solo career. He was Them's talent.

Van was the songwriter, the lead singer, and he put together the arrangements while finalizing the recordings. Why should he share his money with the rest of the group? This attitude spelled Them's end. He had grown up performing with Irish show bands. He was never comfortable in this milieu. He hated the ritualistic show band's direction. The uniforms left Van longing for other musical adventures. He looked for his own musical vehicle. He toured America with Them in 1966. He found a new audience for his music. He also learned a great deal about the entertainment industry. It was his initial education into the music business.

ARTISTIC TRIUMPHS, PERSONAL CONFLICT AND THEM

There were some personal triumphs. He was the guiding light behind one of the most interesting rock groups to come out of the U.K. This group, Them, was in the forefront of the initial British Invasion. Did it make him happy? No! One day Van looked at an old copy of the American magazine **Tiger Beat** and saw the description "beat group." His picture was in the article. He lit the magazine on fire. "Van was complicated," Ray Ruff continued. "I never understood him."

He detested the term "English beat group." He did what he could to deflate it. In numerous interviews, Van lashed out at this description. He became so obnoxious to his manager, Phil Solomon, the London impresario, simply drew up a contract to get rid of Morrison. Solomon told me: "Van was impossible. He was too much trouble."

Morrison's experiences with Them infected his personality. He not only disliked his band mates, he screamed to those around him. He said they were mediocre musicians. They were untalented songwriters. When Them released a series of psychedelic records without him, he smugly pointed out they didn't sell. He hated the management team of Phil and Dorothy Solomon. He disliked the restrictions Decca Records placed upon the group. He hated being labeled a lead singer in a band. He talked at length in various interviews about the seamy side of the music business.

Van's friends remember how carefully and shrewdly he gauged his future. He talked at length about solo success. These confidants were invariably in Belfast. Van made few American acquaintances. That changed after he lived in New York, Boston And Woodstock. By the time he moved to California, Van had a coterie of musical and personal friends.

He looked for sage advice and found it in the older show business icons. The wiser musical types Mervyn Solomon, Phil Solomon, Sir Edward Lewis, Bert Berns, Dick Rowe and Solly Lipsitz listened to Van's dreams. They encouraged him. He learned from Them. He could not get rid of the nightmare from playing in Them.

DID VAN DISAPPEAR IN 1967? NO! WHY?

To the casual observer, Morrison seemed to disappear during a portion of 1967. Nothing is further from the truth. He was simply recharging his creative batteries. He was not in a self-imposed exile. He spent much of the year working productively. He spent his time moving toward a series of new albums. He was often secretive and paranoid about his music. Van was inordinately shy. This contributed to his reclusive nature. He had trouble writing unless there was strict silence and total isolation. Close friends caused him problems. He didn't have much money. He was often aloof and cranky.

His close friends didn't understand Van. Phil Coulter referred to him as "morose and down on his luck." The truth is he was writing furiously, as he considered his career options. Rather than disappearing, he was intelligently planning his future. There was a frenetic drive for success. It was built on years of frustration performing with Irish show bands. Van loved and hated the show bands. Performing in large halls before adoring crowds thrilled him. The constraints and limitations of these venues prevented his original talent from shining through. He had to pursue a solo career. He had to secure a contract with a major label that would appreciate his song poems. For the next five years this was Morrison's daily goal. He became a star. He hated every minute of stardom. He wanted to disappear. He couldn't. He was determined not to be another musician sitting around Belfast coffee shops talking about how he could have made it if not for some quirk in the marketplace. To those around Belfast in 1967 Morrison appeared to be down on his luck. They said he was not ready for success. They were wrong. He carefully planned and worked toward a successful solo career. The naysayers were drinking coffee, smoking cigarettes and stuck in Belfast's dingy clubs. Van had a broader vision.

Although he was torn about his future, the change in living areas inspired him to come up with a defined career plan. One that was necessary to master the unsavory characters populating the inner circles of the record companies. He was determined to learn the business end of the industry.

Morrison made friends with a solicitor, an accountant and key people in a London booking agency. He did all this while performing with Them. He became not only acquainted with tax shelters, taxation laws and how to write off expenses, he developed a concept of what was and what was not a business expense. He was learning future financial tools. It was in London's Notting Hill Gate he found the first certified public accountant. He could take his earnings and expenses and make sense of profits and potential tax obligations. There were other diversions in Notting Hill. One of these was the large number of high-quality record stores. Always a collector of jazz and blues vinyl, Van purchased hundreds of vinyl masterpieces.

THE BUSINESS END OF ROCK AND ROLL

Copyrighting songs and collecting royalties obsessed Van. This was a natural reaction to the problems he experienced with Them. There is a murky history in the accounting of Them's royalties. He has attempted to negotiate agreements that gave him increased rights to the Them material without success.

There were pitfalls in a solo career. Foremost among these was finding the proper management. As he prepared to travel to New York to record for Bert Berns and Bang Records, Morrison was not properly represented. He had very little money. He did not have adequate legal representation. He made some ill-advised business and career decisions. He learned from these experiences. They sharpened his business acumen. He learned a great deal about copyrights, collecting mechanical royalties and being properly booked with an adequate, if not, substantial concert guarantee. It was through no fault of his own he could not find proper management. He discovered his songwriting and arranging skills were ripe to be plucked by unscrupulous copyrighting types. He developed a knack or a sixth sense for selecting managers who could properly represent him. He hired and fired people at will. He was never capricious. It was about business.

The rock and roll business is full of slick management types. Morrison came to recognize them. When Morrison made the decision to leave his garage band, Them, he had little experience in making his way through the rock and roll jungle. By 1970, he learned to navigate these treacherous waters. The results, six decades later, attests to Van's survival skills.

After Morrison signed with Warner Brothers, he battled for creative and financial control. His champion at Warner Brothers, Joe Smith, eventually came almost to blows with Van over the direction of his career.

THE FORCES THAT MADE 1967 A TOUGH YEAR

To understand Van Morrison in 1967, it is necessary to examine the forces shaping his music, his personality and his creative life. The years with Them were at an end. He was making the transition to a solo career. He signed a contract with Bert Berns and Bang Records. Then he flew to New York with Berns' $2500 advance.

When Van met with Berns, he played him acoustic demos. The New York producer loved these songs. Van thought he would record in a folk vein. He envisioned his recording sessions as ones with a simple acoustic guitar.

The shock came on March 28, 1967 when Van began polishing his cache of new songs. He was ready to record. Van did! The results were disastrous. It was as if producer Bert Berns brought in a Mexican mariachi band. This is how the early playbacks sounded to Van. When Berns came up with the "sha la la" portion of "Brown Eyed Girl," Morrison was horrified. It was not surprising he was difficult in the studio. Berns changed the direction of his music. Steve Turner described Morrison as "being uncooperative and moody."

Morrison told Happy Traum in 1970 he wrote "Brown Eyed Girl" for an acoustic folk singer. The partnership between Morrison and Berns was doomed from the first day in the studio. The rift didn't develop over time. It was immediate.

In Woodstock, John Platania and others heard Van perform the acoustic version of "Brown Eyed Girl." They loved it. When the record was released, he disowned the song. He blamed Berns' production interference for turning "Brown Eyed Girl" into a pop hit.

As soon as the Bang sessions ended on March 31, 1967, Berns purchased a ticket for Morrison to return to London. He did this to avoid paying for his food and hotel in New York. He didn't have the courtesy to ask him if he wanted to return to Dublin or Belfast. Van flew into London. He stayed for a time in Notting Hill Gate. Van was seen in the local record stores shopping for blues records. Then he returned to 124 Hyndford Street.

"Van was not about to let the Them fiasco continue," Mervyn Solomon remembered. "He was taking hold of his career." When Berns brought Morrison back to New York in August, he rented a boat and they had a launch party on the Hudson River. "Brown Eyed Girl" was a Top Ten hit. The smiling faces during the launch party hid the hostility that simmered beneath the surface.

THE JANUARY TO AUGUST 1967 BELFAST, LONDON AND DUBLIN INTERLUDE

If there was a low part to Van Morrison's solo musical life it is the January through August 1967 period. He spent much of his time in Belfast. During January and February 1967 Van worked night and day on new material. "I think Van had a vision, he didn't always share it with us," Mervyn Solomon continued. "I think in retrospect he was working hard on **Astral Weeks**. But he hadn't recorded **Blowin' Your Mind**. He was working on those songs and attempting to talk about an album that hadn't been recorded."

On March 10, 1967 Van's appearance at BuitenSocieteit in Deventer in the Netherlands was a concert disaster. Why? You name it. Bad backup band! Inadequate venue! Amateur booking agent! Small fiscal guarantee! With Cuby and the Blizzards as his backup band, Van felt uncomfortable. Van's twenty-one minutes on stage made him long for his own band.

The problem with the BuitenSocieteit show is it was billed as a Them show. The six tunes Morrison performed were all Them numbers opening with "One More time" and closing with "Mystic Eyed." In the middle "Gloria" stood out.

Cuby and the Blizzards were unable to effectively back Morrison. They were also uneasy performing in the venue. They felt like they were in an open-air circus. The six-set song cycle included "One More Time," "If You And I Could Be As Two," "Gloria," "Hey Girl," "Sad Eyes" and "Mystic Eyes." When he was interviewed Van talked about his forthcoming Bang album. The concert venue was more like appearing in the circus. The concert was advertised as the Them Revue. This upset Morrison.

Van Morrison with lead singer Harry Muskee of Cuby and the Blizzards

There were nine appearances from March 10 through March 12 with most of the shows simply media appearances. No one was in charge. Morrison received very little publicity and even less money.

Cuby and the Blizzards tagged along. While they are a great Dutch band, they were out of their league attempting to back Morrison.

After returning from the Netherlands, Van took matters in his own hands. According to Mick Ronson, he made a list of things to accomplish. Bert Berns had no idea Van was becoming business minded.

Then just a week after he returned from the so-called Them Review, Berns flew Van back to New York. He began recording an album at the A & R Studio. The session musicians, along with the Sweet Inspirations, as backup singers, made Morrison feel he was ready for the big time.

At the time the Sweet Inspirations were one of the hottest backup vocalists in the industry. The irony is Berns had trouble placing the trio into the middle of Morrison's music. On "Goodbye Baby (Baby Goodbye)," the Sweet Inspirations demonstrated Van had a soul side. Van was already in a position to influence his music. He had demos with his own spin.

When he arrived in New York, Van went straight to Berns' Brill Building office with his demos. Initially, Berns wouldn't listen to his demos. Van persuaded him. Berns listened. He didn't take the songs seriously. He told Van he would have complete freedom in the studio. He could cut his music his way. These were convenient lies. Berns had no intention of allowing Morrison freedom.

When Morrison arrived at the studio to record "Brown Eyed Girl" he envisioned the March 28, 1967 recording as placing his music in the folk genre. That day he not only cut "Brown Eyed Girl," but also "Ro Ro Rosey," "Goodbye Baby (Baby Goodbye)" and "T. B. Sheets." Morrison was surprised by the post-production alterations.

VAN IS DUPED BY BERT BERNS: "BROWN EYED GIRL"

When Van went into the studio, he realized he was duped. He had no freedom. Berns treated him like the janitor. Berns' suggestions drove Van crazy. Berns loved "Brown Eyed Girl." Van hated it. In 1970 a visibly angry Morrison told **Rolling Stone** he allowed Berns control of "Brown Eyed Girl." He said it was a mistake.

Van Morrison: "Berns, he made it the way he wanted it, and I accepted the fact that he was producing it...." That level of cooperation soon ended. Van recognized it was a hit. He temporarily stood aside as Berns took the song south of the border with its modern mariachi sound. It was a lack of money that drove Morrison crazy.

Berns wouldn't pay a nickel for anything. He failed to listen to Van's advice about promotion. He had little time for suggestions. He had his singer tied up in a contract that was as close to slavery as possible.

When Morrison looked back on "Brown Eyed Girl" in a 1997 interview with Edna Gunderson, he reflected: "The reason I wrote it was to get out of handcuffs. It was to get out of being enslaved." Van complained the Berns' estate sold "Brown Eyed Girl" to CBS. He lamented: "They still aren't paying record royalties." The irony is "Brown Eyed Girl" remains a much requested in-concert song.

In 1971 Morrison remarked to Happy Traum: "Bert wanted me to write a song with him that would be a hit, but I just didn't feel that kind of song." Bitterly and with rancor Van continued telling Berns to have someone else record "Brown Eyed Girl." Poverty made Van outraged. He saw no reason for Berns not supplying funds to live. He also hated the "sha la la" that Berns insisted as a musical interlude. Van complained to close friends the producer was "a manipulative asshole."

Van had a final contract obligation with Bang Records. He decided to do something about it. He cut thirty-one nonsense songs. He handed them over to finish his contractual obligation. They were song fragments unsuitable for commercial release. Van said the songs fulfilled the contract. It appeared the songs would never see the light of day. They did. The Bang Masters have had multiple releases. These nonsense songs were part of a 2017 three CD release marketed as **Van Morrison: The Authorized Bang Collection**. When the 1991 Bang Masters came out Van was flummoxed. He went through the roof and complained to the press, as well as anyone else who would listen, about being ripped off his entire career. The nonsense songs sold. Van was surprised they had a long life.

VAN'S NONSENSE SONGS HAVE A LONG LIFE

There were some strange releases of the thirty-one nonsense songs. In 1994 Charly Records in the U.K. released the album with the ubiquitous title **Payin' Dues**. Charly lacked the proper licensing rights but British law and the small number of CDs printed made it a moot point. The two CD release contained eighteen Morrison tracks from the Bang archives and the second CD was the thirty-one nonsense songs. Charly announced it licensed the material from Lost Gold Records, Inc. Rumor on the street is this is a bootleg label. Maybe! Maybe not! This release was followed by the Burning Airlines and Recall Records releases. The strange case of Recall Records is it is a legitimate independent record label operated by the former head of Castle Communications. I contacted Recall asking about permission to publish. I received an e-mail stating: "Fuck you." It wasn't signed. I backed off.

The European market for anything Van Morrison was demonstrated when in Italy in 2002 the **Fruit Tree** label issued these songs in an attractive bootleg with in depth liner notes. In 1999 the German label Hallmark Records released the material as the **New York Sessions '67**. There is a Hallmark Record label in England. The German release is a mystery. Hallmark Records releases a large number of public domain records.

In Los Angeles an entrepreneur and music aficionado, Brian Perera, had a wide variety of labels releasing some great material. He is known for gothic and industrial music. His Purple Pyramid label is a marvelous source for collectors. The label features progressive and psychedelic rock. He has released material by Asia, King Crimson, the Mahavishnu Orchestra and Van Morrison. The only Morrison release contains the nonsense songs. Whether or not he had copyright permission is unknown.

Because he maintains strict control over his catalogue the nonsense songs have a long history of irritating Morrison. His reaction to the legitimate release of this material in 2017 was understandably over the top. But the Berns estate sold the songs. End of story! Van is still pissed. Did he receive royalties on the re-release? I am still looking for that answer.

The 1967 New York experience was not a pleasant one. From March 12, 1967 until September 18, 1967 Van played twenty-six shows to support himself. All but one show was in New York. He played Cleveland's Convention Hall, and the remainder of his shows took place at the Bitter End or Steve Paul's Scene. It wasn't a happy time. He left for Los Angeles to search for a better fiscal pasture.

Bert Berns and Van Morrison in the studio
(Photo by PoPsie Randolph/Michael Ochs Archives)

THE RETURN TO CALIFORNIA: PLAYING HOLLYWOOD'S HULLABALOO

There were a number of gigs Van contracted for while he was getting himself together in Los Angeles. His first show in September 30, 1967, at the Earl Warren Show Ground in Santa Barbara was not a pleasant experience. The show included the Quicksilver Messenger Service and Clear Light. It was advertised as "The Van Morrison Group" whatever that was. Van's name was at the bottom of the concert poster.

His appearance at a trendy Hollywood club, the Hullabaloo, was a portent of things to come. This small dance venue of 6230 Sunset Boulevard was in the heart of Hollywood's entertainment district. The Whiskey A Go Go and the London Fog, where Jim Morrison and the Doors broke through, were just down the street. Another trendy club, Gazarri's, offered entertainment from the newest and latest rock groups.

The Hullabaloo was the new club on the Sunset Strip. The club owner, Tony Ferra, was a visionary who saw huge profits in booking the right acts. Soon the Righteous Brothers, the Buffalo Springfield, Sam the Sham and the Pharaohs and Roy Head headlined.

The Hollywood club scene was a positive and a negative experience. Van was appalled the crowd wanted the old Them tunes. They had not forgotten the Them gigs at the Whiskey A Go Go. Morrison drew a capacity crowd at the Hullaballoo. It was a club date smoothing his transition into a solo career.

Johnny Rivers walked in one night. No one noticed or cared. He stood in awe at the side of the stage. He gave Van his seal of approval. The irony is Morrison had no idea about Rivers or his live albums. Once Van went solo, Rivers over the years listened intensely to his music. He covered "Brown Eyed Girl," "Slim Slow Slider," "Into The Mystic," "Wild Night" and "Songwriter." When Rivers talked about Van, he confessed he was a fan.

The most interesting early test of Morrison's solo career came when he appeared for two nights with the Daily Flash on October 13-14, 1967 at Denver's Family Dog. He loved the psychedelic poster they handed out. The crowd was inordinately receptive to his new music.

105

The Denver police were intent upon catching dope smokers. They blocked off the street during Van's two shows. This discouraged those wanting to see the show, as they thought it was about to be raided. There was still a sizeable crowd. Canned Heat claimed they had marijuana planted on them by an informant during a show. They wrote a song about it. For Van, the Denver shows were a highpoint. No pun intended! After the Denver shows, Van knew there was a successful solo career in the works.

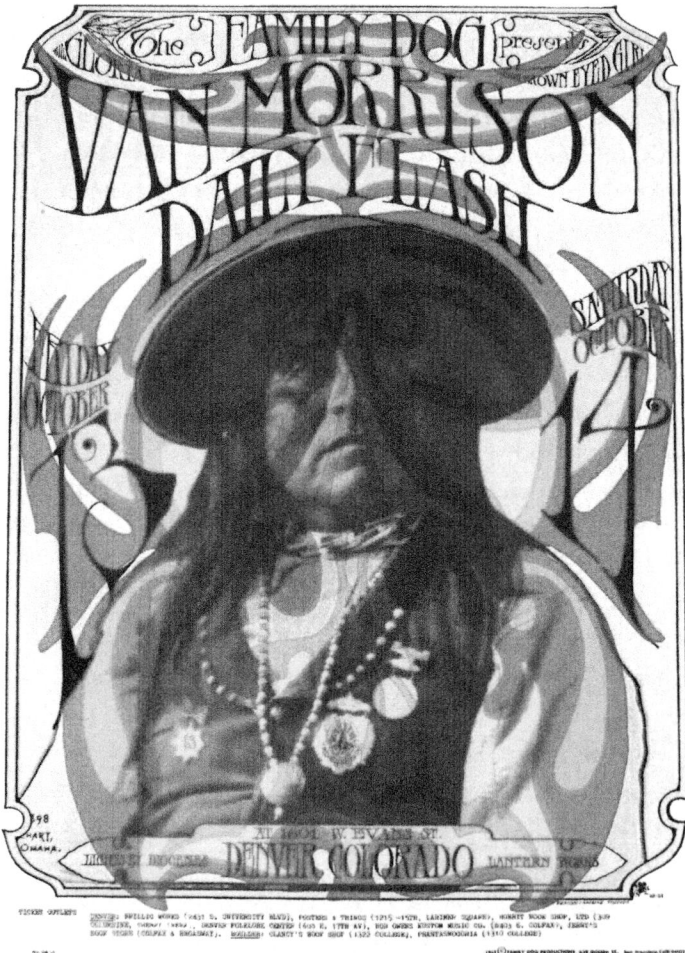

Van-Morrison - Family-Dog-Denver Concert 1967
(Credit: Stanley Mouse and Alton Kelley)

IS THERE A SOLO CAREER FOR ME?

The forces that brought Van Morrison to solo prominence were complex. His rise to stardom was due to his songwriting. Performing didn't come easy. He mastered it for one reason. He fancied himself an interpreter of blues and jazz. It was the creative side of his songwriting that drew interest. Van believed he had to become a lead vocalist to nurture this side of his talent.

There was a brainy carnal thrust to his early songs. The inner workings of Morrison's life provided the grist for his musical phrases. Often his lyrics were tender, then brutal and somehow knowingly sad. There were many streams of consciousness lyrics. They soon find their way into **Astral Weeks**. He learned from his early reading. His desire for variation was tied to reading John Donne, who wrote of what might be in this world and the next life. Van was a Donne disciple. He took this man of letters as one of his early muses.

Business concerns continued to be a driving force. His search for a proper manager was constant. While recording for Decca Records, he had serious problems with the business end of the industry. Van believed Phil Solomon's management style was inadequate. Solomon disputes Morrison's allegations. He offered proof of paid royalties. He said he provided adequate representation. "Van was a difficult person," Solomon remarked to me in his Bournemouth home: "I did everything I could to promote his career. He was impossible. I also paid him." Van differs with this conclusion.

THE BELFAST SABBATICAL AND WHAT IT MEANT

The frequent forays to Belfast were a continuous intellectual sabbatical. He also witnessed the successes and failures of other Belfast musicians. He saw Phil Coulter edging toward a mainstream career. His old band mate Brian Rossi was ensconced in the local cocktail lounge music circuit. He watched Brian Rossi and the Wheels restructure and resurrect their career. It was with limited success. It was a local career. When the Wheels were done, Rossi was playing for old folks in nondescript, decrepit venues singing songs that had had little meaning for his career.

The other problem was the Troubles. By 1972 the presence of British troops, the activity of the IRA and the continual violence forced people to stay at home ending live entertainment. The club circuit, the small rock and roll venues and the places where the bands could expand their talent vanished. Why? He needed time to develop into a solo performer.

The changes in and around Belfast bothered Morrison. The English rock and roll influence, and the battle over the mods and rockers caused Van anguish. He detested popular trends. Particularly, the massive influence of pop culture. The Wellington Street section of Belfast had clothing shops that were a carbon copy of clothes from Lord John's on London's famed Carnaby Street. The John Patrick men's boutique was another example of importing the London styles. Van bought some of these clothes. He was never happy with the local fashion. He was not as the Kinks stated "a dedicated follower of fashion."

WHAT DOES IT TAKE TO MAKE A JUMP TO A SOLO CAREER?

As 1967 ended, Van Morrison was ready for his American adventure. He looked to the blues, to the music of John Lee Hooker and Jimmy Witherspoon and to Boston, New York, Woodstock and San Francisco as cities to articulate his craft.

He remained the son of Northern Ireland. The influence of the Irish show bands was obvious in his songwriting. He blended it with the American blues. When Van used a word like "jellyroll," he placed it effectively in his music. He perfected the blues idiom in a terse Irish sense. He couldn't remain in Ireland to make his mark in the music business. He knew America was the answer.

Life in Belfast was simple. He preferred it to New York or London. Van was realistic. A long-term solo career in Northern Ireland was a virtual impossibility. He knew he had to reside in New York. The decision was delayed until he had enough new material. With the success of "Brown Eyed Girl," his confidence was bolstered.

He had three criteria for jumping to a solo career. One, he was hopeful that he would write and collect the royalties that he had missed with Them. Two, he would be able to write and record whatever he liked. Three, he would be rid of inadequate management and egomaniacal producers. There was a new Van Morrison. He would take charge of his career.

Donal Corvin, a reporter for the Belfast based **City Week**, was an important asset to Morrison. He was one of the few writers Van would sit down with and speak his mind. They were friends. Corvin helped Van to open up to the press. It would be a long time before he was comfortable with the press. The importance of Corvin to Morrison's early solo aspirations is he not only gave him sympathetic coverage, he encouraged Van at a time he needed inspiration.

THE COMMERCIAL SUCCESSES OF 1967 WERE FAILURES

By August 1967 Morrison's single "Brown Eyed Girl" was in heavy rotation on Top 40 radio. He wasn't happy. He recorded an album worth of forgettable songs. At least this is how Van viewed it. Bert Berns and Bang Records began assembling the album. With a hit single, a quickie LP would make everyone money. Van was unhappy with this scenario. His art, not his pocket book, was his mantra.

Van has never been easy to deal with in the studio. "Brown Eyed Girl's" success made him ever more independent minded. There were constant arguments between Berns and Morrison. The New York producer was not only autocratic; he had never been challenged. Van repeatedly pointed out his deficiencies. This was too much for Berns. He couldn't wait to send Van back to Belfast. He repeatedly accused Van of holding back commercial songs. He was! He didn't care for Berns' production methods. He found those around the producer repulsive. He let his feelings be known. Those in the New York record business weren't used to this type of behavior. They didn't know how to handle it. He obviously didn't give Bang his best material. This became a constant source of friction. It was obvious Morrison was now his own man.

Clinton Heylin argues: "Bert Berns death would permanently scar Morrison." Nothing is further from the truth. Van believed it freed him to look to the future. It didn't. There was a long and convoluted road to the Warner Brothers contract.

THE LOOK TO THE FUTURE

What was obvious about Van Morrison in 1967? It is that he was looking to the future. He would continue to look to the future for the remainder of his career. Van was never one to be neither stagnant nor predictable.

He also knew the price of failure. When he signed with Bert Berns and Bang Records, he learned the unscrupulous side of the record business. With Berns' mobster friends hanging around, cracking their knuckles and acting like mob enforcers, Van had material for new songs. He was also scared to death. These guys were heavyweight gangsters. Some were stone killers. This was a bad movie. He had to get out of it. He did! How? He had another way to solve his business problems. He would learn about contracts, mechanical royalties and how to protect his intellectual property. Most rock stars couldn't spell intellectual property. From day one Van went about doing his best to retain copyrights. It was at this point Van decided to become his own guru, develop his own methods and continue to function as his own teacher. He was ready for a new life. Not only a musical one.

VAN COMES TO HARVARD

After recording with Berns, Van moved to Cambridge, Massachusetts, the home of Harvard University, to continue his solo career. What did the area around Harvard offer to Morrison? It was inspiration. He had bookstores where he purchased the William Blake books influencing his songwriting. The coffee shops were a barometer for his political, social and cultural dissent. The war in Vietnam raged and college campuses protested. Van was never political. He was always observant. Harvard provided the laboratory for much of the lyrical beauty flowing into his ever-expanding notebooks. He loved the college bars and restaurants. His Green Street apartment was in a neighborhood filled with aspiring musicians. The nearby Berklee College of Music turned out skilled classical musicians who loved to play rock music. Living was inexpensive.

As Van looked back upon Boston, he saw it as a magical playground to test his music. On the **Astral Weeks** songs Van remarked: "I'd been playing them in dives in Boston and New York, just myself, a bass player and a flute player." Van gets upset when critics suggest the songs were written and produced in final form in Boston. He had worked for half a decade on **Astral Weeks**. "The idea that **Astral Weeks** was some fluke, something done with smoke and mirrors, is complete bullshit," Van remarked to **Uncut** magazine.

The journey to Boston made Van aware Irish music was alive and well in the U.S. Not only were Irish pubs filled with revelers, there were performances by local Irish musicians and the Irish dance clubs kept the culture alive. The annual St. Patrick's Day parade and celebration indicated the vibrancy and political swagger of Irish dominated politics. There was no place more Irish in America than Boston. There was no place more intellectually inclined than Harvard. This college campus, the nearby coffee shops and the scintillating local atmosphere gave Morrison inspiration for his craft. He had a new lease on his commercial life.

WHY 1967 WAS A TRANSITION YEAR

While 1967 was a year of transition, it was the next half decade that led to the emergence of the new Van Morrison. The result created an enduring musical legend.

Van realized he had a potentially large American audience. The Them hits, particularly "Gloria" and "Here Comes The Night," guaranteed concert or club crowds. His solo career was on its way. There were numerous pitfalls. "Brown Eyed Girl" attracted a pop audience Van detested.

The problem with Van's career in 1967 and on into 1968 was a simple one. He was contracted to Bang Records. They failed to record, promote and tour with his product. He had a one-off hit with "Brown Eyed Girl." Rather than promote it, Bert Berns spent three months in Los Angeles searching Laurel Canyon for new talent. His wife had just had a baby and he wanted to sign some new acts. He told Wassel he felt old and out of place in the Los Angeles music scene. By the time he returned to New York he was tired of Morrison. He continued to look elsewhere for talent.

Bert Berns was typical of the industry. He ignored Morrison and worked on other acts. Van had little in the way of personal funds. He received no royalties from Berns. He was learning the intricacies of copyright procedures, the collection of residuals, the signing of contracts, the secrets of management and other facets of the business.

Although he was only twenty-two years old, he had a maturity beyond his years. He had played for years in Irish show bands and then spent two years with the group Them. He was a seasoned music professional. The primary problem was with the industry. In the mid-1960s one-sided recording contracts, shaky management deals and unsavory concert engagements were the norm. These forces temporarily stalled his solo career.

LEAD BELLY AND JACK KEROUAC INSPIRED HIS ARTISTIC DIRECTION: IS MEZZROW THE REAL INSPIRATION?

What prompted Van Morrison's solo career? The answer is a simple one-American poetry and music. It wasn't just the songs but a combination of Jack Kerouac's dreams, Lead Belly's guttural growls, visions of his father's trips to Detroit, American clothing styles, gospel tunes, roots rock and the blues. These influences coalesced to form Morrison's solo persona. Reading was also a part of Morrison's self-education. After he found Jack Kerouac's novels his creativity knew no bounds. Fintan O'Toole asked Van about influential books.

Van Morrison: "Well, three important books for me. A couple of them were given to me by a window cleaner; one was **Dharma Bums**, by Jack Kerouac; the other was **Zen Buddhism** by Christmas Humphreys. And the third one I found myself: **Nausea**, by Jean Paul Sartre."

As a voracious reader, Van was frustrated his early writings had no serious outlet. Soon writing songs became the centerpiece to his voracious reading habit. One book stands out in Morrison's self-education. He found a used, tattered copy at Smithfield Market of the 1946 Mezz Mezzrow book **Really The Blues**. This contains suggestions on how to become a professional musician. Mezzrow was a Chicago kid who learned to play saxophone in reform school. He worked in brothels and bootlegging bars from Chicago to New Orleans while playing with jazz legends Louis Armstrong, Bix Beiderbecke and Fats Waller. Mezzrow's memoir, written with novelist Bernard Wolfe, is a road map to the musical life. Van absorbed it.

BROWN EYED GIRL HAS A LIFE OF ITS OWN

Although Van is fond of stating he has three hundred songs better than "Brown Eyed Girl," it is hard to find one with more airplay and public recognition. In 2000 **Rolling Stone** and MTV published its list of the 100 Greatest Pop songs and Van's tune slotted at forty-nine. In November 2004 **Rolling** Stone listed it was the 109th in the Greatest Songs of All Time. In January 2007 "Brown Eyed Girl" was inducted into the Grammy Hall of Fame. In 2007 it was the fourth most requested pop song amongst disc jockeys.

It wasn't until 1991, in London at the BMI Awards dinner, that "Brown Eyed Girl" was awarded a "Million-Air certificate." This was for air play on the radio. The BMI Awards presenter stated Van had more than nine million radio airplays for "Brown Eyed Girl." No one asked why the late recognition?

There are too many covers of "Brown Eyed Girl" to mention but a few stand out. In 1972 El Chicano charted at forty-five on **Billboard** covering Van's song and in 1982 the Henry Paul Band came in at one hundred and five in a forgettable version. Jimmy Buffet included it on his 1983 album **One Particular Harbour**. In 2009 President Bill Clinton listed "Brown Eyed Girl" as his favorite I-Pod song.

BIBLIOGRAPHICAL SOURCES

See Howard A. DeWitt, **Van Morrison: The Mystic's Music** (Fremont, 1983), passim for a description of Van's transition into the 1970s. Also see Clinton Heylin, **Can You Feel the Silence: Van Morrison, A New Biography** (New York, 2002), chapters 9-11.

Johnny Rogan's, Van Morrison: No Surrender (London, 2005), chapter 10 is a brilliant look at 1967. Rogan attempts to place Morrison within the context of the Irish political-religious troubles.

Interviews with key members of Van's local neighborhood including Molly Fee were important part of this chapter.

Mervyn and Phil Solomon added a great deal to this chapter. An interview with guitarist Chris Michie placed much of the material in this chapter into a clear perspective. The material for an early evaluation of Morrison's career is contained in the Belfast publication City Week. That source was valuable to this chapter.

See B. P. Fallon's article in the **Irish Independent**, June, 9, 1996 for some interesting material on the 1960s. Tony Dey, Van's drummer for a time, provided some important insights into his music. For background material **Melody Maker**, the **New Musical Express** and **Disc** were consulted for 1967. In addition, interviews with Clive Epstein, Joe Flannery, Sam Leach, Tony Sheridan and Bob Wooler helped to reconstruct much of what went on in the English beat movement in the late 1960s.

The BBC Archives in Reading were searched for materials on the British beat groups and the state of the U.K. music industry. A series of interviews with Jesse Hector were important in setting the stage for British music and the London industry in the late 1960s.

Much of the material in this chapter has been covered in more depth and in a different manner in Howard A. DeWitt, **Van Morrison: Them and the Bang Era, 1945-1968** (Fremont, 2005).

Also see Steve Turner, **Van Morrison: Too Late to Stop Now** (London, 1993) for a thoughtful look at Morrison's career with special emphasis upon the problems with the industry. The interviews Turner conducted with Morrison give his book a special feel. A Christian author, Turner is one of few writers to penetrate Morrison natural tendency to avoid or be wary of writers.

Ray Ruff added some important material about Van's early years in California and his relationship to his former band, Them. In Northern California Bill Quarry also established some important material about Van's early American years. The members of Peter Wheat and the Breadmen provided valuable material on Morrison and Them. The drummer, Terry Rissman, was particularly helpful as he kept a diary.

See Matthew Zuckerman, "The Folk Roots of Bob Dylan." http://expectingrain.com/dok/div/influences.html This excellent piece of work on the Internet is an exhaustive look at Dylan's influences and suggests a direction that Van Morrison took.

A 2005 interview with Roy Head added a great deal to this chapter. In the 1980s and 1990s, Lowell Fulson, Bo Diddley and Jimmy McCracklin offered opinions on the English groups and how they changed the industry. Harry Balk, Del Shannon's producer, suggested some important points on the music business and how it shaped Morrison's career.

See Ryan H. Walsh, **Astral Weeks: A Secret History of 1968** (New York, 2018) for material on Van's transition to a solo career. Walsh argues the **Astral Weeks** album was put together in Boston. Hence, the title "A Secret History." It wasn't! What Boston did was to refine Morrison's work habits.

After talking briefly with John Platania in Stockholm when he was on a tour with Chip Taylor, I realized how difficult the early years were for Morrison.

The background to his chapter was helped by **Joel Selvin, Here Comes The Night: The Dark Soul of Bert Berns And The Dirty Business of Rhythm and Blues** (New York, 2015). Selvin's book is well researched, beautifully written and it indicates the depravity of the record business. Selvin does a wonderful job of analyzing how and why Morrison and Berns were at loggerheads from day one. He also shows how Berns' wife carried on the hard-nosed business atmosphere that defined Bang Records and Berns legacy.

See Peter Mills, **Hymns to the Silence: Inside the Words and Music of Van Morrison** (London, 2010), pp. 88-94 for a brilliant analysis of "Brown Eyed Girl."

I interviewed Roy Head for an article that appeared in Blue Suede News and he talked at length about the Boston clubs and he made oblique references with a great deal of admiration for Van Morrison. David Burke, **A Sense of Wonder: Van Morrison's Ireland** (London, 2013) is a brilliant book highlighting Belfast and the Emerald Island's influence. In chapter 6, "American Exile," he places Morrison's American influences upon his music while extolling the virtues of Irish culture. This is a brilliant book. An equally influential study with references to Van Morrison is Gerald Dawe **In Another World: Van Morrison & Belfast** (Newbridge, Ireland, 2017). The Dawe volume is a brief, but brilliant analysis of why and how Belfast is the catalyst to Morrison's songwriting. Dawe is an acclaimed Irish poet and literary figure with close personal ties to Morrison. His writing is much more sophisticated and insightful than the biographers analyze.

For some of the mystery surrounding "Brown Eyed Girl," see, for example, J. D. Nash, "Who Was Van Morrison's 'Brown Eyed Girl?'" American Blues Scene.com, November 8, 2017 https://www.americanbluesscene.com/van-morrisons-brown-eyed-girl/ and Maureen Coleman, "What Inspired Van Morrison To Write Brown Eyed Girl" **Belfast Telegraph**, October 7, 2011. https://www.belfasttelegraph.co.uk/entertainment/music/news/what-inspired-van-morrison-to-write-brown-eyed-girl-28666531.html

For brief comments by Van on Smithfield Market see David Wild, "A Conversation With Van Morrison," Rolling Stone, August 9, 1990. https://www.rollingstone.com/music/music-features/a-conversation-with-van-morrison-232640/ The Wild interview is an unusually candid one for Morrison and the roots of his solo career are revealed in comments about Belfast.

CHAPTER 4

VAN HANGING OUT IN BELFAST: HIS MIND SET, 1967

"Whatever does not destroy me makes me stronger."

FRIEDRICH NIETZSCHE

"I wasn't really happy with it. He picked the bands and tunes. I had a different concept of it."

VAN MORRISON IN CONVERSATION WITH DONAL CORVIN, 1973 ABOUT BERT BERNS' CONTRIBUTION ON THE BANG ALBUM

"What I do is work. It's not magic mirrors."

VAN MORRISON IN CONVERSATION WITH ROLLING STONE'S DAVID WILD, 1990.

❧❧

In 1967, as Van returned home to Belfast, his garage band, Them, came to an abrupt end. They remained in America to record for Ray Ruff's Tower label. Despite new songs and a spate of psychedelic oriented albums, Them could not escape the rock and roll scrap heap.

In 1967 Van lived in Belfast, London and New York. It was a nomadic existence without sufficient funds to maintain a decent lifestyle. As Van's friend Phil Coulter recalled: "I remember Van, in my house in London, after a particular disastrous American tour…. So he went back to Belfast and did very little." Like many of Van's friends who didn't recognize Morrison's career resolve, Coulter never asked

117

about the new songs. His friends offered every opinion available on his future. None were close to predicting his future stardom. There were only a few people who saw Morrison's embryo talent exploding into stardom. "Those who lived Belfast," Mervyn Solomon commented, "had no idea the depth of Van's talent nor the inherent drive in his personality."

BELFAST: A HISTORY THAT IMPACTED THE BELFAST COWBOY

The face of Belfast is a curious blend of the old and the new. A few blocks from the center of town, there is a constant reminder of the violence pervading Van's hometown. As he walked by the facade of the Hotel Europa, Van had no way of knowing it was the most bombed hotel in the world. Protestant schoolchildren in crested blazers laugh as they walk the streets. The hostility from Catholics is everywhere. These ensuing events dominated Morrison's early life.

While Van seldom wandered into Catholic West Belfast, he had little interest in prevailing religious arguments. There is a history to Belfast that has had a dramatic impact upon Morrison. While Van was neither politically nor religiously involved, he was influenced by Northern Ireland's dynamic history. When Morrison walked on Great Victoria Street, he had a sense of how the Troubles impacted Belfast. He kept his feelings about these difficulties to himself. There is no hard and fast evidence he reacted to political problems.

There is a dreary lack of charm in downtown Belfast. It is cold and wet. The twenty plus bombings in 1972 by the IRA were enough to keep Morrison away from his hometown. To this day no one knows how he felt about the bombings. He moved permanently to Northern California.

IRONIC CONTRADICTIONS IN VAN'S PERSONALIITY

In 1967 there were ironic contradictions in Van's personality. He was alternately unhappy and unsure about his future. Then he would experience personal euphoria. He never doubted his talent. He believed his new batch of songs would bring fame and fortune. He was

118

tired. He was confused. He was in need of a reprise. He was no longer interested in performing "Gloria" and "Here Comes The Night." Them was a nightmare he needed to escape.

With the seeds of the new songs, he constructed a solo career. But he needed to rest. He had to find a place where his thoughts could come together. This led to the songwriting producing **Astral Weeks**. In 1964, he began formulating, processing and polishing the material that became the roadmap to his acclaimed album.

When he returned to Belfast, Van told Mervyn Solomon the only way he could forget Them was to pursue a solo career. He also confessed to Mervyn the inspiration he received in his hometown. It was a major force driving his creative energies.

In 1990 David Wild asked Van: "Is music a healing thing for you?" He responded. "Sometimes it is and sometimes it isn't." There was the duality in Van's personality. "You work from the chaos. You just do the best you can do and that's about it," Van concluded.

BACK HOME IN BELFAST

In Belfast, Van felt he could be himself. This explains why he spoke glowingly of his hometown. He had friends who would listen to his ideas and give him positive feedback. The Belfast clubs helped him develop. He experimented with new songs to friendly audiences. He was getting ready to write a concept album or at least a set of topical songs. Bob Dylan's influence was obvious. Few of Van's close associates noticed it. He was full of new musical ideas. They often fell on deaf ears.

Mervyn Solomon: "When Van returned from the American Them tour, he was dour. That ended when he began working on new material." That material was **Astral Weeks**. Back home in Belfast is where Van belonged to be continually creative.

There was an innate cruelty to the local musicians. Brian Rossi believed he would find stardom before Van. There were others who were naysayers. This infuriated Van. It drove him to success. The locals didn't appreciate his prowess on the guitar, saxophone and harmonica. They considered his voice too rough, too bluesy and his songs too contrived.

The idea he had a limited future infuriated Morrison. This thought drove him to new creative heights. To those who said he had failed in America and was returning to Belfast to lick his wounds, he said he was ready for a solo future. Van was a cerebral individual. He had difficulty adjusting to the rock subculture. It was one that didn't celebrate or appreciate an intelligent approach to rock and roll music.

While living with his parents in East Belfast, Van had time to write and listen to music. There was no one who was more influential on Van than Bob Dylan. To his Belfast friends, he talked of Dylan's lyrical prowess. The Belfast Cowboy had time to digest Dylan's lyrics. He also studied his songwriting techniques. Van was too original to mimic Dylan. He was indebted to Dylan's themes. Morrison differed due to his blue-collar work ethic. He was an Irish based singer with poetic insights. How did early Dylan influence Morrison? The comparisons to Dylan were inevitable. Why? Theme, song construction and the overall intellectual impact were similar to Dylan.

JUST LIKE BOB DYLAN

From 1963 to 1972, Van spent a decade listening to Bob Dylan. He loved "It's All Over Now Baby Blue." He searched through Dylan's albums and songs for ideas. He also noted Dylan's lyrical structure and use of musical icons.

It was a combination of folk influences and rock and roll energy Dylan embraced which intrigued Morrison. From the time Van heard **The Freewheelin' Bob Dylan**, he was hooked. He purchased the record at Belfast's Smithfield Market. Soon Mervyn Solomon and Solly Lipsitz were hearing about Dylan from Morrison. When Van recorded "It's All Over Now Baby Blue" on the Them Again album, he paid tribute to his muse.

Van thought of himself as the child of Jack Kerouac. Morrison was a strong believer in the intellectual freedom of the Beats. Why did Van love Kerouac? It had little to do with his writing. Jack Kerouac was the guru for two Irish writers. They were Dublin poet Paul Durcan and novelist and poet Patrick Kavanagh. In his final novel, **Vanity of Duluoz**, Kerouac described his vision of Ireland which Durcan and Kavanagh embraced. They also loved Kerouac's jazz inflected prose as

120

did Morrison. They were poets who listened to the blues. They had a blue-collar working-class mentality. They grew up poor. They identified with and became part of the Van Morrison mystique with a Jack Kerouac twist.

Not only did Van read and appreciate Kerouac, he connected later in life with like-minded individuals. Hence, his friendship and admiration for the work of Durcan and Kavanagh. Kerouac's prose influenced Van's writing to use the stream of consciousness prose characteristic of the Beats.

Paul Durcan is a year older than Morrison. He became a friend. He is a fan. Durcan co-wrote "In The Days Before Rock 'n' Roll" while adding a unique vocal compliment. He is a factotum for Morrison's songwriting. The Dublin born poet in a May 1988 essay in the literary magazine, **Magill**, praised Morrison's intellectual mysticism. Durcan's "The Drumshanbo Hustler: A Celebration of Van Morrison," argued the Irish Minister of Education would do well to include thirty of Morrison's songs in the national curriculum. He listed the Top Thirty of what he labeled "Morrison's poems."

1. Summertime in England
2. Rolling Hills
3. In the Garden
4. Cleaning Windows
5. Listen to the Lion
6. Snow in San Anselmo
7. Rave on, John Donne
8. Alan Watt's Blues
9. A Sense of Wonder
10. Hard Nose the Highway
11. Madame George
12. Queen of the Slipstream
13. Gloria
14. Into the Mystic
15. If You and I Could Be As Two
16. Inarticulate Speech of the Heart
17. Tore Down a la Rimbaud
18. Cypress Avenue
19. Foreign Window
20. Tir na Nog
21. One Irish Rover
22. Ballerina
23. And It Stoned Me
24. The Streets of Arklow
25. T.B. Sheets
26. Ivory Tower
27. Hey Girl
28. St. Dominic's Preview
29. And the Healing Has Begun
30. Full Force Gale

Durcan concluded: "No Irish poet since Kavanagh has produced poetry of the caliber of those thirty compositions." That said it all. He remarked in order to introduce the poems of William Blake one had to be familiar with Morrison's "Listen To The Lion." This was heady praise. Durcan observed: "'Summertime in England,' which to me is an Irishman's Hymn to the Englishness that is in all of us if we care to look inside ourselves - which, of course, so many of us don't...."

Them: featuring Van Morrison
(The DECCA Record Company)

THE NON-CORPORATE LEAD SINGER AS JACK KEROUAC

When people refer to the Belfast Cowboy as part of the English Invasion, he detests the term. He was an outsider. Rod Stewart remarked: "It is amazing that Van Morrison made it, he isn't a corporate kind of record guy."

Mervyn Solomon: "I always believed Van was the non-corporate lead singer with a Jack Kerouac tone."

The non-corporate nature of Van's career was demonstrated when he failed to cooperate with Phil Solomon's management or Sir Edward Lewis' concept of recording for Decca Records. Van would do it his way. He had been the lead singer in a group that was fragmented and operating without his powerful lead vocals. He felt like no one appreciated the power of his voice, his writing and his overall talent. He was rarely featured in the publicity surrounding British groups. His resentment was paramount. The chip so prevalent on Van's shoulder made him difficult.

What was the influence of the Beat Generation and Jack Kerouac on Van Morrison? He acknowledged Jack Kerouac's influence during interviews and in song. In "On Hyndford Street" Van sings of his early influences. It is in language that Kerouac influenced Morrison's songwriting. "Real, Real Gone" is a Morrison song indicating the cadence of **On The Road** in which Kerouac writes someone is "really gone." When he moved to Marin County, Morrison frequently was seen in San Francisco's City Lights Books at Broadway and Columbus purchasing books by beat writers. Kerouac, Lawrence Ferlinghetti and Allen Ginsberg. They were key Beat influences upon Morrison's songwriting. He recalled to Irish journalist Fintan O'Toole his thoughts on Kerouac.

Van Morrison: "Have you read **Dharma Bums** (by Jack Kerouac)? The spontaneity of the writing and just the way it was unfolding." Kerouac's connection to Zen Buddhism influenced Van's religious education.

BETRAYAL: THE MONEY QUESTION AND THEM

The money question angered Morrison. He had other grievances. He was upset with the way his former band mates treated him after he left Them. He was incensed with Billy Harrison's comments to the press. During numerous interviews, Harrison pointed out he organized the Gamblers in Belfast with Alan Henderson and Ronnie Millings. When Eric Wrixon and Van Morrison were added to the Gamblers, they became Them. Harrison said he was the band leader and manager until Phil Solomon came into the picture. He also pointed out Van was the last person to become a member of Them.

I asked Alan Henderson, while he was living in Minneapolis, who founded Them? He said it was he and Harrison. "Anytime you read Van put a group together, he didn't," Henderson continued. "He was the last man in."

Them's royalties vanished. The tensions grew. Morrison's role became the center piece as the band imploded. Van argued he was the brain who put the band together. Them's radio hits featured his distinctive vocals. Them went on tour with another lead singer. This was unforgiveable. He never asked the various musicians who passed through Them to treat him shabbily. They did!

Ray Ruff: "When Van left Them that was the end of the group. I didn't realize it. The band thought he could be replaced. He couldn't."

As Them performed without Van, this angered him. It wasn't so much the money. It was the sense of betrayal he felt toward his old mates. This made for an acrimonious end. He also was hostile to the American promoter, Ray Ruff, who took Them into a psychedelic direction.

The group had a recording contract with the American Tower Record label that went nowhere. Van was vindicated. The group without Morrison did not prosper. The reason was obvious. They missed Van's vocals.

During the post-Them era, many people around Morrison believed his career was over. They told him his music didn't fit into the ever-changing world of rock music. The world was in the midst of the second phase of the British Invasion. There was limited attention paid to Morrison. That would change dramatically in the next year.

VAN'S PSYCHE IN 1967

The drama surrounding his garage band, Them, had a dramatic impact upon Morrison's psyche. He was constantly distrustful of people. He found it difficult to employ the same musicians. His concern about royalties or concert guarantees often turned ugly. He exhibited a kind of professional paranoia about people in the music business. Generally, it was justified.

When he returned to East Belfast his neighbors noticed the difference. He was aloof, diffident and easily provoked. His psyche was a fragile one. He needed to be alone to think and to plot his future.

There were other problems. The music business was undergoing intense change. Record executives began dressing like the musicians. Dan Bourgoise, Bug Music's founder, pointed out double-breasted suits gave way to bell-bottoms and leisure suits. Everyone seemed to be smoking a joint. The prevalence of drugs and the changing structure of record deals clouded the industry. These forces obscured the financial misdeeds of the record labels. The needs of the artist were seldom considered. Van believed he was not receiving his just rewards. He became increasingly difficult. The result was he was shut off from key industry insiders. This contributed to his decision to return to Belfast.

He was exploding with creativity. He wanted to write a concept album. This new album would weave poetic images beyond traditional rock and roll music. **Astral Weeks** was born.

THE FITZROY STREET APARTMENT AND THE SEEDS OF GREATNESS

While he was hanging out in Belfast, Van spent an inordinate amount of time visiting with friends, local musicians and the characters that hung around town. Many images from his Belfast youth appear in his songs.

A group of friends including Janet Martin, Joan McClelland, Gwen Carson, Ann Denvir and a young art student Ursula Graham-White leased a flat that became a party central location on Fitzroy Street. It was a place to party and a premier hangout for beautiful young ladies. Van was for a time a regular. He was looking for material for his solo career. He was hurt by the lack of respect for his new musical direction. Only Mick Cox gave him daily approval.

It didn't take long for Van to tire of these people. He saw himself trapped in Belfast. If he continued the Fitzroy party scene, Van doubted he would work hard on his music. He made the decision to leave as soon as possible for New York. No one, with the possible exception of Mick Cox, realized how serious Morrison was about his career.

Since Van loved to party, he found it hard to leave the Fitzroy flat. He wandered down there frequently. It was at the Fitzroy house Van tried to educate his friends on the joys of listening to Sonny Boy Williamson, Lead Belly or John Lee Hooker. Whoever was in the crowd often looked on in amazement? What the hell was Van talking about?

MICK COX AND HIS BELFAST ROLE

While Morrison was dealing with Bert Berns and Bang Records, Mick Cox was there to help him through the minefield that is the American record business. When Van signed a one-year contract with Bang on January 9, 1967, he had hopes for U.S. hits. Who was better than Berns to deliver hit 45s? Cox said no one.

What Van didn't see was the fine print in Berns' agreement. The contract stipulated a four-year option. Van talked daily with Cox at a local Belfast coffee shop Isabeals. While in Belfast, Van told Cox he was eager to return to New York. The work ethic characterizing Morrison's later career was well and alive in 1967. Van also sat in with local bands as he worked on his songs. Belfast was a ballast to an ego needing reinforcement. Cox was the friend encouraging Morrison's nascent talent.

After Van recorded in New York and returned home for a brief time in 1967, Cox was the person he shared his Bang 45 of "Brown Eyed Girl" with while discussing his experiences with Berns. Cox's

Belfast role was as a cheer leader for Morrison's brilliant original sounds.

Morrison complained Berns' desire to make money made Van's artistic vision a blurred one. The idea of a serious rock artist with a thick Irish accent few could understand did not sit well with Berns. The numerous letters Van wrote to Cox, while in America, suggests an enduring friendship. The willingness of Morrison to accept advice from a peer musician with enormous talent helped Morrison's musical journey

MICK COX ON MORRISON'S CHARACTER: VAN RESPONDS

In many respects, Mick Cox was a role model for Morrison. Van had the success. Cox provided some learning points. It was Cox who suggested London was the place to make it in the music business. Van left for London's Notting Hill neighborhood. Cox visited him regularly.

Where and when did Morrison connect with Cox? It was in Belfast. It was after he signed with Bang Records that Morrison began late in the night conversations in Belfast's numerous coffee shops on the High Street. Soon Cox and Morrison were jamming in local clubs.

Cox was an established Belfast musician. In 1966 Ember Records issued an album with the five top groups from Belfast's Maritime Club. Cox's band, the Alleykatz, was the centerpiece of this attempt to bring Belfast bands into the U.K. mainstream. Their song "Chicago Calling" dominated the album. It appealed to Morrison. It was a piano influenced blues composed by legendary British blues pioneer Cyril Davies.

Van and Cox spent an enormous amount of time writing songs. At the Fitzroy flat, where Cox and Morrison hung out, there were all night writing and music sessions. The locals, who came in and out of the Fitzroy apartment, remember Morrison as shy and reclusive. One local, Janet Martin, recalls Cox and Morrison often talked philosophy. They were as often deep in discussions about music. He educated his Belfast friends on the music of Lead Belly and Sonny Boy Williamson. They were disinterested. Van quickly concluded they were local losers. He had to leave Belfast. His creativity faced a challenge.

It was at Cox's small Limestone Road flat that Morrison hurried to when his **Blowin' Your Mind** album arrived in Belfast. They sat and listened to it. After the euphoria of listening to the album, Van confessed to Cox he lost control of the project. He wasn't happy. Cox and Morrison did like one song "He Ain't Give You None." They played it over and over arguing whether or not it was a blues tune. They were also mesmerized by "T. B. Sheets." Eric Gale's guitar work was another subject they debated.

Without Mick Cox the Belfast interlude would have been more difficult. Van never forgot his friendship. They worked together until Cox died. After Van moved to the U.S., Cox visited him when he was touring with the Jimi Hendrix Experience. Cox had a single on Track records, "Follow Me," and he was in the mist of career advancement. Van invited him to sign on as a session musician for **Astral Weeks**. He couldn't! He had other contractual commitments.

One of the byproducts of Morrison's friendship with Cox is Van wrote a series of revealing letters to his friend. These letters demonstrate Van was working hard on his career. He had a defined vision for his future. The letters are not only an indication of how and why Morrison succeeded, they suggest his literary flair.

The six letters Morrison wrote to Cox offer insight into the Belfast Cowboy's psyche. They suggest his musical vision. Cox had some important observations about Morrison's character. While Van was indifferent to politics, he was an astute observer. The disagreements between local Protestants and Catholics at the clubs piqued Morrison's curiosity. It was never enough to get him involved in politics. He was singularly devoted to his music. Upon returning to London, Van spent considerable time at Cox's apartment. When Van took out an acoustic guitar, he played nothing but original tunes. Ones no one had heard. He didn't pander to the mod musical styles of the day. He was oblivious to current trends. He remained his own man. Even without a hit record and visible means of support, he worked 24/7 on his musical dreams. **Astral Weeks** was on Van's mind. He quietly worked it into a commercial format.

There were others who watched Van's steely resolve. Mervyn Solomon, Phil Coulter, Phil Solomon and Solly Lipsitz talked at length about the mood they perceived in Van's music. He was a solid craftsman with a, blue-collar countenance.

While he was in New York, Van wrote a series of letters to Cox. Van's letters were written from New York's King Edward Hotel. At the time Van was attempting to deal with Bert Berns, Bang Records, while establishing a U.S. music career. An excerpt from one of the letters suggests the pressures of and the lonely, frustrated path of his early music career.

Dear Mick:

"I received your letter a few days ago. As you probably gather from the [address] I've moved again. I'm at present staying at the home of a friend who is interested in management business of some sort. I cannot really say what exactly I've got going as of now because there are about 50 different directions to go. Basically I'm trying to establish something musically and take it from there. ... I want to form a happy harmonious band that grooves with each other and enjoys playing the kind of music which they like playing which sounds very complicated but I'm sure that's the environment I can work well in and produce the best sounds."

This is one of six letters Morrison wrote to Cox while spending time in New York. He was angry. He was bored. He took his hostility out on Bang Records. In another letter he labels Bert Berns the person who "was a Fuck Up." There was also a Christmas card signed "Van and Brenda." The letters, which were put up for auction, illustrate how close Cox and Morrison were in 1967-1968.

BELFAST: GETTING RID OF THEM

No one knows how Van felt stuck in Belfast in 1967. After he established himself as the lead singer in Them, Van guided the group to their U.K. and U.S. hits. "Baby Please Don't Go," "Mystic Eyes," "Gloria" and "Here Comes The Night" charted and the irony was Van didn't have enough money to live in a comfortable manner. It is not surprising he was unhappy. Living with his parent's on Hyndford Street was not a recipe for success. His mother, Violet, was a constant inspiration. She encouraged him to play his saxophone and to write day and night.

Molly Fee recalled it was a tough time for Van. He wasn't sure about his future. He had hit records. He wrote furtively. He played his music loudly well into the night. He nurtured his talent despite the tough times.

Van was stuck in Belfast. He viewed his hometown as a positive influence. It was a place where he could go and be himself. The limited Belfast musical clubs drove him to New York. Jackie Wilson and not Lead Belly was on the Morrison record player. The number of soul artists with Bang Records impressed Van. He was puzzled by key local music people with deep knowledge, notably Solly Lipsitz, Mick Cox, Billy Harrison, Eric Wrixon and Gil Irvine. They lectured Van that the Belfast music scene was an innovative one. It wasn't! He scoffed at this notion. Only Mervyn Solomon told him to leave. In his youth Solomon trained in New York for a business career. "I told Van he would learn more about the record business in a month in New York than a year in Belfast."

DID THE BELFAST SCENE DRIVE MORRISON TO NEW YORK?

Belfast's musical culture was little more than a pale imitation of London's beat music scene. "I don't think the locals realized that we imported London bands to appear in our clubs while many of our local groups didn't receive recognition," Mervyn Solomon said.

It appeared 1967 was a year of musical growth. The arts were blending with the rock and roll revolution. There was speculation among Morrison's friends the lack of depth in the Belfast cultural scene drove him to New York.

Mervyn Solomon: "Van had a vision for his future. He was more complex than his contemporaries."

Had Van spent more time in Belfast, his friends claim, his music would have been even stronger. They argue that it was a time of ferment and change. This is self-serving drivel. Belfast's Jazz Club drew a sophisticated crowd. But few major acts. The patrons were posers not innovators. Brian Rossi presided over a scene that was more copyist than original. Van often pointed this out to Rossi. Van suggested the local musicians were stuck in a time warp. They were playing the easy clubs for the quick money. He told Rossi it wasn't for him.

Mervyn Solomon: "Van saw Belfast as provincial. He loved the town. He loved the people. He realized the limitations of the local music scene."

With many of Van's former Them band mates joining up with a new group known as the Federals, Morrison felt left out of the mix. He continued to write and prepare for a solo career. There was skepticism among many around Belfast as to his chances for success. Local musicians believe his feral personality would hurt his career. Ironically, it helped him. He beat Bang Records and Warner Brothers and the industry. His perennial stage fright and unpredictable nature made solo stardom seem a virtual impossibility to many in Belfast.

WHAT DID VAN TAKE FROM THE ROCK AND BLUES MASTERS?

When Van began his solo career, the blues, folk and rock and roll past masters influenced him. There were lessons to be learned from a wide variety of Lead Belly songs. Equally important was the music of Gene Vincent, Elvis Presley, Jackie Wilson and lesser-known artists like Charlie Gracie, Johnny Kidd and Billy Lee Riley. With the exception of Jackie Wilson, these artists combined rockabilly, country and first-generation rock and roll. The talking blues infatuated him. While Lead Belly was the dominant influence there was material from those who covered this seminal pioneer. Van's genius was to combine and mix genres with an original touch.

As Morrison planned his solo career, he created some unlikely lyrical directions. It was in his early Warner hits that the rock and blues masters had a dramatic impact. When Van's Warner single "Come Running" backed with "Crazy Love" was released in May 1970, it signaled the influence of the talking blues. This is a type of music he was raised on.

The shelves in Van's homes were resplendent with rock and blues masterpieces. It was only natural he crafted his early 1970s hits from this material. Constantly measuring himself against the rock and blues giants, Morrison wrote a large body of work that remains the stuff of legend.

Lead Belly first appears in Morrison's visual imagination when he covered a Lead Belly inspired version of "C. C. Rider." It was Lead Belly's "Make Me A Pallot On Your Floor," which imbued Morrison with the ideas for many of his early 1970s songs.

The manner in which Huddie Leadbetter mixed folk and blues intrigued Morrison. In 1978 Van told Jonathan Cott it was Lead Belly's vocals that inspired his singing style. He also said Lead Belly's royalty problems were much like his own.

Van was analytical looking at other musicians. It is not surprising he found two qualities in Jackie Wilson's music. One was the spontaneity of the vocals. The other was the intense soul quality in his voice. When he wrote "Jackie Wilson Said," Van paid tribute to these influences.

Another important influence resulted from Johnny Kidd's frenetic vocal on "Shakin' All Over." This song not only had an impact upon Morrison's vocal style, he employed Kidd like vocals in his early solo career.

There were two musical obsessions in Morrison's life. One was with the blues and the other was with American roots music. When Gene Vincent sang "Be Bop A Lula," Morrison found a sound in the sweet musical wilderness of Vincent's 1950s hit record. Van tempered Gene Vincent's rockabilly tune with Charlie Gracie's pop vocal style interpreting his songs.

Van realized the blues and rock masters were a life force to be interpreted in a modern light. To Van there was only a future in rock and blues music. The art of the great songwriters and performers, according to Morrison, was to forget the flavor of the day and write for posterity. He believed it was imperative to compose for oneself. There is timelessness to Van's music because of this notion. His songwriting is full of sustaining truth; a lesson he learned from the classic rock and blues musicians.

Van Morrison Contemplating Belfast years later

BIBLIOGRAPHICAL SOURCES

Interviews with Mervyn Solomon and Phil Solomon were important to this chapter. Also see Johnny Rogan, **Van Morrison: No Surrender** (New York, 2005, paperback edition, 2006), chapter11. Molly Fee offered information on the East Belfast area and Van's return to the old homestead.

For Van's journey in and about Belfast see, Clinton Heylin, **Can You Feel The Silence? Van Morrison, A New Biography** (London, 2002), chapters 9-11. Also see Howard A. DeWitt, **Van Morrison: The Mystic's Music** (Fremont, 1983), passim. A useful book on Irish history is Donald S. Connery, **The Irish** (London, 1968), passim.

A lengthy interview with Ray Ruff helped this chapter. Also, Dan Bourgoise of Bug Music provided a great deal of information on the song copyright and collection procedures. Others who contribution to a knowledge of the early 1960s include Bob Wooler, Brian Kelly, Roger Armstrong, Jesse Hector, Sam Leach and Clive Epstein.

See Gerald Dawe, **The Rest Is History** (Dublin, 1998) for a look inside the Irish character and how it influenced Van Morrison. Also, see Benjamin Filene, **Romancing The Folk: Public Memory And American Roots Music** (Chapel Hill, 2000) for an academic look at some influences upon Morrison.

Van's continual search for spiritual enlightenment can be traced in the following superb study, Steve Turner, **Hungry For Heaven: Rock 'n' Roll And The Search For Redemption** (London, 1998).

Some of the material in this chapter has been covered in a much different manner in Howard A. DeWitt, **Van Morrison: Them and the Bang Era, 1945-1968** (Fremont, 2005).

Linda Gail Lewis provided some important material on this part of Morrison's career. Joe Flannery in Liverpool suggested some of the problems that Morrison may have faced in the industry. Also see John Collis, **Van Morrison: Inarticulate Speech of the Heart** (Boston, 1996), passim. For Phil Coulter's comments see the **Hot Press**, April 2000.

See Mic Moroney, **Waking Up in Dublin: Authentic Music and Culture of the Celtic Capital** (Dublin, 2004) for a look at how coffee influences culture. See the 1985 interview with Stephen Davis in **New Age** for Van's take on religion.

For Morrison's reflections on Belfast see, Maureen Coleman, "Van Morrison: Today's Pop Industry Knows Nothing About Music," **Belfast Telegraph**, February 27, 2009. This is an unusually perceptive look at how Van views the recent music scene.

An interview with Lemmy Kilmister in Green Bay, Wisconsin at a rockabilly event prompted him to recall the poverty and despair haunting Van in 1967-1968. The Motorhead icon commented in-depth of the drive, the vision and the commitment to his sound driving Morrison.

See David Fricke, "Van Morrison: The Rolling Stone Interview," **Rolling Stone**, September 26, 2016 for Van's comments on his blues roots. https://www.rollingstone.com/music/music-features/van-morrison-the-rolling-stone-interview-102974/

See the argument that Van Morrison's lyrics should be required reading and listening in Irish schools. This article by an esteemed Irish poet suggests the legendary feel for his poetry, see Paul Durcan, "The Drumshanbo Hustler: A Celebration of Van Morrison," **Magill, May 1988.** http://www.oocities.org/tracybjazz/hayward/van-the-man.info/reviews/durcan.html

For Irish influences in Kerouac's novels, see Michael S. Begnal, "To Be An Irishman Too: Jack Kerouac's Irish Connection," **Studies:**

An Irish Quarterly, Volume 92, number 368, pp. 371-377. Also see Peter Mills, **Hymns to the Silence: Inside the Words and Music of Van Morrison** (London, 2010), pp. 1, 253-255. In 2003 Van told Niall Stokes that Jack Kerouac was a continual major influence. See Niall Stokes, "Van Morrison: Hot Press Interview," **Hot**, October 28, 2003, passim.

The DVD **Van Morrison is Ireland**, which was released in 1981, is a concert recorded in 1979 with images of Belfast and shots of Ireland. The inclusion of Cyprus Avenue and the DVD includes ten songs recorded in Belfast and Dublin in February 1979. This was the first time Morrison played Belfast since 1965. The best review is by Brian Hinton who observed: "The crowd explodes, as do Van's lungs on I've Been Working, blowing the guys out of his harmonica." For the Hinton review see **Celtic Crossroads: The Art of Van Morrison** (London, 1997), pp. 215-216. This DVD included Katie Kissoon's backing vocals on "Moondance" suggesting how important her vocal sound was in altering the original. Kissoon was a backup singer on four Morrison albums. Her artistry is a brilliant addition to Van's music.

For Billy Harrison, see, Richie Unterberger, "Billy Harrison Interview," **Ugly Things**, issues 31-21, 2011.

The close relationship between Van Morrison and fellow Irish musician Mick Cox was a long standing one. The London Bonhams Auction House sold six letters and other memorabilia from Cox's estate. The letters show that Morrison asked Cox while he was living in New York to join his band. But Cox decided to become a member of Eire Apparent and he continued for some time in that ill-fated group. The Morrison letters reveal not only a friendship but a common musical direction. There is also one Morrison letter to Cox written from Boston auctioned off by The Sale Room, The Home of Arts an Antiques Auctions.

For Van discussing Jack Kerouac's influence see Fintan O'Toole, "Being Famous Is Not Great For the Creative Process. Not For Me, Anyway," **Irish Times**, August 29, 2015. https://www.irishtimes.com/culture/music/van/van-morrison-being-famous-is-not-great-for-the-creative-process-not-for-me-anyway-1.2332216 In this interview, Morrison looked back with clarity, honesty and a sense of purpose describing his career. Some of Van's comments are surprising. He saw great optimism after World War II than during the time of the Troubles. He described Belfast as "a quiet village." He didn't find his work ethic surprising, "It's just what people did," Van reflected. When he began reading Morrison realized he fit into the "outsider pattern." He reflected on a recent book he read Seamus Heaney's **Preoccupations**. The influence of American rock and roll is obvious when Morrison remarks: "The Americans were doing it because it was their world – the blues was their world, rock'n'roll was their world – but nobody on this side of the Atlantic was doing that." Thus the reason for Van settling in the U.S.

❦❦

CHAPTER 5

BOSTON 1968: THE BOSTON TEA PARTY AND EXPERIMENTATION

"It's a miracle we played anywhere. It's a miracle we got to any gigs at all."

JOHN SHELDON

"Being a muse is a thankless job, and the pay is lousy"

JANET RIGSBEE

"These were written prior to '68 over a period of five years."

VAN REMARKING TO PASTE MAGAZINE, FEBRUARY 2000 ON WHEN THE ASTRAL WEEKS SONGS WERE COMPOSED.

❦❦

Boston was the final gestation point for **Astral Weeks**. While living in dank, dirty, low-end apartments, Van put the finishing touches on his masterpiece. He continued to work diligently writing his early 1970s hit records that made him a legend. When Van left Boston he had a cache of hit records in his coffee stained notebooks. Had it not been for the Boston environment as well as three young talented musicians, Van might not have made **Astral Weeks** or prepared for the hit records of the early 1970s.

HOW DID 1968 SHAPE VAN MORRISON?

The Morrison's settled in Boston at a momentous time. In 1968, Lyndon B. Johnson announced he would not seek re-election, anti-war protests disrupted government, free peace protests virtually closed down universities and the youthful groundswell against the Vietnam War added to the chaos surrounding the nation. Timothy Leary asked young America to "tune in, turn on and drop out." This led to a politically active youth culture.

In Boston and Cambridge students protests against the war in Vietnam, the rise of the Black Panthers indicated an increased African American political culture, the growing hippie communes and the rise of alternative politics were events that had no influence upon Morrison or **Astral Weeks**. He was oblivious to the political drama surrounding America.

Religion was another matter. The number of religious figures from rabbis, to liberal Episcopalians and other libertine religious activists who crusaded for changes in the American political system intrigued Morrison. The religious synergy in America's radical politics gave Van negative thoughts on the direction of his adopted country. It may have influenced his move to Fairfax California in the early 1970s. It was calm and bucolic in Fairfax.

The 1968 hippies, political radicals and youth culture rejected the 9 to 5 work day. The idea of earning, consuming and working day and night wasn't for youthful radicals. It also wasn't for Van Morrison. The difference was Morrison's blue-collar work ethic drew him to stardom. What was important to the Belfast Cowboy was creative growth and hardworking intellectual pursuits. Van was centered on his music. He never bought the hippie dream. The idea of communes and moving back to the land never entered his mind. He was a student of a movement a decade earlier known as the Beats. He preferred Jack Kerouac to Timothy Leary.

In 1968 Morrison crafted his song from the backdrop of America's tumultuous history. As he lived through the tension, the turmoil and the changes in popular culture, he wrote songs reflecting his view of an evolving nation.

BOSTON 1968: THE BOSTON TEA PARTY AND ...

Morrison rejected much of what defined 1968. When Country Joe and the Fish sang "smoking marijuana is more fun than drinking beer," Van chuckled. He believed happy songs, not hippie, anti-war dirges, provided the key to his successes. As the counterculture dream gave way to disco, leisure suits and Richard M. Nixon, Van settled in Fairfax, California. Some argue his career was defined in the eight months he lived in Boston. How did the Bosstown sound, the presence of Harvard and the freedom to play Boston's small clubs help the evolution of **Astral Weeks**? Boston did have a dramatic impact upon Morrison and **Astral Weeks**.

THE MYSTERY OF BOSTON'S IMPACT UPON ASTRAL WEEKS

For eight months Van and his young wife, Janet, lived in various places around Cambridge and Boston. On Green Street they attempted to find a life as Van worked day and night on **Astral Weeks**. Living was cheap. Life was good. There were music venues providing a meager living.

There is a mystery that evolved while they were in Boston. When **Astral Weeks** appeared there as a strange, perhaps elusive, paean to Boston, Ryan W. Walsh claims there would not have been an **Astral Weeks** album without Boston. **Astral Weeks** was written, the songs were performed in seedy bars and the concept was discussed a half a decade before Morrison moved to his Green Street apartment. Walsh is correct on one point. The **Astral Weeks** material received its final polishing in the shadow of Harvard. Perhaps its intellectual nature reflected the Cambridge bars, coffee shops, bookstores and seedy music clubs.

With his tape recorder, a few days of sunshine, a great deal of coffee and cigarettes, Van practiced, polished and rewrote **Astral Weeks** in the dank, dark, spartan living quarters he shared with Janet and her son Peter. It was a euphoric time for Morrison. He was creative. He lived in a town where there was a large Irish population.

Boston's primary influence was lyrical. The poetic quality of Van's writing intensified. His production increased dramatically. He sat in the backyard sun with an ancient reel-to-reel tape recorder singing, pausing to write and singing again. Intellectual stimulation and solitude brought Morrison's creativity to the fore. The brief time in Boston prompted Van to write effusively of the city, the music gigs, the atmosphere and how it all came together.

Van Morrison:
I saw you coming from the Cape, way from Hyannis Port all the way,
When I got back it was like a dream come true
I saw you coming from Cambridgeport with my poetry and jazz,
Knew you had the blues, saw you coming from across the river …

What this means is known only to Morrison. What it means to the rest of us is Boston had a dramatic impact as his literary muse.

THE IDEA ASTRAL WEEKS WAS CONCEIVED IN BOSTON IS A MYTH

Ryan H. Walsh's **Astral Weeks: A Secret History of 1968**, published in 2018, is a brilliant, well researched and eloquently written history of music in Boston. Walsh claims the origins of **Astral Weeks** is traced to Boston. He suggests it was conceived, the songs were written and much of the final production was worked out in Boston studios and clubs. Not true! Had Walsh read interviews with Van Morrison he would have discovered the songs in **Astral Weeks** date back to 1965. Some might have been fragments in Morrison's early notebooks from the days of the show bands. This does not in any way diminish Walsh's brilliant book. He is right in one aspect. Van experimented and polished the material in Boston. It was here he put **Astral Weeks** in final form.

Van Morrison: "'Astral Weeks' The songs were written over a period of time—some early 1966—and evolved musically. They are timeless works that were from another sort of place." In this conversation with the **Los Angeles Times'** Randy Lewis, Morrison observed **Astral Weeks** was in the planning and formative stages prior to he and Janet settling in Boston. Van continued: "It took a very long time and a lot of thinking and arranging and hard work to structure these songs like I wanted them, like I envisioned them in my head. That was the hardest work, but then I found out I then had to work through the people in the music business, and then the people that come around as a result that you are in the music business, and that was even harder." He was frustrated forty years later explaining **Astral Weeks**. Van made it clear it was not conceived and written in Boston. Perhaps it was polished. That's it!

BOSTON AS MORRISON PREPARES TO SETTLE THERE

What was Boston like as Van Morrison prepared to move into the city? It was a small town with a wide-ranging music scene. Harvard University was next door in Cambridge. There were innovative bands in the clubs. The town was sophisticated and provincial at the same time.

The Boston Tea Party was the club of choice for hip bands. It was the place where the Boston sound was born and thrived. The Boston Tea Party is famous for giving the Velvet Underground the publicity, the adoration and the audience that wasn't always available in New York. The Velvet Underground played the Boston Tea Party forty-three times between 1967 and 1970. How did this impact Van Morrison? He envisioned the club as his potential hit maker. That is, he could experiment with his songs testing audience reaction. He might perform a song five or six different ways. It was a time of total musical freedom. Van loved every minute of it.

When Ray Riepen opened the Boston Tea Party, he was labeled the "hippie entrepreneur." The truth was more complicated. He was a rich kid who loved to party. He moved to Boston to work on a master's degree at Harvard. He already possessed a law degree. His initial interests were in FM radio, experimental music, getting drunk, getting laid and having fun. He had trouble completing any of his interests, but he had fun.

Riepen's mistake was meeting and befriending an heiress, Jessie Benton. She also attended Harvard. They were rich kids playing with their money. Benton convinced Riepen to invest his money in a lease on a Synagogue. But it wasn't a Synagogue. The building emerged in 1870 as a Unitarian gathering place. The long flight of stairs to the main room surprised Riepen. He looked glowingly at a rainbow on the wall with the phrase "Praise Ye The Lord." For a hard-drinking hippie with druggie friends this was the perfect place. But for what?

Benton told him the Ford Foundation would provide her a grant. It never materialized. They talked about how to make money to pay the rent. They opened the Film Makers' Cinematheque. That didn't work. They held dances. Viola! The Boston Tea Party was born. It quickly became the hippest place in Boston. Hippie capitalism worked. Even if it was an accident.

HOW RAY RIEPEN'S VISION CHANGED BOSTON AND INSPIRED MORRISON

When Ray Riepen arrived in Boston it was to pursue a master's degree at Harvard. He was a charismatic dilettante. The name for the Boston Tea Party was coined when Riepen was sitting at Jim Kweskin's kitchen table. In typical hippie mindset they equated "tea" with drugs. The neighbors knew the Cinematheque as a place for non-commercial movies and weird people. No one had a clue it was about to turn into a raucous dance-drug venue. The Cinematheque came to an end when Riepen sat watching a woman's vagina on screen for half an hour. The dance venue quickly took over. Riepen paid money to the local police for protection. The venue was a roaring success.

The Boston Tea Party was Morrison's training ground. Long before he performed there he was in the audience. In late May 1968 when Peter Wolf's band, the Hallucinations, opened for John Lee Hooker, Van was in the audience. He met Hooker, hung out with him at Wolf's apartment, and they talked blues long into the night.

John Lee Hooker appeared at the Boston Tea Party the week before Van Morrison. As Hooker talked about the blues, Van felt validated. There were new literary interests for Morrison. He discovered the work of Alice Bailey while in Boston. She was the author of twenty-seven books on a wide variety of subjects. What was it Morrison took from Bailey's writings? She was a New Age pioneer writing about mysticism. She discussed how a person's personality was determined by an individual's "astral body." Her writing suggested why and how Van believed he was channeling songs. It wasn't until the early 1980s that Morrison used her material. **Beautiful Vision** and

142

Inarticulate Speech of the Heart reflect her influence. The musicians who played with Van remarked he was a walking encyclopedia of philosophical notions and ideas.

The Boston Tea Party was open for eighteen months when Van appeared. The venue was another training ground for the early education of a musician intent upon learning as much as he could about the record business. Ray Riepen was an unwitting guiding force in Morrison's musical education.

THE FIRST DANCE AT THE BOSTON TEA PARTY

On January 20, 1967 the first dance at the Boston Tea Party was held. **Rolling Stone** labeled the opening dance "the most important in Boston Rock and Roll history." The Bosstown Sound was born. Van Morrison arrived at the Boston Tea Party in May 1968. He befriended Peter Wolf. The third night Van sat in the club, Wolf brought him on stage and told the audience he would perform "Gloria" with the Hallucinations. Van didn't perform "Gloria." He went into a cover version of Little Walter's "Mean Ole World," as Wolf's band played the musical riffs to "Gloria." The crowd didn't seem to notice or care. Van was impressed. You could do what you wanted on the Boston music scene.

*Van was living in Boston, and he was a huge Hooker fan. And so I put together this lunch and the interesting thing about it is Van had this very intense Belfast accent…. And John had his own way of talking too that some people could be hard to get. And so here is this guy from Mississippi talking one way, and then this guy from Belfast is talking another way. They were understanding each other perfectly. I couldn't follow nearly a word of it. – **Peter Wolf***

Morrison was quiet and introverted. He spent time analyzing the music scene. He didn't make many friends. Those he did were important to his artistic evolution. It was in Boston Morrison hooked up with drummer Joey Bebo, guitarist John Sheldon and bass player Tom Kielbania. They became his Boston band. It didn't take long to bring the band together. They were talented musicians with a Berklee College of Music pedigree. The lure of the Boston scene brought Van there. The city impacted him. The musicians helped to finalize **Astral Weeks**.

One night when Van Morrison was performing at the Boston Tea Party, he was singing softly and suddenly smoke and flames came from the ceiling. He thought it was part of the act. Van just kept singing.

THE LURE OF BOSTON

When the Morrison's settled in their Cambridge Green Street apartment, Van understood why many of his countrymen migrated to Boston. They left Ireland for economic reasons. It wasn't so different from their homeland. Like Belfast, it had a subdued and old urban tone. Boston was also full of Irish settlers. It was as close to home as Van felt in the U.S. The large number of Irish cultural events was another draw.

Like the Emerald Isle, Boston resisted the twentieth century. The lack of modern conveniences was obvious in the Green Street apartment. The appliances were from the 1920s. The heating was irregular. There was no air conditioning. The plumbing worked sporadically. The peeling walls reeked of incipient poverty.

There were coffee shops, small eateries, smoky taverns with inexpensive drinks, and a large number of bookstores. Van believed creature comforts robbed one of initiative. A man with nothing to risk, Van told Peter Wolf, is a person who will not find success.

Green Street is a one-mile student housing ghetto. Van's apartment was on the street level. He lived one block from the Plough and Stars where he ate a burger and drank a beer for two dollars. This Irish restaurant was like home to Morrison. The O'Malley family founded the pub to pay tribute to Irish literature and music. For a time, Van and Janet lived above Charlie's Tap at 280 Green Street. Wherever Van lived in Boston, he polished **Astral Weeks**. Maybe Ryan H. Walsh is right. He may have given birth to the final version in Cambridge. Van was ready to record the album after an eight-month local residence.

SETTLING IN BOSTON: THE ACOUSTIC THING ON VAN'S MIND

When he arrived in Boston, Van had a concept. He hoped to de-emphasize electric music. He wasn't interested in electric music. This was due to the Them and the solo Bang material. At times Tom Kielbania played an upright bass. John Sheldon was instructed by Van to unplug the electric guitar. Van wanted an acoustic guitar sound.

Van performing at the Spring Sing on Boston common, 1968
(Credit: Dick Iacovello / Penguin Press)

Why the acoustic sound? Van said he had a dream. That dream created a soft, jazz musical direction. The singular picture of ambiguity in Van's instructions to the band created a sense of confusion. They wondered! What the hell was going on? A more plausible explanation is that Bebo's drums were not always nailed down correctly, Kielbania's bass didn't always connect with his inexpensive speaker. Sheldon's guitar had amplification problems. He also loved John Payne's flute. Van's freedom to take the music into new directions intensified the experimental mode leading to **Astral Weeks**.

There was an eccentricity to Morrison's musical dreams. He called Kielbania in the middle of the night, according to Ryan H. Walsh, to tell him he had a dream about an "electric radio." Whatever this meant is unknown. To make his acoustic dream come true, Van rehearsed at times without a drummer.

Mick Cox, Van's Belfast friend, who was recording with his band Eire Apparent in New York, came up to see Morrison. While in Boston they talked about "the acoustic thing." It was while Cox was in Boston, Lewis Merenstein arrived with his management contract. The summer of 1968 finalized **Astral Weeks** while Van and Janet lived close to the fringe of poverty. His acoustic vision was about to become reality.

WHAT IS THE VAN MORRISON CONTROVERSY?

It was at the Spring Sing on the Boston Common where the "The Van Morrison Controversy" was born. Why? It appears the band name fit the times. A local photographer, Dick Iacovello, snapped pictures of Morrison singing to a large crowd. One fledgling musician, Rob Norris, who went on to play in the Velvet Underground without Lou Reed was there and he loved the show.

The Boston Tea Party advertised "The Van Morrison Controversy" appearing on May 30-31, June 1, 1968 as the headliner with Ill Wind opening the show. That was the beginning of "The Van Morrison Controversy." These three nights created one of the questions continuing to surround the Morrison legend. That mystery was the in-progress evolution of **Astral Weeks**. What was the Van Morrison controversy? It was a device to make his show relevant to the times.

Ill Wind was important to Morrison's **Astral Weeks** album. The reason? They worked with producer Tom Wilson whom Van met in Boston. Ill Wind were booked by the William Morris Agency. They were Boston's best-known psychedelic band. The agency took notice of Morrison.

The Boston Tea Party poster advertising Morrison's appearance had a note that WGBH-TV would broadcast the show on May 29 from 7:30 to 8:00. Some say the show aired. Others are not so sure. This is the type of mystery Morrison loves. It added credence to his fledgling career.

Concert Poster - Van Morrison, J. Geils, Peter Johnson, Symphony
Hall Huntington Ave. Boston Ma. Dec. 18, 1970

The legend grew that Van didn't like to play the Them or Bang material. He didn't. In 1968 most of his shows opened with an instrumental riff from "Brown Eyed Girl." We know that because Joey Bebo and Tom Kielbania have repeatedly said they practiced the song. Van was performing some of the Bang material when he felt like it.

While experimenting in Boston, Van attempted to minimize electric instruments. He was experimenting with a new sound. There was money for the musicians. Bebo, Kielbania and Sheldon were confused by Morrison's hand to mouth living conditions. Despite his apparent poverty he paid the musicians, especially Bebo, one hundred and fifty dollars a week to rehearse. They were paid for the shows backing Morrison. Where did the money come from? No one knows. One answer was in New York where a local enforcer and alleged gangster, Carmine "Wassel" DeNoia guided mob money into Morrison's managers coffers. At least that was the rumor. Who knows the truth? When I interviewed DeNoia for my 1983 book **Van Morrison: The Mystic's Music**, he was an overweight thug with a nasty attitude. He was convicted of payola in the 1970s. He hadn't recovered from his alleged mob connected days. He didn't like Van. He didn't like rock music. DeNoia told tall tales. He loved to smoke cigars, drink and party. Did he have anything to do with Morrison's career? Who knows? Here is the speculation.

Carmine "Wassel" DeNoia, a New Yorker, was one of the most unreliable characters talking about music. He was Bert Berns enforcer. None of Berns' artists got paid. Wassel made sure of it. There was a night filled with horror featuring Bert Berns, Van, Janet and DeNoia. Berns chartered a boat for a cruise on the Hudson to celebrate "Brown Eyed Girl's" success. During the night of drinking and partying, DeNoia threatened Morrison. Why? No one knows! DeNoia was a big-mouthed jackass. Van ignored him. He wanted to punch the Belfast Cowboy out. Nobody disrespected "The Wassel."

MONDAY, AUGUST 5th
FREE HOOT

TUES. & WED., AUGUST 6 - 7
SATHER GAIT
ILLUMINATION

the THIRD WORLD
RASPBERRY

FRI. and SAT., AUGUST 9 - 10
VAN
MORRISON
CONTROVERSY
"Brown Eyed Girl"

The Catacombs
1120 Boylston Street 247-8874
NEAR AUDITORIUM MBTA

Van Morrison Poster - The Catacombs
1120 Boylston Street Boston, MA 02215

The 1968 summer shows were important. Joey Bebo remembers practicing new songs. These songs, notably "Moondance," "Virgo Clowns" and "Domino" were perfected over eight months. Van said he

149

wrote these songs in Belfast. The notion Van wrote spontaneously is not true. He did at times. Generally, it was hard work and long hours producing his new tunes. He often spent years crafting his songs. In 2008 Morrison told the **Los Angeles Times** Randy Lewis: "Moondance was written by me in 1965 as an instrumental...." Morrison catalogues his furtive bursts of creativity. He is well organized creating a cache of songs. What he does is not linear. Often, he will go to his personal archive for material. He can spend months or years rewriting this material. On his record releases, Van remarked to Randy Lewis: "I put out records to this day that are not necessarily in a sequence of anything."

In numerous interviews, Van remarked it is not easy to do what he does. John Sheldon observed: "Domino" originated one night at the Boston Tea Party." Others have a similar story. "The story is he took Bo Diddley's 'Mona,' beat," Joey Bebo continued. "Van slowed it down and added Sheldon's guitar sound. The result was the first incarnation of "Domino.""

"Moondance" evolved when Van and his musicians were playing loosely with one another. This instrumental "Moondance" evolved as Joey Bebo said "into a jazz standard." In 1968, Van debuted the unrecorded "Moondance" at various Boston teen dances and the Boston Tea Party.

Morrison was searching for a new sound. He was listening to American jazz. He loved the Blue Note label. While at home in Belfast he came across Grant Green's **Street of Dreams** album. Green's soul jazz sound on **Street of Dreams** intrigued Van. Much of what he finalized for **Astral Weeks** was influenced by Green's work with Elvin Jones, Larry Young and Bobby Hutcherson. One song, "Lazy Afternoon," had a dramatic influence on how Van composed in the late 1960s.

VAN AT THE PSYCHEDELIC SUPERMARKET: THE BASTARD STEP CHILD OF THE UNICORN COFFEE SHOP

The Boston Tea Party was the venue of choice for musicians in the late 1960s. Its closest competitor, The Psychedelic Supermarket, had lackluster management. It was a filthy venue with poor service.

The drinkers didn't bother anyone as college students could barely afford the door charge. On free nights the bar doubled its business. It was a music venue where you smoked dope rather than ordered a beer.

The Psychedelic Supermarket was located at 590 Commonwealth Avenue. The problem is it was in an alley in the back of the street. It was a former parking garage converted to a rock emporium. It was cold, drafty and uncomfortable. It was the brain child of George Papadopoulos who owned a coffee house, The Unicorn, and he was looking to make quick money booking electric blues bands and folk musicians. It was due to the money Papadopoulos made at his coffee shop that he could afford the ill-suited Psychedelic Supermarket.

Why did the Psychedelic Supermarket fail? I attended a concert there in 1968. It was a dump. The floor was concrete. The seating was for maybe two hundred and fifty people. It was uncomfortable as people sat stiffly on the concrete floor. There was no heating or air conditioning. The stage was a makeshift, amateurish affair. Papadopoulos had money and music industry connections. He booked Cream in February 1968, and the same year Janis Joplin with Big Brother and the Holding Company played this freezer disguised as a rock and roll emporium.

Van Morrison played the Psychedelic Supermarket in its earliest incarnation. Papadopoulos wasn't sure the venue would work. He failed to advertise the Van Morrison show. Papadopoulos was a loud-mouthed, entitled arrogant prick. He told Van the group might not be paid. When the Belfast Cowboy walked out on the creaky stage with his three-piece band performing an up-tempo, energetic instrumental version of "Gloria," he looked out at the crowd. All ten of them ignored him. He was astonished. He couldn't believe it. He turned his back to the stage. He had his revenge. He delivered a blistering set without looking at the meager gathering. He was paid.

After the Psychedelic Supermarket show Van retreated to Charlie's Tap Room to nurse his fragile psyche. The comments from the crowd were punctuated with demands for "Brown Eyed Girl." He had enough of the small-time promoters, the hoodlum record label owners and the mobsters hanging around the music scene. But he had no other place to go.

The irony is Papadopoulos's Unicorn at 825 Boylston Street was more than a coffee shop. It funded the Psychedelic Supermarket. Papadopoulos persevered and continued to make money with big name acts. In 1969 Papadopoulos featured James Taylor, Blood Sweat and Tears, Joni Mitchell and Chuck Berry in concert.

WHAT DOES DOUG YULE TELL US ABOUT VAN'S MUSIC?

In 1965 Doug Yule arrived to study acting at Boston University. He was a gifted musician who was a multi-instrumental talent. To make ends meet Yule joined a series of cover bands. By 1967 he was playing in the Grass Menagerie performing at the Boston Tea Party.

When Yule moved into an apartment on River Street, he was in the middle of the local music scene. He met Van Morrison. They talked. Van told him that he needed a multi-instrumentalist. Yule responded he was proficient on the guitar, piano, bass and baritone horn.

Van didn't ask Yule if he was a vocalist. He was! There was something about the depth of Yule's musical knowledge intriguing Morrison. Fate intervened. Yule joined the Velvet Underground. He replaced John Cale. The story didn't end. Van continued to ask Yule to come on board as a paid, permanent member of his band. Yule complained to friends about Morrison's persistence in asking him to join his band. Why did Morrison want him in his various musical groups? The answer was clear. Yule understood **Astral Weeks** before and after it was recorded. What Yule's friendship with Van highlights is the hard working, hard driving nature of Morrison's commitment to the proposed **Astral Weeks** album.

WBCN AND WGBH: BOSTON RADIO-TV AND THEIR REVERED ROLES

WBCN was Boston's first FM radio station to play Morrison's music. He hung out at this underground radio station. When Ray Riepen provided the funds for WBCN, he unwittingly began a rock and roll revolution. Young local kids, like Jonathan Richman, and slightly older rockers, like Peter Wolf of the J. Geils band, gravitated to the station.

Riepen had the commercial golden touch. After the successes of his night club the Boston Tea Party, he believed radio would turn huge profits. He did this by not paying anyone. Riepen raided college radio stations. He found eager would be disc jockeys. Riepen tried to get Peter Wolf to invest ten thousand dollars. Wolff told him he didn't have ten dollars. Riepen responded: "I guess you'll have to be a DJ."

Riepen was an advertising genius. He proclaimed in an ad: "Ugly Radio is Dead." The station was at times pop and commercial and at other times trendy and psychedelic. The WBCN disc jockeys were amateurs. Peter Wolf of the Hallucinations came in the air late in the evening. When he walked from his Cambridge apartment to the station, Wolfe lugged a box of records. No one knew rock and roll better than Wolf.

Wolf had no restrictions on his play list. He loved Them. He featured their music nightly. He did the same with Morrison's Bang material. When the album came out, he played it to death. Soon Van arrived to keep Peter Wolf awake during his late night WBCN shifts.

WGBH-TV was a different medium. It was an experience difficult to master. But it was equally important to the developing Boston rock scene. Riepen filmed Timothy Leary with just an hour's notice. A Leary debate at MIT was an iconic cultural moment as the bard of LSD publicized the freedom that was inherent in the Boston music scene, as well as the drug scene.

WGBH had an eccentric local reputation. It came from an experimental broadcast "What's Happening Mr. Silver?" This program was one where there were no commercials, and it often had a psychedelic tone. If you were a stay at home doper WGBH was for you. The station said there was to be no interruptions from "common sense." The host David Silver sat on the floor. He asks a young woman some questions. She doesn't answer. Then footage of a man talking about producing high school yearbooks babbles on and then Aretha Franklin is heard singing "Respect." No one knew what was going on including Silver. That was the beauty of the show. It meant nothing. It dealt with nothing. You could get stoned and watch David Silver.

Boston loved it. Suddenly, there was a hip countenance to a city with a new reputation for eccentric behavior. There was strange behavior.

BOSTON IS WHERE MORRISON AUDITIONED FOR LEWIS MERENSTEIN AND FINISHED IT, OR DID HE?

At Boston's Ace Studio Morrison auditioned the **Astral Weeks** album for producer Lewis Merenstein. As Merenstein entered the Ace Recording Studio, located near the Boston Commons, he recalled the Kingston Trio recorded their first hit there. Merenstein wasn't sure what he would hear from Morrison. He was a sound engineer turned producer. His new role as producer made him wary of rock and roll. He soon found **Astral Weeks** was not rock and roll. It was a jazz classic with soft rock undertones.

After the Morrison audition, Merenstein said: "My whole being was vibrating. It was Van, alone with a guitar, and he played 'Astral Weeks' the song for me right then and there. I got the distinct feeling that he was going back in time, going back to be born again, and it moved me, spiritually, quite a bit.... It hit me right where I was at that period in my life."

Before he auditioned for Merenstein, Morrison walked over to 304 Columbus Avenue where the National Recording Studio was located. There is no record that he recorded in the studio. Some members of the Boston music community believe he practiced there to perfect **Astral Weeks**. Since Peter Wolf and members of his band, the Hallucinations, lived across the street. It was a destination for beer and music.

THE GIGS IN AND AROUND BOSTON, 1968: WHAT DID THEY ACHIEVE?

If there is a secret to Boston it was in the clubs. Joey Bebo's book, **In The Back Of The Van: The Story of One Unforgettable Summer**, details the hectic and hastily arranged shows as well as the difficulty getting paid. At times Van was conflicted. He didn't like playing "Brown Eyed Girl," Bebo recalled. But he did it. The band opened most shows with an instrumental riff from "Brown Eyed Girl." This is an early insight into how and why Van developed into a legendary concert act. From the earliest point in his career he did what he could to present a sterling show. Bebo recalled the amount of time and the precision in the daily practice sessions. Van was playing his new music in its final stage. **Astral Weeks** was implanted in Van's psyche.

Bebo's insights into Van's creative process, as he sat on the drums watching **Astral Weeks** unfold, were amazing. He saw a rock and roll world turned into jazz. Joey was on board for it.

There was no trouble finding venues. Van's band began every show with the riffs to "Brown Eyed Girl." Even when he didn't sing his hit the band ended the show with this Top 40 radio musical riff. The list of Van Morrison 1968 concerts compiled by Ryan H. Walsh for his seminal book, **Astral Week: A Secret History of 1968** are as follows with some additions. I have added the songs performed, when possible, the atmosphere and the roadies helping with the shows.

MORRISON'S 1968 BOSTON SHOWS: THEIR IMPACT

Rainbow Ballroom, Hyannis Port, MA: This is early April 1968 show where Van began performing "Gloria" and "Brown Eyed Girl." During some of these shows the band worked on new songs with "Domino" being his favorite. Joey Bebo wasn't at this show. Louie Peterson was on drums. John Sheldon was on guitar and Tom Kielbania the bass player. Van may have auditioned Doug Yule.

Throughout the spring and summer of 1968 summer, Van experimented with the musical and then the vocal part of "Domino." Despite his dislike for Them's music, Van performed "Baby Please Don't Go" and "Here Comes The Night" at most club dates. Joey Bebo remarked the band opened with an instrumental riff from "Brown Eyed Girl." During these shows in 1968 John Sheldon's guitar jumped out to other bands. He was a Jimi Hendrix fan and while this guitar sound didn't mesh with Van, the Belfast Cowboy was a pro who followed the band. He told Peter Wolf when he organized another band, they would follow him.

Joey Bebo: "I remember we played with a strong and loud sound behind Van. He could adapt. I was opinionated about music. I was a jazz guy. Our music cooked with Van."

The Electric Circus, Cambridge MA - April 16 (billed as "Van Morrison Controversy") The Electric Circus was the second most popular venue in Boston. It was close to McSorley's Old Ale House which Van loved.

The Boston Commons "Spring Sing" - April 20th, (billed as "Van Morrison Controversy") Joey Bebo said he was not playing with Van yet at this gig. Louie Peterson was the drummer.

The Ark May 1-3: At this gig Rick Philp was one of the musicians performing with Morrison. Philp was a brilliant guitarist. His band, the Myddle Class, was the headliner in 1965 when the Velvet Underground played their initial Boston show. Philp was a local Boston musician who played with Morrison before he recorded **Astral Weeks**.

The Boston Tea Party - May 23 (appears on stage with The Hallucinations for one song) Then Van performs with his group.

Joey Bebo: "This is the first time for me at the Boston Tea Party. Bebo found the high stage muffled his drum sound. The building had a high ceiling, the acoustics sucked. I was trying to play as loud as I could-John Sheldon put a new sound out there-I think Boston finished Van's sound. Van was adaptable. Van talked of listening to John Coltrane and Blood, Sweat and Tears. That when I knew he was a real jazz guy."

WGBH 'Mixed Bag' TV Show - May 29 - Van Morrison's pre-taped appearance airs - Louie Peterson was the drummer.

Wayland High School Auditorium, Wayland MA - Late Spring, Date Unknown

The Psychedelic Supermarket, Boston MA – Joey Bebo: "This was in early May. The cold concrete floor was a downer after the Boston Tea Party. I played terribly. We took a long break. Van said there is no one here. He downed a pint of Southern Comfort. I never saw him get mad. Van laid into George Papadopoulos because no one had showed up." The First Annual Boston Pop Festival was on from May 10 through May 18. The Psychedelic Supermarket sponsored the event and it was a successful festival focusing on psychedelic groups. Harry Chickles was the director. The bands, most of whom played for free, were well known in the psychedelic listening community with the exception of the Colwell-Winfield band appeared and blind blues singer George Leh who the **Boston Globe** described as "under appreciated." The First

Boston Pop Festival was not a commercial success but artistically it was over the top. Some of the best, if unknown psych bands appearing included the Bead Game, Crow, Cloud, Salvation, Eden's Children and the Orphans.

Joey Bebo recalled Van mentioned listening to John Coltrane and Blood, Sweat and Tears. Bebo believes this began Morrison's infatuation with horns in a jazz direction.

The Boston Tea Party - May 30 - 31, June 1 (billed as "Van Morrison Controversy" w/ Ill Wind). Ill Wind was Boston's major psychedelic band.

The Rainbow Ballroom and Rollerdrome, Hyannis, Port MA – June date unknown. Joe Bebo: "The first gig I remember liking was at the Rainbow. I called it a roller rink. We were almost arrested for drinking beer in the van. The police took us into the promoter's office and he talked the police out of pressing charges." A long line of kids with tickets were outside.

Hampton Beach Casino, Hampton, NH - June/July. Joey Bebo: "This was a funny gig. I remember sitting in the back of the van with the equipment. It was a miserably hot day. Once I left the van the hot sun and went into this lounge-it was fun to play."

The Comic Strip, Worcester, MA - June/July-dates unknown. This was a teen club in Worcester founded by two college students. No booze. There was a large dance floor and a huge stage. Van played there at least twice. The guarantee for each show was $500.

"The Cave" @ First Baptist Church, Hyannis, Cape Cod MA - July*Joey Bebo: "This was a horrible gig. It was in the basement, hard wood floor-the acoustics were bad. We were bored and uncomfortable. John Sheldon started bashing my cymbals-I said don't do that-John was great but he could irritate me." This church, located on Main Street in downtown Hyannis Port had a coffee shop in the basement appropriately named "The Cave." The crowd munched on donated popcorn and booze and drugs were brought in to mellow the crowd. Before Van played this gig a young lady, Melisa, sat at the piano singing Joni Mitchell songs.

Rocky Point Amusement Park, Warwick, RI – July-Joey Bebo: "We played some large venues. This was one of the biggest."

Frank Connelly Carousel Theater, Framingham MA - August 4th (opening for The Association) Joey Bebo: "At this show Van drew more attention than the Association with their hit records."

The Catacombs, Boston MA – August 9-10, (billed as "Van Morrison Controversy")

Frank Connolly Carousel Theater-Framingham Mass. Joey Bebo: "We were opening for the Association. At this show we cut loose with "Domino," "Here Comes The Night" and we ended with "Gloria" and "Brown Eyed Girl." Describing the club Bebo recalled: "The Catacombs was a small venue, nightclub, a coffee house where people sat at tables." There is a surviving tape that was placed for twenty-four hours on ITunes in 2018 in the U.K. Payne and Kielbania signed releases prior to the iTunes tape. The Peter Wolf tape on August 9, 1968 the set included "Sit Down Funny Face (aka Virgo Clowns)," "Cyprus Avenue," "Brown Eyed Girl," "He Ain't Give You None," "One Two Brown Eyes," "Beside You," "T. B. Sheets," "Train Train (aka "Stop That Train)," and "Madame George." There is also a longer tape that is in the hands of very few collectors.

The Boston Commons, August 18. Tom Kielbania and John Payne played with Morrison.

In 1968 every Morrison show included "Madame George," "I Need Your Kind of Loving," "Cyprus Avenue," "Beside You" and "Bayou Girl" as well as "Brown Eyed Girl." There are myths and realities developed from Boston obscuring the early part of Van's career. By examining these it is possible to view his artistic development and growth.

RYAN H. WALSH ON VAN: MYTH AND REALITY

Ryan H. Walsh's **Astral Weeks: A Secret History of 1968** is a brilliant book. It is carefully researched, there were more than two hundred interviews as the author mastered the material. It is a potential award-winning book. Walsh in great detail analyzes how the **Astral Weeks** album was polished in Boston. He writes, "Van planned, shaped and rehearsed in Boston and Cambridge." This is true. It is also untrue. Van began writing the songs that became **Astral Weeks** when he toured with his beat rock group Them. He polished these tunes in

158

Belfast, London and New York before moving to Boston. Walsh is correct in his assertion the final phase of **Astral Weeks** took place in Boston.

Van's working method was slow, methodical, overly practiced, overly organized and overly concerned with a sound. Morrison continually altered his lyrics. He worked for years on these songs. Many people in Boston, who heard the **Astral Weeks** material, commented his music changed daily. This suggests Walsh's secret history has a point.

Hunter S. Thompson said when the going gets weird, the weird turn pro. This comment applies to Van Morrison's time in Boston. He had conceived **Astral Weeks** with Them. He continued to polish it while with Bert Berns and finding his hit solo voice in "Brown Eyed Girl." In Boston Van finished the long-awaited song cycle and turned his attention to recording it.

Morrison realized he would have to find musicians who understood his music. When he sang, "If I ventured into the slipstream, between the viaducts of your dream" the backing musicians understood how to place these words in context with the music. When he recorded **Astral Weeks,** he had the right studio accompaniment. It was Lewis Merenstein who put together the jazz musicians that made **Astral Weeks** a masterpiece. After he audition at Boston's Ace Studio, Morrison and Merenstein talked about the Beat poets. Suddenly Jack Kerouac, Allen Ginsberg and Lawrence Ferlinghetti were in the mix. As Merenstein and Morrison talked about the Beats, their words inspired him. He reimagined the beat poetry that became **Astral Weeks**.

Morrison didn't talk about his future. He did have it planned. One person told me "Van was like a ghost in Boston." If he was a ghost, Van was a hard working one.

His wife, Janet, told Ryan H. Walsh he would sit quietly for hours working with a tape recorder. Janet said he would play for twenty minutes at a time. He would stop, listen and rewrite. This is hardly a ghost. This is a serious artist at work on the album defining his genius.

HOWARD A. DEWITT

THE ASTRAL WEEKS MYSTERY CONTINUES: THE CATACOMBS TAPE

As Van performed songs from **Astral Weeks** Peter Wolf taped a few of his shows. What did he tape? Joey Bebo, Van's drummer, said it was much of the material included on **Astral Weeks**. Ryan H. Walsh argues the album was performed in a truncated version at Boston's Catacombs Club. This small, wood paneled jazz club in the basement of a building on Boylston Street was the perfect intimate venue to stretch out and modify tunes like "Madame George" and "Cyprus Avenue." When Van performed these songs bassist Tom Kielbania and flutist John Payne accompanied the Belfast Cowboy.

On the Peter Wolf Catacombs Club tape there is one interesting tune. That song, "Sit Down Funny Face," which is an early version of "Virgo Clowns," which was recorded in 1969. It is an introspective Morrison song. Like all his tunes there is collaboration and input from those around him. Over the years this has prompted tall tales and increased myths. There are some elements of truth to some claims. Walsh concludes Kielbania might have written the bassline for "Cyprus Avenue." He was as Walsh tweeted "over the moon" that the Catacombs material was about to be released as a legitimate CD. Walsh tweeted he believes Kielbania and Payne deserve more credit for their contributions to **Astral Weeks**.

Many of the Van fans were caught flat footed by Wolf's tape. Out of the blue in November 2018 Van Morrison's management announced the release of the "1968 Catacombs Tapes" as a live album on iTunes UK. This is alleged to be the tape from the Catacombs. The conclusion most people came to is Morrison briefly released the material Peter Wolf recorded at the Catacombs as "a copyright dump." That is to preserve Morrison's ownership of the tape. In January 2019 it would slide into the public domain.

Tom Kielbania and John Payne signed releases per the request of Morrison's legal team. They know nothing about the Catacombs tape beyond signing the releases. The live set released on iTunes in the U.K. was on line for twenty-four hours. Its title **Live In Boston 1968** had no artwork, no picture of Morrison and no liner notes. What made Van do this is not known but the rumor is he was concerned about bootlegs

160

that have circulated over the years. Maybe this will force Morrison to continue the **Philosopher's Stone** or to simply release his own bootleg series.

BIBLIOGRAPHICAL SOURCES

For the Van Morrison Controversy see, Ryan Walsh, **Astral Weeks: A Secret History of 1968** (New York, 2018), pp. 175-188. Also see, Joseph W. Bebo, **In The Back Of The Van: The Story of One Unforgettable Summer** (Create Space, 2016) for one of Van's band mates discussing the Boston gigs and those in the surrounding area. Bebo, Van's jazz drummer, is a writer of extraordinary skill. His memoir of that summer suggests how and why **Astral Weeks** emerged, and it is also a history of the local Boston music scene from the inside.

The best overall book on the Boston scene and its impact upon Morrison is Ryan Walsh's. He argued **Astral Weeks** was conceived, polished and finalized in Boston, thus the secret history. This is contrary to the facts. Van had worked on the songs since at least 1964. He continued to polish them in Boston. Walsh's book is a brilliant one and deserves awards. But there is no secret history to **Astral Weeks** in Boston. It was an evolving process and Boston was an important factor.

Mervyn Solomon recalled conversations on the Boston scene and its influence with Morrison. Solomon concluded the **Astral Weeks** album was polished there are it was conceived in Belfast, outlined in more detail in London and worked on the entire time he toured with Them.

An interview with Carmine "Wassel" DeNoia was important to this chapter. In his later years the once robust DeNoia was frail but he never lost his zest for the New York life. He also claimed he put Bert Berns into the record business.

See Howard A. DeWitt, **Van Morrison: The Mystic's Music** (Fremont, 1985), passim for an analysis of how and why the **Astral Weeks** album become a cult phenomenon turned into a mainstream media platinum record seller.

See Eric Von Schmidt and Jim Rooney, **Baby let Me Follow You Down: The Illustrated Story of the Cambridge Folk Years** (University of Massachusetts, 1994, 2nd revised edition) for the development of

Boston's folk scene. There are some important insights into John Payne in a book by his sister, see Sarah Stuart, **My First Cousin, Once Removed** (New York, 1999). This is an insightful examination of the role of genius and mental health in the arts.

For the McLean Mental Hospital see, Alex Beam, **Gracefully Insane** (New York, 2009) for the tales of John Sheldon in the psychiatric ward.

For a recap of the Ryan Walsh book and the impact of Boston on Van Morrison, see, Jeremy D. Goodwin, "In 'Astral Weeks,' A Tale of Van's Time In The Weirder Boston of 1968," March 6, 2018. http://www.wbur.org/artery/2018/03/06/ryan-walsh-van-morrison-astral-weeks Goodwin explains a brief comment on Boston in the **Astral Weeks** liner notes. Before Walsh wrote his book on 1968, Boston and Van Morrison his article in the **Boston Magazine** was a portent of things to come. See Ryan H. Walsh, "Astral Sojourn," **Boston Magazine**, March 24, 2015. https://www.bostonmagazine.com/arts-entertainment/2015/03/24/van-morrison-astral-weeks/

An interesting interview with Ryan Walsh sheds light on Boston's influence upon Morrison as he crafted **Astral Week**. See Matthew Reed Baker, "When Van Morrison Bunkered Down In Boston: A Conversation With Author Ryan Walsh," **Boston Magazine**, March 5, 2018. https://www.bostonmagazine.com/arts-entertainment/2018/03/05/ryan-walsh-astral-weeks/

For WBCN see Carter Alan, **Radio Free Boston: The Rise And Fall of WBCN** (University Press of New England, 2009). For the James Brown Boston concert see the brilliant David Leaf documentary, "The Night James Brown Saved Boston," a 2009 documentary. Also see Chrysanthe Tenentes, "Van Morrison And The Boston Counterculture in 1968," https://kottke.org/18/03/van-morrison-and-the-boston-counterculture-in-1968 for an interesting review of the Ryan H. Walsh book. The best review of the Walsh book is John Williams, "1968 Revisited: A Boston Commune And A Van Morrison Classic," **The New York Times**, April 12, 2018. https://www.nytimes.com/2018/04/12/books/review/astral-weeks-ryan-walsh.html Also see Conor Friedersdorf, "Behind The Masterpiece: Van Morrison's Astral Weeks at 50," **The Atlantic**, April 3, 2018 https://www.theatlantic.com/entertainment/archive/2018/04/behind-the-masterpiece-van-morrisons-astral-weeks-at-50/556472/ This is a brilliant piece of journalism tying Morrison's rising career and the fame and fortune slowly resulting from **Astral Weeks**.

See Karen Marshall, "Boston In 1968: The Birthplace of 'Astral Weeks' A Musical Masterpiece," **WGBH.org**, April 12, 2018. https://www.wgbh.org/news/2018/04/12/arts/boston-1968-birthplace-astral-weeks-musical-masterpiece This is a reasoned and interesting look at the Walsh book.

Clinton Heylin, **Van Morrison: Can You Feel The Silence, A New Biography** (Chicago, 2003 reprint) doesn't examine the Boston period in detail. Heylin does a magnificent job of weaving the **Astral Weeks** album through his book. He shows the album was never far from Van's mind and when the Belfast Cowboy in the 1990s played some songs from it in concert, it was obvious he was reflecting on his masterpiece. No one knew he would perform the album in concert and release a new album and a DVD. In many respects the **Astral Weeks** album is in many ways an albatross around Morrison's neck.

For the unreleased **Astral Weeks** tape cut at the Catacombs in 1968 see Andy Cush, "A Legendary Van Morrison Recording Just Hit The Internet and Quickly Disappeared Again," **Spin**, November 8, 2018. https://www.spin.com/2018/11/van-morrison-catacombs-1968-legendary-recording/ There are a number of posts about this tape from Ryan H. Walsh and his tweets add a great deal of material to the lost **Astral Weeks** tape.

See Jon Michaud, "The Miracle Of Van Morrison's 'Astral Weeks'," **The New Yorker**, March 7, 2018 for a review of how and why the Walsh book helped to clear up a bit of the mystery behind Morrison's intransigent album. Also see Alan Torney, "Van Morrison's Landmark Album Astral Weeks Turns 50 This Weekend. We Tracked Down The Musicians Who Played On It," **The Journal.ie**, October 13, 2018. https://www.thejournal.ie/readme/van-morrison-astral-weeks-at-50-documentary-4279736-Oct2018/ The Tourney article is an intriguing one. He and his team discussed the **Astral Weeks** album and the time before it was recorded. The result is a marvelous view of how and why Van Morrison's musicians believe they should have more credit for his masterpiece. Janet Minto Morrison also provides excellent insight into how the recordings and the background to the album have engendered so much discussion.

An unusually complete and insightful article on Boston's influence and the Peter Wolf tape on **Astral Weeks** is Ritchie Unterberger, "The Road From The Catacombs To Astral Weeks: Van Morrison's Lost 1968 Tape Unearthed," **Pleasekillme.com**, January 3, 2019. https://pleasekillme.com/astral-weeks-van-morrison/

Joseph W. Bebo, **In The Back Of The Van: The Story of One Unforgettable Summer** (Hudson, 2016) is the story of a young twenty-year-old Berklee School of Music student who played the drums with Van Morrison for two months. Bebo is an excellent writer and by recounting his personal experiences with Morrison he reveals some of the problems, pitfalls and eventual successes in the music business. Bebo's book describes the mysterious people around Morrison who may or may not have been mobsters.

The case for Boston influencing **Astral Weeks** is a description from the back cover paying tribute to Belfast and Boston. This poetic verse reads as follows:

> **I saw you coming from the Cape, way from Hyannis Port all the way,**
> **When I got back it was like a dream come true**
> **I saw you coming from Cambridgeport with my poetry and jazz,**
> **Knew you had the blues, saw you coming from across the river, ...**

An interview with Ken Frankel of the Ill Wind band helped to put in place some of the material surrounding Van Morrison's time in Boston and the local club scene. Frankel's group was the first in Boston to perform original psychedelic music. Frankel's observations were particularly helpful in placing the Boston Tea Party material in perspective.

For the First Boston Pop Festival, see, William Phillips "Boston Sound Hits Hip Place," **The Boston Globe**, May 13, 1968, p. 20.

CHAPTER 6

JOEY BEBO: THE MYSTERY OF VAN'S BOSTON ASTRAL WEEKS GANGSTER MANAGEMENT

"There was only three of us and Van, and we had minimal equipment … The small stage was on a low rise stuck in the corner. It was just big enough for the band, the PA, and Van."

JOEY BEBO

"We played a cool version of 'Domino' and a nice song called 'Lorna', … and of course 'Brown Eyed Girl'…. maybe that acoustical session had something to do with Van's next album, Astral Weeks."

JOEY BEBO ON PLAYING AT THE CATACOMBS.

"John Sheldon still plays a bitching guitar and sings good."

JOEY BEBO

"I never saw Van drink casually. Except for a can of beer. The only time I saw him drink was at the Boston Tea Party."

JOEY BEBO

❧❧

As the summer of 1968 approached Joey W. Bebo turned twenty. He had completed two years of study at the prestigious Berklee School of Music. He was an accomplished drummer. He loved to smoke pot and listen to jazz. He loved the ladies. He was looking forward to a summer of drinking beer, smoking an occasional joint, playing in local seedy bars and listening to jazz. Then his parents dropped a bomb. They would only pay for his tuition and books. He would have to find a way to support his living expenses. He was from the small college town of Plattsburg in upper New York. He hated the thought of returning home for a summer job. He was uncertain if he could find work. He decided to remain in Boston. He began looking for a band that needed a sophisticated jazz drummer.

Rock and roll music was not on Bebo's radar. He didn't care for the pop; teenybopper sounds of the day. He didn't listen to local rock bands. He was a serous musician. He criticized the burgeoning rock scene. While growing up in Plattsburgh New York, a college town with plenty of music in a remote section of Northeastern New York, Bebo acquired an encyclopedic knowledge of jazz. He lived in an area where summer jazz dominated the local music scene.

When Bebo discovered Fats Waller's "Blueberry Hill," he sat down with the drum set his dad bought him at ten. He took out the brushes, and he began flawlessly playing along with the song. He listened to jazz day and night in his parent's house. When he discovered Benny Goodman, he found another influence. As the Gene Krupa records hit the family turntable, Bebo could hardly contain himself. He played Krupa's Carnegie Hall concert featuring "Sing, Sing, Sing" almost daily. Why? He was learning jazz technique. Soon he gravitated to Buddy Rich's solos. He became an accomplished jazz drummer before finishing high school. This explains his admission to the prestigious Berklee School of Music.

There wasn't much rock and roll in Bebo's early life. In 1962 he purchased a 45 of Chubby Checker's "The Twist." He took it home. He placed it amongst the Miles Davis, John Coltrane, Dizzy Gillespie and Charlie "Bird" Parker records. Jazz continued to occupy his practice time. Not surprisingly, Joey's jazz background was the perfect accompaniment to Van Morrison in the summer of 1968. His two years at the Berklee School of Music provided experience playing with a wide range of musicians in local music venues. He was only twenty, but he was already an experienced club musician.

THE BERKLEE SCHOOL OF MUSIC DEFINES A JAZZ DRUMMER

Bebo had friends at the Berklee School of Music who jammed with him regularly. One was guitar virtuoso Tom Kielbania. The lanky, quiet, sunglasses wearing Kielbania asked him if he would like to audition for a band. Joey said: "Yes." They went over to the house of a seventeen-year old guitar player, John Sheldon, whose parents looked on nervously at Joey. With his purple shirt and bell bottom pants, Bebo looked like any other 1968 hipster. The problem was John Sheldon's parents weren't impressed. They were traditional middle-class people living with a guitar prodigy son, John, who was a genius in school and as accomplished musically. John and Joey left to drive over to Van's house.

When they arrived at Morrison's dinky apartment, Van was intrigued by Bebo's appearance. In his slightly soiled, always wrinkled, clothes hanging on a body that looked as if he hadn't eaten in a week, Joey and John were smiling. Kielbania looked like a choir boy or a kid who hadn't left junior high school. Van looked at the goofy smiles. He wondered what the hell was going on? They had smoked a good portion of marijuana in the car on the way to Morrison's apartment. They were feeling good. They looked like lost, mismatched college kids.

After some small talk with Morrison the audition took place. Joey didn't know what to expect. He pulled out his best jazz drum solos. He would show this Irishman what he could do. When the audition ended, Van loved Bebo's technical skill. The jazz background, the quiet, cool Bebo emanated and his unflappable personality made him a perfect fit for what became the **Astral Weeks** training ground. Morrison could follow Bebo's drum licks. The kid had an inordinate sense of timing. Did Bebo know anything about Morrison's music? No! Zero! Nothing! He had heard "Brown Eyed Girl" on the radio. He didn't like it. It was teenybopper stuff. He had no idea how to play it. The Them hits "Here Comes The Night," and "Gloria" were not on Bebo's radar. He was strangely disconnected from the rock and roll scene. But the lure of a joint or two, a bottle of beer, getting laid and a regular paycheck ended Bebo's opposition to playing rock and roll. What the hell, he thought, he had to find a way to fund his junior year. He could do that sitting behind this Irishman he could barely understand.

WHAT DID BEBO'S JAZZ PEDIGEREE MEAN?

What did it mean that Bebo was a drummer with a jazz pedigree? His soft strokes helped Van finish the rough demos of "Moondance." He also had a hand in formulating other songs. "We played 'Moondance' all the time at rehearsals," Bebo continued. "We fleshed out the sound over the summer." He looked and acted like any other twenty-year-old kid. His encyclopedic knowledge belied his youthful good looks and playful personality. Suddenly Joey Bebo got serious about performing music. He had to hustle for the first time in his life. He had to make money to return to school.

After Bebo auditioned for and became Morrison's drummer, he played around the Cape and Boston with him for three months. He marveled at Morrison's musical adaptability. "No matter how good or bad we played, Van's vocals were in tune with what we did," Bebo continued. "He was amazing." He received a salary of one hundred and fifty dollars a week and a one hundred and fifty dollars for each show. Bebo had his junior year at the Berklee School of Music financed. The irony is he knew absolutely nothing about Van Morrison when he auditioned. He knew even less about "Brown Eyed Girl" and "Gloria." I heard those songs on the radio," Bebo said. "I wasn't interested." **In The Back Of The Van: The Story of One Unforgettable Summer**, Bebo couldn't identify Van's other hits. He had never heard of "Baby Please Don't Go," which was a U.K. number ten hit, "Here Comes The Night" which charted at twenty in the U.K. and twenty-four in the U.S. or "Mystic Eyes" which was a number thirty-three U.S. chart hit.

As a drummer, Bebo was ready made for Morrison's new music. Bebo broke down a lot of myths and misunderstandings about Morrison. The Belfast Cowboy met with and was gracious with Boston fans. He signed autographs in the streets, in the bars and in the clubs. "There were none of the temper tantrums reported later by the press," Bebo maintained. He did observe the Belfast Cowboy was not easy to get to know. He wasn't a loner. He was shy. He was into music 24/7.

The Van Morrison Controversy was the band that made its way around Boston in the summer of 1968. I asked Bebo: "What did the Van Morrison Controversy mean." He said: "I have no idea." There was an aura of mystery surrounding Van during the 1968 summer. Bebo didn't know the names of the roadies. There were two of them. They looked like they were right out of Mafia central casting. The manager had a first name but Joey had no idea who he was or why he was involved with Morrison. "The manager lived in a mansion and we went there for a party. That's all I know," Bebo said. The summer of smoking dope, bedding the ladies and playing with Van to earn enough money for his junior year at the Berklee School of Music was the only thing on Bebo's mind.

BEBO ON PLAYING WITH VAN AND MOBSTER MANIA

"I didn't realize I was playing with a legend," Bebo recalled. John Sheldon played a guitar that was not like Morrison experienced with Them. Van could adapt to any and all musicians. Sheldon had a Jimi Hendrix style. Contrary to the prevailing myth Van played "Brown Eyed Girl" at many shows. The band had thirty songs down. Van would simply call them out.

There is only anecdotal evidence Van was managed by mobsters The Boston booker, known as Frank, said little to the band. That's it. Nothing else was known. The two roadies were from Boston's Little Italy. The manager, known to Bebo as only Richard, allegedly remarked to Tom Kielbania they were all mobsters. No one paid any attention. It seemed too bizarre to be true.

Bebo recalled the band practiced "Moondance" daily. They attempted to learn a Grant Green jazz number "Lazy Afternoon." That didn't work. On "Moondance" the band practiced it in a number of ways. None were satisfactory for Morrison. They also experimented with "Domino" and "Virgo Fools." Sheldon used some of guitar lines from Bo Diddley's "Mona" on "Moondance" and Van went along with it.

After Bebo passed the audition, there were arduous days of practice. Bebo recalls "Tom Kielbania's bass helped Van formulate his early music. He always stood out distinctively no matter how loud John got," Bebo remarked. John Sheldon played the guitar his way. It was difficult for Van to reign him in. Morrison simply fell in with the guitar riffs. "I could hear Van's voice and noticed it had a distinct quality," Bebo continued. "He used it like a horn, with good power and range."

The practice sessions in Sheldon's basement turned the band into a competent one. A blend of blues, jazz and rock played off Sheldon's guitar. Bebo liked the freedom Morrison gave his musicians. Even in what was at best a garage band, Van worked the group into a smooth, professional unit.

BEBO GETS TO KNOW THE PERSONAL VAN MORRISON

The personal Van Morrison is not known to many people. Bebo got a chance in the summer of 1968 to get close to and understand the Belfast Cowboy. When Bebo arrived at Van's house the first time to pick him up for practice, he met Janet. He noticed the shabby nature of the apartment. He never forgot that day. Van told him to sit down. He and Janet went into a back room. Bebo heard them talking loudly. This wasn't a harmonious home.

Joey Bebo: "Van was a strange dude. Although he was down to earth and friendly enough, he was hard to really get to know." Bebo recalled Van's personal drive for musical success. They did talk. They did become friends.

When Van said Janis Joplin was amongst his favorite singers, Bebo was intrigued. He wondered why? Van hadn't mentioned John Coltrane or Ray Charles. Bebo said Van was nervous. He seldom talked about his past. The present was his only concern. Joey observed he was intensely private. Van had a Boston lawyer and Bebo and Kielbania accompanied Van to the office. He was involved in litigation with Bang Records. "By the looks of it, someone was paying a pretty penny to deal with the thugs who held his record contract," Bebo said. When Van came out of the meeting with the Boston lawyer, he told his band Ilene Berns tied him up legally. He couldn't approach another label.

During his Boston days there was little drinking. "I never saw him drink socially except for an occasional can of beer," Bebo concluded. The band got along well and enjoyed performing with Morrison. Bebo loved to talk about jazz with Morrison. "Van's preference for and knowledge of jazz won me over on that very first day," Bebo continued. "My respect for him as a musician only grew."

Like most American cities in 1968, Boston was filled with youthful eccentrics. Cambridge was a cauldron of Harvard students, drug crazies, hippie burn outs, counterculture entrepreneurs, serious students and musicians looking for fame and fortune. The locals blended with a neurotic set of personalities inspiring the local youth culture. Van was oblivious to much of the circus surrounding Harvard and Cambridge.

Cambridge's uniqueness stemmed in part from the most expensive and famous American psychiatric hospital. It wasn't the nut house, but the locals were intrigued by the famous people who spent time in the McLean Hospital. It is one of the few psychiatric clinics to produce a best-selling book, works by famous poets, a Hollywood movie and celebrity musicians looking to refocus their lives. Ironically two of Van's Boston band mate spent small amounts of time in McLean. With an affiliation with Harvard Medical School, there was a romantic aura to the McLean Hospital.

THE MCLEAN HOSPITAL AND VAN'S BAND: SIGNS OF HARVARD GENIUS?

The McLean Hospital was a mental treatment center in Cambridge. The rich and famous, Sylvia Plath, James Taylor, Steven Tyler, Ray Charles, Marianne Faithful, author David Foster Wallace and poet Robert Lowell received media attention for their treatment. There were musicians, playwrights, poets and novelists who escaped this publicity while residing in this plush psychiatric treatment center. Creative people and their offspring populated the halls. Al Capps daughters, two of Ralph Waldo Emerson's brothers and two of Van's 1968 band members John Sheldon and John Payne had brief stays in McLean. Neither appeared to be a McLean candidate.

Drug and alcohol recovery, as well as behavior modification, made McLean the home of many Boston Brahmins. James Taylor was a high school senior at Milton Academy when he experienced deep depression. He was sleeping twenty hours a day. After ten months at McLean he checked himself out against medical advice. Treating the young was a part of the program. To understand therapy for the young the case of Susanna Kaysen is important. She was the daughter of John F. Kennedy's deputy national security adviser, Carl Kaysen. She spent time for depression at McLean. In 1993 her memoir **Girl Interrupted** became a 1999 Hollywood film starring Winona Ryder. There was no stigma to McLean. It was home to the artistic and talented whose demons were alcohol, drugs and depression. Van's two band mates appear to be less than typical. They had limited issues.

One of the strange rites of passage among Harvard youth, local musicians, actors and rich kids with parents with too much money was the prestige associated with being treated at the McLean Hospital. The 1960s therapy, along with Zen Buddhism and the Maharishi Mahesh Yogi, was the rage.

When Frederick Law Olmsted landscaped this mental hospital to resemble a Tudor mansion, he had no idea he brought Boston psychiatry into the lives of wealthy local Brahmins. There were no fences, no guards and no locked gates. It didn't look or resemble a mental institution. It was also big business. It was for the rich and famous. The presence of musicians and actors gave it a feel-good flow.

The affiliation with Harvard University provided an intellectual aura drawing many who may not have needed psychiatric care. The glamor of having helped some of Ralph Waldo Emerson's proteges and the tales of poet Anne Sexton's erratic behavior obscured the emotional trauma within the walls. Sylvia Plath's **The Bell Jar** wasn't written at McLean, but the aura of her prose fit the institution.

The Pulitzer Prize winning poet Anne Sexton wrote while residing at McLean. She also taught poetry classes and lectured. While in McLean, Sexton became interested in setting her poetry to music. She hooked up later with a jazz group, Her Kind, who added music to her poetry. The level of intellectualism at McLean attracted rich parents. They believed their kids could advance intellectually while healing their psyche. Too much money brought therapeutic craziness. **The Atlantic** labeled McLean "The Asylum On The Hill."

John Sheldon, who was confined to the McLean Hospital, remarked Boston musicians referred to it as "the nut house." Sheldon allegedly suffered from what the doctor's labeled a form of what they termed "teenage malady." He was as sane as anyone. To this day he has a successful music career. He is an acclaimed guitarist.

WHERE DID THE MONEY COME FROM?

In numerous interviews Janet Planet remarked Van lived under the threat of mob violence. Ryan H. Walsh theorized the Mafia threat prompted Van and Janet to relocate to Boston. Fine as far as it goes. Why if Van moved to Boston to escape mob violence did he suddenly have money to pay Joey Bebo one hundred and fifty dollars a week? The answer is the mob moved him there because living was cheaper. The bellicose threats of law suits from Ilene Berns was another reason. How Van lasted through this drama is a miracle. No one has ever said where the money came from to live in Boston and pay the band. Even though Tom Kielbania has commented Van paid him only fifty dollars a week, there was money for the band. There was also money for Van and Janet's living expenses. The source? Who knows! The guess! The mob was laundering its profits.

The one-hundred and fifty dollar weekly salary was one Bebo earned with constant practice sessions and intermittent gigs. This was for rehearsals which were at least five times a week. Van loved to practice. He would stretch out his songs and recast them. The band learned in excess of thirty songs.

THE 1968 CONCERTS WERE NOT WITHOUT THEIR PROBLEMS

The 1968 concerts were not without their problems. Van was a perfectionist. Feedback drove him crazy. A missing musical riff, of which there were many, prompted Morrison to get in the face of unsuspecting musicians. Whether playing for ten people at Boston's Psychedelic Super Market or a full house at the Boston Tea Party, Van was a professional leading his group. It was a portent of things to come.

When the summer gigs began Bebo was not sure what to expect. He was delighted they played regularly. As Bebo performed in and around the Cape and in Boston there were excellent gigs and near disastrous ones. His first show with Morrison was almost this last. The

173

band sat in front of the venue. They were drinking beer. Joey was smoking a joint. There was a line of kids waiting to get into a decrepit looking place resembling a fallout shelter. The beer and the camaraderie eased the tension. As they got mellow there was a rap on the window. The band looked out. A local policeman told them to get out of the car. They were informed drinking beer on the premises violated the law. The promoter came running out the front door screaming "I got a thousand kids who purchased tickets." The band and the police went into the promoter's office. Van and the band were warned but not charged.

BEBO RECALLS THE BOSTON TEA PARTY AND THE PSYCHEDELIC SUPERMARKET

The Boston Tea Party was the apex of local rock and roll clubs. When Bebo entered the club, he smiled. Led Zeppelin and Cream played here. The psychedelic lights gave the venue a hip feel. John Sheldon loved the Boston Tea Party, because he could play as loud as he desired. To commemorate the gig Bebo wore a purple jacket with gold threads running through it with flowered patterns. He called it "my Sgt. Pepper jacket." It was 1968 hip.

The show went well. The raucous atmosphere, according to Bebo, prompted Van to consume copious amounts of alcohol. "This was the first time I had really seen him drink," Bebo said. The two sets went off with, as Bebo recalled, with "a little more passion."

One Boston Tea Party show ended with "Gloria" and "Brown Eyed Girl." Bebo said the audience gave the songs lukewarm approval. "To me they were the worst tunes to play in a club like the Tea Party," Bebo remarked. The next day Bebo was surprised to read the excellent press. Peter Wolf showed up and other celebrities mixed with the crowd. Bebo has fond memories of the Boston Tea Party. The same can't be said for the Psychedelic Super Market. That concert was a disaster. The place was an acoustic nightmare.

Bebo recalled after they set up the equipment there was no one in charge. He thought the place looked like a cold, badly equipped airplane hangar. It was raining. The roof leaked. The weather was foul. No one showed up. Why? There was a baseball game at nearby Fenway

Park. Van complained. The owner, George Papadopoulos, was angry. He told Van if there was a problem it was due to the band. Van worried they weren't going to get paid. Bebo listened. He wondered if they would finish the show. Van put enough pressure on Papadopoulos to guarantee payment. They finished the show. They got paid. The two muscular roadies had a talk with Papadopoulos.

THE MAGIC OF SITTING BEHIND VAN MORRISON

While sitting behind Morrison, Bebo witnessed the magic that would take the Belfast Cowboy from obscurity to the Rock And Roll Hall of Fame. When the band made a mistake, Morrison adjusted to it. The summer wasn't without controversy. When Van made a large sum of money from a percentage of the door the musicians wanted more than their one hundred and fifty dollars. Van said: "No." Bebo recalls this as an early lesson in the fiscal wonders of the music business. Morrison had his business hat on early in his career.

One of the experiments Van conducted in the summer of 1968 was to mix acoustic with electric shows. There were regular visitors from New York coming to see Morrison. They were mobsters. Ilene Berns had taken over her husband's label Bang. She hated Van. She wanted him to record some demos. The visitors she sent frightened the locals. "Don't use my name, man," a Boston musician remarked, "but those guys coming to see Van were scary assholes." Ilene Berns wanted more than the thirty-one songs Van owed Bang to fulfill his contract.

Morrison was not happy with Bang's recording choices. They asked for pop or bubble gum hits. Van ignored them. There was pressure to go into a Boston studio. Bebo said the band ventured into Ace Records to record some demos. Van paid for the recording sessions. Bang Records didn't know about it. The Belfast Cowboy was looking for a deal from another label. Hence, the hush hush recording atmosphere.

Bebo said they cut a "rocking version" of "Domino." He was impressed with "Lorna." They practiced it. Van was working on the lyrics. The song has not been released. It was probably recorded at Boston's Ace studio in the 1968 summer. No one knows for sure.

175

"Lorna" is a studio demo showing up on a number of bootlegs including **And It Stoned Me To My Soul** which was released as an Italian bootleg.

Bebo told his friends he witnessed the genius of Van Morrison. During this session, Van told Bebo he loved his playing. He said to Joey "you are rock and roll enough." A one-armed drummer, Victor "Moulty" Moulton auditioned for Van from the local garage band, the Barbarians. Moulton said Van asked him to become a band member. He declined. Van wasn't interested in hiring him. Why? Bebo's soft jazz shuffle was what intrigued Morrison. It fit his music perfectly.

In 1966 Victor "Moulty" Moulton recorded "Moulty" with musicians that became The Band. It was cut as a joke. When Laurie Records released it, Moulton was infuriated. When the song charted at ninety on Billboard, Moulton became a local celebrity. The Barbarians were breaking up. "Moulty" became a cult song later released on **Nuggets: Original Artyfacts From The First Psychedelic Era, 1965-1966** and later on a 2000 Sundazed Records release of the Barbarians debut album. Moulton was one of many musicians auditioning to play with Morrison. The acoustic sound he wanted favored Bebo, Kielbania and John Payne.

Bebo observed Van went from an electric sound to an acoustic approach. He was getting ready to record **Astral Weeks**. As Van prepared to leave for New York to cut his debut Warner Brothers album, his good friend Mick Cox was in New York cutting an album with Eire Apparent. When Cox came for a long weekend to visit Van in Cambridge, he said Van had put together remarkable music.

BEBO, KIELBANIA, PAYNE REFLECT ON THE CATACOMBS AND MORRISON

What was the summer of 1968 like for Bebo? He started out rehearsing with Morrison. He wondered! What the hell was going on? Joey evolved into a professional musician, and he did a credible job of backing Morrison. When Van came to Boston, he met Peter Wolf, soon to be a member of J. Geils, and they talked about what Van envisioned for **Astral Weeks**. He became acquainted with the local music scene. He also had a plan. That plan was to finish **Astral Weeks**. He had been working on for more than two years and Boston was the final inspiration.

Despite having a manager, a fund to hire musicians and a plan, Van didn't have an adequate apartment. "He'd come over to use my telephone," Peter Wolf told Ryan H. Walsh. John Sheldon claims Van asked to move into his house. Sheldon asked his mother. She told him: "No." Van couldn't move in with a seventeen-year old guitar player. The thought of a recently married musician with a wife and child living in the basement was not on the Sheldon's radar.

It was a rough time for Morrison. But it was in this Irish influenced town of Boston he put his first post Them band together. Sitting behind Van on the drums Joey Bebo had a front row seat to the festivities.

During the eight-month Boston interlude Van was all business. He would come over to Peter Wolf's apartment to call WBCN and other radio stations as well as clubs, producers and managers. There was a 24/7 mania to Van's drive toward musical success. The Belfast Cowboy connected with the local music scene. He learned key future lessons impacting his future. It was time well spent.

Because of the anti-war, hippie, dope smoking times Morrison dubbed his group "The Van Morrison Controversy." Van has never said what the name meant. What the band name meant is it helped secure bookings. Some of these gigs were strange ones. At one club Van and Tom Kielbania began a set with Kielbania's bass guitar providing an eerie backdrop to Van's vocals as Bebo kept a soft drum beat. As the second set began John Payne joined them on stage at the Catacombs. Sheldon thought the music was different. "I was kind of thinking about leaving," Payne told Walsh. Once he was on stage playing with Van, Payne got it. He loved the music. He couldn't believe how easily Morrison blended his vocals with the musical accompaniment. "His phrasing was not independent of what I was doing," Payne continued. "I had ever experienced that. This was alive." When Morrison began performing "Brown Eyed Girl," Payne was perplexed. He didn't realize the short guy with the bad haircut had a Top Ten pop hit. Like Joey Bebo, Payne didn't listen to or care about the Top 40.

The shows at the Catacombs began the Van Morrison Boston legend. Eric Kraft, writing in the underground weekly **Boston After Dark**, set off the siren signal the Van Morrison Controversy was the band to watch on the local scene. The day after the show Kraft sat with Van on the Catacomb's kitchen floor for an interview. During this brief conversation Morrison complained about Bert Berns, his Bang Record deal and he talked at length about his new songs.

FIFTY YEARS LATER BEBO CELEBRATES ASTRAL WEEKS

In 2018 Joey Bebo celebrated fifty years of performing with Van Morrison. As Bebo reminisced about showing up at Morrison's 602 Green Street apartment in Cambridge he entertained a crowd at the Cambridge Public Library where Professor Rob Hochschild of the Berklee College of Music talked about the importance of Boston to **Astral Weeks**. Earlier in the day there was a celebration at the corner of Green and Bay Streets where Van allegedly coined the term "backstreet."

Cambridge Mayor Marc McGovern proclaimed "Van Morrison Astral Weeks Day" as the city celebrated the historic album. Joey Bebo was front and center for the celebration. He experienced a place in musical history with his jazz inflected drum beat, his brilliant clothing and the eye of a historian. He continues to write. He remains a productive author with a superb intellect and a large number of published books. That is too bad as I want to hang out with the 1968 Joey Bebo.

BIBLIOGRAPHICAL SOURCES

See Ryan W. Walsh, **Astral Weeks: A Secret History of 1968** (Boston, 2018), pp. 176-187 for an excellent vie of Joey Bebo's time with Van Morrison. Also see the incisive and well written account by the drummer, Joseph W. Bebo, **In The Back Of The Van: The Story of One Unforgettable Summer** (Hudson, 2016). Bebo is a talented author with a number of fiction and non-fiction books. Bebo's book is a fascinating look from a drummer sitting behind Morrison on his shows. The writing is superb and the story is intriguing.

For the weird, strange and creative atmosphere around Boston in 1968 see, Alex Beam, **Gracefully Insane: Life And Death Inside America's Premier Mental Hospital** (New York, 2003). This book is an important one as many of the local rock and roll figures spent time in this mental hospital. As two of Van Morrison's musical cohorts passed through this hospital the story grew as others like James Taylor made a short stint to sort out his life. The McLean Hospital was an architectural gem with Frederick Law Olmsted planning this elite, expensive and premier mental hospital. Alex Beam makes a connection with Harvard University and he writes in detail about Robert Lowell, Sylvia Plath and Ray Charles spending time at McLean. Also see Sarah Payne Stuart, **My First Cousin Once Removed: Money, Madness And The Family of Robert Lowell** (New York, 1999) for a study of artistic brilliance punctuated my creative madness. The atmosphere in and around Cambridge, Boston and there is a reference to Van Morrison's **Astral Weeks** suggesting early on the intellectual community hung onto the album. Stuart's reference is to John Sheldon who spent four years being diagnosed with depression (p. 200) and she has John Sheldon as a key part of recording the **Astral Weeks** album. When Morrison left for New York to record **Astral Weeks**, he didn't take Sheldon with him. Janet Planet has spoken extensively of this period. She was an observer but remained largely in the background. Her recollection of events is excellent and in a number of interviews she has cleared the air on may subjects. The specter of mental illness surrounded Van in Boston. For a brief period, Van worked with a guitarist, Rick Philp, who was not only a brilliant musician but he was in some of Boston's top bands three years before Van settled in the area. Just before Van recorded **Astral Weeks**, Philp's was beaten to death. For one take on this bizarre story and what it meant, see, Alasdair P. MacKenzie, "'Disgraceland' Could Be So Much Better," **Harvard Crimson**, April 23, 2018. https://www.thecrimson.com/article/2018/4/23/disgraceland-review/
Also see, Joey Bebo, "Exploring The Catacombs With Van Morrison, Music Museum of New England. http://mmone.org/exploring-the-catacombs-with-van-morrison/ A series of lengthy interviews with Joey Bebo formulated this chapter.

Bebo's books are an important insight into how he thinks and how he developed in his non-musical career. See Joseph W. Bebo, **Altered Realities** (JWM Books, 2018) for the story of a brilliant scientist who links a machine and a human in an interesting and well written novel. Also see Joseph W. Bebo, **Lamp of The Gods** (JWM Books, 2015) for a novel of an astrophysicist who is in charge of a deep space telescope. The lead character moves from the 22nd century into the 21st century in what is a unique novel.

For history, Joseph W. Bebo, **Family Legends - The Charbonneau Letter** (JWB Books, 2014) is a lesson in historical fiction featuring one of Bebo's family members who was a participant in the Lewis and Clark Expedition. This is historical fiction at its finest. Also see, Joseph W. Bebo, **Of Lake, Land And Liberty: The Battle of Plattsburgh In the War of 1812** (JWB Books, 2014), passim.

Joseph W. Bebo, **Stricken: Quantum of Revenge** (JWB Books, 2004, 2009, 2016) is an intriguing and often beguiling book. The story centers around a scientist who unleashes a virus on her employers. A drop out computer genius comes to the rescue and the results are interesting and prophetic. This is a must read.

A change of pace in Bebo's prolific writing comes in **Bach Again** (JWB Books, 2014) in which the author centers the story around two skilled musicians who are brilliant and internationally famous composers. A murder mystery unravels which is an exciting story with a preposterous premise that turns into copious reality.

When the Cambridge Mayor Marc McGovern proclaimed December 1, 2018, "Van Morrison Astral Weeks Day," there was a panel discussion with Bebo, Tom Kielbania, Ryan Walsh, and John Payne in which they discussed Walsh's pathbreaking book and the importance of Morrison's eight months living on Green Street and other places in Cambridge and Boston. During this video Payne the soprano sax he used on "Slim Slow Slider." What is intriguing is how accurate and informative the panel was with Professor Rob Hochschild moderating suggested how local influences integrated themselves into Morrison's rapidly emerging cult album. See Amy Saltzman, "Astral Weeks, A Groundbreaking Album with Cambridge Roots, Honored on 50th Anniversary," Cambridge Wicked Local.com, December 3 2018.

http://cambridge.wickedlocal.com/news/20181203/astral-weeks-ground-breaking-album-with-cambridge-roots-honored-on-50th-anniversary

For information on the Cambridge celebration of **Astral Weeks** see, "Van Morrison's Astral Weeks 50th Anniversary Celebration," Cambridge Community Television, January 14, 2019. https://www.cctvcambridge.org/node/612816

For Anne Sexton seen, Diane Wood Middlebrook, **Anne Sexton: A Biography** (New York, 2001) for how McLean helped her poetry. Also see Sage Stossel, "The Asylum On The Hill," The Atlantic, January, 2002 https://www.theatlantic.com/magazine/archive/2002/01/the-asylum-on-the-hill/303058/ for a review of the Alex Beam book. This review goes to the core of the celebrity hospitals successes and failures in a difficult medical field. By the time two members of Morrison's band received treatment the institution was on its downhill slope.

See Ryan H. Walsh, "Astral Sojourn," **Boston Magazine**, March 24, 2015 for a brilliant analysis of why Boston was the key component in the year prior to **Astral Weeks**.

Joey Bebo's recollections are important ones. He believed that Van had turned a corner in his career. The reason for this conclusion is after the group cut some demos at Boston's Ace studio, Van asked how many musicians were remaining with him. Joey decided to return to school. His book details his feelings not only about Morrison but the music business. The band was doomed as John Sheldon returned to high school and Bebo began his junior year at the Berklee School of Music. Both Sheldon and Kielbania went on to professional musical careers. Bebo became a computer specialist and he has over the years established a career as a prolific writer. His books, on a wide variety of subjects, are interesting, well written and fun to read. He no longer plays the drums.

The Boston garage band scene was a brilliant one when Van Morrison was living on Green Street. One of the best bands, the Myddle Class, was endemic to the local music scene. For their history see a wonderful book Kathy West, **A Song For You: The Quest Of The Myddle Class** (Harmonic Notes, 2011). Kathy quotes a letter from guitarist Rick Philp where he talks about playing with Morrison. The Myddle Class released three singles and they were produced by Gerry Goffin and Carol King. They were actually a New Jersey band that relocated to the Boston area. Their manager, Al Aronowitz, was a mover and a shaker in the rock music business. Their influence on Van, other than guitarist Philp is unknown. They represented the vibrant Boston music scene that had its influence upon Morrison. When Rick Philp was killed by his college roommate in May 1969 the Myddle Class as a rock band came to an abrupt end. The author was Rick Philp's girlfriend and she tells the story with warmth, a professionalism and the heartbreak that goes with youthful dreams unfulfilled. Her book is well done.

For a fun read from a Van fan see Patrick Corley, **Vanatic: The Story of A Van Morrison Fan**, (Bath, 2016), pp. 8-27. Corley does a nice job describing 2015 and then reverting to the influence of **Astral Weeks** upon his listening and his life. Also see **Johnny Rogan, Van Morrison: No Surrender** (London, 2005) for how and why Van came to America due to the Troubles. Howard A. DeWitt, **Van Morrison: Them and the Bang Era, 1945-1968** (Fremont, 2005) chapter 20 describes how the term "the mystic's music emerged and what it meant for Morrison's career." Also see **Howard A. DeWitt, Van Morrison: The Mystic's Music** (Fremont, 1983) for an early examination of how and why the **Astral Weeks** album altered the direction of Morrison's career.

CHAPTER 7

THE VAN MORRISON 1970S INTERVIEWS: WHAT THEY TELL US OR DON'T

"Some are Born to sweet delight

Some are Born to sweet delight

Some are Born to Endless Night,"

WILLIAM BLAKE, AUGURIES OF INNOCENCE

"Astral Weeks is still the most adventurous record made in the rock medium, and there hasn't been a record with that amount of daring made since."

ELVIS COSTELLO

"I write songs.... I record them.... I perform them on stage. That's what I do. That's my job. Simple."

VAN MORRISON IN CONVERSATION WITH SEAN O'HAGEN, 1989

❧❧

One of the persistent myths of Van Morrison in the 1970s is he was a difficult, virtually impossible, interview. When I interviewed Tom "Big Daddy" Donahue in 1974 for my book **Van Morrison: The Mystic's Music**, he said: "Van is not difficult if you know his music, if you make him comfortable and you stay away from his personal life." At the time Donahue was San Francisco's most popular FM disc jockey. He also owned a thriving San Francisco club, the Orphanage and the Autumn

Record label. He worked with Van on numerous radio interviews. They got along fine. Why? Donahue talked about nothing more than the music.

Donahue, who passed away in 1975, was a larger than life radio personality. He invented free form radio at KMPX-FM in 1967 when he introduced what he termed "freak-freely radio." He founded the first San Francisco psychedelic night club. He befriended musicians. He also championed Van Morrison.

The numerous Donahue interviews stand as a bulwark against the **Rolling Stone** notion that Morrison was always difficult. He wasn't. The problem was rock and roll journalism. It was in its infancy and only a small number were professional.

There is no ignoring Morrison is at times impossible during interviews. There is no way to defend his at times egregious behavior. There is one caveat. During the 1970s, when he did in-depth interviews. He wasn't always out of bounds with journalists.

The best way to understand why and how some journalists viewed Morrison as impossible is to take a close look at a late 1970s interview with Nancy Horne. This interview is the benchmark for angering Morrison. Van was impossible during this session. During the same years he sat around smoking cigarettes with Donahue and talking openly about his career. He found some journalists impossible. In the Donahue interviews he talked about his life in Fairfax. Van was not a difficult interview for some journalists. For others he was a consummate nightmare. This is not a contradiction. This is simply Van Morrison.

THE 1970S WERE A TIME OF CHANGE: THE NANCY HORNE INTERVIEW

The 1970s was a time of reflection, change and personal growth. This was apparent in numerous interviews. He said repeatedly he despised the press. He hated talking with anyone connected to the media. Despite this disclaimer, he granted at least one major interview a year. He knew how to sell records. Interviews were a key. They were essential to selling albums. The interviews were at times contentious.

He couldn't quiet the inner Morrison. An explosion would take place periodically, as another Van would emerge.

Morrison was criticized in April 1977 when he took his hostility out on Capital Radio personality Nancy Horne. In an on-air interview to promote **A Period of Transition**, he began a tirade. As Dr. John stood nearby nervously lighting one cigarette after another, Van complained about the disc jockey's questions. He even took exception to her tone of voice. To alleviate the tension, Horne brought Dr. John into the interview. This tactic failed. Horne quickly ended the interview by playing "Into The Mystic." Later, she remarked to her producer: "It should have been re-titled into the asshole." This wasn't an isolated incident. It served to remind media representatives of his press difficulties. Yet, there were ten major interviews from 1970 to 1979 that reveal a great deal about Morrison and these encounters highlight an at times friendly Morrison. In a number of these sessions, he was gracious and charming. So maybe there was something that Horne said that set him off. Then again perhaps it was just Van being himself.

CONTROLLING THE ENVIRONMENT AND QUESTIONS: VAN AND THE PRESS

Controlling the environment and the questions is a tactic driving journalists crazy. Morrison has a reason for controls. He has been burnt too many times. He is also notoriously thin skinned. His innovative music brings out the critical journalists. The interviews were at times ones Van viewed as personal attacks. He takes criticism poorly. He does not suffer scrutiny well. Over the years, many have bent to Van's dictates. Others have simply ignored him.

An analysis of key interviews during the 1970s helps to understand the evolution of the Belfast Cowboy from a shy beginner in the music business to the ultimate professional. In the process, Van formed his thoughts and directed his ideas. This allowed him to enter into the musical mainstream. During interviews he either appeared very positive or hopelessly negative. While many view this as a contradiction, it is a reflection of his personality.

The interviews suggest the depth of Van's intellect. He is sharp and quick-witted. His reaction to questions at times sends journalists into retreat. He remains a curmudgeon. He can be alternately charming and diffident. The interviews provide a penetrating insight into his personality.

His first major 1970 interview was with a musician, a friend and a fellow performer-writer who inspired Morrison to open up. That person was the inimitable Happy Traum.

TALKING TO HAPPY TRAUM

When the Happy Traum **Rolling Stone** interview appeared, many Van fanatics asked: "Who is Happy Traum?" The answer was a surprising one. He is a recording artist, teacher, author and folklore specialist. Since 1968 Happy and his brother, Artie Traum, performed folk sets in New York and Boston. They inhabited the same territory as Morrison, if in a narrower vein. They also live in Woodstock.

With his brother, Traum produced two moderate selling albums for Capitol. The **Happy and Artie Traum** LP in 1969 and **Double Back** a 1971 release featuring classics in the folk genre.

Over the years Happy has written more than a dozen guitar instruction books. He founded Homespun Tapes in 1967. He has released more than 500 instructional DVDs, CDs and videos. Happy had no problem with Morrison. They spoke the same language. Music! He also had an impressive 1969 **Rolling Stone** interview with Joni Mitchell which helped to ease Van's concerns. The Happy Traum interview is a gem.

By 1970, **Rolling Stone** was America's premier rock magazine. From the magazine's earliest days in San Francisco, founder and editor, Jann Wenner, shrewdly built a publication that the record labels needed to sell their product. Interviewers with artists like Van Morrison were honest ones. These articles helped to establish the magazines credibility. **Rolling Stone** loved Morrison's music. He didn't always love their stories. That is the essence of the Belfast Cowboy.

In the early San Francisco days, operating out of a warehouse on Third Street, **Rolling Stone** struck up a special relationship with Morrison. It has persisted to the present day. Wenner and his key staff

186

members, notably Ben Fong Torres and Greil Marcus, were Morrison fans, but they were alternately critical and praiseworthy.

When Warner Brothers arranged for Morrison to sit down with Happy Traum, they realized it would sell records in large quantities. **Rolling Stone** promised a cover story. Warner purchased advertising featuring artists other than Morrison. He couldn't believe it. Warner said the interview was enough to merchandize his product. Warner told him he didn't need advertising. Mo Ostin told anyone who would listen that Morrison was a cult, folk rock singer. This wasn't the case. The idea he was a folk troubadour was contrary to Morrison's musical vision. He complained to Warner management to no avail.

Happy Traum lived in Woodstock near Van. He wasn't a professional journalist. At least not in Van's view. This made the Belfast Cowboy comfortable. Traum was knowledgeable. He asked fair and incisive questions. He knew a great deal about Morrison and his music. The interview was a comfortable one in the Sled Hill Café. Van was impressed with Traum's musical body of work.

At one time, Traum edited the folk magazine **Sing Out**, and he was a Greenwich Village personality who appeared regularly in concert in New York. To a close friend, Van referred to Traum as a musician who could write. As a working performer, Traum was sympathetic to Van's media plight.

Traum was the perfect interviewer. He, like Van, admired John Lee Hooker and Lead Belly. The interview went as well as any of Morrison's early press sessions. When Morrison read the final article, he believed there was inaccurate information. He found fault with some of what was written about him. He charged **Rolling Stone** didn't check its facts. This became a common Morrison complaint.

There were no major inaccuracies in Traum's work. Van privately told people at Woodstock's Sled Hill Café he had been misquoted. Van can't stand to read anything about his career or private life that he is not in complete agreement about. Or for that matter he doesn't control. He has a maniacal desire to influence interview content.

The press has skewered Morrison for turning his back in concert. They never asked the reason. Most of the time it was due to the promoter failing to fulfill contractual obligations. Only a small sampling of the articles mentioned Morrison's incredibly shy nature.

He is inordinately shy. His guitarist, John Platania, as well as blues legend John Lee Hooker, have commented it is difficult for Van to come onto the stage and perform. He does so says Chris Michie, because of his respect for Irish music. Tony Dey, Van's drummer in the mid-1970s, told of stories in small clubs where Morrison played late into the night due to his special feeling for these intimate blue collar clubs. "Van would play right up to and sometimes beyond closing time," Dey continued. "There were no ninety-minute sets in those days." He wasn't shy in the small clubs. It was as if Van was once again with a show band serenading the locals.

THE TRADITIONAL IRISH SINGER ON TO AMERICA

During the **Rolling Stone** interview, Van spoke about traditional Irish singers who would often turn away from a visitor or a listener because singing a traditional or historical song was such a private affair. No matter how much he downplayed his Irish heritage, during the early 1970s, Morrison remained loyal to his Irish heritage.

It wasn't until his eighteenth studio album with the Chieftains in 1988 that Morrison commercially embraced traditional Irish music. Working with Uilleann pipe legend Paddy Moloney the **Irish Heartbeat** album was critically acclaimed. It demonstrated how and why Van's Irish roots were important.

Van believes he hasn't gotten acclaim for his songwriting. He vowed to use his solo career to right this wrong. The early publishing deals continued to rankle him. He complained Phil Solomon, Bert Berns and Mo Ostin didn't recognize his lyrical skills. They simply wanted the money. He emphasized they had little interest in developing his songwriting craft.

Van Morrison on American Bandstand 1967
(Youtube - Dick Clark Interviews Van Morrison - American Bandstand 1967)

By the early 1970s, Van learned a lesson from Bob Dylan. He would not be a pliable interview. The inane questions. The inability of journalists to do their homework. The public relations hacks that went along with him for interviews were a constant source of irritation. Van was articulate and honest in selected 1970s interviews. He also had some negative opinions about Top Forty radio.

VAN ON TOP FORTY RECORDS AND HIS EVOLVING LIFE IN THE HAPPY TRAUM INTERVIEW

On Top 40 records, Van complained Bert Berns tried to persuade him to write a series of hit songs. "I just don't feel that kind of song," Van remarked. The songwriting process was alternately easy and difficult for Morrison. He maintains a disciplined writing schedule. He privately complains there are dry periods.

189

For a time, Van lived in Cambridge. His small apartment was near Harvard University. The exciting musical and intellectual climate in and around his Green street apartment drove his creativity. The Green Street apartment was barren and depressing. Many of Van's ideas for songs emerged due to his living conditions. When Van spoke of Van's unhappiness, Lester Bangs urged the Belfast Cowboy to remain unhappy. Bangs believed this was the reason he wrote so many chart friendly songs. He hit upon a key to Morrison's songwriting. It was tension and conflict. It was despair. It was anger. These were the forces that acted as a catalyst to the Belfast Cowboy's songs.

As he discussed songwriting with Traum, Van said he wrote a tune because "it just flows out." This was early in his career. It was a marvelous insight into his creative process. As Van answered Traum's questions, he mentioned his spiritual nature, and his continual search for religious truth.

When Traum's interview got around to why Van hoped to produce his own albums, he pointed out it was a difficult process: "I had to tax my imagination for all sorts of stuff. It was a big job for me...." Van complained he "was stuck with the engineer." This was a veiled criticism of the Schwaid-Merenstein team producing his early Warner albums. These comments suggest more about the difficulties Morrison experienced producing the **Moondance** LP than it does about the engineering. He commented Elliot Scheiner was willing to give him the technical assistance to make the recordings commercial. Who was Elliot Scheiner? He was a producer, a mixer and a sound engineer. Scheiner allowed Van a great deal of studio freedom along with Gary Mallaber to mix the **Moondance** album. At twenty-three years of age Scheiner was a wunderkind beginning a legendary career. Van was not always unhappy with the Schwaid-Merenstein production team. At least not during the making of the **Astral Weeks** album. He was uncomfortable having someone else finalize his music. Van didn't like the final sound on certain songs from **Astral Weeks**. He detested those that had a royalty paid to the Bert Berns' estate. Van praised the work of the session musicians. He thought Jay Berliner, Connie Kay and Richard Davis were excellent. Van believed that he should have had other musicians. This is typical of Morrison. He didn't try to hurt anyone's feelings; he had a simple desire for musical diversity through a wide range of musicians.

As the Traum interview concluded, Van was asked about other performers. Who did he admire? The answer was no one. Even though he talked about Lead Belly being his guru, he couldn't acknowledge other musicians. There was no doubt Bob Dylan remained a significant influence. The Happy Traum piece in **Rolling Stone** was Morrison's first major American cover story. It helped his emerging solo career. But journalists were forewarned. He was not an easy interview.

TALKING TO JAZZ AND POP

In 1970, Van invited Danny Goldberg to dinner at his Woodstock home. The purpose was to publicize **Moondance**. The evolving and relaxed interview provides insights into Morrison's media presence. As his manager, Mary Martin, sat nearby drinking coffee, Van talked about a wide variety of subjects.

"I was surprised by the thickness of his accent," Goldberg recalled. "He explained to me that he was able to sing in an American 'voice' by emulating the pronunciation of Ray Charles…."

During the interview there were veiled comments about Indian gurus giving people advice. Van thought it was ridiculous. The Beatles and the Rolling Stones among others had employed the gurus to help them sort out their problems. Van pointed out you solved your problems by getting up and going to work. The blue-collar work ethic characterizing Van came to the fore repeatedly in this interview.

Van said there was an impromptu nature to his music. He was not a planner. He did not sit down and sketch out an agenda. The music evolved with his moods. On the trappings of rock stardom, he pointed out he never needed an entourage, a limousine or special treatment.

A surprising admittance was Van loved American cinema cowboy stars Hopalong Cassidy, Lash Larue and the Cisco Kid. He often saw their movies at a Belfast theater when he was growing up. He never forgot them. He also loved Leo Gorcey and Huntz Hall in the Dead End Kids movies. Van remarked: "I wanted to be a cowboy."

As Danny Goldberg concluded the interview, Van was running out of comments. They continued to see each other and later

Goldberg wound up as the president of Atlantic and eventually Mercury Records. Van was comfortable with him.

RICK MCGRATH INTERVIEWS VAN IN VANCOUVER, B. C. 1971

Rick McGrath was a counterculture Canadian journalist when he met Morrison as the Vancouver B. C. airport for an interview over bacon and eggs. With long hair and a hippie persona, McGrath made Morrison comfortable. The piece was for the **Georgia Straight**, a counterculture publication, given away free on the streets.

It was an unseasonably cold February 3, 1971 morning when Van dug into his breakfast. He was not only in a good mood; he was forthcoming in his remarks. The grind of recording and touring was telling on Morrison. Yet, he was energetic and upbeat. Not exactly the Van many journalists found. The reason was a simple one. McGrath came prepared with intelligent questions and knowledge of Van's career.

**Ticket stub for Van Morrison concert at
Queen Elizabeth Theater, Vancouver B.C.**

The interview began with Van complaining about the sound and lighting the night before the University of British Columbia student gymnasium. John Platania was part of the interview. He told McGrath the band simply "came in and played."

When McGrath asked Van about his less than inspired stage persona, the Belfast Cowboy educated the reporter on the rigors of the road. Van remarked: "I do other things than playing music." He commented performing was only a small part of his life. McGrath was perplexed. He asked Van to interpret **Astral Weeks**. The band laughed. Van said everyone seemed to be figuring it out. Jack Schroer, the saxophonist, chimed in Van and the band performed the **Astral Weeks** album material live in a different manner. Schroer said it was like the blues. They updated the album. Van performed some songs from **Astral Weeks**, but only a select few. He did so at times grudgingly. When asked about **Astral Weeks**, Van usually had no comment. He talked about it with McGrath. Why? The reporter was a knowledgeable interviewer. The conversation turned away from Van and the band, as Morrison discussed the rock and roll press.

The ever-articulate drummer, Dahaud Shaar, gave his opinions. He chided the rock and roll press for not reviewing Van's material in depth. Shaar commented on the amateur nature of counterculture publications. Van chimed in. He said he read a review in a British jazz journal. They didn't understand **Astral Weeks**. Why should the reporter? Rick McGrath looked flummoxed. He loved being with Morrison and the band, but this was an interview like none other in his career.

Dahaud Shaar aka "David Shaw" (Drummer/percussionist. Member of Van Morrison's band.)

There were a number of positive conclusions from this interview. McGrath pointed out the band was tight. He also complimented the back-up singer Martha Velez for her soaring vocals. When McGrath asked Van where he got her, he replied. "The trumpet player, Keith Johnson, she's married to him."

McGrath suggested Van's stage presence "was less than exciting." Rather than getting angry, he replied he couldn't perform after traveling for six or seven hours and then get up on stage as Mr.

194

Personality. "I can only get into it when I'm comfortable," Van concluded.

ON THE COVER OF ROLLING STONE

In June 1972 **Rolling Stone** sent John Grissim, Jr. to profile Morrison. With Van once again on the cover, there was euphoria at Warner Brothers. They believed the **Rolling Stone** cover would increase album sales. Why advertise? Warner Brothers believed it was a waste of money. When the interview concluded, Morrison said, he had a bad feeling about the article. His concern was soon borne out.

There was a mean-spirited tone to Grissim's article. He talked of Van firing various band members. He claimed Van was continually grouchy and detached from the band. Grissim, without an ounce of evidence, complained about Van's association with Warner. The **Rolling Stone** writer defended the labels nefarious contract. It was a Warner Brothers love-fest ready to hit **Rolling Stone's** pages.

Those close to Morrison said he was furious. Grissim concluded he changed musicians at will. Van was unhappy. He said he did this to vary his sound, create material and prevent his music from being "the flavor of the month." Not only was Morrison's music carefully crafted, he spent more time rehearsing than he did on stage.

Grissim wasn't at the rehearsals. He had no idea how Van created his music. He didn't interview the musicians. He didn't listen to the music. Van wondered how in the hell he could draw intelligent conclusions.

Grissim failed to realize this was just Van Morrison. He concluded Van's "world was crashing around him." Nothing was further from the truth. He was beginning one of his most commercial periods. His world was expanding into prosperity.

As the interview progressed, Van had less to say than Grissim. The finished product was a strange piece of journalism. Purporting to be an interview, it was little more than a journalistic hatchet job. Grissim felt threatened and intimidated. He described Van as being difficult, spoiled and impossible.

Grissim speculated Morrison did not subscribe to a newspaper. He concluded he reads few magazines, and he watches no television.

Grissim said Van read few books. None of this was true. Van had an extensive and defined reading habit. He seldom shares his reading habits with friends. From time to time he will cite a book during an interview. His lyrics are filled with references highlighting an abundant interest in things literary and historical. He has written numerous letters to the editor complaining of inaccurate information concerning his personal life. When you get it wrong, Morrison will call you on it. When you get it right, he will sit down again for a lengthy interview. The **London Sun**, the **London Guardian** and the **London Independent** have heard from Morrison. He writes a literate letter. He did this extensively while living at different times in London, Bath and Belfast.

Where and how Grissim uncovered his misinformation is unknown. In a snippy note, Grissim concluded Morrison did not finish most books. He had to amend his story when numerous photos showed Morrison carrying around different books. His friends said he was a voracious reader. Van often talked about what the books meant to his psyche and songwriting. Morrison challenged Grissim during the interview. The **Rolling Stone** reporter concluded Morrison had a personality disorder. He did! He doesn't tolerate pompous jackasses.

Those who follow Van know his habits. He is a coffee shop aficionado even if he does drink tea. He is not usually approachable. He is not rude. He is private. While living in Fairfax Van would wander at times into the Good Earth for something to drink. His dad's record store was on the main street. He loved Fairfax. Locals remember seeing him carrying around philosophy books. He seemed to be in another world. "Cosmic thought," Chris Michie told me in 1982.

What is interesting about Grissim's interview is if he had listened carefully to Morrison's music, he would have realized Van wrote songs based on his life, newspapers, literature and folk tales. He also had an ear for the American blues. He had an ear and an eye for history.

Grissim reported Van called the Lion's Share in San Anselmo to cancel a booking for no reason. Grissim wrote: "He had evidently agreed to the night ... while under the influence of ... 3.2 suds." This wasn't the case at all. Van had last minute business in Los Angeles at Warner Brothers. Ray Ruff told me Morrison had to rush to Los Angeles due to a contract dispute. The Lion's Share gig was usually at the spur of the moment. The management was happy to have a major star play for a pittance. They weren't upset when he cancelled. They understood. When I interviewed Lion's Share management about the **Rolling Stone** article. They replied: "Who the hell is John Grissim?"

There were some high points in the interview. Van remarked he loved Roy Head's version of "Bit By Bit." He thought Esther Phillips' renderings of "Crazy Love" and "Brand New Day" stood out as faithful interpretations. He also liked Dorothy Morrison's cover of "Brand New Day." Then he talked about how he loved working in the studio.

Van's continual experiments in the studio were evident in the interview. He said originally "Wild Night" was a slow jazz number. "We got fooling around with it in the studio." Van continued: "We ended up doing it in a faster tempo. So they put it out as a single. It works ok that way but I still occasionally sing it to myself in the slow version…."

He also talked at length about despising larger venues. At one such gig at Randall's Island in New York the crowd was sailing paper airplanes. "And so I stopped the band and we all sat down. And we just watched them sail their paper planes. And they didn't even notice that we had stopped playing," Van concluded.

The interview ended as Van lamented his dislike with the process. "Maybe I'm just using this as an opportunity to say some things that have been on my mind," Van concluded. He said the interview process was "bull shit."

SITTING DOWN WITH THE TALK ABOUT POP PUBLICATION

While he was on a brief vacation in Ireland in 1973, Van appeared on an Irish TV show Talk About Pop. The show was one where Tony Johnson of RTE TV in Dublin was supposed to interview Van. The Belfast Cowboy brought along his friend Donal Corvin who joined in the question period. Johnson was unhappy as Corvin replaced him as the questioner. Johnson was an aggressive pretty boy. He had the personality of a wet toilet seat. Van's friend, journalist Donal Corvin, sat down and asked the questions. The Talk About Pop interview was a spontaneous decision by Morrison. RTE-TV management loved it. When Van was announced as the guest, the ratings soared. The station manager called Tony Johnson aside telling him to allow Morrison full freedom.

The show's format evolved into Van being interviewed. Then he would play a record. He also performed some songs. This cut the tension. It allowed for a relaxed evening. It was a coup for Talk About Pop to book Morrison. When the show went on the air in 1973 no one expected a long life for the show. Van not only helped their ratings; he demonstrated his continual appeal to an Irish audience. The inevitable continuation of Talk About Pop, as a major music program, was due to the Belfast Cowboy's guest appearance.

Bill Keating, the Talk About Pop producer, believed by giving Morrison an entire thirty minutes he would get a wider viewing audience. He did! When the show was broadcast on the Irish television network, RTE, the ratings were number one in the time slot. There were some things Morrison didn't like. For some reason he objected to the master of ceremonies Tony Johnson opening and closing the program by asking Van questions. Some of the questions, according to Morrison, were not appropriate. Van tried to be civil. He reluctantly answered most questions. The early parts of the show were not as free flowing, but Corvin saved the day.

At the program's conclusion, Tony Johnson asked seven questions. There was one sticky moment. That was when Van was questioned about Bert Berns and Bang Records. Van hesitated. Johnson demanded an answer. It was apparent why Van wanted Corvin at his side. Johnson answered his own question suggesting Berns and the Bang years were an unfortunate interlude. Van glowered. There was a deadly silence.

Morrison opened up in this interview to Corvin. He talked at length about **Astral Weeks**. Van claimed he hadn't changed his musical direction since **Astral Weeks**. He suggested the critics didn't understand "style is the whole trip." He said he was not about to chase trends.

Donal Corvin's questions provided insights into Morrison's thinking. When Van was asked if he changed his new music. He responded: "Just because I put an album out one way and then put an album out another way doesn't mean I stop singing the other one." Morrison made it clear there was no predictability to his music.

Van did his best to be polite. Johnson remarked Van had a reputation for being difficult. Van responded: "That's the media. The reason you get all that stuff is through the media because people print things without ever talking to the actual people." It irritated Van when the London press said he didn't want to play for the Irish people. Not true! Van addressed this question often. He sometimes became testy. When the subject of Irish music came up Van was cooperative.

He talked at length about the McPeakes. He said they were the only real thing left in Irish music. He discussed a party he went to and watched them perform "Purple Heather." "I don't sing it the way they sing it, but that's what inspired me, it's what turned me on to the song," Van said.

When he talked about the "Drumshanbo Hustle," Van remarked: "I got the title from a town we played when I was with a showband one time. We were getting ripped off in those days, like you always get ripped off no matter what you do if you're a musician. That's where the title comes from and the rest of it is about something else." Van never explained. Why should he? Tony Johnson did not understand anything about Morrison or his music. Why explain?

THE DRUMSHANBO HUSTLE

Van reminisced about the "Drumshanbo Hustle." He joked about running out of things to say. What was the "Drumshanbo Hustle?" It is a song Van recorded for **Hard Nose The Highway** that wasn't released until **The Philosophers Stone**. Van explained why it wasn't released. The subject was how those in the industry took unwarranted songwriting credit, a share of the mechanical royalties and as Van observed in lyrical form: "They were trying to muscle in… on the gigs. And the recording and publishing…." That said it all. The record business was full of crooks. Warner didn't want "The Drumshanbo Hustle" released.

Van discussed his recording career. He told Johnson he loved live studio cuts. He complained by recording separate tracks and overdubbing the music there was a false sense of sound. He preferred to record much like he was delivering a concert. Van hated what the producers did to his music.

199

As the interview progressed things got interesting. Donal Corvin laughingly asked the Belfast Cowboy to walk around the studio on his hands. He did. They all laughed. As the interview ended in a great deal of mirth, Van talked about his mother singing something about "Bops with sugar on top." This interview demonstrated how much fun Morrison could be in the right setting. Unfortunately, that setting was rare. However, he did open up in conversation a few years later when he sat down with Tom Donahue, a San Francisco disc jockey, who was also a friend.

SITTING DOWN WITH BIG DADDY TOM DONAHUE

Throughout the 1970s Van conducted two friendly interviews with KSAN-FM host and local promoter Tom "Big Daddy" Donahue. The first interview was important in changing how the press looked at Morrison's career. The rotund three-hundred-pound radio-concert personality hung out with Van in local clubs. They drank together. They were friends. Donahue booked Morrison in local clubs. He also owned the Orphanage. It was one of San Francisco's premier rock venues.

In a 1974 interview, Van discussed "Bulbs." He had high hopes for the song. The Belfast Cowboy was pleased when Donahue commented the lyrics were as great as the music. When "Bulbs" appeared on **Veedon Fleece** it didn't catch the public's attention. Van couldn't figure out why.

The second interview in 1978 was caught on tape at Donahue's club, the Orphanage. It showcased a relaxed and confident Morrison.

As Van emerged as a solo act Donahue placed his music in heavy rotation on KSAN. When Van played a 1978 gig at Donahue's club The Orphanage, it was preserved as a marvelous bootleg.

The studio interview in 1974 with Morrison is one of the most revealing of his early career. It also goes a long way to challenging the view he was always difficult during interviews. As he sat in a red t-shirt with glasses, Morrison was relaxed. He talked with Donahue about getting used to smoking camels. They laughed.

When Donahue asked Van how long he played the saxophone, he said intermittently. Van thought for a moment and said "only

200

recently." Donahue congratulated him on his skill. When Van discussed the places where he lived, he said he was influenced by where he lived. "I like the contrast," Van said of Fairfax. "I have the best of both worlds." When Van got bored, he drove to San Francisco to eat, drink, shop and listen to music. In the local clubs he could wander in and no one would bother him. Jack's on Fillmore was his favorite haunt. He would show up there and at times jump on stage on perform with Jackie Payne's band. Big Bones, the house drummer and a harmonica virtuoso, recalled the band didn't know who he was but he had the hutzpah to simply come on stage and take over. "I still have tapes," Big Bones remarked.

He said he loved the relaxed Marin County lifestyle. "I am kind of jet setting around," Van told Donahue with a sly smile.

When Donahue played some cuts from John Lee Hooker's 1968 album **Urban Blues**, Morrison brightened. They talked at length about Hooker's lengthy and productive career. This provided a rare insight into Morrison's admiration for the blues legend.

The interview discussed Van's new album tentatively entitled **Highlights**. This LP never saw the light of day. There was another unreleased LP **Mechanical Bliss**. This interview suggests how productive Morrison was in the mid-1970s. He certainly was not entering a period of semi-retirement. When Van went back out on the road extensively in 1977, there were numerous references to the period of retirement. This further intensified Morrison's negative feelings about the media. He had been working on new material. He was playing small clubs. How could the media, Van wondered, ignore his productivity and creativity?

Mechanical Bliss was in its final production stage. To this day no one is sure what happened to the album. The **Mechanical Bliss** album was forty-six minutes with nine tracks. When the album wasn't released the bootleggers went into action. A two CD version arrived with nineteen songs. The bootlegger's artwork and liner notes were superb. Rumor has it Van loved the bootleg. The liner notes remarked the Sausalito's Record Plant was where he recorded nine tracks. The rest were from the New York Mercury Studio in March-April 1974 and the Wisseloord Studio, Hilversum in the Netherlands.

David Chance put together the notes for the **Mechanical Bliss** album. He speculated on the release date as set for February 1975. Johnny Rogan argues, in his 1984 biography, the album's title was changed to **Stiff Upper Lip**. There were two songs from this proposed album "This Is Not The Twilight Zone" and "Mechanical Bliss" that received KSAN radio airplay.

The original cover for Van Morrison's unreleased Mechanical Bliss album. The artwork was never used; eventually being modified and used on Steely Dan's "The Royal Scam" album.

The San Francisco Bay Area maniacs taped the songs. Haik Arakiel produced a bootleg 45. The end result was a great deal of speculation and no conclusive facts on the material or the album. Van told KSAN's Tom Donahue he was working on making the unreleased material available. Eventually, some songs appeared on the **Philosopher's Stone**. "Y'know, various things over the years that I've done that I, I haven't, y'know, gotten on an album," Van remarked to Donahue. That was the first indication of Morrison's plans for collecting unreleased material on an album. The prototype for **The Philosopher's Stone** was born.

Donahue understood Van. He had no problem with him. This was evident when he sat down with a longhaired rock and roll writer who not only listened intently to Morrison. He also wrote the first full-length biography on the Belfast Cowboy. He was a rock and roll guy from Canada. His name was Ritchie Yorke.

STAGE LIFE IN 1977 AND VAN ON ROCK 'N' ROLL

In 1977 Van sat down once again with his initial biographer, Ritchie Yorke. They completed an interview for **Stage Life**. At the time, Van was living in Los Angeles' Brentwood neighborhood close to the University of California, Los Angeles. This upscale community is laden with million-dollar homes adjacent to student housing. He lived in a comfortable manner in what Ritchie Yorke described as "an upper middle class bungalow." While communing with students and drinking coffee near the UCLA campus, Van wrote daily and worked on new music. He was anonymous. He loved it. Van was driving a brown Toyota around Los Angeles with a new sense of personal freedom. Ritchie Yorke asked Van what he had been doing since **Veedon Fleece**? Van said he was working hard on a new album.

There was one reason for the Yorke interview. It was to lay to rest the myth he was retired. He was simply playing small gigs, adding new recordings to his archives, and he was enjoying himself. Van was working furtively. "It wasn't exciting anymore to totally be a singer/songwriter because it wasn't working for me," Van continued. "Then I thought of collaborating with other people which still might happen at this point."

The plan for the **Philosopher's Stone** emerged, according to Chris Michie, and the project turned Morrison into an archivist. Van stockpiled a cache of songs. He felt no need to release new material.

Once again, the Belfast Cowboy cared very little about a commercial product. It was about getting the material out while retaining control.

Van described rock and roll as a primitive art form. He suggested it was the reason the music continued to be popular. It was different. It was eclectic. It was personal. He railed at any sort of categorization. "Labeling me a song poet and all that," Van continued. "I'm not saying I can't do that and that I'm not a song poet." He hated being labeled a song poet. Van didn't like this intellectual tag. Then Morrison talked about being influenced by Jack Kerouac. He suggested that his stream of consciousness prose was closer to James Joyce. This was an accurate description of one of his writing influences. Ritchie Yorke asked Van how the ideas germinated for his songs?

Van remarked as a kid he had visions. They still persisted. These visions fill his songs. A perfect example is in "Fair Play" in which he mentions Edgar Allen Poe's gothic tales. As Van continued, he told Yorke he was tired of hearing himself described as "a man of mystery." He also derided those who said he was a follower of trendy religions. Van remarked: "There's no man alive who has any answers." On his concerts, he told Ritchie Yorke he didn't rehearse before a live show. "I just walk in and we jam on some Bobby 'Blue' Bland tunes for a while to get the groove," Morrison concluded.

On the subject of jazz-rock fusion, Van remarked: "I don't like it personally." However, he went on to praise George Benson's musical style. Van reminisced about the soothing effect jazz had upon him. "Jazz goes into folk music, into rock music," Van concluded.

When he discussed his reading habits, he had wide and eclectic tastes. J. P. Donleavy was the only writer Van confessed to reading consistently. "He's written books that I can definitely connect with," Van continued. "He has amazing insights which other people missed out on." Van confessed that he was "into philosophy."

Perhaps the most interesting comment was obscure blues legend Bo Carter was responsible for a song on the **A Period of Transition** album. The tune Van wrote "You Gotta Make It Through The World," began with a riff from a Carter tune. This insight into Morrison's composing style was an important one. The themes in Carter's records intrigued Morrison. "I found this Bo Carter record and he was just saying something about making it to the woods or something like that...I just picked up on a larger thing about not making it through the woods but making it through the world."

Ritchie Yorke's interview with Morrison was a key one. It revealed a great deal about Van's evolution during the 1970s. What he wrote and why he penned his songs became apparent. He was evolving as a person as well as an artist.

TALKING WITH HOT PRESS THREE YEARS LATER

In July 1977 **Hot Press** published a three-year-old interview with Donal Corvin. The interview was to promote **A Period of Transition**. The only problem was the album fell by the wayside. It got lost in Morrison's complaints. Since Corvin and Morrison were old Belfast friends, the interview was a revealing one. Van's stated his hatred for the Them years, Bert Berns and producer cum lackey, Tommy Scott. Only Belfast friend Phil Coulter is mentioned in a gracious manner. Morrison clearly was uncomfortable with memories from his early career. He loved Belfast. But the hurtful media images haunted him. Van intimated the press failed to recognize how he connected to his home town. It was spiritual and intellectual. Belfast was his muse.

The specter of poverty hung over the Yorke interview. Van confessed to being broke during the early years. He lamented it impacted his drive for stardom. That drive had a fiscal, as well as a commercial, direction. Van stated **Astral Weeks** was not written as a concept album. "I don't think I started to get into, you know, what I do...uh, until '69." He didn't realize that he had written a concept album until after the fact.

Van believes his songs have been overanalyzed. He found it strange a simple song like "Snow in San Anselmo" was prone to multiple interpretations. It was nothing more than a tune about a bizarre weather front in Northern California. He said this was a song not open to interpretation. At least this was Van's viewpoint. "I don't write with an interpretation," Van commented, "that's up to the listener."

"Snow In San Anselmo" deserves credit for innovation. He used the Oakland Symphony Chamber Chorus to open the song. As Erik Hage has noted: "the album suffered a lot of unnecessary criticism."

When he wrote "Madame Joy," Van said he did so as a straight poem with music. As he analyzed his intellectual influences, there was a lengthy discussion about the concept of Caledonia. To Van it represents the notion that soul music originated in Scotland and Ireland. "The structure and roots of traditional Irish and Scottish music has a very strong link with the American negro's rhythm 'n' blues," Morrison observed.

As to his work habits and his Warner Brothers contract, Van remarked: "I'm always writing ... It takes a lot of work and a lot of concentration and a lot of effort." He believes Warner didn't understand how to promote his product. He also complained about songs Warner Brothers excluded from his albums. He said they hampered his career direction.

One of the interesting changes in Van's recording methods took place by the late 1970s. He began looking for ways to improve his vocals. Van stated he was self-critical of his vocals. He remarked to Donal Corvin he would do ten takes of a song. A few years earlier, he had stated the first take of a song was his best one. Van never explained this contradiction.

SITTING DOWN ONCE AGAIN WITH ROLLING STONE: JONATHAN COTT

In 1978 Van sat down with **Rolling Stone's** Jonathan Cott. For much of the decade, Van was unhappy with the magazine's reporting. He needed them to publicize his career. There was a love-hate relationship with **Rolling Stone**. This revealing interview solidified Morrison's attitudes as the 1980s emerged.

When Jonathan Cott arrived in San Francisco, he rented a car and checked into a Sausalito hotel. This small town, located just across the Golden Gate Bridge and just a few miles from Fairfax, was the perfect place for an interview. Van had someone drive him to Cott's hotel. They had dinner. It was October 1978 and the San Francisco Indian Summer created a beautiful night. After dinner, they drove to Bill Graham's sumptuous home. Graham's Wolfgang Productions was managing Van. The setting was an attempt to create the right atmosphere. One Graham hoped would garner the Belfast Cowboy positive publicity. Morrison had not performed nationally or internationally very much in the last three and a half years. Graham was ready to take him on the road.

The interview turned into a friendly one. Van spent a lot of time talking about Lead Belly and the McPeake family. He noted that Da McPeake's use of the pipes influenced him. Cott wasn't interested in talking about Van's approach to music. He was a journalist looking for a sensational story. Van looked at him with a stony silence. Chris Michie recalled Van sitting down and talking about some of the **Rolling Stone** interviews. Van told Michie he had been down this road too many times to listen to journalists ask the questions and answer them. Hence, the stony silence.

When Cott asked Van if he flipped out in 1974, Morrison responded: "No, I didn't flip out. I've never flipped out. It's those who have one kind of fixation that do that." He couldn't believe Cott's gall. Rather than take the bait from questions designed to provoke him, Van took the high road. He calmly said his mind was an evolving one. Van said the William Morris Agency attempted to get him back on the road. He was engaged in explaining his career. Cott yawned. He was not interested in Morrison's career. Van persisted. He explained his musical vision in copious detail. He told Cott: "I will go on tour with the new music when I am ready." It was as if Cott wasn't listening. His next question was: "Why are you not interested in touring?" Van told him he was enjoying himself. This interview suggests Morrison's increasingly normal life in the 1970s.

One wonders if the Cott interview helped Morrison to consider changing his schedule and his means of working. Chris Michie said: "No." He pointed out Van had a long-term commercial goal. There was a change in career direction with an emphasis on future music. "Van was hard working, that was it. Anything else is journalistic hoopla," Michie told me in 1981.

The so-called period of retirement is one of the never-ending myths in Morrison's career. From 1973 through 1977 he concentrated on writing, small club dates, filling his notebooks with new lyrics, and working on a long-term career plan. In 1975 all of Van's shows were in California except for one in Buffalo. He continued to hone his concert act. In 1976-1977 there was a brief period of retreat to a personal creativity with no headlining shows. He did guest at six concerts including the Last Waltz in 1976. There wasn't a single 1977 show of any significance. Van was not retired. He was working 24/7 on new material.

MELODY MAKER AND CHRIS WELCH

The February 3, 1979 issue of **Melody Maker** contained an interview with Chris Welch. On a cold London day, Welch entered London's Royal Garden Hotel. He spotted Van sitting in the corner with a pot of tea. Just two weeks earlier **Melody Maker** had a wanker like headline detailing Morrison running angrily off the stage of New York's Palladium Theater. Another comment about Morrison's apparently weak mental health enraged the Belfast Cowboy. Welch had some trepidation about the interview. Van was ready to explode. The power of the rock press and how it misinterpreted his career angered him.

In the **Melody Maker** interview, Van was polite, often deferential. He was never personally abusive. Welch was shocked. As the interview progressed, Phil Lynott of Thin Lizzy showed up to add his comments. He complained about the insensitive, abusive and generally inaccurate rock and roll press. Lynott said the press misrepresented his career. Welch was flummoxed. He wasn't sure how to respond.

For Van it was one again a chance to demonstrate the media didn't understand his music. They were more interested in his private life. When Welch asked if the new album, **Wavelength**, was about America? Van responded: "It's about everything, it isn't just about America." Van went on to explain as a kid he listened to the Voice of America. This radio station formed much of his early musical knowledge. Morrison declared his recent material was "about Europe."

Morrison said **Wavelength** was about personal change. Van told Welch he was doing this interview to end the continual misinterpretation of his lyrics. Van called the new album "aggressive." He chided Welch for his lack of knowledge. He asked a friend. "Has this critic listened to **Wavelength**?"

Welch's most inane question was whether Van was happy. He responded "Yeah, I feel happier in myself ... I can balance things out more now, between the music business … outside interests." Then Morrison explained how he had total control of his business affairs. There was a long silence. Welch seemed lost in his notes.

The Welch interview was a contentious one. During this lengthy and often strange marathon session there were uncomfortable moments of silence, Van charged: "You're just stroking me." Van was furious with questions having to do with his personal life. He complained Welch needed to learn about the music and his career. One of Van's close London friends told me "Welch wants to fit in. He is mellow and genial. He is a wannabe wanker."

Then Van talked about how punk music was in many ways saving the industry. He said he didn't care for punk music. He loved the attitude. "Music is like a healing thing," Van continued. "Any kind of art or music is involved in healing." The interview concluded as another pot of tea arrived. Welch left. Van pulled out a philosophy book. He ended the afternoon quietly and calmly reading about existentialism while slowly drinking. It was a refreshing break from the interview. Welch was as much a fan as a journalist.

The Chris Welch interview was a milestone in Morrison's career. He consulted a public relations firm in London to smooth over his increasingly volatile media relations. Van hired Keith Altham to handle his public relations. A former **New Musical Express** reporter, Altham had close ties to London's incestuous media market. Chris Welch was a friend. Van was convinced by Altham to agree to Welch's interview. He did. It didn't go well. But Altham remained an important cog in the Van Morrison musical machine.

Some critics see the Welch interview as a major turning point in Morrison's media career. It wasn't. The Welch interview was typical Van. He answered the questions he deemed appropriate. The others he ignored. Welch has an easy interview style. This was the reason he received many excellent quotes.

Despite his problems with Morrison, Altham was a welcome addition to the Belfast Cowboy's commercial camp. He knew how to work the press. It didn't take long for Altham to tire of Morrison. In his book, **No More Mr. Nice Guy**, Altham calls his chapter on Van "A Legend In His Own Guinness." But he was responsible for a new commercial renaissance in Morrison's career. Unfortunately, Altham concluded his chapter on Morrison observing: "The truth is that you are an impossible man." That said Altham has respect for Van's music.

When Morrison's commercial resurgence took place in the late 1970s, it was in part due to Altham's expertise. Suddenly Van agreed to lengthy Warner Brothers photo sessions. He spent more time with Warner marketing people. He attempted to work with his label. When Van missed a photo session to update his label portfolio, he told Altham he had a dental appointment. They exchanged words. Soon Altham was gone. This pattern continued. He often deals directly with the labels. This approach was the result of Van's early 1970s self-education in the music business.

VAN LOOKS BACK ON INTERVIEWS, 2015

In April 2015 Van Morrison sat down with Irish journalist Clive Davis for the **Irish Examiner** to look back on the 1970s. This was the new Belfast Cowboy as he lamented the media's inaccuracies. "They never write about this stuff in the rock magazines," Morrison remarks. What is he talking about? Van told James he is a fun guy who makes jokes, laughs and he claims to be the life of the party. As long as the interviewer stays on music subjects, it is a love fest.

But even in 2015 Van can't pull off his love for the media. "They keep the mythology going — I am grumpy and never have a laugh — because they are so lazy. They might have to get a sense of humor." This comment suggests the new Van Morrison remains the old Van Morrison.

He made it clear to Davis his musical direction has never deviated. "It's about jazz and blues as opposed to rock," Morrison continued. "I didn't grow up on Top of The Pops. It was more esoteric stuff that you had to think about." The leopard doesn't change his stripes.

BILBIOGRAPHICAL SOURCES

Happy Traum, "Van Morrison: The Rolling Stone Interview," **Rolling Stone**, July 9, 1970 is an important source for Van's attitudes at the beginning of the decade. This interview was one of the earliest examples of where Morrison believed that the press treated him unfairly over the years. See Danny Goldberg, "Interview," **Jazz and Pop**, December 1970 for an interesting look into Morrison's jazz roots.

John Grissim, Jr., "Rolling Stone Interview," **Rolling Stone**, June 22, 1972 is a mean spirited look at his early career. It was this interview, which made him reticent to sit down with the press for the remainder of the 1970s. The Grissim interview is the first salvo in the media war between Morrison and the press. The contentious nature of Van's hostility didn't abate until 2008 when he completed interviews for the **Astral Weeks Live** shows. Van's complaint about Grissim is he taped the interview and promised to report the story verbatim from the tape. Van didn't understand interpretation, outside sources and literary license was the way journalism worked. It is intriguing that Morrison complained about Grissim to John Tobler in an interview with **Zig Zag**. In the 1973 Tobler interview Van complained Grissim "changed it all around." He accused Grissim of "Fabrication." The Grissim article was fawning, never critical and praiseworthy of Morrison's talent. What upset Van were tales of how a dream or dreams inspired his music and re-reading of Grissim's brilliant prose doesn't mention or infer a dream was important to Morrison's songwriting genius. Van said to Tobler of Grissim: "He said that I had a dream about a mass in a church. I didn't have a dream." There is no mention of a dream by Grissim. What was the reason for Van's unhappiness? He was articulating his hostility into less than reliable reporting. Van does have a case against the London based press, which has never left his private life alone. But to attack **Rolling Stone** seemed like a strange move. But Van has never flinched in calling the press to task. Even when he cooperates with journalists, as Steve Turner can attest, he can turn with a vengeance on real and imagined false stories. The truth is Van for the first forty years of his career found fault with most stories. There are some excellent journalists who are friends who have written fair and impartial articles. For these stories see the work of Fintan O'Toole, Lester Bangs, John Wasserman, Phil Elwood, Greil Marcus and Donal Corvin among others.

See Tony Johnson, 1973 **Talk About Pop** Interview, a November taping, transcribed by Art Siegel from issue 8 of the **Into The Music Van Morrison** fanzine. This was a November 2, 1973 interview with Morrison. Michael Walsh transcribed the original tape of the show in detail. Art Siegel transcribed it for the Simon Gee Van Morrison fanzine by Art Siegel.

https://www.oocities.org/tracybjazz/hayward/van-the-man.info/reviews/1973rte.html

One of the most comfortable Morrison interviews is with Tom Donahue sometime in the summer of 1974 on KSAN-FM in San Francisco. For the transcript to this interview which runs to fifteen pages and is an excellent one, see the archived Van Morrison Website. http://web.archive.org/web/20091028131621/http://geocities.com/tracybjazz/hayward/van-the-man.info/reviews/1974ksan.html

See the excellent and insightful piece by Ritchie Yorke, "Stage Life Interview," **Stage Life**, June-July 1977, transcribed by David Chances on the archived Van Morrison website. http://web.archive.org/web/20130730035343/http://geocities.com/tracybjazz/hayward/van-the-man.info/reviews/1977stagelife.html Conversations with Ritchie Yorke in Canada and Australia via telephone added a great deal to this chapter.

See Howard A. DeWitt, **Van Morrison: The Mystic's Music** (Fremont, 1983), passim for how the Belfast Cowboy dealt with the media in the 1970s.

Jonathan Cott, "The 1978 Rolling Stone Interview," **Rolling Stone**, November 30, 1978. For a transcript of the interview by David Chance see the full interview on the archived Van Morrison Website. http://web.archive.org/web/20130730034756/http://geocities.com/tracybjazz/hayward/van-the-man.info/reviews/1978rs.html

A series of interviews with Ray Coleman helped me to understand the workings and direction of the British rock and roll press. Also, in Liverpool Joe Flannery, Clive Epstein and Bob Wooler gave their perspective on the British media, which helped to delineate these interviews. Ray Ruff in Los Angeles talked at length about the interview process for rock and roll stars. Red Robinson, the legendary Vancouver British Columbia disc jockey, provided his assessment of the media influence upon Morrison. A telephone interview with Phil Lynott was important to this chapter.

A number of people in the British media helped with this chapter by pointing out the key components of that press. These include Ian Wallis, Bob Denham, Willie Pauwels, Jesse Hector, Rob Hughes and Dave Williams.

Roger Armstrong of Ace Records provided some insight into rock and roll journalism, as did Ian Wallis from his various excellent books and knowledge of the period.

Conversations with Chris Michie, John Platania and Happy Traum were important to this chapter in terms of how Morrison created his art.

An interview with Roy Head was important to this chapter as he helped to clarify the media and the industry in the making of a hit record. Head suggested that Morrison had the soul of an African American singer and he loved all his music.

See Clinton Heylin, **Can You Feel the Silence? Van Morrison: A New Biography** (New York, 2002), passim for key interview information. Heylin fails to adequately interpret the material adequately due to an inherent anti-Morrison bias. Heylin reflects on the Chris Welch interview calling it "surprisingly conversational."

See Danny Goldberg, **Bumping Into Geniuses: My Life Inside The Rock And Roll Business** (New York, 2008) for some incisive observations on Morrison and his career. Goldberg provided a music insider's view of Morrison's complex personality and how he operated within the minefield of the music industry.

Chris Welch, "Interview," **Melody Maker**, February 3, 1979 is an important source for analyzing the changes in Van over the decade of the 1970s. For information on the Talk About Pop show see **Billboard**, September 22, 1973. The press had difficulty talking with Morrison in the early 1970s because they weren't prepared. He was too busy with his career to suffer fools.

Conversation with Ritchie Yorke were important to this chapter in analyzing how and why the interviews are a window into Morrison's thoughts on and method of songwriting. The legendary singer Matt Lucas provided key insights into how Van was able to guide his career through the media minefield.

As he aged Morrison began looking back on his career with vivid insights and calm, if very focused, comments on the highs of his career. He began to reflect on the **Astral Weeks** album in great detail. The best of these later interviews is Fintan O'Toole, "Van Morrison: 'Being Famous Is Not Great For The Creative Process. Not For Me, Anyway'," **The Irish Times**, August 29, 2015. https://www.irishtimes.com/culture/music/van/van-morrison-being-famous-is-not-great-for-the-creative-process-not-for-me-anyway-1.2332216 For a humorous and reflective interview see John Preston, "Van Morrison Interview: People Think I'm Dead Serious But That's Absurd," **London Telegraph**, August 25, 2017. https://www.telegraph.co.uk/music/artists/van-morrison-interviewmy-life-isnt-songs-just-something-do/

For an interview suggesting Van Morrison had a religious experience in Los Angeles and the accompanying story suggests why Morrison continued to be wary of the press. See Ivan Little, "Van Morrison Has Religious Experience During LA Service," **The Belfast Telegraph**, June 27, 2017. https://www.belfasttelegraph.co.uk/entertainment/news/van-morrison-has-religious-experience-during-la-service-35867612.html This is an article delving into a church that Morrison may have had some dealing with and perhaps he was a member. The reporting he took the stage of sing for the Agape International Spiritual Center didn't make Morrison happy. He believed it was an invasion of his privacy.

Tony Dey and Ritchie Yorke were particularly important in discussing Van Morrison and the press. Dey continues to perform in the Sacramento area and he remains an incredible drummer with a legendry history.

For the mysterious and elusive Dahaud Shaar see, Ivan Little, "Drummer Who Kept The Beat For Van Morrison In 1970s Dies," **Belfast Telegraph**, January 29, 2018. https://www.belfasttelegraph.co.uk/entertainment/news/drummer-who-kept-the-beat-for-van-morrison-in-1970s-dies-36539294.html For years Shaw-Shaar played around the San Francisco Bay Area but he was quiet, not necessarily reclusive, and he was a person who was as private as Morrison.

For Van's reaction to the Welch interview see, Johnny Rogan, **Van Morrison: No Surrender** (London, 2005), pp. 321-322. Mervyn and Phil Solomon added material to this chapter. Also see the http://ivan.vanomatic.de/home/home.shtml website for the list of concerts on the so-called period of retirement.

Some of the best writing on Van Morrison in the 1970s came from the facile pen of Donal Corvin. On September 6, 1979 Corvin turned on the oven on his home and he passed away. The suicide caught everyone by surprise. Van was recording in the South of France, and he was, according to the musicians around him, depressed.

See Erik Hage, **The Words and Music of Van Morrison** (New York, 2009), p. 69 for his thoughts on **Hard Nose The Highway**. In 2012 Van discussed "Snow In San Anselmo" in an interview in the November 2012 issue of **Mojo**. Van said: "I was driving and it started to snow and a deer crossed by the lights past the car and there was a drunk who looked like a madman looking for a fight. That's what I saw. That's the song."

See Keith Altham, **No More Mr. Nice Guy** (London, 1999), pp. 75-86 for the brief period Altham handled public relations for Morrison. The Altham book is a gem. It contains his observations on those he was worked for in the music business.

CHAPTER 8

BERT BERNS AND THE BANG RECORD FIASCO: WHY BROWN EYED GIRL WAS THE POP HIT NIGHTMARE

"I don't know where he is buried, but if I did, I would piss on his grave."

JERRY WEXLER OF ATLANTIC RECORDS IN CONVERSATION WITH JOEL SELVIN CONCERNING BERT BERNS.

"You can feel the heat of Morrison's contempt for the poopy fare he'd been pressured to produce for Berns."

DANGEROUS MINDS

Bert Berns is the major figure in creating the critical, raging, occasionally paranoid and generally unforgiving Van Morrison. Since Berns' record label, Bang, brought Morrison to pop stardom with a Top Ten hit "Brown Eyed Girl," Van has never stopped retelling the story of the Bang Record fiasco. He has moaned and groaned about the flamboyant New York producer.

What is it that drives Van Morrison to the brink of interview madness about the Bang years? It is questions about "Brown Eyed Girl." In 2001, an audience questionnaire at Morrison's shows, asked what songs his fans wanted to hear? The answers were invariably "Gloria," "Brown Eyed Girl" and "Here Comes The Night." This irritated Van. After fifty years in the business he did the smart thing. He came to grips with "Brown Eyed Girl." Why did Morrison come to an accommodation with his hit? He realized in-concert favorites kept his career brand alive. Did Morrison enjoy performing "Brown Eyed Girl?" No! Did he realize he had to do it? Yes! Van Morrison: "Let's do 'Brown Eyed Girl' and get it over with." This was a comment Morrison made while performing at the Chester Race Course on July 21, 2001. Why is he reluctant to perform "Brown Eyed Girl?" It is about lost royalties. It is also about remembering gangsters.

There are only a few individuals in the music business Morrison refused to forgive for usurping his royalties. Bert Berns is at the top of the list. Why? The answer is a simple one. Berns allegedly attempted to not just stall Morrison's solo career, he was a demeaning and a threatening individual vowing to ruin Van.

Pure and simple Bert Berns was a record executive jackass. He ignored the artists. He was the ghoul who might have ruined more careers had he not died prematurely. Jerry Wexler at Atlantic Records was still looking to piss on his grave as he passed into rock and roll heaven. When I wrote **Van Morrison: The Mystic's Music**, I contacted Wexler. He had no comment on Berns or Morrison. Two years after the book came out, I sent him **The Beatles: Untold Tales**. He sent me a thank you note with a P.S. "You got Van right; Bert Berns was an asshole."

Berns was also a hit record maker. That infatuated Morrison. As Van told Happy Traum the chance to record with Berns and Bang was his best 1967 option. Van has said it was his only option. The nightmare was about to begin. Why Bert Berns sought out Van was a mystery. It appears it was all about potential profits.

WHY BERT BERNS SOUGHT OUT VAN MORRISON

Bert Berns hung out with gangsters. His right-hand man Carmine "Wassel" DeNoia was a brutal thug. He would stand in Berns office holding a baseball bat and looking around for potential physical violence. In the Bang Records office building Ed Chalpin made bootlegs. One day Berns had Wassel bring him to the office to tell him not to bootleg Bang Records. To make his point Berns looked out his office window as Wassel's right hand gangster buddy, Patsy Pagano, hit

Chalpin so hard the gangster broke his hand. Then they hung Chalpin out the window. He never bootlegged another Bang Record.

Berns made a number of phone calls to London. When he connected with Phil Solomon, they talked about changes in the record business. Solomon suggested Berns could launch Van Morrison solo. "I told him beware," Solomon told me in 1983. "You remember him from the Them tracks you produced and he needs someone he knows." Berns produced some early Them records. He had no idea what happened to Them or Morrison.

Solomon told Berns he had released Morrison from his contract. Van was sitting home singing into a tape recorder. He was living with his parents. He was assembling new songs. Berns immediately sent a recording contract. He told Solomon he was spending time in Los Angeles. If he found a better act, he would release Morrison. Berns wasn't sure Van was the right singer for the rapidly emerging pop market. This eventually led to "Brown Eyed Girl." The contract with Bang Records, a subsidiary of Atlantic, moved Van into the industry mainstream.

WHY VAN WAS INFATUATED WITH BERT BERNS

What was Morrison's infatuation with the New York record mogul? Berns track record working with solo artists was legendary. Long before he recorded solo with Berns, Van worked with Berns when he was the lead singer of Them. Van was proud to be in the studio with the producer who recorded Solomon Burke and Freddie Scott. Soul music was one of Van's favorites.

Berns' first Them recording session on July 5, 1964 had little in the way of commercial prominence. "Don't Start Crying Now" was the closest thing to a hit. There was a version of a Morrison penned song "Gloria." It appears Van and Bert got along during the Them days. When Berns recalled "Gloria," he realized Morrison had a pop voice. When asked about Morrison's songwriting producer Mickie Most, manager Phil Solomon, producer Dick Rowe, arranger Mike Leander and music publisher Robert Mellin described Van as a one hit artist. The reason? He was a bit off the rails compared to other artists. Van was about to change the rock and roll culture by gaining control of his songwriting, publishing, intellectual property, booking and all other aspects of his career.

Bert Berns was brought in from New York. He was placed at Decca Studio Number Two in West Hampstead in October 1964. As Berns sat on a stool strumming an acoustic guitar, Van was impressed. He was a strange guy. Berns reeked of cigarettes, alcohol and cheap cologne. Rumor had it he allegedly married a pole dancer from a strip club. This fit his personality. There was a seedy hip nature to Bern. But he knew soul music inside out. He could produce. Solomon Burke swore by Berns. He was also an excellent songwriter. Van loved the b-side he wrote for the Drifters "I Don't Want To Go On Without You." With hits like "Hang On Sloopy," "A Little Bit of Soap" and "I Want Candy," Van was impressed. He hoped for a chart hit. Van found he was in over his head in dealing with the veteran Berns.

How did Berns impress Morrison? He showed him the guitar part he borrowed from Marv Johnson's "Come On And Stop" to write a hit record. This intrigued Van. The Them song he cut with Berns that impressed Van the most was a cover of "Baby Please Don't Go." It was a song he had listened to many times in his father's record collection. This cover brought a new sense of urgency for Van to pursue a solo career.

As he watched Berns work in the studio, Van was intrigued how he brought in back-up vocalists. There was an intensity to Berns' production Morrison appreciated. He spent his time watching the very subtle nuances Berns employed in the studio. The following week Berns was in the studio recording the same song with Lulu. Jimmy Page's guitar was used once again. This production impressed Morrison.

Celebrating "Brown Eyed Girl" New York 1967: (left to right) Jeff Barry, Bert Berns, Van Morrison, Carmine "Wassel" DeNoia (with cigar) and Janet Planet.
(Photograph: Michael Ochs Archives/Getty Images)

WHAT BERNS DID WITH HERE COMES THE NIGHT

"I think Van was fooled by Bert Berns and he didn't see his dark side," Mervyn Solomon continued. "He admired Berns for writing and producing hits for Solomon Burke." It was Burke's "Everybody Needs Somebody To Love" that Van mentioned in interviews as a song setting the bar for his version of what a perfect rhythm and blues record sounds like. Van also loved Berns' production on The Drifters "Under The Boardwalk" and "Saturday Night At The Movies," Barbara Lewis's "Baby I'm Yours" and the Isley Brothers "Twist and Shout."

From Berns viewpoint Van and Them had to create more coherent vocals. When he recorded "Little Girl," at the end of the song Van sings "I Want to fuck you." No one picked it up. His accent was too stilted and incoherent. The words were incomprehensible. When

220

it was released as a cut on a charity album all hell broke loose. The press in London was never positive for Them. They didn't keep an appointment with **New Musical Express** reporter, Keith Altham, and when he found the group in a bar with Bert Berns, Van said: "Fuck off." Van viewed **NME** articles as hit pieces. A decade later Morrison hired Altham to direct his public relations. Then he fired him.

MORRISON IS DEALING WITH CRIMINALS WHO RAT FUCK EACH OTHER

The level of criminal duplicity amongst Berns and his friends taught Morrison valuable lessons. Today he is one of the most knowledgeable businessmen in the music industry. He owns ninety-nine percent of his musical catalogue. He did this by watching Berns fail to pay royalties. Chris Michie told me Morrison once said those in the music business, "rat fuck" each other. What did Michie mean? He meant the tentacles of corruption in the record industry knew no boundaries.

Early in his career Berns and Jerry Wexler took a vacation to Paris. They met with their French music publisher, Gerard Tournier, who informed them that Bobby Mellin had purchased a large number of Berns' copyrights. He paid $60,000 for the Berns material. Mellin had sent Berns $1400 in royalty checks. Berns sued. Mellin paid $60,000 restitution. Why? The sale was illegal. Berns knew the music business. He sued. He won. How did this impact Van? He watched as the tough as nails Berns navigated the legal waters and won in court. Van never forgot Berns statement. He said never give an inch in matters of song copyrights.

The Bert Berns and Bang Record story was Van Morrison's first in-depth nightmare. Van didn't realize he signed with a record label with mobsters hanging out of every office. Berns, while a legendary producer, was one step from the grave. In this cast of malcontent characters, the press said Van Morrison was difficult.

Berns hung out with gangsters. Whether or not he was one himself doesn't matter, he was a respected producer. When Joel Selvins' brilliant book **Here Comes the Night: The Dark Soul of Bert Berns and the Dirty Business of Rhythm and Blues** appeared in 2014 it normalized Morrison's supposedly illicit behavior. In 1967 when Berns died of heart failure, it was a moment Van Morrison and Neil Diamond embraced. Both were tied up in contracts with Bang Records that verged on servitude when Ilene Berns took over the business. She was smart. She was dangerous in matters of business. She made Morrison and Diamond pay a steep price for signing the Bang agreements.

DID THE HIT SINGLE "BROWN EYED GIRL" BOLSTER MORRISON'S CAREER?

When "Brown Eyed Girl" peaked at number ten on the Billboard chart, this guaranteed an album. Van recorded eight songs for the album in just two days in New York. There was no indication that one song was better than another. None were considered by Berns to be Top 40 hits. This highlights Berns' shotgun approach to an album. Berns reasoned if he released four two-sided 45s one of the eight songs would chart. Voilà, there was an album. None of the songs other than "Brown Eyed Girl" reached the Top 40. Berns was not the genius Morrison envisioned. There was also lyrical censorship for the hastily produced album.

One lyric was changed in "Brown Eyed Girl," due to complaints from radio stations. The line "making love in the green grass" was altered to "Laughing and a running." Van was outraged. Van had an American career. Would he be a one hit artist?

MAKING AN ALBUM WITH BERNS AND THE BANG LABEL: BLOWIN' YOUR MIND

Berns brought Morrison from Belfast to record a quickie album. He had a top Ten Hit with "Brown Eyed Girl." As Van landed in New York City, he was euphoric. He was about to record a solo album. That euphoria soon turned to gloom.

Unseasonably cold weather on March 28-29, 1967 made Morrison think of Belfast. This made him comfortable in the studio. As Van entered A & R Studios on West Forty-Eighth Street, he was in the company of some of New York's finest session musicians. Artie Butler and Paul Griffin were on keyboards, Eric Gale, Hugh McCracken and Al Gorgoni were the guitarists and Gary Chester sat on the drums. Brooks Arthur was the engineer. Jeff Barry wandered around the studio.

The two-day recording process was lengthy. Al Gorgoni was the hidden factor in completing what became the **Blowin' Your Mind** album. Why? He created the guitar riffs making "Brown Eyed Girl" the album's centerpiece. His Gibson L-5 guitar ran through the twenty-two takes necessary to satisfy Berns' studio despotism. Van secretly vowed to make sure he would not repeat the same studio mistakes. As Berns, Jeff Barry and Brooks Arthur sang background on take twenty-two the song was complete. The cold New York weather matched the tension in the two-day recording session. Morrison complained about the Bang contract. It was not a fair one. He was also irritated that the original title "Brown Skinned Girl" was changed to "Brown Eyed Girl."

After Van listened to take twenty-two, he was not happy. The song sounded like a Jamaican vocal with a Calypso beat. The eight songs Morrison recorded in the two-day session were enough for an album.

Blowin' Your Mind was a mixed blessing. Why? The reason is a simple one. The songs didn't seem to fit a pattern, a musical direction or a genre. No one realized this was Van Morrison's warm up for **Astral Weeks**.

THE EIGHT SONGS ON BLOWIN' YOUR MIND SET THE STAGE FOR MORRISON'S MAINSTREAM CAREER: BLOWIN' YOUR MIND AND THE BANG MASTERS

The original release of **Blowin' Your Mind** was a forgettable album. It contained a hit song and little else. It was the beginning of an album odyssey of repackaging and re-releases continuing into the April 28, 2017 Legacy three CD set **Van Morrison: The Authorized Bang Collection**. The sordid tale of the Bang Masters is another chapter in Morrison's war on and victory over Warner Brothers. That victory allowed Van to have some input into the 2017 Legacy three CD release.

The Legacy release was entitled **The Authorized Bang Collection**. With exquisite packaging, in-depth liner notes and remastered songs the ads for the CD proclaimed it was "the first official release" of the Bang material. It also included the much bootlegged "Contractual Obligation Session." The thirty-one tracks from this session were remastered and explained in depth.

For the serious collector, disc one included the original mono mixes of "Beside You" and "Madame George." These tracks were released as a Bang single. On disc one there is also a rare demo version of "The Smile You Smile" which was released on the 1991 compilation **The Bang Masters**. On disc two a mono single mix of "Brown Eyed Girl" is included with a version of "Ro Ro Rosey" with backing vocals. The rarities conclude with previously unissued studio cuts of "T. B. Sheets," "Midnight Special," "Beside You" and some outtakes of "Brown Eyed Girl." The packaging and presentation makes the Legacy release the premier one for the Bang material.

Van's rendition of "The Midnight Special" owes it roots to Lead Belly but the Sweet Inspirations provided a backup rendering young Morrison into a blues place. He continued that direction with the slow, dreamy blues in "Beside You" with an organ following his vocals. It was a magic moment on this re-issue.

There were some brilliant moments for Berns and Morrison. "T. B. Sheets" was an improvisational song unique for the times. It was about a prolonged slow death. It was not Top 40 material, but the song established Morrison's reputation as a serious songwriter. The cover of Solomon Burke's "Goodbye Baby (Baby Goodbye)" was one in which Morrison felt constrained. He told Berns he "should be freer." Berns ignored him.

The album was finished in late March 1967. By August, 1967 Van returned from his Belfast exile and began living with his girlfriend Janet Gauder a divorced, beautiful California vixen. Her son Peter was in tow. Things looked rosy. They weren't. Van was broke. Berns was a cheapskate. "Wassel" and other gangsters were in the background causing mayhem.

Van Morrison poses for a portrait in 1970 in Woodstock, New York.
(Photo by David Gahr/Getty Images)

THE BLOWIN' YOUR MIND ALBUM AND VAN LEARNS ABOUT ARTISTIC INTEGRITY

Once Van listened to the finished product he was horrified. There was nothing that could save **Blowin' Your Mind** from being an album disaster. It was produced and released hastily. with everything done in a less than professional manner. He found the cover embarrassing.

To complicate matters, Van signed the Bang contract without scrutinizing it. He had other concerns. When Berns wrote the liner notes, they were infantile. Berns said on the album cover: "Van Morrison...turbulent...today...insider...a multi colored window through which one views at times himself and his counter self. Van Morrison...erratic and painful...." Morrison was upset by this juvenile description. Welcome to the record business. This was not a long-term solution for stardom.

To celebrate the album and the Top Ten hit, Berns rented a Circle Line Cruise boat and the ensuing raucous cocktail reception drew gangsters, low life types and industry wannabes. Van was uncomfortable. As Tiny Tim walked around playing his ukulele Wassel grabbed him and threw him overboard. A drunk reveler picked him up. Everyone laughed.

Van with two backing musicians, performed a short set on the boat. One of the benefits of working with Berns was meeting Charlie Brown, a legendary New York guitarist, who Van played with the next week at the Bottom Line. At this show a New York media outlet commented on "T. B. Sheets." The newspaper called it "evocative with a primitive nature." These early New York shows were excellent ones. At this point Van and Janet were living in the City Square hotel. It was a dump near Times Square with hookers, transvestites, drug dealers, illegal immigrants and the urban poor running through the halls.

THE SORDID TALE OF THE BANG MASTERS NEVER ENDS

The deal Morrison signed with Berns was iron clad. The Belfast Cowboy has spent fifty-plus years complaining about the manner in which Berns recorded his material, compiled and released the singles and the album. In matters of business it was akin to chattel slavery.

The best way to understand the Bang Masters is to realize there is no shame in the record business. When Morrison turned in his thirty-one nonsense songs to fulfill his contractual obligation, no one realized the Bang Masters were destined to become commercial. The nonsense songs sold. The earliest release of the material came from bootleggers. The insatiable appetite for anything Van Morrison quickly caught the attention of Ilene Berns and what was left of Bang Records. She watched as the fans marveled at the crude songs and eagerly purchased them. What was she to do? The obvious answer was to find a buyer for the first Van Morrison album. The demos, the outtakes and anything left in the can were preserved for future sales. Ilene Berns had gold in Van's catalogue. She didn't realize the extent of Van's musical popularity. Columbia Legacy certainly did.

Columbia's Legacy imprint, after purchasing the material from Ilene Berns, released the 1991 compilation album **The Bang Masters**. The centerpiece was "Brown Eyed Girl." The album consisted of eighteen songs plus an alternate version of "Brown Eyed Girl," (Take 6). Columbia Legacy remixed the original multi-tracks. They were enhanced with a wider stereo sound. There were also alternate versions of "Spanish Rose," "He Ain't Give You None" and "Joe Harper Saturday Morning." Bill Flanagan's extensive liner notes explained how and why the project was completed. Was Van happy? No! Why? He wasn't consulted. Robert Christgau described the 1991 release as a "Hungry young Irishman spouts blues poetry in a roomful of session pros." He gave it a three-star rating.

THE BANG MASTERS LEGACY EDITION 2017 AUTHORIZED

The April 2017 Bang Masters was a three CD reissue. There were amazingly sixty-three tracks. When the Legacy edition was compiled in 2017 the deft hand of a Grammy Winner, Andrew Sandoval, created three CDs with sixty-three marvelous tracks with remastered sound. This material was a primitive forerunner to **Astral Weeks**. There were also some brilliant songs. He was receiving royalties.

Why did Morrison cooperate on the 2017 Bang Masters? He believed Columbia Legacy spent the appropriate sum for the reissue. It may be because of working with reissue musicians like keyboardist

Paul Griffin who was a presence on Bob Dylan's early electric material. Griffin consulted on the reissue. The care and quality Legacy took in releasing the Bang material inspired Van. The "Band Session And Rarities" is the second CD. It contains some of the best of the rarities. Van loved it. CD3 includes the so-called nonsense songs They have been remastered with a romantic aura reflecting the times.

BERNS' LEGACY TO VAN MORRISON

What was Bert Berns legacy to Van Morrison's career? Van respected Berns as a songwriter. His songwriting hits included the Jarmals "A Little Bit of Soap," the Exciters "Tell Him," Garnet Mimms and the Enchanters "Cry Baby" and Solomon Burke's "Goodbye Baby." This was an impressive resume.

In the U.K. Berns work with Freddy Scott, who created a legendary Norther Soul presence. Scott's "Hey Girl" was a Morrison favorite. On **Them Again**, Van wrote an original song that had nothing to do with the Scott tune. He called it "Hey Girl" in tribute to Scott's soul vocals.

Freddy Scott performed regularly in the U.K. on the Northern Soul circuit. Along the way he talked at length with Bert Berns about Van Morrison. The result was Scott recorded "He Ain't Give You None." In 1973 Scott cut "Brown Eyed Girl" for the 2003 **Vanthology** album.

It appears Scott's 1967 album **Are You Lonely For Me** was a Morrison favorite. How much it impacted his songwriting, his performing and his career is lost to history. Every indication is Van listened to it. Scott's influence? Probably more as a song stylist as Scott didn't write his songs.

What was wrong with **Blowin' Your Mind**? When rock music buyers purchased the album, it didn't sound like Van Morrison. The flamenco production on "Spanish Rose" was straight out of a New York nightclub. There were some songs with hints of Van's future genius. "Ro Ro Rosey" was a forgettable tune with a reference to a sixteen-year-old girl. The subtle genius of Morrison's future songwriting hung in the lyric's balance. In the eight songs there were references to London's Notting Hill Gate and Curzon street indicating how Van wove his environment into his songs. In "He Ain't Give You None," the lyric: "You can leave now if you don't like what is happening" is a Dylanesque line.

The use of Belfast, friends from his early days and the importance he attached to his fight for stardom evoked lines in "Who Drove The Red Sports Car." He sings of one of his early girlfriends, Jane Adams, without mentioning her by name. She was an upper-class girl with a fine education. Her pedigree was one Morrison was uncomfortable with over a long period of time. In lyrical fashion, Van spoke to her writing: "I know you ain't gonna like it. But I'm stepping right out in your world." That said it all. Van spent a few months with her and "Who Drove The Red Sports Car" ended with the line "Goodbye Baby hmm...baby good bye." Jane Adams set the tone for the girls Van dated in Belfast. He wanted a young vixen, well-educated with a quiet, thoughtful beauty.

Van remarked the eight songs on the Bang album were little more than rough demos. He cut these tunes for the 45 singles market at Berns' insistence. There were some gems. "He Ain't Give You None" was an early indication of how Van envisioned the blues. Eric Gale's guitar solo made it a radio friendly tune. One song from **Blowin' Your Mind** was a precursor to **Astral Weeks'** brilliance. "T. B. Sheets" was a maudlin tale of a young girl succumbing to tuberculosis. The song may have been about one of Van's girlfriends during the last days of Them. It could also have been about Gloria Gordon who was his cousin. John Collis concluded Van broke down and cancelled the rest of the session. Why? She was in ill health. She may have been dying. It is open to conjecture.

What is the importance of "T. B. Sheets?" It is a song establishing Morrison's avant-garde song writing. It was more than a song about death. It was a poetic tale in which Morrison sings: "The sunlight shining through the crack in the window pane numbs my brain." This is a portent of things to come in **Astral Weeks**.

HOWARD A. DEWITT

THE CRIMINALS AND THOSE WHO HUNG ON TO MORRISON'S COAT TAILS

There are a lot of lessons from the Bert Berns and the Bang years. None stands out more than the hangers on, think Carmine "Wassel" DeNoia. He was one of those who took advantage of Van. Bert and Ilene Berns claimed to be an influence on his future music. They sucked every nickel out of his career. They have remained in the story driving Morrison crazy for more than fifty years. Now both are dead. The daughter runs the company. She is still collecting royalties from the Belfast Cowboy.

In numerous interviews, Van answers questions concerning influences that never existed. Those who have attempted to ride to fame and fortune on Van's coattails are numerous. This explains his at times reticence to deal with people. It also defines his moods.

One of the myths of Morrison's career is that Gary Sherman, who worked for Bert Berns, arranged songs on **Astral Weeks** that helped Morrison. He didn't. Van has stated Sherman was in the studio. He offered nothing. In an interview in January 2019 with **Uncut's** Andrew Male, Van said: "I didn't learn anything from Gary Sherman. He was just the arranger. Who did you hear that from?"

Record label heads suffered Morrison's moods. It was not without reason. He became manic early in his career to control his music. He never forgave Warner Brothers for owning portions of his first three albums. In 2008, when he announced **Astral Weeks Live**, Van still was complaining about lost royalties. Much of this he blamed on Mo Ostin. As I interviewed people in and around the music business it appears the only person who didn't like and respect Ostin was Van Morrison.

Mo Ostin is respected and adored to this day for the way he handled Warner Brothers. He legitimized the growing group of songwriters in the late 1960s. At least a dozen industry figures told me he hated Van. They also said he had good reason. When Warner ended their affiliation with Morrison after the **Wavelength** album it was a blessing. His creative energies reached new heights. Warner Brothers said they fired him for poor sales. Van shot back. He fired them. Whatever the reason when the label head hates you, it is just a matter of time until you hit the road. The list of criminals and those who hung on Van's coat tails would make a good book.

BIBLIOGRAPHICAL SOURCES

For Bert Berns see the brilliant biography by Joel Selvin, **Here Comes The Night: The Dark Soul of Bert Berns And The Dirty Business of Rhythm And Blues** (New York, 2014), chapter 7. Also see, Peter Mills, **Listen To The Silence: Inside the Words and Music of Van Morrison** (London, 2010), pp. 88-94 for an analysis of "Brown Eyed Girl." Also see Clinton Heylin, **Can You Feel The Silence? Van Morrison, A New Biography** (Chicago, 2002), pp. 160-179, 266-268.

See Ryan H. Walsh, **Astral Weeks: A Secret History of 1968** (New York, 2018), pp. 4, 13-15, 268-288 for Van Morrison in Boston and how the city influenced the eventual album. Joey Bebo was important for this chapter. Bebo's **In The Back Of The Van: The Story of One Unforgettable Summer** (Hudson, 2016) is a marvelous account of Bebo's time drumming with Morrison in Boston. The book is detailed, well written and presents a side of the Belfast Cowboy that is personal and it shows how some excellent, if unheralded, musicians were important to Morrison's rise to fame and stardom. Bebo is a professional musician. After attending the prestigious Berklee College of Music, Bebo graduated with a degree in Arranging and Music Composition in 1971. His story with Morrison and his subsequent career after playing the summer of 1968 with Van is a tour de force in what is right and what is wrong with the music industry. Bebo's book deserves careful attention.

There are a number of Janet Morrison Minto interviews regarding Boston. See, for example, Louis Sahagun, "Janet Planet: Van Morrison's 'Brown Eyed Girl' The Clouds Have Lifted, Those Tumultuous Years Behind Her, The Astra; Angel Lives A Quiet Life And Still Writes Music," **Los Angeles Times**, November 17, 1998 and the hit piece By Barry Egan, "Love Lost In The Myths of Time," **London Independent**, January 30, 2000. The Egan article is an attempt to curry favor with Van and his take on Janet Morrison Minto to closer to fiction than the truth.

For interpretations of "T. B. Sheets," see, for example, John Collis, **Van Morrison: Inarticulate Speech of the Heart** (New York, 1996), pp. 84-85 and Brian Hinton, **Celtic Crossroads: The Art Of Van Morrison** (London, 1997), pp. 80-82.

Ritchie Yorke after interviewing Van a number of times was convinced **Blowin' Your Mind** was an illegal album. Morrison made a strong case to him that the contract did not specify an album. Van was incorrect, he was tied into a one-sided deal. See Ritchie Yorke, **Van Morrison: Into The Music** (London, 1975), p. 188.

Phil and Dorothy Solomon talked at length about their relationship with Morrison and their interaction with Bert Berns. Mervyn Solomon talked at length about this period and his brother, Phil, made the decision to release Morrison from a management agreement.

The material on Jane Adams comes from Mervyn Solomon. Molly Fee and Solly Lipsitz. Also see, Johnny Rogan, **Van Morrison: No Surrender** (London, 2005), pp. 90-91, 174-175, 203-205. For background information on Belfast and Northern Ireland see, Donald S. Connery, **The Irish** (London, 1969). Also see Donal S. Corvin, "Van Morrison Interviewed," **City Week**, September 22, 1966.

The **Blowin' Your Mind** album was Morrison's first solo LP. He was not only unhappy with it, the Bert Berns experience was a roadmap for his future career. Of all the songs on the album "T. B. Sheets" has drawn the most attention. In numerous interviews Janet Planet has stated "T. B. Sheets" was based on a real-life experience. Violet Morrison said that the song came from a nightmare. The operative wisdom is "T. B. Sheets" was about his cousin Gloria Gordon. Van said the song was fictional. From his youth Van was told of the dangers of T. B. and this was a memory he could not escape.

Andrew Male, "It's About Time: Who Kidnapped Van Morrison And Replaced Him With this Guy," **Uncut**, January, 2019, pp. 60-65 is a reflective look back by Van in and open and friendly manner. He corrected many myths about his music, those who influenced and those who didn't have much of a say but claim influence. This is a brilliant, introspective interview.

A brief 1982 conversation with Jerry Wexler added key information to this chapter. Steve Rowland provided key material on the mid-1960s London record industry and the role of Robert Mellin songwriting and publishing. Rowland also analyzed how and why Mickie Most and Phil Solomon were important to the music business.

When the critics reviewed the re-release of **Blowin' Your Mind** there was universal praise for the album. For the best review see, Bob Cannon, "Blowin' Your Mind," **Entertainment**, February 10, 1995. https://ew.com/article/1995/02/10/blowin-your-mind/ He gave it a B rating but the comments overall were praiseworthy of an early effort. Van said it best when he commented his initial view of caused him to "throw up."

PART II

ASTRAL WEEKS AND THE LEGEND DEVELOPS IN WOODSTOCK

Van Morrison (© Warner Brothers)

CHAPTER 9

NEW YORK AND THE GENESIS OF ASTRAL WEEKS: VAN CHANGED THE INDUSTRY

"I've never denied rock 'n' roll. My roots are also in rock 'n' roll and rhythm 'n' blues. They are my musical family. I've always denounced what was called rock after that. Rock 'n' roll is Fats Domino, Little Richard, Carl Perkins. This music was a liberating force for body and soul."

VAN MORRISON IN CONVERSATION WITH HUGO CASSAVETTI, FOR TELERAMA, FRENCH TV GUIDE, 1997

"When Astral Weeks came out, I was starving, literally."

VAN MORRISON QUOTED IN THE BRIAN HINTON BIOGRAPHY

"Astral Weeks was like a religion to us."

LITTLE STEVEN VAN ZANDT

Van Morrison believed he spent years taking verbal, personal and monetary abuse from those who directed his career. He has never escaped the feeling he is being persecuted for his artistic vision. His special kinship with words placed his songs into a creative zone few understood. He said his style and his frame of reference weren't appreciated. Van ignored the critics who persistently, and often unfairly, speculated on his music. As Van remarked: "fact not fiction" needed to be emphasized. He saw press criticism as fiction.

He had a fierce determination to be paid for his music. It was contrary to the times, and the prescient standards of the music business. The rock music business is filled with artists who never received proper royalties. The notion of being ripped off remains a continual theme in Morrison's life. He was obsessed with people who sold him out, stole his music, exposed his private life or censored his thoughts. It was as though Van practiced a daily psychodrama. When did his feeling about artistic persecution begin? How did it influence Van's approach to his label?

When **Astral Weeks** failed to sell it was a positive. Why? It allowed Morrison to focus on new releases. Hence the hit making **Moondance** album. It prompted him to craft his club and concert appearances to perfection. He also challenged industry practices. To Warner he became a pariah. He wouldn't allow the nickel and dime charges on royalty statements to limit his royalties. He threatened to sue Warner for excessive fees for storing his demos. Ray Ruff told me Van sent a long letter to Warner about the miscellaneous charges on his royalty statements. Van noticed the larger the royalty check, the bigger the miscellaneous charges. Morrison single handedly altered industry practices by combating Warner Brothers.

For other Warner singer-songwriters their royalties increased. By questioning self-serving house producers, like the former surfer Ted Templeman, Van changed the corporate culture. It was no longer totally weighed against the artist.

He told close London friends few people understood his music. He wondered if Warner Brothers knew how to sell his music. Van realized **Astral Weeks** was not Top 40 material. This is precisely the reason he wrote it. The challenge was to merchandize his product. He had the drive, the talent and the fortitude to pursue his dream. He looked around for a proper producer and manager. He didn't find one. He had no choice. He was his own producer and quasi manager.

By 1968, Van no longer trusted anyone. It wasn't paranoia. It was the pressures of the music business. He outlined a plan to record hit records. He would write the music, compose the lyrics and produce the material. This is not how it was done in the late 1960s. In Van's mind, it was post production that caused his career to flounder. Bert Berns destroyed his lyrics, made his music sound like a mariachi band backed him and the post production changes were the final insult. Nothing changed at Warner Brothers. When strings were added to one of his **Astral Weeks** songs, Van was upset. His negative early comments on **Astral Weeks** resulted from Lewis Merenstein's post-production touches.

He believed Warner Brothers didn't treat him with the same respect as Joni Mitchell. On the surface, the Warner Brothers deal appeared to be an equitable one. It wasn't. There were red flags. The Warner Brothers contract assigned him to independent production teams. This bothered Van. After that Warner could replace them with an in-house producer. Van was understandably nervous.

Producers didn't understand his creative mantra. They bastardized his musical vision. He was infuriated over signing a contract where he split a portion of his songwriting and publishing royalties with producers who didn't write a word. It was a better deal than he had with the London Decca or the New York Bang label.

In the genesis of **Astral Weeks** one can see the future of Van's legendary writing and recording career. He withheld some songs from Bert Berns' Bang label. "Ballerina" was saved for a Warner Brothers release. "The Queen's Garden" was another tune that was not only in Van's notebook, it was ready for the recording studio. Just not with Bang.

In 1966, when Van wrote "Ballerina," he was in the midst of the Them recordings. No one took the song seriously. Phil Solomon told Van: "It was crap." Berns didn't care for it. The other musicians in Them laughed at the song. Morrison filed it away for future use.

Prior to Berns' untimely death, he and Van continually had a studio war. Morrison objected to Berns' constraining charts. They cut into Van's studio freedom. He also had no input on studio musicians. The production techniques and the lack of studio freedom made it difficult for Morrison. He didn't want to be a teen idol. He had serious songs. Van decided to record one for Berns. Maybe he would understand the type of songs Morrison wrote.

It was after Van cut "Madame George," he realized he would never convince Berns of his talent. It was all about how Berns envisioned the songs. Bang Records controlled the product to the point of destroying it.

Van Morrison: "I had previously recorded 'Madame George' and 'Beside You' well before the '68 Warner release." Van made the point Berns and Bang Records didn't know how to produce these songs. "The arrangements were nothing like I had in mind for these songs," Morrison told the **Los Angeles Times**' Randy Lewis.

When Berns placed a group of female singers in the background to "Madame George," Van vowed to break the contract. This cut the emotional heart out of the song. As Berns demanded a new set of songs, he was stuck in New York. He longed to return to Belfast. He couldn't return home for lack of money. Van did the next best thing. He wove images of his hometown in lyrical form. He continued to develop the material that became **Astral Week**s.

IF YOU WANT A SONG IT HAS TO BE ABOUT BELFAST

The New York experience had not been what Morrison expected. He didn't have many American friends. He wrote or reworked tunes that celebrated his Belfast roots.

When Van cut "Madame George" and "Beside You," he had a strong sense of his Warner Brothers future. The lyrics indicate Morrison was homesick. He was living out his life in lyrical verse. He vowed to record these tunes in a completely different manner for **Astral Weeks**. It was "Joe Harper Saturday Morning" which allowed Van to rethink his roots. This tune about the janitor at Belfast's Maritime Hotel was filled with nostalgia. There is a line suggesting one has to go ask Joe Harper to find out what really happened at the Maritime Hotel. The images in and around Belfast were important ones. He used them to retain his sanity in the cutthroat New York music business.

IS IT CHANNELING OR IS IT MUSIC?

One of the eerie aspects of **Astral Weeks** is when Van stated he channeled the music. He said a spirit came into his body. This created the earliest signs of his musical genius. Van talks of channeling to convince the critics to stop asking what his songs mean. The songs making up the **Astral Weeks** album gestated for a long time. When Van said a spirit came to him during the early Warner Brothers sessions, he was defining his **Astral Weeks** creative process. Van has said repeatedly freedom is what made the album work. Creative isolation was his mantra.

Astral Weeks benefited from the session musician's freedom. The recording sessions were in the evening. There was a relaxed atmosphere. The musicians were able to have a nice dinner, relax with a few drinks and then play with enormous creativity. Van was singing in an enclosed booth. He had no contact with the studio musicians. This is the hidden genius in Lewis Merenstein's production. Despite Van's description it wasn't channeling. It was a free form musical format. This is what produced the genius of **Astral Weeks**.

How important was channeling? Van commented many times a spirit comes to him intermittently. This spirit channeled his songs.

In an interview with Andrew Male in **Mojo** in January 2019, Van spoke reluctantly about **Astral Weeks**. "People always bring up Astral Weeks, but almost every track on that is based on a 12-bar blues…." Van is tired of talking about **Astral Weeks**. He wants journalists to concentrate on his version of what he thinks about the album. It is an idiosyncratic character trait.

VAN ON ASTRAL WEEKS AND WRITING

"Cyprus Avenue is a pretty real place. If you're ever over in Belfast, I'll take you to see it. It's not a jive place, it's real. A lot of things I do are real."

VAN IN CONVERSATION WITH HAPPY TRAUM, 1970

"Astral Weeks was a whole concept from beginning to end…. It was all thought out up front. Originally it was supposed to be an opera. By opera, I mean multiple visual sketches. When I had written the songs, there was talk of a film. So it was visual sketch oriented."

VAN IN CONVERSATION WITH RITCHIE YORKE, EARLY 1970S.

"I don't have a clue what I'm writing about. If I knew I'd tell you. But I don't. It is unknown."

VAN IN CONVERSATION WITH JONATHAN COTT, 1978

New York's Café Au Go Go was the most important vehicle in Morrison's development. This was due to the freedom it gave folk types. There were no rules. There were few expectations. This is what Morrison desired. "Some nights we'd go down there and they'd just put his name out on the marquee," John Payne recalled. "If some people would show up, we'd do a show for just a few people." There were also gigs at the Scene where Steve Paul presided over an ultra-hip club near Times Square. It was at the Scene musicians like Janis Joplin and Jimi Hendrix casually showed up to gig or simply hang out. One night when New York journalist Bob Sarlin walked into the Scene, he heard Van playing with Kielbania and Payne. He was instantly smitten.

What was it that took a seasoned critic like Bob Sarlin by surprise? It wasn't just Morrison's lyrics. Sarlin, like other critics, praised the unique musical direction and the voice. It was how Van interacted with the musicians and the lyrics creating a new song form. These comments came before he went into the studio to record **Astral Weeks**. To this day Tom Kielbania and John Payne believe they should have received more credit. When the Boston Catacombs tape surfaced on iTunes in 2018, and, before that on the bootleg circuit, the question of their input was not discussed. That is still the case.

New York journalists loved Morrison's trio. Many record moguls and music industry insiders believed he had moved beyond rock and roll's boundaries. He used these club dates to convince media moguls **Astral Weeks** was commercially viable.

There were five songs Van performed at virtually every 1968 show after he left Boston. From September 25 until November 24, he played "Madame George," "I Need Your Kind of Loving," "Cyprus Avenue," "Beside You" and "Brown Eyed Girl" in virtually every New York show. Why? He was auditioning songs for **Astral Weeks**. There would not have been a Warner album had it not been for Joe Smith.

JOE SMITH IS THE HIDDEN HERO IN THIS GANGSTER DRAMA

Joe Smith, now in his nineties and retired in Beverly Hills, is the hero in this part of Morrison's career. He discovered his music in Boston and liberated it in New York. He was a savvy industry insider realizing Morrison was in over his head. The gangsters, hoodlums, bozos, wannabes, hookers, drug dealers and shysters were part of the New York music business. They surrounded Van. They almost suffocated him. Smith's goal was to clean up the personal management. He also secured an equitable recording contract. To get rid of the hoodlums and nefarious record industry types was a tall order. Smith did it.

Van, recently married to Janet, was in the midst of a nightmare when Smith arrived as the savior. Just six months earlier he had a Top Ten **Billboard** hit "Brown Eyed Girl." Bert Berns failed to pay royalties. Van was stuck in a cheap New York hotel. Things were not looking good. Van kept working. Janet Planet recalled he had a tape machine he worked on constantly. From this source **Astral Weeks** emerged.

Janet Planet: "Because it was really streamlined and easy for Van to sit with his guitar, and sing and play, and I could sit very close to him with the machine and I could record about twenty minutes at a time." This is exactly the method that intrigued Smith. **Astral Weeks** was like something he had never heard. It was a new kind of jazz.

Why is Joe Smith the hidden hero? He not only paid the gangsters, cum managers, the $20,000 to release Morrison from a management contract, he convinced Warner Brothers to sign him. Why? His championing of **Astral Weeks** initially hurt Smith's credibility with Warner. It almost derailed his career. Over time Warner recognized Smith's insights and Van's genius.

Smith operated in a harrowing time. When he was finished with what he described as the "Van Morrison Soap Opera," he remarked: "He was a hateful little guy, ... I still think he's the best rock and roll voice out there."

NEW YORK'S INFLUENCE: PREPRARING FOR BOSTON

While in New York, Van was lost in the excesses of the late 1960s. He had no interest in visiting the Chelsea Hotel where all the hip musicians, stoned aristocrats and hangers on gathered. It wasn't Van's scene. There was a void in Van's life. He needed a space to work on his music. That space would emerge during the Boston sojourn.

Van would not leave New York. Why? He feared immigration authorities. There were rumors of a drug bust. These rumors were untrue. It was Bert Berns' attempt to intimidate him. He found out it didn't work. It was just that a rumor. Van had never been busted on drug charge. This insidious rumor prevented Morrison from taking advantage of lucrative European touring opportunities.

Van believed his New York connections were important ones. He needed to be in the Big Apple to secure a new record deal. There was also the problem with the Bang Record contract. Van wasn't released from it. He was working on it.

As August 1968 came to a close, Van had written and recorded rough tapes of four of the songs for **Astral Weeks.** He had worked for more than a year to perfect what became his cult classic songs, "Cyprus Avenue," "Madame George," "Beside You" and "Astral Weeks." They all bore the marks of his Belfast youth. Before he could put the finishing touches on **Astral Weeks**, he needed a recording contract with a major label. That label turned out to be Warner Brothers.

THE UNSTEADY ROAD TO THE WARNER BROTHERS: ANDY WICKHAM IN THE BACKGROUND

As Van worked in the small New York clubs, the major record labels were signing every available singer-songwriter. When acts like James Taylor and Joni Mitchell came to the forefront, there was a mania to publicize their commercial songs. Van more than fit this bill. Mitchell had jazz roots. "She was tame compared to Morrison," Ray Ruff continued. "Mo Ostin knew it and did little for Van. He hated him." Warner Brothers had no idea about the wide range of Van's talent.

It was an Englishman, Andy Wickham, working in New York as an A & R man, who was mesmerized by Van's club gigs. Who was Andy Wickham? He looked like a British hanger on. He wasn't. He knew his music. He dressed and talked like an aristocrat. His white suit had the air of a spoiled dandy. After moving to Los Angeles, Mo Ostin hired Wickham as a talent scout. He was a cool dude with expensive suits, Beatle boots and a stylish speaking manner. He was an English dandy. He became Warner's aristocratic house hippie. A shrewd judge of talent, he brought many of the new folk-rock acts to Warner's attention.

For $200 a week, Wickham provided a window into the Laurel Canyon homes where future rock and roll legends plied their wares. Wickham was a genius when it came to promotion. He originated the Pig Pen lookalike contest that brought the Grateful Dead enormous publicity. He convinced Joni Mitchell to draw her **Clouds** album cover. She was brilliant artistically. Why was Wickham a favored employee? He found ways to save Warner Brothers production money. **Rolling Stone** described Wickham as the "company freak." "He was more than that," Ray Ruff continued. "He could make or break an artist." The Englishman as house hippie had a shrewd business mind. That impressed Mo Ostin who was always an accountant.

With his stylish glasses, a sly smile and a boyish charm, Wickham is credited with contracts for Joni Mitchell, Eric Anderson, Jethro Tull and Van Morrison. He schooled Lou Adler on obscure aspects of the music business. He also had a knack for bringing back long forgotten artists. When the Everly Brothers recorded **Roots** for Warner in 1968, it was due to Wickham.

Mo Ostin didn't understand rock music. Ostin told Wickham to find as many singer-songwriters as possible. Warner signed everyone. He depended upon the bespeckled Englishman. Soon Warner signed Van Dyke Parks and Randy Newman. Their contracts weren't equitable. Most music artists were happy to have a record deal. Money? It would come later.

Wickham was not out of place in the Laurel Canyon homes. He thrived in the small coffee shops and shanty eateries. He had a strength of personality few possessed. He could spot a hit performer in an instant. Wickham described himself to those at Warner Brothers as being interested in dissecting "the new music." He told the Warner Brothers brass, notably Mo Ostin and Stan Cornyn, the young kids they could sign weren't interested in money. Nothing was more important than greed to the Mo Ostin's and those who ran Warner Brothers. During his first week at Reprise, Wickham convinced the label to sign Joni Mitchell.

Wickham liked to travel. He went to Boston. It was there he saw Morrison with two backing musicians. He discovered a rough version of **Astral Weeks**. In Wickham's mind, Van fit into the evolving FM radio format. His eclectic songs, the raspy, melodic vocals and the subtle jazz inflected music provided the perfect back drop for the late-night FM disc jockeys.

The problems of the Bang contract persisted. Ilene Berns wanted big bucks to release Van. This scared off the major labels. She had a sustained hatred toward Van. Ilene believed he didn't show the proper respect over her husband's death. The bad blood persisted. Ilene blamed Morrison for Bert's death. It was a tendentious time. Morrison opted not to attend the funeral. He later said it was a mistake.

JOE SMITH, GEORGE LEE AND THE FINAL STEP TOWARD WARNER BROTHERS: BOSTON IS A KEY

No one understood Van's contract dilemma better than Warner Brothers executive Joe Smith. He had come of age in the industry in and around Boston. He had a vision of musical change. Van fit that image. He understood the garage bands. He also had a strong affection and appreciation for the singer-songwriter. He was interested in the burgeoning group of singer-songwriters performing in the small cubs. When and where he first heard Van Morrison is unclear. It was probably at Boston's Catacombs Club. He was immediately attracted to the Belfast Cowboy's intimate, jazz-oriented style.

Early on, Smith may have cooled on Van because of the Bang Record contract. It was iron clad. Ilene Berns was rumored to want big money to release him. After a show at the Catacombs, Van talked at length with Smith about a new contract. Smith appeared reticent. He wasn't sure Morrison would sign. He was struck by the commercial direction of Van's new music. It was a gold mine. Someone had to bring him into the mainstream. That turned out to be George Lee.

Who was George Lee? He was a Vice-President heading the Warner Brothers Music Publishing Division. He also supervised the Warner Rhythm and Blues label Loma. Van loved Lee's connection to the label. He listened to and purchased some of its product. An unsung, but important, executive Lee was important for bringing tapes and sheet music sales to a profitable level at Warner. He was a Van Morrison supporter from 1968. He had only good things to say about Van. Lee told the Warner brass the hits would arrive.

George Lee was the final catalyst to signing Van. Why? He held a unique position at Warner. He had the dual titles of Vice President of the East Coast and head of Warner music publishing. In these positions, he judged what songs and which artists would have a long-term future. He believed Morrison had a long-term career. Before he recommended the signing, Lee took a short trip to Boston.

He attended a show at the Catacombs. He talked with Van. It was a strange meeting. Unlike others who had dealt with Van, Lee found him opinionated but willing to take advice. The level of intelligence concerning the music business Van displayed was a critical factor in Warner's decision to sign him. Lee believed his future client would produce marketable music. He saw a person who wanted to make it big in the business. Van was serious and talented. Lee praised his music. He also loved his attitude. Lee saw Van's feisty demeanor as an indication of future success. The stories spreading about Morrison's lack of professionalism were just tall tales, according to Lee.

George Lee reported to Warner Brothers executives the Bang Record contract difficulties. He said they could be ironed out. He warned a new agreement had to satisfy Ilene Berns. The buyout was the most important aspect. Lee convinced Ilene Berns Van had a bleak future. Berns was a brilliant businesswoman. She went on to success with other artists and genres. She knew she had no chance of producing future Morrison records. That is why she sold Van's contract at an equitable price.

Warner never considered allowing Morrison to produce his material. They gave him disingenuous verbal assurance. They believed he needed a production team due to "his raw demos." "I was everywhere around Warner attempting to help Them without Van Morrison," Ray Ruff commented. "It was war for Van."

The irony is demos are raw recordings. Mo Ostin was in Van's face at every turn. He quickly became tired of Van's theatrics and complaints. The arguments were testosterone driven. Even Joe Smith had trouble with Morrison. "There were points when he was certifiable," Smith said of Morrison. Things became so testy Mo Ostin refused to talk to Morrison. In a 1996 interview with Robert Hilburn in the **Los Angeles Times** Ostin commented of Van: "He was as difficult as anyone I have ever dealt with."

For **Astral Weeks** the Inherit Productions team provided Morrison a jazz direction. This company was the brainchild of Van's manager Bob Schwaid. The Warner Brothers publishing group had previously employed Schwaid. There were hints of conflict of interest. There is a rotten, symbiotic nature in the record business. Van fought this force for half a decade. Schwaid and his producer-partner, Lewis Merenstein, recognized Morrison's long-term commercial potential. They acted as Van's managers. Schwaid teamed up with Merenstein to form Inherit Productions. Like most music moguls they presented Morrison with a contract friendly to Inherit Productions. The ensuing contract legally controlled and owned a portion of Van's early Warner albums. No wonder Van was angry. Inherit Productions and the Schwaid-Merenstein partnership looked like an ideal solution to his management problems. This didn't turn out to be the case.

As the contract spelling out Van's rights and that of Schwaid-Merenstein was finalized, Van reconsidered his Bang Record mistakes. In 1968, Schwaid-Merenstein was an acceptable option. Van told Mervyn Solomon he came to regret his decision to sign with them.

In Boston, Lewis Merenstein took Van into the Ace Recording Studio at 1 Boylston Place. They recorded the early demos for **Astral Weeks**. He loved the depth and emotion in Morrison's work. He also grasped the lyrical poetic quality of the music. Merenstein believed the material would sell. When it didn't immediately jump off the shelves, he argued it would eventually sell. That is exactly what happened. The **Astral Weeks** songs overwhelmed Merenstein.

Merenstein, Smith and Morrison discovered a common musical bond. They both liked King Pleasure's "Mood For Love." Morrison loved the way King Pleasure blended and featured the saxophone. A photograph of Morrison holding the 1952 album **King Pleasure Sings** tells one all they need to know about his influence. The King Pleasure album cemented the Merenstein-Morrison working relationship.

Clarence Beeks, aka King Pleasure, had a vocal style providing a training ground for Morrison. As Van listened to "Moody's Mood For Love (I'm In The Mood For Love)," he noticed Blossom Dearie's backing vocals accentuated Beeks' lead. He has over the years employed this influence most notably with Brian Kennedy. "The New Symphony Sid" provided Van with an education in allowing your side men more freedom. When Elliott Landy shot a picture of Van in Woodstock for the **Moondance** cover, he was captured rapturously holding the King Pleasure album. Van introduced King Pleasure's jazz sound to the rock and roll world.

The question of whether or not Merenstein and Morrison had a good working relationship is an insoluble one. John Cale, who recorded in the next studio, while Merenstein was producing **Astral Weeks**, said: "No one can work with Van." Connie Kay had the opposite view. As did Jay Berliner.

In numerous conversations, Merenstein recalled his favorite jazz recordings. Van was intrigued. They talked about what made the jazz sound important. Morrison increasingly incorporated this direction into the plans for his new album. There was a silent observer in the studio. His name was Tom Wilson.

Merenstein recognized the musical genius of producer Tom Wilson. He produced such diverse acts as Sun Ra, the Velvet Underground, Frank Zappa and Bob Dylan. The notion of including Wilson in the recording process intrigued Morrison. Wilson provided suggestions on the production direction. Wilson's defined jazz roots added a great deal to **Astral Weeks**.

As plans for **Astral Weeks** took shape, there was concern over the insidious Bang contract. Warner Brothers needed to break Van free of Bang contractual obligations.

HOW BANG RECORDS ALMOST DESTROYED MORRISON'S CAREER

Van Morrison signed an agreement with Bang Records favorable to the label. It gave Bert Berns creative control. He provided little in the way of royalties. Berns and Morrison were about to re-negotiate a deal. Berns died suddenly. Van believed he was free of the Bang contract. He wasn't. Bert's wife, Ilene, came at Morrison with a vengeance. Even though Bert Berns was dead, he still haunted Morrison. He would continue to do so from the grave for half a century. Van's Web IV Music contract explains the nightmare he experienced.

The business side of Berns' Web IV Music was a sophisticated one. Too much attention has been paid to the differences between Berns and Morrison. The business structure at Web IV Music educated Van on the intricacies of the industry.

The Web IV Music contract Morrison inked wasn't the work of amateurs. It was set up with Atlantic Records distributing the records and Berns providing the songs. With Garnet Mimms, Ben E. King, the Drifters and Freddie Scott among others recording Berns' tunes, it was a profit-making enterprise.

On September 12, 1968, Van signed a lengthy agreement with Web IV Music. It finalized Berns' rights to the Bang material. Berns owned it. Van was unaware. Web IV Music was the publishing arm of the Bang Record empire. There was no quick way Van could get out of this contract. He gave up a portion of his songwriting to Ilene Berns to move on to Warner Brothers.

Web IV Music was a company Berns formed with legendary insiders Jerry Wexler, Ahmet Ertegun and Neshui Ertegun. They were the owners of Atlantic Records. Web IV Music's contract allowing them to control "Brown Eyed Girl."

The songwriting credits and mechanical royalties were part of Berns' Web IV Music. Berns' corporate structure tied Morrison up contractually for decades. At Warner Brothers, Joe Smith wanted to go slow and create the impression the label was not interested in Morrison. Smith did this to buy out Ilene Berns. It worked. Bang settled for less than $100,000. She was a no-nonsense businessperson.

Berns was out of her element dealing with Joe Smith. He devised a plan to free Morrison from the tentacles of the Web IV agreement.

These negotiations soured Morrison. He was outraged by the way his royalties were so cavalierly treated. He decided to get even. One of the stipulations to end the Bang Record contract was for a thirty-one-song tape.

What were Morrison's Bang royalties? He never received a complete accounting. When he asked Bert Berns about royalties, he was ignored. Carmine "Wassel" DeNoia told Van not to think about royalties. The Wassel was holding a baseball bat as he talked to Morrison. The threats and intimidation from the Berns camp clouded Van's future.

He hired a New York based lawyer, Herb E. Gershon, to represent him in a case involving Bang royalties. The office of Goldberg and Gershon assigned Martin E. Silfen to the case. He argued that Web IV Music owed Morrison $50,000 for post songwriting royalties. They also owed another $25,000 in record royalties. He allegedly didn't recover any of Morrison's royalties.

The nonsense songs are a window into Morrison's psyche. Van got even with songs like "Want A Danish." It is a paean to Van arguing with Berns over whether a Danish or a sandwich was more appropriate. After Berns died on December 31 1967 Van wrote: "I'm waiting for my royalty check to come, ... it's about a year overdue.... I guess it's coming from the big royalty check in the sky." Ilene Berns was not amused.

She countersued alleging Morrison's nonsense recordings were commercially worthless. She alleged the songs damaged Bang Records' reputation. She argued Van acted contrary to the agreement. This countersuit took place in 1973. The law suit dragged on for almost half a decade. Not surprisingly, Berns' legal action prompted Morrison to cut back on large scale, well-paying concerts. One wonders if he expected to lose this case?

This case suggests Morrison's growing business sophistication. His publishing companies, Van-Jan Inc. and Caledonia Music, were placing his cache of original songs into a protected legal framework.

When the thirty-one songs were cut at the Mastertone Studio in New York, Van felt a sense of relief. He finally got even with Bert Berns.

It was a nice feeling. The recording quality made them unsuitable for release. The irony was the tunes were released on a double CD. They were often coupled with other Bang songs. They sold very well. Van's fans had to have everything. These non-commercial tunes brought in millions of dollars to everyone except Van.

After Bert's death, his wife had other concerns. With two young children and her husband's business affairs to straighten out, she gave up pursuing Van. She was still angry over what she considered to be the violation of the basic contract agreement. The thirty-one nonsense songs bothered her. Eventually they turned Web IV music a nice profit.

The nonsense songs are a major part of Morrison's war on the music business. The idea behind the thirty-one short songs was to leave Berns and the Bang label with a tape that wasn't commercial. These songs were released on a bootleg **Van Morrison: New York Sessions '67** with copious liner notes by a noted Morrison scholar. Over the years there have been numerous releases. Finally, Van explained his feelings in the classic song "Why Must I Always Explain." In the **Hymns To The Silence** album, Van wrote: "Get up in the morning and I get my brief, I go out and stare at the world in complete disbelief." "There are hypocrites and parasites and people that drain. Tell me why I must always explain."

When the nonsense songs were released, Van didn't know about it. When he found out he told a friend: "I saw it and I almost threw up." He turned on Ilene Berns with a vengeance. He argued his reputation and his career were in jeopardy.

Morrison's idea in the studio was to make fun of Berns' productions. When he wrote and cut "Hang on Groovy" it was a way of singling out the McCoys' "Hang On Sloopy" criticizing its syrupy pop sound. The Belfast Cowboy wasn't a fan of the Isley Brothers' "Twist and Shout." He wrote three songs "Twist And Shake," "Shake And Roll" and "Stomp And Scream" to let the world know he didn't care for the Isley Brothers.

Van thought Ritchie Valens' "La Bamba" was pop slop. He wrote "La Mambo" to express his distaste. What Van didn't expect was the fans would purchase the material.

The liner notes to the 1999 release of the Bang sessions by an Italian bootlegger, licensed from the Charly label, was the first to have

250

historically accurate liner notes. Whoever wrote the notes was a stone Morrison fan with in-depth knowledge. The literary asceticism of the liner notes is shown when the relationship between Berns and Morrison is described as deteriorating "beyond help…." This suggests Clinton Heylin wasn't involved. The two CD bootleg is brilliantly packaged. The liner notes written in March 1997 by a noted Los Angeles college professor, as well as the sound quality, offers a tribute to Van's emerging talent.

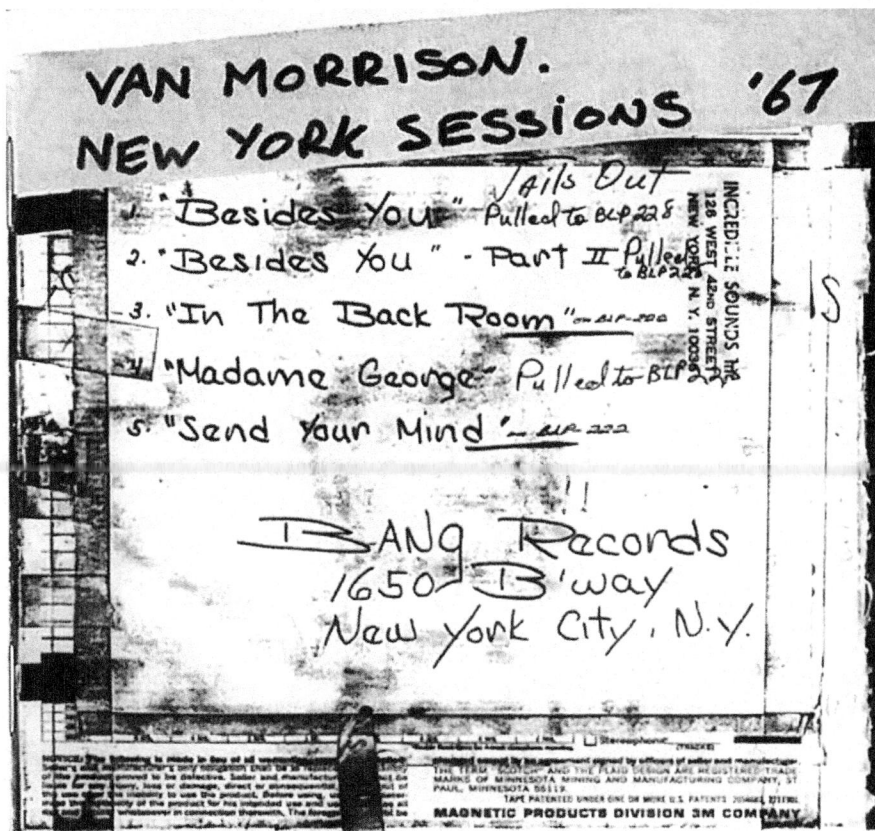

1999 bootleg packaging of New York Sessions '67 CD Cover (Bang Records)

The eighteen tracks on disc one are for a bootleg wonderfully produced with session sheets. The liner notes point out in the final settlement with Ilene Berns, Van agreed that the publishing rights to ten Morrison songs was included in the settlement. When some of this material was released as **The Best of Van Morrison**, he called it the worst of Van Morrison.

BERT AND ILENE BERNS (Bang records)

The battle between Berns and Morrison escalated into a full-blown legal war. By the early 1970s, Ilene's continual attacks occurred at a time when Morrison had enormous chart success. He believed it was a vendetta. His earnings were excellent. He viewed Ilene Berns as someone trying to cash in on his fame. She was!

Ilene arranged for a number of reissues of Van's Bang material. The subpar quality of the Bang re-releases angered Van. The war was on and not about to end. The controversy over the release of the Bang songs continued to haunt Morrison. It is in the basic agreement with Web IV Music that Van fumed about his inability to control his product. In 2017 EMI Legacy prepared the nonsense songs for release. They packaged the original Bang material in two discs and the third disc contained the nonsense songs. It sold at Amoeba in Hollywood for twenty dollars. The store manager told me they reordered it six times in the last year. What does Van think? He is tired of the controversy. He is mum on the recordings.

THE WEB IV AGREEMENT AND VAN

1.	The agreement granted Web IV specified rights on Morrison's career for a one-year period.
2.	Web IV was to receive 50% of the copyright of any song written and released by Van on a 45 single within a one-year period from September 12, 1968.
3.	Van was required to submit to Web IV three original compositions each month with thirty-six songs required. Web IV had the right to accept or reject the songs submitted to the publishing company
4.	Two songs written by Van with copyright control from Web IV Music must be included in a subsequent long-playing album.
5.	Web IV Music will have overseer rights to all Morrison albums for a one-year period.
6.	A cash settlement was agreed upon based upon a sliding scale of Van's future earnings.

Why this agreement angered Morrison was obvious. He signed a document guaranteeing the inclusion of songs Web IV Music had the rights to on the **Astral Weeks** LP.

When "Madame George" and "Beside You" appeared on **Astral Weeks**. Van was beside himself. He had agreed to a settlement with Ilene Berns. He couldn't stop raging about lost royalties. Warner Brothers did not release a 45. By not releasing a 45-single to properly market an album, sales were dismal. In an attempt to appease Van, Warner launched an aggressive advertising campaign suggesting the singer songwriter would have his product judged by the album. FM radio stations picked up **Astral Weeks.** It took a decade before steady sales emerged. Their marketing did little, if anything, for the album.

LIVING IN NEW YORK AND LOST DEMOS

The time Van and Janet spent in New York was far from idyllic. They had a romantic sense of their future. The early hotel rooms offered little comfort as the romantic illusion faded. The reality was something quite different. As Janet remarked she was a creative muse without a salary.

As a studio rat, Van couldn't wait to get into the studio booked by Warner Brothers. At Century Studio in New York Morrison cut endless hours of tape. Soon Warner had a batch of songs. He spent enough time to accumulate more than six hours of tunes. One bootleg, **Gypsy Soul,** provides a window into this period of recording creativity.

The **Gypsy Soul** bootleg is a 1996 release of demos from the **Astral Weeks, Moondance, His Band and the Street Choir** and **Tupelo Honey** albums. The eighteen tracks also include from the 1968 to 1971 period unissued cuts of "Nobody Really Knows," "Bit By Bit," "I Need Your Kind Of Loving," "Lorna," "Rock and Roll Band" and "(Sit Down) Funny Face, Virgo Clowns." The sound quality is superb. The packaging makes you forget it is a bootleg. This bootleg consisted primarily of publishing demos. The majority of these demos were released on **The Genuine Philosopher's Stone (disc 3)**.

THE CLUBS IN AND AROUND GREENWICH VILLAGE

The New York clubs in and around Greenwich Village and on Bleecker Street were important to Morrison's continual development. He listened to folk acts, like Tim Hardin and Tom Paxton. He also played in a number of coffee shops showcasing new material. What were the significant clubs Morrison played?

The Café Au Go Go was located in the basement of the New Andy Warhol Garrick Theater at 152 Bleecker Street. It was here Morrison found his most receptive audience. From August 29 through 31, 1968, he had a three-night engagement with the Holy Modal Rounder's as the opening act. He also played the Bitter End at 147 Bleecker Street, and he hung out with owner Paul Colby who was a friend of John Lee Hooker. Van was interested in learning about the blues legends. He deepened his education on Lead Belly and John Lee Hooker.

As Van prepared to enter the studio to record **Astral Weeks** there were some strange sidebars. John Payne had to borrow a flute for his part on the title track. The musicians were given chord sheets. But not lead sheets. As the sessions unfolded, Van didn't always follow the chord sheets.

There was uncertainty in Van's life as he entered the studio. "It was a very scary time," Janet Planet continued. "We were in a terrible position. We had no money. Still Van wanted to continue to make his music." It was his wife, Janet, who provided the atmosphere to write **Astral Weeks**. She sat by his side as he sang into a tape recorder. She dutifully transcribed the lyrics. Not an easy task considering his Irish accent.

Janet Planet was interviewed by RTE Ireland for a fifty-year special on **Astral Weeks**. As she looked back there was a fondness in her voice. It was a time of penniless joy. From her home in Los Angeles, she remarked: "Because it was really streamlined and easy for Van to sit with his guitar and sing and play, and I could sit very close to him with the machine and I could record about twenty minutes at a time really. Then we'd go back and listen to it. Then he would decide: he'd say I like that, ... I don't like that.... And then I'd say, 'Well I like this'. Then I would re-write those parts, and then he would do the whole process again."

In **Astral Weeks** Janet is a working partner. She did more than lend spiritual support. She was a co-writer. After she talked with a documentary film maker Alan Torney, Van had a fit. He complained her comments invaded his private life. It had been fifty years since **Astral Weeks**. He still had issues with the album.

**Van Morrison - 1968-1971 - Gypsy Soul Lost Demos (STU/FLAC)
1996 bootleg front and back CD cover**

RECORDING ASTRAL WEEKS: THE EARLY BACKGROUND TO
A CLASSIC ALBUM

The background to **Astral Weeks** is a long and arduous one. The LP didn't simply emerge. A Warner Brothers publicity representative appeared on Los Angeles and San Francisco radio, and this industry factotum said Van wrote and recorded the material on the spot. This established the myth of Van's songwriting spontaneity. Morrison spent long inordinate periods crafting his songs. The truth is **Astral Weeks** percolated in Morrison's mind for years.

In New York's Century Sound Studio at West 52nd street the recording sessions began on September 25 and lasted until October 15, 1968. **Astral Week** was released in November 1968. There were three sessions necessary to completing the album. The reason for three sessions was bass player Richard Davis had so many sessions booked, and other performing commitments, Merenstein had to work around his schedule. Due to Davis' legendary stature, the other musicians would wander in and practice with him.

256

ASTRAL WEEKS SESSION ONE: SEPTEMBER, 25,1968
- **Cyprus Avenue**
- **Madame George**
- **Beside You**
- **Astral Weeks**

Larry Fallon, the album's arranger, put in the string and horn section overdubs. He also played harpsichord on "Cyprus Avenue." He said Van was the key to piecing the package together. "He was a great arranger," Fallon continued. "He understood the importance of the chord sheets, as well as the needs of the session players." The musicians recalled Morrison told them next to nothing. This was the genius of the album. Morrison let the musicians follow their instincts. It was spontaneous. **Astral Weeks** was the product of pure unintended genius.

With Jay Berliner on guitar, Richard Davis on bass, Connie Kay handling the drums, Warren Smith, Jr. on percussion and vibraphone and John Payne providing flute and soprano saxophone, Morrison was ready to break new musical ground.

No one realized Van was about to make history. Jay Berliner kept a diary. It reflected the moment. Berliner wrote: "I had just recorded jingles for both Noxzema and Pringles potato chips before showing up to start work on one of the most celebrated albums of all time." There was no project title. In Berliner's personal diary the note simply read: "Van Morrison." None of the musicians had heard of him. They treated it as much like any studio gig. They showed up on time. They were professionals.

During the first night of the **Astral Weeks** sessions, Century Sound was booked from seven to eleven. It had an isolated vocal booth for Van. Some say this was the key to the intimate vocals. Van was at his best cutting "Cyprus Avenue," "Madame George," "Beside You" and "Astral Weeks." The isolation in the recording booth personalized his vocals.

The most interesting session took place on October 1st when two separate out takes were combined with a finished version of the plaintive ballad "I've Been Working." For some reason it was labeled "Train" in the Warner Brothers filing system. The irony was there was an unreleased tune called "Train." This was an innocuous blues tune that Van didn't care for. He had no trouble vetoing it for the Warner Brothers album. There was further confusion when another version of "Train" was rumored to be a twenty-minute cut. This song is now available on ITunes live.

On October 15th the session musicians cut "Sweet Thing," "Ballerina," "The Way That Young Lovers Do" and "Slim Slow Slider." As Van recorded his cult masterpiece, some key musicians remained in the background. A drummer, Ray Lucas, smoked and a pianist, Paul Harris, were also in the studio. Neither was used on the album. The detail to which Schwaid-Merenstein went to make the album a classic is often overlooked.

This session also produced a tune entitled "Royalty." It is a song Van believed had no commercial appeal. Van agreed this song was little more than a rough demo. The session also produced "Going Around With Jesse James." This was another throwaway.

During the mixing of **Astral Weeks**, Larry Fallon provided string overdubs and a harpsichord on "Cyprus Avenue." The session musicians had little idea about Morrison's music. Jay Berliner, the guitarist, was unaware he contributed to a cult album until the late 1970s. Berliner didn't play on "Cyprus Avenue" or "Madame George," because he didn't arrive at the studio until nine o'clock, the time he was contracted to appear.

JAY BERLINER ON ASTRAL WEEKS

"I played a lot of classical guitar on those sessions and it was very unusual to play classical guitar in that context. What stood out in my mind was the fact that he allowed us to stretch out. We were used to playing to charts, but Van just played us the songs on his guitar and then he told us to go ahead and play exactly what we felt."

JAY BERLINER QUOTED IN MOJO MAGAZINE

Jay Berliner made the **Astral Weeks** album special. His quiet presence created a unique guitar sound. His classical guitar helped to set the stage for his contribution to Van's magnum opus.

The key to **Astral Weeks** was the easygoing recording atmosphere. A case in point was "Slim Slow Slider." There is a version with an extended saxophone solo. This did not sit well with Van. He had jammed in an improvisational solo with John Payne and then Richard Davis joined him on the bass. Van loved Davis's version of "Slim Slow Slider." This is how he wanted the song.

ASTRAL WEEKS SESSION TWO OCTOBER 1, 1968
- **The Way Young Lovers Do**
- **Outtakes: Train (aka: On A Rainy Afternoon)**
- **I've Been Working**
- **Madame George**

There was a Dylanesque quality to **Astral Weeks**. This reflected the times as much as Dylan's influence. To Morrison the album was a "song cycle" following a story line. In the title song the bond between Van and his new wife, Janet, suggests he was finding happiness. In "Beside You" and "Sweet Thing" he exhibits his euphoric look at life. One wonders if Van's problems with immigration, Ilene Berns and the music industry temporarily subsided. The two songs the critics loved "Cyprus Avenue" and "Madame George" were a portent of things to come. They boded well for his future songwriting.

ASTRAL WEEKS SESSION THREE OCTOBER 15, 1968
- **Sweet Thing**
- **Ballerina**
- **Slim Slow Slider**
- **Outtakes: Royalty and Going Around With Jesse James**

THE 45 MINUTE ASTRAL WEEKS MYTH AND OTHER CUTS EXPLAINING VAN

During the **Astral Weeks** sessions, there was a rumor a forty-five minute song was cut. The initial story was it was the title song. Van told Ritchie Yorke this rumor wasn't true. "The truth is that I had a song at that time that was about forty-five minutes long," Van recalled. Then Van told Yorke: "It wasn't recorded for the album." Speculation is it is in the Warner archives. What this epic story suggests is Van was a studio rat. He haunted the recording studio. His prolific nature was the direct result of his desire to experiment musically.

There were a number of tunes that never made **Astral Weeks**. Such songs as "Magic Night," "I Need Your Loving," "Bayou Girl" and "Hey, Where Are You" were relegated to the scrap heap. Or perhaps more accurately to the private Morrison archive.

No one paid attention to Morrison's taping obsession. He loved to cut songs spontaneously. In doing so he created a sense of his historical, literary and musical vision. He realized his material had long-term financial implications. Van built up a huge tape collection. This cache of unreleased songs allowed him the freedom to mix new and old material.

There was a great deal of personal reflection upon the release of **Astral Weeks**. A reference to Huddie Ledbetter has Van talking about staring at the picture he kept of Lead Belly on his Belfast bedroom wall. He could write and sing about love and warm relationships. He would then shift in mid-stream to jazz or blues. This wasn't the norm in the late 1960s. **Astral Weeks** was a strange combination of euphoria and pessimism.

Richard Davis, the bass player, recalled "Van was not communicating personally with the musicians, he certainly did so musically." This was Van's genius. In person he was shy and difficult to get to know. In the studio he knew how to work with and use the musicians to implement his sound. Van and Schwaid-Merenstein urged the session musicians to follow their instincts. Connie Kay, the drummer, recalled the ease with which the sessions progressed. The upbeat mood of the musicians was reflected in the final product. This created the freedom and easy-going atmosphere infusing **Astral Weeks** with a mystical quality.

The brilliance of the session musicians was the hidden ingredient. The flutist, John Payne, was extraordinary. He was more than a musician. His intellectual integrity, and his powers of observation were keen. He commented Van had trouble communicating. Payne spoke of Van being on an "astral plane."

JOHN PAYNE ON THE VARIOUS ASTRAL WEEKS ALBUM SESSIONS

When Payne was asked what recording sessions the Astral weeks album came from, he replied: "It was the first and the third. The second one nothing was ever used - the second one was done in the morning. And it just didn't really happen, it's not a good time for musicians. So they didn't use anything from the second session. It was all the first and the third."

Source: Thomas C. Palmer, Jr., "John Payne: Astral Days, Wavelength, number 23, March, 2000, p. 10.

Payne realized Tom Kielbania knew where Van was headed musically. He found it intriguing. Payne's flute and soprano and saxophone on "Slim Slow Slider was important to the final product. "Beside You" and "Cyprus Avenue" benefitted from Kielbania's musical insights. Both musicians deserve more credit and perhaps royalties.

Astral Weeks established Morrison as a song poet. He didn't like the title. Reflecting on the LP in a December 1970 interview with Danny Goldberg, he didn't mention **Astral Weeks**. Why? Van hated the post-production addition of a string section. This suggests the problems Warner Brothers had convincing Van strings made it commercial. Van knew it was a magnificent album. Just not one with strings.

TALKING TO RITCHIE YORKE ABOUT ASTRAL WEEKS

When Van Morrison sat down with Ritchie Yorke the result was the 1975 book, **Van Morrison: Into The Music**. It was an inside look into his career. This biography was unique. It remains the only book containing in-depth interviews reflecting Van's career point of view. Yorke, a hip Canadian journalist with long, flowing blonde hair, knew Morrison's music inside out. He traveled from Toronto to Woodstock to interview Morrison.

Matt Lucas: "No one wrote better than Ritchie Yorke. He came to my Toronto gigs. He hung out with Ronnie Hawkins and Levon Helm. He understood the music. He was one of us. This is why Van Morrison cooperated on a book with him."

When Yorke spoke of the "vulgarity of the music industry," he was quoting Van. There was also discussion about making **Astral Weeks** into a movie. Van has been quiet about this rumor. Warner's movie division took a look at the project. The movie division was one of the reasons he signed with Warner. They ignored **Astral Weeks: The Movie**.

The most revealing part of Yorke's book is when Van and the author interact to explain how Warner maintained artistic control. Creative accounting! Non-existent expenses! Bogus contract charges. These were a major concern. The Schwaid-Merenstein production team was doing everything to retain control. This prompted a festering resentment. Lewis Merenstein is listed as the producer on **Astral Weeks**. He said he bent to some of Morrison's wishes. He said Van was the producer. In August 1973 John Tobler sat through an interview as Van took credit for everything. Merenstein never contradicted his statements.

TENSION IN THE STUDIO: WHY?

In the studio there was frenetic activity. Lewis Merenstein had no idea which session musicians to hire. He was conflicted until he talked with Richard Davis who recruited Jay Berliner, Warren Smith and Connie Kay. As the session musicians gathered, Tom Kielbania stood by looking out of place. He was. He did teach Davis the bass lines to

"Astral Weeks" but Merenstein wanted studio veterans in the recording studio.

As the **Astral Weeks** sessions progressed, Davis evolved into a quasi-producer without credit. Davis was perplexed by Van's shy nature. He thought the closed in recording booth was perfect to overcome Van's studio nervousness.

During the first two sessions, Merenstein suggested there were studio tensions. This was a reference to an early morning October 1, 1968 session. Nothing was accomplished. Jazz musicians and creativity were not in the mix. At least not in the morning. It was two weeks before another session. During the October 15, 1968 session Barry Kornfeld was brought in to play acoustic guitar on "The Way Young Lovers Do." This set the tone for side two dubbed "Afterwards."

It was in the final session, Van urged "Slim Slow Slider" be included. John Payne recalled Morrison never performed it in the clubs. He wasn't sure he could do justice to it in the studio. There was no problem. Payne's soprano saxophone gave the song the studio groove Van needed. "Slim Slow Slider" was so relaxed, so smooth and so lengthy Merenstein edited it down. Van disagreed. As much as a five-minute instrumental break was eliminated as Merenstein said the songs had to be commercial.

On "Slim Slow Slider," Payne recalled: "We went through stages (until) we got to avant-garde kind of weird...." Merenstein countered the song endlessly wandered. Van believed Merenstein's cuts took away is original intent.

THE GENESIS OF ASTRAL WEEKS RECONSIDERED BY VAN

Astral Weeks genesis was a long and complicated process. He wrote fragments in a notebook. Mervyn Solomon remembered reading his early song musings in a coffee stained little pad. He had recurring discussions with a number of Belfast musicians. Solly Lipsitz and Mick Cox heard about the project two years before Van recorded the album.

When he was asked how he came up with **Astral Weeks**, Van recalled: "It took a very long time and a lot of thinking and arranging and hard work to structure these songs like I wanted them." The **Los**

Angeles Times asked Van about when and where these songs were written. He replied: "**Astral Weeks** songs were written over a period of time — some early 1966 – and evolved musically. They are timeless works...."

Van is angry there have been numerous books written about him without his input. "It's a funny feeling that you actually have the courtesy of asking me about my songs. Did you know there have been numerous books written about my music where none of the authors were interested in my take on my music? None of the authors have ever had the courtesy of asking me to elaborate on my own music—500-page books and not one word did they want from me...."

This comment was a reference to Johnny Rogan's **Van Morrison: No Surrender**, which appeared in 2005. It offered the thesis how and why Northern Ireland was the key influence in the Belfast Cowboy's career.

Van Morrison said of his biographers: "I have tried to offer up help and I am refused. They have flat out refused all insight from me." This comment in an October 31, 2008 interview with the **Los Angeles Times** Randy Lewis demonstrates a change of heart for the Belfast Cowboy toward the press. The truth is Van Morrison, until the early 2000s, was one of the most difficult interviews in rock music. In the last decade he has been more gracious and forthcoming.

MORRISON GETTING SERIOUS ABOUT ASTRAL WEEKS IN NEW YORK

Where did **Astral Weeks** begin? It began with Morrison moving with his musical partners, Tom Kielbania and John Payne, to New York. The roots of **Astral Weeks** were more suited to the New York avant-garde scene. While in New York, the trio played the Café Au Go Go opening for Tim Hardin. There was no difficulty getting gigs. At times when the name Van Morrison was placed on the marquee, only a few dozen people showed up. Van was playing and working toward signing with a new record label. He didn't want to perform "Gloria," "Here Comes The Night" and "Brown Eyed Girl." He let the promoters know he wasn't an oldies act.

He also had a new musical format. It is one designed for small coffee houses. He experimented with three new musical directions, none of which had a commercial foundation. His lyrics were intellectual ones. Everyone wanted to hear "Brown Eyed Girl." This brought an innate frustration fueling Van's drive for a jazz sound as far from rock and roll as possible. Industry insiders who watched Morrison mesmerize small crowds weren't sure what to do with his talent.

WHAT IS SIGNIFICANT ABOUT ASTRAL WEEKS?

Few rock and roll albums received as much scrutiny as **Astral Weeks**. It was a departure like no other. There is a sense of Lead Belly mixed with Jimmie Rodgers. Mention of these artists is enough to ensure immortality. The folk music influences mixed in with the blues were unique. This allowed Van to reinterpret his songs in his manner. He is much like an old blues artist.

"Cyprus Avenue" reflects Van's Belfast roots. As a young man he wandered down to this tree lined street and fantasized about a better life. "Cyprus Avenue" was a tune about being upwardly mobile and successful. The expensive homes, the good-looking girls and the upper-class pretensions along "Cyprus Avenue" made an indelible impression.

There was an artistic ambivalence to Van. During the **Astral Weeks** sessions, John Payne recalled Van was in "personal pain." Perhaps this is why there was only one take of the title song. The Belfast Cowboy's lyrics fit into the cultural milieu of late 1960s. Morrison lived the title song for many years. His close friends agreed. They heard the song for three or four years before the jazz-based musicians recorded it. It was a treat to play with no charts and few artistic restrictions.

The best way to describe the significance of **Astral Weeks** is to take Van's conversations with Ritchie Yorke and interpret them. He told the Canadian writer there was a sense of energy or perhaps synergy in the songs. He maintained there was a free flowing, channeling effect. The title song, Van maintained, was "like transforming energy, or going from one source to another with it being born again like a rebirth. I remember reading about you having to die to be born." Van was talking about the dual death he experienced with the Solomon Organization and later with Bert Berns and Bang Records.

WARNER BROTHERS AND THE HIDDEN ROLE OF STAN CORNYN

When Van signed on with Warner Brothers, he was concerned about proper advertising and aggressive promotion. Warner would spend large sums to promote their artists. Van was not one of them. Morrison's marketing budget was cut in half. No one in top-level management believed he would sell in large numbers. The advertising budget centered around Joni Mitchell's albums. Van was not happy. Van believed Stan Cornyn, would further his career. He talked to Cornyn regularly.

Stan Cornyn was in charge of Warner's Creative Services. He was a marketing genius. His plan was to break Morrison on FM radio, college radio, the counterculture press and the Fillmore East and West concert venues. Bill Graham was important in maintaining Morrison's concert draw. Tom "Big Daddy" Donahue, the rotund 300-pound KSAN-FM disc jockey, played Morrison daily. One day riding around in a car with Greil Marcus, Van heard his songs every hour. This was due to Stan Cornyn.

ASTRAL WEEKS IN RETROSPECT

In 1974, Van looked back nostalgically on **Astral Weeks**. During an interview with Irish writer Donal Corvin, Van remarked **Astral Weeks** was "full of sketches and that's why people read more into it." He said he didn't write with a sense of interpretation. He left that up to the listener. He called "Madame George" a straight poem with music. Much of what he wrote, Van told Corvin, was consciousness prose. It was as if Van identified in lyrics with the American outlaw literary tradition.

He informed Corvin **Astral Weeks** remained his favorite album. Then Van talked at length about his belief soul music derived much of its influences from Scotland and Ireland. Hence the name Caledonia. "The structure and roots of traditional Irish and Scottish music has a very strong link with the American Negro's rhythm 'n' blues," Van continued. "The structures are very similar and the chordings are in the same mode."

Donal Corvin's interview showcased the Belfast landscape and Irish influences that were predominant in Van's music. He mentioned he listened to Dolly McMahon's album with the uilleann pipes. The music of the traditional Irish folk family, the McPeakes, and other Celtic influences on Van's music were evident in the interview.

BIBLIOGRAPHICAL SOURCES

For the events surrounding 1968 see Clinton Heylin, **Can You Feel The Silence? Van Morrison: A New Biography** (London, 2002), chapters 11-12. Also see, Brian Hinton, **Celtic Crossroads: The Art of Van Morrison** (London, revised edition 2002), chapter 4, Howard A. DeWitt, **Van Morrison: The Mystic's Music** (Fremont, 1983), pp. 27-33, Johnny Rogan, **Van Morrison: A Portrait Of The Artist** (London, 1984), chapter 5 and Ritchie Yorke, **Van Morrison: Into The Music** (London, 1975), Chapter 5.

See Thomas C. Palmer, Jr., John Payne: "Astral Weeks," **Wavelength**, number 23, March, 2000, pp. 8-14 for the early New York years. Mark Naftalin, formerly of the Paul Butterfield Blues Band, helped with the dissection of the **Astral Weeks** album.

An interesting analysis of Van's music is Ben Cruikshank, **Into The Sunset: The Music of Van Morrison** (Andover Hampshire, 1996), pp. 22-25.

See Tony Johnson, "Talk About Pop," RTE Television, Dublin, November 1973, transcribed by Art Siegel from issue 8, 1992 of the Van Morrison fanzine **Into The Music**. This interview is one of many taken from the Van Morrison Website. This was a television show that Morrison performed on and he began the program singing "Wild Child" followed by an interview.

Conversations with Bug Music founder Dan Bourgoise helped in understanding and interpreting the Web IV contract agreement. Harry Balk, formerly Del Shannon's producer, helped in understanding the production and marketing process.

The Bang Record story was important to this chapter, see, for example, Mike Callahan and David Edward, "The Bang Records Story," https://www.bsnpubs.com/nyc/bang/bangstory.html for an in depth account of the Bang Record experience. Even more significant is the excellent and fact filled year-by-year accounts of Them's activities compiled by David Chance, "Van Morrison With The Monarchs/Them Chronology 1947-1969.

http://www.oocities.org/tracybjazz/hayward/van-the-man.info/miscellaneous/themchrono.html

Also used in this chapter were selected issues of the Belfast based **City Week** magazine from copies located at the Colindale Library, London. See Peter Frame, **The Beatles and Some Other Guys: Rock Family Trees from the Sixties To The Beat Boom** (London, 1997) for the genesis of who passed through Van's various bands. Select issues of the **New Musical Express**, **Disc** and **Melody Maker** were consulted for this chapter.

See "Sloopy II: The Music of Bert Berns," for his official web site maintained by his son. It is an excellent source of information and it is at http://bertberns.com/biography/

Howard Johnson, "John Platania: Astral Weeks," **Wavelength**, number 23, March, 2000, pp. 20-22 examines the career of a major guitar influence upon Morrison's early career.

Danny Goldberg, "Interview With Van Morrison," **Jazz and Pop**, December 1970. Goldberg is a music insider. He has headed major record labels. Morrison was comfortable with him during the interview.

A series of interviews with John Lee Hooker in his Redwood City, California home gleamed some brief references to Van's music. Also, Mervyn Solomon provided some excellent suggestions on how Irish influences shaped the **Astral Weeks** album. The roots of the **Astral Weeks** album were explained by reading the Belfast based newspapers for the years 1965 to 1968. Phil Solomon also helped with descriptions of Belfast and its musical direction.

See Donal Corvin, "Van Morrison Interview", **Hot Press**, July 7, 1977. This interview was probably conducted in 1974.

For some interesting **Astral Weeks** reviews, see, for example, "Discs," **Music IT**, December 4-17, 1969 and two reviews in **Van Morrison Magazine**, volume 2, n. p., n. d., p. 17.

A number of interviews with Ray Ruff helped to understand not only the music business but also the recording industry.

A conversation with Seattle disc jockey and promoter Pat O'Day put the late 1960s and Van's place in it in historical perspective. Ron Peterson of the Frantics provided some interesting ideas to this chapter. A number of other Pacific Northwest music figures including George Palmerton, Little Bill Engelhardt, Rich Dangel, Jim Manolides, Grady McCartt, Tom McMillan, Ron Peterson and Don Fulton gave important information. Jim Bashnight added elements of the Seattle scene. Also, the detailed explanations of Don Wilson were important to understanding Seattle and when Wilson's Ventures emerged as one of the hottest instrumental acts of the late 1950s and early 1960s, they owed their success to the Pacific Northwest clubs where they began their career.

The Pacific Northwest influence on Van Morrison is an unexplored one. He is a music student and it was more than a coincidence he began listening to some Seattle and Portland bands. What exactly was the influence? That question is one that remains to be answered.

For Van channeling songs see Steve Heilig, "The Old Weird Ireland And The Young Weird California: Van Morrison As Channeled by Greil Marcus," **Anderson Valley Advertiser**, June 17, 2010. http://theava.com/archives/7088 When Van performed "Astral Weeks" in Los Angeles in 2008 he talked at length about channeling, see Randy Lewis, "Van Morrison's Full Q & A On 'Astral Weeks'," **Los Angeles Times Blog.** October 31, 2008. http://latimesblogs.latimes.com/music_blog/2008/10/van-morrisons-f.html

Conversations with Roy Head, Ritchie Yorke and Horst Fascher were important to this chapter.

For Van looking back on the press and explaining his attitudes towards the print media, see, for example, Clive Davis, "And He Stones Us To Our Souls: The Van Morrison Interview," **Irish Examiner**, April 11, 2015. https://www.irishexaminer.com/lifestyle/artsfilmtv/music/and-he-stones-us-to-our-souls-the-van-morrison-interview-323139.html Also see Jon Pareles, "Review: Van Morrison Finds New Meaning In Extensive And Nostalgic Catalog," **The New York Times**, June 21, 2015.

https://www.nytimes.com/2015/06/22/arts/music/review-van-morrison-finds-new-meaning-in-extensive-and-nostalgic-catalog.html?action=click&module=RelatedCoverage&pgtype=Article&region=Footer

See Jon Michaud, "The Miracle of Van Morrison's Astral Weeks," **The New Yorker**, March 7, 2008, for an article placing Ryan H. Walsh's book on the making of the **Astral Weeks** album in context. The book is examined in detail and Boston is given an inappropriate amount of credit for Morrison's creativity.

George Lee's industry importance is shown in **Billboard**, February 13, 1965, p. 4, August 21 1965, July 20, 1968, p.8 p. 4, June 6, 1970, p. 3, June 13 1970, p. 1 and January 16, 1971, p. 4. For the Loma Record period see Kirk Silsbee, "Revisiting Loma Records, The L. A. Soul Label That Launched Ike and Tina Turner," **Los Angeles Weekly**, April 26, 2016. Also see Robert Hilburn, "Mo Ostin Interview," **Los Angeles Times**, June 6, 1996. Roy Head sat for a lengthy interview on how and why he liked Van Morrison's music.

For some reflective comments looking back on his career, see Andrew Male, "It's About Time: Who Kidnapped Van Morrison and Replaced Him With This Guy?" **Mojo**, January, 2019, pp. 60-65. This is an excellent and telling interview where Van attempts to set the record straight on his career, his music and his future planes. The reflecting comments on past influences help to identify the key musical and career influences. For a decade Van has been cooperative and open with the press. Now in his mid-seventies he is attempting to answer writers like Clinton Heylin and Johnny Rogan who he believes have steered his career in the wrong direction. Van also talks at lengthy about Jimmy Witherspoon's influence and the tragedy of King Pleasure leaving the music business. The influence of jazz vocalist Jon Hendricks is another interesting aspect of the article as Van mentioned seeing Hendricks in Paris when he was just past ninety singing in his vocalese style that influenced Morrison. It is as if Van was writing his autobiography in this interview.

❧❧

CHAPTER 10

WHY ASTRAL WEEKS WORKED: THE EQUATION

"The lesson of our time is that Irish writers cannot any longer go on writing about Ireland, or for Ireland within the narrow confines of the traditional Irish life-concept; it is too slack, too evasive, too untense,"

SEAN O'FAOLAIN, FIFTY YEARS OF IRISH WRITING STUDIES, 1962

"I am into a completely different thing now. Now there is no limit to what I can do. I plan to use the type of instrumentation I like and be completely free. This is only the beginning for me."

VAN MORRISON ON ASTRAL WEEKS

"It made me trust in beauty."

BRUCE SPRINGSTEEN COMMENTING ON ASTRAL WEEKS

❧❧

The irony of Sean O'Faolain's statement that Irish writers cannot go on writing about Ireland, may or may not have been known to Van Morrison. What is ironic is Morrison employed a Belfast background. He has never stopped employing Irish themes. His Irish subjects make **Astral Weeks** poetic. The stream of consciousness lyrics have a sense of drama.

To understand why **Astral Weeks** worked one must comprehend the equation. That is Morrison's music emphasized spontaneity combined with themes uncommon in previous rock music.

271

VAN AND HIS SONGS

Why has **Astral Weeks** worked for fifty plus years? What is the equation? "The approach was spontaneity," Morrison recalled. As Brooks Arthur mixed **Astral Week**, he told Lewis Merenstein he was lucky to have his hands on the mixing board. "A cloud came along, it was called the Van Morrison sessions," Arthur continued. "We all hopped upon that cloud, and the cloud took us away for a while." What did Arthur mean? He was one of many participants who mentioned what he labeled "the **Astral Weeks** creative tension." He suggested a "special atmosphere" developed. That said it all. Everyone who worked on **Astral Weeks** reacted like Brooks Arthur. That is, they said the sessions were something surreal. Morrison's songs were uniquely creative. The session musicians loved Morrison's mysticism.

Van Morrison describes the album in more pragmatic terms. "I didn't have time to sit around pondering or thinking all this through. It was just done on a basic pure survival level. I did what I had to do," Morrison concluded.

There have been too many interpretive essays on **Astral Weeks**. Lester Bangs came closest to describing the angst, the bittersweet lyrics and the convoluted phrasing of Morrison's brilliant mind. Van hates interpretive essays on the album. "It's not about me," Morrison continued. "It's totally fiction. It's put together of composites, of conversations I heard — things I saw in movies, newspapers, books whatever. It comes out as stories. That's it." This is Van's view. For Morrison **Astral Weeks** is an early phase in his musical journey. He is too busy with the future to worry about the past. He continues to collect, catalogue and cut demos.

Van hoarded songs for years. He also reworked them. It is the time and care he took with **Astral Weeks** that makes it special. This is not to suggest his other albums didn't have the same focus. **Astral Weeks**, however, had a tight, lilting direction due to the make or break circumstances surrounding his career.

WHY ASTRAL WEEKS IS THE ULTIMATE CULT LP

Astral Weeks is the ultimate cult album driving the first wedge into his Warner Brothers contract. Van was outraged Warner didn't pick up on the rave **Rolling Stone** review. He has said they failed to publicize the album. When **Astral Weeks** didn't sell upon its initial release in November 1968, no one took notice. Then when the San Francisco based fledgling rock magazine **Rolling Stone** labeled it "the album of the year," Van believed Warner would intensify its advertising. It didn't. He was pissed.

When people asked where **Astral Weeks** came from? One answer might be Boston's Green Street. It was at this apartment the finishing touches were put on the lyrics and music. While he lived on Green Street, Van loved to walk down to Hancock Street to Peter Wolf's apartment at nearby 122 Mount Auburn Street. It was here they talked at length. Some say the streets of Boston created the **Astral Weeks** album.

The 122 Mount Auburn Street apartment in Cambridge Massachusetts intrigued Morrison. Why? It was built as a brick dwelling in 1890. It is located a stone's throw from the Harvard Kennedy Government Center. The apartments were turned into condos. It is now a very elegant address. It wasn't when Morrison visited Wolf. The John F. Kennedy Park and the Harvard University Winthrop Square are nearby. These disparate sources intrigued Morrison.

THE STREETS OF BOSTON CREATED ASTRAL WEEKS, OR DID IT?

It was while Van and Janet were living in Cambridge, he trekked over to Boston to play the small clubs. It was here **Astral Weeks** took its final form. He worked daily on the new songs. At night, he could play his new tunes and gauge the audience response. He wanted the material to be an intelligent rock opera with literary meaning.

The drive for a successful mainstream record consumed Morrison. He realized lyrics were the key to future success. The writing came fluidly. The folk clubs, the presence of singers like Tim Hardin, Tom Paxton, Tom Rush and Fred Neil, as well as the ever-expanding folk music scene helped him develop his art. It was in the midst of this energy he came upon two musicians, John Payne and Tom Kielbania. They helped to finalize his jazz-folk sound leading to **Astral Weeks**.

It was the Van Morrison Trio with Payne and Kielbania that gave final form to **Astral Weeks.** As he performed in and around Boston, Van was ending his concerts with "Cyprus Avenue." It was a psychological tool to recall Belfast. It also gave him the belief his hometown still had a presence in his life. Always a history buff, he was able to appreciate the rich texture of Harvard's nearby history. **Astral Weeks** created a sense of his lost educational opportunities. He realized self-fulfillment was a means of creating a strong intellectual foundation. The coffee shops in and around Cambridge reinforced his belief in reading thoughtful analysis and continually revising one's thoughts produced intellectual awareness. It also produced **Astral Weeks**.

QUOTATIONS FROM CHAIRMAN VAN

"I didn't really want to be in the rock 'n' roll scene."

"I think I opened up an area with Astral Weeks that hit a lot of people's nerves. But you can't really say that they're my favorite songs."

"I think Astral Weeks was definitely the transitional album."

"I wasn't into any romantic interludes when I recorded Astral Weeks, but when I wrote the songs I probably was."

"When Astral Weeks came out, I was starving literally"

"Astral Weeks was a breakthrough for me creatively, but then again I didn't have any particular rapport with those musicians."

"I was really happy with the album (Astral Weeks). The only complaint I Had was that it was rather rushed. But I thought it was closer to the type of music I wanted to put out. And still is, actually."

NORTHWEST RELEASING & KINK PRESENT
IN CONCERT

VAN MORRISON

THURSDAY, FEB. 4, 1971 - 8:30 PM
PARAMOUNT THEATRE
TICKETS: MEIER & FRANK, STEVENS & SON,
MUSIC MILLENNIUM, TODAY SHIP

ENTER LEWIS MERENSTEIN: WHAT WAS HIS ROLE?

Initially, Van didn't like recording for producer Lewis Merenstein. Morrison felt the Schwaid-Merenstein management and production company didn't have any idea where his music was going. They had never met an artist like the Belfast Cowboy. Their company, Inherit Productions, had a vision. It was to hire Van the best session musicians. They were to be older with jazz or classical backgrounds. This would enable Morrison to stretch his music into new directions. Merenstein was positive and often underappreciated in Morrison's nascent career. His background and decision making were decisive in **Astral Weeks**.

Merenstein was a Baltimore recording engineer working on jazz records. He was also a sophisticated jazz fan. He moved to New York to work with producer Tom Wilson. Before he met Morrison, Merenstein produced Miriam Makeba and Gladys Knight among others. He was well respected as a sound engineer and producer. He was also laid back, mellow and relaxed.

Bob Schwaid managed Morrison. When Schwaid proposed a production partnership, it was agreeable to Merenstein. They envisioned Van's creative genius. They formed Inherit Production. Merenstein had Morrison's best interests at heart.

Inherit Productions was confident they could produce the **Astral Weeks** album to cut a new niche in the rock music market. It was Merenstein's commitment to the material that made the partnership work. Merenstein told Clinton Heylin when he listened to the album: "I started crying." Merenstein was determined to get Van's music out to the marketplace.

That Merenstein was a jazz guy is well known. His influence upon Morrison's jazz direction is greater than suggested. He taught the Belfast Cowboy how to interpret jazz. Van disputes this. Merenstein told Clinton Heylin Van was not a jazz person when he met him. Merenstein said he

VAN MORRISON   ASTRAL WEEKS

In The Beginning

1 ASTRAL WEEKS
7:00
2 BESIDE YOU
5:10
3 SWEET THING
4:10
4 CYPRUS AVENUE
6:50

Afterwards

5 THE WAY YOUNG LOVERS DO
3:10
6 MADAME GEORGE
9:25
7 BALLERINA
7:00
8 SLIM SLOW SLIDER
3:20

PRODUCED BY LEWIS MERENSTEIN FOR INHERIT PRODUCTIONS
Division of Schwaid-Merenstein

FRANCE WE 835
US: 1768-2
EUROPE: 246 024

WARNING: The music on this Compact Disc was originally recorded on analog equipment, prior to modern noise reduction techniques. This Compact Disc preserves, as closely as possible, the sound of the original recording, but its high resolution also reveals limitations in the master tape, including noise and other distortions.

Warner Bros. Records Inc., a Warner Communications Company ℗ All Rights Reserved. Unauthorized duplication is a violation of applicable laws.

0 7599-27176-2 5

Astral Weeks Back Album Cover
(Warner Bros. Records, Inc)

educated his protégé in a sound culminating in a number of classic jazz-rock tunes like "Moondance." Van demurred.

Lewis Merenstein, producer on Van Morrison's classic 'Astral Weeks' and 'Moondance' LPs, (The estate of Lewis Merenstein)

There were other Merenstein contributions. He realized Tom Wilson, a producer cum musician, was perfect to bring the studio musicians together. Since the musicians were not familiar with Van's music, they had little, if any, expectations. They needed Wilson's input. Wilson said: "This album will be historic." There is no direct evidence Wilson influenced **Astral Weeks**. There is anecdotal evidence he spent hour talking production with Merenstein. His suggestions were important to the final product.

MERENSTEIN LOOKS BACK AT ASTRAL WEEKS

Lewis Merenstein looked back on **Astral Weeks** with fondness. He said he formed Inherit Productions for the sole purpose of bringing Van Morrison into the mainstream. It was a risky ploy. His friends said Schwaid-Merenstein would regret this decision. Merenstein didn't. He listened to the **Astral Weeks** songs as Van sat on a stool in Boston's Ace Studio. He realized he was listening to incipient genius.

"We took Van back to New York. I had an office with a little rehearsal room out back, and we'd sit around while he'd play tunes. I'd write down the songs I thought would go together in the album, because I sensed a story, like a little play," Merenstein concluded.

Merenstein speculated on Van's experiences with Bert Berns and Bang Records. "He had obviously gone through a rebirth," Merenstein continued. "I knew I needed people who could pick up that feeling." What did Merenstein mean? He said the studio musicians were selected because they could pick up on what Van wanted to do. "They were all super pros, but also open souls who played from the heart," Merenstein concluded.

Jay Berliner recalled his guitar work on **Astral Weeks**. "This little guy comes in and goes straight into the vocal booth. He doesn't have any contact with anyone. We could hardly see him." Berliner labeled the first session "off the cuff." Berliner said to Van: "Keep going, it sounds great!"

On some songs like "Madame George," Berliner remarked the music went on for a long-time allowing Van to stretch his vocals. The critics remarked Morrison opened up to feel the song. On the final session Berliner remarked: "a song called 'Royalty' didn't make the final cut." He called the **Astral Weeks** sessions "special." As he left the last session, Berliner remarked he had a soap product commercial the next day. He said he never forgot the magic of recording with Van Morrison.

Lewis Merenstein: "The funniest thing was that Warner Brothers, when they first heard it, didn't know what to make of it. They said, 'This is not Brown Eyed Girl.' … I said, 'You go ahead and you take 'Astral Weeks' and you make that into 'Brown Eyed Girl.' Don't you get what he…?" They didn't.

When Morrison recorded "Brown Eyed Girl," Arthur was the sound engineer. He praised Van's talent as a songwriter and as a recording artist to Wilson. Arthur concluded the Belfast Cowboy was the future voice and lyrical genius of rock music.

Why was Brooks Arthur's opinion important? He owned a studio, Century Sound, on New York's 52nd Street. He talked daily with executives from every New York major and minor label. His opinion mattered. As musicians, producers, industry insiders and label heads talked to Arthur, they realized Morrison's enormous talent. Brooks Arthur never got along with Morrison. That was a tragedy. He respected the Belfast Cowboy. He did everything he could to further his career. Van ignored him.

If there is an unsung hero to **Astral Week** it is Brooks Arthur. He was more than a sound engineer. The Brooklyn born Arthur wrote songs with Tony Orlando recording "At The Edge of Tears," Erma Franklin covered "Hello Again" and Arthur's "Memories, Memories" was covered by Jeanie Sommers. He had an ear for hit records. He engineered the Angels' "My Boyfriends Back," as well as the Raindrops "What A Guy." He was nominated for twenty Grammy's. He won three. When **Astral Weeks** was completed, Arthur speculated it would be a hard sell to the rock and roll crowd. He also said it was a priceless piece of music. He said it would endure for generations. Arthur's wisdom was paramount.

In order to understand how and why Van worked in the studio, it is necessary to examine one of his key collaborators Jeff Labes. He was there in the aftermath of **Astral Weeks** to help Van morph into a mainstream artist.

JEFF LABES REFLECTS ON THE AFTERMATH OF ASTRAL WEEKS

The piano-organ sounds characterizing Van's early music was due to Jeff Labes. He lived in Woodstock. He would drive up to the home on top of Ohayo Mountain and rehearse with Van. He wasn't in the studio for the **Astral Weeks** album. He had a close connection with Van. After Morrison returned to Woodstock after recording the album, he spent time working with Labes on the **Moondance** material. They talked at length about **Astral Weeks**.

Labes was one of many musicians who told Van to move away from the **Astral Weeks** sound. Van demanded Merenstein change the studio musicians for **Moondance**. Van was adamant. Merenstein relented. "He definitely wanted to create something radio-friendly," Labes continued. "He owed that to the record company and himself. A lot of the sound was kind of a tribute to The Band."

A simple musical formula with expressive lyrics and music is how Labes described Van's writing beyond **Astral Weeks**. As Labes reflected in the aftermath of **Astral Weeks**, he believed in the commercial mantra that was Morrison. He also realized in the studio **Astral Weeks** was a masterpiece. Labes was around before and after **Astral Weeks**. His observations suggest how varied and experimental Van was in the studio.

One of Labes most interesting observations is Van was much like Sinatra. He wanted to sing live. He wanted to make albums live. "Van loved to have a first take vocal," Labes concluded.

Labes moved from Boston to Woodstock, and he relocated to Marin County to continue the friendship and musical journey with Morrison. Some say Labes was the midwife for Van's cult sound in **Astral Weeks** and eventually his commercial breakthrough in **Moondance**.

A MASTERPIECE IS PRODUCED

For years, Van talked about how he conceived **Astral Weeks**. According to Morrison, it was "an opera, at the beginning…." What he did with the material was to take his childhood experiences; his early adult years and mold these into a potpourri of his life.

The studio was the place where the album was created. He had taped demos. He had experimented with these songs for friends. He worked hard on **Astral Weeks** for years before it was completed. The idea **Astral Weeks** is spontaneous is a myth. Van doesn't work that way. He is a slow, meticulous, careful craftsman. The intimate studio helped to create the atmosphere producing this classic album.

THE NINE COMMANDMENTS
OF THE ASTRAL WEEKS ALBUM

1.   Warner Bros. does not publicize Van's signing and he gives no interviews.

2.   Van is put on the sampler albums Warner sold through Rolling Stone. For one or two dollars a record or sometimes a two-record set provided 11 to 22 of the new Warner releases. Van was featured prominently on these LPs.

3.   No 45 record or single release was planned.

4.   Most of the promotional activity was directed to FM radio.

5.   San Francisco disc jockey Big Daddy Tom Donahue was the key person publicizing the Astral Weeks album.

6.   Van was one of many artists to have stardom without a 45 or hit single.

7.   Greil Marcus, noted Rolling Stone critic, called Astral Weeks "profoundly intellectual," thereby opening a new form of recognition to Van and to rock music in general.

8.   The initial sales were so poor that some predicted Warner Bros. would terminate his contract.

9.   "Slim Slow Slider" was left off the album because Van believed that it was the wrong song to end the LP. This began his resurgence as a producer.

ASTRAL WEEKS SESSION MUSICIANS

- **Richard Davis, bass**
- **John Payne, flute**
- **Jay Berliner, guitar**
- **Connie Kay, drums**
- **Warren Smith, percussion**
- **Larry Fallon, harpsichord on "Cyprus Avenue"**
- **Barry Kornfeld, guitar on "The Way Young Lovers Do"**
- **Van Morrison, guitar, keyboards, sax, and vocals**

During the **Astral Weeks** sessions, Van wasn't in charge. This led to a change in one studio musician. Richard Davis replaced Morrison's bassist. Van apologized to Tom Kielbania. It was Lewis Merenstein's decision not to use Kielbania. Van felt bad for his partner. He also learned a valuable lesson. If you wanted a specific sound, you had to experiment with the session or concert musicians. It was a lesson Van never forgot.

Astral Weeks has a number of themes and ideas common in Morrison's work. One of these is the use of Irish place names and isolated vignettes from the history of Northern Ireland. Belfast is a starting point for Van's vision. It is also useful way of interpreting his poetic dreams.

The use of jazz musicians helped to make Van's lyrical direction non-rock and roll. The calm and understated music is one-reason rock critics initially had trouble interpreting and understanding the album. Van didn't sound like the other musicians and other albums in 1968. This is exactly what he intended.

WHERE DID THE MAGIC FEELING COME FROM: LESTER BANGS TELLS US?

If there was a magic feeling in the recording studio, one wonders how the **Astral Weeks** album became an underground hit despite poor sales. The answer is a simple one. FM radio and the underground press trumpeted the album's unique strengths. When the New York based **Village Voice**, the **Los Angeles Free Press**, the San Francisco based **Oracle**, the **Haight Ashbury Tribune** and the **Berkeley Barb** praised the album, there was immediate artistic recognition. One critic, Lester Bangs, accentuated the drift toward cult success. His review of **Astral Weeks** is one of the most quoted in rock history.

As rock critics go, Lester Bangs is an anomaly. He was at times a clown. He was more often a serious voice. When it came to Van Morrison's **Astral Weeks**, he wrote with a facile pen. It was a decade after the album was released when Bangs sat down at his typewriter. He analyzed Morrison's music in scrupulous detail.

Like many people, he identified **Astral Weeks** with watershed periods in his life. This is the beauty of the album. It allows the listener to identify a crisis in his or her life. The beauty of Morrison's music is it is so different from anything else in the rock music marketplace it is open to wide and varied interpretations.

According to Bangs, Van is "obsessed with how much musical or verbal information he can compress into a small space...." He also points to the beauty of the material. To Bangs' credit, he is not interested in interpreting the lyrics.

When Bangs suggests **Astral Weeks** is an album that deals with truth, he makes it the central focus of his review. **Astral Weeks** was an album difficult to duplicate. Van is tired of answering questions about how he created it. In 2008 he decided to recreate **Astral Weeks Live**. He hoped that would end the need to interpret it. This would eventually turn out to be a double-edged sword.

THE LYRICS IN THE ASTRAL WEEKS ALBUM

Van Morrison is the only person who truly knows what is going on with the lyrics to **Astral Weeks**. These songs provide important clues to his life, his art and his mindset. With the title track, "Astral Weeks," Van speaks of Lead Belly. He brings us into his youthful bedroom and points to Lead Belly's picture on his wall. There is an intimate feeling. Then he switches the mood and talks about his mother taking good care of him with clean clothes and red shoes. The slipstream in this song is his introduction to the music business. His progression in the various showbands is a subtheme. The end of "Astral Weeks" highlights the religious symbolism that is so much a part of the Morrison mystique.

The musical changes in "Beside You" make the song work. A previous recording for Bang was a dud. With Warren Smith's vibes and Jay Berliner's soft guitar, the lyrics remain the same. The music evokes a primitive subtlety. "Beside You" is a literary form of pop music. This became Morrison's trademark.

"Sweet Thing" is a love song to Janet Planet. Van describes her special smile. He sings of her natural beauty. He sings about her eyes. He describes her sweet disposition. "Sweet Thing" captures the joyous nature of Morrison's new life. He is on the road to success. He is happy with America. His new surroundings inspire him. It is his wife who is his muse. "Cyprus Avenue" is his most famous paean to Belfast. He tours the neighborhood in lyrical fashion. In "The Way Young Lovers Do," Van completes a song that became a staple of his concerts. "Madame George" remains the quintessential song about Belfast. It explores his literary concerns. There are so many interpretations of this tune; it is impossible to figure out what Morrison meant. One thing is certain, the songs evoke Belfast's literary influence on the artist as a young man.

"Cyprus Avenue" is a literary masterpiece as Van transforms an ordinary Belfast street into images of hope, inspiration and his future. As Morrison points out in countless interviews, it is a song about the average Belfast denizen. When "Cyprus Avenue" ended the first side of the **Astral Weeks**, it finished what Morrison termed "In The Beginning."

"Slim Slow Slider" employs images of London's Ladbroke Grove. He said he would walk over to Notting Hill Gate to clear his head. In Ritchie Yorke's biography, Van refers to Ladbroke Grove as "that brick road." The illusion is a telling one. Van is walking from a dirty metro stop into a tourist-oriented part of London. He did this to remind himself of Belfast's lack of comforts. He needed this contrast to write. Van was comfortable in London. He realized his commercial future was in America. He employed commercial symbols necessary to the American record buying market.

INTO THE MYSTIC

The mystic's music had its origin in the **Astral Weeks** album. The Irish past was everywhere on the LP. Belfast dominated his music. It is striking how different this material is from his previous efforts.

Astral Weeks remains elusive. There is an aura of mysticism to it. "Some people are really disillusioned when I tell them about making the record," Richard Davis continued. "I don't remember any conversations with him." The admission he didn't talk to Van bears out the notion Lewis Merenstein deserves at least half the credit for **Astral Week's** brilliance. It was Van's material. He had the best production a young man could have in the early stages of his career.

Morrison's images were in an embryo stage. Few people recognized his literary forces. They were everywhere. "Into The Mystic" is a term, as well as a song, that Van told Chris Michie resulted from extensive reading. It was a literary cocktail distilled into song. One author, W. B. Yeats, stands out as an influence on Morrison's early material.

WAS MADAME GEORGE THE CONNECTION TO W. B. YEATS?

"Madame George" is the singularly most debated song on **Astral Weeks**. Of the eight selections on the LP none is more poignant than "Madame George." It has been the subject of many guessing games. Was Madame George a Belfast transvestite? Was Madame George a composite of some local characters? Was Madame George a historical figure?

The origin or meaning of "Madame George" remains elusive. There is one theory. It leads directly to W. B. Yeats wife. To some observers she is the muse to "Madame George." Everyone agrees Morrison employed literary influences. He quotes Irish writers as primary literary inspirations. They were half of his inspiration. The other half were the San Francisco beat writers Jack Kerouac, Lawrence Ferlinghetti, Allen Ginsberg and Lew Welch.

The Irish poet William Butler Yeats was one key figure who fascinated Morrison. Like Morrison, Yeats was rigid and possessed a mania to control the Irish theater. As a critic, Yeats was difficult and uncompromising. Van never envisioned he had a critical aura like Yeats. He does. There is one Yeats' play that not only intrigued Morrison, he used it extensively in his songwriting.

Cathleen ni Houlihan was Yeats' third play. Some critics claim it was only his idea, and he did not write it. This doesn't matter. Yeats' dream produced the play. It is in line with Van's use of dreams in the creative process. It was at Coole, in the summer of 1901, that Yeats recalled he had a dream "almost as distinct as a vision, of a cottage where there was well-being and firelight and talk of a marriage...." This play has intriguing parallels to Morrison's life. His courtship and marriage to Janet Planet, his new cottage in Woodstock, his temporary residences in Boston, his hotels in New York and finally settling in Fairfax, California all contained elements of Yeats' life. Like W. B. Yeats, Van envisioned writing would lead to fame, fortune and a new musical direction. It did!

Van employed images of Yeats' wife to compose "Madame George." When Van wrote "Rough God Goes Riding," it was a tribute to Yeats' rough beast gone slouching. It was Yeats wife from 1917 to 1939, the infamous Madame George Yeats who inspired Morrison. Yeats's mysticism and imagery had a direct bearing on Van writing "Madame George."

The blend of Yeats and Lead Belly created Morrison's unique musical direction. When Bob Dylan was asked if he could recreate his early body of work?" He replied with a curt "No!" Van would answer that question. "Yes!"

It was Morrison's creative Anglo-Irish heritage that gave him the impetus to write a distinguished body of work. Like William Butler Yeats, he became cranky, introspective and uncooperative at times. This personality trait is necessary to his art. He needs isolation to create.

VAN AND THE JOHN MCCORMACK FACTOR

John McCormack appears to be an unlikely influence upon Morrison's music. As a vocalist McCormack made his operatic debut at Covent Garden in London in 1906 appearing in Mascagni's **Cavalleria Rusticana**. He left the opera stage. He became a much sought after concert performer. His five hundred and forty-one recorded songs left a brilliant legacy. His transition from an operatic voice to international stardom, performing Irish songs, was seamless. He appeared with American singer Bing Crosby. James Joyce was a fan. When Joyce's ambition to be a singer didn't materialize, he mentioned McCormack in **Ulysses**.

Peter Costello's **The Irish 100: A Ranking Of The Most Influential Irish Men** includes McCormack along with Van Morrison. Like Van, he kept a notebook with his thoughts, his writings and his observations. Like Morrison, McCormack also had an American career. Like Morrison, he had a way with words. He had a sense of intimacy with his audience.

Van Morrison: "My father loved John McCormack, and he had lots of John McCormack records. So it was always part of the picture. And I always liked those sorts of songs anyway." The decision later in his career to cover Irish songs was due to his appreciation for McCormack's music. Van remarked he married McCormack's songs and sound with that of the Chieftains. This began his drift into Irish music. It was Northern Irish music. That is what attracted Van.

T. B. SHEETS: AUTOBIOGRAPHICAL LIKE JIMMIE RODGERS

"T.B. Sheets" is a haunting song. Was it autobiographical? Some say it was akin to Jimmie Rodgers. Who knows! Perhaps! Perhaps not! The similarities are overwhelming. Like Rodgers, Morrison is an excellent guitarist. Morrison is as gifted a songwriter and musician as Rodgers. The similarities remain in their music.

Like Rodgers, Morrison is a student of the blues and country music. "T. B. Sheets" suggests his infatuation with not only Rodgers' unique country blues style, but the tragedy is inherent in Rodgers' work.

How much did Van listen to Jimmie Rodgers? Plenty! In later years, Rodgers' "T. For Texas" inspired Van to write lyrics to "Foggy Mountain Top" suggesting Rodgers' impact. When Van cut the song in 1974 in Holland, he was questioning his place in the music business. In the next three years, he would lighten his schedule and pull back from the major concert venues. Perhaps Morrison looked at Jimmie

Rodgers brief life and decided it was time to think about the quality of his life.

Financial freedom was one of the main decisions revamping Van's career. He didn't care for Warner management. He didn't trust his production team. To ensure his future, however, he remained at Warner Brothers. He had to create a series of Top 40 hits to achieve fiscal independence. Was he happy? No! He was uncomfortable with fame and fortune.

Van thought for a long time about moving to San Francisco. His wife, Janet, grew up north of San Francisco in the small town of Fairfax. When Van visited the San Francisco Bay Area his records were played regularly on the radio. His albums in the San Francisco Bay Area had strong sales. But he didn't immediately re-locate to California. When he finished **Astral Weeks**, he moved to Woodstock. It was due to the musicians, the musical influences and the country ambiance. After he tired of Woodstock's hippie culture, he relocated in Fairfax, California. The experiences on the East Coast were important ones. The aftermath of **Astral Weeks** was an interesting time. Van pursued a more commercial direction. He didn't want to be a cult artist. It was time for fame and fortune. Then he spent fifty years complaining about it.

AN IRISHMAN WORKING AS A GUEST IN ENGLAND AND AMERICA

Finalizing the songs for **Astral Weeks**, Van was an Irishman working as a guest in England and America. If you asked Morrison whether or not he was English or American, he replied: "To the contrary." No one was sure what he meant. He used Irish themes in his songwriting. They were often disguised so well people didn't recognize the depth and level of his Irish imagery.

Like James Joyce, Morrison had a suspicion of mass politics and mass movements. He was never a joiner. When he flirted with the Jehovah's Witness sect, the mindless message of the cult perplexed him. The same can be said for brief stints with Scientology, evangelical Christianity and Buddhism. Van is not a person of the masses. He is an insular and singularly creative force. Nothing proved that more than **Astral Weeks**.

Van's Joycean obsession with ordinary people, their themes and their mores are a hallmark of his music. His writing practices the cult of the commonplace. He found the English pompous and arrogant. The snobbery inherent in British and American letters never influenced him. When the Universities came with their honorary doctorates, Van accepted with humility. The same could not be said for those who evaluated his work. He remains a blue-collar songwriter in a doctor of philosophy body.

In February 2009, as Van talked of the pleasure of recording **Astral Weeks Live**, he pointed out he established **Listen To The Lion Records** to promote the **Astral Weeks Live** CD. He talked about his distribution deal with EMI. He remarked coyly: "I just left Universal, because basically they didn't do anything except coattail me…." He also pointed out he owned the **Astral Weeks Live** material. He could license it. The smile on his face told it all. Morrison remained angry with Warner Brothers. Revenge was sweet after forty years. He got his money.

Van labels **Astral Weeks Live** new material. He left the original album behind. He told a close friend it was time the critics quit analyzing it. They won't. That analysis is one of the enduring parts of his legend.

THE YARRAGH AND VAN

Ralph Gleason, the noted San Francisco music critic, remarked that John McCormack has "yarragh in his voice." What Gleason meant is that "yarragh" defined the brilliant voice. The notion is that as McCormack said: "is the song singing you?" That defines how Van approaches his vocals.

Greil Marcus wrote Van "strikes a note so exalted you can't believe a mere human being is responsible for it." As Marcus explains the "yarragh" is reason for extraordinary blues-jazz vocals defining Morrison's vocals.

Van explains: "The only time I actually work with words is when I'm writing a song."

BIBLIOGRAPHICAL SOURCES

Chris Michie, Mark Naftalin, John Goddard, Howard Axelrod, Joey Bebo and Rick DeMeis also contributed material for this chapter.

See the Dan Goldberg interview in **Jazz & Pop**, December, 1970, David Reitman and Jackie Solomon in **Sounds**, December 12, 1970, Rick McGrath in the Vancouver B. C. alternate newspaper the **Georgia Straight**, April 15, 1971 and the Happy Traum interview in **Rolling Stone**, July, 1970 for various comments on the **Astral Weeks** album.

Clinton Heylin, **Can You Feel The Silence? Van Morrison, A New Biography** (London, 2002), chapters 11-12 is excellent on the **Astral Weeks** album. Also see Brian Hinton, **Celtic Crossroads: The Art of Van Morrison** (London, 1997), chapter 4 contains some key points on the literary side of the **Astral Weeks** album.

See Lester Bangs' essay on the **Astral Weeks** album in Greil Marcus, editor, **Psychotic Reactions And Carburetor Dung** (London, 1988), pp. 20-28. This is an important interpretation of the **Astral Weeks** album. It combines serious analysis with deft writing.

See John Collis, **Van Morrison: Inarticulate Speech of the Heart** (London, 1996), chapter 5 for a look at the **Astral Weeks** album in which Collis suggests Morrison reached "stellar heights" with the LP.

Some interesting comments on this period come in a discussion with Mick Brown. See Mick Brown, "The Interview Album," (Mercury Records, 1986). Also see Howard A. DeWitt, **Van Morrison: The Mystic's Music** (Fremont, 1983), pp. 27-33.

Don Stevenson of Moby Grape talked about playing with Morrison and how he performed in the early years. Folk, blues and rock singer Alice Stuart added her reminiscences of appearing with Morrison early on in his career.

See John Grissim, Jr., "Interview with Van Morrison," **Rolling Stone**, June 22, 1972. for some interesting comments on the **Astral Weeks** album.

A brilliant book that suggests that perhaps Van Morrison's "T. B. Sheets" had its roots in Jimmie Rodgers "T. B. Sheets" is Hugh Barker and Yuval Taylor, **Faking It: The Quest For Authenticity in Popular**

Music (New York, 2007), chapter 3. Also see, Nolan Porterfield, **Jimmie Rodgers: The Life And Times of America's Blue Yodeler** (Urbana, 1979), passim.

For an excellent article connecting Morrison to W. B. Yeats see Tom Nolan, "Who Was Madame George?" **Wall Street Journal**, April 14-15, 2007, p. 14. Also, on Madame George see, for examples, the brief comments in Vladimir, et. al., **All Music Guide To Rock: The Definitive Guide To Rock, Pop and Soul** (San Francisco, 2001, 3rd edition), p.762.

See Eavan Boland, ed., **Irish Writers On Writing** (San Antonio, 2007) for an excellent academic look at Irish writers. The similarities in themes and direction between W. B. Yeats and Van Morrison are imprinted all over this volume.

For Van's youth and the impact of Belfast upon the **Astral Weeks** album, see, for example, Martin Buzacott and Andrew Ford, **Speaking In Tongues: The Songs of Van Morrison** (Sydney, 2001), pp. 21-25.

The most inclusive interview given by Van on the **Astral Weeks** is Scott Foundas, "Van Morrison Interview," **London Telegraph**, February 25, 2009 during the aftermath of live re-creation at the Hollywood Bowl. Foundas also writes for the **LA Weekly** and he is a self-described "Vanhead." His writing was thoughtful and incisive on the new **Van Morrison Live** album.

On Van Morrison's Harvard years on Green Street there is a dearth of information, however, interviews suggest that he may also have lived near or on Pearl Street. A more likely scenario is that this is where the clubs where and he was seen hanging out there. Peter Wolf lived for a time on Pearl Street and this may suggest why there were Morrison sightings.

See Hank Shteamer's interview with Lewis Merenstein. "Goodbye, Lewis Merenstein" which he conducted on October 29, 2008 at a New York Upper West Side restaurant for some cogent remarks on the **Astral Weeks** album. http://darkforcesswing.blogspot.com/2009/03/in-full-lewis-merenstein-producer-of.html After Merenstein's passing in 2016 the interview was updated. This is the best critique of **Astral Weeks** by a person who sat in the studio and quasi produced this masterpiece.

For insight into how Van viewed his career over time, see Fintan O'Toole, "Van Morrison: Being Famous Is Not Great For The Creative

Process. Not for Me," **The Irish Times**, August 29, 2015. https://www.irishtimes.com/culture/music/van/van-morrison-being-famous-is-not-great-for-the-creative-process-not-for-me-anyway-1.2332216

One of the best interviews where Van talks about **Astral Weeks** is Josh Gleason, "Van Morrison: 'Astral Weeks' Revisited," **National Public Radio**, February 26, 2009. https://www.npr.org/templates/story/story.php?storyId=101249415 See Tom Pinnock, "Van Morrison-The Secret History Behind 10 Of His Best Albums," **Uncut**, August 28, 2015. https://www.uncut.co.uk/features/van-morrison-the-secret-stories-behind-10-of-his-best-albums-70516/2 This article is important for some excellent analysis and comments on Morrison's music. The brief section on **Astral Weeks** is brilliant. Why? Pinnock was one of the few writers to talk about Bob Schwaid and what he did for Morrison's career. He also interviewed Lewis Merenstein who was unusually candid.

For John McCormack's influence see David Burke, **A Sense of Wonder: Van Morrison's Ireland** (London, 2013), pp. 39-42, 76, 88, 128, 158, 168, 171-177 and Peter Mills, **Hymns to the Silence: Inside the Words and Music of Van Morrison** (London, 2010), pp. 61-68, 70-77.

Ed Thrasher handled the art direction for the **Astral Weeks** album, and his role has never been fully explained.

Rolling Stone did an unusually excellent job of eliciting information from Morrison. When editor David Wild inquired what the **Astral Weeks** album, Morrison replied: "It received no promotion from Warner Bros. That's why I never got to play the songs live." That explained in a simple sentence why Van never forgot the degrading treatment he received from Warner Brothers.

The **Astral Weeks** album has been reviewed so many times it is redundant to consider the analysis. What is not redundant are the over the top reviews that are either too praiseworthy or those reviews condemning Morrison's innovative product. Some reviews are simple an exercise in frivolous word play. The best example of this is Peter Reilly, "Astral Weeks," **Stereo Review**, volume 22, issue 112, 1969. Reilly writes: "This is another free verse mind-bender of an album performed by Mr. Morrison in a style that is something like an electric blender operating without its lid." Reilly went on to say **Astral Weeks** made no sense. "Mr. Morrison is heard howling away...." Reilly concludes. What does this insipid review tell us? It suggests rock criticism was in an early infantile stage. Peter Reilly was the head infant. In 1974 famed New York critic Robert Christgau echoed similar sentiments when he wrote: "Astral Weeks is still unlistenable obscure by many astute observers." Christgau hadn't gotten the message. Legions of Van fans did. See Robert Christgau, "Another Moving Van," **Newsday**, March 18, 1974. Reilly and Christgau are typical of mainstream reviewers as they have preconceived notions of what is and what is not a hit album. They have little empathy for adventurous music.

See Greil Marcus, "How Van Morrison Surrenders to the Yarragh", **The Irish Times**, August 29, 2015 for an excellent analysis of how and why the Belfast Cowboy employed the yarragh.

❦❦

CHAPTER 11

THE AFTERMATH OF ASTRAL WEEKS AND ON TO WOODSTOCK JANUARY-MARCH, 1969: A NEW LIFE

"In all fairness to Van, he was the one who was directing the taping, I thought it was a great record at the time, but initially it was a failure. I don't think we did 20,000 copies. It wasn't until years later that people started to come up to me and tell me that their lives had been changed by Astral Weeks."

ROBERT SCHWAID, MORRISON'S MANAGER.

"I do not consciously take the listener anywhere."

VAN MORRISON

"There's nothing here but dope, music, and beauty. If you're a woman, and you don't make music and you don't use dope, there's nothing here at all."

DOMINIQUE ROBERTSON, WIFE OF THE BAND'S
ROBBIE ROBERTSON ON WOODSTOCK.

❦❦

Once **Astral Weeks** was released, Van Morrison's initial euphoria turned to gloom. The Schwaid-Merenstein production team believed they had a jazz blockbuster They soon realized **Astral Weeks** was not a commercial success. Merenstein recommended a house producer for future Morrison recordings. He believed he had failed. That led to Ted Templeman, who Van despised, taking over future productions. Van developed a reputation for being impossible. This tag was due to Templeman. Van defended his actions. He suggested he had a vision for his music. No one at Warner understood. Templeman was a surfer from Santa Cruz. He didn't have a clue about music with a literary bent.

In the lexicon of rock and roll production, Templeman is credited with producing a number of Morrison albums. Van tells another tale. He was stuck with Templeman. He got credit for the production. Van produced it. The Morrison biographies pay very little attention to a Santa Cruz surfer who began working at Warner as a seventy-five dollar a week apprentice who went on to become a Vice President. His production credits for Morrison include the **St. Dominic's Preview**, the **Tupelo Honey** and the **It's Too Late to Stop Now** albums. Templeman was intimidated by Morrison. This made for an uneasy relationship. Templeman was laid back, calm and non-confrontational. He soon became disenchanted with the Belfast Cowboy. Templeman had some production strengths. He was organized in the studio. He had a deft production touch. He was smart and a quick learner. There were those who swore by him in the studio. Van didn't.

THE TED TEMPLEMAN INFLUENCE: WHAT WENT WRONG?

After Ted Templeman played drums with Harper Bizarre, Lenny Waronker, who produced their hits, offered him a job. No one was sure what he did. He was training to become a producer. He sat in on Frank Sinatra and Elvis Presley sessions. "I stayed in the studio a lot and watched engineer Lee Hirschberg work," Templeman told David Gans. This led to producing the Doobie Brothers second album **Toulouse Street**. The first song on the album, "Listen To The Music," became a hit. This led to him working with Morrison.

David Gans asked Templeman what he learned from working with Van Morrison. "I learned the value of a good, spontaneous performance from working with Van," Templeman said. He indicated Morrison taught him a great deal about producing. When Van walked into the studio he would ask: "Is the tape rolling, Ted?" That unnerved Templeman. "I was a rookie producer, and he made me very nervous." As a person, Templeman liked Morrison. "He's irrational. And he's no fun to work with." Templeman went on to observe he would never work with Morrison again "even if he offered me three million in cash." The problems in the studio were never ending. "He's a marvelous talent, a fantastic singer, but he's fired everyone who's ever worked with him," Templeman concluded. It appears Templeman had a love-the relationship with the Belfast Cowboy that morphed into abject hatred.

One reason for Templeman's dislike of Van is the final mix for "Tupelo Honey." Templeman spent hours remixing the song and after Van heard it, he said put out "the rough mix."

Then after the album was released, Templeman said Van called him in the middle of the night and told him: "You know, you were right about that mix." Templeman reflected: "I almost cried." Working with Van aged Templeman ten years, he remarked to David Gans.

Ted Templeman's unflattering opinions have influenced Morrison biographers. This may be his only contribution to the story. John Collis is a prime example. He takes Templeman's word on all things about Morrison. Sad! David Gans profiling Ted Templeman said he had evolved from a seventy-five dollar a week joke at Warner Brothers into an acclaimed producer. Not all of us agree with Gans. The reason? Templeman's opinions vary with the facts. He seldom talked to Van. He had thoughts on productions he never articulated, and he was more inclined to Van Halen than Van Morrison.

TED TEMPLEMAN CHANGES THE STORY: 2019

In 2019 Ted Templeman recalled his time with Van Morrison. Time had erased the bitterness. He no longer talked about the problems he had with Morrison in the early 1970s. Templeman told **Billboard** that Van gave him his start in the producing business.

Here is the story Templeman spun. He said he was nervous when he manned the production desk for **Tupelo Honey**. "I was working as a listener at Warner Bros. Records," Templeman remarked to **Billboard**. The label assigned Templeman as a house producer for

Morrison after Lewis Merenstein left. He did turn into a brilliant and acclaimed producer working with the Doobie Brothers and Van Halen. That wasn't the case when he sat at the recording console with Morrison.

When Templeman drove from San Francisco to Fairfax to talk with Morrison about his next few albums they got along. Van was not temperamental. He listened politely to Templeman's ideas. He has never said what he thought of the blonde haired surfer. Van was willing to work with him. What happened to sour the relationship? No one knows.

"Van was quiet, polite and self-effacing, and I took an immediate liking to the guy," Templeman continued. "His Irish brogue was hard to understand sometimes, but I could tell he was a super-smart cat." After they talked and Templeman returned for a second visit, they developed "a common interest in jazz."

Then Templeman skewers the story. He said Van looked at him and remarked: "Wanna work on a record with me?" Templeman said Van wanted to "give this young rookie a shot." Those I talked to inside Warner Brothers said it was common to assign a house producer to new acts. Van Morrison was a new act. Recalling Van's comments forty eight years later is dangerous. Templeman alleges Van said in the studio: "Ted are we getting a good sign in there?" In his Irish brogue, he was saying "sound", Templeman concluded.

When Templeman claims Van joined him in the hospital while his wife had a baby, he clinches the deal for their friendship. "He was a very sensitive cat," Templeman continued. "He was there for me in a time of need. And he gave me my first hit record. I will never forget that. Van gave me my start in the music business."

When **Billboard** ran the story in 2019 of how Van broke Templeman as a producer there was a photo of him in a production session at Western Studios on January 27, 1969 standing over the mixing board. Yet, two years later he said he was just getting into the business. Hopefully one day Van will tell his side of the story. Templeman's sound like a piece of fiction. It is a respectful, praiseworthy reminiscence. It is another story that may or may not have Van seething. He has seen this movie too many times. "Mo Ostin assigned Ted Templeman to produce Van as punishment," Ray Ruff recalled. Templeman's later recollections are at odds with his earlier statements as well as statements by others.

The story is true if you look at Templeman's early career. Van did help Ted's career. Templeman looked back fondly on working with the Belfast Cowboy, and he is right that there was a sense of personal accomplishment working with Van.

THE MYSTERY AND UNCERTAINTY OF VAN AND ASTRAL WEEKS: WICKHAM, LEE AND RALFINI'S ROLES

It took some years before **Astral Weeks** sold steadily. The mystery and uncertainty surrounding **Astral Weeks** was mitigated by the actions of Lewis Merenstein, Joe Smith and the Warner house hippie, Andy Wickham. They preached patience. George Lee and Ian Ralfini were other industry figures urging the Warner brain trust to remain calm. Van would eventually be a cash machine. That happened shortly after **Astral Weeks** flopped.

The first Van Morrison Warner Brothers album passed into the commercial abyss virtually unnoticed. At least for the first two years. Then, with a boost from FM radio, the album sold steadily. Cult status arrived a decade later. The events surrounding America took the emphasis away from music as the Vietnam War raged. There was a peace march upon Washington D. C. The nation was preoccupied with a contentious presidential election. Warner Brothers changed its advertising to meet the national mood. The youth culture was increasingly political. Warner advertised their artists were counterculture icons. They were opposed to the Vietnam war. Van blanched. He wasn't political. His music didn't fit into Warner's preconceived singer-songwriter syndrome. While Diana Ross and the Supremes topped the charts, Van sat back and waited for his time in the spotlight. He knew he had a winning product.

There were internal concerns at Warner Brothers over the commercial quality of **Astral Weeks**. As the executives in charge of advertising attempted to use FM radio to publicize Morrison's album, they ignored more conventional outlets. These executives sent cover letters to disc jockeys extolling the virtues of Morrison's singer-songwriter capabilities. Warner Brothers refused to purchase large-scale advertising for **Astral Weeks**. This irritated Morrison. At Rolling Stone, Jann Wenner was unhappy about Warner's business practices. In a fit of pique, he allegedly screamed: "Cheap screws." Eric Isralow, known years later in the San Francisco Bay Area as Dr. Rock, attempted to influence Morrison's career for his position teaching at the State University of New York, Buffalo.

Eric Isralow: "I was working on my doctorate and I came to San Francisco to talk to **Rolling Stone** about Morrison. I said this guy is the next big thing. They ignored me." Isralow, who later went on to mainstream radio success in San Francisco, was one of many San Francisco music people extolling Van's music. Isralow had to work hard to get paid as Dr. Rock. "I worked with Warner on promotion. They said it is good for your career." Isralow continued. "I said to the secretary, 'Do you get paid?' She said: 'Yes' so I said: 'Then fucking pay me'." Isralow continued. "They never did and I was done with Warner Brothers. They wanted me to play a cut from each of their promo records. Fucking amateurs are killing the record business."

The best explanation why Van was disparaged, ignored or pigeon holed as a Warner artist came from a March 1, 1969 **Rolling Stone** article by Greil Marcus. He reviewed Morrison's music prior to **Astral Weeks**. Marcus concluded: "Van Morrison, who seemed to have been captured by Donovan's 'freedom in a lie,' has now released a unique and timeless album called Astral Weeks." The dimwits at Warner read this and came to the conclusion Donovan had the folk mantle. Why spend money on Morrison?

Marcus wrote: "Van sings in and around what might be called a modern chamber orchestra…." This frightened the Mo Ostin's and his ilk. They believed Morrison's fan base was not a rock and roll one. After all Van said he was not a rocker. Marcus reinforced this notion writing of **Astral Weeks** "the music is not rock and roll in any ordinary or hyphenated sense…." Marcus continued to frighten Warner executives as he prattled on his prose. "Not everything works; there are poor lines like 'the viaducts of your dreams,' awkward moments, shouts of 'breathe in, breathe out'…." that Morrison wrote. Warner executives photocopied the **Rolling Stone** article as the publicity budget for **Astral Weeks** went south. Van was right. No one, including Greil Marcus, knew what he was doing.

After Marcus wrote this article, he went to San Francisco's Avalon Ballroom and watched Morrison perform the **Astral Weeks** songs. He loved the set. After the show Van and Greil talked at length. The Belfast Cowboy went on about how unhappy he was with the **Blowin' Your Mind** album. Van's frustration with Bert Berns and the Bang label was clear during the interview.

Van Morrison: "It was the producer who did it, and that record company. They had to cover it all with the big electric guitar and the drums and the rest. It all came out wrong and they released it without my consent."

VAN IN JANUARY-MARCH-15 1969: WHAT TO DO WITH THE NEW ALBUM

In January 1969, Van did his best to promote **Astral Weeks**. He appeared on radio shows, he did in store record events, and he took phone calls from disc jockeys. This was a new Van Morrison. The old one associated with "Gloria," "Here Comes The Night" and "Brown Eyed Girl" was a thing of the past. Many of his fans expected the old rock and roll material.

This made the first few months of 1969 a difficult time. Van's career changes hadn't caught on with the public. He was an opening act for artists like Jeff Beck. There was no rancor from Van in Chicago when they appeared at the Kinetic Playground. The March 14, 1969 shows were ones where Van honed his in-concert act while visiting with old British friends. The hidden influence in the two-day gig was a California based band Sweetwater.

Sweetwater was a Los Angeles psychedelic group who had little mainstream success. They were booked to perform at Woodstock. They were scheduled to be the first band to appear. The New York State Police stopped them on the way to Woodstock. This allowed the Ritchie Havens Trio to open the festival. Sweetwater still retained the title of the first full rock and roll band to perform at Woodstock. Things looked good for their career. They were signed to a major label. The beautiful lead singer sounded like an angel on acid. They built their sound on the fusion of folk and psychedelic rock with an assist from early Jefferson Airplane recordings.

Then six months later disaster struck. The lead singer, Nancy Nevins, was injured in an automobile accident. She was placed into a coma and years of physical therapy, as well as alcohol and drug problems, took her away from music. The group was lost to history.

Sweetwater album cover 1968 (REV-OLA)

What was the reason Van liked Sweetwater? They were a typical Los Angeles hippie band with one difference. They had an incredible flutist, Albert Moore, and a cellist, August Burns, who brought their music into a surreal place. To Van they were a band with the **Astral Weeks** sound, as well as a full roll and roll conventional set of instruments. He was intrigued. They blended psychedelic sounds in a jazz direction. The clothes, the instrumentation, the stage presence and the quirky music appealed to Morrison.

WHAT DO WE DO WITH VAN MORRISON?

Warner had no idea what to do with Morrison. He was independent in the studio. He was difficult. He had his own ideas about promotion. The first sign Van was different from other artists occurred on September 25, 1968 when he entered New York's Century Sound Studios carefully outlining his songs. This was not the industry norm.

Where were the lead sheets? They didn't exit. Van would explain the direction of the music. Warner Brothers demurred. Van held his ground.

This was the beginning of his relationship with Warner Brothers. He showed no signs of compromising with the Warner corporate mentality. As the material for **Astral Weeks** took shape, Morrison violated previously sacrosanct studio rules. Warner claimed he gave the musicians too much interpretive leeway. Lewis Merenstein said he was too relaxed. Van was a strange mix of charm, naivete and conceit. It took a great deal of confidence for him to work with some of New York's legendary studio jazz musicians. Van's music inspired the jazz legends. Connie Kay remarked Van led the session musicians down a new interpretive path. This comment shows a great deal of respect for Morrison's embryo talent.

Connie Kay, of the Modern Jazz Quartet, was on drums. The vibraphonist, Warren Smith, loved the **Astral Weeks'** sound, and how its musical idiosyncrasies were interpreted. He took to Van's musical direction. The end product was a sophisticated jazz sound.

"When Warner executives listened to the final cuts in Van's breakthrough album, they were divided. They weren't sure if it was unrequited genius or hippie excess. They didn't know where he fit into the musical landscape," Ray Ruff observed.

WHY WARNER PACKAGED ASTRAL WEEKS

Astral Weeks' packaging made it appear Morrison had written a rock opera. It wasn't. At least not in the conventional sense. Nothing Van did was in the conventional sense. This drove Warner executives crazy. Joe Smith loved Morrison. When Mo Ostin took over the label, Van's days were numbered. Ostin was a cipher or perhaps, more accurately, an accountant.

It was Mo Ostin, some years later in the 1980s who asked: "What the hell do we do with Van Morrison?" The answer was a simple one. Leave him alone as his back catalogue still sells. The worries about his commercial future and his alleged erratic behavior became an immediate concern. It shouldn't have as Van had a straight-ahead musical vision. Ostin vowed to fire him.

VAN MORRISON ON ASTRAL WEEKS

"It wasn't meant to be like that … it didn't really surface the way it could have … I didn't have the same mood in mind for the whole album … The way I wrote it … as an opera …" 1970

"I think I opened up an area with Astral Weeks that hit a lot of people's nerves. But you can't really say that they're my favorite songs." 1977

"I didn't really want to be in the rock and roll scene. Then the critics started saying that Astral Weeks was a rock album … the whole point was not to make a rock album." 1986

"I think Astral Weeks was definitely the transitional album … coming from a deeper unconscious level, getting more in touch with the unconscious." 1990

There was nothing erratic about Morrison. That was the spin Warner executives placed on his work and personality. It wasn't true. Warner sent an inordinate amount of time convincing the media he was impossible. Whether or not there was a reason depends on your source. He made so many Warner executive angry they fought back by cutting promotional funds taking long lunches when he visited and ignoring his requests for sales support.

WHO WAS VAN MORRISON IN 1969?

On January 1, 1969 Van Morrison was twenty-three years old. He had left his Belfast mates in Them with bitterness and rancor. Like James Joyce's **Ulysses**, he had gone into exile to write his musical thoughts.

Who was Van Morrison? There are as many answers. By 1969 he had a burning zeal to achieve solo stardom. He worked night and day on that dream. There were complaints from record executives. His songs ran against the grain. Mo Ostin remarked this defined his personality. A more obvious answer is he was one of the hardest workingmen in show business. The irony is Warner management never fully appreciated his willingness and ability to promote his records. Nor did they recognize the care he took crafting his songs, his productions and his concerts.

WARNER BROTHERS DIDN'T UNDERSTAND MORRISON

Warner Brothers executives didn't listen carefully to Morrison's music. Had they paid attention they might have understood his concepts. **Astral Weeks** didn't chart in either the U.K. or America. When the London based **New Musical Express** labeled Van's effort a mediocre one, he moved permanently to America. He didn't return for fifteen years. **Rolling Stone** made it the album of the year. Van found his home in the San Francisco Bay Area. It was there he intensified his hit record sound.

Van has never handled criticism well. He was crushed with the lack of a commercial reception. The irony is he continued to work on redoing the lyrics, the direction of his music and the mystic feel of **Astral Weeks**. His close friends say he was obsessed with the album's failure. As the critics reviewed **Astral Weeks**, Greil Marcus and Lester Bangs praised Morrison's in-studio magic.

The genius of Greil Marcus should not be overlooked in the slow, but steady, sales. His advocacy moved the album into the cult mainstream. Marcus observed: "What might seem arty at first proves to be a new place to go, a new kind of music to hear...."

A decade later, when Marcus edited Lester Bangs' essays, the praise for **Astral Weeks** was the centerpiece of this popular book. It was as if Marcus and Bangs conspired to bring Van's album to the mass consumer. When Warner announced **Astral Weeks** went gold, it wasn't due to their marketing or belief in the product. Royalties! They were miniscule. Van fumed over what he believed to be fiscal slights, as well as inaccurate sales figures.

SEQUENCING ON ASTRAL WEEKS AND LECTURING MO OSTIN

The final product benefited from Lewis Merenstein's shrewd post-production direction. When the eight songs were put together Merenstein had one word in mind. He told Van it was sequencing. He argued the counterculture would not purchase a record that had no sense of order. Van agreed. Merenstein did his best to make the album look like a rock opera. The **Berkeley Barb**, the **Village Voice** as well as the **Los Angeles Free Press** reviewed **Astral Weeks** highlighting its intellectual direction. This sold the LP on college campuses. The **Berkeley Barb** observed; it was: "poetry within the rock music framework."

Merenstein believed visual packaging was important. The album cover had a mystical quality. To make sure there were no problems, Van didn't see the LP cover until it was in the stores. The album began with side one labeled "In The Beginning." This was an unusual but effective way of introducing a concept album. By labeling side two as the "Aftermath," Merenstein created an aura of mystery. He reinforced the notion Van was a mystic. These qualities intensified over the years. The mystic became Morrison's moniker.

Van observed **Astral Weeks** was only thirty minutes of a longer work. He told Mo Ostin and others this would be the standard for the concept album. He looked into his notebooks. He spent an hour lecturing Ostin on what was important about **Astral Weeks**. Mo was chagrined. That may have been the day Ostin decided to do as little as possible to promote Morrison. Van let Ostin know he was a rank amateur musically speaking. Van suggested Ostin needed to return to the ledgers on profits and losses. He should leave the music decisions to the professionals. Ostin never forgot this slight. Ray Ruff, who managed the later incarnation of Them, told me Ostin had "a deep-seated anger with Morrison."

Jon Gershen, who played with Van and lived near him in Woodstock, recalled Van had little interest in discussing **Astral Weeks**. Gershen said Van was unhappy with the final product. It was not the album he hoped to complete. Van argued Schwaid-Merenstein compromised his concept album.

Van believed there was a commercial direction to his music. He intended to take it to the bank. He told close friends he needed to "stretch the music out and not make commercial pop ditties."

The small rehearsal hall Merenstein built in his office impressed Van. When Morrison constructed a home recording studio in Fairfax, he used Merenstein's model. The home studio allowed Van to focus his music. He would sit and play his guitar. His house became the practice hall. Then it quickly morphed into the recording studio.

In the aftermath of **Astral Weeks**, Van was angry. He got even with Warner spending three years writing one hit record after another. Mo Ostin wanted to fire him. He never forgave Morrison for disparaging his management style. He vowed to get even. As 1972 drew to a close, Morrison's Top 40 hit making potential was recognized. Van Morrison detested Top 40 hits. He reluctantly produced a string of hits.

Merenstein told Ostin he stumbled upon a raw talent in Morrison. He seldom takes credit for the first two Warner Brothers albums. He augmented Van's expertise in the recording studio. Van began his education with Bert Berns at Bang Records. He finished it with Merenstein. Then he informed Warner Brothers he would do it on his own. He has! This was enough training to produce material for the rest of his life. Van was adamant. Neither Berns nor Merenstein understood his production direction. He had to rid himself of producers.

The mania to produce his material resulted from changes Merenstein made to **Astral Weeks**. He believed his masterpiece was compromised. The initial press comments on **Astral Weeks** angered Morrison. He realized his musical vision needed more time to seep into the cultural milieu. In time, the peculiar and often nasty early reviews gave way to praise. He came to grips with it in 2008 taking

Astral Weeks Live to appreciative audiences. That was not the case in the year after the album's release.

PRESS COMMENTS ON THE ASTRAL WEEKS LP

"This album is as far removed from Them as possible, Morrison sounding for all the world like Jose Feliciano's stand-in on eight of his own compositions. The comparison rather deadens the impact of the album because Morrison can't better or equal Feliciano's distinctive style. The songs themselves aren't very distinguished apart from the title track, and suffer from being stuck in one groove throughout."

NICK LOGAN, NEW MUSICAL EXPRESS, SEPTEMBER 27, 1969

"Van Morrison … has now released a unique and timeless album, called Astral Weeks. The limits and restrictions are no more in evidence than on the previous record, but the limits of the blues, as they exit for Van Morrison, have been abandoned as well…. Astral Weeks is serious and it is also a profoundly intellectual album."

GREIL MARCUS, ROLLING STONE, 1969

"Rather Dylanesque."

BEAT MONTHLY, 1969

"It sounded like the man who made Astral Weeks was in terrible pain, pain most of Van Morrison's previous works had only suggested … there was a redemptive element in the blackness … It did come out at a time when a lot of things that a lot of people cared about passionately were beginning to disintegrate … Astral Weeks was also the product of an era."

LESTER BANGS, STRANDED: ROCK AND ROLL FOR A DESERT ISLAND (NEW YORK, 1979)

Over the years, as the critics finally praised **Astral Weeks**, Van grudgingly acknowledged Merenstein's contribution. The initial residue of bitterness took place because of a lack of sales.

Touring was something Van liked as long as it was brief and filled with musical freedom. The large arenas, the television shows, where you lip-synched, the disc jockey bashes in roller skating rinks and high school gyms were not Morrison's forte. He had to go out on the road for financial reasons. He picked places he liked to play. It was in New York Van found the perfect venue.

ON THE ROAD AGAIN: A MIXED BLESSING

The Scene in New York was one of Van's favorite clubs. He loved its atmosphere. The crowd was quiet, reverent and stoned. The Scene was situated in the basement at 301 West 46th Street. This was in New York's Theater district. Every rock act of significance such as the Lovin' Spoonful, Fleetwood Mac, Traffic, the Velvet Underground and the Doors played there. The first performance by the Jimi Hendrix Experience in June 1967 was at the Scene. The club closed in 1970 when Steve Paul refused to pay protection money to the Mafia. The Mafia started fights in the club. They alerted the New York Liquor Board for violations. Paul closed the club.

Steve Paul presented Van Morrison at the Scene for three nights January 22-24, 1969 and then on a Monday night January 27. Each night there were two performances. Tom Kielbania accompanied Van on bass. Artie Kaplan was on saxophone and flute. These eight shows were a practice session for **Astral Weeks**.

The Scene was ultra-hip with Spirit appearing before Van and the Savoy Brown Blues Band closing the show. The press was everywhere. The reporting failed to pick up on Morrison's new sound. Looking back on The Scene, in an interview with the **New Yorker,** he recounts how important New York was to putting **Astral Weeks** in motion. The January 27th 1969 show was a party hosted by Warner Brothers to celebrate the new album and Morrison's coming journey with the label. It was a festive night.

DANCING-BLUES-CONCERT

(WED. JANUARY 22)
(THUR. JANUARY 23)
LAST 2 NIGHTS!

SPIRIT

TONIGHT THRU SUNDAY

VAN MORRISON
HOLY MODAL ROUNDERS

HAL WATERS

SUN. THRU THURS. SAVOY BROWN BLUES BAND

JAN. 27 - FEB. 2   N R B Q

JAN. 31 - FEB. 2   SOFT WHITE UNDERBELLY

FEB. 3 - FEB. 6   LEAD ZEPPELIN

FEB. 9 & 10   PENTANGLE

FEB. 24 - MAR. 2   FLYING BURRITO BROS

MARCH 17   JERRY LEE LEWIS

FEB. 4 MARCH 2   A MONTH OF SPECIAL
SIGNIFICANCE — BETTY CARTER

NEW EARLY and LATE, LATE SHOWS
Uninhibited Dancing & Listening Encouraged

STEVE
PAUL'S   SCENE   JU 2-5760
                 301 WEST 46th ST.

Steve Paul's Scene 1969 Ad

Then Van and Janet flew to San Francisco to play three shows at San Francisco's Avalon Ballroom. These appearances were followed by four nights at Los Angeles' Whiskey A Go Go. The Whiskey gig was one where the audience wanted to hear "Brown Eyed Girl" and the old

Them hits "Gloria" or "Here Comes The Night." Van was performing the **Astral Weeks** material. At the Whiskey A Go Go the Flying Burrito Brothers shared the bill with Morrison. The trip to California rekindled fond memories from Them's 1966 tour. It also made Janet Planet nostalgic for her old hometown north of San Francisco. Everyone expected "Here Comes The Night," "Gloria" or "Brown Eyed Girl." The patrons at the Whiskey A Go Go complained they were treated to chamber music. It was **Astral Weeks** material. While Tom Kielbania and John Payne provided an excellent soft jazz back up, the audience was flummoxed. No one in the hippie community could figure out what was going on. What had happened to Van Morrison? Where was "Brown Eyed Girl?"

BOSTON AND GETTING READY FOR A CHANGE TO THE COUNTRY

While he was in San Francisco and Los Angeles, Van was urged by a Boston friend Dick Waterman to remain living on Boston's Green Street. As a photographer, Waterman shot all the blues greats. He eventually morphed into an industry insider. Van was taken with Waterman. They spent hours talking about the blues. Waterman had extensive knowledge of Mississippi John Hurt and Son House. He knew everything there was about Charlie Patton and Robert Johnson.

Dick Waterman was a writer, photographer and concert promoter living near the Morrison's on Franklin Street in Cambridge. Van loved to come over to Waterman's place to talk about the blues. His street, Franklin, ran parallel to Green. Van walked over a block, and he was at Waterman's front door. One day Waterman found Morrison sitting on his doorstep. He was perplexed. He needed a manager. Van convinced him to walk over to the Harvard Library. They did. Van sat in a large leather chair and Waterman sat on the arm. They talked. Van carried an acoustic guitar. He started to sing every song from the forthcoming **Astral Weeks** album. Waterman told Van to get a real manager and a lawyer. The rest was history. Waterman said: "The Band and Bob Dylan were in Woodstock."

Woodstock was two hours north of New York. It was perfect for a young couple living on a meager income. The image of California's sun and old friends made Janet nostalgic for the West Coast. Van thought of performing in the San Francisco area as a homecoming for his bride. Van loved Marin County, and the small town of Fairfax. He would eventually move there. For the moment there was very little money to relocate. They had relocation on their mind while moving to Woodstock. Van increasingly had California on his mind.

THE SAN FRANCSICO SHOWS AND WHAT THEY DID FOR ASTRAL WEEKS

It was at San Francisco's Avalon Ballroom that Van put on his best West Coast shows. The Avalon was a small movie theater converted into a concert hall. Located just off Van Ness Avenue near San Francisco's Tenderloin, it had a seedy countenance. Van loved it. The bathrooms lacked the usual comforts. It was filled with posters advertising past shows. Psychedelic posters replaced the movie posters on the theater walls and the admission charge of $2.50 wasn't collected if you couldn't pay. The owner, Chet Helms, at times presented free concerts.

It was a counterculture dream. The free concert emphasized personal freedom. Or at least this was the message from Helms. There were also new forms of entertainment. None was more interesting than the psychedelic light shows. The Little Princess 109 light show brought in a bevy of free loaders and druggies eventually prompting Helms's bankruptcy. The free-flowing entertainment philosophy was important to artists like Van. He believed he could experiment with his music in front of a friendly audience.

Van loved San Francisco's hip subculture. Greil Marcus' review of his shows reflected the Belfast Cowboy's performing acumen. To Marcus the new Van Morrison delivered "a brilliant set." Marcus, who earned a PhD in American Studies from the University of California, Berkeley, intrigued Morrison. He talked openly and at length with Marcus. The talkative academic Marcus was driving the Belfast Cowboy around the San Francisco Bay Area while lecturing on rock and roll. Van was mute.

When Van performed at the Avalon Ballroom there were some special songs. As much as he hated Bert Berns and the Bang Record material, Van surprised everyone by performing "Who Drove The Red Sports Car" and "He Ain't Give You None." Along the way "Gloria" and "Here Comes the Night" were not included in his concert repertoire. On "Who Drove The Red Sports Car," Van took it into a blues direction.

These tunes were at times performed, but they were altered into a style consistent with **Astral Weeks**. Anything associated with Bert Berns was altered beyond recognition. Van was making it clear; he was performing songs his way. There were many critical reviews. The worst was by a London exile living in Los Angeles, Judy Sims, who was a pop music critic with a penchant for purple prose. Van vowed not to talk to these reporters. Sims was a prissy, self-important reporter whose idol was Rona Barrett. The press was something Morrison hated to deal with on the road. He considered it an unnecessary impediment to his art. It was an unwelcome intrusion into his touring schedule.

Judy Sims claimed Morrison altered his music beyond recognition. She asked what the hell was going on with **Astral Weeks**? Sims failed to listen to most of Van's music. She forwarded her stories to London where they appeared in top music magazines.

Judy Sims: "Poor Van Morrison. He opened at the Whiskey last night and played to a big crowd which was feted by his record company; lots of important people crammed into booths and tables, drinking and talking and generally ignoring Van on stage. After three numbers I wished I could ignore him-it was simply awful." Sims wrote a column "Hollywood Calling" for London's **Disc And Music Echo** while living near Sunset Boulevard. Her writing was akin to a primary student learning the alphabet. She knew very little about the music. Free drinks! She loved the perks. She caught Van on one of his worst nights.

There is no evidence Sims' reporting in **Disc and Music Echo** had an impact upon Morrison's career. Sims described Van as "simply awful … loose, rambling songs that all sounded alike. They went on forever and Van's nasal voice did nothing to vary the pace or inflection. We left after a solid hour of this torture." Van didn't respond. He needed to write new material and get back into the recording studio.

After the California tour, John Payne got married. He gave up life on the road. He was replaced by Graham Blackburn, who had traveled with Van to California. An Englishman, he was a skilled musician. He was connected in the music industry. Blackburn did as much as anyone to alert those in the industry to Morrison's talents. As a flutist, Blackburn's style had a defined rock and roll direction. This helped round out Van's sound. Blackburn attended the Julliard school of music and he built two homes in Woodstock.

When the California concerts ended, Van moved on to Detroit to play the Grande Ballroom for three nights from February 21-23, 1969. The second floor Grande Ballroom was a miserable venue. It had an inadequate sound system. The seedy neighborhood reeked of poverty. Van didn't enjoy the night. He left as soon as his set concluded. The Jeff Beck Group was the headliner. The Michigan crowd gave Van rapturous applause. Why? They appreciated his acoustic sound.

Matt Lucas: "When I played the Grande in 1969 the cops would ask me if I had any drugs. I didn't. So the rent-a-cop gave me some. It was a place to get stoned. I don't think anyone listened to the music. That is except for Van Morrison."

Van decided to move to someplace less expensive. The price of Boston's housing remained a constant problem. He also hoped to find a place with the serenity necessary to productive songwriting. Van discovered the upstate community of Woodstock. At this time, it was the home of Bob Dylan and a host of itinerant musicians including "The Band."

LITERARY ILLUSIONS IN VAN MORRISON'S WORK

William Blake's Song of Innocence is the Structural theme for the first side of the Astral Week album entitled In The Beginning.

William Wordsworth's Prelude and Excursion is the book, which helps to set some of the themes for the Astral Weeks LP.

James Joyce, Ulysses was a model for Van's stream of consciousness writing.

Van listened to Graham Blackburn's idyllic description of Woodstock. It was one of the catalysts to moving to Woodstock. He was shifting into a new direction. His social life had a new dimension. His confidence soared.

The diverse bands in Woodstock were what Van needed in the late 1960s. He had to separate from the Them sound. He had to establish his musical identity. In Woodstock, Van experimented with an electric rock band. He made the decision to search for chart hits. It was once again a temporary phase. Van vowed to reinvent himself every few years. He loved the notion of different musical formats. Morrison searched out new and innovative musicians. This time they were of the electrical rock and roll and boogie-woogie variety. He was getting ready for **Billboard** chart hits.

For days at a time, Van would have Janet drive him down to East Saugerties. He would visit with "The Band" at their communal home. They were hard at work on new music. They were creating a new form of country rock. One that would make them international stars. From his home on the Ohayo Mountain, Van looked over the valley surrounding Woodstock. It didn't take long to tire of this rural paradise. From time-to-time, Van would have Janet or someone drive him into New York or Boston. In Woodstock, there were bigger stars. Van was left alone. He reveled in this period of anonymity.

The end for the Morrison's in Woodstock came in the summer festival that brought the counterculture raging into this small, rural town. Van never forgot the turmoil. He vowed to leave Woodstock, as soon as it was economically possible.

Van realized he didn't fit into the East Coast social milieu. New York, Boston and Woodstock hadn't worked out. He began casting about for a new place to live. He recalled Janet's hometown, the bucolic feel to the Mill Valley-Fairfax communities, and the wonders of the San Francisco Bay Area.

While Van continued to work on new songs, he was surprised by the lack of interest in the **Astral Weeks** album. When Los Angeles folk rocker Johnny Rivers cut a version of "Slim Slow Slider," it received FM radio play. The song was placed in Top 40 rotation. Van was unfailingly complimentary to Rivers. He told close friends no one could cover the material in the **Astral Weeks** LP better than Johnny Rivers. In an

314

interview with Ritchie Yorke, Morrison praised Rivers for doing "it like himself." Yorke couldn't believe it. "I realized I was wrong about Van," Yorke told me in 1982. "He praised musicians he believed were original." The notion of originality prompted Van to recreate **Astral Weeks** in 2008.

BIBLIOGRAPHICAL SOURCES

Ray Ruff helped to recall the Whiskey A Go Go performances. See Steve Turner, **Too Late to Stop Now** (London, 1993) for photos of Van at the Whiskey A Go Go and an excellent description of the four days there and why the shows were not particularly successful.

The legendary rockabilly singer Johnny Powers helped with the material on Detroit's Grande Ballroom. Matt Lucas was also instrumental in recreating the Motor City concerts and musical atmosphere. Shirley Westover, Matt Lucas, Harry Balk, Dan Bourgoise, Dick Parker and Maron McKenzie provided important information on the area in and around Detroit.

For the aftermath of the **Astral Weeks** album see, for example, Brian Hinton, **Celtic Crossroads: The Art of Van Morrison** (London, 1997, revised edition 2000), chapter 4, Ritchie Yorke, **Van Morrison: Into the Music** (London, 1975), chapters 5-6, Clinton Heylin, **Can You Feel the Silence? Van Morrison, A New Biography** (London, 2002), pp. 162-202 and Howard A. DeWitt, **Van Morrison: The Mystics Music** (Fremont, 1983), pp. 27-33.

See Bob Sarlin, **Turn It Up (I Can't Hear The Music)** (New York, 1973) for an excellent interpretive essay on Van's growing musical reputation.

An excellent source for the late Them and early Van period is David Chance, "Van Morrison With the Monarchs/them Chronology, 1968-1969," on the archived Van Morrison Website http://web.archive.org/web/20091028131621/http://geocities.com/tracybjazz/hayward/van-the-man.info/reviews/1974ksan.html

See Clinton Heylin, **Bob Dylan: Behind The Shades Revisited** (New York, 2000), chapter 9 for a description of Woodstock.

Thomas C. Palmer, Jr., "John Payne: Astral Days," **Wavelength**, number 23, March 2000, pp. 8-14 is an important source for the **Astral Weeks** sessions and Lewis Merenstein's role in this cult album.

The **San Francisco Chronicle**, the **Los Angeles Times**, the **Berkeley Barb**, the **San Francisco Oracle**, the **Seattle Post Intelligencer**, the **Seattle Times**, the **New York Times** and the **Los Angeles Free Press** were consulted for this chapter. Equally important was the Belfast based **City Week** which occasionally reported on Morrison's American journey.

In Belfast Mervyn Solomon provided a great deal of material on how Van handled the transition to a solo act and dealt with the fame of the **Astral Weeks** album. Phil Solomon also added material to this chapter.

An interview with Corky Siegel added important information to this chapter. Art Siegel was an important source for this chapter. Also, the Van Morrison list helped as the fans reported many intimate details of the 2008 recreation of the **Astral Weeks** album.

The management at Santa Monica's KCRW was an important source for material.

In a 1984 interview Russ Solomon added some important comments on Tower Records and its relationship to Morrison. Solomon, who founded Tower Records, lived until he was ninety-two watching record stores slip into the abyss. He told me Van Morrison had a strong following and his vinyl sold steadily and by the late 1980s the fledgling CD market brought Morrison the old audience and a new one. "I think Van sold more quietly in the 1990s than any artist," Solomon remarked to me in Sacramento.

A brilliant look at the **Astral Weeks** album is Joel Brodsky with Greil Marcus, "Into the Mystic," **Mojo**, issue 202, September 2010, pp. 50-55.

For the paste interview see Jessica Pilot, "Catching Up With... Van Morrison, **Paste**, February 10, 2009. https://www.morrissey-solo.com/threads/van-morrison-interview-about-live-performance-release-of-astral-weeks.95824/ For a warm and friendly review of the Hollywood Bowl shows see Randall Roberts, "BFF: Van Morrison, **Astral Weeks Live**, and LA Weekly," **LA Weekly**, August 18, 2009. https://www.laweekly.com/music/bff-van-morrison-astral-weeks-live-and-la-weekly-2411350

See the incisive interview by Greil Marcus in the January 3, 1969 issue of **Rolling Stone**. Also, see, Lester Bangs, Greil Marcus, editor, **Stranded: Rock And Roll For A Desert Island** (New York, 1979) An interview with Russ Solomon of Tower Records was important to this chapter.

Insights into Lewis Merenstein can be gleaned from Randy Lewis, "An Appreciation: Lewis Merenstein, Producer of Van Morrison Masterpiece 'Astral Weeks'," **Los Angeles Times**, September 13, 2016. https://www.latimes.com/entertainment/music/la-et-ms-lewis-merenstein-producer-obituary-appreciation-20160913-snap-story.html

For the Dominique Robertson quote and a brilliant article on **Astral Weeks**, the album's impact on popular culture and Woodstock see, Lindsay Zoladz, "Van Morrison's 'Astral Weeks' Is 50, But It Never Ages," **The Ringer.com**, November 28, 2018. https://www.theringer.com/pop-culture/2018/11/28/18115313/van-morrison-astral-weeks-album-50th-anniversary-review

Interviews with Eric Isralow in 1983 and comment from Ron Kovac and Richard Boyle were important to this chapter.

See the in-depth review-article by Travis M. Andrews, "The Rage of Van Morrison And the Battle Behind His Masterpiece, 'Astral Weeks'," **The Washington Post**, November 30, 2018. https://www.washingtonpost.com/lifestyle/the-rage-of-van-morrison-and-the-battle-behind-his-masterpiece/2018/11/29/38d67a88f32e1108bc79-68604ed88993_story.html?utm_term=.67bf3345fa10

The **Astral Weeks** period was a tough one for Van. His manager, Bob Schwaid, made comments to the press that the Belfast Cowboy was not only difficult to know but he charged Van wasn't open to compromise. Schwaid talked about how strong and well-adjusted Janet was, thereby causing Van to become enraged. The people interviewed in this period describe Schwaid as even more elusive. He wouldn't allow his picture to be taken. Carmine "Wassel" DeNoia suggested he was a gangster. He did this in good humor.

See David Gans, "Ted Templeman Interview," **Bam, The California Music Magazine**, October 9, 1981 for information on how and why Morrison and Templeman found it difficult to work in the studio. Templeman has a net worth of one hundred million dollars. He is credited with producing hit albums by Van Halen, Carly Simon, Aerosmith, Eric Clapton, Cheap Trick, Joan Jett, Bette Midler and the

Doobie Brothers. The people interviewed for this book described Templeman as laid back, non-confrontational and a good guy. He found his difficult to co-produce with Morrison.

The tough part of the **Astral Weeks** period was Morrison's embryo career. He had few guarantees concerning his commercial future. For the uncertainty of this period see, Howard A. DeWitt, **Van Morrison: The Mystic's Music** (Fremont, 1983), passim. For Ted Templeman's look back at his time with Van Morrison see, Katherine Turman, "Ted Templeman Explains How Van Morrison Taught Him To Produce Records," **Billboard**, October 2, 2019.

CHAPTER 12

THE ARTISTIC TRANSITION: WARNER AND ATLANTIC RECORDS, MARCH-DECEMBER 1969

"We all want to be famous people, and the moment we want to be something we are no longer free."

JIDDU KRISHNAMURTI

"Morrison claims to have discovered a certain element of soul."

RITCHIE YORKE IN CONVERSATION WITH HOWARD A. DEWITT 1982

"Astral Weeks would herald the clear, bright, brilliant voice of a truly unique talent, one which would survive and continue to independently produce great songs, music and, of course, performances that are second to none."

PROFESSOR GERALD DAWE

The competition between Atlantic Records and Warner Brother for new talent had a direct impact upon Van Morrison. In the late 1960s the two labels were intent upon signing every major British rock group or singer-songwriter. They were also spending large sums of money on signing bonuses. This intrigued Van. He believed it would give his solo career a much-needed boost.

Because Bert Berns founded the Bang label with his Atlantic Record partners, Van reasoned after Berns passed away, Atlantic would come calling. They didn't. He preferred Atlantic over Warner Brothers.

The competition amongst the major labels for new talent provided Van with complaints. His signing bonus was not big enough. His studio time was controlled. His production team was inadequate. The publicity department ignored him. His complaints festered. They caused Morrison to periodically explode.

The irony is Morrison entered the mainstream of the American rock music marketplace with his Warner contract. He was in an artistic transition, as the rock music industry searched out singer-songwriters. This spelled an end to song factories like the Brill Building. It portended a new era in rock music. Morrison believed there was only one first rate label, Atlantic.

When he lived in New York, Van observed the record industry with a keen eye. As he watched Atlantic Records make millions with new acts, Morrison seethed with anger. He had signed with the wrong label Bang. He used the Atlantic Record model as a barometer for his discontent. He had visions of a future with Atlantic Records.

ATLANTIC RECORDS AND THE NEW MUSIC

The Atlantic label was undergoing a dramatic transition. It was a business method that most other labels copied. They signed groups to highly specific contracts to limit their expenses, control copyrights and produce terms favorable to the label. Ahmet Ertegun sent a note to Jerry Wexler pointing out the English rock acts, even five years after the Beatles invaded America, were still the dominant sound. Atlantic made a decision. It was to sign every British rock and roll act available.

When the London-based New Yardbirds were given a $75,000 contract advance for the North American rights to their songs, the group changed its name to Led Zeppelin. They became the largest grossing act on the Atlantic label. The money flooded in from album sales. "The industry changed by the late 1960s," Dan Bourgoise of Bug Music, remarked, "suddenly there was a second influx of British bands. The singer-songwriter began to dominate."

As Van watched not only Led Zeppelin, but also other English acts, he believed he would receive the same treatment. When he didn't, bitterness ensued. He reluctantly signed with Warner Brothers. Then his demands escalated. Van asked Warner Brothers to increase his songwriting royalty rate. He said his songwriting was worth millions. Warner said he had a contract. They told him to live up to it. This began the off and on-again relationship with the label. Van said he fired them. Morrison talked of signing with Atlantic. It didn't work out.

Why didn't Atlantic offer Morrison a contract. Bert Berns was the reason. He told his friends at the label of the difficulties with Morrison. Warner signed Van.

WARNER BROTHERS AND THE NEW MARKETING

There was a promotional mania to the Warner label bordering on the obsessive, as they advertised their new signings. A large number of giveaway albums, parties for disc jockeys and special events featuring the label's artists heightened sales. The usual payola was in effect as sex, drugs and hookers flooded the business. Rock and roll slowly matured into a mainstream industry. Cheating the artist and filling the corporate pocket book was the mantra for the times. It was accomplished with industry friendly contracts. Most of which were legal. Van didn't fit into the promotions.

When Van hired Woodstock resident, Mary Martin, to represent him, his career soared. She was an assistant to Bob Dylan's manager, Albert Grossman. She learned the attack and demand technique that brought millions to Dylan's coffers. She employed these tactics representing Morrison.

Mary Martin suggested Warner wasn't giving him his due. Martin observed the obsessive mania for artists like Joni Mitchell. It didn't match what the label was doing for her client. She sent Warner a letter with Morrison's name in bold letters suggesting they ignored him. Warner responded they gave each singer equal promotion. They did so through the promotional albums. A series of inexpensive records were released featuring one cut from every artist. These records sold for one or two dollars and they included a biography of each artist.

Warner signed so many artists it was hard to keep track of their musical direction. In 1969-1970, Warner Bros. completed contracts with Black Sabbath, Doug Kershaw, Jethro Tull, Gordon Lightfoot,

James Taylor, Fleetwood Mac, Ry Cooder, Deep Purple, Alice Cooper and the Small Faces featuring Rod Stewart. Van was signed prior to this mélange of entertainers. He wondered where he fit into the Warner Brothers hierarchy? He frequently quizzed Warner executives about their plans for him. "I remember Van coming down the elevator at Warner," Ray Ruff recalled. "He didn't look happy. He also didn't acknowledge me." The reason was a simple one. Sporadic sales of Morrison's material fueled his anger. When Ruff brought Them to America in 1966, he remembered Van as gregarious and happy. "The industry weighed on him," Ruff concluded.

VAN AND THE PSCYHOLOGICAL MALAISE: SPRING 1969

The pressure of the music business was taking its toll on Morrison's marriage. As Janet Planet told Joel Selvin, "Van's rages were frequent and generally directed toward those in the music industry." In 1969 Van was at an important turning point. The next year would tell whether or not he would remain a long term mainstream artist. Warner worried Morrison didn't aim for the hit record market. He told Warner he didn't care about having pop hits. Then he abruptly shifted into the hit record mode. He became something he detested. A mainstream artist.

Initially, Van did not select his musical cohorts with the idea of hitting the pop charts. When he performed with Tom Kielbania and John Payne the audiences were small. They were also not very enthusiastic. The crowds hollered for "Gloria," "Here Comes The Night" and "Brown Eyed Girl." Van ignored them. Peter Wolf remembers the Belfast Cowboy had little, if any, interest in performing the Them or Bang songs. Most people wanted indulgent hippie music. Morrison would not bend to their wishes.

There was a quiet and moody side to Van. Many people had trouble accepting him. He was also a night person. He would frequently call his band members at three o'clock in the morning for a recording or practice session. "I lived in Sacramento and it took more than two hours to drive to Fairfax," drummer Tony Dey continued." That was Van's genius. When the muse called, we recorded."

Van had a way of remaining aloof. He was not easy to know. He was more difficult to remain friends with over the long term. This was due to the secrecy surrounding his writing and music. Van needed isolation as well as instant rapport with his band.

Van Morrison (1993 - Rock & Roll Hall of Fame Rock Hall Library and Archive)

IAN RALFINI: ONE OF THE INDUSTRY GOOD GUYS

By 1969, Van experienced a Warner Brothers management reorganization. When Warner opened a London office in 1969, they persuaded an ex-bandleader, Ian Ralfini, to manage a London public relations branch at 69 New Oxford Street. From this office they hoped to break Warner products in the United Kingdom. Ralfini became a life-long friend of Van's while working at multiple labels and winding up as a senior corporate official at EMI Blue Note. He eventually became the label president. He had Morrison's best interests at heart.

Ian Ralfini was a hidden gem at Warner's London office. An experienced record man with an eye for talent, he had a role in breaking Aretha Franklin, Chaka Khan and Norah Jones in the United Kingdom. An elegantly dressed man with impeccable manners, Ralfini was in every way the opposite of Morrison. He stayed behind the scenes providing Van with excellent promotion.

Ralfini's knowledge and credentials were evident as he worked with Neil Young, the Grateful Dead, the Rolling Stones, Yes and Led Zeppelin. He also worked closely with Atlantic Records. He was pushing for Van to sign with Atlantic. Ahmet Ertegun loved Morrison's music. He realized Van was becoming too savvy about business. This cooled him on signing the Belfast Cowboy. The urbane, intellectually inclined Ralfini made a strong impression on Van. Ralfini was at heart a jazzman.

When Morrison returned to EMI with his 2009 album **Astral Weeks Live At The Hollywood Bowl**, Ralfini was a principal figure in negotiating the deal. "I brought these records to EMI because they seem to have people with vision...." Morrison remarked.

In order to make Warner Brothers a U.K. household name, Ralfini shrewdly planned a series of promotional events. Warner flew New Orleans singer Clarence "Frogman" Henry to London to play at promotional shows. This was not the music Warner should have promoted in the U.K. Van Morrison was never asked to appear on one of these promotional junkets.

Van had his first lesson in corporate decision-making. The label spent hundreds of thousands of dollars sending executives and obscure artists to London, rather than the more popular singer-songwriters.

The Warner Brothers hierarchy was openly unfriendly toward Van. He never felt appreciated. There was constant friction between Van and key executives. This was due to the continual change in management style, public relations campaigns and sales tactics. This did little to help his career.

The reason for Warner's inability to properly merchandize Van is traced to Mo Ostin. When he took over as the head of Warner Brothers, he was an accountant. He had little knowledge of the music side of the industry. He was out of touch with the sounds of the day. In many ways he was good for some artists. For whatever reason he had a grudge against Van. There is no doubt he was an excellent label head. This was due to his business expertise. Artistically? Forget it!

When Warner signed the Electric Prunes in 1967, it was to demonstrate how knowledgeable the label and Mo Ostin were in discovering untapped talent. Ostin told Morrison he was on top of the key sounds of the day. He pointed to the Electric Prunes signing as his coup de grace. Morrison laughed in his face. While "I Had Too Much To Dream Last Night" was something of a cult hit, Ostin's signing did little to alleviate Morrison's belief he was an accountant with little knowledge of the musical side of the industry. There were others at Warner whom Morrison admired. Andy Wickham was one of his favorites. It was Andy Wickham that cemented Van's relationship with Warner. Had it not been for Wickham, things would have been even more difficult. Mo Ostin was brilliant for everyone but Morrison.

MO OSTIN A BRILLIANT FISCAL MIND, FORGET THE MUSIC

Prior to signing Van Morrison, Mo Ostin took over at Warner/Reprise. After working for Frank Sinatra at Reprise, Ostin came over to head what became Warner/Reprise. He held the top spot for thirty-two years. Generally, he was loved and trusted by most artists. There is little doubt when Van threatened to fight him in his home, he made an enemy. Ostin was successful despite a minimal knowledge of rock, pop, folk or hit songs. Ostin's training was in accounting. He never met a nickel he didn't like to squeeze. Rock music was the perfect venue for a penny-pinching executive.

Ostin was a brilliant businessman. When he was retained as the Reprise label manager they were in heavy debt. He brought them out of the financial malaise. He moved to Warner Records. He began the onerous task of creating Warner/Reprise. Ostin cut back on Reprise releases. The label had Frank Sinatra. Ostin helped orchestrate one of the biggest commercial comebacks for any artist with Sinatra. Lee Hazlewood brought Nancy Sinatra into the Top 40. Warner acquired the rights to release the Kinks and the Jimi Hendrix Experience.

Ostin formed Loma Records in 1964 to focus on rhythm and blues acts. He hired former King Records promotion man Bob Krasnow to run it. By November 1966 Warner was finically sound. While Loma folded in 1968, it left a legacy of excellent soul record releases. This little-known Warner Brothers subsidiary appealed to

Morrison. Van has never stated that he preferred Loma artists, but he loved the music.

ON THE SOLO ROAD IN LOS ANGELES AND SAN FRANCISCO

On February 1, 1969, Rolling Stone's Greil Marcus went to the Avalon Ballroom to hear Van Morrison. Marcus described Morrison as "a unique and forgotten figure in the history of rock and roll." In a sympathetic review, Marcus praised Van's enormous talent. He also provided a mini-history of Them.

Greil Marcus wasn't sure what to make of Tom Kielbania and John Payne as backing musicians. Consequently, Marcus' review concluded Van needed a little more in the way of musical accompaniment. The review suggested Kielbania and Payne obscured Morrison's talent. Marcus praised the Avalon Ballroom show. He envisioned Van as a future hit maker. He didn't change that perception after driving Morrison and his wife, Janet, around the San Francisco Bay Area. When Morrison discussed Lawrence Ferlinghetti and Jack Kerouac, Marcus realized he was dealing with a different rock star. Van was one with literary aspirations.

Marcus said Van was a misunderstood original talent. His mystical lyrics intensified that talent. This reference to **Astral Weeks** initially pleased Morrison. Van didn't care for the trite and fawning rock and roll press. The erudite and highly intellectual Greil Marcus was an exception to most journalists. He didn't write fan based reviews. It was an intellectual view of the music. Van loved it.

It was a strange pairing, the quiet Irish singers and the son of San Francisco furrier who wrote books everyone praised but didn't understand. Along the way Marcus did some of the best reporting on Van. They had a mutual love fest.

After the 1969 Avalon shows, Marcus and Morrison talked backstage. Van continued to bemoan how producers bastardized his music. He told Marcus: "I've got a tape in Belfast with all my songs on that record done the way they're supposed to be done." Van was referring to **Astral Weeks**.

Greil Marcus lived in the Berkeley Hills in a palatial home. It is fit for a corporate mogul. He is also America's foremost intellectual rock critic. Van Morrison is the son of an electrician. Marcus has a University of California, Berkley PhD. Morrison dropped out of school at fourteen. John Wasserman, the late San Francisco Chronicle entertainment editor, recalled listening to Morrison and Marcus backstage. Wasserman observed: "They talked to each other but each one had no idea what the other said."

WARNER BROTHERS RENTS THE WHISKEY A GO GO TO PROMOTE VAN: IT BACKFIRES

Warner Brothers and A and M Records decided to rent the Whiskey A Go Go to bring Gram Parsons and the Flying Burrito Brothers into the mainstream. Warner reasoned Morrison would benefit from being paired with this up and coming country rock band. The intimate relationship with the audience at the Whiskey was the perfect venue to impress reporters. The diminutive stage and the cage for the go go dancers made for a showcase venue. Van wasn't the headliner. He vowed to do what he could to wow the crowd.

The Whiskey A Go Go had a policy of two or three bands playing nightly to draw a varied crowd. The first week in February 1969 was to showcase the country-rock sound of the Flying Burrito Brothers. Why did Warner decide to book Van Morrison for a series of shows from February 5 through 9th, 1969? Warner may have believed the Sunset Strip would be the place to take Van into the commercial mainstream.

When Van came on stage at the Whiskey A Go Go the shows were well paced, carefully crafted and the audience increased nightly. To the audience's surprise there were only two backing musicians. The word was out on the Sunset Strip. There was a new Van Morrison.

The Whiskey A Go Go shows were interesting ones. They provided Van with the means to not only experiment with the **Astral Weeks** material live, but it gave him the opportunity to gauge the audience reaction. It didn't take long for Van to realize a five or six-piece rock and roll band was necessary to maintaining his career.

Van played the Whiskey A Go Go in 1966 with Them. Now, three years later, he saw it as a testing ground for his new sound. The ad for the show by a young Detroit artist, Dennis Loren, had Morrison as the headliner. Van realized if he opened the show he could play for as long as he desired. The crowds with their California cool often ignored the bands.

Jim Morrison and Van Morrison onstage at the Whiskey-a-Go-Go, jamming on "Gloria" 1966. (Photo by George Rodriguez)

These sets were an excellent opportunity for Morrison to showcase his avant-garde music. The country-rock types were surprised to see Van standing on stage with John Payne on flute and sax and Tom Kielbania on bass. They wanted a rock and roll band. They heard the songs from **Astral Weeks**. The Whiskey A Go Go staff was mystified. How well was Van received? There was a quiet reverence. There was interest. Or perhaps it was California cool.

This Whiskey A Go Go gig was one of Morrison's strangest performances. When he played an hour beyond his allotted time, the Whiskey management simply smiled and sold more liquor. The Flying Burrito Brothers didn't care; they were too busy partying backstage. Michael Vosse, an A and R person for A and M Records, did his best to get Morrison offstage. It didn't work.

The flute, bass and saxophone were a far cry from Them's "Here Comes The Night" or "Gloria." They complained about the lack of intelligible lyrics. Van found that weird. He made an artistic transition that no one, except Greil Marcus, understood.

VAN AND THE ARTISTIC TRANSITION AND LEAD BELLY

By March 1969, Van was in the midst of an artistic transition. He realized his ability to continue as a major recording artist depended upon producing a series of hit records. He was upset Warner Brothers paid so little attention to his new demos. Van believed he had new commercial tunes. Van said these new tunes would place him on the **Billboard** Hot 100. He was right. The management hierarchy at Warner did not agree. This further strained his relationship with the Schwaid-Merenstein production-management team. Then in-house producers were assigned to Morrison. This upset him.

There was talk inside Warner of having Morrison cover tunes for a folk album. Warner paid very little attention to his original compositions. He said he wouldn't cover other artists. Warner had no idea Van was no longer interested in commercial folk music. This is one of the contradictions in Morrison's approach to music. He was so broadly based in musical styles he couldn't be categorized.

He informed Warner Lead Belly was his idea of the perfect folk singer. He said he was not the new Lead Belly. No one at Warner seemed to understand. They didn't care about Van's interest in Huddie Ledbetter better known as Lead Belly. They should have paid attention. By the mid-1970s Morrison's covers of Lead Belly "John Henry" and "Western Union" drew small, appreciative audiences.

In numerous interviews, Van paid tribute to Lead Belly's influence. He also did so in song. In "Cleaning Windows," Morrison sings: "Lead Belly and Blind Lemon on the street where I was born."

What did Morrison see in Lead Belly? He equated his music with the essence of the blues. Van also identified these songs with Irish music. When the **Philosopher's Stone** was released, Lead Belly's covers were a quixotic look at a Morrison influence. He recorded some of these songs in 1975. They weren't released until 1998.

By the spring of 1969, Van had written a large number of new songs while producing rough demos. One song in particular, "Domino," had strong commercial possibilities. As Van toured and performed in the spring and summer of 1969, there was not the same concert approach as there had been with "Gloria," "Here Comes The Night" or "Brown Eyed Girl." He continued to experiment with up-tempo songs. He realized these were the easiest to place on the **Billboard** Top 40.

THE NEW BAND AND COMMERCIAL MANIA

Van knew he had to write songs closer to the contemporary rock and roll sound to last commercially. He hired a six-man band. The maudlin strains in **Astral Weeks** gave way to traditional rock and roll. Van's new band played music akin to the Marin County boogie-woogie style. The sounds of Commander Cody and the Lost Planet Airmen, Clover, the Youngbloods, the Quicksilver Messenger Service and the New Riders of the Purple Sage was the Marin musical groove. It was youthful piano virtuoso, Mitch Woods and His Red-Hot Mamas, who intrigued Morrison. When Woods arrived in Marin County, as a twenty-one-year-old piano protégé, he quickly united with singer Gracie Glassman. Their act intrigued Van. Woods' originality and ability to adapt to old time blues and rock and roll influences with a boogie-woogie piano beat drew large crowds. Other groups like Stoneground and Alice Stuart and Snake were also in their embryo stages. They all had a rock-blues sound. These diverse musical acts helped Van find his musical niche. "I came to Marin County and found all this musical energy," guitarist Chris Michie remarked, "and I saw Van at local shows long before I played with him."

Suddenly there was a honky-tonk, good time quality to Morrison's music. As he experimented with new musical ideas, Warner Brothers management realized he had hit record possibilities. He still liked to play material from **Astral Weeks**. In concert, "Cyprus Avenue" was a favorite. He increasingly combined traditional rock and roll with poetic lyrics. A new and more complicated Morrison emerged. These changes and his evolving artistic outlook perplexed Warner executives. They tried to classify his sound. They wanted him to produce the same type of music for each future release. He resisted. One day in a meeting with the Warner brain trust, Ostin talked about Gary Puckett's success on a rival label. Van looked on in astonishment.

They just didn't get it. He wouldn't follow their dictates. Shortly after this discussion Puckett's hits ended. Van made his point. He would never be the flavor of the month.

In this hectic atmosphere, Van put together the material for **Moondance**. While he was on the road, he paid close attention to of all people Elvis Presley. Somewhere he read about the Sweet Inspirations, who backed Presley in his Las Vegas shows. Van hired three backup singers Judy Clay, Emily Houston and Jackie Verdell to provide the hard driving rhythm and blues back-up that made the February 1970 **Moondance** album a dramatic departure from **Astral Weeks**.

Judy Clay's hit record with Billy Vera, "Country Woman, City Man," impressed Van. He hoped to use her soul-oriented backup vocals to augment his sound. When she stepped into the studio with Morrison, Judy Clay had little knowledge of his music. "I couldn't believe it, Van was literally a one take, in concert artist in the studio," Clay continued. "He has an extraordinary level of his talent." Judy Clay recalled Morrison was easy to work with, she couldn't believe the stories that he was difficult. Touché.

Mitch Woods: Boogie-Woogie Piano Legend
(Photo by Jay O'Neil)

IF IT'S JUNE IT MUST NOT BE TIME FOR A FOLLOW UP ALBUM

By June 1969, Van was working diligently on a new album. He didn't like the idea of a follow up LP to **Astral Weeks**. At least not an album that went in the same direction. Morrison was intent upon maximizing his music. Warner found out there was more than one Van Morrison.

The Warner Brothers hierarchy let Van know he was expected to turn out a decidedly commercial product. He balked. In the midst of these discussions, the Schwaid-Merenstein production team gave up dealing with Morrison. Thing got worse when Ted Templeman was brought in as the house producer. They argued from the moment the collaboration began. Templeman vowed never to work again with Van. The differences were over production, as well as the length of songs and the type of tunes. One Warner executive remarked: "They couldn't decide on Coke or Pepsi, so the music was even more of a problem."

Morrison didn't understand the necessity of completing a three-minute hit record. One of his strongest 1969 songs "Listen to The Lion" was too lengthy for release, Templeman remarked to David Gans. This song from the **St Dominic's Preview** album initially was recorded for **Moondance**. The reason is it was eleven minutes. In 1971 Van re-cut "Listen To The Lion" with Van playing guitar alongside Ronnie Montrose with Connie Kay on drums and Gary Mallaber handling percussion and vibraphone. After two takes it was decided that the recording with the live vibes and Morrison playing guitar was the best take. Ritchie Yorke remarked: "Van used his voice so superbly … it seemed to become part of the instrumentation…." "Listen To The Lion," Johnny Rogan argues "re-creates the sound of an unleashed lion within himself." Van considers the song sacred. When he finished the 2008 **Astral Weeks Live** show, he used the tune for an encore. The title was altered to "Listen To The Lion-The Lion Speaks."

In 2005, in an interview with Nigel Williamson, Van looked back upon how and why he wrote "Listen To The Lion." He was reading a great deal of material on the Phoenicians. They became the inspiration for this song. Van reminisced how the Phoenicians had lions carved on their boats when they landed in Ireland. This inspired him to write the song. Templeman thought Van was nuts.

THE ODYSSEY OF THE 1969 SUMMER

"Van Morrison was in a class by himself," Tommy Boyce continued. "I knew that our songs and some of the song factory writers at the Brill Building were done. It was a new day." The singer-songwriter still dominated the industry. The spotlight was increasingly on the artist.

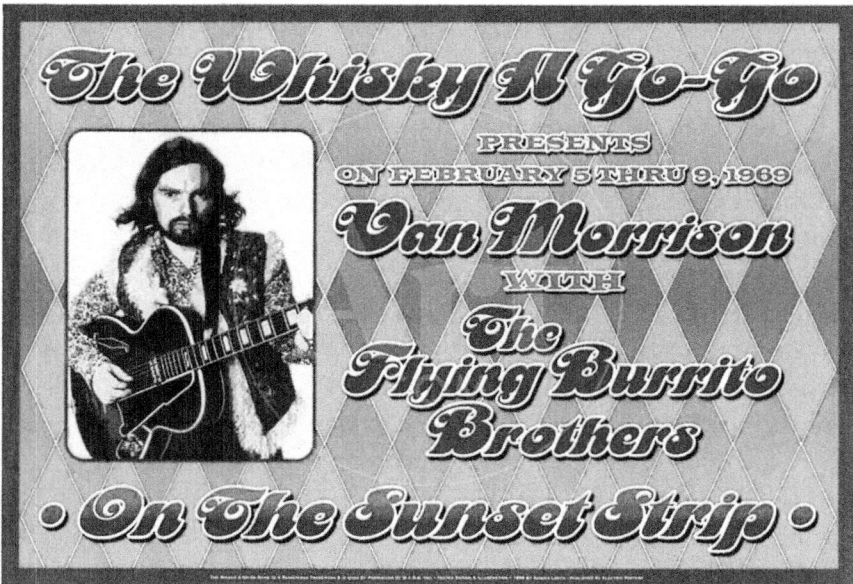

Van Morrison at the Whiskey A-Go-Go
(By Dennis Loren)

Van was making progress. He was getting his future in-concert act in place in small clubs. He wrote furtively. He worried that his contract with Warner Brothers might be terminated. Consequently, with Janet's inspiration, he wrote some of the best music of his career.

Throughout 1969 Van planned and carried out a program for his professional future in Woodstock. He had a careful sense of what he needed to do to be successful. When he went for lunch, he walked down a small road in Woodstock to the Sled Hill Café. This small Woodstock eatery was just a block off the main street. Van even performed there. He wrote many of his early 1970s songs in a booth at this small eatery. The Sled Hill Café staff dreaded Morrison's arrival. He was unfriendly and invariably grumpy. What was obvious to the staff was that he was under enormous pressure. Hit records were needed. They were coming.

As Van slid into a Sled Hill Café booth with his notebook, he searched for commercial themes. Unwittingly, myths and realities began to surround the Belfast Cowboy's career in the transition from the laid-back music of the late 1960s into the hit years of the early 1970s. Fame and fortune was about to intrude on his life in a big way.

BIBLIOGRAPHICAL SOURCES

For analysis of the **Astral Weeks** album see, for example, Brian Hinton, **Celtic Crossroads: The Art of Van Morrison** (London, 1997, revised edition 2000), chapter 4, Ritchie Yorke, **Van Morrison: Into the Music** (London, 1975), chapters 5-6, Clinton Heylin, **Can You Feel the Silence? Van Morrison, A New Biography** (London, 2002), pp. 162-202 and Howard A. DeWitt, **Van Morrison: The Mystics Music** (Fremont, 1983), pp. 27-33.

The complexity of the music business is revealed in Fred Goodman, **The Mansion On The Hill: Dylan, Young, Geffen, Springsteen And the Head On Collision of Rock And Commerce** (New York, 1998), pp. 30, 77, 102, 224, 263.

See Bob Sarlin, **Turn It Up (I Can't Hear The Music)** (New York, 1973) for an excellent interpretive essay on Van's growing musical reputation.

An excellent source for the late Them and early Van period is David Chance, "Van Morrison With the Monarchs/Them Chronology, 1968-1969", which appeared on the on the archived Van Morrison website http://web.archive.org/web/20091028131621/http://geocities.com/tracybjazz/hayward/van-the-man.info/reviews/1974ksan.html

See Clinton Heylin, **Bob Dylan: Behind The Shades Revisited** (New York, 2000), chapter 9 for a description of Woodstock.

Thomas C. Palmer, Jr., "John Payne: Astral Days," **Wavelength**, number 23, March 2000, pp. 8-14 is an important source for the **Astral Weeks** sessions and Lewis Merenstein's role in this cult album.

The **San Francisco Chronicle,** the **Los Angeles Times**, the **Berkeley Barb,** the **San Francisco Oracle,** the **Seattle Post Intelligencer**, the **Portland Oregonian,** the **Seattle Times**, the **New York Times** and the **Los Angeles Free Press** were consulted for this chapter. Equally important was the Belfast based **City Week**, which occasionally reported on Morrison's American journey.

In Belfast Mervyn Solomon provided a great deal of material on how Van handled the transition to a solo act and dealt with the fame of the **Astral Weeks** album.

Mark Naftalin provided some information on this period as did Corky Siegel and Chris Michie.

See Stan Cornyn with Paul Scanlon, **Exploding The Highs, Hits, Hype, Heroes and Hustlers Of The Warner's Music Group** (New York, 2003), passim for the intricate management tactics that drove Morrison into a frenzy.

Dan Bourgoise of Bug Music and Harry Balk, Del Shannon's producer, explained a great deal about the industry in extensive conversations. A lengthy conversation with Opal Louis Nations on the nature of British rock and roll and the transition to the American marketplace helped this chapter.

Johnny Rogan, **Van Morrison: No Surrender** (London, 2005), chapter 14 was useful to reconstructing the events surrounding 1969.

For Van's comments on "The Lion This Time," see Nigel Williamson, "2005 Interview With Van Morrison," The archived Van Morrison website.
http://web.archive.org/web/20130628140615/http://geocities.com/tracybjazz/hayward/van-the-man.info/reviews/2005june.html

Happy Traum and Tom Pacheco helped to sort out Van's living period in Woodstock. Chris Michie related some stories that Morrison told about the Woodstock days. Some comments from John Platania helped the chapter.

Tony Dey provided some important material for this chapter.

See informative review of the **Gypsy Soul: Lost Demos From A Classic Period** bootleg and the analysis of its cuts on the archived Van

Morrison website http://www.oocities.org/tracybjazz/hayward/van-the-man.info/discography/gypsy.html

A 1980s interview with Judy Clay added important material to this chapter. Art Siegel was an important source on Van's transition to Warner Brothers and his subsequent musical changes.

An interview with Tommy Boyce when I was working on a Del Shannon book led to some interesting comments on Van Morrison.

On Van and the Whiskey A Go Go appearance see, David N. Meyer, **Twenty Thousand Roads: The Ballad of Gram Parsons and His Cosmic American Music** (New York, 2007), p. 285. Ray Ruff also talked at length about his experiences at the Whiskey A Go Go.

Alice Stuart and Sal Valentino added information on this period in Morrison's life and the Marin County rock and roll scene in general. An interview with Judy Clay was important to this chapter. Ron Sexton added some important conversations as did John Goddard of Village Music.

For Andy Wickham's place in the record business see, for example, **Billboard**, June 24, 1967, August 18, 1973, September 1, 1973, February 11, 1978 and January 22, 1983 and John Collis, **Van Morrison: Inarticulate Speech of the Heart** (Boston, 1996). Pp. 91-92. Also, for background on Andy Wickham see, Andrew Loog Oldham, **Stoned: A Memoir of London In The 1960s** (New York, 2001), passim.

For a brief mention of Ian Ralfini's influence see, for example, "Van Morrison Returns To EMI With Live Astral Weeks," **Jambase.com**, December 22, 2008. https://www.jambase.com/article/van-morrison-returns-to-emi-with-live-astral-weeks

For Stan Cornyn at Warner Brothers and his influence upon Van Morrison, see, for example, Stan Cornyn, **Exploding: The Highs, Hits, Hype, Heroes, And Hustlers of The Warner Music Group** (New York, 2002), passim.

Van's comments on Lead Belly can be seen at a Royal Albert Hall concert, see, Robin Denselow, "Van Morrison: 'People Who Say Others Are Difficult Are Usually Difficult'," **The London Guardian**, June 4, 2015. https://www.theguardian.com/music/2015/jun/04/van-morrison-people-who-say-others-difficult-are-difficult-themselves-lead-belly-lonnie-donegan

For "Listen To The Lion," see, for example, Ritchie Yorke, **Van Morrison: Listen To The Music** (London, 1975), p. 96 and Johnny

Rogan, **Van Morrison: No Surrender** (London, 2005), p. 276 Also see Toby Creswell, **1001 Songs: The Great Songs Of All Time And The Artists, Stories and Secrets Behind them** (New York, 2006). For other versions of "Listen To The Lion," see the 2006 DVD **Van Morrison: Live At Montreux 1980/1974** and the limited three CD compilation **Still On Top-The Greatest Hits**.

For an interesting look at Morrison's music inspired by "Listen To The Lion," see Andy Whitman, "Listening To Old Voices: Van Morrison, the Lion In Winter," **Paste**, November 14, 2005. https://www.pastemagazine.com/articles/2005/11/listening-to-old-voices-van-morrison.html

When Whitman gets to "The Lion This Winter" he observes of Van's redoing of "Listen To The Lion" as "the lion in winter is on the loose." That is Van is now sixty but still at the top of his musical game.

CHAPTER 13

MYTHS AND REALITIES OF THE TRANSITION FROM THE LATE 1960s TO THE EARLY 1970s

"My heart beats faster and faster,

And I say To The Drunk by the door

I'm Like You; my life's a disaster,

And I Can't Go Home anymore,"

SERGEI ESENIN

"Too Many Myths, People just Assuming Things That Aren't True."

VAN MORRISON

"If the listener catches the wavelength of what I am saying or singing, or gets whatever point whatever line means, … I guess as a writer I may have done a day's work."

VAN MORRISON IN CONVERSATION WITH RANDY LEWIS, 2009

The transition in Van Morrison's career from the late 1960s into the early 1970s brought dramatic change. This was a period of enormous personal growth. It was reflected in his music. The bad news is it was a strain on his marriage. The music business brought fame, fortune and grief. He went into periodic rages, according to his wife Janet. She needed to find a calm life.

Janet told close friends she couldn't endure the frequent outbursts. He was never a violent man. Nor was he an abuser. He wrote new songs constantly. He was in his home studio every spare moment. He was overly concerned with his career. He was a person who wanted success. It drove him mercilessly. His marriage was a casualty to fame and fortune.

He had a plan for his career making compromise difficult. His past dealings with Phil Solomon, Sir Edward Lewis and Bert Berns soured Morrison on the music industry. He paid close attention to business. The industry prompted Morrison to write songs that showed his disaffection with the business. Such phrases as "copycats ripped off my songs," as well as "professional jealousy started a rumor" suggests his innate hostility.

Van evolved from a lead singer associated with the Irish band, Them, into a musical icon. Fame was a bitter pill. This was largely due to his first Warner Brothers album **Astral Weeks**. The critical acclaim for this LP didn't propel sales. It brought Morrison to the precipice of fame. When the genius tag was attached to **Astral Weeks**, Morrison's music became the stuff of legend.

Being a legend translated into a livable wage. A music publishing company, a home with an affordable mortgage, a home recording studio and a Mercedes filled the Morrison household. A horse named Domino and other assorted investments mitigated the pain of dealing with the industry. But money remained a key factor. He believed Phil Solomon, Sir Edward Lewis and Bert Berns had cheated him. According to Mervyn Solomon, this wasn't the case. "I called Sir Edward and asked him to sign the boys," Mervyn Solomon continued. "Van never seemed to understand there were expenses associated with his career." Before his death Sir Edward Lewis remarked to me: "I spoke with Mervyn Solomon about the boys in Belfast, I wasn't impressed but as a favor to Mervyn I signed the group. I can't understand Van Morrison's criticism of Decca; we did what we could for the boys." The problem, as Van saw it, was the lack of a basic understanding of rock and roll music by Sir Edward Lewis.

There were other problems. Van was upset the Rolling Stones received most of the recognition and promotion at Decca. Morrison watched as the pugnacious and insulting Allen Klein bullied Sir Edward Lewis. Some say the Belfast Cowboy learned some valuable lessons witnessing Klein renegotiating a Stones contract.

Another problem was Van didn't like the slogans the label placed on him. Such terms as "a musical genius" or "a cult artist" infuriated him. It didn't matter. He was stuck with these tags. He worried fame eroded his creative freedom.

There was also the matter of Morrison's personality. He didn't suffer fools very well. He was outspoken. The Belfast Cowboy made enemies. He didn't like to socialize. He became increasingly reclusive. With his complicated personality, relationships were fragile. His managers, journalists and business friends find him an on again and off again personality. This partially explains the cataclysmic changes in Morrison's life.

FROM 1968 TO 1972 CATACLYSMIC CHANGES

From 1968 to 1972, Van experienced personal and professional growth. He signed with Bert Berns and Bang Records. He had a hit with "Brown Eyed Girl." He got married. He signed with Warner Brothers. He had a daughter Shana. Not a bad set of accomplishments.

Van moved from New York, to Boston, to Woodstock and finally settled in Fairfax, California. Eventually, he moved to Mill Valley where he still owns a home. Shana lives in it.

Personally, Van remained shy and introverted. He doesn't like crowds. He hates to perform at venues where there is talking or excessive drinking. He quit playing San Francisco's Great American Music Hall because some drunks sat in line all day for tickets, and then they interrupted his concert with requests.

He complained, in an interview with Al Jones for Danish radio, about the difficulty of living in Woodstock. He said the area became too commercial. "So, there was like two Woodstock's," Van continued. "One of them was sort of the commercial entity." It was the other Woodstock Van loved. It is a calm and quiet lifestyle. It appealed to him. He loved the lack of pretension. By the spring of 1971 Marin

County was a refuge. He lived in Fairfax and later in Mill Valley. It was the perfect place to craft hit records and play local clubs.

THE HIT RECORDS: WHAT THEY MEANT TO MORRISON'S CAREER

When Van recorded a series of hit records, he did so to establish longevity in the music business. In a period of five years, he evolved from a rhythm and blues singer with a penchant for a garage band sound into a hit making artist. He wrote mystical tunes. These songs eventually turned him into a hit-making singer-songwriter. With songs like "Domino," "Wild Night," "Moondance," "Jackie Wilson Said (I'm In Heaven When You Smile)," "Sweet Thing," "And It Stoned Me" and "Old Old Woodstock," he established a commercial portfolio. He was a multi-talented performer who desired obscurity.

Van Morrison: Boston
(Photo by AJ Sullivan)

In 1970 **Moondance's** success was a curse and a blessing. This was the first album guaranteeing regular royalties. He also appeared in larger concert venues for bigger paydays. **Moondance** gave Morrison some clout and power in the Warner hierarchy. It turned out to be a mixed blessing. He had finally gotten some control of his product.

Much of Van's energy in this period was devoted to breaking the contract with Schwaid-Merenstein. His manager, Mary Martin, was a witting accomplice. She quickly helped Van gain his artistic freedom. Then he fired her.

Martin was hostile to Schwaid-Merenstein. She saw them as the old guard. The type of rock and roll management team that worried about the profit line not the music. In a shrewd management move, Martin guaranteed Van's next album would be radio friendly. To their credit Schwaid-Merenstein announced that they had enough of Morrison and wished him luck. They released him.

WHAT THE EARLY 1970S MEANT TO VAN

The irony is fame and fortune turned Morrison into an increasingly reclusive personality. After achieving a string of pop hits in the early 1970s, he retreated to his Fairfax, California home to plan his lengthy, productive career. He searched for a means to prolong his music. That is to create a musical direction not dependent upon hit records.

He pined for a normal life. This didn't seem to be in the cards. The demands from Warner Brothers, the press and his fans placed Morrison into a difficult position. He couldn't satisfy everyone. So he satisfied himself.

As the strain on his marriage led to divorce, Morrison needed to take a break. From 1973 to 1977 he didn't retire, as some have suggested, he took a relaxed approach to recording and touring. The royalties from the first three Warner albums provided a comfortable lifestyle. He recovered from his divorce, financially speaking, but the emotional trauma of his wife's departure was another matter.

There was another reason for the period of retirement. He needed to put his business affairs in order. After Mary Martin re-negotiated his Warner contract, he had the money and the time to pursue his craft. Then he fired her. As **Tupelo Honey** followed Moondance, this gave Morrison a place in the pantheon of rock and roll stars.

By the time **Tupelo Honey** was released, Van called it a series of "leftovers." After co-producing **Tupelo Honey**, Ted Templeman, vowed he would never work with Morrison. When **Tupelo Honey** was released in October 1971, Van had worked himself into frenzy. He was spending too much time in the recording studio, too many days on the road, and he had little in the way of a personal life. He was exhausted. He was in the Warner Brothers prison. He wasn't happy about it.

BIBLIOGRAPHICAL SOURCES

For the aftermath of the **Astral Weeks** album see, for example, Brian Hinton, **Celtic Crossroads: The Art of Van Morrison** (London, 1997, revised edition 2000), chapter 4, Ritchie Yorke, **Van Morrison: Into the Music** (London, 1975), chapters 5-6, Clinton Heylin, **Can You Feel the Silence? Van Morrison, A New Biography** (London, 2002), pp. 162-202 and **Howard A. DeWitt, Van Morrison: The Mystics Music** (Fremont, 1983), pp. 27-33.

See Bob Sarlin, **Turn It Up (I Can't Hear The Music)** (New York, 1973) for an excellent interpretive essay on Van's growing musical reputation. Sarlin does an excellent job pointing out how and why Morrison's music was so much more poetic than his peers.

An excellent source for the late Them and early Van period is David Chance, "Van Morrison With the Monarchs/Them Chronology, 1968-1969," on the archived Van Morrison website http://web.archive.org/web/20091028131621/http://geocities.com/tracybjazz/hayward/van-the-man.info/reviews/1974ksan.html

See Clinton Heylin, **Bob Dylan: Behind The Shades Revisited** (New York, 2000), chapter 9 for a description of Woodstock.

Thomas C. Palmer, Jr., "John Payne: Astral Days," Wavelength, number 23, March 2000, pp. 8-14 is an important source for the **Astral Weeks** sessions and Lewis Merenstein's role in this cult album.

The **San Francisco Chronicle**, the **Los Angeles Times**, the **Berkeley Barb**, the **Seattle Post Intelligencer**, the **Seattle Times**, the **New York Times** and the **Los Angeles Free Press** were consulted for this chapter. Equally important was the Belfast based **City Week**, which occasionally reported on Morrison's American journey.

In Belfast, Mervyn Solomon provided a great deal of material on how Van handled the transition to a solo act and dealt with the fame of the **Astral Weeks** album.

Mark Naftalin provided some information on this period, as did Corky Siegel and Chris Michie. Some of the key conclusions on Morrison and his personality were provided in interview with folk cum blues legend Alice Stuart.

See Stan Cornyn with Paul Scanlon, **Exploding The Highs, Hits, Hype, Heroes and Hustlers Of The Warner's Music Group** (New York, 2003), passim for the intricate management tactics that drove Morrison into a frenzy.

Dan Bourgoise and Harry Balk explained a great deal about the industry in extensive conversations.

Johnny Rogan, **Van Morrison: No Surrender** (London, 2005), chapter 14 was useful to reconstructing the events surrounding 1969. For the early 1970s a number of key interviews with musicians and friends close to Morrison helped.

For Van's comments on "The Lion This Time," see Nigel Williamson, "2005 Interview With Van Morrison," The archived Van Morrison website http://web.archive.org/web/20130628140615/http://geocities.com/tracybjazz/hayward/van-the-man.info/reviews/2005june.html

John Platania offered some important information and Tony Dey were helpful in Morrison's adjustment to California. Also, John Goddard of Village Music provided local color and Art Siegel helped to identify key changes in the local music scene.

A series of interviews with Sir Edward Lewis in London helped this chapter. Also see Victor Bockris, **Keith Richards: The Unauthorized Biography** (London, 2002) for useful information on Decca and Sir Edward Lewis.

A series of interviews with John Lee Hooker at his Redwood City, California home helped to clarify the material in this chapter. John Lee spent two afternoons telling me about his interaction with and love for Morrison. Guitar Mac was an important source providing me entre to Hooker and it was Guitar Mac who pointed out how close Van and John Lee were over the years.

❦

CHAPTER 14

WOODSTOCK'S LEGACY AND THE PEOPLE

"It's taken me twenty years before I really starting working with music."

VAN MORRISON IN CONVERSATION WITH PAUL VINCENT

"Van found peace and contentment in Woodstock."

TOM PACHECO IN CONVERSATION WITH HOWARD A. DEWITT

"Well I get up in the morning and I get my brief. I go out and stare at the world in complete disbelief…. There are hypocrites and parasites and people that drain."

VAN MORRISON'S SONG "WHY MUST I ALWAYS EXPLAIN?"

❦

Woodstock's New York countryside influence was a positive one. It formed the basis of Van Morrison's early 1970s songwriting. It helped him refocus his life. His life style, combined with the country ambiance, prompted his creativity to reach new heights. Woodstock's influences crept into Morrison's songs in many ways. He had written or finished old tunes for **Moondance**. The hits of the early 1970s were crafted in this rural New York retreat. Van wrote furtively. In the spring of 1971, Van moved to California. For a year and a half Woodstock was the perfect please to encapsulate his burgeoning creativity.

Van's wife, Janet Planet, said she hoped her husband and Bob Dylan would become best friends. That didn't happen. What took place is Van bonded, like Dylan, with other musicians in this fertile musical climate. New ideas! New musical directions! New themes! These were the rewards for the move to Woodstock. The legacy it left Morrison was in his new maturity and the depth of his lyrics.

VAN'S MOVE TO WOODSTOCK, THE SOUND OUT FESTIVAL AND OLD OLD WOODSTOCK

Why did Van and Janet move permanently to Woodstock? It was a combination of inexpensive rent, cheap food, the presence of local musicians and the love of the countryside. Or was it? Did the move bring Van and Janet momentary happiness? Did it provide added stability? Who knows! They loved Woodstock. They made friends. Janet purchased an old car to drive Van around the scenic area.

Happy Traum remembers Van performed at Woodstock's less-publicized 1968 Sound Out Festival. There was, Traum believed, another draw to the area. Van had talked to other musicians about Dylan and The Band. He moved to the area largely due to the local musicians. Others spoke of seeing him in town before the infamous Woodstock Festival in 1969.

The 1968 Woodstock Sound Out was the brainchild of a local roofer John "Jocko" Moffitt. He was also an amateur drummer. He had the connections, the organizational skills and a local farmer's field, which wasn't even in Woodstock, to promote a laid back and free festival. He envisioned less than a thousand people in a bucolic pasture.

The 1968 Woodstock Sound Out was the model for Woodstock. The Sound Out featured Paul Butterfield, Tim Hardin, Happy and Artie Traum, the Colwell-Winfield Blues Band and an overjoyed Van Morrison. Michael Lang, the Woodstock Festival promoter, said the Sound Out shows were a precursor to the infamous Woodstock gathering.

The lyrics to "Old Old Woodstock" offer important clues. Van sings of the "cool breezes" that "blow all around your coat." While weather is generally not a hit record topic, Van said the countryside inspired him. He refers to the downtown as "old Woodstock" and as

Tom Pacheco remarked: "Nothing was better than hanging out in downtown Woodstock."

While in Woodstock, Van loved to walk. His house was up on a hill overlooking the city. As he sings about walking around town, it is a window into his increasingly mellow personality. Life was good. His writing was superb. Fame was around the corner.

SMALL TOWN TALK: WOODSTOCK'S MYSTERY AND LURE

What was Woodstock's mystery and lure? Barney Hoskyns' **Small Town Talk: Bob Dylan, The Band, Van Morrison, Janis Joplin, Jimi Hendrix & Friends In The Wild Years of Woodstock** answered many of the questions. The title, "Small Town Talk" was adapted from a song written by Rick Danko and Louisiana song legend Bobby Charles. It is an in-depth analysis of how and why the Woodstock music scene grew into a mainstream rock and roll phenomenon.

The depth and breadth of musicians living in Woodstock was amazing. Such big names as Charles Mingus, David Bowie, Jimi Hendrix, the members of The Band and Paul Butterfield called the area home. Many lived here for only a brief period. Visitors like George Harrison found the tree lined streets and local shops a welcome relief from New York.

When The Band released **Music From Big Pink** fans identified West Saugerties in the liner notes with Woodstock. The stampede was on. The fans arrived looking for rock stars. The Bearsville General Store was where everyone shopped. It was not uncommon to see a member of The Band going in or coming out of the store.

Woodstock didn't give birth to Americana music. It publicized this form. Van Morrison drank in the influences. Some artists, like Todd Rundgren and Jackson Browne, didn't fit into the Woodstock milieu.

You could get a hard liquor drink for fifty cents downtown as an eighty-year-old woman played Beatle songs with George Harrison and Bob Dylan sitting at the piano bar. Booze, not drugs, dominated the early Woodstock scene. Then by 1970 cocaine and heroin ruled the local music scene. It was in Albert Grossman's recording studio that some of the best, if often not very commercial, music was produced.

The proximity of Albert Grossman's Bearsville recording studio in nearby Bearsville was another important draw. Grossman also built a restaurant there. He had so many business interests he lost his desire to manage Dylan. A series of lawsuits over copyrights estranged Dylan and Grossman. No one could deny Grossman's influence on late 1960s and early 1970s music.

Jesse Winchester made his debut album there. The Band's third album **Stage Fright** was cut in Bearsville. Ian and Sylvia came down from Canada to record. Dylan wrote "Bringing It All Back Home," in a barely furnished room that looked like a dungeon above Woodstock's Café Espresso. Dylan said Woodstock was the place where: "We stop the clouds, turn time back and inside out." This comment explains the draw Woodstock provided for the fledgling, as well as the established artist.

WOODSTOCK AND THE BYRDCLIFFE ARTS COLONY

When Van Morrison visited Woodstock's Byrdcliffe area, he found an artist's colony with America's oldest Arts and Crafts Club holding weekly meetings. Since 1903, the 1500 acres of land that is home to the art colony, provided a haven for recalcitrant artists. It was also for a time home to Bob Dylan.

For Morrison the significance of Byrdcliffe was immediate. Van was intrigued by the concept of utopian living. Janet was interested in the arts and crafts movement. Woodstock appeared perfect. "Solace for songwriting," Van remarked.

The Byrdcliffe Theater offered plays with actors like Joanne Woodward. Lee Marvin had his first role in the area in a stage play. There was an active dance troupe. It was inspired by a performance years previous by Isadora Duncan. In the past, educator John Dewey and author Thomas Mann were frequent visitors. Van and Janet embraced the intellectual aura of the Byrdcliffe Arts Colony.

Byrdcliffe inspired Morrison to create lyrical poetic images. Living in Woodstock changed Van's songs as well as in life. It had a profound impact upon his psyche. There was also an unseen influence from singer-songwriter Fred Neil who lived in Woodstock. When Neil left in the mid-1970s, the Woodstock era lost its rock and roll luster.

Neil had a series of brief conversations with Van in local coffee shops. They talked about the difficulties of the music business. When Morrison moved to Marin County, he met one of Neil's musical friends in a Mill Valley coffee shop. That person turned out to be John Cipollina. Van discovered Neil recorded with the Quicksilver Messenger Service. He loved QMS's music.

When I interviewed Happy Traum, a folk musician living in Woodstock, he still had a handmade poster of the Sound Out Festival on his office wall. The 1968 Woodstock Sound Out Festival, Traum recalled: "Van came to the first Woodstock Festival and gave a great performance. He relocated to the area shortly after this festival."

JANET PLANET ON WOODSTOCK

Janet remarked to Louis Sahagun her daughter, Shana, was born in three feet of snow in Woodstock. "Given that it took a mile of narrow road to get down our hill," Janet continued, "a recurrent nightmare was that Van would have to deliver our baby." A week after Shana was born Janet and her daughter were on a three-week tour with her husband. Van wouldn't go on the road without her. She recalled how quickly Woodstock changed as busloads of fans emerged to make life hell for the locals.

"By then," Janet told Sahagun, "our life together was very traumatic and horrible." Janet was at a crossroads. "I couldn't stand any more of this rage as my daily reality. I worried about its impact on the children."

There was a quirky flower child persona to the young Janet Planet. When they moved to Marin County, she had a baby sitter who told her that California might fall into the ocean due to an earthquake. She demanded they pack up and leave for New Mexico. Van complied with this craziness. In her interview with Sahagun, Planet remarked it was Van's time not hers. "Looking back, it all seems part of a 'fabled love lived'...." Planet concluded.

It was a tough time for the young girl calling herself Janet Planet. She recalled; "I couldn't reconcile the fragile dream with the emotional chaos which kept intruding and crashing everything down," Planet told Sahagun. The divorce was a casualty of those times.

In an interview with a **London Independent** reporter, Barry Egan, Janet talked at length about Woodstock. She said: "Van fully intended to become Dylan's best friend, but the whole time we were there, they never met." They would drive by Dylan's house. Van would stare plaintively at the gravel road. It was a strange ritual. Van loved it. Janet hated it. "He thought Dylan was the only contemporary worthy of his attention. But back then, Bob just wasn't interested in him," Janet concluded.

Barry Egan's article on Janet Planet was a hit piece to curry favor with the Belfast Cowboy. Then he interviewed the Belfast Cowboy. "For my own part, the Van I got to know some years ago socially bore scant resemblance to the nettlesome character Planet describes," Egan wrote. What Egan missed is he had a few brief encounters in the 1990s with Morrison then happily married to Michelle Rocca. Egan unfairly skewered Janet Planet. Van had this hapless reporter in the palm of his hand. He interviewed the star struck Egan.

Van asked Egan's girlfriend Sonja: "What's your sign?" She said: "Gemini." Van responded: "Jesus! That was my ex-wife's star sign! She was trouble." What is wrong with this story? Egan said the story took place at a dinner. Van doesn't go to dinner with journalists. He doesn't make small talk. It is a great story. It has little relationship to the truth or Morrison's life. This is what happens when a reporter, like Barry Egan, takes a 1998 interview that Janet did with the **Los Angeles Times'** Louis Sahagun and interprets it. The result is a form of hagiography appealing to Van Morrison.

THE MUSICAL INFLUENCES IN WOODSTOCK

The reflective creativity in and around Woodstock acted as a catalyst to Morrison's frenetic songwriting. Woodstock's bucolic countryside is reflected in Van's writing. He would walk down the country road where he and Janet lived for lunch. He would find one of the quaint downtown cafes. After copious amounts of coffee and after smoking a half of pack of cigarettes, he outlined half a dozen tunes. Over the next few years the Woodstock notebook turned into gold.

It was at the various coffee shops and eateries in Woodstock, and later in Marin County, Van carried his notebook and worked diligently on his early 1970s material. When he sang of "Gypsy Rose" and "Sweet Amarou" they were real people. He not only met them. He immortalized them in song. The musicians in and around Woodstock provided a musical legacy defining Morrison's early career. Marin County continued the songwriting bonanza.

Paul Butterfield settled into Woodstock in 1968. He was often seen about town with his trademark jeans and baggy sweater. From time to time, Van would run into Richard Bell who played piano with Janis Joplin's Full Tilt Boogie band. Bell, a Canadian, played with Ronnie Hawkins and the Hawks. He was a much sought after piano artist. When the Hawks moved to Woodstock and became "The Band," Bell followed them to this rustic New York community. Although he never recorded with Morrison, Bell talked music with him. He listened to Van at an impromptu acoustic gig at the Sled Hill Café. He was everywhere. He knew everybody.

Richard Bell was connected to the Ronnie Hawkins band. This interested Morrison. Such Hawkins's songs as "Mary Lou" were among Van's favorites. Van was not only intrigued by Bell; he found his music knowledge outstanding. As a piano player, Bell owed more to Jerry Lee Lewis than to current musical trends.

Richard Bell moved to Woodstock permanently after Janis Joplin died. He went on to become a replacement member in The Band. His relationship with Van remains a murky one. The reason is Bell lived for only a short time in Woodstock. Those who remembered Bell talking frequently to Van about music suspected they were discussing ways to incorporate the piano into Morrison's music.

John Platania was a significant musician in the Woodstock area. He was born near Woodstock and early on his band, Silver Byke, signed with Bang Records. He met Morrison in New York. Platania was the perfect guitarist for Morrison. He could play from the charts. He could also accompany Van simply following his musical direction. He began his career with Van as the guitarist on **Moondance**.

Later, he contributed songs to the 1997 **The Philosopher's Stone**. He played with Morrison's band at the Montreux Jazz Festivals in 1980, 2006 and 2007. He also co-wrote two songs with Van "Try For Sleep" and "There There Child." There are few artists who have lasted as long in Morrison's band. His talented guitar virtuosity, and his quiet nature are the reasons he survived in various Morrison aggregations. Platania has appeared on ten Morrison albums.

In Woodstock, Platania and Morrison played small bars as a duo. These small club-bar dates allowed Van to practice the **Astral Weeks** material for larger venue dates that seldom materialized. While Van performed some of the material from **Astral Weeks**, he never felt comfortable with it until the 2008 Hollywood Bowl shows. Peter Mills points out Platania's guitar work is an example of how to "keep things simple and make them work."

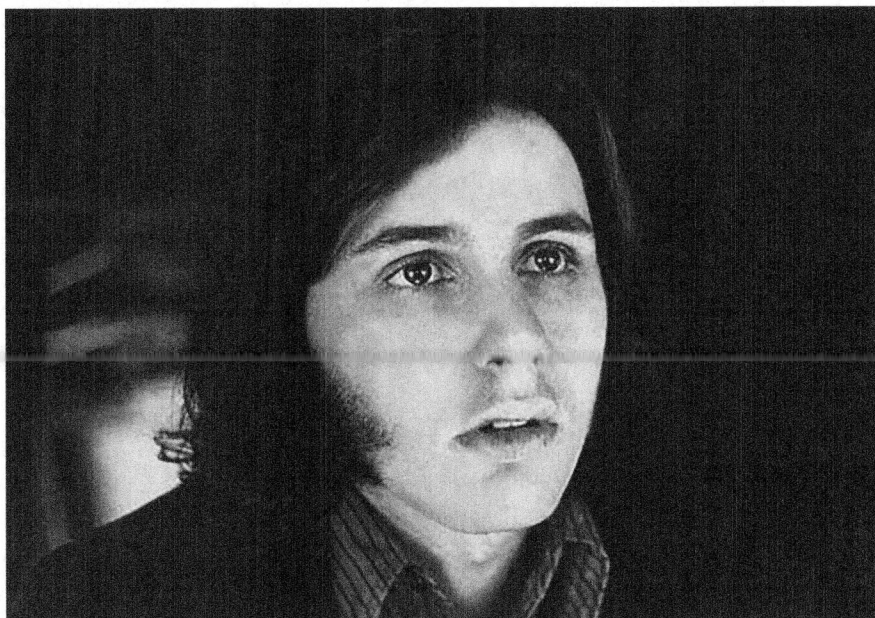

Gary Mallaber 1969
(Gary Mallaber Fan Photos)

THE GARY MALLABER FACTOR: A HIDDEN GENIUS

While living in Woodstock, Van worked extensively with Gary Mallaber. At the time Mallaber was playing in and around New York with Raven. A roadie gave Mallaber Van's **Astral Weeks** album. He loved it.

Gary Mallaber: "I decided to track him down, and I found that he was working in a folk club in New York on MacDougal Street. I went to see him play, and twenty people were there. I offered to sit in and to make a long story short, two months after that, we were making **Moondance**. We started rehearsing up at Van's house in Woodstock, ... a lot of the material was developed in the A&R studio."

Mallaber sought out Morrison and met him at Steve Paul's New York Club, The Scene. He was mesmerized by his talent. After watching Van perform at New York's fabled Café Au Go Go, he wanted to make music with him. What was it that caught Mallaber's attention? When he went to see Morrison in the New York clubs there were small crowds. One weekday concert showcase featured Van as well as the Holy Modal Rounders and two folk singers Cathy Smith and Tim Brimm. As Mallaber watched he saw Morrison's musical genius unfold, there were maybe twenty people in the club. That night Van hired Mallaber on the spot for the **Moondance** album.

When he played drums on **Moondance**, Mallaber commented: "Van was the kind of artist who really didn't worry about anything. He went at it more like a jazz recording." There was a level of understanding from Mallaber for Van's music. He was on the same wavelength.

Who was Gary Mallaber? He was born on October 11, 1946 in Buffalo, New York, and early in his education he trained for a life as a drummer and percussionist. In addition to drums, he plays a mean keyboard. He was a talented vocalist. His skill in the recording studio made him an in-demand session musician. He played with Bruce Springsteen, Peter Frampton, Poco, Paul Williams, Eddie Money, the Steve Miller Band and even backed up Kermit The Frog in the recording studio. He has also written and performed songs for more than thirty major Hollywood movies.

He appeared on six Van Morrison albums. He offered a musical backup Van loved. Mallaber's influence extends beyond the recording studio. He was from day one a professional musician who made good music deals. Wittingly or unwittingly, he was a major influence upon Morrison's developing music persona and emerging business skills.

When Mallaber moved to Woodstock, it was to work with Morrison. He began rehearsing for the **Moondance** album. "It was folk music, mixed with jazz," Mallaber commented. He was intrigued by Morrison's wide musical influences. He believed they "made Van's music so special." For a time Mallaber left Van to move to England where it was rumored George Harrison would sign his band, Raven, to the Apple label. This didn't materialize. Mallaber returned to play on the **St. Dominic's Preview**, the **Hard Nose The Highway** and the **Beautiful Vision** albums.

Van's California look

JOHN KLINGBERG AND THE MOONDANCE INTERLUDE

John Klingberg was a brilliant bass player who began his musical career in Dario and the Rainbows. In Boston he also played in the cult band Third World Raspberry. He was also in a cover band Randy and the Soul Survivors. He hooked up with local Woodstock musicians where he played in the Colwell-Winfield Blues Band. He played around Boston in cover bands in 1965-1966 after dropping out of the

Berklee School of Music. J. Geils considered Klingberg Boston's most accomplished bassist.

Like Van, Klingberg was shy. When he played with Van at various venues, he stood behind the speakers. That may be why Morrison loved the guy. He eventually left the music business after moving in with his girlfriend, Cathy, who had six children. In the early 1980s Klingberg lived in Austin attempting to break into the local music scene. That didn't work out. He moved to Oklahoma where he worked as a physical laborer in the oil fields. He passed away at thirty-nine. Cathy took his ashes and spread them on Tinker Street where they had lived in Woodstock. His work on **Moondance** remains the stuff of legend.

It was during the production of Van's third solo LP, **Moondance** the musical expertise of bass player John Klingberg stood out. As a member of the Colwell-Winfield Blues Band, Klingberg was no stranger to the studio. His soft electric bass added a great deal to a number of Van's songs. It was on "And It Stoned Me" Klingberg's bass set the stage for a beautiful song retaining a nostalgic feel.

Klingberg was more than a low-key personality. He was a perfect friend. He understood where Morrison was musically. Klingberg was on the same wavelength. His interest in the blues was such that he could talk at length with Morrison. He left the music business with a drug problem. Klingberg, like many musicians around Woodstock, was a local who hated the road. He despised the music business. He wanted a home life. A career as a professional musician wasn't in the cards.

The John Klingberg story is a tragic one. He was a talented musician who made the wrong choices. The Jack Schroer story followed the same tragic lines.

JACK SCHROER: SEVEN BRILLIANT ALBUMS WITH VAN AND BATTLING ADDICTION

Jack Schroer was one of the musicians closest to Van Morrison from the early Woodstock years until 1974. He first appeared on **Moondance**. Jack relocated to California when Van purchased his Fairfax home. While in California, Schroer toured with the New Riders of the Purple Sage, Boz Scaggs and Stoneground. He was an in-demand saxophonist. Like Mallaber and Klingberg, he was shy, quiet, and he wasn't interested in the spotlight. He was a musical prodigy that didn't feel comfortable talking about his scholarship offers from every major U.S. music university.

After studying at the Berklee College of Music in the Fall of 1963, Schroer moved to Boston where he performed in cover bands with John Klingberg. When Schroer met Morrison the saxophonist-playing musician moved to Woodstock stepping in as one of Morrison's closest musical cohorts.

When he relocated near Van in Marin County, the California landscape inspired his musical life. Schroer was recognized for his genius with the Caledonia Soul Orchestra. "I was a music professor," Nathan Rubin remarked, "but Jack had a way of cutting through the problems and he sounded wonderful behind Van."

Although Schroer appeared on seven LPs with Van, he continued to shun the spotlight. One of Schroer's rare interviews took place in February 1971 when Rick McGrath interviewed him along with Van and the band for the Vancouver, British Columbia counterculture newspaper **The Georgia Straight**.

The February 24, 1971 **Georgia Straight** was a free underground newspaper. The reporter, Rick McGrath, was treated fairly by Van and three members of the band. He couldn't understand why Van wasn't recording songs like "Brown Eyed Girl." Van was polite. He answered all his questions. The band couldn't believe the reporter's lack of knowledge about Morrison.

During this interview Schroer scolded McGrath for asking if he expected all the **Astral Weeks** songs to be the same. Van loved his friend stepping in and putting the reporter in his place. Van hated stupid questions. This interview was one where Dahaud Shaar, Van's drummer, also chimed in with the same observation. In 1971 Van's band was like him. They believed **Astral Weeks** could be performed in different ways. When the reporter asked how the band came together? John Platania looked at the reporter with exasperation. He had never heard such a stupid question. He commented: "I just came in and played." For once Van and the band turned the tables on a press that had no clue about Morrison. It was a sweet moment.

Schroer and Morrison talked music. It was Schroer who alerted Van to the 1973 solo Art Garfunkel album **Angel Clare**. From this LP, Van listened to and began performing "I Shall Sing." Schroer played saxophone on this album.

The tragedy of Jack Schroer's life was drug addiction. Drugs were a curse on his family. He married Connie Schroer, a flight attendant, and they moved to Albuquerque, New Mexico. He dropped out of music. He worked as a truck driver. His family moved to Albuquerque when he was nine and he graduated from high school there in 1963. He was an All-State musician who won a scholarship to the prestigious Berklee School of Music. There he met John Klingberg. This began the musical journey that killed him by fifty-one.

Schroer's wife, Connie, died the same year. They both battled drug addiction. Their son Sonny (John) Schroer passed away September 22, 2016 from an overdose of drugs and alcohol. He was thirty-one years old. He was an internationally acclaimed snowboarding instructor who taught life skills to at risk kids. Sonny simply couldn't face the world. His parents, his grandparents, his Uncle Ken Schroer and Sonny's best friend, Chris Meinsohn, proceeded him in death. The sad end of the Schroer family was a blow to Van Morrison. After seven albums Jack Schroer was one of Morrison's closest musical cohorts and a good friend.

ELLIOT LANDY: PHOTOGRAPHING WOODSTOCK AND THE MOONDANCE ALBUM

As Van prepared **Moondance** for release, Elliot Landy came into town to shoot album and promotional photos. At the time Landy received accolades for his cover shot for Bob Dylan's **Nashville Skyline** album. It was difficult for Van having the photographer around. Landy realized Van was shy and introverted. He decided to photograph Van and Janet in and around their house.

The Elliot Landy photos paint a much different picture from that of Van in Clinton Heylin's brilliant biography. Heylin writes of Van: "As a private person ... he was hardly able to cope with life ... he was a complete failure just able to write songs and sing them." (p. 211) There isn't an ounce of truth to this conclusion. Happy Traum found

Van congenial. He said at times he was boring. Albert Grossman's office talked of Van being timid. His friend in The Band, Richard Manuel, said Van needed a couple of drinks to have a long-term conversation. What Heylin misses is Morrison worked 24/7 on his music. When he left Woodstock for Marin County, he had a notebook full of potential hits. There were a number of poems be turned into songs with literary references. The best way to examine the Woodstock period is it was Morrison's university training. Landy's photos demonstrate that fact.

BIBLIOGRAPHICAL SOURCES

One of the more interesting Landy photos is Van holding an album. It is by the jazz artist King Pleasure. Many of the photos show the rural setting that Van and Janet lived in at the time. The mood surrounding the photos was one of a happy marriage. Landy wasn't sure what to make of Morrison. He knew that Woodstock was an important influence. 380-383 and Bob Spitz, **Dylan: A Biography** (New York, 1989), 382-386 for another side of the Woodstock story.

Also see Howard A. DeWitt, **Van Morrison: The Mystic's Music** (Fremont, 1983), pp. 34-42, Clinton Heylin, **Can You Feel the Silence: Van Morrison, A New Biography** (London, 2002), chapter 13, Ritchie Yorke, **Van Morrison: Into the Music** (London, 1975), chapter 6 and Brian Hinton, **Celtic Crossroads: The Art of Van Morrison** (London, 1997, revised edition, 2000), chapter 4.

Michael Gray, **Song And Dance Man III: The Art of Bob Dylan** (London, 2000), pp. 94, 131, 161, 212, 266, 269, 288, 310, 356 provide some interesting influences by Dylan and Van on each other's art.

See Ken Brooks, **In Search of Van Morrison** (London, 1999) for some interesting comments on the **Moondance** album. Interviews with Simon Gee, Roger Armstrong and Mark Naftalin helped in analyzing the music. Interviews with Rob Dunham helped to shape material for this chapter.

A brief interview with Elvin Bishop helped to recall the details of the 1970 NET show. A special edition of **Wavelength** magazine detailed the television shows and was helpful to this chapter.

See Elliot Landy's website for the photos that he took during the **Moondance** album. Tom Pacheco added a great deal of material on the local scene during a Woodstock interview.

Van in two interviews in the 1990s reflected on his earlier career, see, for example, Polygram Interview CD, promotional for the CD **How Long Has This Been Going On: Van Morrison With Georgie Fame and Friends** (London, 1996) and John Kelly, "Interview," **Irish Times**, April 11, 1998.

A number of interviews with Mervyn Solomon added a great deal to this chapter.

A series of interviews with Bobby Blue Bland at Seattle's Jazz Alley helped to formulate some of Van's personality and musical traits.

An interview with George Morrison at his Fairfax record store in 1983 helped to form the basis of many points in this chapter.

For a review of the Gaslight show see, John Lombardi, "Van Morrison On MacDougal Street," **Rolling Stone**, February 21, 1970, p. 10.

The Colwell-Winfield Blues Band album **Cold Wind Blues**, Boston Sound, 1968, Comets Records Italy, 2001 reissue is a must to listen to for an obscure influence upon Morrison.

See Johnny Rogan, **Van Morrison: No Surrender** (London, 2005), chapters 12-14.

The bootleg CD **Van Morrison: The Genuine Philosophers Stone**, 3 discs, GPS 7 has three versions of "Domino" which suggest that Lewis Merenstein was more important to Van's sound than he may have realized. Other bootlegs helpful to this chapter were **Van Morrison: Unplugged In The Studio**, OP 8 Music and **Van Morrison: No Stone Unturned**, n. p., n. d.

See Rick McGrath, "It's Too Late to Stop Now": The Van Morrison Interview, **The Georgia Straight**, February, 1971. See this archived in depth interview on http://www.oocities.org/tracybjazz/hayward/van-the-man.info/reviews/1971_straight.html

Johnny Rogan, **Van Morrison: No Surrender** (London, 2005), chapter 13 is a brilliant look at the post-**Astral Weeks** career problems.

See the Gary Mallaber interview on the archived Van Morrison website http://web.archive.org/web/20091028131615/http://geocities.com/tracybjazz/hayward/van-the-man.info/reviews/mallaber.html

A series of conversations with Tom Pacheco, Happy Traum and Corky Siegel helped to put this period in focus.

For Mick Ronson see, for example, the following website https://www.mickronson.co.uk/mrbio.shtml

A 1982 interview with Nathan Rubin at California State University, Hayward helped this chapter.

On John McCormick's influence see Niall Stokes, "Interview," **Hot Press**, March 2000 and Peter Mills, **Hymns to the Silence: Inside the Words and Music of Van Morrison** (New York, 2010) pp. 61-65, 68-77. Also see John Glatt, **The Chieftains: The Authorized Biography** (New York, 1997), passim.

For an insightful Gary Mallaber interview, see an interview in April 1995 **Modern Drummer** and Michael Limnois, "Gary Mallaber: The Wizard of Rhythm," **Blues GR**, February 24, 2012. http://blues.gr/profiles/blogs/brilliant-drummer-songwriter-gary-mallaber-talks-about-van

Ritchie Yorke's thoughts on the Woodstock musicians, the first three Warner albums and how he viewed Morrison's artistry were an important influence over the years on my thinking. From phone calls to Canada and Australia, Yorke provided a fresh vision for Van's often difficult to understand talent. Yorke was more than a journalist; he had the ear and eye of a talented musician.

For an extensive interview with Janet Planet see Louis Sahagun, "Janet Planet: Van Morrison's 'Brown Eyed Girl' The Clouds Have Lifted, Those Tumultuous Years Behind Her, The Astral Angel Lives A Quiet Life and Still Writes Music," **Los Angeles Times**, November 17, 1998. Also see Barry Egan, "Love Lost In The Myths Of Time," **London Independent**, January 30, 2000. https://www.independent.ie/woman/celeb-news/love-lost-in-the-myths-of-time-26253156.html The Egan interview is a particularly revealing one and word has it among Morrison's friends that he was upset with the **Los Angeles Times** and the **London Independent** articles. He complained for more than a year to his daughter, Shana, and the mere mention of the articles sent him into an angry tirade.

For an interesting revisionist account and a long look back on the Morrison's in Woodstock see, Peter Stone Brown, "The Long Not So Idyllic Descent Of Woodstock, New York," **Counterpunch**, March 11, 2016. https://www.counterpunch.org/2016/03/11/the-long-not-so-idyllic-descent-of-woodstock-new-york/ The Brown article is an exceptionally insightful review of Barney

Hoskins' Small **Town Talk: Bob Dylan, The Band, Van Morrison, Janis Joplin, Jimi Hendrix & Friends In The Wild Years of Woodstock** and in the process, he clarifies some of the mystery surrounding the Morrison's Woodstock period.

Mick Ronson was the King of Glam Guitars. He was known as Davie Bowie's guitarist but he was also a friend to and musical compatriot with Van Morrison. See Chris Salewicz, "Obituary: Mick Ronson" **London Independent**, May 4, 1993 for an overview of his life. For Mick Ronson with Bowie, see Dylan Jones, **David Bowie: A Life** (New York, 2017), passim. Ronson is described as the missing piece in Bowie's early career.

Van Morrison

CHAPTER 15

WOODSTOCK: THE MUSIC, LATE 1969 AND MOONDANCE FEBRUARY 1970

"It's taken me twenty years before I really started working with music."

VAN MORRISON IN CONVERSATION WITH PAUL VINCENT

"The Woodstock period lasted only two years, but its influence is unmistakable...."

ERIK HAGE

"That was the type of band I dig,"

MORRISON ON THE MOONDANCE SESSIONS

The move to Woodstock changed Van Morrison's life. He was living in a rural upstate New York community with a sense of ecology, and a laid back lifestyle. He had an atmosphere conducive to full time songwriting. In his brief time in Woodstock, Van wrote, recorded and placed into notebooks the songs for the next decade of his career. He was living in the midst of some of the best rock musicians with Bob Dylan and The Band heading the list. In the midst of this fertile musical environment, Morrison wrote his strongest material.

When Janet and Van relocated to Woodstock, the counterculture was about to take over this small, upper New York state farming community. The Woodstock Music Festival was a year in the future.

Van and his bride were able to live in a quiet, rustic setting. He never cared for the hippies. The counterculture types or the radical political activists had a message he abhorred. He was about the music nothing else.

Since Van seldom drove, he had to live near old town Woodstock. This necessitated finding a place that was close to one of the local restaurants. His house was within walking distance to town. "I think everything was in walking distance to town," Happy Traum remarked. The Sled Hill Café was a happening place. It was located near the Café Espresso and Morrison frequented both eating spots. Maggie Whiteside, a waitress, recalled that Van was "hard to understand and cranky."

The isolation, the musical environment and the relaxed atmosphere were what Van needed to escape the Bert Berns nightmare. He concentrated upon his writing. He spent a great deal of time reading. It was a connection to promoter Sid Bernstein that brought Morrison to Woodstock. He was much more than the promoter who brought the Beatles to America. Bernstein was an entrepreneur who knew everyone from Albert Goldman to Bob Dylan. He was a close friend to Lewis Merenstein telling him to get Morrison out of New York City. He had just the place to stash Van. He owned a home on a hill in Woodstock. He would let Merenstein rent it for next to nothing. Woodstock was the next step for Van, Janet and Peter.

THE SID BERNSTEIN CONNECTION

Everyone wanted Morrison away from Bert Berns gangster buddies. There was a rumor Berns sold a portion of Morrison's contract to gangsters. If they couldn't collect on their investment, Van might vanish. The story everyone spun is The Band lived nearby Woodstock and Van rented their old house to be near them. Completely inaccurate! It was music promoter Sid Bernstein's home Van's management group rented. Bernstein was one of Lewis Merenstein's best friends. They often talked about the problem of keeping rock artists afloat financially. The other nonsense story spun is Van believed Woodstock had magical musical qualities. Wrong! He wanted a quiet place to write songs. It was the cheapest place to live.

As he prepared to move to Woodstock, Van had no idea about Bernstein's home. He and Janet were surprised. It was isolated, run down, but beautiful. It was a typical weekend cabin. It appealed to well to do New Yorkers. The large bay windows looked out on the valley. The back yard was scenic, comfortable and a perfect place to write. The single-story home was built into a rock cliff. Woodstock was the catalyst to a new burst of creativity.

Van loved the low-key Woodstock life style. He had total freedom walking around the town. Then things changed. The new Woodstock brought by the 1969 festival prompted Van to look toward San Francisco. His close friendship with rock impresario Bill Graham, and the number of friends he made in the San Francisco Bay Area influenced his decision to relocate. His wife, Janet, was on board.

By 1971 Van had learned everything he could in Woodstock. His notebooks were filled with future hits. He had a large number of demos. When he visited San Francisco and Los Angeles, he was impressed with the local music scene.

VAN MORRISON - Lost California Performances Riverside 1975

A good example of the Woodstock ambiance is "Caravan." Van spent a good deal of time with The Band. He thought about his career. He also concentrated upon new songs. "Caravan" is a good example of this period. "Caravan" is a song celebrating the gypsy lifestyle. Van writes at length about the radio. This is a key inspiration for many Morrison tunes.

The English writer Nick Hornby's book **Songbook** celebrates his thirty-one favorite songs. Hornby lists the live version of "Caravan" from the **It's Too Late to Stop Now** album as one of his key influences. The reason? He wants it played at his funeral.

THE IDYLLIC WOODSTOCK LIFESTYLE: GEORGE LEE, JOE SMITH, CLINTON HEYLIN ALL TRYING TO UNDERSTAND VAN

Van found Woodstock idyllic. He was prone to call Warner executive George Lee for money. Lee, acting as Vice President of Warner Brothers East Coast operations and now head of the music publishing division, kept Morrison happy and productive.

George Lee told Clinton Heylin Van called on a daily basis. The reason was a simple one. Lee came to believe Van did not fit into the Woodstock scene. Lee urged Van to move to California. Lee, like many others, described Van as reclusive and prone to angry outbursts. The Warner Brothers executive found Van difficult. Lee was a good friend early on to Morrison. That friendship soon faded.

George Lee was a Warner Brothers executive working under Joe Smith. Lee, in his own words, described his Warner position in a strange and convoluted manner. "I was originally with the record company, as VP of the East Coast, and then I became the head of the music publishing. I still retained my position at the record company as well."

George Lee was angry at times with Morrison. But at other times he supported him. Over time something happened. No one knows what.

VAN IN WOODSTOCK: WHAT WAS LIFE LIKE?

While Dylan was in his last days in Woodstock, Van hung out with The Band. The drinking and musical sessions did a great deal to focus Morrison's music. He also learned more about the Southern roots of rock and roll. Van had an entrée into a million selling group that recognized his nascent talent. He made the most of it.

By the summer of 1969, The Band rented a house near the lush Ashokan Reservoir. They began setting up a rehearsal space to record a solo album. Before they cut the album there were many impromptu jam sessions. Van and Janet sat around with Tim Hardin, Paul Butterfield and a host of session musicians who dropped in to play. When he wasn't hanging out with The Band, Van was down at the Café Espresso enjoying himself.

While he was searching for a permanent home, Bob Dylan lived upstairs at the Café Espresso. He would come downstairs and pound on the piano in the corner. Some of Dylan's early music was composed on this piano. Van loved the story. He often went down to simply look at the old relic. The piano that is, not Dylan.

Happy Traum and his brother, Artie, hung out at the Café Espresso performing their folk music to appreciative locals. Paul Butterfield wearing jeans, a dark sweater and wool knit hat often sat in a corner reading and quietly playing a harmonica. Tim Hardin often came in to write in a dark corner. Fred Neil read voraciously looking plaintively around the cafe. There was a small stage or rather a makeshift one at the Café Espresso. No one knew who would get up and gig on stage.

The Cafe Espresso was a meeting place for folk musicians. There were community meetings. In addition to Dylan, Ramblin' Jack Elliot and Joan Baez frequented the place. Bob Dylan brought in his typewriter and sat in the corner writing songs. John Sebastian, soon to form the Lovin' Spoonful, was another songwriter frequently seen with a note pad. Van used this atmosphere to create a flourish of songs lasting into the late 1970s.

Rod Hicks, who played bass with Aretha Franklin, was typical of the musicians who hung out at the Cafe Espresso. Hicks told Van it was the serious musicians and the lack of groupies that brought him to Woodstock.

The Café Espresso served hard liquor, beer and wine. It was a rite of passage to get drunk there. Paul Butterfield talked about his new album with a **Rolling Stone** reporter, as the Traum brothers provided soft acoustic on the Café Espresso stage.

Despite all the famous musicians, the Café Espresso was a place for privacy. No one bothered anyone else. It was the perfect setting for Morrison.

THE CHANGES IN VAN DUE TO THE BAND

Jon Gershen told Clinton Heylin Van hoped to become close to The Band. The Band's chief employer, Bob Dylan, lived in a secluded house in Byrdcliffe. Soon Dylan moved his family to another location. The raucous 1969 Woodstock Festival was the reason for the bard's relocation.

Van lived and hung out in Woodstock until 1971. He remained influenced by local musicians, the beautiful landscape and the lessons he learned from Albert Grossman's management style of taking no prisoners.

There were also local clubs Morrison either drank in or performed casual gigs on small stages. The White Water Depot and Rose's Cantina were venues musicians played while fine-tuning their albums. One of the ironies of the early Woodstock days was a teenager named Cindy Cashdollar who followed Van Morrison around town. Later, she played steel guitar and dobra with him. She hung around Rose's Cantina. When she toured with Morrison in support of his 2006 **Pay The Devil** album, she recalled the Woodstock days warmly.

When the 1969 Woodstock Festival took place, Van changed his mind about the area. In 1973, Morrison told Richard William about Woodstock: "When I first went, people were moving there to get away from the scene. Then Woodstock itself started being the scene." Van never liked to live near the scene. He began reconsidering his options.

As he was completing **Moondance**, Van dropped in to say good-bye to The Band's Robbie Robertson. He and Janet were preparing to move to Northern California. The result was they shared credit for writing a song about two musicians stranded in Hollywood. The inspiration for this tune was a fifth of whiskey. The song, "4% Pantomime," evolved in a one take session for The Band's **Cahoots** LP. It featured a drunken duet between Van and drummer Richard Manuel. This may have been the first time the term, the Belfast Cowboy, was used to describe Van.

There is a strange literary connection between Robertson and Morrison in the lyrics to "4% Pantomime." When they use the line "Richard, tell me, if it's poker" and in another lyric Manuel exclaims: "Belfast Cowboy, lay your cards down on the table." This suggests a symbiotic relationship.

HOW LIFE INFLUENCED THE MUSIC IN WOODSTOCK: THE COLWELL-WINFIELD BLUES BAND

Woodstock for a time offered Van the life he desired. The area's rustic qualities appealed to his artistic soul. The home Van rented from Beatle concert promoter Sid Bernstein was on a huge hill overlooking the valley. It was a beautiful setting. It prompted him to sit in his front room playing the piano for hours while working on new music.

The Colwell-Winfield Blues Band lived in the area. They became an integral part of Van's new backing band. With Jack Schroer on alto and soprano sax, Mike Winfield on bass, Chuck Purro on drums, Bill Colwell on guitar, Collin Tilton on tenor sax and flute and Charles "Moose" Sorrento on vocals and piano, the Colwell-Winfield aggregation had a sound made for Van's music. Their musicianship was first rate. They had been on the road backing Boz Scaggs after he left the Steve Miller Blues Band.

A number of replacement musicians came into the Colwell-Winfield Band. Jeff Labes was one of them. Exactly when Labes played with the group is uncertain. He was there from time to time. This influenced Morrison's decision to hire him for recording sessions and concerts. Labes did not play on the Colwell-Winfield album **Cold Wind Blues**.

It was Chuck Purro, the drummer, who was helpful in Morrison's musical direction. Purro introduced Jeff Labes to Van. They began jamming. They practiced the material, which would make up a great deal of Morrison's subsequent Warner Brothers albums.

When Van brought in Jeff Labes on keyboards, along with drummer Gary Mallaber, and conga percussionist whiz Guy Masson, he completed the new sound integral to his hits. With these musicians, Van was ready to record his second Warner Bros. album. The bucolic life in Woodstock not only aided his creativity, it placed his music into a new perspective. Lurking in the background the Colwell-Winfield sound was an important influence.

When the members of the Colwell-Winfield Blues Band practiced with Van they helped finalize **Moondance**. The Colwell-Winfield Blues Band provided the foundation for this new and updated Morrison sound.

THE COLWELL-WINFIELD BLUES BAND: COLD WIND BLUES

In 1968, the Colwell-Winfield Blues Band released an album **Cold Wind Blues**. Its music was straight ahead rock and roll with poetic lyrics and a blues tinge. There was a decided influence from Blood Sweat and Tears. The use of horns was excellent throughout the LP. Few people heard the album. Even fewer purchased it. Van hired them. He let the group know that he wanted to tour with them. Morrison was a shrewd judge of talent. He liked their sound, and the easy way they followed him.

Cold Wind Blues was a strong album with Collin Tilton's tenor saxophone and Jack Schroer's alto, tenor and soprano saxophone portending much of Van's future sound. After Morrison ended his **Astral Weeks** experiment, he went into a straight-ahead rock and roll direction.

It was the blues-jazz roots in the Colwell-Winfield Blues Band's music Morrison appreciated. Bill Colwell's "Got A Wind" presaged some of Morrison's romantic ballads. Charles "Moose" Sorrento's vocals were much like the ones Van would employ in the mid-1970s. His bluesy inflection and soulful feel were the band's signature sound.

Collin Tilton's flute had an eerie sound. This was a musical direction Morrison incorporated. The group's signature song "Cold

Wind Blues" was a soulful tune. Van listened to intently while writing new material.

The instrumental jams on the **Cold Wind Blues** album intrigued Van. The use of horns prompted him to hire a number of horn players. He employed Jack Schroer who became a key element in Van's horn sound.

Tilton's songwriting intrigued Van. One song, "Govinda," became the prototype for a number of Morrison tunes. There was a dreamy mystical quality to this tune. It was seven minutes long. It had a measured jazz elegance. Schroer and Tilton's horns dueled in such a way it stuck in Van's mind. By the 1980s he used a similar sound on **Common One** and **Beautiful Vision**.

Morrison was intrigued by "Govinda," which blended Middle Eastern influences with rock music. Tilton's saxophone work on **Moondance** remains a quintessential contribution. After he toured with Etta James and the Rolling Stones on their 1978 tour, Tilton joined Clarence Clemons and the Red Bank Rockers. He eventually opened the Bar None Recording Studio in New Haven, Connecticut where he resides to the present day.

THE GERSHEN BROTHERS, THE MONTGOMERIES AND VAN MORRISON

Many people marveled at Van's musical ingenuity. None were more complimentary than Jon and David Gershen. They played in the Montgomeries. Eventually, they recorded two albums as Borderline. When the Gershens saw Van perform at the 1968 Woodstock Sound Out, they were sold on his unique talent.

The Gershen Brothers, along with Jim Rooney, performed around Woodstock. They were a marvelous band with a country rock sound. They attracted other musicians. In the recording studio, The Band's Garth Hudson and Richard Manuel joined the Gershen Brothers. They recorded a great deal of material at Albert Grossman's Bearsville Studio. They became Borderline. Their 1973 album **Sweet Dreams And Quiet Desires** was scheduled for release by a major label. It didn't happen. Toshiba Japan released **Sweet Dreams and Quiet Desires** from 1973 on EMI Japan in 2001. Sales were abysmal. What did this have to do with Van Morrison? Plenty. Borderline's versions of "Clinch Mountain" and "Handsome Molly" suggest Van's Irish influence on Borderline.

The Gershen Brothers from left, David Gershen, Jon Gershen, and Jim Rooney
(photo by Stanley Knap)

Soon the Gershens were jamming with Van in their home studio. Van taught them how to play "Friday's Child." They were enthralled with his songs. The Gershens tried to get to know Van. His protective shield prevented in-depth personal contact. It was a musical connection. Nothing more. Nothing less. Relationships are not always in Morrison's psyche.

The Montgomeries were a band the Gershen Brothers put together. They continued to help Van craft a country-blues sound. Somewhere along the line the Gershen Brothers advised Van to hire a good lawyer. Soon Morrison was in New York talking with the Gershen brother's lawyer. This began the sorting out of the Belfast Cowboy's business affairs and legal problems.

Van Morrison and the Montgomeries, Woodstock, NY - 1970: Van, Tony Brown, Joe Ciera, Dave Gershen, Mike Estes (Kneeling), and Jon Gershen
(Photo by David Gahr)

The Montgomeries were a band that developed a country-rock sound before it was popular. They wrote their material, while living in New York City. They soon tired of the urban sprawl. The brothers hung out in Greenwich Village. Mississippi John Hurt, Doc Watson and Charlie Mingus influenced them. It wasn't until 1969 they relocated to Woodstock and began working with Morrison. The New York based brothers were looking for a record deal. They were intent upon commercial success. They had an education in the ways of the music business. They were not exclusively rock musicians. They had many styles, many influences and played a creative, original eclectic music. This appealed to Van.

When they moved to Woodstock in 1969, it was ostensibly to interest Dylan's manager, Albert Grossman, in their career. They hoped to cut a deal with his Bearsville label. It didn't work out. Van introduced the Gershen Brothers to Jim Rooney, who had previously managed the Club 47 in Cambridge. He wasn't interested in their music.

Jon Gershen had a special relationship with Morrison. He moved to Marin County. He settled into the California lifestyle to perform and record with Morrison. Van trusted him musically. They talked at length about Van's likes and dislikes. The taboo song, "Brown Eyed Girl," was something Morrison complained about. One night when Jon was sitting in Van's Fairfax home, the Belfast Cowboy began playing the song in a slow, folk vein. He told Gershen that is the manner in which it should be performed. He was still angry Berns ruined it.

There were many ironic tales associated with Jon Gershen. Just after **Moondance** was released, Van went to watch the Gershen Brothers perform at Saugerties High School. He loved the way they blended folk, jazz, country and jazz into a commercial musical package. After three years of playing in and around Woodstock, the Gershen Brothers formed a new band as Morrison moved to California.

When the Gershen Brothers evolved into the band Borderline, their musical expertise as an Americana band was highlighted. The two albums by Borderline are important influences upon Van's ever evolving sound.

How did Van interpret the Americana genre? It was a combination of music Morrison knew and practiced with one new ingredient. Americana records had a gospel sound combined with country, blues, rhythm and blues and roots rock. Van organized the Street Choir. Why? He believed a gospel-oriented background would add commercial appeal. This was a direct result of the Woodstock music culture.

When the Montgomeries single "Don't Know Where I'm Going" backed with "Marble Eyes" came out, Van was praiseworthy. The United Artists' Avalanche label didn't do a thing with the song. Even with Morrison's endorsement the Montgomeries were doomed. They did provide a country-rock sound encouraging Van to move into this direction. One Woodstock observer told me: "The Montgomeries album was a road map for Van's future sound." The Montgomeries Jim Rooney evolved into an acclaimed producer.

THE VAN AND JANET MARRIAGE: AN IDYLLIC INTERULDE

The story behind Van's marriage to Janet Rigsbee, née Janet Planet, is an enduring tale of love and devotion derailed by the rock and roll world. After he met her while performing with Them at Bill Quarry's Roller Arena in San Leandro, California, they got into a serious relationship. She had been married for a brief time. "There were a lot of girls backstage that night," Terry Rissman, the drummer for Peter Wheat and the Breadmen, remarked, "but Van was smitten with this blonde with a Texas accent and the looks of a California surf bunny." When Rissman and his band went to play in the San Joaquin Valley, as an opening act for Them, he saw Van backstage with Janet. This was 1966. The courtship continued for the next two years.

When Van returned to San Francisco, Janet followed him. He flew home to Ireland. They spent time writing letters. She waited for him to arrive in New York. When he did fly into America to record for Bert Berns, she relocated to the Big Apple.

By the time Janet moved to New York to be with Van, her earlier marriage was over. She had a son, Peter, who accompanied her everywhere. It was the times that prompted her to change her name to Janet Planet. She wasn't the space case that the name suggests. She was a centered young girl determined to make Morrison happy. She was also a talented artist and songwriter. In time, this would cause problems. She had an idyllic outlook on life. It wasn't long before her optimism clashed with Van's pessimism. In the beginning this had little bearing on their relationship. They were in love.

For a time, Janet and Van had an idyllic marriage. Their rock and roll life evolved into problems not suitable to a young couple. They were primarily money issues. The demands of the music business prompted Van to rage periodically. When his parents came to visit, Van's father, George, thought that this was a union much like his own. Van's parents were highly individualistic and different people. "I just worried my son was too artistic," George told me in his Fairfax record store. At this point, no one had any doubts about the marriage. Woodstock's rural setting, the presence of other talented musicians, the lack of daily stress and a wife who doted on him made Morrison into a new man. His life was one where songwriting took on a romantic and peaceful direction. All of this led to the **Moondance** album.

As he wrote in the rustic and quaint Woodstock countryside, Van's had a cutting edge creativity. Before he recorded **Moondance**, he took his musicians into a New York studio to cut some demos. With a cache of old songs, Van had plenty of material. There were twenty tunes he made demos of. He began shaping these songs into a romantic cycle. Warner Brothers rejected most of the material. He knew they were potential hits. He re-worked two songs, "Come Running" and "Domino," for later commercial release. He spent a year on these tunes. Not all these songs appeared on **Moondance**. They provided a starting point for **His Band and the Street Choir** and **Tupelo Honey**.

THE TWO VAN MORRISON'S

There were two Van Morrison's during the Woodstock years. One was the meticulous studio craftsman. The other was the itinerant and often misdirected performer. When he performed in Woodstock, Van was known for his brilliant, but often erratic, sets. This set up a pattern he followed for the remainder of the 1970s.

Jon Gershen told Clinton Heylin Van didn't like sound checks. He wasn't always prepared to go on stage. That said what Gershen forgot to mention was the hundreds of hours of practice prior to these early 1970s shows.

It was at the Woodstock music weekend in 1968, known as Sound Out, that Van established his reputation among local musicians. He was known as a gregarious craftsman. He could stand up and perform at will. Everything Van did was calculated and crafted to perfection. No one recognized his fear of going on stage.

Around Woodstock, Mallaber was considered the most accomplished local drummer. He was in a number of popular lounge groups. He had a steady style that fit Van's music. Mallaber told Clinton Heylin he was getting ready to record with a group, Raven, for CBS Records. Then he joined Morrison. He was also in a better-known band, Chrysalis, that made some noise in the rock music business.

Mallaber continued on to a legendary sideman's career. He went on to record with Bruce Springsteen, Steve Miller, Bonnie Raitt, Bob Seger, Eddie Money, Warren Zevon, Peter Frampton, America, Poco, Cher, Los Lobos, Tom Rush and Johnny Rivers among others. Not surprisingly, Van recognized that Mallaber added a great deal to his music.

JEFF LABES IN WOODSTOCK

Jeff Labes is one of the heroes of the Van Morrison story. As a musician he is enormously talented. As Van's friend he was on the same wavelength. He knew how and when to enter the Belfast Cowboy's musical mainstream. He lived in Woodstock. He moved to Marin County. He married. He raised a family. He remains a resident of the county north of San Francisco home to the musically hip.

Labes began his career in a Boston cult band, the Apple Pie Motherhood Band, as the group's piano-organist. He also wrote four songs for their debut album **Apple Pie** released in 1969. The band disbanded. Labes joined Morrison's group of Woodstock musicians. He was a key session player on **Moondance**.

In 1971 Labes worked with Jonathan Edwards on his debut albums adding what he called his "rural-flavored piano licks." The following year Labes and Edwards worked with Orphan on their debut album. Both Edwards and Orphan were favorites of critics. They failed to achieve mainstream commercial success. Morrison was attracted to Labes' skill in arranging strings, working with a synthesizer and performing live. He worked with Morrison on eight albums. The Ivan.vanomatic.de website lists Labes as being on one hundred and forty various Van Morrison projects.

The toil and turmoil of traveling from Woodstock to New York to record **Moondance** took its toll on Labes. He left Morrison and traveled to Israel to find meaning in his life. Labes continues to live in Marin County with his family. He is an entrepreneur with some wealth. Recently, he purchased a forty-seven percent interest in the Sandals Resort International. He is a principal in the Mill Valley based Bright Antenna Record label. He continues to write, produce and perform.

Every indication is he is in touch with and ready at any time to work once again with Van Morrison.

VAN AND THE BUSINESS SIDE OF THE INDUSTRY

While living in Woodstock, Van took take charge of his business affairs. His past record contracts with Decca and Bang Records, as well as the management deal with Schwaid-Merenstein left a bitter taste. He was determined to solve these problems. He didn't have a lucrative recording contract. He had little clout in the industry. He needed help. He knew it. One day he talked at length to the Gershen Brothers about their business. He found out that they had an excellent New York lawyer. Van hired him.

After talking with his newly acquired New York lawyer, Van realized Warner was holding a large portion of his songwriting and publishing royalties. He signed a business deal that turned out to be a disaster. He blamed the Schwaid-Merenstein management and production arm for this unmitigated financial disaster.

It wasn't long before Van was in Bob Schwaid's face concerning publishing royalties, copyrights and percentages taken for collecting his requisite royalties. This established a pattern that has continued throughout his lengthy career. In Woodstock, he found a new manager who was also a skilled industry person. She was a person trained in the Albert Goldman school of intimidation. Enter Mary Martin!

ENTER MARY MARTIN: SENDING HIS CAREER INTO THE MAINSTREAM

Van began looking for new management. He was very aloof. He began talking with Lewis Merenstein. Van saw Merenstein's jazz studio roots as a positive sign for the music. On the business side he wasn't sure. While Van recorded **Moondance**, Mary Martin, entered the management sweepstakes. Morrison told her to do what she could to right the contract wrongs.

When he hired Mary Martin, Van had no idea as to her expertise. She was skilled. She managed Leonard Cohen, Rodney Crowell and

Vince Gill at important junctures in their careers. Her specialty was taking the reins of a moderately successful singer and bringing the artist into the mainstream. Her contemporaries described her as outspoken, rash, brash, passionate and eccentric.

As a college student at the University of British Columbia she was seen at Vancouver's Commodore Ballroom and a local blues bar the Yale. She hated school and left for Toronto where she met Ronnie Hawkins and the musicians who became The Band.

She quickly became a friend to the group calling itself the Hawks. She was there when they became The Band. She was smitten with Richard Manuel. She was close to drummer Levon Helm. When they moved to Woodstock, she came along.

She remarked of Van's contract: "It was as close to slavery as I've ever seen." She straightened out Van's business affairs. She told him to put together a touring band. She would take care of his business needs. As Martin predicted; "The rest would fall into place." She appeared to be a good choice.

After guiding Leonard Cohen to the music mainstream, Martin, at the suggestion of The Band's Richard Manuel, listened to **Moondance**. "I was blown away." She quickly moved in to help Van with his career. Martin complained to local Woodstock residents Van would not tour. He was personally difficult. He was perpetually angry. She helped him escape penury contracts. That was it.

Because she managed Leonard Cohen, she called Morrison and asked him if he was interested in collaboration. "Nothing came of it," Martin remarked. Years later Morrison's **Veedon Fleece** album occupied a special slot on Cohen's personal jukebox.

In 1975 Cohen was asked to name "those he admired on the contemporary music scene." He responded: "I ... like Van Morrison very much, including his **Veedon Fleece** effort."

Martin and Morrison never signed a management contract. In a 2009 interview she told Tori Tarvin that Van told her he didn't have any money. He couldn't pay her. Martin promptly sent a telegram to Morrison firing herself. She sent Van a telegram. It read: "I quit." The next day a note arrived from Van: "You're fired!" The truth! Who knows!

379

Martin's value to Morrison was immediate. She forced Warner Brothers to renegotiate his contract. This helped soothe Van's feelings. Martin was instrumental in the creation of Caledonia Productions, which became Morrison's publishing arm. It eventually evolved into Vanjan Music. Martin warned Van the Warner demo sessions resulted in the label owning more than its share of his tunes.

LEWIS MERENSTEIN MYSTERY: HELP OR HINDRANCE?

Van's relationship with Lewis Merenstein remains a mystery. When he signed with Inherit Productions, there was no doubt Merenstein's successes with Brill Building type songwriting helped him recognize Van's talent. He had worked with jazz greats Art Farmer and Thelonious Monk. This impressed Van. An understated personality with a small ego, a fair man and a family man, Merenstein seemed to have no faults. Van soon found fault with his production techniques.

The initial Schwaid-Merenstein deal appeared like a good one. It wasn't. Inherit Productions signed Van to a multi-album production deal with Warner. They would produce him. They would control his music through their company Inherit Productions. Schwaid was the business guy. He was a former Brill Building regular who signed acts to control their production and royalties. He took a share of their songwriting and dictated the choice of record companies. Why would Van agree to work with Schwaid? He was broke. He was desperate. He didn't have any other choices. Schwaid had connections to major labels. Schwaid knew everyone in New York. Van relocated to Woodstock. Schwaid drove him. The drive to Woodstock, with Janet sitting in the backseat, was one where the Belfast Cowboy said very little. He may have been rethinking his options in Woodstock. Morrison referred to Schwaid as "a creature."

Schwaid-Merenstein moved their New York offices due to their business successes. Van paid close attention. He was impressed. They handled Miriam Makeba's business matters, managed soul singer Walter Jackson, as well as rising blues artist Barry Goldberg. Long before he signed with Schwaid-Merenstein, Van checked out their new offices at 57 West 56th Street. It was one of New York's premier addresses. When he signed with Inherit Productions, Van's vision was one of a firm business guidance. He was quickly disappointed. It was the Brill Building with a fancy office.

They hoped to make as much money as possible. Van embraced artistic integrity. To get out of his contract, Van began to bicker with Bob Schwaid. As the partnership with Inherit proceeded, Lewis Merenstein worked on the final **Astral Weeks** tracks. He was uncomfortable. Merenstein took a reduction in title. He was no longer the main producer. There was no mystery about the process, Van had taken charge. He was the producer.

WAS DOMINO A HARBINGER OF THINGS TO COME?

The experimental nature of Van's music is reflected in "Domino." When this tune appeared on the **His Band and the Street Choir** album, it was a window into Morrison's creative process.

Graham Blackburn recalled in Woodstock Van spent almost a year finalizing the song. The musicians in and around Woodstock couldn't figure out what Van had in mind. They didn't realize he was experimenting. He hoped to blend acoustic and electric music.

He went to New York City to cut some demos. By experimenting with "Domino," Van refined his production techniques. The studio versions of "Domino" included three separate approaches to the song. There was a harmony demo. There were two versions with a repetitive almost rapping sound. Merenstein found the "Domino" demos uninspiring. He let Van know his feelings. It was a mistake. The three demos were nothing like the original. They lacked the hit record sound. It was Van's concept of jazz.

The period with Merenstein is one Van has talked about in retrospect. In recent years, he has shown great respect for Merenstein's production techniques. Morrison learned from him. The problem was if Van couldn't feel it in the studio, he couldn't produce the record he wanted. It took Warner Brothers a decade to recognize this trait. When they did, they released Morrison from his contract. This was a big mistake.

According to Merenstein, part of the problem with "Domino" was Van was infatuated with the flute, the stand-up bass and the horns. Merenstein said the vocals suffered.

While living in Woodstock, Van heard one tale after another about Bob Dylan's songwriting. When he wrote "Domino," Van had Dylan in mind. "Domino" was a paean to Dylan's unseen intellectual influence. The lyrics suggest a time of great joy. It was a harbinger of things to come. Van wrote new songs that had a hit quality. The four albums after **Astral Weeks** featured chart friendly music. Van retooled his musical direction from 1973 through 1977. Some years, in the mid-1970s, he performed primarily in California. While in other parts of this five-year period he had forays into Europe. There was no predicting where and when Morrison would perform.

THE 1970 WARNER DEMOS

After three demos of "Domino," Van experimented with "When The Evening Sun Goes Down" in a country western style. The finished product reflected The Band's influence. A version of "Lorna" indicated Van was moving away from the Bang Record material. This tune talks about a young schoolgirl with a folk-rock direction. "Wild Night" was the last of the six demo tracks he cut in 1970. This version was one where the harmony opening was too slow. He didn't have the drive or feel of the finished product.

These six demos indicated Van needed a producer. No better case could be made for Lewis Merenstein's role than his ability to create a hit sound. He did so out of a maudlin demo of "Domino." When "Wild Night" appeared on the **Tupelo Honey** album in 1971, the post-production work by Merenstein made it hard driving rock and roll.

INTRODUCING SHANA CALEDONIA MORRISON

In July 1969, Janet found out that she was pregnant. She and Van were overjoyed. They had wanted a child for some time. Peter, Janet's boy by a previous marriage, was a young man. They doted on him. They eagerly welcomed another sibling. For a time, the Morrison's

382

thought of having a mid-wife come in for the birth. Their pediatric doctor convinced them to go to a Woodstock hospital.

Those around Van and Janet remember how happy they were with the pregnancy. On April 7, 1970, Shana was born in the Woodstock, New York hospital. The Morrison family now included two children. Friends who dropped by spoke of the joy Van experienced being a father. He was also carefully pondering his future by building a cache of unreleased songs. It was fatherhood that made Van proud of his life, his wife and his career.

LEWIS MERENSTEIN: THE ATTITUDE BEHIND THE THRONE

One of the session musicians who played on the early Warner Brothers material described Lewis Merenstein as "the attitude behind the throne." What he meant was the atmosphere was not right for Morrison's experimental musical nature. He needed a producer who understood his music.

Merenstein set up a special rehearsal space the musician's dubbed "the Van room." Here Morrison could use any type of instrumentation. This helped provide a sense of what the music would be in its final form. This helped Morrison to begin with three styles for each song. As a studio rat, Van was in heaven. He could experiment with tempo, pace and style.

There was a hidden motive in the Warner Brothers contract. As Lewis Merenstein told Clinton Heylin: "Warner's had us go back in because they had put up money for the publishing portion and they wanted to feel that they had enough publishing to warrant giving advances." This translated into making Warner excessive profits from a portion of Morrison's publishing and songwriting. No wonder Van was difficult. This corporate attitude prompted Van to reconsider the wisdom of signing with Warner. He had trouble coming to grips with Warner's business decisions. He viewed them as arbitrary, capricious and blatantly unfair.

Merenstein attempted to lead Van into a more commercial direction. He realized **Astral Weeks** was a one-time musical odyssey. Morrison told Warner executives he would take his songs into the commercial mainstream. The July 30, 1969 session that began the

Moondance LP was one where Merenstein appealed to Morrison's ego. This ensured a hit sound. The studio musicians recalled Merenstein whispering into Van's ear. He told him a series of hit records brought freedom. He appealed to Van's musical snobbery by introducing drummer Buddy Salzman along with Warren Smith, Richard Davis and Jay Berliner. Van knew these musicians were top of the line session giants. Their jazz roots dramatically impacted Morrison. Van said years later to Chris Michie "they were old jazz guys." He wanted young musicians in his future sessions. He insisted Jeff Labes be hired for **Moondance**. Labes was a friend and confidant. Van needed his affirmation.

Labes' inclusion was a smart move. He became the first in a long line of quasi-bandleaders to translate Morrison's ideas into completed songs. When Labes instructed the musicians, they understood how the songs should sound. His work as a keyboardist, arranging strings and woodwind instruments paved the way for Van's hits. He was also low key with a normal family. To this day he lives quietly in Marin County. Labes has talent only a small number of musicians possess. He demonstrated his skill when he wrote out alternate arrangements. Van used what appealed to him.

THE IN-FIGHTING OVER THE MOONDANCE ALBUM

After recording **Astral Weeks**, Van realized his career could be over if he didn't take charge of producing his music. The album wasn't what he envisioned. The musicians he worked with in Woodstock understood what he wanted. Why? They practiced his original compositions for six months. Van had written some of the songs as far back as the Them days.

The idea Morrison simply wrote his music quickly and furtively rankled him. It was one of the favorite ploys of the Warner Brothers public relations gurus. He couldn't stand the suits, the middle-aged jerks who ran the label and the fawning, often at times critical, press. He made demands. He did things other musicians were too timid to do. This further strained his relationship with Warner Brothers. All Van wanted to do was make good music.

There was a tremendous amount of tension and in-fighting during **Moondance**. When Jeff Labes was brought along to the sessions, it was Morrison's way of regaining control. The inclusion of guitarist John Platania was another move reducing Lewis Merenstein's production power. Morrison believed if he didn't control his music it would be destroyed.

The in-fighting was over. **Moondanc**e established a pattern that continued throughout Van's early career. Because he is such an inordinate perfectionist, Van evolved into his own producer. He used techniques that were much like an in-concert performance.

John Platania, in an interview with Michael Walsh for the second issue of the fanzine **Into The Music**, recalled Van manipulated the sessions to take control of the album. At the time no one realized how serious the differences were between Morrison and Merenstein.

Van came to believe the older musicians on **Astral Weeks** looked and played like jazz relics. Van wanted a young, fresh sound. It was when Van came in to cut the album single, "Moondance," the difficulties came to the surface. The Belfast Cowboy insisted he select the songs, the arrangements and the musicians. Lewis Merenstein relented. Things calmed down. Van took control of the remainder of the **Moondance** album.

MOONDANCE: WHAT WILL IT BE?

When Van selected material for his second Warner Brothers album, he was in a contented frame of mind. Why? He realized **Astral Weeks** was a masterpiece. It never dawned on him it would not sell. He used the lyrics to "Moondance" to joke about what a marvelous time it was to make an album. No one in the studio got the joke. Morrison was having fun. He was artistically free. It showed in the songs. They had a good time, honky-tonk appeal. It also began the hit-making phase of his Warner Brothers career. Mo Ostin, asked: "What will **Moondance** be?" Van responded: "The work of a bunch of new musicians who understand what I am doing." Ray Ruff said the exchanges testifies to Van's intransigence. Ruff blamed Ostin for this acrimonious atmosphere.

385

There is a great deal of conflicting information on Mo Ostin. Most artists, including Maria Muldaur, praised Ostin as an "artistic friendly executive." That is true. But somewhere along the line Ostin and Morrison had personal difficulties. No one knows the cause. But there was no love lost between them. Their differences appeared to have little impact on the **Moondance** album. Van was too busy crafting a hit album.

The new musicians had a different outlook. This was evident in John Platania's guitar. He played in a traditional rock and roll mold. This was the direction Van was headed. It would guarantee his fiscal, as well as artistic future. Collin Tilton's flute added a sound that was more commercial than John Payne's. It was rock and roll as opposed to classically influenced sounds. Tilton was a brilliant instrumental performer. He was also a gifted arranger. He was a calm presence in the studio, in the rehearsal hall and in concert.

It was Jack Schroer on alto and soprano saxophone that was closest to Van in musical styling. Jeff Labes rounded out a musical menagerie that was reinforced by three well-known back-up singers Judy Clay, Emily Houston and Jackie Verdell. These seasoned musicians were in place to make **Moondance** a success. Van was now a hit artist. He was a permanent part of the rock and roll hit machine. The only person who was unhappy was Van Morrison.

As Van finalized the **Moondance** material, he cut the album quickly in late 1969 for a February 1970 release. There was always the question of money. He needed a hit to guarantee continuing his Warner contract. He had no idea the "Moondance" single, with its jazz inflections, would spend four weeks on the Billboard Top 100, even if it only reached number 92. There was another hit with "Come Running" in the Top 40 at number 39 for eight weeks. Friends recall that Morrison was surprised with these hits.

Moondance's commercial success surprised Warner Brothers. They didn't publicize the LP. It took a considerable amount of time to get the album on the charts. It wasn't until a month after its release the album charted. The staying power of **Moondance** was extraordinary. It remained on the Billboard Hot 100 album listing for twenty-two weeks. While not having a top ten single, the LP sold steadily for more than five years. This was a dramatic improvement from **Astral Weeks**. It was an indication Van's songwriting was one reason for his success.

Russ Solomon, of Tower Records, told me his San Francisco store **Astral Weeks** sold out in a few days. "I knew the **Moondance** album would be a blockbuster," Solomon said. Tower Records was the flagship for California record buyers with stores in Los Angeles, San Francisco, Berkeley and Sacramento. Their sales made new artists. They featured Van Morrison in window displays. The bootleggers were also busy turning out concert vinyl albums. When he came to Marin County to visit Janet's family and friends, Van was in the midst of his commercial renaissance. This would influence him to relocate to the Golden State.

MOONDANCE: SOME THOUGHTS ON VAN AND THE ALBUM

The biggest change in Van Morrison while recording **Moondance** was as Tom Kielbania said: "He was playing hardball." What did Kielbania mean? It was simple. Van charged everyone was stealing from him. Mary Martin was on the scene to attack producer Lewis Merenstein. She also criticized Warner management. In this chaotic and contentious atmosphere, Morrison recorded one of the most commercial albums of his career.

How much chaos was there in the recording process? Plenty! Van took to booking studio time without consulting Merenstein. To his credit, Merenstein went to the sidelines turning things over to Morrison.

When I interviewed people at Warner, they demanded anonymity. To a person they complained of the difficulty of dealing with Morrison. He didn't forget sleights. He didn't forget bad business deals.

Merenstein was listed as the co-producer on the album. Gary Mallaber mixed the album as Merenstein, who was a recognized mixing genius, left the sessions angrily. Mallaber said **Moondance** turned out as a wonderful album due to Van's insistence on studio freedom. Mallaber commented the songs were "a tour de force of almost every style rock music could currently contain."

Mallaber and other musicians loved the songs that weren't included on **Moondance**. When they recorded "Listen To The Lion," Van kept it unissued. It appeared on the **St. Dominic's Preview** LP.

The musicians I interviewed for the Moondance sessions said Morrison was not totally comfortable in the studio. This is why Mallaber mixed the LP.

Van Morrison: "I can't stand playing with knobs, levels. It's out of my domain. I supervise it but don't have to be there twenty-three hours a day." This was a comment Van made during a 1984 interview concerning **Moondance**. This explains why Mallaber and engineer Elliott Scheiner spent so much time in the studio. They mixed the final production.

VAN SHOULD HAVE THE LAST WORD ON MOONDANCE

Over the years Van has been candid about his likes and dislikes concerning **Moondance**. What he dislikes is he doesn't own 100% of the album. He liked the studio musicians, the recording atmosphere and grudgingly over the years he has come to praise **Moondance**.

Van Morrison: "Two horns and a rhythm section - they're the type of bands that I like best." He should! He put the band together. Why did he like it? Van could blend influences from jazz, blues, rhythm and blues and poetry to fit his musical mélange. **Rolling Stone** observed: "The title track and 'And It stoned Me' and 'Caravan' felt like a lucid dream."

He had to share credit with others. **Moondance** is a Morrison production. He remains angry about others who had production credit. Van never forgets sleights. To this day he complains about **Moondance**. When Warner reissued the album, the old grievances surfaced.

When Warner Brothers released the publicity on the **Moondance: Deluxe Edition**, Van hit the roof. The reason? The press reported Morrison liked the 5 disc special package. He reminded the press he didn't condone the reissue. He was not receiving his fair share of royalties. His ex-wife, Janet, sent an Internet tirade telling Van to get over it. She pointed out he owned more than ninety-five percent of his material.

Van Morrison: "I didn't authorize it … it's being stolen from me again." Then Van ceased criticizing Warner. He made his point.

MOONDANCE: THE PATH ON THE CHARTS AND THE CRITICS WEIGH IN

The original February 1970 release of **Moondance** demonstrated Van's staying power. It wasn't until November 1976 the album was certified gold. When this took place Morrison was miffed Warner Brothers didn't recognize his accomplishment.

Billboard reviewed **Moondance** positively. They suggested **Astral Weeks** "was overlooked." Billboard praised **Astral Weeks** as "the aesthetic success of '69' throughout the underground." This review mystified him. He told a friend there wasn't mention of the songs.

Greil Marcus and Lester Bangs in the March 19, 1970 issue of **Rolling Stone** cut through to the essence of Morrison's album. They wrote: "**Moondance** is an album of musical invention and lyrical confidence; the strong moods of 'Into The Mystic' and the fine, epic brilliance of 'Caravan' will carry it past many good records we'll forget in the next few years."

Robert Christgau's 1981 **Record Guide** was equally praiseworthy. He suggested Van's Irish roots were intact. Many critics missed the Belfast influence. Christgau used the term "Gaelic poetry" to describe Morrison's masterpiece. He got it right. The enduring strength of **Moondance** was shown when a December 2003 issue of **Rolling Stone** stated it was the 65th best album in rock and roll history.

VAN MORRISON ON NEW YORK'S MACDOUGAL STREET: THE GASLIGHT'S INFLUENCE

Greenwich Village's Gaslight Club was New York's premier folk club. As the urban folk revival of the 1960s faded in the early 1970s, Sonny Terry and Brownie McGhee, John Hammond, Tom Paxton, Tom Rush and Ramblin' Jack Elliot played the club.

On a chilly Friday night on February 1, 1970, Morrison came into the front door of the Gaslight Club on New York's MacDougal Street. Down the block at the Fillmore East Janis Joplin and the Paul

Butterfield Blues Band were packing the house. The Village folkies turned out in large numbers to see Van. The irony is he was a bigger draw on the folk circuit than in the trend setting Fillmore East.

As the crowd filed into the Gaslight, Van Morrison wandered out from the kitchen to grab a glass of beer. He stood in the back of the small club. He smiled. It reminded him of the old days at Belfast's Maritime Hotel. Van was totally accessible to the fans. They didn't seem to notice him. Van loved the anonymity.

The show opened with a young folkie, David Nichtern, coming on stage and performing a short set. When the Morrison band came on and started to play, they were more of an upbeat jazz unit than a rock and roll band. Then Morrison wandered on stage. Everyone expected the songs from **Astral Weeks**. He performed only two numbers from the album, "The Way Young Lovers Do" and "Ballerina." It was time to test out the new material. When Van swung into "I Shall Sing," and then during "Everyone" the crowd quietly clicked their fingers to his jazz direction. He performed a much applauded "And It Stoned Me." Then he explained why he wrote "Ordinary People." There was an eerie silence. No one knew anything about "Ordinary People." This wasn't surprising. The song wasn't released. When Van wrote it, the melody came from "Joe Harper Saturday Morning" which was on the **Blowin' Your Mind** album. Van said the song was about a time of turmoil in his life. It was one of Morrison's leftovers.

Van's six piece band featured John Platania's guitar, Jeff Labes on keyboards, John Klingberg on bass, Gary Mallaber on drums and saxophonists Jack Schroer and Collin Tilton. This seasoned, professional band stunned the Gaslight crowd. Van was in a blues mood. He finished with a John Lee Hooker medley. He was still finding his way in the studio. In the clubs, he was a seasoned performer.

VAN IN THE STUDIO: THE EARLY LESSONS

In the Warner Brothers studio, Van enhanced his writing, conceptualizing and producing talents. Lewis Merenstein was the initial guiding force behind **Astral Weeks**. He was less of a force on

Moondance. Van took over the album production. The records that came out after 1970 bore the Belfast Cowboy's distinct stamp.

What were the lessons learned in the studio? One was Van needed someone to write the charts. He could explain what he wanted. There were translators. Graham Blackburn and Jeff Labes did it for a while. Later in his career, Van depended heavily upon Pee Wee Ellis. This transformative intermediary was a necessary part of Morrison's production genius.

There were minor problems with the mixing process. Van did not feel comfortable mixing the final product. It was the improper mixes, which persuaded Van to produce his albums with an in concert sound.

On **Moondance** drummer Gary Mallaber had an enormous impact upon the final cuts. Van handed over a great deal of the mixing to him. When Mallaber need advice, he went to the engineer, Elliott Scheiner.

WHAT WORKED BEST FOR VAN ON MOONDANCE?

Because Van didn't have charts or a written guide for the musicians, this turned out to be a blessing. Studio spontaneity was evident. Ralph J. Gleason, the noted San Francisco critic, observed of Van: "He strikes a note so exalted you can't believe a mere human being is responsible for it...." Why Gleason didn't point out Van's distinctive vocal style is mystifying. After the strong reception for **Moondance**, Morrison wrote furtively. He spent every waking hour crafting new music. When a rock critic, Lester Bangs, suggested that Van get divorced so that he could write some new hits, he missed the point. Van wrote those hits in the midst of a happy marriage.

"Moondance" with its jazz oriented pseudo-Frank Sinatra cadence, wowed the critics. Van was no longer the person who belted out "Brown Eyed Girl." He had grown into a mature Song Meister. Van's music reflected his new sophistication. The soprano saxophone on "Moondance" give it a jazz inflection crossing over into the pop market. When he wrote "Caravan," Van was outside his Woodstock home listening to a neighbor's radio. The soothing sounds of the radio prompted him to rush into the house to write "Caravan." Suddenly characters like Gypsy Robin and Sweet Amarou, (Ammaro), (Sweet

Emma Rose) filled his songs. "Into the Mystic" demonstrated that for all his material, Van was still true to the **Astral Weeks** concept. But in a more commercial manner.

CARAVAN DEFINES VAN'S THOUGHTS ON WOODSTOCK AND RADIO'S INFLUENCES

"Caravan" is a window into Morrison's mind. He loved Woodstock. After he moved to California, he performed "Caravan" to recall the pastoral, bucolic Woodstock countryside. "It was like sticking a pin in Janet," Chris Michie continued. "Van used the song to suggest that he didn't like living in California."

Michie, who was Van's guitarist from 1981-1986, told me Van loved to perform "Caravan." Why? Michie said it was to recall "Van's lost Woodstock days." Michie observed it was one of many ways Morrison synthesized his past. "Van often found contentment and happiness in the past when it may not have existed," Michie concluded.

When he wrote "Caravan" Van conveyed many images. His Woodstock home sat by itself. There was no sound except the loud radio from far down the road. "I could hear the radio like it was in the same room," Van continued. "I don't know how to explain it. There was some story about an underground passage under the house I was living in…." This mystical story found its way into "Caravan." The radio was a key to many of Van' early songs.

In popular culture "Caravan" was an unexpected hit. Disc jockey Johnny Fever on the television show WKRP in Cincinnati played it during the first episode while singing along with it. When Morrison was inducted into the Rock And Roll Hall of Fame, he was conspicuously absent. The Counting Crows took the stage performing "Caravan."

When Morrison wrote "These Dreams of You," he had a dream about Ray Charles. Van remarked: "The song is essentially about dreams." "Brand New Day" was written after Van heard a number of songs on FM radio. He purposely made it a five-minute plus song to poke fun at the AM radio play list. Van said The Band was the inspiration for "Brand New Day."

Van Morrison reflected: "I was in Boston and having a hard job getting myself up spiritually." Then Van heard a Bob Dylan song on the radio. He took out his notebook. But it wasn't Dylan singing. It was The Band. He scribbled a quick lyric: "When all the dark doors roll away." He looked at it. He quickly finished the song. It was the summer of 1969. The song turned into "Brand New Day." One musical cohort remarked "it was magical, almost mystical." When the song appeared on **Moondance**, it was a window into his life in Boston and Woodstock.

Not all songs had a mystical quality. When Van penned "Everyone," it was simply an optimistic song about eternal joy. It would be a long time before he would feel that way again. When the album ends with "Glad Tidings," Van expresses his feelings about New York. This should have warned everyone. He was ready to move on. He still couldn't afford to relocate. That came after he wrote the **Moondance** album. His new manager, Mary Martin, secured the money Warner Brothers owed in back royalties. There was about to be a brand new day. It was more than just in song.

ELLIOT LANDY AND THE MOONDANCE COVER

If rock music is an art form, the cover to Morrison's **Moondance** album is a Monet. Elliot Landy shot a large number of photos in and around Woodstock. He had previously provided album covers for The Band and Bob Dylan. Landy has a way of capturing the spirit and essence of an artist.

Landy was the official photographer at Woodstock. His photographs adorned the covers of **Rolling Stone**, **Life** and the **Saturday Evening Post**. The critics praised his cover for Bob Dylan's **Nashville Skyline** LP, as well as the Band's second album. In the late 1960s, he traveled with and photographed Jimi Hendrix, Janis Joplin and Jim Morrison.

Elliot Landy: "Van Morrison was living in Woodstock NY. When I went to his home on the day of the photo shoot Van had a large pimple on the top of his forehead. The extreme close up was in contrast to the portraiture used on albums up till then." Among the photos Landy shot there was one depicting the Belfast Cowboy's record collection. The photo of Van holding a King Pleasure vinyl album: "Original

393

Moody's Mood With Quincy Jones" included references to musicians who played on it. They were Lucky Thompson, Kai Winding, J. J. Johnson, Blossom Dearie, Betty Carter and Jon Hendricks. Van told Landy he was familiar with every musician on the cover.

The **Moondance** album wasn't the beginning of album cover art. It enhanced the genre. Landy attempted to shoot some typical photos of Van. He found it difficult. Why? He couldn't get Van to relax. He was reticent to pose. He had trouble concentrating.

Later that year, Van talked at length about his relationship with Warner Brothers to anyone who would listen. A Warner Brothers executive told me he complained about the time that the cover art took and the demands made by the label. Warner executives didn't understand Van was upset over a contract that gave his label ownership of his first three albums. That was the issue.

Elliott Landy was the perfect choice to photograph Van's cover. Landy, like Morrison, had a vision of Woodstock. It came through in the album's production. He also understood how to work with the reclusive Morrison. The art in the **Moondance** was a tour de force of the new rock and roll album cover genre.

VAN WEIGHS IN ON MOONDANCE

"Somewhere along the line I lost control of that album. Somebody else got control of it, and got the cover and all that shit, while I was out on the West Coast. I knew what was happening to it, but it was like I couldn't stop it. I'd given my business thing over to somebody else ... they just went ahead and did the wrong thing."

Van Commenting About The Moondance Album IN 1974.

ON THE ROAD WITH VAN MORRISON, 1970

The venues Van played in 1970 were varied ones. The concert business was undergoing radical changes. The Bill Graham Organization was gaining a stranglehold upon booking acts as well as controlling the venues.

Graham and Morrison were old friends. He regularly played the Fillmore auditoriums in New York and San Francisco. He preferred these smoky, free form venues because the audiences were laid back and appreciative. They also didn't want the hits. It wasn't cool to listen to the radio oriented songs.

Van could do as he pleased. He could bring along any band. He could perform any type of music. He had the freedom to venture into jazz solos. Of these venues, Van loved the Fillmore West, because it was close to the Mill Valley-Sausalito area north of San Francisco. It was here Morrison hung out.

On April 26, 1970, Van performed at the Fillmore West. It was located at Market and Van Ness Street in San Francisco near the Castro district. This was the second Fillmore West. The first one having been abandoned at Fillmore and Geary after a dispute with the landlord. The new Fillmore location was on the second floor of a large building with an automobile dealership downstairs. Climbing the stairs to go through the front door, Van loved his anonymity. It was either drugs or a heavy cool attitude keeping people from bothering Morrison.

The April 26 show was less than an hour. Van responded with a stunning live version of "Moondance." This set was broadcast over an alternative San Francisco Bay Area radio station, KPFA. The bootleggers quickly turned out a vinyl album. The headliner, Joe Cocker, also had his set broadcast. One of the earliest vintage Crocker bootlegs emerged from this show.

VAN MORRISON APRIL 26, 1970 PLAY LIST

From April 23-26, 1970 Morrison and his band played a four-night engagement at San Francisco's Fillmore West. The following list is from the April 26, 1970 show.

Set List

Moondance • Glad Tidings • Crazy Love • Come Running • The Way Young Lovers Do • Everyone • Brown Eyed Girl • And It Stoned Me • These Dreams of You • Caravan • Cyprus Avenue and Into The Mystic

Band Personnel

- John Platania, guitar
- Jack Schroer, saxophone
- Collin Tilton, saxophone and flute
- Jeff Labes, keyboards
- John Klingberg, bass
- Gary Mallaber, drums

Source: Into the Music Archives

At the Fillmore West Van's musical depth was apparent. John Wasserman and Ralph Gleason, two of San Francisco's premier newspaper critics, noticed Morrison played the saxophone, the guitar and the harmonica. He also directed the band. He had three superb backup singers. A bootleg LP, **The Moonlight Serenade**, suggests Morrison developed into a top concert act. This bootleg also came out under the title **Van Morrison: Rocks His Gypsy Soul**.

One of the ironies of early Van Morrison bootlegs is he allegedly collected them. One day in Berkeley a shocked Rasputin's Records employee looked up. He was selling a bootleg to the Belfast Cowboy. After all this was Berkeley. Anything was possible.

Van was unhappy with stardom. The requirements of stardom didn't seem worth it. He told Chris Michie: "I can't walk into City Lights and buy books." This was a reference to the famed North Beach bookstore in San Francisco that Morrison frequented. It was not uncommon to see Van and poet Lawrence Ferlinghetti browsing the book stalls oblivious of one another.

Then Van would walk for an Irish coffee next door to Vesuvio's. He could enjoy the city. For a time Morrison traveled between New York and San Francisco. He was in demand for concerts thanks to **Astral Weeks** and **Moondance**. He wasn't keen on performing. Money was a factor. Over time his stage fright lessened. The shows were increasingly pleasing to his legion of San Francisco Bay Area fans.

WEIGHING IN FOR THE CONCERT FRAY: VAN DIDN'T LIKE IT BUT HE DID IT

When he performs there is often a mystical quality. This is due to his well-defined spiritualism. The result is an in-concert magic. An example of concert magic was a four-minute "Come Running." On July 17, 1970 at New York's Randall Island Van made an appearance with Jimi Hendrix, Dr. John, John Kay of Steppenwolf and a host of other bands. He was up to the task. After the Randall's Island Pop Festival, the press took an increased interest in Morrison's music. Van brought along a seasoned band. It included John Platania on guitar, Jack Schroer on alto sax, Jeff Labes on piano and the creative Dahaud Shaar on drums. It was a magic moment. The question of whether Morrison could perform in concert was never an issue. The question was whether he desired to perform. The Randall Island show was one Morrison hated. He gave a top-notch live performance. Why is this important? Van's view of the concert is a business window into his mind.

From Van's point of view, Randall Island was a failure. He was the fourth act listed on the bill behind Mountain with Joe Cocker and Dr. John. The crowd was intent on dancing in front of the stage and throwing objects at each other rather than listening to the music. As paper planes and Frisbees flew through the air, Van vowed to avoid future hippie festivals. When this show was broadcast on public television, it was a ratings blockbuster. The film, known as "Free," was an attempt to explain the hippie culture. It failed. The film showcased Morrison's in-concert charm. Although he hated this appearance,

Warner Brothers and Bill Graham convinced the Belfast Cowboy his future earnings would be increased by television exposure. Morrison agreed to tape a program for the Public Broadcasting System. In America PBS is a commercial free outlet with an intellectually based audience. It was a smart move on Morrison's part.

New York Pop Festival, Randall's Island 1970 - Poster ad

THE PUBLIC BROADCASTING SHOW AND THE MORRISON MYSTIQUE

On September 23, 1970 Van was part of a Public Broadcasting System special entitled "Welcome To the Fillmore East." It was broadcast on November 10 over local public television. Bill Graham came on stage to introduce the acts. Graham remarked: "Sit back and say hello to our friends from Macon, Georgia." The Allman Brothers came out and performed a fiery set. Van followed. Morrison's brief appearance stole the show.

Van's two songs "These Dreams of You" and "Cyprus Avenue" were a highlight. The taping, which was broadcast over WNET in New York City, also included the Byrds, Elvin Bishop, Albert King and Sha Na Na.

Elvin Bishop recalled how brilliantly Van worked the audience. He was amazed at his stage show. Bishop heard rumors of Morrison being difficult in concert. The rumors were not true. The New York music scene was a positive one for Morrison. He was booked into New York's Academy of Music with Linda Ronstadt and Tim Buckley. It was a four-day concert from November 13-16 sponsored by **Rock Magazine**. The shows were poorly attended. The opening act, Linda Ronstadt, debuted her new back up group Swampwater. At the urging of Warner Brothers executives, Van performed "Moondance," "Domino" and "Come Running." It was to sell product. He disdained these requests for specific songs.

WHERE WAS VAN AT THE END OF 1970: IS THERE A NEW VAN?

In 1969, Van toured with a six-piece band. That is when he could afford to pay the musicians. He had to keep the group together to work on a third Warner album. His musicians, some of whom had a pedigree from the Berklee School of Music, were established performers. They had an inordinate influence upon his music. Suddenly, there was a honky-tonk good time sound. **Moondance** was the beginning of that musical direction. In the next two albums **His Band and the Street Choir** and **Tupelo Honey,** he would take this sound to the bank. As Van experimented with his musical ideas, he analyzed the charts and wrote Top 40 hits. He did this to survive in the business.

The proof of the new Van came in the next few years when five of his 45 releases and three of his albums charted. Van had arrived as an artist. There was only one person unhappy with his success. That was Van. He didn't want to be the flavor of the month.

By 1970 Morrison's shows underwent dramatic change. There were some mild theatrics. He would turn the microphone off. He would pause. He would throw it to the floor. He would stare at the crowd. He would turn his back. Then he would turn around and finish the song. A band member told me Van wanted the audience to listen to the music. He wanted to avoid the adulation. While 1970 was a busy year, it was also a period of reordering his priorities. He made the decision to move to San Francisco. He called Bill Graham continually. Graham had no idea Van was contemplating relocating to the West Coast. He was too busy with his own ventures to spend enough time on the Belfast Cowboy's career.

One of Bill Graham's faults is he never listened. He did all the talking. Had he taken the time; he would have seen Van longed for the San Francisco Bay Area. The Woodstock days were coming to an end. He would take his life and music to the small town of Fairfax, north of San Francisco.

BIBLIOGRAPICAL SOURCES

The best description of Woodstock is in Barney Hoskyns, **Across The Great Divide: The Band And America** (New York, 1993), chapter 2. Also see, Robert Shelton, **No Direction Home: The Life And Music of Bob Dylan** (New York, 1986), pp. 261-265, 380-383 and Bob Spitz, **Dylan: A Biography** (New York, 1989), 382-386 for another side of the Woodstock story.

Also see Howard A. DeWitt, **Van Morrison: The Mystic's Music** (Fremont, 1983), pp. 34-42, Clinton Heylin, **Can You Feel the Silence: Van Morrison, A New Biography** (London, 2002), chapter 13 and pp. 151, 181-182, 198-199, 215-224, Ritchie Yorke, **Van Morrison: Into the Music** (London, 1975), chapter 6 and Brian Hinton, **Celtic

Crossroads: The Art of Van Morrison (London, 1997, revised edition, 2000), chapter 4.

On Schwaid-Merenstein see, John Collis, **Van Morrison: Inarticulate Speech of the Heart** (Boston, 1996), pp. 97-100 for an account of their management and production. Also see Erik Hage, **The Words and Music of Van Morrison** (New York, 2009), pp. 40-48,127. Professor Hage is a specialist in media and he is an Assistant Professor and Journalism, Mass Medic and Cultural Criticism at SUNY Cobleskill. His book on Morrison is an important insight into how and why Morrison became and has endured as a cultural icon. Hage also analyzes the music industry and he is able to show that Morrison's extraordinary skill as a businessman was a reason for his continued success in an industry filled with vipers and corporate snakes.

Michael Gray, **Song And Dance Man III: The Art of Bob Dylan** (London, 2000), pp. 94, 131, 161, 212, 266, 269, 288, 310, 356 provide some interesting influences by Dylan and Van on each other's art.

See Ken Brooks, **In Search of Van Morrison** (London, 1999) for some interesting comments on the **Moondance** album. Interviews with Simon Gee, Roger Armstrong and Mark Naftalin helped in analyzing the music. Interviews with Jesse Hector helped to shape material for this chapter.

Peter Mills, **Hymns to the Silence: Inside the Words and Music of Van Morrison** (New York, 2010) is a brilliant work and for this period see chapter one "Imaging America" for a new twist on the Woodstock-California influences.

A brief interview with Elvin Bishop helped to recall the details of the 1970 NET show. A special edition of **Wavelength** magazine detailed the television shows and was helpful to this chapter.

See Elliot Landy's website for the photos that he took during the **Moondance** album.

Van in two interviews in the 1990s reflected on his earlier career, see, for example, Polygram Interview CD, promotional for the CD **How Long Has This Been Going On: Van Morrison With Georgie Fame and Friends** (London, 1996) and John Kelly, "Interview," **Irish Times**, April 11, 1998.

An interview with Mervyn Solomon added a great deal to this chapter.

A series of interviews with Bobby Blue Bland at Seattle's Jazz Alley helped to formulate some of Van's personality and musical traits.

An interview with Van's father, George Morrison, at his Fairfax record store helped to form the basis of many points in this chapter.

For a review of the Gaslight show see, John Lombardi, "Van Morrison On MacDougal Street," **Rolling Stone**, February 21, 1970, p. 10.

The Colwell-Winfield Blues Band album **Cold Wind Blues**, Boston Sound, 1968, Comets Records Italy, 2001 reissue is a must to listen to for an obscure influence upon Morrison.

The bootleg CD **Van Morrison: The Genuine Philosophers Stone**, 3 discs, GPS 7 has three versions of "Domino" which suggest that Lewis Merenstein was more important to Van's sound than he may have realized. Other bootlegs helpful to this chapter were **Van Morrison: Unplugged In The Studio**, OP 8 Music and **Van Morrison: No Stone Unturned**, n. p., n. d.

Johnny Rogan, **Van Morrison: No Surrender** (London, 2005), chapters 12-14 is a brilliant look at the post-**Astral Weeks** career problems.

For the **Moondance** album and its chart and review progress, see, for example, Robert Christgau, **Rock Albums of the 70s: A Critical Guide** (New York, 1981), Paul Gambaccini, **The Top 100 Rock 'n' Roll Albums of All Time** (New York, 1987), Rick Clark, **The All Time Music Guide to Rock** (1995) and the **Zagat Music Survey-1000 Top Albums of All Time** (2003).

For the **Moondance** album photos see Elliott Landy's website at https://elliottlandy.com/portfolio-items/van-morrison-gallery/

See **All About Jazz**, February 2007, no. 58 for information on the Gaslight Club. Nick Hornby, **Songbook** (London 2002) talks of the importance of the song "Caravan."

For the Café Espresso see Peter McCabe, "Mellow Down Easy In Woodstock," **Rolling Stone**, March 4, 1971. For the story of Bob Dylan's piano at the Café Espresso and Van, see Haven Jones, "If These Old Keys Could Talk ... Bob Dylan's Piano Looks Back," at http://www.hvmusic.com/writers/werewolf/misc/piano.shtml

On the influence of American music on the British scene, see, for example, Mo Foster, **Play Like Elvis! How British Musicians Bought**

The American Dream (London, 2000) and L. Cooper and B. L. Cooper, "The Pendulum of Cultural Imperialism-Popular Music Interchanges Between the U.S. And Britain, 1943-1967," in G. Crnkovic and S. Ramet, editors, **Kazaam! Splat! Ploof! The American Impact On European Popular Culture Since 1945** (New York, 2003), pp. 69-82.

On "4% Pantomime" and the Band's relationship with Morrison see the erudite article by Peter Viney, "Van Morrison & The Band, **Wavelength**, Issue 7, March 1996 and it is also on the web at http://theband.hiof.no/articles/van_morrison_band_viney.html

A brief interview in the late 1970s with Mary Martin in Woodstock was important to this chapter and my two previous books on Van Morrison.

Also see Elliott Landy, **Woodstock Vision: The Spirit Of A Generation: Celebrating The 40th Anniversary of the Woodstock Festival** (London, 1997, reprint 2009).

For the Gershen Brothers and Borderline's influence upon Van's early 1970s music, see, for example, Matthew Lewis, "Music From Big Pink's Neighborhood," **Big O Magazine**, n. d. Singapore, Ritchie Unterberger, "Liner Notes To The U.S. Release of 'Sweet Dreams And Quiet Desires'/The Second Album," Real Gone Music, 2013, Bob Sarlin, "Album Review," **Crawdaddy**, July 1973 and Steve Ditlea, "Review of 'Sweet Dreams And Quiet Desires," **Rolling Stone**, September 13, 1973.

See Sean O'Hagan, "All I Really Want To Do," **London Guardian**, August 26, 2000, for a glimpse by Van back into the Woodstock era. This was the beginning of more forthcoming and retrospective interviews from the Belfast Cowboy. He wanted to set the record straight.

For Mary Martin, see, for example, Tori Tarvin, "Louise Scruggs Memorial Forum: Marty Martin," **Country Music Hall of Fame**, November 17, 2009 and Dr. H. Guy, "Into The Mystic: Leonard Cohen - Van Morrison Connection," October 15, 2015 Also see, Michael Oberman, "Music Makers: Van Morrison," **The Washington Star**, October 23 1971.

One of the more analytical reviews of **Moondance** and what it meant after the fact with details from 1970 is Ryan H. Walsh, "Van

Morrison: Moondance," **Pitchfork.com**, November 25, 2018. https://pitchfork.com/reviews/albums/van-morrison-moondance/ Walsh demonstrates the differences between Van and Warner Brothers exploded due to the February 1969 Whiskey A Go Go gig and how these differences festered into a brutal and open hostility that might have derailed Van's career.

On the evolution of "Moondance," Joey Bebo, the drummer for Van Morrison in the summer of 1968, discussed in an interview with me how the song came together in the months he played with Morrison in and around Boston. In its initial phase John Sheldon played a very defined, almost Jimi Hendrix like guitar and Van adapted to the band. Bebo was impressed with the way Morrison blended in with this band which played small clubs, roller rinks and high school auditoriums. Bebo said the group practiced "Moondance" regularly but didn't perform it in local shows.

One of the sidelights to this chapter that I fail to analyze is the number people who were institutionalized in Boston's McLean Hospital. These included fifteen year old John Sheldon who was diagnosed with "adolescent turmoil" whatever that meant. McLean was a mental hospital that looked like a college campus. James Taylor, Sylvia Plath and Ray Charles were treated at the facility. When asked was McLean did for him, John Sheldon replied he learned to smoke pot. Van's flute player, John Payne, was for a time at the hospital. Why is this important? Van distanced himself in the studio and from some of these musicians as he wrote the **Moondance** album. Why? Only Van can tell us. Maybe he didn't do it. Who knows! What is known is John Sheldon in Alex Beam's **Gracefully Insane** observed that Van showed up at his house one day saying he had a dream to get rid of the electric instruments? They fired the drummer and became a three piece group. (Beam, p. 197). See John McCarthy, "Did Ye Get Healed? - How Van Morrison's Music Helped Me Recover My Life," **BBC News**, January 21, 2017 for a poignant report on how Van's song "Wonderful Remark" made one reporter recall a tough time in his life with psychological implications. 'Wonderful Remark" helped the reporter overcome demons and view a window from insanity into sanity. Mental health cleansing and "Wonderful Remark" went hand in hand according to John McCarthy.

For an interesting analysis of **Moondance**, along with other albums, see Alan Light, "The All-Time 100 Albums: Moondance by Van Morrison, **Time**, November 3, 2007.

❧❧

CHAPTER 16

MOONDANCE'S SECOND LIFE: WARNER MAKES A LOT OF MONEY AND THE FANS GET A BONUS: WHAT DOES VAN THINK?

"I wrote the melody first. I played the melody on a soprano sax and I knew I had a song so I wrote lyrics to go with the melody."

VAN MORRISON IN CONVERSATIONS WITH RITCHIE YORKE

"Crazy Love' was part of his deliberate attempt to make more of a commercial mark with the Moondance album…."

PETER MILLS

"Moondance was always an exquisite experience and this remaster brings back the fact, that even if this album is overly familiar to me, it's one of the best collection of songs assembled in one place at one time. Van built with his bare hands what we still can't do today."

PAT THOMAS

❧❧

Van Morrison April 1970 in Woodstock, New York.
(Photo by David Gahr)

Uncut, one of the U.K.'s premier music magazines, announced Van Morrison was going to release a five CD revised **Moondance Deluxe** edition with a DVD that contained virtually every studio outtake. Van was the only person who didn't know about the release. Morrison's management responded he had nothing to do with the project. They complained the early publicity indicated the Belfast Cowboy approved of the release. He didn't. He was unaware. Van was furious with Warner Brothers.

Van Morrison: "Yesterday Warner Brothers stated that 'Van Morrison was reissuing **Moondance'**. It is important that people realize that this is factually incorrect. I did not endorse this; it is unauthorized and it has happened behind my back."

There was also a two-disc reissue with the centerpiece being a previously unreleased version of "I Shall Sing," as well as three previously unreleased versions of "Moondance." The two-disc release contained eleven previously unreleased songs. All were remastered.

The day after Warner Music announced the release of the deluxe reissues of **Moondance**, Morrison took to his website to denounce both the five disc and two disc reissues. He claimed his management company gave the album away forty-two years ago. "Now I feel as though it's being stolen from me again," Van concluded.

There were some interesting songs on the re-release. A lost take of "I Shall Sing" in a Caribbean type musical direction, which was a hit for Art Garfunkel, is one of the best cuts. Judy Mowatt also recorded this song, as well as Miriam Makeba, attesting to Morrison's wide ranging musical influence.

It is the second disc on the two CD release that contains gold. There are eleven tracks, which includes a version of "Into The Mystic" without horns. The jazz oriented "Nobody Knows You When You Are Down And Out" recalls a record that Van may have heard his father play. There is a funky version of "I've Been Working." "Glad Tidings" is another gem. The ability to take songs he recorded previously and make them into new versions is one of Morrison's strengths.

MOONDANCE: THE 5 DISC DELUXE PACKAGE

If you could find a mystical way to introduce a five-disc reissue of **Moondance** it would be Janet Planet's original liner notes to the album. That is one of many things Warner got right releasing **Moondance: Deluxe Edition** with Janet's lucid and literary illusion. Her introduction to Van's music provides a roadmap to understanding the album. She describes the essence of Van's soul. "The young man remained quiet for a long while. His hands and breath were quiet, his eyes lowered in deep contemplation," Janet wrote. There is no better description of the twenty-five year old Morrison.

Moondance deserves a multiple disc release. Why? The album was inducted into the Grammy Hall of Fame in 1999. **Rolling Stone** rated it number sixty-five in the "500 Greatest Albums" listing. The Allman Brothers, Jerry Garcia, Michael Bolton and Michael Bublé covered songs from the album.

After he began "Moondance" as an instrumental, Morrison realized he had more than a song for his soprano sax. "I knew I had a song, so I wrote lyrics to go with the melody," Van recalled. The lyrics provided him with his most popular early Warner recording. The critics noted the imagery, and the manner in which Morrison blended rock and roll with jazz and the blues.

The 2013 **Moondance: Deluxe Edition** was praised by critics. It was quickly snapped up by Van's fans as well as a new generation. **Record Collector** called it a "marvel." On "And It Stoned Me" and "Crazy Love" the re-mastered production made these tunes new ones. It was included in an April 2018 Record Store Day vinyl release.

The five-disc package includes eighty songs and the fifth disc is a Blue Ray audio version of disc one in 24-bit/192 kHz high resolution with 5.1-surround sound. The remastering includes mono remixes, alternate versions, as well as eight takes of "Caravan" and thirteen takes of "I Shall Sing." You come away from the album with a working blueprint of Van in the studio.

The **London Independent** observed the re-mastering "strips away centuries of digital compression and makes the music sound as if you've never heard it properly." For the fan this is the reason to purchase the five disc reissue. Will Hermes, writing in **Rolling Stone**, observed the bonus tracks created "an intimate quality."

Hal Horowitz, writing in the **American Songwriter**, called the release "bloated." Ouch! He gave it a two star rating. Horowitz argues the five disc set was "never meant to see the light of day." This critic speculated "so many working versions of these songs can be a trying, time consuming yet occasionally enjoyable experience." Horowitz couldn't decide if the liked the reissue. What did he miss? The fifty unreleased tracks have some unexpected gems beginning with an eleven minute rehearsal of "I've Been Working" and including twelve versions of "Glad Tidings." These songs provide a road map into how Morrison's musical genius works.

Hal Horowitz: "Morrison has been adamant in his opposition to this barrel scraping reissue and his typically curmudgeonly trait might be on target." Hey Hal! Van is going to love your attitude. The problem is you are a critic without brains. Your homework assignment is to go back and actually listen to the five discs. You will be surprised. Morrison's brilliance almost half a century after this re-release is a tribute to his lyrical magic.

JANET PLANET'S ORIGINAL LINER NOTES AND WARNER IGNORING HER TALENTED FABLE

When Warner Brothers made plans to reissue **Moondance**, they didn't consult Morrison. They owned the album. Their attitude was "fuck Van." They also didn't consider paying Janet Planet royalties. She wrote the liner notes. She made a contribution to the mood and the tone of this brilliant album. Why didn't they compensate her? Who knows!

Janet's liner notes are a brilliant look into the life she had with Van. Using a medieval fable as her structure Janet wrote of how Van gave away his "gift." One assumes that gift was songwriting. Her liner notes, using a parable form, telling us all we need to know about Morrison's troubles with the recording business.

The liner notes abruptly shift tone and direction when the young man with gifts finds his lover pale and in poor health. The remainder of the liner notes suggest the difficulties between the young maiden and the young man with the gifts.

Janet concludes her notes asking a question. "Who will quiet the aching in your heart, the ache which you have quieted in mind?" What is Janet portending? She knows! We don't!

Why did Janet Planet have to hire a lawyer to get paid for the liner notes on the reissue? No one knows. She did get paid thanks to her lawyer. The fact she had to threaten to go through the courts, hiring a sophisticated, urbane, suave, well known San Francisco lawyer, tells one all they need to know about Warner Brothers. The aura of Mo Ostin continues to stink up the corporate offices.

ALAN LIGHT'S REISSUE LINER NOTES AND ELLIOT LANDY'S BRILLANCE

Alan Light wrote the liner notes for the **Moondanc**e reissue. They are brilliant. Light recognizes the extraordinary work of Jack Schroer on alto and soprano sax and Collin Tilton on tenor sax and flute. He weaves a story of those who were instrumental in Morrison's breakthrough commercial album. The backup singers were important to the album. On the re-release they stand out due to Wyn Davis, Brian Keweh and Craig Anderson's re-mastering.

Shelly Yakus, one of five engineers employed on the album, observes on the first six songs Van never uses the same voice twice. It is as if he reaches into his past history, his record collection and his feel for the music to bring out a wide variety of vocal interpretations. That is the way he intended it. Alan Light's booklet and information distills what is a one of the classic albums in rock history.

THE STUDIO CHATTER, SPECIAL SONGS AND THE MUSICIANS

For the serious listener there is an endless amount of studio chatter. The difficulty recording a final take of "Caravan" is shown as Morrison says: "I can't feel nothin' in here … there's just nothin' I feel at all." Whoa! That tells it all. He wouldn't stop recording until he had the song down right. The frustration in Van's voice was obvious.

"Nobody Knows When You're Down And Out" is a 1923 song popularized by Bessie Smith. There is an unfinished version on the reissue. Why? No one has ever explained it. Perhaps Jimmy Cox's lyrics were ones Van identified with and he sees his life in this song. "Nobody Knows When You're Down And Out" has a message. The song ruminates on success, failure and the nature of close relationships. Van identified.

"I've Been Working" is a special song. The tune is referred to as an old Irish working man's song. The three versions on this reissue are intriguing. Van saved it. He redid the song for the **His Band and the Street Choir** album.

The sampling of thirteen takes of "I Shall Sing" tells a story. How? The experimental studio mood that was Van is shown in reworking this song. After sampling the thirteen cuts on the **Moondance: Deluxe Edition** there is a completed version. It is like sitting in the studio and listening to Morrison create. Jack Schroer's saxophone stands out. Not surprisingly Art Garfunkel brought Schroer into the studio for his 1973 solo debut album **Angel Clare**.

There are seven experimental takes of "Into The Mystic." This is another window into Morrison's creativity. As the song develops there are horns and a saxophone. There are versions without these instruments. Van loved to explore and extrapolate. This album allows you to follow him in the studio.

Surprisingly, there are only two takes of "Moondance." Why? He had played this song extensively in shows in Boston in 1968. It was ready for the recording studio. The inclusion of takes 21 and 22 suggest how hard and how long Morrison worked on "Moondance."

VAN ON THE MOONDANCE REISSUE: JANET MORRISON MINTO'S ROLE

When asked about **Moondance**, Van remarks: "Songs are just ideas, concepts and you just put the mic there and go." This comment, according to Alan Light, suggests the new and mature Van Morrison. He is tired of being asked what his songs mean? He now answers this missive with hyperbole.

Janet Morrison Minto, who Warner did pay reluctantly for her contribution to the re-release, was an important part of the original album. She is a talented writer with a sense of what is commercial in the rock marketplace. She was unpaid during the initial **Moondance** release. Her original liner notes were used in the reissue. She received a check.

Janet Morrison Minto is a person who writes music, poetry, makes jewelry, and she was a quiet fountain of wisdom in the midst of Van's rock and roll world. Her poetic liner notes suggest the influence of fantasy fiction. She writes of her love for her husband and his music. It is a touching moment. She ends her liner notes with a literary flair: "As the sun began to set, he and his beloved went out into the garden to await the coming of the moon." That said it all tranquility and artistic accomplishments were in the air.

The three discs of session materials is a bonus for the serious collector, the historian and those who wonder how and why Morrison can create such lyrically sophisticated, and beautiful music. The DVD presents **Moondance** in a sound previously unheard with the Blue Ray High Resolution Stereo and Surround Sound mixes making the album sound like Van in playing in your living room. The **Moondance: Deluxe Edition** reminds the listener Morrison's roots are in folk, blues, soul, jazz, pop and rock. Somehow, he combines these disparate elements in what is arguably his most brilliant album. With apologies to **Astral Weeks**, this is the best window in the multiple talents making up Van Morrison.

MOONDANCE LIVE: RARE CREATIVE INSIGHTS INTO VAN'S RECORDING METHODS

What does one get from fifty unreleased tracks plus two finished versions of **Moondance**? There are numerous versions highlighting how he worked in the studio. The mono remix of "Caravan" is a brilliant version. The studio conversation goes a long way toward showing how and why Van is a studio genius. There are only subtle changes in most of the songs.

Why spend fifty dollars on the **Moondance Deluxe edition**? That is the question. Here is the answer. The remastering is worth the price.

The previously unreleased outtakes tell one all they need to know about Morrison's creative drive. Not to mention his lyrics and music are crystal clear.

BIBLIOGRAPHICAL SOURCES

For a five star review see, Will Hermes, "Moondance (Deluxe Edition)," **Rolling Stone**, October 18, 2013. https://www.rollingstone.com/music/music-album-reviews/moondance-deluxe-edition-102832/ Also see John D. Luerssen, "Van Morrison 'Moondance' Reissue Full of Rarities-Album Premiere," **Rolling Stone**, October 17, 2013. https://www.rollingstone.com/music/music-news/van-morrison-moondance-reissue-full-of-rarities-album-premiere-71076/

For the best review of what the original **Moondance** meant and the re-releases prior to the 2013 deluxe edition, see, Pat Thomas, "Now I Can Die in Peace, They Have Finally Remastered Van Morrison's **Astral Weeks**, **His Band and the Street Choir** And **Moondance** Albums On CD," **East Portland. Blog**, October 6 2012. Thomas is an unusually perceptive Van critic. With the eye of a trained musician, he is a drummer, his writing on Morrison provides deep insight into how and why the Belfast Cowboy explores his musical terrain. Also see the review by Hal Horowitz, "Van Morrison: Moondance - Deluxe Edition," **American Songwriter**, October 22 2013. https://americansongwriter.com/van-morrison-moondance-deluxe-edition/ Horowitz labels the reissue "a Barrel scraping reissue" and says that you still buy if you want an "overstuffed package." One wonders if Horowitz listened to the five CDs? Probably not!

For Elliott Scheiner's role in **Moondance** see, Clinton Heylin, **Van Morrison: Can You Feel The Silence? A New Biography** (Chicago, 2002), pp. 228-229, 239.

For an excellent review of the album see Jeff Burger, "Van Morrison-Moondance Deluxe Edition," **No Depression**, November 19, 2013 https://www.nodepression.com/album-reviews/van-morrison/ The Burger review is one of the best analyzing Van in the studio and how and why he recorded.

Also see, Doug Collette, "Van Morrison: Moondance Expanded," **All About Jazz.com**. November 30, 2013. https://www.allaboutjazz.com/moondance-expanded-van-morrison-warnerarchives-review-by-doug-collette.php The Collette review reminds the listener of the "relative simplicity of the material" and he goes on to praise the re-mastering. In particular, he points out the "hypnotic bass lines, the subtle touches of percussion … and the depth of emotion." Also see, Joe Marchese, "Review: Van Morrison, 'Moondance: Deluxe Edition'," **The Second Disc**, October 28 2013. https://theseconddisc.com/2013/10/review-van-morrison-moondance-deluxe-edition/

For an excellent review of the reissue see Martin Chilton, "Van Morrison Moondance Outtakes Are Hidden Gems," **London Telegraph**, October 16, 2013. https://www.telegraph.co.uk/culture/music/rockandpopfeatures/10367638/Van-Morrison-Moondance-outtakes-are-hidden-gems.html

The reviews for the reissue are uniformly terrific on the vinyl release suggesting Warner went to a great deal of trouble. The most important negative comment is the 5 disc reissue fell apart due to inadequate packaging. There are no complaints concerning the music.

PART III

THE WARNER YEARS HURLING INTO THE MAINSTREAM WITH HITS

CHAPTER 17

THE VAN TRANSITION: HOW WARNER BROTHERS, THE LAST WOODSTOCK DAYS, AND THE CALIFORNIA MOVE ACTED AS AN ARTISTIC CATALYST

"Meanwhile back in San Francisco - We're trying hard to make this whole thing blend."

VAN MORRISON, ST. DOMINIC'S PREVIEW

"Everybody feels so determined not to feel anyone else's pain.... No one's making no commitments to anybody but themselves."

VAN MORRISON, ST. DOMINIC'S PREVIEW

"Woodstock was getting to be such a heavy number.... Everybody and his brother started showing up at the bus station ... that was the complete opposite of what it was supposed to be."

VAN MORISON IN CONVERSATION WITH RICHARD WILLIAMS.

❧❧

In the spring of 1971, Van Morrison began the transition from Woodstock to Fairfax California. His life turned upside down. He had a contract with Warner Brothers allowing for creative freedom. He had a young daughter, and his wife described herself as "a muse without money." The transition to California was in the works.

417

One of the ironies of Van moving to Northern California caused Van to recall his Belfast days. For whatever reason, he reconsidered his Irish past. He wrote furtively. How much of it was about Ireland? No one knows! What is known is he frequented the San Francisco Irish community. The owners of the Irish bars and restaurants were not surprised when he showed up for a pint or a meal. One told me: "Van is Irish to the core." While he was writing Americana music there were major Irish influences. He seldom felt his Irish roots in Woodstock. This is one of many reasons for relocating to California.

As Van prepared to move to Fairfax, Tupelo Honey was in the works. He finished writing the songs before the move to Marin County except for "You're My Woman." He wrote that song in the midst of the recording sessions. The studio time for the album began in the spring of 1971 in San Francisco at Wally Heider's Studio. By May he was completing it in the city at the Columbia Studio. The new atmosphere brought a good time rock and roll tilt to the songs. His home in Fairfax was the catalyst to a free, easygoing set of chart friendly songs. The last Woodstock days were important for the writing. The San Francisco experience made the album musically.

THE HOUSE IN FAIRFAX AND HOW IT TRANSFORMED VAN

When you arrive in Fairfax California it is a small town between San Anselmo and the San Geronimo Valley. It is a quiet town of just over five thousand. It is a small city where people do things their own way. It is only sixteen miles from San Francisco. It is a touch of heaven in the bustle of the San Francisco Bay Area.

If you ask a local what defines Fairfax? The answer is "music and art." When Van settled into Fairfax, he had come into some money. The home he Janet, Peter and Shana lived in at 89 Spring Lane in Fairfax was a three thousand plus square foot residence with six bedrooms and four bathrooms. It was built in 1927. It was stately, quaint and well maintained. It sits on 2.3 acres with a rustic, quiet romantic countenance. The property sold on March 1, 1977 for $130,000. It was at that point Morrison purchased his Mill Valley home. He still owns it. Shana lives there pursuing a musical career.

The home studio Van built in the back of his Fairfax home was a ballast to his songwriting. His parents, Violet and George, eventually moved to Fairfax. They opened Caledonia Records. Van's daughter Shana was frequently behind the counter working the cash register and listening to Kiss.

WHAT THE MOVE TO MARIN COUNTY MEANT TO VAN'S ART

When Van moved to Marin County, he found like-minded musicians. He brought with him musical friends from Woodstock. He attempted to adjust to the new Warner Brothers contract and to forget the heartbreak over the commercial failure of **Astral Weeks**. He had critical acclaim. The money was coming. The transition almost destroyed his psyche. When he went into what his biographers call "the period of retirement: from 1973 to 1977," he was far from retired. He was working 24/7 on his music. He was gigging as much as he could in the San Francisco Bay Area, then without warning, he was surprised by a divorce.

When Van's wife, Janet Planet, packed up the car, scooped up Shana and left for Los Angeles, Van was shocked. It wasn't what he expected. In typical Morrison fashion he went to work to solve the problems in his life. This accounts for the so-called period of retirement.

The question of who wanted to move to the San Francisco Bay Area has intrigued biographers. Some say it was Janet Planet's decision. Others say it was Van's. He addressed the issue in a 1972 interview with **Rolling Stone's** John Grissim.

Van Morrison: "I'd always wanted to move to California. I didn't plan on staying in the East so long after leaving Boston. But we ended up living in New York City because of all the business. And then we rented a place in Woodstock for quite a while. I really liked it there."

The interpretive biographical machine never ends when it comes to Van Morrison. The chief mythmaker is Clinton Heylin.

CLINTON HEYLIN'S MYTHS ABOUT VAN

Clinton Heylin's Van Morrison biography is arguable the best one. It is unfortunate in one aspect. He continues to develop the myth Van was enraged, angry, out of control and simply not a good human being. This is not true. He introduces chapter fifteen: "1971-1972 Listen To The Lion" with a 1998 quote from Janet Planet: "By the time we moved to California, our life was very traumatic and horrible." That may be true but may also not be close to the truth. Divorce was imminent. Janet was not in a friendly mood.

No one denies Van has his moods. He does! He also wasn't the maladjusted, miscreant Heylin portrays. The truth is in the middle. When he moved to Fairfax his life didn't implode. It didn't get worse. It improved. There was a divorce. That was on the table in the later Woodstock days.

Van loved living in Fairfax. So did his wife. He had a decade of friendships, local music triumphs, huge record store sales and he was close to a number of key executives in the industry. When asked why he moved to Fairfax Van might have said: "It's the music stupid." If he didn't say it, he thought it.

WHY DID VAN MOVE TO FAIRFAX? IT WAS THE MUSIC STUPID

If you drive around Marin County and exit into the small town of Fairfax, it is much like Belfast. His dad founded Caledonia Records in Fairfax. Van lived a stone's throw from the record store. Marin County in the 1970s was filled with musicians. On any given day members of Commander Cody and the Lost Planet Airmen, Clover, the New Riders of the Purple Sage, Santana, the Grateful Dead, the Paul Butterfield Blues Band, the Youngbloods and solo acts like Bonnie Raitt, Maria Muldaur, Ramblin' Jack Elliott, Elvin Bishop, Mark Naftalin, Charlie Musselwhite, Norman Greenbaum and a host of others jammed in local clubs.

The clubs like the Inn of the Beginning and others in Marin County became home to Morrison when he wanted to test out his new material. He would call up a club. They would agree to have him perform the next day or two. FM radio would announce Van at the Inn of the Beginning. The show sold out in an hour. In San Francisco Van appeared regularly at the Great American Music Hall.

In 1968 the Inn of the Beginning in Cotati Ca. began booking rock music acts. It was a coffee shop serving Sonoma State College students. Over the next two years it evolved into a folk music club. The nightly bands were some of the San Francisco Bay Area's best.

THE VAN MORRISON BOOTLEG INDUSTRY

One of the joys of moving to Marin County was playing in the small local clubs or in the bowling alleys with a cocktail lounge, the former dance halls turned seedy nightclubs, the half dozen music clubs in and around the University of California, Berkeley, and the fly by night promoters trying to be Bill Graham. The area intrigued Morrison. From these clubs a Van Morrison bootleg industry emerged. Without these bootlegs a large part of the Morrison story would be lost to the clouds of obscurity. The fervent Morrison bootleg collectors intensified the mystery of the mystic's music.

What was the key Morrison bootlegs? This is a subjective matter. But some stand out. What are the ones that tell us about his life and his music? By examining key bootlegs that fit into the 1968 to 1972 scope of this book significant aspects of Van's life come to mind.

Bluesology, 1963-1973 was an early seminal album for Van collectors. The fifteen tracks include six songs from Them, eight studio outtakes and a rare single where Van plays saxophone "Boo Zoo Hully Gully" and "Twingy Baby." This bootleg album arrived from Luxembourg. The second vinyl masterpiece is **Buona Sera Senorita**, which contains the Pacific High Studio recordings of September 5, 1971. Some of the other boots of this show include bonus songs. The Desert Land bootleg combines the Pacific High shows with the Rainbow Theater concert of July 24, 1973. **Friday's Child** is a double album bootleg of the Pacific High shows along with tracks from a Rock City TV show in 1978 (This was actually a Don Kirshner TV special) as well as some rare cuts from Deventer Holland in 1967. **Friday's Child** is a rare treat and in 1978 a repackaging included "Flamingos Fly," which was a much different version from the original.

The Genuine Philosopher's Stone, from the Scorpio label, in September, 2000 was a three-disc masterpiece with studio demos and outtakes. This was material not previously bootlegged. The interview booklet, the photos and the identity of where and when each song was recorded made the Scorpio label a major bootlegger. For acoustic versions of Van's early material see **Van Morrison Gets His Chance To Wail**, which are tracks from 1969 to 1971. This is one of the best albums for sound quality. The tracks are mainly demos for **Moondance, His Band and the Street Choir** and **Tupelo Honey**. Another bootleg much like this is **Gypsy Soul: Lost Demos From A Classic Period**. Some interesting studio chatter suggests why the flute was left out of "Domino."

The large number of live concerts bootlegged could fill a book. The best early 1970s are **Into the Man**, which is the April 26, 1970 Fillmore West show, and **Moonshine Whiskey**. This bootleg CD is a compilation including the Pacific High Studio cuts.

The Inn of the Beginning - A bootleg cover of Van's May 14, 1971 show

When Van arrived in Marin County the local clubs were the catalyst to bringing his music together. He needed diverse Americana musical samples. He found them in the post-hippie, dark and dank, small clubs like the Inn of The Beginning and the Lion's Share.

LOOKING BACK ON THE TRANSITION FROM THE PERSPECTIVE OF 2018

In December 2018, in a brief interview with the **Irish Examiner**, Van reflected fifty years later on the transition in his career to Warner Brothers. He told Miriam O'Callaghan how the **Moondance** album didn't provide economic rewards. The album did define him as a major music act. Then the money arrived. Van remarked he was paid: "$100 a week ... just enough to kind of survive but not survive very well." Then the money flooded into Fairfax.

One of the intriguing aspects of Van's interview concerns Them. He said: "So I was the lead singer but I had to get paid as a session singer, not as an artist, because I wasn't getting anything as an artist, so the only way to get money was fill in the forms, send off the forms and they would get the money from the record company and pay ... it was very basic, it was a session fee so that's what I was getting for those records."

When O'Callaghan asked Van why he was still working hard at seventy, he responded: "It's what I do." Looking back on **Astral Weeks** he confessed he didn't know what he was doing. Van reflected: "It's very difficult to relate to it now, because it keeps coming up, but it's a great album."

Van sat quietly. He was in deep thought. He reminisced about the old days. "I'm not the same person, I was a kid then. I didn't know anything about anything, I was just spinning off the top of my head." Miriam O'Callaghan is a presenter for Irish RTE Radio 1 and her interview with Morrison was a fan favorite highlighting the new, reflective and friendly Morrison. Eventually, Van left Fairfax and purchased a Mill Valley residence. This home is on a bucolic road leading to Mt. Tamalpais. The brown, two story singled Mill Valley home sits on a non-descript street with a battered mailbox that simply states: "Morrison." There is a tall picket fence leading to the house and a chain-linked fence covers the property. It is not a fortress, but it is private. The only paean to luxury is a rectangular swimming pool. Privacy is a must.

There is no sugar coating Van's personality in the early1970s. He was at war with Warner Brothers and when I attempted to interview top-level Warner executives, I was met with a stone wall of silence except for Ray Ruff. The reason was a simple one. He had some low-level publicity people fired. One told the press Van was "unstable."

Ted Templeman is another source of Morrison's perpetual irritation with Warner Brothers. Not only was he a blonde haired, blue eyed surfer, he as full of himself in the studio, according to Van.

The irony is Morrison is easy to work with in the concert hall or the recording studio if his vision is not compromised.

BIBLIOGRAPHICAL SOURCES

See Miriam O'Callaghan, "I Hadn't A Clue What I Was Doing: Van Morrison Talks money and Music In Rare Interview," Irish Examiner, December 23, 2108. https://www.irishexaminer.com/breakingnews/entertainment/i-hadnt-a-clue-what-i-was-doing-van-morrison-talks-money-and-music-in-rare-interview-893833.html This is a particularly revealing interview as Van talks briefly, but with clarity, about the transition to Warner Brothers and how and why it was not financially or artistically beneficial. Also see Miriam O'Callaghan, "Van The Man Was An Absolute Joy," RTE News, January 9, 2019. https://www.rte.ie/culture/music/2018/1219/1018088-miriam-ocallaghan-van-morrison/

The O'Callaghan interviews represent another major turning point in Morrison's sometime acerbic relationship with the press. With the right questions, the proper interviewer and the right setting with a cup of teach there is a new Van Morrison. Is it maturity in his mid-seventies? Probably!

An interview with Dan Hicks at the Phoenix Musical Instrument Museum was important to this chapter. John Goddard of Village Music provided important information on the local clubs. Art Siegel helped to reconstruct the Marin County and San Francisco musical venues. Ray Ruff provided insights into the early Warner years and he blamed both Van and top Warner executives for the contentious relationship. A 1982 telephone interview with Nick Clainos who was in the management side of Bill Graham Presents was an interesting one. Clainos said Van was not that difficult and he claimed Bill Graham Presents loved booking Van. Later BGP managed Morrison for a brief time. But, like his previous management agreements, it was a short lived partnership.

There are many in-depth Van Morrison interviews. One of the best is Michael Goldberg, "Van Morrison Breaks His Silence (sort of), Rolling Stone, February 18, 1982 for an in-depth look at Van's Marin County home and his tenuous relationship with Warner Brothers. During the interview a generally cooperative Morrison discusses why he is wary of the press. As the interview was in progress Morrison either wouldn't answer some questions and he called out the inappropriate questions. When asked if he was happy? Van replied" "What does that have to do with anything?"

This chapter depends heavily upon interviews. At Bill Graham Presents blue coat Larry Catlin described the reaction by Morrison to Graham and his management tactics. Nick Clainos answered a number of questions on the Morrison-Graham relationship.

The continuing prominence of Van Morrison bootleg CD's suggests his continued popularity. One of the best sources for all sorts of bootlegs used to be the Midnight Café website which was shut down in April 2019. When Van does unadvertised shows, as he did with an unannounced performance in early 2006 at Rancho Nicasio, the owner, Bob Brown, was ecstatic. So was the bootlegger. The Rancho Nicasio show at four in the afternoon due to Van now being sixty years old. There was an announcement that only a couple of hundred tickets were available. It sold out in minutes. The bootlegger must have scored a ticket as the CD was an excellent soundboard production.

Also see extensive and well described list of Van bootlegs at Bootlegpedia http://bootlegpedia.com/en/product/G.R._932 One of the best from this site, which is also a best seller in European and U.K. stores is Van Morrison: Deep In Your Heart which is the much bootlegged April 26, 1970 Fillmore West show. This bootleg goes so far as to add four bonus tracks using Van's Warner Brothers demos. Godfather Records even has an advertisement on the website so you can order the CD and they have been doing this for almost five years.

CHAPTER 18

HIS BAND AND THE STREET CHOIR AND TUPELO HONEY, 1970-1971

"Hindsight is the bane of biography."

BRENDA MADDOX

"I wasn't very happy with Tupelo Honey."

VAN MORRISON

"Like Kerouac, some of his prose stuff, how can you ask what it means? It means what it means ... that's rock & roll to me."

VAN MORRISON IN CONVERSATION WITH CAMERON CROWE, ROLLING STONE 1977

During his last days in Woodstock, Van crafted the **His Band and the Street Choir** album. When the album was released on November 15, 1970, Morrison was inching toward stardom. Jon Landau called the album "the other side of Moondance." In sharp contrast, John Tobler reviewed it as "even if it's inferior to **Moondance** it is still better than eighty percent of the records you've got in your collection." Brian Hinton said it reeked of Bob Dylan's **Nashville Skyline**. Johnny Rogan labeled it "a severe disappointment." Maybe Van was right. It was time to confuse the critics.

Van headed into a new musical direction. He formed an ensemble of vocal musicians he dubbed the Street Choir. Van remarked he conceived **His Band and the Street Choir** as an a cappella work. He confessed he lost control of the album. Fortunately, Morrison's vision quickly translated into a pop-rock direction. Some critics described it as an unfinished product. The reality is quite different. It is the quintessential Americana album. The last vestiges of the counterculture flow through the lyrics.

The **His Band and the Street Choir** album was a celebration of Van and Janet's life. The album cover with a stoner hippie tone was a paean to Van's relaxed, bucolic life. Janet organized the visuals for the fold out album cover. She wrote the liner notes. She produced the album's graphics. She selected the pictures. With Van's hair in a long fashionable cut, the cool hippie style clothes, the tie dyed kaftan robe and an image of serenity there was a new Belfast Cowboy. Van quickly disavowed the clothes and the horse, Domino, in the picture. Morrison claimed he didn't own a horse. He did. It is listed as an asset in the divorce proceedings.

Janet remembers Woodstock as a positive experience. She talked with a **Los Angeles Times** reporter, Louis Sahagun, in a lengthy interview. She said the break up was difficult. "When I left everybody got real mad at me because I had become an important cog in a music industry machine that was starting to make so much money," Janet continued. "On the other hand, I just had to find peace and my own voice." She did. She went on to found a thriving jewelry business. She wrote original songs. She released an album with Pam Barlow. The album, on German MTM Music, is a collection of her thoughts in musical form. Janet's album was released under the name "Fake ID." She never attempted to exploit Van Morrison's name. He thought otherwise and years later he attempted to shut down her jewelry website. He failed. The title of Planet's 1997 album **Dreaming Ezekiel** was never explained. It was AOR with some heavy metal music. Janet was proud of it. She explained in detail to the **Los Angeles Times**.

Janet Planet: "This is not so much a review as a remembrance of what is was like to create these songs and performances. My songwriting partner Pam Barlow and I were at the top of our game during these years, we had perfected every aspect of the path from inspiration through the recording process, with the enormous help and assistance of world class engineer Chris Minto. You have to remember - this was back in the days when there were no Pro-Tools, no auto-tune, no digital, minutely manipulatable recording. We recorded to tape - in this case a Tascam 8-track. We had to actually be able to sing and play. Big difference these days. Each of these songs was lovingly crafted after being meticulously and often contentiously decided upon and written. These are the best of the best, many of them subsequently recorded by other bands and used in various TV show soundtracks. Thanks so much for listening and for loving our work. You are the reason we worked this hard." This is only one of many music projects Janet completed. She remains a burgeoning talent.

Janet looked back on Fairfax. She recalled: "Van was at his most relaxed and contented in his personal life." Janet said she found happiness with Van in Fairfax. Why the divorce? That is a question only Van and Janet can answer. The culprit in their personal difficulties was the music business. Van had a take no prisoner's mentality. He would not be bullied. He would not be pushed around. He would not allow the Warner Brothers' accountant, Mo Ostin, to derail his career.

The move to Fairfax was a smart one. The reason? Van's Protestant work ethic kicked in prompting him to make his home tranquil and private. He worked 24/7 on his music. He didn't like to socialize. Janet did. The chasm developing in the marriage became a breach without a solution.

When Janet left Fairfax, she retired her hippie name. "Janet Planet was never my name," she told Joel Selvin. "Pretty much the minute we parted and divorced, that was the end of Janet Planet."

As the battles with Warner Brothers escalated, the internecine strife that accompanied doing business with a major record label took its toll. While his daily life was pleasant, Warner blocked his artistic vision. Van told Ritchie Yorke: "I lost control of that album." This reference to **His Band and the Street Choir** was one where Van complained he had written the songs, brought the musicians together and produced the album. Then Warner took over. They altered and ruined his concept. He confessed to Yorke he detested the final product.

Van was bitter about Ted Templeman's co-production on **Tupelo Honey** and **St. Dominic's Preview**. Van complained about Templeman for years. He said Templeman added little, if anything, to his albums. Van inferred he was simply lining his pocket book.

The problems between Morrison and Warner Brothers surfaced when they vetoed his original album title, "Virgo Fools." The problems escalated in April 1970 as Morrison went into the studio to cut the LPs demos. In a small Woodstock church, Van worked on simple arrangements and minimalist music. Warner had a fit. They listened to the demos and declared them unsuitable for commercial release. For a moment they treated Morrison like an amateur.

This infuriated Morrison. His music was selling well. Warner demanded he hastily finish the album. Van demurred. In Woodstock, his musical friends, notably John Platania and Jack Schroer, noticed Morrison was unusually cantankerous. The trip to New York was tension filled. The label didn't understand his negative feelings. Van sent a demo tape to the New York studio. There was also a copy sent to Los Angeles. Mo Ostin listened. He exploded. He didn't like the demo tapes. It would be some weeks before Morrison found out Ostin's reaction.

On the way to New York to record the album, Van was angry. He was in the throes of a major crisis. There was a reason for his anger. Warner Brothers complained about the lack of quality. The Warner hierarchy criticized two instrumentals on the demo tape as filler. They reminded him he was a vocal artist. He responded. He was a multi-instrumentalist who could write, arrange and produce his albums.

The demos were cut in a Woodstock church. The leftovers from **Astral Weeks** and **Moondance** were marvelous songs. The demos for "Crazy Face" and "Give Me A Kiss" prompted one musician to remark: "Van seemed to pull these songs together effortlessly." That wasn't the case. They were in coffee stained notebooks. Dahaud Shaar attested to the demos care and precision. Van exploded at Warner for failing to recognize his work ethic. Or his talent.

ON TO NEW YORK

When Van entered New York's A & R Studio to record the album, he was ready. The Warner brain trust had no idea how prepared Morrison was prior to recording an album. There was a great deal of free form creativity to the **His Band and the Street Choir** LP. It is typical of Morrison to allow his musicians total studio freedom.

Warner complained about the inclusion of back-up singers. The label wanted him to be a folk singer. Van challenged long held rules and studio practices. Warner Brothers ignored him. They didn't recognize many of his perceptions were on the cutting edge of future technology. He pioneered the in-concert recording technique.

According to **Rolling Stone**, when Van began production on the LP in June 1970, he spent an inordinate amount of time redoing the tracks. This had nothing to do with the musicians. It was Morrison's desire for perfection. By 1970 his perfectionist nature took over in the studio.

The **His Band and the Street Choir** album saw the musical aggregation of John Platania, Jack Schroer, Daoud Shaar, also known as David Shaw, and John Klingberg return to form Van's musical core. At the time Shaw was getting to know Morrison. He went on the produce and drum on **It's Too Late to Stop Now**, **Veedon Fleece** and some of his work appeared on **The Philosopher's Stone**.

As a drummer, Shaar was innovative and low key. He was a mystical character everywhere but in the recording studio. He was a multi-instrumental performer who could play woodwind instruments. He was given the title of assistant producer on the **His Band and the Street Choir** album.

As David Shaw, he performed with Jerry Garcia and Etta James. During the first two years of Saturday Night Live, he was the drummer on this national television show. He also is a producer and spent much of his time in Philadelphia at Radio Active Productions. Shaar's skills are as a producer-musician. Van found he had innovative ideas.

MARY MARTIN PLAYS HARDBALL

Because his manager, Mary Martin, played hardball with Warner Brothers, Morrison received substantial royalties. Martin addressed another issue. It was to protect his songwriting. The Schwaid-Merenstein agreement was not artist friendly. Inherit Productions did nothing that was criminal. Like most other record moguls, the contract Van signed was weighed heavily in their favor. That is, they received an unwarranted cut of his songwriting and publishing royalties. Martin rewrote his management agreement. Van's songs were placed in the Vanjan Company and other Morrison business entities.

As Morrison prepared his follow up to **Moondance**, Martin reminded him to remain on schedule. Van never had a schedule. The word was alien to his character. She also began setting up concerts to garner maximum exposure for the new material. Van was making a nice living. He wanted to relax in Fairfax. He wanted to play small local clubs. Martin was fired.

When Van went into the studio to produce **His Band and the Street Choir**, there was no shortage of material. The themes in Morrison's music took on an increasingly lighthearted direction. These songs had Top 40 potential. Warner was concerned only about immediate commercial possibilities. This bothered Morrison. He wasn't a hit record machine.

Warner had Van continually demo songs. He worked up a mammoth catalogue of unreleased material. The positive reception for **Moondance** created problems. Van was in demand for concerts, disc jockey interviews and record store appearances. Warner set up a series of press conferences, promotional appearances and intimate one-on-one interviews. He didn't like to meet the press. He didn't want a timetable for completing a new album. For the first time in his career, Van displayed signs of writer's block. Fortunately, it quickly vanished.

IT IS TIME TO LEAVE WOODSTOCK AND NEW YORK

The Woodstock days were drawing to an end. Since the Woodstock Festival, the weekend hippies had taken over. They arrived in their suits, work clothes and new cars. These weekend hedonists quickly changed into t-shirts, beads and bell-bottoms. Out came the joints. Everyone got high. The weekend visitors littered the streets and went home. It was the ultimate act of hypocrisy, as weekend hippies coming to Woodstock altered the local culture. It didn't take long for this to drive Van toward the San Francisco Bay Area.

Before he left Woodstock, Van performed in a series of farewell concerts. He was the only person who knew they were final appearances. The venues he loved were in New York City. It gave him an excuse to travel to the Big Apple and earn a nice paycheck. The Fillmore East was the ultimate rock concert venue.

The Fillmore East operated from 1968 to 1972. This concert hall was New York's premier rock venue. Van's April 3-4, 1970 shows at the Fillmore East were not artistic triumphs. He was tired. He performed listlessly. The middle band, the Quicksilver Messenger Service, played a set highlighted by a Bo Diddley style beat. They were roundly cheered.

There was a reason for Van's foul mood. A group of 133 British journalists were flown into New York by Warner to interview the opening act, the Brinsley Schwarz band. Nick Lowe stood backstage and held court. Van was not happy with the two nights. The $72,000 spent to hype Brinsley Schwarz never translated into commercial success. Van was all but ignored. Warner refused to spend money to promote him.

Warner Brothers got it wrong once again. "Van Morrison was a hero," Nick Lowe remarked. As the bass player-vocalist for Brinsley Schwarz, Lowe was mystified with Warner Brothers. Why were they treating Morrison so poorly? Lowe remarked of that night: "I watched Van's show, ... because they were incredible, and I had a mounting sense of dread that we'd made a terrible mistake." Van was gracious and congratulatory to Lowe. This eased his concerns. Warner Brothers didn't get it. Lowe did.

THE PRELUDE TO THE NEW ALBUM

Woodstock's isolation impacted Morrison's songwriting. He needed calm to write. When he moved to Fairfax, he had the same tranquil atmosphere. Van and Janet's daughter, Shana, was born in Woodstock's Kingston Hospital, while Van was sorting through the material for the next two albums **His Band and the Street Choir** and **Tupelo Honey**.

Because of Shana's birth, Van wrote songs which were a paean to Janet's goodness and life influences. In the lyrics to "I'll Be Your Lover Too," Van suggests the overwhelming debt to his wife.

When Warner Bros executives visited with Van, they discussed his album cover concept. Morrison believed his wife's pictures should appear on the next few albums. She not only wrote liner notes, Van pointed out, Janet had a feel for what he was doing. Warner agreed. They also didn't have to pay her. The publicity over his idyllic marriage continued.

This created a false sense of marital bliss. The wholesale impression of good times on the albums **His Band and the Street Choir** and **Tupelo Honey** was an illusion. Morrison had trouble living with during the next few years. As Janet penned the notes to the **His Band and the Street Choir**, Van's career reached a new plateau. Commercial success arrived. His moods darkened. The pressures of stardom, combined with a need for continual productivity, drove a wedge in the marriage.

COMING TO CALIFORNIA: THE PERMANENT MOVE TO MARIN COUNTY

The Marin County music scene was a tonic to Morrison's performing development. He honed his performing skills in the small clubs like the Inn of the Beginning and The Lion's Share. From April 15, 1971, until the end of the year, Morrison played thirty-three intimate shows in the San Francisco Bay Area. By September 1971 Van settled permanently in Northern California.

The September-October 1971 dates are interesting ones for the live selections. The most played song for Van in concert in 1971 was

"I've Been Working." "Domino" was another in concert favorite. These were followed by "These Dreams of You," "Tupelo Honey," "Moonshine Whiskey," as well as covers of Bob Dylan's "Just Like A Woman," a Big Mama Thornton inspired "Hound Dog" and a Louis Prima influenced "Buona Sera." Van was smiling, having fun and engaging with the fans. In venues like San Francisco's Winterland and the San Jose Fairground Expo Hall the fans mixed with the musicians.

With a seven-person band and three backup singers the shows were precise. The ninety-minute sets were flawless. This was not the norm in the hippie inspired musical mélange that was the San Francisco Bay Area.

On October 3rd Van and a band featuring Woodstock exiles John Klingberg, John Platania, Jack Schroer and Collin Tilton backed him at the University of California, Riverside. This was the smallest University of California campus. It was located near a seedy looking downtown with a student population of future teachers, out of focus liberal arts types, perpetual students and those who didn't have a clue about their future.

The next night at UCLA's Pauley Pavilion, which was the universities basketball court, Van featured his recent material. Both shows sold out. For these shows he brought along the Street Choir his wife Janet as well as Ellen Schroer and Martha Velez. The band also included keyboardist Alan Hand and drummer Dahaud Shaar.

The UCLA Pauley Pavilion show featured a set highlighted by "Tupelo Honey," "Wild Night," "Moondance" and covers of Bob Dylan's "Just Like A Woman" as well as a truncated version of Big Mama Thornton's "Hound Dog." The concert at Pauley Pavilion featured Linda Ronstadt as the opening act.

FINALLY RELOCATING TO CALIFORNIA

By the spring of 1971 the Morrison's relocated to Marin County. At this point temporarily they lived in a San Francisco and later a Los Angeles hotel. Then they purchased a beautiful home in Fairfax. This small city north of San Francisco didn't manifest the ostentatious wealth of Mill Valley or Sausalito. It was perfect. With two young children, the rural ambiance was conducive to raising a family. It was a relaxed atmosphere for Van's songwriting. The house was located within thirty minutes of a large number of small clubs.

It was in his early trips to San Francisco, and during his first few years in Fairfax, Van saw his future. It was in the Marin County musical landscape. He loved the bands playing in the local clubs. He listened to the New Riders of the Purple Sage, Clover, the Quicksilver Messenger Service, Terry and the Pirates, Elvin Bishop, Commander Cody and the Lost Planet Airmen, Billy C. Farlow's band, Alice Stuart and Snake, It's A Beautiful Day, Huey Lewis and the American Revolution and Stoneground.

In November 1970, when the **His Band and the Street Choir** album appeared, the plan to relocate to the San Francisco Bay Area intensified. By 1971, the **Tupelo Honey** album was Morrison's last Woodstock LP. In "Old Old Woodstock" he expressed his feelings that he didn't want to leave upstate New York. "See the water flowing way beneath the bridge. And my woman's waiting. By the kitchen door. I'm driving along. In my old beat up car," Van wrote. Why did the Morrison's move? Van needed to be near the Los Angeles Warner Brothers corporate office. He had a war to fight against corporate malfeasance.

By early 1971 Warner believed there was no need to publicize **Tupelo Honey**. College radio station airplay indicated a strong FM presence. At Carnegie Mellon University WRCT's program director Bob Simon reported the album was in constant rotation. Chuck Lackner at KCLC-FM at Lindenwood College praised **Tupelo Honey** as number one at the station. Not surprisingly, KUSF the University of San Francisco college radio station had the album in constant rotation. Mo Ostin ordered a reduction in Morrison's advertising budget, according to Ray Ruff, who remarked Ostin never forgave Morrison for challenging him to a fight at dinner party in his home.

MARIN COUNTY: A RURAL PARADISE DESPITE THE PRESS

Van and Janet left one rural paradise for another. The similarities of Fairfax to Woodstock became apparent to those who visited the Morrison's. They left Woodstock to ensure their privacy. In numerous interviews, Van talked about how the 1969 festival altered their lives.

The journalistic intrusions were beginning to wear thin. Van hated interviews. He abhorred the insipid journalistic questions. He despised the lack of knowledge amongst the media. Still, he had to meet the press. Van seldom warmed to journalists. He didn't have to worry. The negative press and the London wankers who hounded musicians for sensational stories were constant. **Moondance's** popularity ended Morrison's privacy. The acclaim for the album led to a rush of journalists analyzing the album. The counterculture press: the **Los Angeles Free Press**, the **Berkeley Barb**, the San Francisco based **Oracle** and a host of college newspapers requested interviews. **Rolling Stone** was a welcome publicity arm for Morrison's albums and live shows.

The **Marin Independent Journal** (MIJ) reported Van's every move. When he performed at an unadvertised show the MIJ reported it a day before it took place. In 2006 Van was visiting his daughter Shana, he decided to perform at four in the afternoon at the Rancho Nicasio. The owner, Bob Brown, alerted the press the day before the show. The show sold out. As Van arrived there were more people in the parking lot than in the club.

Brown said Van contacted him and setup the show. "It was entirely his idea," Brown recalled. Morrison said he wanted to open his American tour of seven dates as this small club. "That was cool," Brown concluded.

Tickets to the Rancho Nicasio sold for one hundred and fifty dollars on line or through e-mail. The last time Van play the Rancho Nicasio was 1979 with Huey Lewis and the American Express opening for him.

As he entered his most commercial phase, Van was content to ignore the media. He viewed himself as an outsider. He was happy with that role. His press was generally respectful. He was referred to as "quirky." This bothered him.

Throughout his career, Van criticized the press. He's incensed over inaccurate coverage. In a 2003 song, "Goldfish Bowl," Van sings: "Newspaper barons are scum of the lowest degree. And they prey on everybody." In an April 2018 interview with BBC News, Van said: "I've been talking about fake news from day one."

VAN'S FAIRFAX BAND: MUSICAL GENIUS FOR NEW ALBUMS AND CRAZY LOVE

After relocating to California, Van assembled a semi-permanent band. He did this to complete his future albums. He also had a band ready to play club dates. He wanted a band he could have on call for rehearsal or a concert. His confidence level, while increasing, still needed the boost that comes from close musical friends.

The Woodstock musicians who relocated to Northern California blended with the local musical talent. This helped Morrison add new components to his music. An increasingly free form jazz sound emerged. The presence of horns made for an up-tempo sound. Jack Schroer's saxophone, John Platania's guitar and Jeff Labes keyboard made for a pop sound. They had played with him long enough to follow his very nuance.

The pop tones in Van's music led Helen Reddy to chart with "Crazy Love" in 1971. Then twenty five years later Aaron Neville hit the charts with the same song. Michael Bublé's fourth studio album, in 2009, contained "Crazy Love."

In 2003, when Van was inducted into the Songwriters Hall of Fame, Ray Charles accompanied him on "Crazy Love." In an astonishing moment Charles played piano and sang the first verse and chorus before Morrison made his entrance. "It meant a lot to me to sing 'Crazy Love' on stage that evening with Ray Charles," Morrison remarked.

Ray Charles included the duet with Van on "Crazy Love" that evening on his 2004 album **Genius Loves Company**. "Crazy Love" is a song that kept having a second life. This attests to Morrison's staying power as a contemporary songwriter.

What is it that makes "Crazy Love" an epoch? One phrase stands out "I'm running to her like a river's song." The gospel sounds of Cissy Houston, Judy Clay and Jackie Verdell added a soulful touch to a romantic pop song. That tells it all.

VAN: HIS WRITING, THE CRITICS AND THE NEW MUSIC

Van reads everything about himself. He developed a defensive strategy with the press. To this day, he is infatuated with the written word. He complains about it continually. He grants interviews with stringent conditions. There is invariably a time frame.

Joe Smith, who was instrumental in signing Van at Warner Brothers, tried to smooth over his press relations. He informed the press Morrison danced to the beat of a different drummer. He was uncomfortable during interviews. The media countered he wanted to write the story his way. They alleged he was spoiled and temperamental. In London **Melody Maker**, **Disc** and the **New Musical Express** were his strongest critics. They pilloried Van for his quirky, unpredictable nature.

In his songwriting, Van skewers the critics for their lack of knowledge. He asks them to leave him alone. He has written songs asking his interpreters to avoid the arcane language the French describe as "la langue de Bois." This is a phrase that describes the reviewer as having a wooden tongue in which nothing useful is said. During interviews, he describes how and why the critics analyze his music. When Brian Hinton's biography appeared, Morrison's song "Brand New Biography" skewered his attempt to place Van's life into a literary perspective. He remains aloof. He believes his music is his personal fiefdom. He is the overlord of his written domain.

It doesn't matter who writes about Van. He dislikes most of the critics. Those who have gotten along with him are the exception. Even those he respects, like **San Francisco Chronicle** critics John Wasserman and Joel Selvin, S. F. jazz expert Phil Elwood or **Rolling Stone** writer, Greil Marcus have all experienced Morrison's wrath. There is no predicting how Morrison will react. He can be friendly one moment. He can be difficult the next. To protect him from the media, the intrusion of Warner Brothers executives and the uncertainty of the music world, Van has a tightly constructed management team. He works best with Belfast connections.

THE FORMATION OF HIS BAND AND THE STREET CHOIR: HOW IT CHANGED THE MUSIC

When **His Band and the Street Choir** was released on November 15, 1970, Van was pursuing another musical direction with an a cappella tinge. That was the pedigree for his musical advancement. He feared creative stagnation to the point of being obsessively creative. The **Street Choir** helped his sound. Van's wife Janet Planet joined with Ellen Schroer, Martha Velez, Larry Goldsmith and Andy Robinson to form an a cappella group enhancing his sound.

Martha Velez and her husband, trumpet player Keith Johnson, were more than musicians. Martha was opera trained attending the High School of Performing Arts in New York City. During her career as an actress and musician, she earned a PhD. from the Pacifica Graduate Institute in Cultural Mythology and Depth Psychology. She is a founding member of the Imaginal Institute of Ojai, California. She also recorded a blues-rock album **Friends and Angels** with a stellar lineup of musicians including Eric Clapton, Stan Webb of Chicken Shack, Paul Kossoff of Free, Christine McVie of Fleetwood Mac, Jack Bruce and Ginger Baker of Cream. Velez has eight albums including one in 1963 with The Gaslight Singers. She has appeared in numerous TV shows and movies.

Van has never commented if Velez and Johnson influenced his study of religion. They constantly talked about meditation, poetry, religion and spiritualism. This obviously had an influence upon Morrison's intellectual makeup.

The musicians in the **His Band and the Street Choir** album were among the most celebrated in the recording business. John Platania surfaced on guitar with new members Alan Hand on keyboards and Keith Johnson on trumpet and organ. They were all seasoned musical veterans. The remaining Morrison friends were Jack Schroer and John Klingberg. They were inordinately familiar with his music. It was a band of like-minded cohorts who worked extensively to interpret Van's music. When Van played a song a different way, they followed him.

This band eventually became known as the Caledonia Soul Orchestra. It helped him adjust to the American lifestyle. He blended his understanding and knowledge of American roots music with his Belfast youth.

There was a retooling of old songs. "I've Been Working" was an attempt to create a Lead Belly direction. Hit sounds such as "Domino," which charted at number 9 for twelve weeks on **Billboard**, "Call Me Up In Dreamland," charted at number 95 in a brief two-week stint, "Blue Money," rose to number 23, "Sweet Jannie" received consistent FM airplay but failed to chart. These were tunes Van reworked from demos into a commercial vein. The initial demos were quite different. With his rewriting touch, these songs became radio oriented. Van said he didn't like the album. He told a number of interviewers business decisions often cut into his artistic persona. His friends couldn't believe Morrison was unhappy. The commercial direction of **His Band and the Street Choir** made it a strong seller.

Janet Planet was one of the unsung heroes of the **His Band and the Street Choir** album. She brought the back-up singers together. She gave advice on lyrics and musical direction. She created an atmosphere conducive to creative and successful recording. Her pay? Nothing!

Too much has been made about the eventual divorce. The hippie environment in and around Woodstock and Marin County had nothing to do with it. Janet nurtured the proper atmosphere for her husband's creative genius. It was the marriage that didn't work. On the creative side, Van and Janet were on the same page. In a number of interviews, she described herself as naïve and sweet. She told Clinton Heylin her efforts went on as long as they helped the music. She recalled: "For me, Street Choir was a musical manifestation … to real happiness…."

ON THE ROAD WITH VAN AS A STAR: HE HAD THE BAND AND PEDIGREE

Van Morrison was a star. His concert appearances gravitated to larger venues. For a few years, he played small clubs, an occasional concert hall, a teen dance or a college date. Van was into an uncomfortable transition. When his manager, Mary Martin, and Warner Brothers executives came to him with a list of venues there were too many large halls. Van wanted to remain in the small clubs. He believed the show band days were still intact. He would pick the venue. He would pick the songs. He was in total charge. Warner wasn't used to this behavior. Most artists were compliant. They were happy to have a recording contract. Van wanted equity. He wanted freedom in the studio. He wanted to be paid.

He decided to take his musical aggregation out on the road. Van said: "finances come before artistry." The economics of the rock music industry made this a perilous undertaking. Then Van met a friend of Graham Blackburn's who changed the Belfast Cowboy's view on the music business. Blackburn's friend, Ed Fletcher, a Marin County resident, understood the economics of the music business. He helped Van plan the logistics to build a long-term career. His ability to organize kept Van on a comfortable touring schedule. In 1973 Van's appearances were carefully crafted. Fletcher was the final ingredient in developing Morrison's in-concert genius. He planned the tour, secured the financing and took care to make the concerts comfortable. His attempts to manage money on the road were on again off again due to the intricacies of the business. The band was too large. The expenses were too great. The venues were too small. Van took notes and learned from these experiences. The musicians loved these tours. They benefited from coming into contact with major recording executives. Soon some of Morrison's sidemen left him to sign recording contracts.

A case in point was when Gary Mallaber's group signed with Columbia Records. He left Van's employ to make his stab at stardom. Another drummer, Bob Mason, came into the group but his sound wasn't a commercial one. For a time, Mason was the Fugs' drummer. His erratic, experimental style was not what Morrison needed.

HIS BAND AND THE STREET CHOIR: WHAT DID IT SAY?

The **His Band and the Street Choir** album surprised those close to Van. Despite Warner's meddling, Van held firm on song selection. Warner wanted him to perform in a more defined folk vein. He resisted. Morrison held out for a hit record direction. His vision worked. The LP produced three hits The conscious decision to

441

produce pop hits was contrary to everything in Morrison's character. His ability to achieve a permanent position in the rock and roll world depended upon hit records. The LP was packaged in such a manner to guarantee royalties. It worked. On the **Billboard** album listing, **His Band and the Street Choir** album peaked at number 32. It remained on the listing for seventeen weeks. This was due to Morrison's shrewd input in the selection of a hit 45, "Domino."

Personal freedom is "Domino's" message. Van's lyrics mention Jesse James and his weapon. What is the point? It is Van's story about a person free of societal shackles. Unbridled creativity remained a theme. On the next song, "Give Me A Kiss (Just One Sweet Kiss)," Van returns to rollicking good time music. This is characteristic of the LP. When Van sings in Jackie Wilson style "That's all I want...I'm satisfied." This is a portent of things to come.

"I've Been Working" disavows touring. He complains he has been working too hard. The pressures of marriage, fatherhood and the music industry were weighing on him. The marriage was still a positive one. He sings about Janet making him feel good.

"Call Me Up In Dreamland" highlights Van's growth as a songwriter. It has a riveting message. He sings he hopes to withdraw from the nine to five hubbubs of life. This is a surprising lyrical statement, since he never had a day job. The image Van presents of standing in his yard and then having to go out on tour suggests his dissatisfaction. He is tired. He is ready to stay home.

Side one closes with the poignant love song "I'll Be Your Lover Too." Van lets everyone know his strong feelings for Janet Planet. He sings of never growing too old while complaining about traveling.

The second side of the **His Band and the Street Choir** album is a fan favorite for the up-tempo songs. "Blue Money," which hit number 23 on the Billboard Hot 100, remained on the chart for three-months. This is a jazz inflected rock song. Van was now played regularly on AM and FM radio. Not bad for an artist who disdained commercial success. Other strong songs included "Virgo Clowns," with its acoustic guitar lead, "Sweet Jannie" with moonlight walks Van took with Janet. "Gypsy Queen" was a tribute to legendary Impression lead singer and solo soul giant Curtis Mayfield.

"If I Ever Needed Someone," suggests how important his wife was to the finished product. The final song, "Street Choir," embraces the message the album was a lot of fun. A notion Van later disavowed.

When the LP was completed, it was not what Van envisioned. He said he hoped to cut a record with a total a cappella sound. He lost this concept. That was a good thing. This is Morrison's most accomplished early album. Then again Van remained his own best critic. He ferreted out what was unacceptable while nurturing his songs.

Van was worried there was a stale quality to some tunes on the early Warner albums. Morrison did his best to fight the corporate ignorance of turning out the same LP. Van realized his longevity depended upon moving away from **Astral Weeks**. While Van embraced his fanatical fans, he refused to be forced into a commercial rut. He worked for the hits. Then he immediately disassociated himself from the process. Van remains a contradiction. Chris Michie remarked Van was: "an ornery little bastard with a sense of musical genius." When he played with Van Morrison, Michie began to formulate his own solo career. He told me Morrison was very supportive.

VAN ON THE HIS BAND AND THE STREET CHOIR ALBUM

"I've got stuff in the can that's got nothing to do with the mood of those particular albums ... What I'm trying to say is that when I'm doing an album, I'm just not doing an album. I may be doing four albums.... I mean, I've got stuff in the can from the Street Choir album that was totally uncommercial."

VAN MORRISON IN 1973

Van had some commercial leftovers from the **His Band and the Street Choir** album. He wrote many songs that were so intensely personal Warner Brothers pressured him to leave them unreleased. Many turned up in **The Philosopher's Stone**. Among these songs "Really Don't Know" expressed his current feelings. It chronicled his disaffection with everyday life. Warner Brothers didn't want any

443

depressing songs. They feared it would ruin the upbeat tempo of the **His Band and the Street Choir** LP. He stood up to the corporate pressure. Then Warner Brothers responded by cutting back on promotional funds. "I never understood what Warner was doing," Ray Ruff continued. "One minute they supported Van. The next time I talked to Mo Ostin he pulled money from Morrison's promotional fund."

THE HIS BAND AND THE STREET CHOIR LP CHANGES THINGS

The **His Band and the Street Choir** album brimmed with Americana. This was due to the Colwell-Winfield musicians. As Morrison flew to California and prepared for the move to Marin County, he picked up key American phrases. His off the wall references and radio friendly tunes suggest a more commercial artist.

"Domino" is a song highlighting Van's straight ahead hit mentality. Strangely, the song was written about his horse Domino. Some critics argue he paid tribute to Fats Domino. Chris Michie told me this was Van's way of getting back at the pompous, imperious writers analyzing his every word. They had no idea what he meant or intended to portray. "Van loved to tweak the critics," Michie remarked. Some of Van's references demonstrated his intuitive understanding of American history. A good example is references to Jesse James in "Crazy Face."

The blues were never far from Morrison's mind. On "I'll Be Your Lover Too," he uses John Platania's plaintive acoustic guitar to trade off his vocals. The three diverse songs in the album "Virgo Clowns," "Gypsy Queen" and "Sweet Jannie" are among his strongest. The reason is that "Virgo Clowns" is so original it brings the Belfast Cowboy's music into a new realm. As "Sweet Jannie" ends this trio of songs it suggests the diversity in Van's writing.

When the album concludes with "Street Choir," it is as if Mahalia Jackson went into the studio to help Van produce the material. He used so many different stylistic directions, there was a new Van Morrison. Some critics concluded the **His Band and the Street Choir**

444

album was a "mixed bag." In reality, it was a "Welcome to America" album.

TUPELO HONEY: ARE THE HITS ENDING?

When **Tupelo Honey** was released in October 1971, reviewers said it reflected Van's marital bliss. Nothing was further from the truth. He periodically raged over his recording contracts, the difficulty of touring and the business intrusions into his creative life. It was increasingly taking a toll on his marriage. Janet commented Van's continual rage drove her out of the marriage.

The songs for **Tupelo Honey** were written in Woodstock, except for "You're My Woman," which was composed hurriedly in the studio while recording the album. From this song erroneous tales of how rapidly Morrison wrote were circulated by the press.

The Woodstock songs were magnificent ones. Although Van composed most of the song for the **Tupelo Honey** album before they moved to California, the Golden State provided the final inspiration. When Morrison cut some songs at Wally Heider's San Francisco studio they had a free flowing, blues-rock direction. In May 1971, Warner booked San Francisco Columbia Studio to put the finishing touches on **Tupelo Honey**.

The American sales for **Tupelo Honey** surprised Morrison. By 1974 it outsold **Moondance**. When "Wild Night" charted at twenty-seven on the Billboard singles listing, collectors realized the b-side "When That Evening Sun Goes Down" was a rare alternate cut. In 1990 Polydor Records released the record on CD. After a 1997 reissue a remastered 2008 CD contained two bonus tracks with an extended version of "Wild Night" was issued.

The pressures in Van's life prompted him to withdraw from the hit-making syndrome. This was typical Morrison. His moods ruined his relationship with surf guru, popmeister turned producer, Ted Templeman who was no help in the studio.

Van didn't like Templeman's pedigree. He was from Santa Cruz, California. He broke into the business with Harper's Bizarre in 1966. In 1970 he went to work for Warner as an in-house producer. He immediately brought the Doobie Brothers to stardom. He also produced Ronnie Montrose. He was considered one of the easiest producers to work with in the business. That is until he landed in the midst of Morrison's early 1970s career.

As the Warner Brothers house producer assigned to Morrison, Templeman helped make **Tupelo Honey** amongst his strongest LPs. Once he finished with Morrison's album, Templeman remarked to San Francisco's **Bam** magazine he would never work with the Belfast Cowboy again. What started out as an idyllic producing project, turned into a nightmare.

Part of the reason was Van's production. He talked about making a country and western LP. Then he veered into another direction. He said he didn't need a producer. He had every song precisely crafted. He also had a concept. **Tupelo Honey** would be a country-western album. This was a musical path Templeman could not understand. If Morrison wanted to cut a country LP, Templeman told him, he had the wrong producer. This strained relationship became irreconcilable.

The music explosion in and around Marin County gave a new vibrancy to Morrison's sound. Ronnie Montrose's rock and roll guitar riffs were neither jazz oriented nor counterculture cool. Montrose was a rocker. "Wild Night" is the purest expression of his rocker mentality.

RECORD WORLD ON TUPELO HONEY AND MEETING JOHN LEE HOOKER

The backbiting and arguments over **Tupelo Honey** and Warner's reticence to publicize it had little impact upon sales. It sold well. The November 13, 1971 **Record World** reported Van's album was the number one seller in retail shops for the last week. When Van complained to Warner about lack of promotion, an executive said: "look at the November 13, **1971 Record World** weekly singles chart." This executive said Van didn't have a Top Ten hit. He failed to realize "Wild Night" was twenty-eight on **Billboard**. Ray Ruff commented: "The old wounds and grievances with Van never ended."

Record World reported Van had more airplay on Am Top 40 or AOR radio stations than he did on FM radio. This surprised Warner executives. This was an early indication he was a mainstream artist. The

November 13, 1971 issue of **Record World** contained a full page ad for a Rod McKuen tour. Van was flummoxed.

To broaden his appeal in 1971, Van recorded the first of many duets with John Lee Hooker. He would show Warner Brothers the full scope of his talent. John Lee Hooker remarked that Morrison was a "guy who knows it. And he can do it." That was heady praise from John Lee Hooker.

Hooker met Van in Berkeley one night when he was playing the Keystone Korner. He struck up a friendship that lasted until John Lee passed. One of the surprising points is Van recalled to **Rolling Stone** that Hooker told him: "Man, I loved that song 'T. B. Sheets." Hooker recorded it.

THE RONNIE MONTROSE FACTOR

In 1971 Ronnie Montrose was a twenty-three year old guitar player looking for his first break. He played with a San Francisco band, Sawbuck, and his guitar wizardry was well known among local musicians. It was the Bill Graham Organization that brought Montrose into the studio to record on **Tupelo Honey**. Van wanted a different guitar sound. Montrose had it.

Ronnie Montrose: "Bill Graham called. He told me Van Morrison needed a guitarist. I showed up at the Lion's Share. There were ten other guitarists with small amps. Before he called me, I knew I had the job."

On **Tupelo Honey** Ronnie Montrose brightened and enlightened the tempo of Morrison's songs. He created a party-time atmosphere. This was borne out on "Wild Night." The song was written about New York City.

Van incorporated Montrose's unique style. Montrose was one of rock music's most accomplished and innovative guitarists. His work with his band, Montrose, as well as with Sammy Hagar, established him as an important industry figure.

GIMME THAT BAR BAND SOUND

When he played drums with Van Morrison, Sacramento's Tony Dey remembers a few years after **Tupelo Honey** was released that the Belfast Cowboy would turn to his back musicians smiling and exclaiming "gimme that bar band sound." The bar band sound in the **Tupelo Honey** album was all over the LP. Not only did "Wild Night" have that direction but also "(Straight To Your Heart) Like A Cannonball." had a honky-tonk feel that was part of Morrison's new sound. In "Starting A New Life" Van paid lip service to his newfound Marin sound. The incipient happiness it produced. On "I Wanna Roo You" he reflects on his Irish past. He suggests he still has a longing for Belfast.

The **Tupelo Honey** album is a glimpse into the increasing serenity of Van's life. "When That Evening Sun Goes Down," suggests this tranquility. Then he is off to boogie-woogie land in "Moonshine Whiskey."

"Moonshine Whiskey" displays his recently acquired American roots. In Woodstock most people said he wrote "Moonshine Whiskey" after seeing and hearing Janis Joplin. With a soul and country rock tinge, "Moonshine Whiskey" inaugurated a new phase in Van's career. It was one where he was making good time music. The use of electric and steel guitar sounds suggests a future country direction.

Tupelo Honey's sales surprised Warner management. With numbers close to 400,000 by June 1974, Van was an established best seller. He was also making a very good living. He would need the money. An expensive and emotionally exhausting divorce was on the table. There was still solace in the music.

VAN WEIGHS IN ON TUPELO HONEY: THE CRITICS LOVE IT, HE HATES IT

For reasons no one can explain, Van was unhappy with **Tupelo Honey.** He said in numerous interviews the stable on the album cover was not real. "I didn't live there," Morrison continued. "We just went there and took the picture and split. A lot of people seem to think album covers are your life or something." Van said the album consisted of "leftover songs. It wasn't really fresh. It was a whole bunch of songs that had been hanging around for a while." The irony is it was his best-selling early career album.

He made the same remarks about **His Band and the Street Choir**. "I never really listen to **Tupelo Honey** much," Van continued. "I just don't connect up with it. I've got a bad taste in my mouth for both the Street Choir and Tupelo Honey albums," he told Jeff Giles in 2016. What is going on? Van is still pissed over royalties.

Jon Landau, writing in **Rolling Stone**, came closest to understanding what Van meant. He pronounced the album was "a synthesis of what has preceded it and a statement of something new." Landau concluded: "Tupelo Honey is … an album of beautiful themes, dazzling musical motifs, and exquisite performances." Van should have been happy. He wasn't. When the critics weighed in on the 2008 reissue, they loved the alternate take of "Wild Night" and the unreleased version of "Down By The Riverside." Chris Jones, writing in **Uncut**, concluded **Tupelo Honey's** re-release was the album "the fans deserve." There is no word from Morrison on this review.

RAY CHARLES SAVES THE DAY

Why Ray Charles? When Van saw what Charles did with horns, strings and country music in his early 1960s album **Modern Sounds In Country And Western Music**, it became a road map for Morrison. Ray blended soul and jazz. As early as 1971 Van worked in this direction.

Van listened to so many Ray Charles records, he thought he was Ray. In many ways, Charles saved the day. He gave Van a reason and a rationale for continuing his experimental journey. Van stayed with a specific set of Charles' tunes. That is in the blues and R&B songs. He listened intently to Charles' early Atlantic Records. In particular, he loved Doc Pomus's "Lonely Avenue."

He explained to Chris Michie; Charles saved his artistic life. The importance of Charles was shown when Van had a dream about someone attempting to end Charles' life. This awe-inspiring nightmare brought Van out of a temporary writing funk. He composed the 1968 song "Come Running" while reflecting on Charles.

When Morrison released his version of "Lonely Avenue" on the 1993 **Too Long In Exile** LP and included it on **A Night in San Francisco**, one critic remarked: "Van had sung this song his entire life." Van told Chris Michie that Doc Pomus inspired a medley with Jimmy Witherspoon featuring "4 O'clock In The Morning/Try For Sleep." Van said this was in appreciation of "Lonely Avenue." "I asked Van to explain the inspiration," Michie told me. "Morrison suggested that he had been on many a lonely avenue at four in the morning."

CLEARING VAN'S BRAIN AT THE INN OF THE BEGINNING

Cotati California is a sleepy and iconoclastic settlement with a nineteenth century ambiance. The nearby college, Sonoma State University, gives the town a liberal to radical tinge. In the late 1960s, when students needed a place for coffee, booze, music or a safe place to smoke a joint, they gravitated to a local club, the Inn of the Beginning, for music. When a band, known as the Bronze Hog, opened the venue it became instantly popular. Van Morrison soon discovered this venue.

The Bronze Hog, a legendary local band, played largely for Sonoma State University students. They also opened for Janis Joplin's Big Brother and the Holding Company. Frank Hayhurst was a talented guitarist and one of Marin's most creatives musical innovators. He established the club to help itinerant musicians.

On September 28, 1968 the Inn of the Beginning opened its doors for business. For the next two years the club attracted not only the best San Francisco bands but blues and folk legends Bukka White, John Lee Hooker, Dave Van Ronk, Lightnin' Hopkins, Charlie Musselwhite and Sonny Terry and Brownie McGhee. When Van was handed a flyer of the Inn of the Beginning, he couldn't believe artists in his record collection were playing near his new home.

Morrison called Frank Hayhurst to bring his band to play there for a night. The Inn of The Beginning owner said no. But if Van wanted to perform for three nights the answer was yes. Because of his advertising and good business sense, Hayhurst booked and publicized the shows professionally. When Van took the stage with his band at the

Inn of the Beginning it was after Sonny Terry and Brownie McGhee completed three nights performing at the venue.

Van's three nights at the Inn of the Beginning resulted in more people standing outside listening to the music than watching him play from inside the club. The May 14, 1971 show at the Cotati produced a bootleg highlighting his continual development on stage. The bootleg album "Live At The Inn of the Beginning," had some interesting cuts. The show began with "I've Been Working" and by the time Van was into the third song he combined "Beautiful Obsession" with "Let The Cowboy Ride." It would be seven years before some of these songs appeared on the **Wavelength** album. The ability to experiment with his music was the reason for playing the Inn of the Beginning. The other was to pay tribute to his blues idols. No one cared what he played. The crowd didn't holler for "Brown Eyed Girl." An eight-minute version of "Let The Cowboy Ride" was perfect for Morrison. He could whittle it down later.

The ads in San Francisco counterculture newspapers, flyers with crude drawings of who would appear at the club, flooded Marin County. In Berkeley and San Francisco, a loyal crowd of followers ensured sold out shows. There was excellent food. A ticket price of less than five dollars guaranteed sell out shows. For the locals the drinking started in the afternoon. If you were in the bar drinking by two o'clock you never paid a cover charge.

On nights that didn't have a name act the club had a dinner with a local folk singer. Invariably, Joan Baez, Pamela Polland, Patti Santos of It's A Beautiful Day or any other local singer would wander in for the dinner. Van came in once for the folk dinner night. The beauty of the Inn of the Beginning is you never knew who would be sitting next to you.

Van enjoyed the small clubs. Why? He was left alone. He could play what he wanted. During one engagement at the Inn of the Beginning a telegram from a Warner executive to the front office complained he had trouble understanding Van's singing. The Warner Brothers executive was in Mendocino to check out Cat Mother and the All Night News Boys who recorded for Polydor. Cat Mother's album **Street Giveth & The Street Taketh Away**, produced by Jimi Hendrix, prompted many record labels to look at the group. Ray Ruff said

Warner looked to sign other Marin County groups. Ruff believed Warner Brothers had little, if any, understanding of Morrison and his music.

Ray Ruff laughed when he read the telegram. He told me the Warner executive was confused. The telegram read: "Why did Morrison play this small venue?" The answer was obvious to Van's band. He wanted audience friendly gigs. He hated the pressure of larger venues.

Van took his band into Cotati's Inn of the Beginning, this small Northern California venue, for the appreciative audience. The small room and funky décor mixed with a laid-back audience created a perfect showplace.

When the Inn of the Beginning opened in 1968 it was a highly political venue. This club was the brainchild of twenty-two-year-old Greg Cochrane and his Sonoma State University buddy David McNair. It was opened in an unlike place. The Inn of the Beginning began in a former Italian restaurant. Cochrane said he named the club while on LSD. When Cochrane sold the club in 1970, he complained of burn out. There was too much music, too much food, too many drugs and only twenty-four hours in the day. The sale was fortuitous. The new owners, Ward Millard and Sonoma County artist Elizabeth Quandt, had a defined commercial direction.

The Inn of the Beginning was so hip the Mayor Richard Cullinen tended bar there in the mid-1970s. "Van Morrison popped in frequently," Cullinen recalled. If the Grateful Dead weren't on the road Jerry Garcia was at the bar or on the bandstand. Garcia and Merle Saunders often wandered in when an act wasn't booked. He played for the locals. It was in this atmosphere, Van Morrison created some of his best work. Cotati inspired the Belfast Cowboy.

The liberal creative atmosphere was shown when a youthful Jackson Browne was denied entry because he said he was from Orange County. One time Van called the Inn of the Beginning to book a gig, the bartender couldn't understand him. He had one of the band members call back to inquire about a show for Morrison. Van's band was aware of the quirky bookings.

There were some unlikely bookings. Waylon Jennings, George Winston, the Cramps, Ricky Skaggs and Hank Williams Junior played the club. The Meters, Clifton Chenier, Doc Watson and Etta James were other acts playing the club. When Joan Baez showed up, she sold more tickets than Bukka White. Such bluesmen as Lightnin' Hopkins, Sonny Terry and Brownie McGhee, Clarence "Gatemouth" Brown, Buddy Guy, Taj Mahal and John Lee Hooker performed to reverent crowds. Van Morrison was at times in the audience.

Cotati is a town where responsible hippies migrated. It is also a college town. Rents were low. Soft drugs were plentiful. The town was filled with interesting characters. There was a free store in town where Vito Paulekas, after he moved from Los Angeles's Sunset Strip, handed out old clothes. Irving and Irene Lipton opened the Cotati Company Number 2 store where young entrepreneurs rented space for as little as ten dollars a month to sell albums, comic books, pipes and rolling papers.

THE MAGIC OF THE INN OF THE BEGINNING

There was magic to Morrison's Inn of The Beginning shows. The four nights he played there from May 13 through 16, 1971 were performances that belied his youth. He was already a performing veteran. He was only twenty-five.

One show stood out. It was the May 14, 1971 performance featuring a lengthy set list, including a version of Them's "Mystic Eyes," and a Hank Williams' inspired "Jambalaya." This was one of the keys to Van's small venue concerts. He loved to perform songs he didn't include in larger concert halls.

The Inn of The Beginning was so hip in 1972 **Rolling Stone** sent a reporter, Tim Findley, to report on the scene. The first assignment was to interview Mayor Annette Lombardi. The twenty-five-year-old Mayor sat in front of the **Rolling Stone** reporter. The reporter wore a sport coat, a designer white shirt, a fancy tie, pressed slacks and shined shoes. Mayor Lombardi took out her pipe. She filled it with an unknown substance. She lit it. She sucked on it. She exhaled. Findley looked on in astonishment.

Lombardi told the reporter her confidence in the locals was supreme. He had no idea what she was talking about. Mayor Lombardi made it clear. The counterculture had taken over the town. The five member Cotati City Council was youthful and looking to make sure the free-flowing local lifestyle wasn't endangered. The Peace and Freedom Party elected three of the five members on the City Council. The hippie takeover was complete. Smoking dope in the city was almost a requirement. There was more than music to Cotati. They boasted the town was the "Wrist-Wrestling Capital of the World." They held a yearly competition with foreign entrants as numerous as their American counterparts. Mayor Lombardi was a business booster. She owned the Eeyore Bookstore which Van frequented. The Cotati City Council also voted against the war in Vietnam. They protested the Veterans of Foreign Wars selling poppies to raise funds.

Cotati's five-man police force, headed by twenty-eight year old Chief Olindo (Tony) Locarnini, took a liberal stance on dope smoking, nudity and the selling of pipes, papers and drug paraphernalia. It was much like Berkeley with a rustic setting. The city council mandated the local police give up their uniforms to wear blue jeans and tie-dyed t-shirts. At this point Chief Locarnini put in his letter of resignation. Then two other officers quit. The hippie revolution in Cotati was in full swing.

The Inn of the Beginning thrived in this atmosphere. The club announced they formed their own record label. This was a way of selling bootlegs legally. The music flowed freely as did sex, drugs and rock and roll. Van Morrison was just another guy. Few people bothered him. He was free to create. He did!

> **INN OF THE BEGINNING, COTATI, CA - MAY 14, 1971**
>
> From this show the most intriguing songs are a version of Them's "Mystic Eyes" and the old Hank Williams country standard "Jambalaya."
>
> **Set List**
> *I've Been Working • He Ain't Give You None • Beautiful Obsession • Give Me A Kiss • Mystic Eyes, (inst.) • Jambalaya • Rock Me Baby • I Want To Roo You • Moonshine Whiskey • And It Stoned Me • Blue Money • Domino • Bring It On Home To Me*
>
> **Lineup: Alan Hand - piano, John Klingberg - bass, John Platania - guitar, Dave Shaw - drums, Jack Schroer - saxophones, Collin Tilton – flute**

When Van returned to the Inn of The Beginning for two nights and four shows on April 8-9, 1975, it was a Tuesday and Wednesday night. In the San Francisco Bay Area clubs didn't book big acts for these nights. Morrison was the exception. Van wanted to play for a small audience. That didn't happen. The four shows sold out with more people in the parking lot listening to the music than were in the club. The Inn of the Beginning was a musical fairyland. In 1971-1972 the reality of dealing with Warner Brothers was contrary to the magical life in Marin County. Reality set in when he performed outside of the San Francisco Bay Area.

WHILE RELAXING: CALIFORNIA TENSIONS REAPPEAR IN IRELAND

For much of his performing life, Van expressed dissatisfaction with managers, booking agents, musicians and record label executives. He abhors intrusions upon his performing and artistic life. That said he delivered excellent shows. He does not suffer fools well. A case in point took place in March 1971 when a Warner Brothers executive committed Van to a Dublin Ireland show. When tickets sold out there was considerable bad feelings when Morrison cancelled. He said he hadn't agreed to the booking. Warner booked it without his consent. Ray Ruff said Warner was testing Van. They did! They lost!

This misunderstanding angered Van. Fame was constantly intruding upon his life. There was a rumor he would return to Ireland to direct a film. That rumor turned out to be untrue. Van found himself all over the Irish newspapers. He was irate. He felt helpless. He laid the blame on his management and Warner Brothers.

On May 15, 1971, London's premier music newspapers, the **New Musical Express** and **Melody Maker**, announced Van would not be returning to Ireland or England for a series of shows. At this point Ron Harriman was booking Van. He couldn't give anyone an answer as to why the dates were cancelled. Warner executives were also mum on the question of Van's tours. Harriman was fired. Warner was criticized by Morrison.

Finally, the reason came out. Van couldn't find a proper backing band. This didn't satisfy anyone. His manager, Mary Martin, did her best to control the damage. Van fired Martin once again over this incident. He began looking for new management. He was spending more time in Fairfax. He wanted someone locally to handle his affairs. He didn't like the fact Martin was critical of his small California club shows. Why did he play these clubs? She pointed out he often paid the band out of his own pocket. This opened the door for Bill Graham.

Bill Graham's Fillmore West management team was after Morrison. They made a pitch to manage him. Bill Graham could book the larger venues. He could also indulge Van's yearning to play in small, funky San Francisco clubs. Graham convinced Van he would send his career into a new orbit.

Nick Clainos, Graham's chief assistant, told me the partnership didn't work. There were too many other concerns for Graham. "Van seemed happy to play our venues. That was it. He liked an informal management agreement."

The brief partnership between Bill Graham Presents and Van was a tempestuous one. It did bring Morrison into new venues. The irony is Morrison and Graham didn't have a formal management contract. They had a handshake. Van told people he was working with Bill Graham Presents when he felt like it. It wasn't until 1978 that Graham legally had a contract to manage the Belfast Cowboy. But Graham's name and support was important to Van's unfolding career.

On May 6-8, 1972, Morrison persuaded Bill Graham to book a date in Berkeley, California. Then Van changed his mind. He wanted three nights and five shows. Even Graham was mystified. The venue Morrison selected was the New Orleans House. This small musical bar held only 150 patrons. Van asked only a $3 door charge. For the five shows he collected $1500. So much for the greedy rock star image!

At the New Orleans House, he brought in a seven-piece band and three backup singers who were introduced as the Street Choir. They included Ellen Schroer, Martha Velez and Janet Planet. The gate receipts didn't come close to paying the band. Van did so out of his own pocket. Then management issues with Bill Graham surfaced.

Ralph J. Gleason, writing in **Rolling Stone**, pointed out Bill Graham's Fillmore West and his Winterland venue were charged by the San Francisco Musicians Union with not paying union scale. The irony was Van paid his band above union scale. The New Orleans House gig was a money loser but a creative winner. Gleason sat in the audience smoking his pipe taking furtive notes. No one noticed the college professor taking notes.

Why did Morrison play this venue? The answer is a simple one. He wanted close contact with his audience. There were also other things Van loved about the New Orleans House. The most important one was Kitty's Kitchen, where a series of aspiring chefs prepared some of the best food in the San Francisco Bay Area.

As one entered the New Orleans House, the ticket taker, Gretchen, danced to the gyrating sounds of the jukebox. The owner, Kitty, carefully counted the crowd. When attendance reached one hundred fifty, Kitty closed the doors. That night Boz Scaggs was standing outside. He finally convinced Gretchen to allow him inside. He stood near the kitchen eating a pulled pork sandwich listening to Van.

While the crowd ate and drank, Morrison strolled out from backstage and went up to the bar to order a glass of wine. This was a cool Berkeley crowd. No one bothered him. He came on stage. He worked the crowd just three feet from the tables. There was no band when Van came out on stage. He began to sing a cappella and then one by one the backing musicians sauntered out on stage. It was a magic moment.

On stage with a harmonica and guitar, Van took control of the show. Ralph J. Gleason called it "magic." He performed for ninety minutes as the crowd stood up to give him continuous ovations. That night, as always, he was testing new material for the larger venues.

There was only one review of substance for this show. It was virtually lost in the back pages of **Rolling Stone**. As Ralph Gleason noted: "Music does not have to be totally big business unless you insist on making it so." Van Morrison agreed. This is why he continued to play the small clubs.

WAS THE RADIO ANOTHER STUDIO AND DID TOWER RECORDS HELP?

FM programming provided a wider audience. Van convinced Warner Brothers to increase advertising for **Tupelo Honey**. The label reluctantly agreed. Van was now increasingly on the **Billboard** and **Cashbox** charts. The Tower Record chain, largely a California one, had a special merchandising deal with Warner Brothers. They agreed to feature Morrison as part of their in-store promotional campaigns. Russ Solomon, the founder of Tower Records, recalled: "Van was my employee's favorite artist. We played him all the time in the store." Tower Records sweetheart deal with Warner Bros. distribution arm gave the record store a one hundred eighty-day credit cycle. If they had any albums left, the Tower brain trust returned them on the one hundred and seventy ninth day. Van was never a loss leader. In San Francisco, Berkeley, Sacramento and Los Angeles he outsold all the local bands except the Grateful Dead.

Warner executives sent Van letters, made phone calls to him and dispatched representatives to encourage him to increase his promotional activity. Van didn't want to leave his Fairfax house. Finally, he agreed to a concert over the San Francisco FM radio station KSAN. The show was due to disc jockey buddy Tom "Big Daddy" Donahue. In this setting, Van had the freedom to play any musical set he desired. It was more like being in the studio. He was comfortable with it.

This show was broadcast from the Pacific High Studios. This studio was located in a diminutive room in a desolate part of San Francisco. It was perfect for the hermit musician. The small recording studio held about 175 people. It had a radio station ambiance with a concert persona. This is why Tom "Big Daddy" Donahue selected it for Van's live radio performance. There were egg cartons on the ceiling to muffle the sound. Van commented as he walked into the studio, it was like going back to his Belfast days.

The sound equipment was first rate. With a sixteen-track Dolby sound system capable of creating quadraphonic sound, it was a first class studio. There were also five echo chambers. Tom Donahue spent a great deal of time on the air heralding the importance of what he termed "concerts for the people." This became a Warner Brothers marketing ploy. They attempted to make Van a hippie, folk singer with a common person's bent. He hated labels. Warner, like Van's previous labels, had not learned their lesson. He needed low-key promotion without the hype. Van would not take part in ridiculous promotional programs. He used the Pacific High radio broadcast as a means of suggesting the promotional activity he approved of and why he sold records.

When he went into the Pacific High Studio for an impromptu radio concert, he told Warner Brothers he had a better way of promoting his material. As the September 5, 1971 Pacific High Studio concert began, it was an example of how tight Van was in concert. Why? For all practical purposes, it gave birth to the Van Morrison bootlegging phenomena. While there were earlier bootlegs, this was the one that made the fans rabid collectors.

At the Pacific High Studio there were songs that hadn't found their way onto a Morrison album. With covers of Elvis Presley's "Hound Dog" or Louis Prima's "Buona Sera, Senorita," Van demonstrated his musical diversity. This aspect of his career would be lost to posterity without the bootlegs. Presley's "Hound Dog" cover and Bob Dylan's "Just Like a Woman" were keys to the growing interest in Morrison's San Francisco Bay Area appearances. The fans loved the covers.

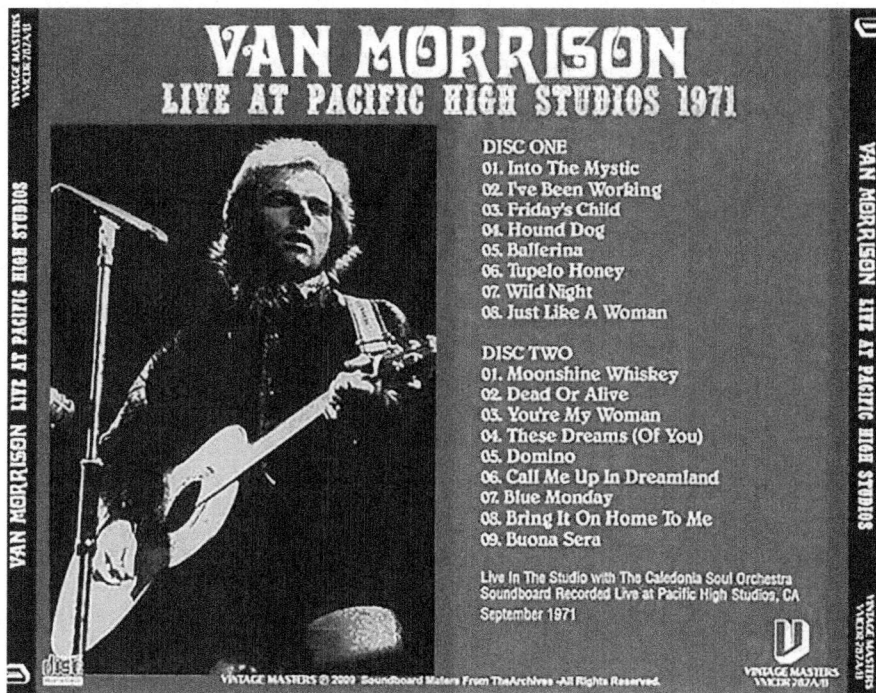

Van Morrison Live at Pacific High Studios 1971 - CD back cover

---

PACIFIC HIGH STUDIO CONCERT SEPTEMBER 5, 1971

SET LIST

Into The Mystic • I've Been Working • Friday's Child • Hound Dog • Ballerina/Tupelo Honey • Wild Night • Just Like A Woman • Moonshine Whiskey • Dead or Alive • You're My Woman • These Dreams of You • Domino • Call Me Up In Dreamland • Blue Money • Bring It On Home To Me • **Buona Sera • Senorita**

A vinyl bootleg **Van The Man** came out from a Sausalito based bootlegger; it went on to mainstream record success. It also intensified the Morrison bootlegging industry. In Los Angeles, a medical doctor set up a home studio. He began producing a wide variety of Morrison bootlegs. In San Francisco Haik Arakiel distributed Morrison bootlegs

461

to the record stores and the record swaps in Los Angeles, Oakland, Berkeley and San Francisco. In the pricey East Bay suburb of Danville, Zaire operated a bootleg company.

BACKING MUSICIANS ON THE PACIFIC HIGH RECORDING STUDIO SHOW SEPTEMBER 5, 1971

- **Alan Hand, piano**
- **John Klingberg, bass**
- **John Platania, guitar**
- **Daoud Shaw, drums**
- **Jack Schroer, saxophone**
- **Collin Tilton, flute**

VAN AT WINTERLAND AND SAN FRANCISCO'S FILLMORE WEST

On November 5-6, 1971 Van played a two-night engagement at San Francisco's Winterland Auditorium. He was in a great mood. This was a recently opened venue for Bill Graham's Organization. Winterland was a large concert hall in the predominantly African-American Fillmore district. It was around the corner from the original Fillmore Auditorium. For a time, a second Fillmore Auditorium, located above a car dealer's showroom and adjacent to the seedy City Center Motel, was open for concerts. The second Fillmore at Market and Van Ness was a safety hazard. It was always packed to capacity. Across the alley from the back entrance, Fillmore bands hoping to save money stayed at the City Center Motel. It was a seedy, hooker favorite off Market street. It was a dump with stained carpets and a reputation for ignoring loud music, dope smoking and partying. Chuck Berry stayed there each time he played the Fillmore. The riotous after concert parties were a benefit to fans who wandered into the rooms. But the second Fillmore gave way to Winterland.

At Winterland Van gave his more memorable concerts. The venue was a large one with wonderful acoustics and a balcony in which fans hung over and cheered the acts. It was Van's favorite. It was a block off San Francisco's Fillmore in a residential neighborhood. For rock concerts it was a luxurious palace.

For Van's appearance at Winterland, Graham went out of his way to make it a perfect night. Bill Graham personally put together a bill including It's A Beautiful Day, the Elvin Bishop Group and Grootna. The headliner, Van Morrison, was Graham's favorite local artist. The Fillmore was an exciting area at night. For years it was the center of an African American jazz and blues culture. There was no shortage of rib joints, blues bars and good time cafes. Winterland became an immediate success.

This five-hour Winterland show was highlighted by Van's encore version of "Gloria." Elvin Bishop remembered when the audience hollered out for Them hits, Van turned his back to the throng and scowled. Backstage Bishop recalled Van talked at length about Ireland. Bishop remarked Van missed Belfast. He longed for the Irish countryside.

The search for new musical venues was one of Van's favorite pastimes. He didn't need to worry. In the San Francisco Bay Area there were many small clubs, bowling alleys and off beat concert venues that loved to have Morrison perform. In turn, he charged a fee that didn't always guarantee a profit. It did guarantee a strong and loyal fan base. The musicians loved the gigs.

ON TO FRENCHY'S IN HAYWARD CALIFORNIA AND ON TO SACRAMENTO

The good feelings from the Pacific High recording studio were still with Van as three cars full of musicians and an equipment van pulled into the back lot of a seedy club, Frenchy's, that needed paint on Mission Boulevard in downtown Hayward, California. The September 8, 1971 gig at Frenchy's was special for Morrison. The former roller skating rink had a magnificent sound system, a kitchen to feed the band steaks and a clientele of bikers, druggies, college students, hookers, businessmen and local ne´er do wells who didn't care what kind of music you played. They were there for the $2.95

steak, and fifty cent hard drinks. The plentiful supply of ladies was another asset.

At one time in 1967 Sly and the Family Stone was Frenchy's house band. Early in 1971, Huey Lewis played regularly on a Monday night jam. Tower of Power frequented the club. Emilio Castillo, Tower of Power's founder and his co-founder friend Mick Gillette showed up for the Monday night jams. It was the type of venue with its roller rink décor that local bands loved to play. Alice Stuart, Clover, Sly and the Family Stone, Stoneground, the Beau Brummels, the New Riders of the Purple Sage and Elvin Bishop were a few of the acts gracing Frenchy's stage. It was a huge club. Bill Quarry, formerly of the Rollerarena venue in Castro Valley, booked many of the acts. The East Bay, south of Oakland, was a musical potpourri Morrison loved. It was the city of Hayward that was his favorite. This down home funky city had two country and western bars with live music, a blue-collar persona where alcohol, cigarettes and greasy food were preferable to drugs.

BILL QUARRY'S ROLLERARENA: QUARRY WITH TINY TIM

For his show at Frenchy's, Van pulled out a cover of Bob Dylan's "Just Like A Woman," as well as a spirited version of Elvis Presley's "Hound Dog." It was a great night as Van ended with a raucous version of "Brown Eyed Girl." After the show, Van and the band stopped at a local hamburger drive inn. He got out. He was talking and laughing with the locals.

After Van and Janet moved to the San Francisco Bay Area, Van showed signs of being burnt out. When he accepted a booking from Bill Graham at Winterland, he told the San Francisco impresario it would be his last concert for a time. He was tired. He was adjusting to a new life. "I was serious about it," Van told **Rolling Stone** reporter John Grissim, Jr., "I wanted some time to get acquainted with the scene around Marin."

It didn't take Van long to find the local clubs. He went to the Lion's Share in San Anselmo and found Ramblin' Jack Elliott on stage with only a guitar playing to a full house. Van was mesmerized. A few nights later Van returned to find Alice Stuart and Snake performing.

He noticed Ramblin' Jack Elliott in the audience enraptured with the show. Van decided to do some small venue gigs.

When he performed at the Lion's Share on November 26-27, 1971, Van showed up with a harmonica and guitar. He went through a long set and finished with a rousing version of "Ballerina." During the night, Ramblin' Jack Elliott and guitarist Bobby Neuwirth joined him. Neuwirth was an old friend from Boston, via Woodstock, and he was a guitarist, banjo and mandolin player. Van loved Neuwirth's use of the blues in his folk oriented songs. Morrison found the San Francisco Bay Area a hotbed of musicians, and the rabid fans loved his music. Bob Neuwirth is one of Morrison's most interesting friends. He was six years older than Van. He had hung out on the fringes of the Cambridge music scene. He was friendly with Janis Joplin and beat poet Michael McClure. He co-wrote "Mercedes Benz" for Joplin with his friend Kris Kristofferson. Neuwirth eschewed commercial music. Perhaps this is why Morrison loved to talk to him. He was also interested in film. He had no thoughts of wanting to ride on Morrison's musical coattails. He was a friend who wanted nothing from Van. In some ways, Neuwirth was not typical as he developed an artistic side apart from the music. As a commercial artist and folkie, Neuwirth was never a dull companion. Neuwirth was one of Bob Dylan's closest friends.

From September 5 until November 5-6, 1971, when he finished up at Winterland, the Belfast Cowboy performed only ten shows. Van missed Ireland. He needed to return home. He hoped to get his writing inspiration into what he termed "the Gaelic mode." Fame and fortune slowed Morrison's writing.

On September 7, 1971, Morrison and the band, which included drummer Tony Dey, played a small club in Sacramento. The set list, provided by Dey, had Van starting out with "Dead Or Alive," followed by "Moonshine Whiskey," "You're My Woman," "These Dreams of You," "Domino," "Call Me Up In Dreamland," "Blue Money," "Buona Sera," "Into The Mystic," "I've Been Working," "Friday's Child," "Just Like A Woman" and an encore of "Caravan" ended this show.

Tony Dey recalled: "I can't even remember the name of the club but Van loved playing it because it had egg cartons on the ceiling to help the acoustics." Dey continued: "Van said it reminded him of his days with the showbands in Belfast."

ON THE ROAD WITH VAN IN CALIFORNIA, SEPTEMBER-OCTOBER 1971

From his Fairfax, California home, Van continued to experiment musically. He spent September and October performing for audiences who appreciated his music. The college audiences were among Van's favorites.

VAN'S ITINERANT CONCERT SCHEDULE SEPTEMBER-OCTOBER 1971

September 5, 1971: Pacific High Studios, Marin County

September 7, 1971: Memorial Auditorium, Sacramento, Ca.

September 8, 1971: Frenchy's, Hayward (with Lexington opening)

September 17-18, 1971: Winterland (with It's A Beautiful Day and the Elvin Bishop Group)

September 19, 1971: San Jose Fairgrounds.

September 25, 1971: Fairgrounds Expo Hall, San Jose, Cal.

October 3, 1971: UC Riverside Student Center, Riverside, Ca.

October 16, 1971: Pauley Pavilion, UCLA, Los Angeles, Ca. (Linda Ronstadt is the opening act)

November 5-6, 1971: Winterland, San Francisco, Ca.

As 1971 came to an end, Van worked hard to maintain his place in the music business. True to his muse, he continued to work on new music. Was it to make a sound that emphasized commercial hits? Or was it to experiment with the genre? This led to the **St. Dominic's Preview** album.

In concert, Van performed a large number of songs from his recent catalogue. Such tunes as "I've Been Working" and "Domino" were his in-concert favorites. He also followed these songs with "These Dreams of You," "And It Stoned Me" and "Blue Money." To demonstrate his musical independence he didn't perform "Gloria," "Brown Eyed Girl" or "Here Comes the Night" during most 1971 shows. "Van wondered if Warner got the message," Chris Michie remarked: "They didn't."

CONCLUSIONS TO HIS BAND AND THE STREET CHOIR

One of the myths surrounding the album is it didn't sell well. It did! On both sides of the Atlantic, it was a hit with a chart position of eighteen in the U.K. and thirty-two in the U.S. Van for a few years complained about its lack of sales. Not true! It was a hit album.

He told Ritchie Yorke he simplified the product. That is he didn't consider the LP on par with **Astral Weeks**. "I really didn't think that album is saying much," Van told Yorke who showed up for the interview with no shirt, socks or shoes. Van was comfortable with him. They talked for hours leading to Yorke's 1975 biography.

When "Domino," the single from the LP, was released it reached number thirty-two on the **Billboard** 200. The single was released prior to the album, thereby spurring sales. The two other singles, "Blue Money" and "Call Me Up In Dreamland" charted at the lower end of the **Billboard** Hot 100. Warner was trying to promote Morrison's material. They were doing their best despite his reticence about self-promotion.

Dahaud Shaar was one of the hidden factors in the completion of the **His Band and the Street Choir** album. Why! He was the studio guru calming Van, smoothing over the differences with Warner and bolstering Morrison's confidence. How did he do this? When the album stalled, due to differences between Morrison and engineer/production coordinator Elliot Scheiner, Shaar stepped in to engineer six songs.

There were other problems with the **His Band and the Street Choir** album. The Street Choir grew to six, and then was redefined as three singers. Of these two were wives. Van remarked: "The old ladies got involved and this changed the album's direction." These distractions drove Morrison crazy.

HOWARD A. DEWITT

WHAT WAS WARNER'S VIEW OF THE HIS BAND AND THE STREET CHOIR?

By this point in Morrison's career his relationship with Warner was an uncertain one. Warner created problems when the publicity department, anticipating a Christmas break, mislabeled the songs on the album in the promotional material. At the conclusion of "I'll Be Your Lover, Too" there is a small snippet of conversation. Peter Mills landmark interpretive book observed this highlights the lack of skilled production. It also points to inept promotion. Brian Hinton doesn't view this as a problem. He calls the album one that "you must sing with, dance to...."

His Band and the Street Choir failed to bring a ringing endorsement from the Belfast Cowboy. The cover photo of Van in a full length Kaftan looked like something out of a Japanese movie. Van called the large number of album photos "rubbish."

What was Morrison's complaint? It was about everything. He wanted to record a simple a cappella album with only a guitar background and a well-defined set of vocalists. That didn't work out. He took exception to Warner marketing the album as a "hippie product." This was not his intent. This wasn't his music.

When Van sat down with Ritchie Yorke in 1973, he commented the album didn't "mean much in terms of where I was at ..." Dahaud Shaar disagreed. He believed it was brilliant. Janet Planet's album design was right for the times. Van was not on board. "Somebody else got control of it and got the cover and all that shit while I was on the West Coast," Morrison told Ritchie Yorke.

BIBLIOGRAPHICAL SOURCES

On Van's difficulties with the media, see, for example, Johnny Rogan, **Van Morrison: Portrait of The Artist** (London, 1984), chapter 7 and Vivien Goldman, "Van Interview," **Sounds**, March 30, 1974. The Goldman interview is an example of sending the wrong writer to conduct an interview. It says more about her ineptness than about Morrison's moods.

468

See the Richard Williams interview with Van in **Melody Maker**, July 28, 1973 for Van's reflections on how Woodstock changed after the festival. The Williams interview is also important as Van explains why he moved to Fairfax, California.

For the background and recording of **His Band and the Street Choir** see Clinton Heylin, **Can You Feel The Silence: Van Morrison, A New Biography** (London, 2002), chapter 14, Howard A. DeWitt, **Van Morrison: The Mystic's Music** (Fremont, 1983), pp. 36-39, Johnny Rogan, **Van Morrison: The Portrait of The Artist** (London, 1984), chapters 7-8 and Brian Hinton, **Celtic Crossroads: The Art of Van Morrison** (London, 1997, revised 2000), chapters 4-5. Hinton's analysis of the **His Band and the Street Choir** album remains one of the best interpretations of an LP Morrison at times criticized.

Interviews with Mark Naftalin, Elvin Bishop, Chris Michie and John Goddard helped to fill out portions of this chapter. These musicians and record store owner Goddard lived near and interacted with Morrison. His daily life was pieced together using their reminiscences as well as a dozen sources requesting anonymity. Alice Stuart and members of her band, Snake, also had a series of positive comments on Van in Marin County.

Interviews with Eric Isralow, aka Dr. Rock, helped to provide key points for this chapter. Also San Francisco disc jockeys Paul Vincent and Russ "The Moose" Syracuse helped with key information.

See Ralph J. Gleason, "Perspectives: Van Morrison Does It Right," **Rolling Stone**, June 24, 1971, p. 26 for the New Orleans House show in Berkeley, California. An interview with Larry Catlin of Bill Graham Presents helped this part of the chapter. Bill Graham spoke at length with me about how much he liked Van as an artist but he confessed managing the Belfast Cowboy was difficult. He also confessed he never understood Van's musical journey.

On Tom Donahue and FM radio see Ben Fong Torres, **The Hits Just Keep On Coming: The History of Top 40 Radio** (San Francisco, 1998), pp. 199-210.

A brief interview with Corky Siegel aided this chapter. In Chicago a number of support people who worked with Van added detail, these people included Junior Wells and Wayne Jancik.

Cleve Duncan of the Penguins shared his memories of playing at Frenchy's. Jimmy McCracklin and Lowell Fulson provided information on clubs in the East Bay and they also suggested how and why Morrison's music was embraced.

Tony Dey provided information on the Sacramento gig. For the Inn of the Beginning concert set list see the https://www.setlist.fm/setlist/van-morrison/1971/the-inn-of-the-beginning-cotati-ca-43f72be7.html

An interview with Ronnie Montrose was important to this chapter. Happy Traum provided important information on Woodstock. Nathan Rubin spoke at length about this period.

For an excellent analysis of the **His Band and the Street Choir** album see, Martin Buzacott and Andrew Ford, **Speaking In Tongues: The Songs of Van Morrison** (Sydney, 2005), pp. 110-115.

For the Fillmore East shows see the Fillmore East Preservation Society website for a listing of shows. http://www.fillmore-east.com/showlist.html

An excellent review of the **His Band and the Street Choir** is Dave Marsh, **Creem**, October 1971.

See Jon Landau, Review of **Tupelo Honey**, **Rolling Stone**, November 25, 1971 for some interesting thoughts on the new album. John Collis, **Van Morrison: Inarticulate Speech of the Heart** (Boston, 1996), pp. 233-237 is important to understanding "Moonshine Whiskey." Ray Ruff added material on Morrison's relationship with Warner Brothers.

An interview with Chuck Steaks, aka Charles (Chuck) Schoning, of the Quicksilver Messenger Service in 1974 was important to this chapter. Conversations with Pacific Northwest musicians Jim Manolides and George Palmerton were helpful as was Frantics leader Ron Peterson.

The press for his three post **Astral Weeks** albums was uniformly excellent and Van was at times very accessible. The San Francisco Bay Area shows in 1970 and 1971 were ones where Van was often accessible to the fans. Frenchy's in Hayward California was a former big band dance hall and by 1970-1971 it was a venue where all the local bands played and one night you might have Sly Stone, the next night local bands, like Peter Wheat and the Breadmen, and then a headliner like Van Morrison. There was little to no security, dope smoking was casual and accepted and the entrance was maybe five dollars. This was the

470

type of atmosphere Van loved. The guarantees for bands were also small ones. See Peter Mills, **Hymns to the Silence: Inside the Words and Music of Van Morrison** (London, 2010), pp. 38-46 for comments on **His Band and the Street Choir**. Ritchie Yorke, **Van Morrison: Into The Music** (New York, 1975) p. 89 argues Van lost control of the **His Band and the Street Choir** album.

For Janet Planet's in-depth thoughts on the move from Woodstock to Marin County and how this changed their life and Van's music, see Louis Sahagun, "Janet Planet: Van Morrison's 'Brown Eyed Girl' The Clouds Have Lifted, Those Tumultuous Years Behind Her, The Astral Angel Lives A Quiet Life and Still Writes Music," **Los Angeles Times**, November 17, 1998 http://articles.latimes.com/1998/nov/17/news/cl-43498 This is one of Janet Planet's more in-depth interviews suggesting the coming problems in their marriage. Over the years Van has made it clear he did not want Janet or his daughter Shana to talk with the media. He continues to rant and rave whenever an interview takes place. He is committed to his privacy and for that reason he has a mercurial relationship with the press.

For recent interviews with Van Morrison where he has looked back upon his life and his relationship with the media, he has maintained he is cooperative with the press. There is an element of truth to the statement. In 2008 when the **Astral Weeks Live** project debuted in Los Angeles, Van had an unusually open and friendly interview with Randy Lewis, "Van Morrison's Full Q & A On 'Astral Weeks'," **The Los Angeles Times Music Blog**, October 31 2008 https://latimesblogs.latimes.com/music_blog/2008/10/van-morrisons-f.html and Fintan O'Toole, "Van Morrison: 'Being Famous Is Not Great For The Creative Process. Not For Me, Anyway'," **The Irish Times**, August 29, 2015. https://www.irishtimes.com/culture/music/van/van-morrison-being-famous-is-not-great-for-the-creative-process-not-for-me-anyway-1.2332216 Coverage by Fintan O'Toole changed the quality of journalists interviewing Morrison. O'Toole was not a music reporter. He is a premier Irish news analyst. Van was being interviewed by major hard news journalists. O'Toole's questions were serious, informed and in line with serious news inquires. The old days of **Melody Maker**, **New Musical Express** and **Disc** sending insulting journalists lacks information on Van's music and life was at an end.

In the last twenty years Van has gone into a damage control mode with the press. He says he is mystified over those who write about him without contacting him for an interview. This is my third book on Van. Except for some backstage conversations in the 1970s and early 1980s when I lived in the San Francisco Bay Area his management has ignored a dozen requests for interviews. Fortunately, his musicians, two of his managers, a dozen close associates and members of the Bill Graham Organization have worked with me since the late 1970s.

See Jeff Giles, "45 Years Ago: Van Morrison Clears Out His Vaults With 'Tupelo Honey'," **Ultimateclassicrock.com**, October 15, 2016. http://ultimateclassicrock.com/van-morrison-tupelo-honey/ The Giles article includes a number of quotes from Van about how and why he didn't care for the **Tupelo Honey** album. For the reissue of **Tupelo Honey** see the January 23, 2008 review by David Cavanagh in **Uncut** which beautifully dissects the songs, the album cover and why the curmudgeonly Morrison disliked the album. Also see Jon Landau, "Tupelo Honey," **Rolling Stone**, November 25 1971. https://www.rollingstone.com/music/music-album-reviews/tupelo-honey-101911/ This review is the single best one and suggests what and why Morrison was doing with his music. Another excellent and well written review of the 2008 reissue is Chris Jones, "Van Morrison: Tupelo Honey Review," **BBC Music**, 2008. http://www.bbc.co.uk/music/reviews/d3bd/

For insights into **Tupelo Honey's** impact on college radio see, **Record World**, November 13, 1971, p. 8. Also see Ken Brooks, **In Search Of Van Morrison** (London, 1999) for an analysis of each of his songs. An important source for Morrison's songs is Becker Gunter, "Van Morrison Song Database." http://ivan.vanomatic.de

The influence of the song "Tupelo Honey" is an important indication of not only the song but also the album upon popular culture. Peter Fonda's movie "Ulee's Gold" brought Morrison's song to the general public once again in 1997.

For Cotati and the Inn of the Beginning see, Tim Findley, "Grassroots Saga: A 25-Year-Old Mayor In Action," **Rolling Stone**, September 14, 1972. https://www.rollingstone.com/politics/politics-news/grassroots-saga-a-25-year-old-mayor-in-action-118805/

Lote Thistlethwaite, one of the owners of Eeyore Books in Cotati, provided important information on the local culture and how Van Morrison reacted to it. On Brinsley Schwarz appearing with Van in

New York, see Will Birch, **Cruel To Be Kind: The Life And Music of Nick Lowe** (New York, 2019), pp. 71-77. The question of Van's temporary writer's block was brought up by more than twenty people interviewed for this book. Paul Vincent, a KSAN disc jockey, alerted me to this area of investigation. It appears there was very little down time for Van as far as writing and producing is concerned. But it was talked about due to his prolific nature.

Van Morrison - Kingdom Hall - Live in Berkeley 1979

CHAPTER 19

ST. DOMINIC'S PREVIEW: DO THE HITS KEEP ON COMING OR IS IT EXPERIMENTATION? 1972-1973

"I'm an inspirational writer, … I've always got bits and pieces hanging around…. If I didn't have a contract to do an album, I wouldn't do it."

VAN MORRISON IN CONVERSATION WITH SAN FRANCISCO RADIO PERSONALITY PAUL VINCENT

"Spirituality is one thing…. I don't really like to use the word, because that's what it really means. It really means this church or that church … but spirituality is different, because that's the individual."

VAN MORRISON

The changes in Van Morrison's life by 1972 were cataclysmic. Irish themes, while never absent in Van's life, took on an increasing role. He has never said how "The Troubles" influenced his life. He is Irish to the core. He was thinking more about Belfast. That would eventually prompt him to relocate to the U.K. and then to Belfast.

John Platania, Van's guitarist, spoke to Clinton Heylin about Van's marriage stating: "She was a strong person. People used to offer her modelling assignments and acting roles, but Van flatly refused to allow her do these things."

When Janet described her marriage as a happy one, she pointed out to a San Francisco journalist that Van was "incredibly Irish to live with…."

The tensions from constant creativity took its toll. Heylin claims Van didn't like performing. The opposite was true. From the moment he moved to Marin County there were continuous small club appearances. By the Winterland show for The Band's 1978 farewell, Van led the tightest band in rock music.

Ed Fletcher, Van's road manager, was instrumental in the development of the new Morrison. He wasn't fond of the shows at the Inn of the Beginning or the Lion's Share. Why? They were a logistical nightmare. When the band and the roadies showed up it was difficult to get into the club. There were more people outside than inside listening to the music. It was a zoo.

The busy life Morrison experienced in the early 1970s made **St. Dominic's Preview** special. As one band member told me: "We were all running out of gas. Van would call the band in the middle of the night for practice or to announce a last moment small club dates." Everyone was young and having fun. But it was wearing on Morrison and the musicians.

The good news was Van pulled out past influences. Celtic folk became a mantra for his songwriting. He spent more time in the studio working on the final product. It was 1972. Van hadn't had a day off since **Astral Weeks**. He was tired. He was also reflective. Thoughts of Hyndford Street and Belfast persisted. He was tired being asked about Ireland. Was he Irish? What was the Irish influence? In **St. Dominic's Preview** Van answered these questions.

TO THE IRISH OR NOT TO BE IRISH: THAT IS THE QUESTION?

The **St. Dominic's Preview** album represents another turn in the Morrison saga. He was aware of "The Troubles," while not actively speaking of Northern Ireland's turmoil. His friends let him know the Belfast club scene was shrinking due to the violence. How did this influence Van? The hints of his Irish nature and the missing Belfast symbols are shown in the lyrics to the title song. Van sings: "It's a long way to Belfast city too."

While sitting home one day in 1971, Van read the **San Francisco Chronicle** about a peace rally at San Francisco's St. Dominic's Church. He took this as a sign. He drove into S. F. and looked at the church. Unwittingly, this was the inspiration for the album title. Some attribute the story to Van getting ready for a Reno, Nevada concert and picking up the newspaper. There were no Reno concerts prior to the album's release.

As he finished a whirlwind string of albums from 1970 through 1972 Van was tired. He needed a break. This suggests why St. **Dominic's Preview** appears truncated. One example of this change is "Listen To The Lion," which is described as a leftover from the **Tupelo Honey** sessions. "Listen To The Lion" is a step child of the **Astral Week's** sound. It was initially recorded during the **Moondance** sessions. Warner said it was too long and overly experimental. When Van went into the San Francisco studios to re-record it there was a sense of personal liberation. There were only two takes to a tune in which Van's voice blends with the instrumentation and the influence of the repetitive rhythm and blues records to create one of the more unique musical vocals.

Morrison's guitar playing alongside Ronnie Montrose with drummer Connie Kay and Gary Mallaber adding percussion and vibraphone, completed "Listen To The Lion." "I did one (take) and Connie Kay did the other," Mallaber continued. "They used the one with the live vibes, which is what I played live."

LISTEN TO THE LION: PERHAPS VAN'S GREATEST SONG

In July 1972, Van Morrison's sixth album **St. Dominic's Preview** was released in the U.S. to steady sales. Because of a mixed reception for Van's albums in the U.K., Warner increased its London advertising budget. This release featured elaborate advertising in the **New Musical Express**, **Disc** and **Melody Maker**. Ray Ruff said Mo Ostin was trying to heal the promotional rift with Morrison.

The gestation period for "Listen To The Lion" was a long and convoluted one. The initial version of the song was cut during the

Moondance sessions. The idea was to preserve it for the **Tupelo Honey** album. Ritchie Yorke called it Morrison's premier rhythm and blues songs. One that placed his voice, according to Yorke, within the instrumentation. Johnny Rogan wrote of Van it "unreleased the lion within himself." For Van it was a time he considered and reconsidered and talked about with his musical friends. In the 2005 album **Magic Time** one song, "The Lion This Time", showed the tune was on his mind. He also played it during the **Astral Weeks Live** performances. Greil Marcus wrote: "He breaks away from language and speaks in Irish tongues. He is not singing it is singing him." Why "Listen To The Lion" resided in Morrison's psyche is unknown. On the **It's Too Late to Stop Now** album there is a magnificent live rendering. The 2007 three CD **Still On Top-The Greatest Hits** featured a remastered version. The **Live At Montreux 1980/1974** DVD has **Common One** band members backing him on the song. Van was intrigued by "Listen To The Lion" because it provided him with a good reason to show Warner Brothers' ineptitude in judging his music. The corporate suits didn't like the song from day one. He showed them multiple times they were wrong.

St. Dominic's Preview melded Celtic folk, blues, jazz and rhythm and blues into a mainstream pop sound. Van was influenced by Woodstock's bucolic beauty and the free-spirited Marin lifestyle. The album touched a wide variety of subjects. He sang about cleaning windows, W. B. Yeats poetry, country music, William Blake's influence and Edith Piaf's Paris life. These themes were not exciting to rock and roll aficionados. While he was never overtly political, Van sings for the first time of "The Troubles" in Northern Ireland. It was as if to apologize for leaving Belfast. He had no interest in living through "The Troubles." Marin County was his home.

Many songs in **St. Dominic's Preview** had a defined commercial tone. Others were personal tunes. He could become a serious wordsmith while turning out commercial songs. One critic remarked **St. Dominic's Preview** was much like **Moondance** in tone and timbre. It befuddled the critics. Some said it was a rare treat. Others complained it was recycled Morrison.

Rolling Stone called it the "best produced, most ambitious Van Morrison yet released." Why? Reviewers remarked the album was "a blend of soul and funk." There were hints of **Astral Weeks** in "Listen

To The Lion" and "Almost Independence Day." Connie Kay's drums recalled Astral Week's soft jazz ambiance.

There were changes in Morrison's working habits. He spent more time in the studio. He still worked 24/7 on his music, but the frenetic pace was as much due to his home studio and the burgeoning San Francisco recording industry. The number of S. F. recording studios increased dramatically. It was to meet the demand for musicians who wanted to cut demos. The major labels began looking to San Francisco to develop new studios. Columbia was the first to build one for their new acts. Wally Heider was the Godfather to the studio explosion.

HOW WALLY HEIDER HELPED MORRISON IN THE STUDIO

In 1969 Wally Heider opened a recording studio in San Francisco. Why? His time working in Los Angeles convinced him he had a gold mine in the emerging San Francisco sound. The Fillmore West, the rise of small music clubs, and the increased interest in signing local rock bands made it difficult to find a recording studio slot. With **Rolling Stone**, America's premier rock magazine, located in the South of Market industrial area there was demand for new music as **Rolling Stone** deified the local record scene. Tower Records in San Francisco for time was open twenty-four hours a day. At the 1967 Monterey Pop Festival, Heider found his calling as he engineered this rock music event. His remote recordings were used in the documentary. This experience prompted him to leave Los Angeles opening a recording studio near the Fillmore West. The Hyde Street location was in the midst of the Tenderloin with hookers, drug dealers and low life denizens populating the streets. The studio brought in Crosby, Stills, Nash and Young, as well as the Creedence Clearwater Revival who recorded **Cosmo's Factory** there.

The sudden influx of recording studios in the late 1960s was due to the expanding San Francisco sound. In addition to Heider's facility at 245 Hyde Street, Columbia Records opened a recording studio at 827 Folsom Street as the bands grew in numbers and popularity. Carlos Santana and Paul Simon recorded at this facility.

Coast Recorders was another studio in the 1960s designed by Bill Putnam. Coast Recorders was founded before the San Francisco

478

Sound exploded. The company began in North Beach as Columbus Recorders in the late 1950s. It was owned by the Kingston Trio's manager Frank Werber. Jazz and folk acts recorded here.

There was also Golden State Recorders where the Beau Brummels cut "Laugh Laugh" and Tom "Big Daddy" Donahue brought in his Autumn label artists. The Grateful Dead and Sly Sound recorded at this facility.

IN WALLY HEIDER'S STUDIO

Not surprisingly, **St. Dominic's Preview** took longer to complete than previous albums. In Wally Heider's studio a crowd of friends assembled making Morrison at ease. There was a hit record quality to the album. While "Jackie Wilson Said (I'm In Heaven When You Smile)," "Redwood Tree" and "Gypsy" charted, none reached the Billboard Top 40.

"Jackie Wilson Said" charted at sixty-one, "Redwood Tree" at ninety-eight and "Gypsy" at one hundred and one. Van was happy. He didn't need Top 40 hits. His increasingly deep interest in his business affairs was a sign of fiscal and artistic freedom. The pressures of the music business conflicted Van. He was often testy and irritable.

The lengthy period recording **St. Dominic's Preview** worked to Morrison's advantage. After spending the Fall of 1971 in the studio and taking a break until January 29, 1972, when his touring band assembled in Wally Heider's studio, his writing and music continued to mature. This session led to a commercial breakthrough as "Jackie Wilson Said (I'm In Heaven When You Smile)" was cut with Mark Naftalin's brilliant piano. It was Naftalin's work with the Paul Butterfield Blues Band that made it essential for Morrison to hire him. He was more than a session musician. Naftalin was a composer, arranger, band leader, promoter and radio host. Morrison was intrigued by the large number of hats this skilled musician wore.

Jackie Wilson's "Reet Petite" was the model for Morrison. Van took a little bit from Louis Jordan's "Reet, Petite and Gone" to craft this personal seminal rocker. In 1982 Dexy's Midnight Runners had a chart hit peaking at five on the U.K. singles chart. The influence of Lee Michaels was evident as his Mill Valley Studio with Doug

Messenger on guitar, Michaels on piano and Van's guitar flushed out the early demos. By the time Van arrived at Pacific High Studio the tribute to Jackie Wilson was in its final form.

As Morrison finished **St. Dominic's Preview**, he wasn't sure about the album's appeal. "I am pretty confused right now, but, y'know, I've got a feeling that everything's starting to come together ... I think it's all going to work out," Morrison concluded. It was his best-selling album until 2008 when **Keep It Simple** arrived at ten on **Billboard**.

Most Morrison biographers pay little attention to Ted Templeman. After all Van said he produced the albums not the blonde-haired surfer from Santa Cruz. The truth is a bit more complicated. Templeman was a hands-on producer. He continued to play a role in Morrison's sixth studio album. What did he do?

When Van was asked about Templeman, he remarked: "I gave (Templeman) co-production credit for things I didn't want to do ... (like) making sure it was mixed. I'd send him the tapes back and tell him and I wanted it mixed. I could be anywhere, like on holiday, and I'd ring up and tell him I want it mixed like this." This comment explains itself. The year after **St. Dominic's Preview** was released, Van told **Zig Zag**, Templeman was "a technical adviser."

Janet Planet saw Templeman as a studio asset. She said Templeman organized the studio and made it comfortable for the musicians. She described him as "hands on." "He had lots of suggestions," Janet told Peter Wrench.

St Dominic's Preview was an album with new band members. Templeman's role was to integrate the new musicians with Morrison.

What did Van intend in **St. Dominic's Preview**? He was personalizing his work. The turmoil in American politics, the free form youth culture and changes in musical tastes had little impact upon Morrison. What did impact him? It was 1950s rock and roll and Jim Henson's Muppets.

He was more interested in paying tribute to Jackie Wilson or Bobby "Blue" Bland than he was singing about Vietnam or the travails of President Richard M. Nixon. With Van it was about his music. Nothing else! This was the beginning of a period in which he had little, if anything, to do with rock music. He didn't consider himself a rock and roll act.

VAN ON THE ST. DOMINIC'S PREVIEW LP

"In terms of my own music, I've always thought about it in terms of jazz. I don't mean 'jazz' in the sense of chord structures. I mean that my approach to music is jazz. Like Louis Armstrong said, 'I never sing or play the same way twice.' Every time Armstrong sang something, it was different. He didn't believe in the idea of playing a wrong note…. I love that idea. That's the basic approach of jazz and blues."

VAN MORRISON IN CONVERSATION WITH JON WILDE, UNCUT, JULY, 2005, P. 58

ST. DOMINIC'S PREVIEW: WHAT IT SAID

St. Dominic's Preview combined different styles. The paean to the 1950s is "Jackie Wilson Said." It is one of the most adventurous tunes in Morrison's career. Van combines his fascination with roots rock with a careful historical eye. As a 1950s rock and soul act, Wilson moved effortlessly as a soul balladeer into the 1960s and 1970s. He was signed to Brunswick Records. The label was allegedly owned or influenced by the mob. Wilson never got paid. This is a theme Van embraces. The resulting song rang true concerning the excesses of the music industry. "Jackie Wilson Said (I'm In Heaven When You Smile)" has an emotional countenance striking a raw nerve. The song evokes dark images of corruption in the music industry. In this song Wilson combined pop, rhythm and blues, jazz and blues into an up-tempo rocker.

There were several other musical departures. On "Gypsy," Van uses an acoustic guitar to weave a simple, soft lyrical folk tale. He follows it with "I Will Be There" combining Kansas City blues reminiscent of Big Joe Turner with Van's intricate view of that genre.

On the b-side a church of the same name inspired the title track. It is one of Van's more autobiographical tunes with references to such diverse cities as Buffalo and Belfast. While America and Ireland were continents apart, they were a big part of Morrison's songwriting psyche. The influence of American themes is obvious. When Van sings nostalgically about Safeway supermarkets in "Redwood Trees," he uses sublime images of California's natural resources. He demonstrates a keen eye toward historical forces.

The final song on **St. Dominic's Preview,** "Almost Independence Day" is a cogent comment on his personal life. With Bernie Krause's moog synthesizer turning out cocktail lounge background music, Van sings of another musical time. In its simplest form the song is much like a Byrds tune. Not surprisingly, Krause played the moog synthesizer on the Byrds "Space Odyssey." It is Mark Naftalin's seductive solo piano genius, which shines through. His subtle piano mastery adds a depth making "Almost Independence Day" a classic. **St. Dominic's Preview** is a major experimental turning point. It continued Van's mystical qualities.

The album's co-producer, Ted Templeman, was confused by Van's music. Once again, he announced that he would never work with Van. It was Van who would never work again with Templeman. Genius has its problems. Morrison remained a curmudgeon in the studio. He is a difficult person to produce. As he wrote the songs, recorded the album and prepared to go out on the road, producers, journalists and band members wondered if there was a hidden Irish side to the album. There was!

WAS THERE A HIDDEN IRISH SIDE TO ST. DOMINIC'S PREVIEW?

Van said it best when he told Ritchie Yorke **St. Dominic's Preview** had nothing to do with James Joyce. "He's not even in it," Van continued. "People were intellectualizing their own interpretations…." Van emphasized he is a stream of consciousness songwriter. "What I'm trying to get across is misinterpreted," Van concluded. It had nothing to do with James Joyce. Once again, he reminded the critics he was the only interpreter of his music. He warned the critics not to judge his work. That is my domain. You must abstain, Van warned. They ignored him. The media war was on.

The tendency to read literary influences into Morrison's music is the critic's favorite past time. Many of them envisioned stream of consciousness writing akin to James Joyce. Van simply laughed. He had a writing style incorporating many influences. Joyce was foremost amongst them. His writing was his own unique method.

By the early 1970s Van Morrison was a star. Yet, he remained unhappy. Career pressures plagued him. Fame and the cult of personality were robbing him of personal freedom. He solved that problem by taking off almost three years from the music business. He performed in small, select venues. He wasn't retired. He was retooling his career. He had to take control of his life. Van's mental health was more important than hit records. This is the only part of his career where he discussed writer's block with friends.

WAS THERE A HIT POTENTIAL TO ST. DOMINIC'S PREVIEW?

Van told close friends the hit potential in **St. Dominic's Preview** was unlimited. He believed he was being given signs in his song writing. Perhaps even divine intervention.

The critical barbs began when the single "Gypsy" backed with "Saint Dominic's Preview" (W. B. 7665) bubbled under at 101 on the **Billboard** 45 chart. It didn't help Warner pressed only 5,000 singles. The January 1973 release was cut to three minutes ten seconds, as compared to the four minute and thirty second album cut. It is one of Morrison's rare 45s. It was a mono release. Ironically, it sold better in Germany than the U.S.

Although **St. Dominic's Preview** had limited chart success. The lyrical direction of the LP pleased Van. While "Jackie Wilson Said" reached number 61 on the **Billboard** Hot 100, there was concern expressed from Warner Brothers executives about the lack of Top 40 hits. When "Redwood Tree" reached number 98 on the **Billboard** Hot 100 there was some snide comments made by Mo Ostin. Van ignored these critical barbs.

ST. DOMINIC'S PREVIEW IN RETROSPECT

St. Dominic Preview is a character trait defining Van. Chris Michie, who played with Van in the early 1980s, was around the Marin music scene. He watched Van grow and mature. "Those who write about rock music don't realize Van needs constant change to create,"

Michie concluded. What does Michie mean? He said Van fires musicians to change his musical direction. It is not for vindictive reasons. He fires some of the road crew due to sheer superstition. It shows Morrison's musical thematic revolution. To Van it is simply business as usual. "To get a new sound you need to change musicians, the atmosphere surrounding your music and your management. That was Van's goal," Michie concluded.

This volatility is reflected in his music. **St. Dominic's Preview** was no exception. The album vented his feelings. His images included his love for the redwoods, his view of people he described as local gypsies and he skewered those around him for failing to understand his artistic mission. He also aimed barbs at the critics questioning his ever-changing musical direction.

Van defends hiring new musicians, producers, roadies, business managers, booking agents and lawyers as a way of remaining fresh and vibrant. Some suggest it is simply a personality trait. He loves to work. Part of his work ethic is to find new sources of inspiration. His ever-present coffee-stained, tattered notebook is filled with scrawls of future songs. By the end of 1972 writing was not as easy for Morrison. He was showing the strain of constant creativity. He told close friends he was frightened. He might have writer's block. Fortunately, he didn't.

VAN IN CONVERSATION WITH ROLLING STONE

"I'd been working on this song about the scene going down in Belfast. And I wasn't sure what I was writing but anyway the central image seemed to be this church called St. Dominic's where people were gathering to pray or hear a mass for peace in Northern Ireland. Anyway, a few weeks ago I was in Reno for a gig at the University of Nevada. And while we were having dinner, I picked up the newspaper and just opened it to a page and there in front of me was an announcement about a mass for peace in Belfast … at St. Dominic's church in San Francisco. Totally blew me out. Like I'd never even heard of a St. Dominic's church."

VAN MORRISON TALKING WITH JOHN GRISSIM, JR., ROLLING STONE, JUNE 22, 1972

This was a tough time for Van. He had to maintain his writing schedule. His marriage was crumbling. He also had a daughter, Shana, he adored. She was seen everywhere with her father. He doted on her. The divorce made **St. Dominic's Preview** an album with some sour moments and acrid comments.

The primary inspiration for **St. Dominic's Preview** was a church in either Belfast or San Francisco. This led to an emphasis on the spiritual. It was while he thought of and viewed the San Francisco church images of Belfast abounded. He missed Belfast. His thoughts on returning home ruminated as his career exploded.

Van was concerned about not being Irish enough. He created songs professionally Irish. There wasn't a political position taken in his music. There was only a reflection of Northern Ireland, if a troubled one. There were a few moments of tenderness and a couple of love songs in **St. Dominic's Preview**. It was a workman like approach to a series of songs that had uneven connections or themes.

There was also a conscious attempt to expand the length of his songs. On "Listening To The Lion" and "Almost Independence Day," Van spent twenty-one minutes highlighting his primal vocal style. Peter Mills path breaking book, **Hymns to the Silence: Inside the Words and Music of Van Morrison**, published in 2010, devotes a chapter to Van's vocal style with the title "Listening To The Lion." This brilliant essay concludes "Morrison's musicianship is both distinct from and unbreakably connected to his singing and to his roots...." If that is the case then the **St. Dominic's Preview** is a tour de force inside Van's mind.

WHAT DOES ONE MAKE OF ST. DOMINIC'S PREVIEW?

St. Dominic's Preview is the album that brought Morrison attention not only as a unique songwriter, but one whose visual, lyrical picture depicted his life. He also began creating the Caledonia Soul Orchestra. He worked in isolation at his home-based Caledonia Studio. The final tracks for **St. Dominic's Preview** were cut in a number of San Francisco studios. The message was clear. He wouldn't overdub. He wouldn't spend hours on mixing. By working out intricate demos at home, he had a finished product when he entered the studio.

One track stands out from **St. Dominic's Preview**. That cut is "Listen To The Lion." It is an eleven plus minute tune suggesting the raw emotion in Morrison's vocal range. The growling vocals owe more to Bobby Blue Bland than to anyone else.

By the time the **St. Dominic's Preview** album appeared, Van had moved on to other creative areas. Yet, the LP brought a number of innovations. Bernie Krause's moog synthesizer, the blues-jazz fusion of the single, "St. Dominic's Preview," the Big Joe Turner inspired "I Will Be There" and the manner in which he shunted producer Ted Templeman to the side indicated there was a new Van Morrison. One who was in charge. He was taking control of his music. The best was yet to come.

When Michael Maggid shot the album cover for **St. Dominic's Preview**, he selected a small, elegant church in San Anselmo California. Then Maggid took Van over to the San Francisco Theological Seminary in San Anselmo to shoot the remainder of the photos. Initially, Van wanted to title the album "Green." Warner Brothers considered this non-commercial. The publicity department put out some promo material pointing out the title track came to Morrison in a dream. They were selling "the mystic's music."

There were changes in the musical direction. Van was not as concerned with "love" and "relationships." This was not surprising. During the interviews for the album, Van was tired of answering questions about where the songs originated and what they meant. The absence of his wife, Janet, caused the critics to ponder his personal life. This enraged Van. He isolated himself as much as possible from intrusive interviews. Warner Brothers did its best to assuage Morrison. The press was positive. The noticeable change in themes built Morrison growing reputation as a brilliant songwriter and a performer who continued to draw in new fans.

The increasingly rhythm and blues tone to **St. Dominic's Preview** intrigued reviewers. Another change was the absence of Janet. She was no longer in the mix. Her art, her liner notes, her beauty, her calm nature and her obvious support for everything her husband accomplished was absent from the final product. Janet was now a muse without portfolio or royalties. She was also a muse living with Shana in Los Angeles.

BIBLIOGRAPHICAL SOURCES

For a description of the **St. Dominic's Preview** album see, Howard A. DeWitt, **Van Morrison: The Mystic's Music** (Fremont, 1983), pp. 90-91, Clinton Heylin, **Can You Feel The Silence: Van Morrison, A New Biography** (London, 2002), pp. 255-259, Brian Hinton, **Celtic Crossroads: The Art of Van Morrison** (London, 1997, revised edition 2000), chapter 5 and Johnny Rogan, **Van Morrison: The Portrait of The Artist** (London, 1984), chapter 10. Also, see Johnny Rogan, **Van Morrison: No Surrender** (London, 2005).

Peter Wrench, **Saint Dominic's Flashback: Van Morrison's Classic Album, Forty Years On** (FeedARead, 2012) is an exhaustive and well written book on the album. Interviews with Mark Naftalin, Ron Eliot, Tony Dey and Ronnie Montrose were important to this chapter.

See Peter Mills, **Hymns to the Silence: Inside the Words and Music of Van Morrison** (London, 2010), pp. 95-96, Ritchie Yorke, **Van Morrison: Into The Music** (London, 1975), pp. 90-96 and Greil Marcus, **When The Rough Gods Go Writing** (New York, 2010), p. 65. Erik Hage, **The Words and Music of Van Morrison** (London, 2009), pp. 65-69. The Hage volume is an important analytical source with brilliant interpretations of Morrison's music.

Steve Turner, **Van Morrison: Too Late To Stop Now** (New York, 1993) is a friendly, but insightful look, into Morrison's music with a Christian approach. The work of Ritchie Yorke is important for understanding Morrison as a creative entity.

See Stephen Holden, "Saint Dominic's Preview," **Rolling Stone**, August https://www.rollingstone.com/music/music-album-reviews/saint-dominics-preview-93093/ for a rave review in which Holden says Van's album is: "The best-produced, most ambitious Van Morrison record yet released." While mentioning esoteric lyrics and a penchant for new themes, Holden points out the album has a "thrilling mystical presentiment." With tributes to Count Basie and Big Joe Williams, Holden concludes Van's "Rhythm and Blues-jazz roots" dominate.

Mitch Woods, Art Siegel, John Goddard, Paul Vincent, Larry Catlin, Chris Michie, and Nick Clainos helped me to understand how Marin County influenced Morrison.

CHAPTER 20

JACKIE DESHANNON INTERLUDE, FINALIZING COMMERCIAL SUCCESS, A NEW CREATIVITY AND A NEW VAN

"I was fortunate enough … to work with Van. He's an amazing talent."

JACKIE DESHANNON

The seminal changes in Van's life in the early 1970s were ones where he increasingly worked producing other artists, writing songs others could cover and polishing his stage show. By the time he began the **Hard Nose The Highway** album, Van was only twenty-eight, but he was a grizzled veteran of the music business. He was also in demand as a producer leading him to pop-folk chanteuse Jackie DeShannon.

In 1972 Jackie DeShannon released an album with a cover of Van's "I Wanna Roo You." Her **Jackie** album showed an interest in Morrison's songwriting. When he began working with DeShannon it was to find a new muse. The 1972 DeShannon sessions did not find immediate mainstream success. This was due to business differences between Atlantic and Warner Brothers. But the real problem is Morrison feared he suffered from writer's block. Was it real or imagined?

She also sang back up on Van's **Hard Nose The Highway**. But the collaboration didn't lead to commercial success. It did extend both artists creativity.

WRITER'S BLOCK: REAL OR IMAGINED?

When I conducted the research for my 1983 book **Van Morrison: The Mystic's Music** I was intrigued by the number of people close to Van who discussed his fear of writer's block. Nathan Rubin said Morrison believed he might not be able to continue to write. Others observed pressures from Warner Brothers for hit songs was constant. Morrison needed peace of mind. He found it on the printed page. "I think Van took to a heavy reading schedule to fortify himself mentally," Rubin told me in his office at California State University, Hayward. He continued: "I remember Van telling me the small clubs gave him the freedom to delve into his musical bag and experiment." Chris Michie, Mark Naftalin Jack Schroer, and a host of other musicians agreed with Rubin. There is a split among those close to Van. Some thought he was drained from writing too much. Others said he had a case of writer's block. He was also exhausted.

Nathan Rubin: "I think there were too many distractions for Van. It wasn't writer's block. His life was encumbered."

"The constant demand for interviews drained Van," Chris Michie remarked. Van needed a vacation from the press. Van trusted few journalists. In Belfast, Donal Corvin had his ear. Joel Selvin of the **San Francisco Chronicle** was a trusted confidant. Tom "Big Daddy" Donahue and the **San Francisco Examiner's** Phil Elwood were a part of Van's inner circle. Greil Marcus was a friend.

He despised the print media. He believed his free will was compromised. The press didn't understand him. They didn't understand his music past or present. Van complained constantly about the Them re-releases.

WILL THEM GO AWAY?

The Them recordings and the Bang Masters continued to be a point of irritation. Why was he angry? He didn't control the music. He didn't receive royalties. He didn't have artistic control. He didn't feel the industry respected his talent. At times he would react to these past transgressions, real and imagined, impinging his current production.

As Van prepared to release another Warner Brothers album, the ghost of Them haunted him. There had been periodic Them releases. None were satisfactory. Usually, these records were designed to cash in on whatever level of popularity Van had at the moment. They were unattractive releases with minimal or no liner notes. This changed in 1972 when a Parrot double album arrived with Lester Bangs' superb liner notes.

The album, **Them Featuring Van Morrison Lead Singer**, was a marketing device with remastered cuts, superb liner notes and a large advertising budget. It infuriated Van. His present success prompted the re-release. He scurried to lawyers. There was nothing they could do. He let it be known that the double album didn't make him happy.

Lester Bangs' liner notes added some credibility to the twenty tracks. Van should have been happy as two of Tommy Scott's songs were taken off this anthology. Morrison said Scott was a rank amateur. He disavowed his work. He intimated industry insiders like Scott could destroy his career. For Van fans, this was an excellent compilation. It included songs from the first two Them albums. It was attractively packaged. Van ranted and raved about it. The album sold well. The reissues and repackaging of the Them material continued to bother Morrison. The **St. Dominic's Preview** LP was what was on everyone's mind, not the Bang or Them material.

JANET PLANET'S SEMINAL INFLUENCE AND RE-DIRECTED CREATIVITY

When Janet Planet moved out, Van was in a quandary. He had to begin a new life. His future tunes had a maudlin, sometimes sentimental, and often they veered into a critical direction. The freshness in his songs came from exploring new themes. The result was a chaotic quality to **St. Dominics Preview**. One that presaged not only Van's divorce, but his retreat into the Marin countryside. His writing became more mature and at times more esoteric. It remained personal.

He was the subject of cranky critics who found him unfashionable in the rush of disco and pop drivel derailing his rock and roll credibility. Van laughed at the critics. By 1973 he was ready for what the critics called "a period of retirement." Once again, the critics got it wrong. Van wasn't retired. He was retooling his songs, his concert act and his life. He was doing it his way. It was a period of re-directed creativity.

The boneheads running Warner Brothers disdained him. What did Mo Ostin miss in Van Morrison's music? Everything! Ostin didn't understand a talent continuing to grow. Unlike Gary Puckett, Van refused to sound the same on every record. That is why he is still relevant and Puckett is playing with six other oldies acts in small venues in Des Moines, Iowa or Fargo, North Dakota.

Morrison talked directly to his fans in song. Conventional ideas of success did not impact his music. His fans loved this aspect of his art. The remote persona that is Van Morrison is a feature his fans love. They remain with him to the present day. He is an original talent who is an outlier.

WHAT THE DIVORCE BROUGHT IN A CREATIVE SENSE

Divorce is traumatic. The creative artist either benefits from it, or it is an impediment. In Van's case, his divorce led to a period of creative isolation. That is he didn't go out on tour. He did play local clubs. He was far from retired. He spent an increasingly large amount of time in his recording studio. He continued to write in a small notebook. The house was filled with books. He drank in the aroma of intellectual ferment. He reinvented himself. He was formulating, organizing and perfecting the Caledonia Soul Orchestra.

It was in the planning for the Caledonia Soul Orchestra Van placed his energy. He wanted to make new music. He continued to work with guitarist John Platania, drummer Daoud Shaar and ever-present bassist David Hayes. They were friends, as well as musical cohorts. They helped him get through the divorce.

Van's eight-track recording machine was old, inexpensive but perfect for his needs. Often, he would summon the musicians at two or three in the morning for a session that might begin a few hours later. Van was as mercurial in the studio, as he was in his private life.

Tony Dey recalled joining Van in the studio. He would drive from his Sacramento home fueled with coffee and early in the morning

491

unload his drum set. He would sit in Van's home studio. They would turn out great music.

The idea for the Caledonia Studio, as Van labeled it, became the focal point of musical experimentation. A week after the **St. Dominic's Preview** album was released Van began working on his next set of tracks. It was an unseasonably hot August night when Van went into the studio with songs for a new album. He was also working on a film treatment of "Madame George." The project was tentatively entitled "Madame Joy." He indicated an interest in pursuing movie soundtracks. Warner refused to back a movie.

Van hoped to produce other artists. He got a chance to demonstrate the depth of his production talents when he hooked up with Jackie DeShannon. Atlantic Records had recently signed DeShannon. She desperately wanted to collaborate with someone to produce hits. That turned out to be Van Morrison.

Her career paralleled his in many ways. She had difficulties with labels, producers and agents. Like Van, she was a marvelous songwriter with multiple talents. The industry pigeonholed her into the folk singer-songwriter mode. She resisted the cloistered industry maneuvering pursuing a wide-ranging sound combining pop, folk and blues.

INTRODUCING THE JACKIE DESHANNON INTERLUDE

In 1970, when pop-folk chanteuse Jackie DeShannon departed from Liberty Records, her frustration with the label was evident. They viewed her as more of a singer-songwriter than a performing-recording artist. It was as if she signed a contract solely to write hit tunes for others. She turned to Van Morrison for advice. He urged her to find another label. He was instrumental in convincing her to go with another producer. He had one in mind. Himself!

DeShannon signed a deal with Atlantic leading her to Morrison. The Atlantic producers Jerry Wexler, Tom Dowd and Arif Mardin mapped out her next musical venture. They wanted DeShannon to record cover versions that matched her style. A version of Neil Young's "Only Love Can Break Your Heart" is replete with an accordion backdrop. Another song selected to bring DeShannon back was Van's

"I Wanna Roo You." The Atlantic Record brain trust didn't feel comfortable producing a Morrison tune. They asked the Belfast Cowboy to come aboard. It was a golden opportunity. It also began a musical friendship that was beneficial to both performers.

As she sang backup on **Hard Nose the Highway**, Van schooled her on production techniques. DeShannon convinced Atlantic to allow Morrison to produce her album. Somewhere in the murky business transactions the album was lost. When it was finally released in 2003 the **Jackie…Plus** LP was a strong effort. There is also a DeShannon 45, written by Morrison, "Sweet Sixteen" that attests to Morrison's production genius and DeShannon's pop hit voice.

Jackie DeShannon

What did Morrison offer DeShannon? His lyrical magic drew her to him. She was an accomplished songwriter moving into a new direction. Her lyrics were brilliantly pop while Morrison's were more cerebral. Another difference was theme. She recognized the complex thought in Van's songwriting. It was unique. Her pop songs lacked

Van's creative direction. They were equally brilliant in a pop vein. She recognized that in a decade with Liberty she was no longer a pop princess. She was looking for a new musical life. She found it temporarily with Morrison. DeShannon felt used and abused by Liberty, Atlantic and Capitol. She had that in common with Morrison.

When Liberty released her **Splendor In The Grass** album, she was furious. The songs were little more than demos with her backing band, the Byrds, providing little in the way of a finished product. Then she signed for two years with Capitol. That didn't work out. Her Capitol album, **Songs**, had no impact. After one album and two singles DeShannon left Capitol. She signed with Atlantic. This created the Van Morrison interlude.

The lyrics to "Sweet Sixteen," offer insight into Morrison. He sings of a vision of a young girl at sweet sixteen and his lost love for her. It was a commercial song with a theme of unrequited love. Not exactly what one would expect from Van. That is why it is so special. The album Morrison and DeShannon collaborated on remained in the Atlantic archives for almost thirty years. In 1973 a DeShannon single "Sweet Sixteen," backed with "Speak Out To Me" (Atlantic 2919) was released to tepid sales. Warner Brothers threatened to sue if Atlantic released a limited edition. It was pirated in the marketplace. Mo Ostin was the culprit behind this decision. Finally, three decades later the album appeared. Sales were dismal.

When the **Jackie...Plus** LP finally was released, **Rolling Stone** called it one of the best reissues of 2003. The main reason it was so good was her choice of songs. She not only had the Morrison tunes but John Prine's "Paradise" and Alice Stuart's "Full Time Woman." These were cover tunes made for her voice. It was the six-minute plus song "Laid Back Days" the critics loved. Using the American Sound Studios in Memphis, Morrison brought out the best in DeShannon's sultry vocals.

The Rhino Handmade reissue of the material from 1972/1973 featured ten unreleased songs of which four were Morrison's. These songs "Sweet Sixteen," "Flamingos Fly," "Santa Fe" and "The Wonder of You" were designed to present her to a wider audience. The album also included her cover of Morrison's "I Wanna Roo You." The release of "Sweet Sixteen" as a DeShannon single indicated Van's commercial production touch.

Jackie DeShannon: "I went to Van's house to work on material. We had done a little bit of a baby tour together. While I was there, we started writing some stuff. They spent a month working on new songs. "I think we came from the same spiritual plane," DeShannon continued. "So it wasn't a very big reach."

The interest in the Morrison songs and other lost DeShannon recordings prompted the label in 2015 to release **Jackie DeShannon: All The Love, The Lost Recordings**. The four Morrison cuts were listed as bonus tracks. When DeShannon looks back on these songs she is unhappy. Much like Morrison, she despised an industry refusing to showcase her multiple talents.

Jackie DeShannon: "People try to put me in a box and they just couldn't." She told anyone who would listen she picked "And It Stoned Me" from the **Moondance** album and "I Wanna Roo You" from **Tupelo Honey** as a tribute to Morrison's talent. Her distinctive vocals on "Warm Love" suggest her easy working relationship with Morrison. "There is no containing Van," Jackie continued. "We rehearsed in his living room and guys were setting up elsewhere. He had a studio in the back, and we just left and went back.... I always loved his music because I felt there was so much freedom there. He's such a great writer. He stuff is so interesting. Who else but Van could think of some of these things?"

Morrison and DeShannon found it easy to write together. They composed "Santa Fe" which appeared on Van's 1978 album **Wavelength**. Of the four songs Van produced, DeShannon observed: "They are feel-good songs. The emotion is so raw and so close. You identify with it as if it were your own."

When Van performed at the Los Angeles Troubadour, DeShannon opened for him with the Caledonia Soul Orchestra backing her. At the time Morrison's manager, Ron Gibson, told the press a joint tour was planned. He also talked of duets album. Nothing materialized.

Jackie DeShannon: "I think it was all out of my hands." It was! Blame Atlantic and Warner. They were like kids fighting over the spoils. DeShannon and Morrison were disgusted. It was the music business. What could they do?

Jackie DeShannon - Jackie (LP with Van Morrison songs)

"Santa Fe's" lyrics suggest Van had taken the train to this trendy New Mexico town. He imbibed too much wine and he consumed too much food. He concludes the song is nothing special. It is a song of isolation. It is a requiem for lost love. He wrote it after Janet Planet's babysitter dreamed an earthquake prompted California to slide into the Pacific Ocean. This caused Van to relocate for a few weeks in Albuquerque. While there he wrote "Santa Fe." Living in New Mexico even for a few weeks was a disaster. Van and Janet quickly returned to Fairfax. "Santa Fe" is primarily a tune of rejection. As Morrison wrote "Santa Fe," he acknowledged his failing marriage.

The song demonstrates Van's ability to use inspirational images. The setting was American with the trains, the mountains, and the casual laidback attitudes surrounding New Mexico mesmerizing him. When "Santa Fe" appeared on the **Wavelength** album it was coupled with "Beautiful Obsession," to create a window into Morrison's extraordinary psyche. He hated the brief period of living in New Mexico. California was his home. As Chris Michie observed: "The Jackie DeShannon sessions brought Van sanity as his marriage crumbled. He had to work day and night to ease the tension." He was now in a production mode. The Jackie DeShannon sessions were extraordinary ones if not commercially successful.

Jackie Deshannon

Musicians have their code of ethics. They have their sense of what is commercial. They have their feel for what they should record. The problem is the record company, the producer, the pressures of the commercial marketplace and the corporate profit plan that influences what an artist records. Van Morrison and Jackie DeShannon are two examples of how the corporate structure restricted their artistic direction.

JACKIE DESHANNON: THE PERSONAL SIDE

The Jackie DeShannon interlude remains a mysterious side of Morrison's career. It was all about music, nothing else. As a singer-songwriter in 1971, DeShannon hit the charts with "I Don't Need You Anymore." Her career at twenty-seven appeared once again on the rise. She previously had a major hit with "What the World Needs Now Is Love" and "When You Walk In the Room." She also toured with the Beatles.

While silly rumors of a romance with Van surfaced, DeShannon and her future and still husband Randy Edelman were engaged in a lengthy courtship. She eventually married Edelman on June 3, 1976. His career as movie soundtrack writer eclipsed hers. The marriage is a strong one enduring to this day.

When Van invited DeShannon to sing background, he unwittingly influenced the gossipmongers. Van was quiet but pissed. The rumors accentuated his bitterness toward the media. Lush words could not erase Van's distaste for the press.

JACKIE DESHANNON: AN UNSUNG HERO IN VAN'S WORLD

The Jackie DeShannon interlude is an unexplainable part of Morrison's career. It is really rather simple. She was a folk-rock-lyrical performer blending her self-penned classics "When You Walk In The Room" and "Put A Little Love In Your Heart" into Top 40 hits. She was more of a songwriter than a performer. She also didn't care for the spotlight.

Another problem was her songs charted for other artists. The Searchers' "When You Walk In the Room" peaked at thirty-one in the U.K. and thirty-five in the U.S. There have been numerous other artists covering her material.

Jackie DeShannon: "I'd write all week, then on Friday I'd pop upstairs in Liberty's little studio above the publishing office and arrange and produce my demos." She brought Glenn Campbell, Leon Russell, Hal Blaine and James Burton in to help her cut demos that were released as chart friendly 45s.

Her 1969 album **Put A Little Love In Your Heart** caught Morrison's attention. When he worked with her it was as much about her songwriting, as it was her ability to cover his songs. She never achieved mainstream success. During the 1972 Jackie DeShannon sessions Van recorded "Spare Me A Little," which turned up in 1997 on The **Genuine Philosopher's Stone**. "Spare Me A Little" is a poignant Morrison song with lyrics reaching into his inner soul. When he sings: "Why not lie here. In my arms. And Just listen To the Night," Van is commenting on the torturous days as his marriage ended. It is a song of forgiveness. Van repeatedly sings "spare me a little." Janet didn't. He never forgave her.

How does one conclude the Jackie DeShannon interlude? It is much like his other partnerships. The meeting of the minds musically. Van produced DeShannon's cover of "And It Stoned Me." Jackie had another thing in common with Morrison. Her record companies ignored her best efforts. "They didn't know what to do with me, because I could do everything," DeShannon continued. "I came up at a time when marketing for an artist like myself was not even in its infancy, it didn't exist." This is why Morrison loved working with DeShannon. She was a soul partner ignored by Liberty, Atlantic and Capitol Records.

ON TOUR IN 1972: SORT OF

He kicked off the 1972 tour with a January 22 show at San Francisco's Boarding House. He played four shows in two nights January 14-15, 1972 with an eclectic set. College students were an integral part of Morrison's audience. Stanford University students were amongst Van's most loyal followers. The **Stanford Daily** on January 19, 1972 featured Chris Peck's article "Wild Night With Van Morrison." Peck wrote: "Many lovers and would-be lovers have left Van's live performances wishing they had stayed home next to the stereo because Morrison live sometimes isn't as good as Morrison on vinyl. For the lucky few who saw Van Morrison at the Boarding House Theater in San Francisco over the weekend however, there was a special musical treat." The reason for Van's stupendous show is the Boarding House had a three hundred-seat capacity. It was filled. The audience sat in rapt silence. Van rewarded them. He performed almost two hours of wonderful music.

Dave Allen, the rotund owner of San Francisco's Boarding House, loved booking Morrison. "The shows sold out in a few days. He was a prince. He came in quietly. He did his show and left. A little booze for the band, some of the guys smoked a joint on Bush Street and Van's shows were great. I heard he was difficult. Not for me," Allen concluded.

The Boarding House show featured guitarist Doug Messenger, bass guitarist Bill Church, former Paul Butterfield keyboardist Mark Naftalin, and saxophonists Jack Schroer and Boots Houston. Van performed some surprises including a cover of Big Mama Thornton's "Hound Dog." On the Friday show when he exited the stage the raucous applause brought him back for an encore featuring "Wild Night."

Phil Elwood, the Dean of San Francisco music critics, reviewed the Boarding House shows. In the Sunday January 15, 1972 **San Francisco Examiner**, Elwood observed: "Morrison's live renditions usually bear little resemblance to his exquisite and popular recordings. Last night, however, was an exception." That said it all. The doyen of San Francisco Bay Area critics placed his stamp of approval on the Belfast Cowboy. For more than a year Van practiced diligently with his band for live shows. The results were evident to Elwood.

The next weekend Van performed at San Francisco's the Village. This was a trendy gay nightclub with a large dance floor. The club had an intimate feel. It was just the sort of venue Morrison preferred. A February 18th concert at San Anselmo's Lion's Share was a warm up for later Los Angeles appearances.

The Lion's Share was a small club located on Red Hill Avenue in San Anselmo. There was a previous club in Sausalito. It opened in 1970. When Janis Joplin died her will stipulated that $2500 be set-aside for a farewell party for her friends at the Lion's Share. This covered the $1600 bar bill. The Grateful Dead provided the music. Van regularly hung out there.

Van took a few weeks off from live shows before appearing for two nights at Santa Monica's Civic Auditorium. The April 28, 1972 show saw Van remark: "Here's a new one." He performed "St. Dominic's Preview." The show ended with "Brown Eyed Girl." It was during this concert that Van looked around for a Los Angeles rental house. He wanted proximity to Warner Brothers' corporate offices. He needed to work on new material. It wasn't until later in 1977-1978 he lived temporarily in Brentwood. There were pluses and minuses in the Los Angeles area for Morrison.

Brentwood was next to the UCLA campus and Van was seen regularly in Campbell's Bookstore. He spent hours perusing the religious and philosophy books.

Van didn't like the trendy Beverly Hills or Malibu locations. He needed coffee shops to write. He liked to hang out in small sandwich cafés. He could observe people and titillate his mind. He looked for a few drinking spots to loosen his shy nature. He gravitated to the area around the University of California, Los Angeles. One section in particular, Brentwood, caught his eye. It was upscale but close to working class eateries and blue collar drinking establishments. He didn't rent a small house in the area until 1977. But he found a renewed creative drive in the Los Angeles area. It was a short drive to some of his favorite venues the Santa Monica Civic Auditorium, Doug Weston's Troubadour Club, the Whiskey A Go Go and Sneaky Pete's a seedy night club near the Whiskey.

As he experimented with live sets, a smooth in-concert perfection developed. He continued to feature original songs. The seeds of cover songs in concert and eventually in the recording studio took root in Los Angeles. The only cover record that Van practiced in Los Angeles, according to one band member, was Erroll Garner's "Misty." Why? Van's needed to explore his jazz roots. He finalized a tight concert set that made his live performances among the best of his career. Show business demanded perfection. Van was working on it.

SANTA MONICA CIVIC AUDITORIUM, SANTA MONICA, CA – APRIL 27 & 28, 1972.

Set List – April 27
Moondance • Come Running • Blue Money • Caravan • He Ain't Give You None • I'll Be There • Misty • Jackie Wilson Said • Tupelo Honey • Moonshine Whiskey • Domino • Wild Night • Brown Eyed Girl

Set List – April 28
Moondance • Come Running • Blue Money • Caravan • He Ain't Give You None • Old Old Woodstock • I've Been Working • I Will Be There • Misty • Tupelo Honey • Moonshine Whiskey • Domino • Wild Night • Brown Eyed Girl • St. Dominic's Preview

---

It was the play list for the Santa Monica Civic Auditorium shows of April 27 and 28, 1972 that provides interesting insights into what Van liked to play. The Warner executives attending the concerts were mesmerized. Van played his tunes in a mainstream, pop manner. The resulting letter of congratulations from Warner Brothers, Ray Ruff said, was an attempt to remind Van to keep aiming for the mainstream.

The Belfast Cowboy In Repose. May 22, 1970 Capitol Theatre Port Chester, Port Chester, NY (Photo by Joe Sia)

At Santa Monica he played the hits. The set list for each night was similar with "Old Old Woodstock" and "I've Been Working" added the second night. During the first show at the Santa Monica Civic Auditorium, Van closed with "Brown Eyed Girl." On the second night he bellowed "Brown Eyed Girl" to the band. Then the encore "St. Dominic's Preview" sent the audience home happy. One band member remarked: "Warner Brothers executives were in the house. He demanded they do more to publicize the new album. They ignored him." Van sang the title track and left the stage.

On May 5, 1972 Van appeared at Seattle's Paramount Theater. A Marin County folk group, Lamb, opened the show. During this performance Van realized Lamb guitarist Chris Michie played instrumental riffs that fit into his music. The other members of Lamb Tom Salisbury on keyboards, Dan Aarhus on guitar and congas, Tom LaVarda on bass and David Perper on drums provided lead singer and guitarist Barbara Mauritz with a solid gospel inflected folk-country sound. Van was impressed. He hired Michie on the spot.

This was typical of Van. When he heard musicians that would add to his sound, he approached them. There were more pressing problems. The Seattle show was an important one. It was the first time the Seattle promoter, Pat O'Day, doubled ticket prices. The promoter's rock and roll profit margin decreased due to the need to pay the bands a fair wage. The Paramount Theater tickets for Van's performance were raised from $2.50 to $5.00. Van recognized the change. He put together a set that stunned the audience. There were no complaints about the increase in ticket prices. The Paramount Theater was the perfect venue for an intimate show. The art deco look and the balcony with the perfect acoustics the Paramount Theater had built in, remains to this day a wonderful Seattle venue.

After the Seattle concert there were two other venues Van appeared in with Lamb. The Marin County folk-rock group rented a minibus to drive Morrison to the other concerts. Van's musicians followed in a rental truck. Chris Michie, Lamb's guitarist, rode in a large station wagon. He told me it was hippie touring. "We were young, we loved it," Michie said.

Lamb wanted to show Van the Oregon countryside. The next concert was at the Salem Oregon Armory. This town, located halfway between Portland and Eugene, is the state capital and a capacity crowd turned out. Pat O'Day, a Seattle radio station disc jockey at KJR, booked the gig. There was a great deal of pre-concert publicity. O'Day recalled Van loved the Salem show. It was because the large armory reminded him of the shows he performed with Irish showbands.

Then they loaded up on a cold Salem morning and drove north for six plus hours to Vancouver, British Columbia. That night Van appeared at the Queen Elizabeth Theater. In Vancouver there was no liquor on Sunday. There were few things to do. The town has a church atmosphere except for the raucous Yale Hotel presenting the blues. Van loved it. The Queen Elizabeth Theater opened in 1959. The ornate stage and the first rate sound system prompted Van to spend some time before the show admiring the building. The art deco lobby accentuated the high-end feel for the show.

Then Lamb drove home to San Francisco. Van boarded an airplane to Denver, Colorado. He and his band played two nights in Boulder before flying to Oklahoma City for a one-night gig. Two days later Morrison performed at Washington D. C.'s Constitution Hall. On May 18, he was at New York's Carnegie Hall. The following night he returned to greet some old friends at Boston's Aquarius Theater. This was followed by an appearance on May 20 in Providence Rhode Island. The next night he closed his touring at Philadelphia's Walnut Theater. He flew home exhausted. Touring and Van Morrison did not go hand in hand.

Van had a plan. He was toying with the idea of putting together a larger band. The genesis of the Caledonia Soul Orchestra took place during this time. Chris Michie said he talked about it after the Salem show.

Why was this mini-concert tour important? The musicians addressed the question of how and why Van's shows grew increasingly tighter. Reviewers noticed a change in his shows. They were tighter. Don Heckman, in the **New York Times**, called Morrison's Carnegie Hall show one of the best "jazz-rock-folk" concerts of the year. Even though Van eschewed rock music, he was on top of that genre.

AQUARIUS THEATRE, BOSTON, MA– MAY 19, 1972

One of Van's best concerts with "Astral Weeks," "He Ain't Give You None," and "Misty." "He Ain't Give You None" is played with a slow bluesy shuffle. A bootleg tape from the audience is interesting. The sound quality suffers, but the tape catches of Van's live performances at its peak. This took place just before he went out on the road with the Caledonia Soul Orchestra– John Platania and Jack Schroer adding their amazing talents to the mix.

Set List
I've • Been Working • Astral Weeks • Caravan • I Will Be There • Moondance • Misty • Tupelo Honey • Listen To The Lion • He Ain't Give You None • Wild Night • Domino • Cyprus Avenue

---

Boston's Aquarius Theater show was the best of Van's mini-tour. He was inspired to be back in Boston. He performed extended versions of "Astral Weeks," "He Ain't Give You None" and he covered Errol Garner's "Misty" with a smoky jazz vocal. John Platania and Jack Schroer were key backing musicians. He closed the Boston show with a rousing version of "Cyprus Avenue." Van's up-tempo version of "Moondance" brought the audience to its feet.

These concerts provided a training ground for the soon to emerge Caledonia Soul Orchestra. The CSO was important to Van's continued artistic development. Images of Ireland swirled in his head. He planned a 1972 American tour combining small club dates, with University appearances, and some in the round or small theater shows. Along the way there were a few larger venues like the Santa Monica Civic Auditorium or Seattle's Paramount Theater. The 1972 concert appearances brought Morrison into the commercial mainstream.

THE 1972 AMERICAN TOUR

January 14-15: The Boarding House, San Francisco (2 shows a night)
January 21-22: The Village, San Francisco (2 shows a night)
March 3: Berkeley Community Theater
March 25: Convention Hall, San Diego
April 14: Freeborn Hall, University of California, Davis
April 16: Stockton Civic Auditorium, Stockton
April 19: Travelodge Theater in the Round, Phoenix, Arizona
April 26: Granada Theater, Santa Barbara
May 4: Civic Auditorium, Santa Monica, California
May 5: Paramount Theater, Seattle, Washington
May 6: Armory, Salem, Oregon
May 7: Queen Elizabeth Theater, Vancouver B. C.
May 12-13: Boulder, Colorado
May 14: Oklahoma City, Oklahoma
May 16: Constitution Hall, Washington D. C.
May 18: Carnegie Hall, New York
May 19: Aquarius Theater, Boston
May 20: Providence, Rhode Island
May 21: Walnut Theater, Philadelphia, Pa.
May 22: The Field House, Villanova University
May 26-29: Winterland, San Francisco
August 1: King's Beach Bowling Alley, South Lake Tahoe, California
November 17: Bermuda Palms, San Rafael, California

Sources: Nathan Wirth's article, newspapers and posters and Howard A. DeWitt, Van Morrison: The Mystic's Music. Mark Naftalin and Chris Michie added material, and most importantly the magnificent Gunter Becker website: http://ivan.vanomatic.de

Thank you Gunter.

Because he loved to be near his Fairfax home, Van spent four nights in familiar territory. From May 26 to 29, 1972 he played Bill Graham's Winterland Arena. After each show Van walked over to Jack's Jazz Bar. One night he bounced up on stage for a number with the house band. Sometimes the musicians had no idea who the white cat was jumping up on the stage. Once they heard him, they murmured approval. Jackie Payne played Jack's at this time. He remembers how the audiences loved his impromptu numbers. Van was appreciated and not by his cult coterie of fans. Big Bones, the drummer in the Jackie Payne Band, recorded one of Morrison's appearances.

During these years a former pimp, Fillmore Slim, often came into the bar and he was one of many who saw Van perform. Big Bones laughs at this period in the Fillmore history. "There were more white people there than Negroes," Big Bones continued. "Fillmore Slim was an icon. No one knew who the little Irish guy singing on the stage was or why he was there."

Payne was the lead singer for the Johnny Otis Show for fifteen years. Then he relocated to San Francisco. Van loved his music. Payne was a fan of the Belfast Cowboy.

Morrison's career was taking off. The media, particularly **Rolling Stone**, turned out glowing reviews on the bursting creativity of his sound. For years, Jann Wenner, the founder of **Rolling Stone**, trumpeted Morrison's career.

ROLLING STONE ON VAN IN 1972

On June 22, 1972 America's premier rock magazine, **Rolling Stone**, profiled Morrison. As he appeared on the cover, there was no doubt he was moving into a more commercial direction. **Rolling Stone** assigned one of its first string reporters, John Grissim, Jr., to the story.

In preparation for the article, Grissim previewed Morrison's recent Winterland shows. This San Francisco venue was one of Morrison's favorites. It provided **Rolling Stone** with some graphic descriptions of the Belfast Cowboy's quirky personal nature on stage.

When Grissim wrote descriptively of Van finishing "Moondance," he recounted a story in which Morrison's stage mike malfunctioned. He walked in a huff off-stage. Immediately, a band member ran to get him. When piano wizard Mark Naftalin urged Van to return for some encores, he did and performed "Blue Money" and "Domino" to an enthusiastic and appreciative audience. He informed Bill Graham, after the final Winterland show, that he was taking some time off.

Morrison and Graham discussed a management deal. The Graham production schedule was hectic and it would be another five years before Wolfgang Productions, Graham's management arm, directed the Belfast Cowboy's career.

There was a strange relationship between Morrison and Graham. The Fillmore impresario booked him regularly. They didn't agree to a formal management contract. Both had big egos. Both wanted to run the show. Both had a view of the future. Unfortunately, none of their ideas meshed. It made for a tempestuous and temporary working relationship.

When they met at Graham's sumptuous Marin County home, Van had little to say. Graham did all the talking. For this reason, any permanent management agreement was in jeopardy. In some strange way, Van needed Graham. He was the King of American bookers.

Van Morrison and Bill Graham

It was just after this concert Van disbanded the group he labeled: "His Band and the Street Choir." The entire time this aggregation was together, Van was working up the musical direction of the Caledonia Soul Orchestra. It was early in his career. The notion of constantly changing musicians persisted. As he sat down with **Rolling Stone**, it was the usual cantankerous Morrison.

This interview revealed some interesting aspects of his career. After he disbanded the musicians who recorded **His Band and the Street Choir**, Van rethought his career. Throughout 1971 he continued to change his musical ideas. Van remarked: "People have told me that I have this cult following, but I don't think that's true at all." Van denied this notion. There was no doubt that it was true. He had a loyal and fanatical following.

Happy times with Bill Graham

As Van talked to Grissim, he complained he was going through a career epiphany. Van had had this epiphany in November 1971, when he was convinced a William Blake vision portended bad things. His reluctance to go on stage increased. He continued to be universally annoyed with the media, drunken fans, his labels and the pressures of hit records.

HANGING OUT IN BERKELEY IN 1972

In 1972, Van often hung out at Berkeley's Keystone Korner. He loved the positive vibes from the laid back University of California students who flooded the club nightly. The crowd would show up five minutes before Van went on stage. They always gave him a rousing reception. He loved it. Music critic Greil Marcus could walk from his house to see Van perform. It was a special place and time. John L. Wasserman and Phil Elwood were critics who wandered into the club with Joel Selvin waiting in the wings. Some nights John Lee Hooker walked in with his entourage. Sometimes the critics wrote a review, other times they enjoyed the show. For a time, Van appeared at ease with the critics. The San Francisco musical atmosphere was so mellow it made for great sounds. It was the unique ambiance of the local clubs that brought the locals to these relaxed venues.

Berkeley's Longbranch Saloon was another one of Van's favorites. It was here he discovered Ray Benson and his country group Asleep At The Wheel. When **Rolling Stone** interviewed Van, he talked at length about Asleep At The Wheel. They were signed to the United Artists label. Van was one of their staunchest supporters.

One local folk singer, Judy Mayhan, met Morrison there. She opened for him during a number of shows. She was a folkie who first opened for Van in 1970 in Los Angeles. This was typical of Van. He befriended and helped local musicians. Huey Lewis and the American

Revolution played these clubs opening for Morrison. There was a sense of musical camaraderie Morrison loved.

Judy Mayhan was a special performer. She trained as a classical musician until she caught the New York folk bug. After signing with Horizon Records in 1962, she released her first album **Rockin' The Cradle**. Later, the Tradition label under the title **Songs of Old Eire** reissued it. Mayhan's inclusion of "Rich Irish Lady" and "Lass of the Low Country" inspired Morrison to rethink his Irish roots. While Mayhan's albums for Atco/Atlantic in 1970 and one for Decca in 1971 didn't sell well, they established her as a first rate folk talent. She moved north of Morrison to the Mendocino Coast in the 1970s. She remains active in the music business. As a classically trained musician who turned to traditional folk music, she had Van's ear.

From time to time, Van would hang out at Berkeley's Freight and Salvage Coffee House. This venue began in 1968 as a folk music enclave, but it quickly developed into a rock and roll, blues and country venue with Asleep at the Wheel, Country Joe and the Fish, Alice Stuart, Barbara Dane, Lightnin' Hopkins and Bruce Duncan "Utah" Phillips among others playing nightly. The key to this club was an eclectic booking policy. One night Van sat in the audience watching Lightnin' Hopkins' deliver a dynamite hour set. Chris Strachwitz, the founder of Arhoolie Records, sat nearby tapping his foot.

The Freight and Salvage, located in an old Berkeley furniture store at 1827 San Pablo Avenue, was an 87 seat coffee house. It was the club, as well as the ambiance, which made the place special for Morrison. When he was through listening, Van often wandered down to Ruthie's Inn to hear some soul music. One night as Van wandered into Ruthie's Inn, he caught Bobby Blue Bland belting out a soulful set. The music scene was so strong in the San Francisco Bay Area, Morrison didn't go out on the road extensively for much of the mid-1970s.

He learned a great deal not only about music but also the industry from watching the locals wander into new directions. He was an eclectic musician. This tendency took a dramatic turn for the better as a result of his experiences. His songwriting was influenced by the various clubs and tourist sites in and around San Francisco. **St.**

Dominic's Preview bore the unmistakable stamp of Van's new home town.

BIBLIOGRAPHICAL SOURCES

Interviews with Simon Gee, Art Siegel, Sal Valentino, Ray Ruff, Ron Thompson, John Goddard, Jesse Hector, Roger Armstrong, Tony Dey, Mitch Woods, Pat Thomas, Ron Sexton and Bill Graham were important to this chapter. For the genesis of the Caledonia Soul Orchestra see Nathan Wirth, "The Road Goes On Forever: Van Morrison On Stage, 1967-1984," **Wavelength**, volume 16, June 1998, pp. 14-18. For Van's comments on the critics and what they have said about **St. Dominic's Preview** see, for example, Ritchie Yorke, "Stage Life Interview," **Stage Life**, June-July, 1977, see the transcribed manuscript by David Chance on the Van Morrison Website, http://web.archive.org/web/20130730035343/http://geocities.com/tracybjazz/hayward/van-the-man.info/reviews/1977stagelife.html

On the Jackie DeShannon sessions, see Howard A. DeWitt, **Van Morrison: The Mystic's Music** (Fremont, 1983), p. 69. A series of interviews with Mark Naftalin helped to ferret out material about the state of American rock and roll and its impact upon Marin County where Van lived in the 1970s.

The **Seattle Post Intelligencer**, Datebook, May 5, 1972 describes the Paramount Show. An interview with long time Seattle musician George Palmerton helped to pull some of the material together for this show.

See John Grissim, Jr., "The Rolling Stone Interview," **Rolling Stone**, June 22, 1972 for an interview this is lengthy and informative. This interview is excellently transcribed by super Van Morrison fan David Chance who placed it on the archived Van Morrison website http://www.oocities.org/tracybjazz/hayward/van-the-man.info/reviews/1972rs.html

Interviews with Mark Naftalin helped to clarify some of the 1972 shows. John Goddard of Village Music also provided some important material on the 1972 tour. Chris Michie provided his comments on the state of Morrison's music during this time period. Mervyn Solomon helped in analyzing aspects of Morrison's personality changes during the early 1970s.

Ronnie Montrose provided important comments on the **St. Dominic Preview** album. Alice Stuart and Barbara Dane added material to this chapter. Pat O'Day of Seattle's KJR provided his reminiscences on Morrison's Washington and Oregon appearances.

Jackie Payne provided some comment on Morrison at Jack's Bar. This was a bar on Fillmore Street that Morrison often came into for the blues. He also jumped up on stage a few times and there are tapes of Van at Jack's Bar that have yet to surface.

The San Francisco music scene was described by a number of people including Opal Louis Nations, Bonnie Raitt, Juice Garcia, Charles Brown, Gino Landry, Pee Wee Thomas, Lee Hildebrand, Guitar Mac and Jimmy McCracklin.

On Jackie DeShannon see Peter Lerner, "The Story of Jackie DeShannon, Part 3." http://jackiedeshannon.tripod.com/jdsas7b.html Chris Michie was helpful with the Jackie DeShannon material.

Key biographical material for this period is located in Luke Crampton and Dafydd Rees, **Encyclopedia of the Blues** (University of Arkansas, 1997) and Patricia Romanowski, **The New Rolling Stone Encyclopedia of Rock and Roll** (New York, 1995).

See the **San Francisco Chronicle**, April 4, 1973 for a review of Van's Lion's Share show.

See the brilliant article by Ulrich Buehring, "Jackie DeShannon," **Wavelength**, no. 3, March 1995, pp.8-9 for her collaboration with Morrison. See Peter Lerner, "The Story of Jackie DeShannon, Part 3," http://jackiedeshannon.tripod.com/jdsas7b.html for her interaction with Morrison. Jackie DeShannon had said little, if anything, about working with Morrison. There is no doubt they were magic on stage and in the studio. But materials on the collaboration are slim and unreliable.

See Erik Hage, **The Words And Music of Van Morrison** (New York, 2009), chapter 4 for a brilliant interpretation of this period. Also see, Lauren Onkey, "Ray Charles On Hyndford Street," in Diane Negra, editor, **The Irish In Us" Performativity And Popular Culture** (Durham, 2006); Richard Williams, "Van Morrison Gonna Rock Your Gipsy Soul," **Melody Maker**, July 28, 1973 and Ritchie Yorke, "Van Morrison: A Van For All Seasons," **New Musical Express**, February 23, 1974.

See Don Heckman, "Morrison Concert of Jazz-Rock-Folk Among Year's Best," **New York Times**, May 20, 1972 for the Carnegie Hall show.

For a lengthy and interesting review of the Boarding House shows see Chris Peck, "Wild Night With Van Morrison," **The Stanford Daily**, January 19, 1972. https://stanforddailyarchive.com/cgi-bin/stanford?a=d&d=stanford19720119-01.2.21# The Peck review is an interesting one. Van's shows were generally superb, but there are times when he stormed off stage, he was moody or he simply wasn't up to performing. While Peck alluded to these shows, he failed to describe them in detail.

Also see Phil Elwood, "Hard Working Gospel-Blues of Gideon," **San Francisco Examiner**, January 15, 1972, p. 7 for a review of Morrison's Boarding House show. Dave Allen, the Boarding House founder and owner, described Morrison during 1980 and 1981 interviews.

CHAPTER 21

VAN MORRISON: THE MAKING OF A LEGEND, 1968-1972

"These similitudes are charming and entertaining, and who does not enjoy playing with analogies?"

Goethe

"Three of Morrison's songs appear in the Rock And Roll Hall of Fame Top 500 Songs That Shaped Rock And Roll. They include 'Brown Eyed Girl,' 'Madame George' and 'Moondance'."

Rolling Stone

How does one analyze the transition in Van Morrison's music from the late 1960s into the early 1970s? The answer is he became an accomplished solo artist. His ability to write and translate his music into live dramatic performances. He remained shy. As a performer he continued to grow and mature in this half decade from **Astral Weeks** through **St. Dominic's Preview**.

The theme in this period is Van experienced conflict while ultimately finding resolution. He worked out his business difficulties. He continued to add depth and character to his music. By 1972 his band, his stage presence matured and he became a top flight concert act. It was playing small clubs in and around the San Francisco Bay Area that created a level of in concert professionalism that continues to define Morrison.

WHAT WAS MUSIC TO VAN MORRISON?

Van Morrison believes music is the essence of existence. This was the mantra he developed in his Belfast youth. He has lived by it his entire life. The bursts of creativity that brought him into the music business were honed into a fine edge. By 1972 he was at the top of his commercial game.

His early **Billboard** Top 100 chart hits provided vindication. He had fiscal stability. He wondered if this would negatively impact his art. It didn't. He still worried. He went about the music business by his own rules. He desired and sought out hits. He worried about becoming a predictable artist. The fear of losing his original voice haunts Morrison.

The Warner Brother contract was not an equitable one. The slights from the industry, real and imagined, the feeling many didn't believe in his talent and the continual search for new musical directions intensified Van's contrarian nature. He is a perfectionist. He could develop a new musical style only to abandon it. Changing musical themes turned his vision into a prescient literary rock and roll. The snubs from his early life drove Van to new intellectual directions with critical insights.

MORRISON'S YOUTH: STEPS TO STARDOM

During Morrison's Belfast youth his talent was nurtured by many forces. He had diverse musical interests from listening to his dad's record collection. He interpreted any type of music. Blues, jazz and rhythm and blues records were Morrison's primary influences.

"I think Van was too quirky and too dependent upon American music to interest many of the British labels," Phil Solomon continued. "Van Morrison was difficult to pigeon hole." Others, like producer Mickie Most, took a dim view of the early Van Morrison. Most observed: "Van was volatile and for this reason he had to go to Bert Berns and the Bang label." This was of course hindsight from Solomon and Most. The truth is Van was suited to the British market. His Irish experiences put him in the middle of it. He was grounded in so many types of music, it was impossible to categorize Van. This confused the labels. The producers and the A & R people didn't know what to do with him. He found stardom in America.

After playing with Irish show bands and for three years with Them, he was a walking jukebox. Morrison said if he didn't feel it, he couldn't play it. He had the soul of the African American artist. Others described him as having a jazz soul. John Lee Hooker remarked: "Van, he had all different music in him." Hooker thought he was complicated musically. "This made Van a special player," Hooker concluded. Like the classic bluesmen, he never plays a song the same way. He has a different interpretation of each tune. He learned from classic blues performers like Little Walter whom he befriended in the early Them days. When Van sat in a London hotel near Russell Square talking with Little Walter, he learned a great deal about the blues. As Little Walter performed in the U.K., Van paid special attention to his music, his act and his persona.

This was only a small part of Morrison's musical mystique. Van's infatuation with musical instruments created the backdrop to his early success. He learned to play the saxophone, the guitar, the piano and the harmonica with proficiency. He entered a fantasyland of music as he listened to the timeless classics of the blues, jazz, rhythm and blues and soul. Morrison was a walking encyclopedia of musical influences. He felt he was different from other kids. He was! His devotion to the music of King Pleasure suggests one esoteric influence.

There is one King Pleasure vocal Van spent hundreds of hours listening to in his formative years. "'Jumpin' With Symphony Sid" was not only a King Pleasure, it was one of Morrison's favorites. Who was King Pleasure?

KING PLEASURE AND VAN: WHAT IS THE INFLUENCE?

King Pleasure is not well known. He was a singer born in Oakdale, Tennessee. His name was Clarence Beeks. He moved to New York in the mid-1940s working as a bar tender while playing New York's be-bop jazz clubs. He was a singer of unusual talent who covered Eddie Jefferson's "I'm In The Mood For Love." James Moody created an improvised solo known as vocalese. This was a jazz singing style that includes words added to a soloist. This was a style jazz singer Jon

Hendricks employed after hearing the song. Hendricks said his commercial success was due to "Moody's Mood For Love." The song failed to chart until 1954 when King Pleasure's "Moody's Mood For Love" was a popular seller with accompanying vocals from Blossom Dearie.

The irony is Clarence Beeks didn't use his given name on records. Symphony Sid was actually Sid Torrin who hosted a live jazz radio broadcast out of New York's Birdland in the 1940s and 1950s. Beeks took that name. Symphony Sid's goal was to popularize jazz. The radio theme song "Jumpin' With Symphony Sid" is another Morrison favorite. Beeks added the vocals. He didn't receive full writers' credit and royalties. Van early on identified with this injustice. As he turned thirty King Pleasure cut his first album for the Prestige label. He teamed with jazz pianist-vocalist Blossom Dearie. Then he worked with Betty Carter on a version of "Red Top." He became a cult jazz artist.

How did this obscure jazz artist influence Van Morrison? On **Astral Weeks** Morrison has said he drew inspiration from King Pleasure. After listening to King Pleasure, Van discovered in his dad's record collection one song stood out. It was "Moody's Mood For Love." He was mesmerized by the saxophonist James Moody. There was also a 1949 instrumental Eddie Jefferson recorded of Jimmy McHugh's 1935 song "I'm In The Mood For Love" with new lyrics. King Pleasure made it into a cult masterpiece.

THE FIRST STEPS TOWARD THE LEGEND

From 1968 to 1972, Van solidified his legend. This half-decade musical journey was highlighted by his most commercial work. Van wasn't a star in the making when he recorded **Astral Week**. Warner considered him an important songwriter. Not a recording-performing artist. The Warner Brothers brass believed Joni Mitchell and James Taylor were more commercial.

Ray Ruff: "When I talked with Mo Ostin, he told me Van was a songwriter. No more. No less."

As Joe Smith signed Van and shepherded him through the hard times and the good times, he was never thanked for his efforts. Why not? Van saw it as Smith's job. As Van told a friend: "It's a business, they get money not thanks." After listening to Van's early tapes, Smith became a champion of the Belfast Cowboy. He vigorously defended his musical direction. Smith envisioned a literary form of rock and roll.

As Morrison and Smith talked from 1968 to 1972, they agreed communication was the key to Van's music. When he asked Smith where his music fit, the Warner executive smiled and replied: "Van doesn't fit." To Smith that was the beauty of Morrison. His creative energies went where no one had gone previously.

VAN AND LITERARY REALISM

Van created a sense of literary realism. The illusions to William Blake, James Joyce. W. B. Yeats and John Donne surprised the critics. The elusiveness of his thoughts made Morrison's songwriting brilliant. His cryptic and ever changing body of work created a new direction for rock music. Van's genius was not lost on Bruce Springsteen, Bob Seger or John Cougar Mellencamp. They took the Morrison formula to the bank. Van still appears to be pissed.

While writing songs in America, whether in New York, Cambridge, Boston, Woodstock, San Francisco or Los Angeles, his work incorporated the symbols of what was and what wasn't right or wrong with his life. The five-year period from **Astral Weeks** through **St. Dominic's Preview** suggests a continued songwriting maturity. Van understood the subtle nuances of lyrics, the interplay of music and the manner in which the audience needed to interpret his music. Morrison's frame of reference was one that immersed itself in a lifelong passion to point out what was and what wasn't important in his life. Van was his own biographer.

ENTER JANET PLANET: A MUSE TO LYRICAL SYMBOLISM

Enter Janet Planet. Initially, she was more than just a wife. Janet was a source of inspiration and a ballast to Van's erratic personality. She became inspiration and nemesis. She was a marvelous and devoted marriage partner. She couldn't cope with the demands of Van's career. His erratic moods, periodic rages and diffident personality ended the marriage. Van had trouble coping with the pressures of the music business. His marriage was the casualty.

From 1968 through 1972 Van was embarking on establishing a distinguished musical career. It is one defining his concept of lyrical beauty. This poetic direction came from many sources. It was a fusion of religious symbolism and the problems of everyday life that created the lyrical beauty transcending Van's music. Much like a novelist, he sets down a story line that reaches an ultimate conclusion. He reports on daily and habitual occurrences in his life in song form. Those who like his songs view them as sermons, epistles or novels. They tell a story that is near and dear to one's heart.

When Van stood outside his Fairfax, California home, he saw a plain old house. He saw a horse named Domino. He saw a Mercedes Benz. He saw a defined life. He liked it that way. In the night he watched the blue sky and luminous stars settle over Marin County. Life was idyllic.

By 1972 life couldn't get much better for Van. He was happy. He was making money. He was content. He had a seasoned professional backing band. He decided to slow down the money making machine. He felt like he was created and led by Warner Brothers. Van was always his own man. In the good old days, he would gear up for another tour. That was no longer the case. He was now financially independent. He was in excellent health. He was able to play small clubs. Van chose lifestyle over money. He temporarily cut back his big venue appearances with large fiscal guarantees.

THE NEW VAN IN THE STUDIO

In the studio, he remained as obsessed as ever with the recording process. He continued to turn out more demos than Warner Brothers was interested in releasing. It was time to sit back and enjoy his hard earned financial independence. The natural progress of his talent brought out some of his best music. As Van looked out over the Marin County nights, he realized the trees looked different, the air smelled of fresh pungent odors and he saw inspiration. Later, he told a Marin friend, the countryside inspired him to write a series of new songs. Not surprisingly, these tunes turned up in the 1973 **Hard Nose The Highway** album.

It was moments like this in the California night Van thought of Belfast, of Ireland and of his Celtic roots. These forces surfaced during the next half-decade as his touring was sharply curtailed. His song crafting continued unabated. From 1973 to 1977 he wasn't semi-retired, he was writing, performing when and where he desired. It was not a vacation. He was continuing to work on his musical direction.

He was moving into another career path. This was one where finely crafted song lyrics met an imaginative musical score. The result was personal songs. Van was an oblique songmeister who sometimes let you in on the subject. At other times he confused the listener with his non-grammatical lyrical prose. Van knew what life was about. He also knew how to mix his metaphors. As an observer, Van has few equals. To close friends, he remarked the best songs are "the ones that fail." For when they are rediscovered, their importance and commercial appeal is amazing. To Van, lyrics were his property. This explains his tirades against Warner management. He had a contract that was label friendly. While it wasn't fraud, Warner took advantage of an inexperienced musician. The attitude in the industry is this is how it is done. Warner told Van to make his money in concert. This further exacerbated him.

As 1972 concluded, Morrison looked back upon his career with a sense of accomplishment. He had completed a series of studio albums placing him into a special category. He had hits. His music played steadily on FM radio. He was increasingly popular in the rapidly expanding adult music market. He continued to be in search of new sounds.

VAN ON HIS ACCOMPLISHMENTS, 1968 TO 1972

As Van looked back upon his first half decade with Warner Brothers, he had good reason to feel proud. He had turned out albums that rank among the best of his career. Although he was only twenty-three when **Astral Weeks** was released, the music created a slowly evolving legacy. As the group of jazz musicians played at night in the New York studio on **Astral Weeks** they turned out a classic album which mixed Celtic, folk, jazz, rhythm and blues and pop sounds with stunning lyrics. Joe Smith was one of the executives at Warner Brothers who appreciated Morrison.

While V. P. of Warner's East Coast's Operation, Smith championed Van's music from the time he saw him perform in Boston. The fact that very few people bought the album didn't faze him. He informed Warner executives that Morrison's material would jump off the shelves.

In February 1970 Smith looked like a prophet. The **Moondance** LP created a broad based audience that remains to this day. **Moondance** was recorded with rock musicians. It helped Van to hit the charts. The jazz artists who were on **Astral Weeks** were relegated to the background.

To ensure his continued success in January 1971, Van spent an inordinate amount of time creating the **His Band and the Street Choir** album. This was an obvious attempt to write a series of hit records. It worked. When "Domino" reached number 9 on the Billboard, it signaled a new phase in Morrison's career.

There were brilliant, but undiscovered, musicians who broke out after working with Morrison. In the **His Band and the Street Choir** LP, Martha Velez sang backup vocals. She later went on to work with Bob Marley and make an acclaimed, if poorly selling, solo album.

As 1973 dawned, Van Morrison was ready for change. He had displayed his hit record potential. He was quietly working on another career change. The making of the Morrison legend continued and during the next five years, he released only two albums.

As 1972 ended, Van was conflicted about his future. He had his hit records. He was making decent money. He successfully toured. He decided to launch the most ambitious tour of his career. As he put together the **It's Too Late to Stop Now** LP and the subsequent tour, Morrison reached a new level of professional achievement.

THE MUSICAL POET IN EXILE

There are many ways to look at Van Morrison's early career. During the late 1960s and the early 1970s, he was the musical poet in exile. That is his Irish roots initially were not evident in the U.S. market. Rock and roll musicians behave like conquistadores. They roam and perform in their bastion. That is the arenas and clubs that are home to their music. Much of Van's best music was written in Belfast. He also wrote, while on tour with Them, and in quiet moments of reflection. He wrote a great deal of the **Moondance** album in New York, Cambridge and Woodstock. Would Morrison have been the same songwriter without these American cities? Probably not!

Jonathan Cott in a 1978 **Rolling Stone** article "Van Morrison: The Poet" highlighted what he termed the contribution of one of the "few originals in rock...." Cott concluded Morrison is a performer who "seems almost possessed." Cott concluded Morrison channels the poet William Blake. He does so with a personal touch. In a subsequent interview with Van in a Sausalito California restaurant, Cott continued his questions about a singer he viewed as "a scholar and a poet." The result is a conversation demonstrating Van Morrison by 1978 was a musical poet in exile.

Where did the musical poet of exile begin? The answer is Belfast. To a young man born in Belfast, the rhythms and intonations of the American experience energized him. He saw symbols. He saw themes. He saw truth. He saw hypocrisy. He saw industry malfeasance. He had a vision of his future. His American exile was the glue bringing his art together.

The language of the blues titillated Van. It created words turned into rock and roll poetry. The **Astral Weeks** album reflected the ambiguity of American and British life. Van's themes were ones that amused, that mocked, and that were mildly filled with strange images. They were themes universal for the times. In other words they were commercial songs in the making.

A powerful maker of phrases, Morrison often uses obtuse language to craft his experiences. Much of what he has written is autobiographical. With the help of the American landscape, he created an enduring set of songs.

He realized to change his lyrics he had to alter his life. Van arrived in America to add depth and deep themes to his songwriting. His most fluid work, **Astral Weeks**, was a blessing and a curse. It became the bar by which his music was judged. He wouldn't be stuck in a chamber rock mode with its ubiquitous lyrics and a moribund direction. There was only one **Astral Weeks**. He didn't need to repeat it.

The songwriter in exile is the best way to interpret the first half dozen years Morrison spent in America. It is a songwriting career beginning in sorrow and ending in commercial success. The lack of money and hostile feelings toward his old band, Them, drove Van into the Top 40. He proved he belonged in the pantheon of hit record artists. Then he left as soon as he was accepted. This was a personality trait that continues to define Morrison's future work.

THE RECORD LABELS: THEY GET A GRADE OF "F"

The place of the American record labels, Bang and Warner Brothers, occupy a prominent place in Morrison's first half decade as a solo artist. The clashing egos in the board rooms, the inflated opinions of producers, the nefarious activities of business departments and the inability of the public relations arm of the record companies to understand Morrison accentuated his difficult personality.

There was more intrigue within the record labels than Morrison could stand. It was the role of the obscure executive who knew little, if anything, about rock music that infuriated him. The corporate nature of the music business was like a jungle that Van did learn in time to navigate.

As he became sophisticated in business matters, Van remarked to Belfast journalist, Donal Corvin, the record labels received an "F" in personal dealings. He wanted his voice heard and his opinions respected. The record labels were more interested in the profit margin. Art was seldom, if ever, a consideration.

Van failed with Warner Brothers because he tried to be overtly literary. Mo Ostin confessed that he couldn't understand Van when he talked. Van had trouble dealing with him. Soon Van's strongest supporter at Warner Brothers, Joe Smith, and his early producers, no longer talked to him. Many observers believed that it was Morrison's fault. The truth lies somewhere in the middle as Van seethed over a scrupulously unfair contract. Both sides were at fault.

Van Morrison and Jim Morrison share the stage of the Whisky-A-Go-Go in 1966 (Photo by Don Jung)

FROM THE SLIPSTREAM TO THE MAINSTREAM

From 1968 to 1972 Morrison went from the slipstream into the mainstream. Along the way there were enormous changes in his music, his personality and his life.

Astral Weeks changed Morrison's life. He no longer had anonymity. He increasingly became a wealthy man, despite his protestations of poverty.

The argument that Van was a literary songwriter took shape and only Johnny Rogan poured cold water on this idea. The critics uniformly loved "Cyprus Avenue." They pointed to it as the product of the new Van Morrison. Van was his usual moody self with brief moments of sociability. The problem was he was writing furtively and working toward entering the music business mainstream. The slipstream was a thing of the past.

BIBLIOGRAPHICAL SOURCES

See Brian Hinton, **Celtic Crossroads: The Art of Van Morrison** (London, 1997), chapters 4-5 for personal insights into the Belfast Cowboy. Also see, Tony Clayton-Lea and Richie Taylor, **Irish Rock** (London, 1992) for important background material.

John Collis, **Van Morrison: Inarticulate Speech of the Heart** (Boston, 1996) contains some interesting insights into Morrison's personality.

Ben Cruikshank, **Into The Sunset: The Music of Van Morrison** (London, 1996) is an important source for analyzing the music.

Charlie Gillett, **The Sound of the City** (New York, 1970, revised edition, London, 1983) puts the industry into perspective. Also see the excellent academic tome David Hatch, **From Blues To Rock** (Manchester, 1987) for a hybrid description of where Van fits into the music marketplace.

See Howard A. DeWitt, **Van Morrison: The Mystic's Music** (Fremont, 1983), passim. Peter Mills, **Hymns to the Silence: Inside the Words and Music of Van Morrison** (New York, 2010), chapter 4 addresses the themes in Morrison's music.

The themes to Morrison's early 1970s music are varied ones, but he occupied a highly commercial place in the Warner Bros. pantheon of artists. For one journalist there was a tribute to "Vanlose Stairway." Laura Barton writing in the **London Guardian** was inspired by the song that told the story in the early 1980s of Van spending time in Copenhagen with his then girlfriend Ulla Munch. What is intriguing is that many people have sought out this small apartment building. This shows the power of Van's lyrics. See Laura Barton, "And Your Stairway Reaches Up To The Moon," **London Guardian**, April 1. 2011. The London press spends much of its time delving into Morrison's private life and the result over the years has been an often-contentious relationship. That said in the last decade the U.K. press has been more circumspect than in the previous four decades.

For later reflection on his life and the media see John Preston, "Van Morrison Takes Swipe At 'Absurd' Media Portrayal of Him," The **Belfast Telegraph**, August 26, 2017. https://www.belfasttelegraph.co.uk/entertainment/news/van-morrison-takes-swipe-at-absurd-media-portrayal-of-him-36069873.html This interview was part of the publicity for the 2017 release of **Roll With The Punches**.

Van Morrison & The Band – Caravan Live (1976 – The Last Waltz)

CHAPTER 22

VAN MORRISON ON BIOGRAPHY

"A great thinker is 'capable of being in uncertainties, mysteries, doubts, without any irritable reaching after fact and reason'."

JOHN KEATS

"The reason I don't like interviews is that I seem to react violently to personal questions. If the questions are about the work, I try to answer them. When they are about me, I may answer or I may not, but even if I do, if the same question is asked tomorrow, the answer may be different."

WILLIAM FAULKNER

"Some years ago, Van Morrison wandered into a press launch as the party was breaking up. The receptionist took one look at the stout, truculent figure in battered tweed jacket and flat cap, and called out. 'Anyone order a minicab?' Never a rock Adonis, Morrison would be the last Sixties survivor who could be accused of sliding through life on his good looks. Or on his sweet, warm personality."

CHARLES SHAAR MURRAY

Van Morrison has a phobia for privacy. He is adamantly opposed to any and all biographies. He reads everything written about him and his career. He finds all of it inaccurate. After Steve Turner's **Van Morrison: It's Too Late to Stop Now** came out Van was at a party with John Lee Hooker at his Redwood City, California home where he found the book. He sat down and began underlining Turner's mistakes. A person at the party told me Van screamed: "This is wrong." He turned a page. "Here is another mistake." Then he went home and wrote a lengthy letter to the publisher. He also included a list of every mistake, erroneous conclusion and spurious fact. The irony is Van cooperated with Steve Turner. Even his in-depth interviews didn't dispel Morrison's rage. A decade later, Van attended a party where Turner's book was on the coffee table. He grabbed it. He took out a pen. He began marking up the book. Van shouted: "Wrong, wrong, wrong." The owner of that book still has it. Whether or not it is a pleasant memory no one knows. It is an insight into Morrison's mind set. Biographer beware! The owner of the Turner book is considering selling it on e-bay. What about an official biography?

Morrison won't commission an authorized biography. More than two decades ago his representative shopped a proposal for an autobiography. A number of publishers were interested. Talks ensued. Jon Walsh writing in the November 20, 1997 **London Independent** reported Morrison produced an autobiography "self-penned ... provisionally entitled In My Own Words." Morrison's literary agent, Sheil Land, asked for half a million pounds for the publishing rights. This was a reasonable sum. There were no offers from anyone at the Frankfurt Book Festival. Why? That is the question. It remains unanswered.

The **Irish Times** reported: "Van Morrison is writing a book about his childhood and influences, and is looking for a publisher at the Frankfurt Book Fair. Van Morrison, In My Own Words, ends his usual reticence about his private life, and has received international interest at the fair." Rumor has it, Van withdrew the book proposal. But an outline surfaced.

Speculation among those close to Morrison was the director of the Frankfurt Book Fair publicized Van's name in brochures, press interview and TV commercials. It was to hype the fair. He was not happy about it. He hoped for a quiet, private deal. He didn't get it. He returned home.

What did Van's proposed autobiography offer? The book's outline contained forty-four chapters. Those who have looked at the outline, and the few who claim to have seen a portion of the manuscript, conclude it was impersonal. It lacked a defined biographical direction. The key turning points in Morrison's career were not discussed. He left out his marriages. His rich personal life was ignored. Much of his fight against the music business was missing. What did the book conclude? No one knows. One critic told me it was beautifully conceived but it lacked "the inner Van Morrison."

THE TWO-PAGE EXTRACT

The selling point for Morrison's autobiography was a titillating, well-publicized two page extract Van coyly labeled "influences." This document tells one how Van learned to play the guitar, and how and why he wrote the lyrics. Interested publishers asked for information on dating the former Miss Ireland Michelle Rocca. Van demurred. Then one publishing executive complained his private life, his business life and his musical life weren't discussed in the proposed autobiography. This executive asked: "What the hell is he talking about?" The consensus was little to do with his life in book form. The proposed autobiography failed to sell to a publisher. Perhaps Van withdrew it. That remains unclear. What is obvious is Morrison is working on his life story. Stay tuned.

After the autobiography project cooled, Van's lyrics were published by the San Francisco based City Light imprint. The notion of Lawrence Ferlinghetti's press publishing his lyrics appealed to Morrison. The literary recognition excited him. The autobiography was quickly forgotten.

IF THERE IS A CRAW IN VAN'S PSYCHE IT IS CLINTON HEYLIN

In 2002 Clinton Heylin's monumental biography came out to glowing reviews from establishment newspapers and magazines. There was carping criticism from a portion of the rock and roll press. The London daily newspapers unloaded on Heylin. They called the book a hit job. It was! The accused him of character assassination. It wasn't! Van's prickly nature and desire to control the story was woven throughout Heylin's high level prose. Heylin fired back when Van criticized him. His depth of research and conclusions made for a verbal war between Heylin and Morrison. That war produced what can only be described as "Van Morrison on Biography."

Morrison believes his private life is off limits. He points out biographers don't understand his music. The press is another story. He believes they have engaged in career assassination for decades. In 2002 the press was kind to Morrison and uniformly critical of Heylin's book.

Kevin Mitchell, writing in the **London Observer**, complained Heylin made Morrison seem ordinary. "It is not a biography; it is a quibble ... humorless snarl of a book," Mitchell concluded. Charles Shaar Murray, writing in the **London Independent**, pointed out Van threw an ashtray at Mo Ostin, the Warner president, at a dinner in his home. Murray writes: "... Or tour with the distinguished Irish folk group the Chieftains and tell them, moments before taking the stage, that they'd be nothing without him." Van may have hit the roof. The proof for this statement is vague and anecdotal.

Those who write about Van complain he wants to direct the story. He does. Murray describes Heylin as a brilliant researcher with "clunky prose." London journalists, they are the story not the rock and roll singer. When I find mention of Lou Reed in a review of Van's life, I realize Charles Shaar Murray has other things on his mind. Van Morrison is not on his mind.

What is it that prompts the raging in Van's soul when he hears the words "Clinton Heylin?" Van's rage comes from numerous stories in Heylin's biography he labels "fiction." One might say factual fiction. When Van called Sacramento drummer Tony Dey to appear in his house for a 3:00 am recording session then slams the door in his face, he gets the story right but it wasn't Dey who spun that story. It was an anonymous source. It turns out it was bullshit. The method of using anonymous sources is a staple of modern journalism. To Morrison it is creative fiction.

Another story Morrison disputes is he threw an ashtray at Warner Brothers president Mo Ostin while having dinner in his home. Ray Ruff pointed out the disagreements between Ostin and Morrison are well known in the industry. No one had heard of the ashtray incident until the Heylin book. The truth? Who knows!

Is Heylin's book is a hit piece? Kevin Mitchell, writing in the **London Observer**, thinks so. He doesn't mince his words about it. Mitchell praises Heylin's research and writing. In the Murray and Mitchell reviews there is a common theme. That theme is Morrison is a massive contradiction. Perhaps the best way to solve this dilemma is to go to the source. What does Van Morrison think? He has never told us.

There is no sugar coating Morrison's venom. A close friend told me he was still raging about Heylin's book. This was two years after it sold well enough to make it the premier Van biography. Then in 2019 this person mentioned Heylin and Van's lawsuit. His lawsuit against Heylin went nowhere. He soon had a new target Johnny Rogan. The person telling me this story was kicked out of Morrison's inner circle.

A Van fan in Utrecht in 1991 remarked: "Van looked at me and wanted me kicked out of the venue. He is truly a world class asshole." That is not the common perception. What it suggests is Van should write his autobiography. In some ways he has in the last decade during key interviews.

SITTING DOWN WITH TIME MAGAZINE, 2009

As Van basked in the glow of **Astral Weeks Live**, he sat down to answer ten questions for **Time**. Morrison now appeared in major newspapers and magazines. The acrid rock and roll press was a thing of the past. Van confessed he didn't own full rights to the original **Astral Weeks** album when he decided to perform it live. "We don't know where the record business is going," Van responded to a question about future productions. It was all about royalties, control and interpreting the material.

"I listen to the stuff that got me into it," Van said. What that meant is he takes his inspiration from listening widely to music and connecting with new artists who become temporary sidemen. It is a formula for continual success. He didn't think "Brown Eyed Girl" was any more than a throwaway. He also said no groups in 2009 interested him. Van remarked he had three hundred songs better than "Brown Eyed Girl." There was a new and friendly Morrison during interviews. That is until it came to the question of his biographers. He had some firm opinions on the qualifications of his biographers, as well as the veracity of their work. None of his opinions were pleasant ones. The new Van Morrison couldn't hide his disdain for those who write about him.

What is it that bothers Morrison about biography? He didn't believe his biographers have in-depth knowledge of rock and roll. He questioned their credentials. He remarked many are lazy. He said he was ripped off "time and time again." His biographers, he intimated, don't understand his fight with the industry. Van stated he had to become someone he didn't want to become. Biography is one of Morrison's pet peeves. He hates the idea of it. Why? He is fiercely protective of his privacy. That will remain. The lawsuits may still be on the horizon. I hope this is not the case.

BIBLIOGRAPHICAL SOURCES

Much of Van Morrison's late in life irritation with biographies on his art came from reading Clinton Heylin's, **Can You Feel The Silence? Van Morrison, A New Biography**, published in 2002. Van was angry with this superb rendering of his life. He sued Heylin. The British authors book is a towering feat in rock music journalism. Despite its warts, Heylin comes closest to describing the personal Morrison while going to recording studio notes to tell us all he can about the interior of the Belfast Cowboys music. The reviews and criticism of Heylin's book further opens up penetrating analysis of his life and art. Along the way Van's comments created what I term "Van on Biography." There are many gifted writers who have reviewed Heylin's book, perhaps the best is Charles Shaar Murray, see Murray's, "Can You Feel The Silence? Van Morrison, A New Biography," **The London Independent**, November 28, 2002. https://www.independent.co.uk/arts-entertainment/books/reviews/can-you-feel-the-silence-van-morrison-a-new-biography-by-clinton-heylin-129620.html Murray is a critical, often testy, seldom praiseworthy, rock and roll writer with a literary pedigree. He is the U.K.'s equivalent of his American powerhouse critic and Memphis based rock music observer Stanley Booth.

Murray's review of Heylin is much like a secondary biography. That is he takes the meat or telling points from Heylin's work weaving his review into a new direction. As Murray begins the review with a disparaging story of Van wandering into a press party where someone mistakes him for a cab driver, Murray uses the quote: "Anyone order a minicab?" This seems disrespectful to Morrison. It isn't. What Murray is doing is making it clear he views Van's music is that of blue collar, working class poet. That is exactly a brilliant description of the Belfast Cowboy. Murray calls him "one of the most perplexing and contradictory individuals ever to participate in the music business." Murray is a brilliant literary stylist so it is not surprising he accuses Heylin of "clunky prose." For other poignant reviews see Keith Phipps, "Clinton Heylin: Van Morrison: Can You Feel The Silence," **Aux.avclub.com**, October 21, 2013 https://aux.avclub.com/clinton-heylin-van-morrison-can-you-feel-the-silence-1798198989 and the rather hostile review by Kevin Mitchell, "How To Make Van Ordinaire," **London Guardian,** December 2, 2002. https://www.theguardian.com/books/2002/dec/08/biography.vanmorrison

The most significant comments by Morrison on biography comes from the facile interviews conducted by Fintan O'Toole and the work of poet Gerald Dawe contains important insights into how Van thinks of and reacts to the biographical process. See, for example, Fintan O'Toole, "Bittersweet Insights Into Van Morrison's Belfast," **The Irish Times**, December 16, 2017. https://www.irishtimes.com/culture/books/bittersweet-insights-into-van-morrison-s-belfast-1.3322104 This article reflects on Gerald Dawe's book on Van, **In Another World: Van Morrison & Belfast**. Since the early 1990s Dawe has written about Morrison suggesting how and why East Belfast created Morrison's legacy. For insights into Van's writing, his way of thinking, his thoughts on Belfast and London and other influences, see **Lit Up Inside**, published by City Light Books in 2014 with a brilliant forward by Ian Rankin, as well as another forward by David Meltzer and an introduction by Eammon Hughes. The selected lyrics in this volume are simply Van's songs with no interpretation. He has over the years talked about seminal influences. The title came from "On Hyndford Street" where he used the term "lit up inside." Ian Rankin said Van's book showed "the arc of a life." Morrison said: "Why Must I Always Explain" tells the story of his life. Van told Rankin that in 1965 he played an instrumental of "Moondance" with Mick Fleetwood playing drums and then Van said in 1968 the lyrics came to the song in a stream of consciousnesses moment.

William Blake's influence is all over Morrison's interviews. In a conversation with Ian Rankin on November 14 1974 at London's Lyric Theater, Van talked in depth about Blake's prose and how he connected it to his songs. Oscar Wilde and Samuel Beckett were name checked in songs and this suggests how and why Belfast influenced his art. Rankin asked Van what was his most significant influence. Morrison said "the poetry of the blues." He also said Hank Williams was a big influence as well as Leroy Carr and Lightning Hopkins. These were the influences Van said was "very Elizabethan." When Van said Lightnin' Hopkins couldn't read but he told Rankin to listen to his music. The most interesting comment from Van is when he says what he wants to say in a song the rest is instrumental. When he was asked about "Brown Eyed Girl," Van said it was not based on a particular person. He said his songs were a composite. They are much like writing fiction.

For reviews of Clinton Heylin's biography and the barbed criticism from the London press, see, for example, Kevin Mitchell, "How To Make Van Ordinaire," **London Observer**, December 7, 2002 https://www.theguardian.com/books/2002/dec/08/biography.vanmorrison and Charles Shaar Murray, "Can You Feel The Silence, Van Morrison A New Biography, by Clinton Heylin," **London Independent**, November 28, 2002. https://www.independent.co.uk/arts-entertainment/books/reviews/can-you-feel-the-silence-van-morrison-a-new-biography-by-clinton-heylin-129620.html See the **Irish Times**, October 18, 1997 for the Frankfurt Book Fair proposal and the surrounding controversy or using Morrison's name to increase attendance. Charles Shaar Murray comes closest to defining Morrison when he writes: "Van Morrison takes pride of place: he's indubitably the most awkward of them all." In clunky prose Murray speaks the truth.

☙❧

EPILOGUE

"There have been many lies put out about me and this finally states my position. I have never joined any organization, nor plan to. I am not affiliated to any guru.... I don't have a teacher either."

VAN MORRISON IN CONVERSATION WITH ANTHONY DENSELOW OF THE LONDON OBSERVER.

"No white man sings like Van Morrison."

GREIL MARCUS

"It's hard to explain.... Sometimes it's really hard to get (onstage). Like, y'know I almost withdraw five minutes before I go on."

VAN MORRISON IN CONVERSATION WITH ROLLING STONE

☙❧

By 1973 Van Morrison was not only an established rock star, he had taken his management reins and solved his fiscal problems. The years from 1968 to 1972 were a watershed in his career. He left a small label, Bang, to sign with one of the five major labels Warner Brothers, he married, he divorced, he built a recording studio, and he settled in half a dozen different towns. He became one of the premier singer-songwriters in rock music.

The future was bright. He had control of his songs. His touring was handled professionally. He had no illusions about those who controlled the rock music marketplace. They were sharks who would rip off your soul.

As 1972 came to an end, Van had one album on Bang **Blowin' Your Mind**, issued in 1967, and five albums from **Astral Weeks** in 1968 until 1972 when **Saint Dominic's Preview** was released. The three albums in-between **Moondance, His Band and the Street Choir** in 1970 and **Tupelo Honey in 1971** placed Morrison in the center of the commercial marketplace. He should have been happy. He wasn't. Here is where it gets strange. Van was not the maladjusted miscreant Clinton Heylin's biography suggests. After talking with a hundred of his close friends and musical associates there is no doubt, he is quirky. He is not the person Heylin describes.

When 1972 came to an end Morrison experienced five years of excellent sales and respectful reviews. He was finally making a living in the music business. When **St. Dominic's Preview** was released in July 1972, with its combination of Celtic folk, blues, jazz and rhythm and blues, the critical reception was positive. The album charted at fifteen on the **Billboard** 200 it was Morrison's best-selling album until 2008 when **Keep It Simple** reached number ten on **Billboard**.

The five years from 1968 through 1972 was a transformative time. What did Van Morrison learn? He discovered he needed to become tough as nails to deal with the sharks in the music business. The result was an at times abrasive style, a search for proper management and an attempt to create new music while he juggled his marriage with touring. He didn't secure proper management. He straightened out his business affairs. His personality remained distant, often abrasive, but he was never rude, inconsiderate or angry with close friends. It was the music business that fomented his anger.

Did the turmoil of constant changes in living conditions, the demands from Warner Brothers and the touring alter Morrison's life and personality? These forces molded the curmudgeon that his fans took to heart. Van survived the entry into stardom from 1968 to 1972.

A book could be written on the artists influenced by Van Morrison. From the early years there are some intriguing influences. When Jimi Hendrix recorded "Gloria" he talked in various interviews about the Belfast Cowboy. The Doors Jim Morrison discussed Van's stage moves at Los Angeles's Whiskey A Go Go. He claimed Morrison helped his stage persona.

Bruce Springsteen, John Cougar Mellencamp and Bob Seger have discussed how Van's early material shaped their early solo songs. There are many other artists taking Morrison's musical formula to the bank.

MORRISON MELLOWING SITTING DOWN WITH FINTAN O'TOOLE

After fifty plus years in show business, Van Morrison sat down with **Irish Times** reporter Fintan O'Toole to look back on his career. O'Toole was nervous. He didn't have to worry. Van was in a good mood. O'Toole is not a rock music reporter. He is a respected mainstream journalist. Van loved talking to him.

As Morrison reminisced, he was asked about "The Street Only Knew Your Name." O'Toole picked a phrase from the song "the view of the street from your window pane," and he wondered what Van's memories were of the Belfast streets. Morrison replied: "I remember after the war they used to take the railings away. That's the first thing I remember in relation to when people were talking about the war." Van said the phrase came from his youth.

When Van looked back on his life, his career and life in Belfast, he remarked. "I find in retrospect a lot of it is romanticized, and mythologized but early on there wasn't any of that." Morrison was addressing the dangers of his legend. As he turned seventy, he became more introspective and less inclined to think about the past.

When he talked about his place in the world Morrison was unusually direct. He said early on he realized he was not a follower. "I realized that I'm more fitting into this outsider pattern," Van observed. On the use of words and word play Morrison credited Seamus Heaney's book **Preoccupations** with schooling him on word usage. A local window cleaner gave him books that influenced Van's developing intellect. Jack Kerouac's **Dharma Bums**, Christmas Humphreys' **Zen Buddhism** and Jean-Paul Sartre's **Nausea** were seminal intellectual influences. It was from Kerouac's writings, Van maintained, he discovered a free flowing writing style akin to jazz. Of Kerouac, Van said: "His writing actually had a lot to do with jazz, because that's what he was listening to at the time and that's what got me too...."

Not surprisingly, he has done it for decades, Van denied he is a part of the rock and roll industry. "I was never on that track," Van said of rock music. "It doesn't really matter if other people thought I was, you know. That was their problem."

On business, Morrison recognized early in his career you had to own the music to survive. He told O'Toole: "You never really got ahead of it until you could manipulate the situation to actually get control by owning the product."

When Van looked back on his burst of creativity in the 1970s, he credited it to re-reading Jack Kerouac and discovered William Blake. He also dabbled in Allen Ginsberg. Why did it take until the 1970s to re-discover his voice? Van said with Them and the Bang material he was controlled by "the puppet masters." He had to work day and night to keep food on the table and a roof over his head. Morrison said the industry kept artists on a subsistence level. It made them easier to control.

DID VAN PRACTICE THE AMERICAN LIE? DAVID BURKE'S BRILLIANCE

As thought pieces go David Burke's **A Sense of Wonder: Van Morrison's Ireland** provides significant insights into his character, his mind, Ireland, his music and at times his personal life. There are some interesting chapters that fail to recognize the American influence. In chapter six, "American Exile," Burke brilliantly encapsulates what he terms "exile" in the colonies."

One of Burke's theories is the violence in Belfast from 1970 through 1972 drove Morrison to America. Not true. He had been with Them in the mid-1960s touring the states, and he realized the only way to forge a mainstream music career was in New York or Los Angeles. That is what drove him to New York, Boston, Woodstock and Fairfax. It was about his career. It was not about Belfast or Ireland. He was intent at beating the bastards at their own game.

Morrison was more like James Joyce or Samuel Beckett, preferring exile to a chaotic countryside destroying his artistic vision. While Burke views Morrison as a lost and desolate figure in California, the truth is, he found innovative, talented, aggressive and influential musical collaborators. Without the Fairfax experience Morrison's early music would not have been as commercial. Of course, the notion of this direction infuriated the Belfast Cowboy.

In 1972 Caledonia Productions hired Stephen Pillster. He became Morrison's new manager. Why is he important in the final year that Morrison beat the industry bastards and began his long, ascendant run to mythical stardom?

WHAT IS BELFAST TO VAN MORRISON?

Gerald Dawe is a respected, award-winning poet who looked at Belfast's influence, and he concluded it was the key to Morrison's art. Dawe suggests written history and art combine in the Belfast Cowboy's songs. The blue collar city that produced a working class musician is indelibly stamped all over Van's music. The musical influence of Morrison's Protestant neighborhood is an undeniable influence upon his lyrical magic.

Gerald Dawe, unlike Clinton Heylin, ignored Van's fame. He sees no problem with it. Why? It is what drives Morrison's productive machine. Dawe proposes the reader-fan consider Morrison's music. The rest of his life and persona is insignificant. Van would agree. Dawe says to view Morrison in the context of his times. That is he reacts to his environment. Perhaps he wasn't as angry as he appears with Warner Brothers. When he stormed Joe Smith's house on Christmas eve or attempted to fight Mo Ostin in his home at a dinner party, Van was venting the frustration of the record business. That doesn't serve as an excuse for his wanton behavior. It does explain why Morrison was at times the most difficult man in show business.

Rapture not radicalism is Dawe's theme in his book **In Another World: Van Morrison & Belfast**. When Otis Redding died in a plane crash in 1966 young Belfast rockers wore black armbands. We have no idea if Van wore one. But this symbolic gesture is one his compatriots believe he approved of and perhaps took in the arm band as a sign he should move to New York. Much of Dawe's book centers around a 1995 interview where Van talks at length about Belfast.

When Van sings in **St. Dominic's Preview** "And it's a long way to Buffalo," he followed it with "It's a long way to Belfast City too." This tells it all. Van is recalling what influences his song writing. Where Dawe's book excels is in analyzing how and why Belfast provided "the poetic path" to greatness.

Van Morrison and Irish music is the theme Dawe's propounds. He has a point. For much of his career the Belfast Cowboy had employed Irish themes to define his intellectual direction. Dawe's makes the case if you listen to "Astral Weeks" the mystery that is Van Morrison is explained.

WHY AND HOW VAN PROVED HE WASN'T A ONE HIT WONDER OR THE PRODUCT OF HIS GENERATION

In the rock music field one hit wonders are the norm. To have a large fan following, to release hit records, to have albums that sell regularly over a fifty year period is not the norm. Van Morrison has accomplished that goal. This is why the years from 1968 through 1972 provide the foundation for his continued success. He had a hit with "Brown Eyed Girl" in the mid-1960s and he continued into 2020 to place albums on the charts. How did he survive fifty-two years in the nastiest business known to mankind? He survived due to his cranky, contrarian nature combined with a talent no one could ignore.

At seventy-five Van has lived long enough to have the last laugh. Rather than gloat and scream "I told you so," he remains a productive musician. Today rather than mobsters and assholes calling the record industry shots, it is accountants, bean counters and hipsters chasing every new trend run a record business. One almost wants the mobsters hanging people out of ten story New York buildings again. It would make things more interesting and more fun.

Surviving the music industry was as important as Morrison's talent. Had he not survived the A & R people, the insipid label heads and the sex, drugs and booze minions that worked for the major labels, Van's brilliant songs might not have captured such a dominant audience. The sleazy and corrupt industry was not only a challenge to Morrison, he single-handedly changed the rules for artists. Now he negotiates with the label heads. Other artists have personal and artistic freedoms in the studio unknown at the time Van began his career. Thank you Van Morrison.

VAN OPENS UP ABOUT THE EARLY YEARS

At the Riverside Theater at the University of Coleraine, on April 20, 1988, Van sat down for an interview with an old musical friend Derek Bell of the Chieftains, as well as with Martin Lynch and Professor Bob Welch. He was relaxed. In an hour show filled with intelligent, knowledgeable questions, Van opened up concerning his early life. This program was a relaxing one. Why? Van was relaxed in conversation while performing a number of songs including a Lead Belly cover. When Van sang "Celtic Ray" his Irish roots were on display. He also performed songs with Bell's piano and a guitar backing him. The live audience was rapturous.

The five songs Van performed also included "Foggy Mountain Top," a cover of Lead Belly's "Out On The Western Plains," "A Sense of Wonder," "In The Garden" and a cover of the Dubliners "Ragland Road."

When Van was asked about his use of the "mystic," Van said Alice Bailey was an inspiration for his songwriting. Van said he gave an Alice Bailey book to the sound engineer on the **A Sense of Wonder** album. Van quoted Carl Jung in this interview stating one had to come to grips with the dark side of his life.

An intimate performance of "In The Garden" highlighted how Van's lyrical beauty needed little more than Bell's piano and a soft guitar. As Van sang "No guru, no method, no teacher" he made it clear his music was his alone. There was no need to interpret it. As he sat down the conversation came back to his songwriting and poetry. Van said when he wrote "In The Garden," he was reading a book on meditation. Van said he realized in the 1960s his roots were important. He suggested the 1960s was about rejecting roots, but this was not Van's mantra. He held onto these roots. He said Wordsworth's poetry and Joseph Campbell's thoughts were important to his song poetry. "The older poets wrote songs," Van concluded.

Van spent some time talking about Carl Jung and how he defined the creative life. Then Van talked about recording with the Chieftains emphasizing his Irish roots but the traditional Irish songs were done in a unique, creative way that differed from the original. Derek Bell said this created new interest in traditional Irish music.

VAN ON SPIRITUALISM AND THE RECORD COMPANIES

A persistent question surrounding **Astral Weeks** concerns it spiritual nature. The critics, the fans and even Van debate this issue. "My spiritual understanding has grown only to the extent (of my knowledge) about myself," Van said. The foray into Scientology, the Jehovah's Witnesses, the Los Angeles based Agape Church and other faiths helped to form this spiritual countenance.

As he concluded the **Los Angeles Times** question and answer session he talked about the industry. He paid tribute to Sam Phillips and Ahmet Ertegun while disparaging those who run the present day industry. "For the record business to win and win big it has to have people within it that have ears for music and who understand the old greats...." The record company executives who wait for the "famous (to) come in the building," receive Van's wrath. He was as combative in 2008, when he made this remark, as he was from 1968 to 1972. Along the way he freed his music from the industry predators.

Van has beaten the record companies at their own game. **People** magazine reported in 2018 that Morrison held the number one position among the ten highest paid musicians. "In 2016 it looked like the musician's spectacular career was winding down," **People** observed. They reported from November 2017 to November 2018 he made an incredible forty-six million dollars and this was twenty million more than his closest competitor. With a net worth of almost one hundred million dollars, Van's careful investments, his savvy dealings with the music industry and his non-rock star lifestyle make for his fortune increasing dramatically.

There is more to Morrison than the music business. He has a lucrative endorsement deal with Cover Girl cosmetics to use his music. He owns several restaurants including the Fat Morrison Burger Chain in Dublin. He has invested in a football club the Belfast Angels. He has his own brand of Vodka known as Pure Wonder Morrison. A best-selling perfume With Love From Van is partnered with a fashion line labeled "Van Morrison Seduction."

The next phase of Morrison's career from 1973 to 1980 provides a new and wonderful story. Stay tuned.

ACKNOWLEDGEMENTS

I sat at a table smelling of cigarettes and beer at Frenchy's in Hayward, California watching Van Morrison and his band perform. It was the early 1970s. I had just finished a PhD in American history and I was a fan of Morrison since the Them days. I decided to start collecting Van bootleg vinyl albums. Then I searched the San Francisco Bay Area for memorabilia. Then I started to make notes. In 1983 my first book **Van Morrison: The Mystic's Music** arrived and in 2005 the first volume of a multi-volume biography **Van Morrison: Them and the Bang Era, 1945-1968** came out as I became a Professor Emeritus. That is after thirty-five years as a college professor I opted for retirement. From 2006 to 2017 I wrote the next four volumes of what is now five book and 3000 pages on Morrison's life. Why the biographer's obsession? The reason is a simple one. Van is as much a literary-historical figure as a rock musician.

In this book I have recreated concerts, meetings with musicians, industry differences and a few personal stories influencing Morrison's music. One critic, living in Ashville, North Carolina, professor B. Lee Cooper said: "Did you jump into a time machine to recreate so many vivid memories?" "No," I answered. At the end of each chapter "Bibliographical Sources," tells the reader my conclusions are tethered to the facts. The story I tell is to bring life to Morrison's story and make it personal as far as the music is concerned. It is not personal about his life. That I have ignored. The factual tidbits and obscure people in this book tell the story of the real Van Morrison. For the settings that Van lived in, I have many people to thank. Mervyn Solomon on Belfast, Nick Clainos on San Francisco, Joey Bebo on Boston, Mark Naftalin on Marin County and Happy Traum and Tom Pacheco on Woodstock provided the foundation stones on which to build this book. Van was a powerful new voice in the music business.

Van is a haunting figure. Many of his fans wanted nothing personal in books. Others want the whole story. So how do I proceed? I decided to leave out the gossip, the personal stories and the ennui to concentrate this volume on how and why Morrison battled the music industry. He did. He won. It is now a new ball game thanks to Van. This book would have been impossible without the people listed below. All mistakes are mine.

Pat Thomas was the catalyst to finishing this book, which I began in 2006. Thank you, Pat, for the push. Also thanks for critiquing the manuscript. Michael Fishman also looked at and offered suggestions on the manuscript. His work is appreciated. Art Siegel answered all my phone calls, met for lunch and he was a fountain of information since the 1980's.

Joey Bebo, the drummer for Van in Boston in the summer of 1968, helped to correct misconceptions and he provided key information. Joey us a brilliant writer, a great storyteller and I urge everyone to read his books.

In reconstructing these five years Simon Gee provided copies of his magazine. Russ Dugoni offered suggestions. Pat Corley's wit and wisdom helped, as did Bernard McGuinn's knowledge. The late Haik Arakail was my favorite bootlegger as was Zaire in the East Bay. John Goddard at Village music was a constant source of new material. Ron Sexton, aka the Dude, helped with his memories of various shows. Opal Louis Nations provided information and background material. Michael Saltzman's online postings were a constant source of information. Dave Williams in the U.K. was a source of information on the early days of the British blues. Mike Sanchez offered some thoughts at a birthday party for Dave Williams.

The late Chris Michie was important describing Van's positive relationship with his musicians. Neil Skok added to that knowledge as Neil provided concert tapes, memorabilia and insider knowledge. Mike Stax at Ugly Thing was an unwitting conspirator. Ken Burke was a constant source of music, critical thinking and Ken's observations on writing make him one of rock music's great critics. Dennis Loren at RPM in Detroit published my early rock and roll pieces and my first article on Van was in RPM.

ACKNOWLEDGEMENTS

There were many San Francisco musicians recalling these days. Mark Naftalin of the Paul Butterfield Blues band went solo in the San Francisco Bay Area. He was instructive and helpful concerning Marin County clubs. Elvin Bishop added his thoughts on Morrison. Tony Dey talked at length about playing with and recording with Morrison.

My good friend Steve Rowland helped me understand the music business. Budd Albright added to the tales. Shel Talmy provided useful information on the industry. Conversations with Dan Bourgoise clarified copyright issues as did Harry Balk. Ray Ruff added material on Them after Morrison left the group. Ruff was helpful for insider Warner Brothers material, and he shared internal Warner memos on Van Morrison's career.

A conversation with Steve Turner helped to change my attitude toward the place of religion and philosophy in Van's life. The work of Professor Peter Mills was important in focusing my attitude on Morrison's intellectual achievements.

Mervyn and Phil Solomon provided material from the 1980s until they passed. Mervyn and his lovely wife Ann took me all over Belfast and Phil and Dorothy treated me to lunch in their Bournemouth pent house apartment. They also introduced me to Sir Edward Lewis for a brief interview. In Liverpool Bob Wooler spent time with me in the 1980 analyzing how and why Van Morrison and the Beatles were alike and different. This helped my 1983 book **Van Morrison: The Mystics Music**.

In Woodstock Happy Traum and Tom Pacheco led me on a tour of the area. A brief interview with Levon Helm at his "barn home" led to some interesting anecdotes. The staff at the Sled Hill Café fed us for two weeks as they recounted tales of Van Morrison.

A chance encounter with Dahaud Shaar at a Grateful Dead show led to a discussion of the **His Band And The Street Choir** album.

The groundwork for this book was laid in the 1980s in Liverpool when the late Clive Epstein mentioned to me that Van Morrison's work ethic would make him amongst the most productive rock musicians.

Marc and Gaby Maag Bristol at **Blue Suede News** published my articles, encouraged me and along the way became good friends. My brother, Dennis DeWitt is an excellent writer and I have benefitted from thirty years of his interpretive writing.

Scott Amonson reshaped, designed, criticized, and he produced the final version of this book. He is responsible for editing, layout, providing visuals, original art work, photo processing, digital transfers, cover design, technical assistance and the overall design of this book. Thank you Scott!

Michael Seltzer is a good friend who gave good advice and support for this book. Thank you Michael!

Dennis Loren and Mick Gray – Thank you for your support over the years.

Simon Gee – I am continuing your journey. Thanks for your support and your wonderful fanzine.

ABOUT THE AUTHOR

Howard A. DeWitt is Professor Emeritus of History at Ohlone College, Fremont, California. He received his B. A. from Western Washington State University, the M. A. from the University of Oregon and a PhD from the University of Arizona. He also studied at the University of Paris, Sorbonne and the City University in Rome. Professor DeWitt is the author of twenty-five books and has published over 200 articles and more than 200 reviews in a wide variety of popular and scholarly magazines.

DeWitt has also been a member of a number of organizations to promote the study of history. The most prestigious is the Organization of American Historians where he was a reviewer for a decade.

For more than forty-five years he has taught full and part time at a number of U.S. colleges and is best known for teaching two college level courses in the History of Rock n Roll music. He continued to teach the History of Rock and Roll music on the Internet until 2011. In a distinguished academic career, he has also taught at the University of California, Davis, the University of Arizona, Cochise College and Chabot College. In addition to these teaching assignments, Professor DeWitt was a regular speaker at the Popular Culture Association annual convention and at the National Social Science Association meetings. He has delivered a number of addresses to the Organization of American Historians.

DeWitt is an award nominated writer. His 2017 book Searching or Sugar Man II: Coming From Reality, Heroes and Villains was a finalist for the best pop music book by the Association for Recorded Sound Collections. This was DeWitt's eleventh book on rock music.

He wrote the first book on Chuck Berry, which was published by Pierian Press under the title Chuck Berry: Rock N Roll Music in 1985. DeWitt's earlier brief biography, Van Morrison: The Mystic's Music, published in 1983, received universally excellent reviews. On the

English side of the music business DeWitt's, The Beatles: Untold Tales, originally published in 1985, was picked up by the Kendall Hunt Publishing Company in the 1990s and is used regularly in a wide variety of college courses on the history of rock music. Kendall Hunt also published Stranger in Town: The Musical Life of Del Shannon with co-author Dennis M. DeWitt in 2001. In 1993's Paul McCartney: From Liverpool To Let It Be concentrated on the Beatle years. He also co-authored Jailhouse Rock: The Bootleg Records of Elvis Presley with Lee Cotten in 1983. His two books on Sixto Rodriguez are benchmark studies of the record business and how it is difficult for obscure performers from collecting their royalties.

DeWitt is working with Ken Burke on a study of Gary S. Paxton, Kim Fowley and how they had success despite the music industry.

Professor DeWitt's many awards in the field of history include founding the Cochise County Historical Society and his scholarship has been recognized by a number of state and local government organizations. DeWitt's book, Sun Elvis: Presley In The 1950s, published by Popular Culture Ink, was a finalist for the Deems-ASCAP Award for the best academic rock and roll book. His first book on Sixto Rodriguez was a finalist for a Michigan Notable Book Award.

In his research for any and all of his books, Professor DeWitt employs the Gay Talese method: interview everyone around and connected to the project!

Professor DeWitt is a renaissance scholar who publishes in a wide variety of outlets that are both academic and popular. He is one of the few college professors who bridge the gap between scholarly and popular publications. His articles and reviews have appeared in Blue Suede News, DISCoveries, Rock 'N' Blues News, the Journal of Popular Culture, the Journal of American History, California History, the Southern California Quarterly, the Pacific Historian, Amerasia, the Western Pennsylvania Historical Magazine, the Annals of Iowa, the Journal of the West, Arizona and the West, the North Beach Review, Ohio History, the Oregon Historical Quarterly, the Community College Social Science Quarterly, Montana: The Magazine of the West, Record Profile Magazine, Audio Trader, the Seattle Post-Intelligencer and Juke Box Digest.

For forty plus years DeWitt has combined popular and academic writing. He has been nominated for numerous writing awards. His reviews are combined with articles to form a body of scholarship and popular writing that is frequently footnoted in major works. As a political scientist, Professor DeWitt authored three books that questioned American foreign policy and its direction. In the Philippines, DeWitt is recognized as one of the foremost biographers of their political leader Jose Rizal. His three books on Filipino farm workers remain the standard in the field.

During his high school and college years, DeWitt promoted dances in and around Seattle, Washington. Such groups as Little Bill and the Bluenotes, Ron Holden and the Playboys, the Frantics, the Wailers and George Palmerton and the Night People among others played at such Seattle venues as the Eagle's Auditorium and Dick Parker's Ballroom.

Howard and his wife Carolyn have two grown children. Darin is a Professor of Political Science at California State University, Long Beach and Melanie is a Special Education teacher with two children Natalia and Katarina. They both live in Los Angeles. Howard's wife of forty-seven plus years, Carolyn, is an educator, an artist and she continues to raise Howard. She is presently retired and vacationing around the world. The DeWitt's live in Scottsdale, Arizona. That is when they are not in Paris looking for art, books and music. Howard is working on a book on Portugal's Secrets, That is a year or two away.

His book on the president Obama's Detractor's: In The Right Wing Nut House is a marvelous look at the radical right and the tragedy of Fox TV News, right wing book authors and political kooks like Laura Ingraham and Ann Coulter. His novels Stone Murder and Salvador Dali Murder feature a San Francisco P.I. Trevor Blake III and a gay mobster Don Gino Landry, and much of the story line will evolve around crimes that DeWitt witnessed while working four years and two days as an agent with the Bureau of Alcohol, Tobacco and Firearms. He was a street agent for the BATF and his tales of those years are in manuscript waiting for publication. He was also a key figure in the BATF Union.

Meeting Hitler: A Tragicomedy, published in 2016 was a best seller with excellent reviews. In 2017 Sicily's Secrets: The Mafia, Pizza and Hating Rome was a number one best seller for travel books on Amazon. DeWitt is working on a like-minded book on Portugal. In 2018 DeWitt's Trump Against The World: A Foreign Policy Bully, Russian Collusion was the first in-depth examination of his European foreign policy and how it impacted American domestic politics.

Any corrections or additions to this or the subsequent volumes that will follow this study can be sent to Horizon Books, P. O. Box 4342, Scottsdale, Arizona 85258. DeWitt can be reached via e-mail at Howard217@aol.com

Printed in Dunstable, United Kingdom